MW01045415

SACHA SAUDA
GURMAT PARCHAR SOCIETY
2575 STEELES AVENUE EAST, UNIT No. 18,
BRAMPTON, ONT. L6P 5TI CANADA
TEL. : (905) 459-8351
FAX : (905) 459-5986

A Historian's Approach to
GURU GOBIND SINGH

A Historian's Approach to
GURU GOBIND SINGH

SURJIT SINGH GANDHI

Singh Brothers
Amritsar

A Historian's Approach to
GURU GOBIND SINGH
by
SURJIT SINGH GANDHI

ISBN 81-7205-306-1

First Edition March 2004

Price : Rs. 450-00

Publishers :
Singh Brothers
•
Bazar Mai Sewan, Amritsar - 143 006
•
S.C.O. 223-24, City Centre, Amritsar - 143 001
E-mail : singhbro@vsnl.com
Website : www.singhbrothers.com

Printers :
PRINTWELL, 146, INDUSTRIAL FOCAL POINT, AMRITSAR.

Offerings At The Lotus Feet
of
Sri Guru Gobind Singh
who is my ever-lasting succour
and
comes unseen to me in my dark despair

To
My Dearest Sons
Gurmit Singh
and
Navneet Singh

CONTENTS

—Imprimis 9

1. Heritage 15

2. Early Life in Bihar 65

3. At Anandpur 79

4. Paonta Period 124

5. The Battle of Bhangani 145

6. Return to Anandpur 1688 156

7. Emergence of the Khalsa 189

8. Alleged Worship of Goddess Durga 241

9. Onslaught of Hindu Conservatism
   and Islamic Imperialism 251

10. The Guru's Escape Towards Malwa 278

11. Damdama Period 303

12. From Damdama to Agra 316

13. From Agra to Nanded 331

14. Culmination and Beginning 364

15. A Multidimensional Personality 376

16. Guru Gobind Singh's Literary Activities 391

Part-II

Guru Gobind Singh's Vision of Metaphysics, Polity and Social Ideals

17. God, Universe and Man   419

18. Sikh Polity   443

19. Sikh Social Ideals   467

20. Epilogue   484

   —Appendices   499

   —Bibliography   507

   —Index   515

IMPRIMIS

The present study aims at presenting an objective account of Guru Gobind Singh's life, his response to the contemporary spiritual, political, social and economic conditions, his contribution to metaphysics, social engineering and polity, his attitude towards Muslims as well as Hindu orthodoxy—the former was nourished, promoted and made hegemonic by *Ulemas* of *Naqshabandi* sect and other varieties and the Mughal state, while the latter was nurtured, and spearheaded by Brahmins, the Hindu priestly class hand in glove with the Rajput Hindu rulers, especially of Shivalik and Kumaon Hills, his proactive role to save Sikhism and Sikh society from internal erosions caused by dissentient sects and *Masands* and taking concrete and positive steps to bring about social compactness among the Sikhs, his resetting of the goals at all levels and in all fields of activities and his formulating of fresh structures and strategies to promote the cause of Sikhism even amidst varied serious challenges, his floating of the Order of *Khalsa*, a new model of man as well as of society, his providing of fresh insights and fresh stimuli to make the people dynamic, forward-looking and transcendental in their approach and out-look, ever yearning and striving for a global fraternity, built on social equality, mutual respect, non-exploitation and superseding caste system and the principle of fixity and discrimination inheriting it, his urgings and his polemics for multi-culturalism, universalism, and religious pluralism, his special accent on the principle of struggle as the means to ensure and promote welfare of the people, his understanding of *Pursh* and *Parakriti* nexus, his engendering of the spirit of ascending higher and higher, his heralding of new era of enlightenment, righteousness, equitable justice and freedom from fear, restrictions on speech, expression and worship.

True, a number of studies have already broached this

subject but their findings were sketchy or tinged with prejudice. Kavi Santokh Singh's Magnum Opus *Gurpartap Suraj Parkash* is more a book of devotional poetry than of history. The author's approach is not analytical; it is primarily theological. Whatever information is embedded in his work, is not objective and reveals that he was more after the adoration of characters than the evaluation of events which form matrix of history—so much so that at times, he prunes the facts to suit his predetermined themes. At places, the events are so much soaked in mythology that they lose their identities.

M.A. Macauliffe wrote on the life of Guru Gobind Singh but he, too, failed to do justice in spite of being an erudite scholar and a zealot researcher. His writing, at best, was a record of events as they were presented to him by his hired Punjabi assistants.

Gurbilas by Sukha Singh and *Gurbilas* Koer Singh are far away from objective historiography. Their accounts are more marked for the adulation of their characters than for presenting analytical study. Not only this, they, at places, had given currency to the views which were clearly contrary to the teachings of the Guru.

A Short History of the Sikhs by Teja Singh and Ganda Singh gave too meagre information; although in style and objectivity, it can be ranked quite high. Strangely enough, very few pages are devoted to Guru Gobind Singh's life which was fabulously rich in terms of his landmark achievements.

Even some recent biographies, especially the one written by Professor Kartar Singh and the other by Bhagat Lakshman Singh fell short of the requisite standard. They were neither fully documented, nor were they objective. The intrinsic history of the Guru's life had been left untouched due to lack of a sound historical methodology.

Giani Gian Singh, the celebrated author of *Twarikh Guru Khalsa* and *Panth Parkash*, worked hard to write a detailed history of the Gurus including Guru Gobind Singh. But his drawn portrayals suffer from two snags : one, it did not take into reckoning the socio-economic forces operating during the Guru period, and second, his inclination towards rhetoric made his study lop-sided and tainted.

In the recent past, late Dr. Indubhushan Banerjee wrote *Evolution of the Khalsa* with detailed account of the Sikh Gurus. Even this work could not provide the whole information. Probably, the scope of the book was limited and the study was confined only to find out details in regard to the visible and the manifest, not comprehending that the manifest and the unmanifest, both are needed to grasp the whole truth. After the annexation of the Punjab by the British the Western scholars developed keen interest in the history of the Sikhs. Broadly, we come across three categories of books written by them. In the first category, are all those works written mainly to acquaint the British administration with the habit, customs and varied reactions of the people to different challenges. In the second category come those which were produced with a view to bolstering up racial pride among the Jats so that they might become ego-centric enough to deny the good influence of Sikhism on them. Through this device, the British had designs to weaken the Sikh unity. The works comprising both the aforesaid categories obviously could not be assumed as the real history of the Gurus.

In the works comprising the third category, the authors tried to write down objective history, as exemplified by Cunningham's *History of the Sikhs*. Even then, majority of the authors of this category could not think above racial prejudices and conqueror's complex.

In view of all this, I decided to rewrite the biography of the Guru, and soon I embarked upon the errand with a view to collect requisite facts on the project. In the course of my work, I was faced with innumerable difficulties. The appropriate original material was not available. There was *Bachitter Natak* (Wondrous Drama) written by the Guru himself, but that dealt with a very few events of his life. Sainapat and Bhai Nand Lal, the two court poets of the Guru, had written *Sri Gurusobha* and *Zindgi Nama* respectively, but these were not sufficient and did not narrate all important events and aspects of the Guru's life. Bhai Nand Lal's accounts intended to eulogize the Guru than to put forth a true biography. *Sri Gurusobha* is scrappy and its narratives were, self-concieved and partly legendary. *Guru Kian Sakhian* by Swarup Singh Kaushish, *Bhat Vahis*,

Khafi Khan's *Muntkhab-ul-Lubab, Bahadur Shah Nama, Amar Nama, Ahkam-i-Alamgiri, Maasar-i-Alamgiri, Hukamname* were also scrutinised but these sources too provided very little information. *Akhbarat-i-Durbar-i-Mualla* did make a mention of about one or two incidents relating to the last phase of Guru Gobind Singh's life, and that too from the Imperial point of view. We have also gone through the poetic works of numerous court poets of the Guru, especially those mentioned by Devinder Singh Vidyarthi in his book *Guru Gobind Singh Abhinandan* as well as in *Darbari Ratan* by Piara Singh Padam. Almost all of them have underlined that Guru Gobind Singh was a protector of the Hindus and he fought relentlessly against the Mughals whom he regarded as oppressors, unrighteous and tyrants, thus projecting the Guru as a champion of the Hindus and a determined foe of the ruling Mughal class. This inference is not true because the mission of Guru Gobind Singh was world-wide. Persian sources, although meagre in quantity, also failed to assess appropriately the work of Guru Gobind Singh. Most of the Muslims were under the influence of Sheikh Ahmed Sirhindi, the spiritual guide of the *Naqshbandi* the Muslim sect who continuously nourished the thought that Islam alone could save humankind from being swallowed by Satanic forces. They were not ready to study Guru Gobind Singh's attitude and mission in right perspective. Therefore their inferences smacked of partiality.

Notwithstanding these difficulties, I continued to collect facts. I also screened traditions, legends and myths regarding Guru's life. I went through the mythic poetic works of the contemporaries, especially those contained in *Dasam Granth*. This exercise was done to know the mind of the Guru. My approach was that facts unfold the outer life while myths and legends reveal the state of consciousness. Therefore both are useful while constructing history, although care has been taken that non-historical and imaginary facts do not affect the conclusions.

I was aware that history is not a linear series of events but has depth as well as surface. An event is an abstraction from the matrix of history and has significance only in its concerns. Guru Gobind Singh fought the Battle of Bhangani on

18th September, 1688 against the Hindu Rajas of Shivalik hills and won it. This is only a narration denoting his temporal uprising. It is the political and ideological conflict leading to the facts that make a history.

In the present work, attempt has been made to treat all the facts pertaining to the life of the Guru, as they took place, and indeed, it has been a matter of great satisfaction.

In the main narratives of the book, I have followed the synthetic method of history while in the comments I have followed the analytical method, thus combining the two. The intrinsic history of the Guru's life has been revealed as much importance as the external history.

Dealing with a stupendous work like the present one in the hands of the reader, the author makes no pretension to have gone whole hog by himself. Help and guidance were sought with humility and gratitude from many individuals as well as organisations.

First and the foremost, I would like to place on record my debt of gratitude to Dr. Kirpal Singh a doyen of history of the Punjab, who was kind enough to share with me the product of his investigative research. I can never forget Prof. Prithipal Singh Kapur, Editor, *Encyclopaedia of Sikhism*, for seeding the idea in my mind of taking up the present study.

My special thanks are due to S. Manjit Singh 'Calcutta' (Former Cabinet Minister, Higher Education and Languages Punjab). Himself an eminent scholar of Sikh History and theology, his comments proved of immense inspirational value for motivating me to break fresh grounds and make indepth study of hitherto untrodden labyrinths.

Equally grateful I am to Dr. Jodh Singh and Dr. Dharam Singh who allowed me to use their researches on the subject. I am beholden to Dr. Kharak Singh, Former Secretary, Institute of Sikh Studies, Chandigarh for his stimulating cooperation, to Dr. Harnam Singh Shan for providing a lot of relevant material especially from Persian sources besides his blessings which he showered on me so liberally. I can't forget the names of Dr. Ranbir Singh, Prof. Surinder Pal Singh of Mastuana, Dr. Charanjit Singh Udari, Dr. Gurnam Kaur and Dr. Balwant Singh Dhillon for keeping me on the track in ways more than one.

I am failing in my duty if I do not express my heartfull gratitude to Col. Devinder Singh (Retd.), who very keenly, went through the whole manuscript, improved its diction and made useful suggestions which I readily and gladly incorporated in the present study.

The work of both word-processing and preparation of the type-script was carried out most conscientiously by my aide Mr. Gurcharn Singh 'Premi'. He also prepared a General Index in a short time. For all this he can legitimately lay claim to my thanks.

My wife Daljit Kaur also deserves my thanks. Her positive outlook has always been reassuring.

My mind will not lighten of its burden without expressing my sincerest thanks to my publishers, Singh Brothers, Amritsar, especially S. Gursagar Singh, a brilliant youngman, for evincing his keen interest in the publication of the book. No social organization or government agency has financed this project. Only, my sons Navneet Singh and Gurmit Singh have rendered their help.

258, Nanak Pura   **Surjit Singh Gandhi**
Sangrur

CHAPTER I

HERITAGE

The medieval Hindu society was in the grip of an awful social malaise. It looked like a person on the verge of death, crying and shrieking for survival. It had lost its elan vital, without which no society is able to respond to different challenges which it is bound to face from time to time. The Brahmins or the Hindu nobles whom the social structure had assigned the job of fashioning creative responses to different challenges and to lead the masses along with them had ceased to play their role; rather they had circumscribed their activities to safeguard, sustain and promote their own interests. Naturally all their activities centred around this purpose.

They had created symbols, rites, traditions, religious and social precepts to tame the people's psyche to make them follow blindly and even used coercive methods—force of social boycott and physical violence in order to achieve their aim. Social discipline of which rites and rituals etc is an integral part, is a necessity for a society to forge ahead. But mechanical social drill is no good as it curbs initiatives. This was exactly the malady with the social system evolved by the men at the helm of affairs of the medieval Hindu society. Such men, who in the opinion of Toynbee were to act as a creative minority reduced themselves to a dominant minority alienated from the people whose interests they looked upon with gross indifference. The ultimate result was that the people, whether they belonged to the Hindu society or lived on its fringes, became rudderless and became the victim of the waves of different challenges.

The people reacted to the situations and tried to create a response outside the dominant minority. They threw up different types of reactions but none could come forth not to overcome the crisis and stimulate the society to move further towards progress. Some of the reactions were even retrogressive and repressive, thus socially detrimental. *Nathism* and *Baulism* etc are such examples. These cults gave a speculative philosophy unrelated to the social problems, exhorting the people to become self-centred and withdraw within themselves. Such withdrawal as part of the process of self-discipline is not considered bad in India. But, withdrawal within oneself never to come out to serve the society was more harmful. More dangerous than these responses were those which recommended a life of renunciation. A streak of this type of thinking is clearly visible in *Sehjyana Vaisnavism*. Abandon in the sense of looking detachedly at the problem would have been positive but abandon in the sense of indulging in it as the end in itself was certainly a devitalizing factor. A few responses were obviously good and useful, as for instance, one fashioned by some of the reformers of Bhakti Movement but even these were sporadic and incomplete attempts. These could vaguely be described as comprehensive and touched only the periphery of different problems.

The Hindu society already suffering from the crisis of faith and of social disintegration, suffered another blow at the hands of Islamic society which established its political hegemony during the 12th and 13th centuries and had chosen to stay in India. The Muslims had a civilization of their own, which laid stress on two points which were sure to attract the Indians. One was social equality and the other was the faith in the oneness of God and brotherhood of mankind. Both these points were complementary to each other on the social plane. Besides, the Muslims had political predominance and were in a position to use ample means of patronage. As a result of that situation coupled with caste based division of Hindu society, many Hindus, particularly from the lower strata, chose to go into the fold of Islam.

In the course of time, the Islamic society also developed many weaknesses. Islamic leaders alienated themselves from the general masses and reduced themselves to a group interested only in their individual welfare. The religion and the social laws were all harnessed to buttress the aforesaid tendency. Thus, the Muslim masses were also thrown in the vortex of confusion. Though, the *Sufis* amongst the Muslims continued to show the right path yet even they could not stem the rot that was gradually creeping in.

Sikhism was the product of the social dichotomy and political situation that had thus been created. It was an organisation to meet the social and religious challenges thrown up by the situation as also to provide a solution to the varied socio-politico-religious problems likely to emerge in future. It originated with Guru Nanak (b. April 1469, d. 1539). He was followed by a continuous line of nine successors who for nearly two centuries guided the destiny of Sikhism the followers of Guru Nanak ideology. The institution of the Guru ended with the demise of Guru Gobind Singh in 1708, who bestowed it on Sri Guru Granth Sahib for ever.

The ultimate objective of Guru Nanak was to regenerate the individual and the society. To achieve this object, he evolved a program of action. He advocated strict monotheism which was totally different from that of Hinduism.

The concept of Godhead of Hinduism is expressed through plurality of deities, whereas Guru Nanak believed neither in gods and goddesses nor even in the reincarnations of God. His God was infinite, beyond time and space, and self-existent. He never dies nor is He ever born. Nanak disapproved of the worship of idols because people tended to look upon them as God Himself. Nanak believed that God is *Sat* (Truth and Reality), Fearless and Beyond animosity. This being so, he not only made God a spiritual concept but also based his principles of social behaviour on his concept of God. Since He is Truth, Beyond Fear and Enmity; to speak untruth, to nurse enmity and to act coward-like is irreligious. A good Sikh, therefore, must not only believe that God is one and the only one, Omnipotent and Omniscient, but also conduct himself towards his fellow-beings in a manner that should not look untruthful, filled with prejudice or animosity towards anyone. He should always be merciful towards his fellow beings, ever ready to forget and forgive.

Nanak believed that the power that is God, cannot be

defined because He is *Nirankar* (formless)[1]. All descriptions of God are consequently admission of man's inability to define Him :

> Thou hast a million eyes, yet no eye hast thou.
> Thou hast a million feet, yet no feet hast Thou.
> Thou hast a million forms, yet no form hast Thou.
> Thou art without feet, yet no feet are without Thee.
> Thou art without odor, yet millions of odors emanate from Thee.
> With such charms, O Lord, hast Thou bewitched me.
> Thy light pervades everywhere.   (*SGGS*, p. 663)

Nanak addressed God by a variety of names, such as *Pita* (Father), *Pritam* (Lover), *Khasam* (Master), *Data* (The Great Giver). Nanak did this to show human dependence on God rather than invest him with anthropomorphic qualities. Although Nanak used both Hindu and Muslim nomenclatures for God such as *Ram, Govind, Hari, Murari, Rab* and *Karim* etc., yet the attribute he usually ascribes to Him was of *Sat Kartar* (True Creator) or *Sat Nam* (True Name).

According to Nanak, the Guru's help is essential for the realization of God. But who is the Guru ? Nanak uses the term Guru in three senses : (i) The Guru is God; (ii) The Guru is the voice of God; (iii) The Guru is word, the truth of God. How can one reconcile these three senses of the term Guru ? Apparently these terms do not reflect any identity. But on probing deep into the matter, one would find the basic identity which these three senses possess. The Guru in the sense of a perfect man who has realized God answers to all these different connotations of the term. He is the voice of God, the word of God, indeed God Himself. Such a perfect man's guidance is indispensable for any progress on the road to realization of the Truth.

The ultimate object of a man is to be God-like, capable of enjoying the Absolute into himself, in the fullness of its self-consciousness. Thus he must imbibe all those qualities which emanate from the Truth, such as love, humility, honesty, compassion, contentment, truthfulness etc.

The greatest enemy of a man towards the realisation of

---

1. *Nā tis(u) rūp(u) na rekhiā kāī.*   (*SGGS*, p. 750.)

Truth is *Haumai*[1] (Egocentricity) which involves him in worldly attachments, creating impediments in his path of seeking Truth. All the activities of an unregenerate man are guided by *Haumai*. Even that which a man calls right or good is done only if it is in accord with his *Haumai*. And if it is not in keeping with it, it is rejected. Without getting rid of *Haumai* the path to ultimate realization cannot be recognised.

The mind of the unregenerate man expresses itself in the evil impulses which are : *Kam* (lust); *Karodh* (anger); *Lobh* (greed); *Moh* (attachment to worldly things); and *Hankar* (pride).[2]

To him the best course to control the surges of these evil forces was to practice meditation on *Nam*, ever remembrance of God, realization of His presence everywhere and in all objects, inanimate and animate. *Nam* is the remedy for the sick or diseased world. *Nam* is realization, the coming of God's grace within oneself which obliterates the sense of duality and makes one not only himself, but be a part and link of God.

In order to realize Him through *Nam*, one will have to observe its discipline. He must lead an ethical life, offer prayers, enjoy the company of *sadh sangat* (holy men) and develop an attitude of *seva* (selfless service).

The person who realises *Nam* makes no distinction between the individual and the universal. He becomes *Gurmukh* who always have good of His creation at heart. He does not abjure the world but lives in it like a lotus in water. He is a *Panch*, Plato's philosopher King, a *Brahm-giani*—one who has realised God and has acquired Divine Knowledge. Such a person does not fear anybody. The *Panch* is an ideal man in the concept of the Guru. His qualities have been described by Guru Nanak in his composition titled *Japji*. He is a saint in religion, a true statesman in politics–all his actions are guided by *Bibek Budh* (Sense of Discrimination). He is *Jiwan*

1. *Hau vich(i) āiā hau vich(i) gaiā.*
   Hau vich(i) jamiā hau vich(i) muā.
   Hau vich(i) ditā hau vich(i) laiā.
   Hau vich(i) khaṭiā hau vich(i) gaiā. (SGGS, p. 466)
2. *Is dehī andar(i) panch chor vaseh kām(u) krodh(u) lob(u) moh(u) ahankārā.*
   Amrit(u) looteh(n) manmukh nahī būjheh koe na sune pukārā. (SGGS, p. 600)

mukt (Liberated in Life) enjoying perfect release while living in the world. He attains perfection in virtue and happiness. Although the limitations of the body and the world are there, yet they do not restrict this perfection which is more of the soul than of the body. For him, perfection does not come after death. It is attained while the *Panch* is alive. He negates the influence of *Haumai* and feels one with the nature. This type of person always operates within God's *Hukam* (Divine Order). Guru Nanak believed in the traditional theories of *Karma*, Rebirth and Transmigration of soul. But he also believed that the bondages of Karma are capable of being conquered or surmounted through self-exertion and divine grace.

Guru Nanak preferred a householder's life to the life of a recluse. The Guru himself led a householder's life and impressed upon the people that this life is not an impediment on the pathway to bliss and self-emancipation, thus bringing out clearly the importance of living a full-fledged and fullsome life in the world.

The poetic compositions of Guru Nanak are replete with vitriolic criticism of meaningless superstitions, Brahmanical rituals, caste prejudices, untouchability and religious expatiations. The society which the Guru envisaged stemmed from his personal experience of the unity of mankind and oneness of God. The three basics of his social philosophy were *Kirt karo, Nam Japo* and *Wand chhako. Kirt karo* means that one should earn one's livelihood by honest creative labour. *Wand chhako* signifies that one must share the fruits of one's labour with one's fellow creatures who could be devoid of basic necessities of life. Such acts instil the spirit of selflessness or sacrifice. *Nam Japo* means meditate on *Nam*, i.e., no one should lose sight of the cosmic process and the divine will permeate everything in the world.

Besides this, if the society is to endure and overcome successfully the stress of different challenges, it is imperative for its members to be ethical in their attitude and behaviour at all levels. The Guru roundly condemned the unethical attitude of the people.

No changes can be brought about by creative thoughts alone. Requisite institutions have to be created to give a local habitation and endurance to it. Guru Nanak created institutions such as *Sangat, Pangat* and *Kirtan* for further promotion of his cause. *Sangat* was an assembly of like-minded people engaged in the pursuit of Truth. This organisation was open to all persons irrespective of their social status and cast-affiliations etc. As a matter of fact, the Guru used it as an instrument to shape the Sikh psyche and promote the Sikh ideals of a casteless, classless and egalitarian society. It was also to be an organization to knit the Sikh together to give them a corporate character. *Guru Ka Langar* (community kitchen) was another important institution created by the Guru. This institution possessed the potentiality of a valuable instrument of social reform in a setting where caste taboos prevented people from sitting and eating together. Therefore, from the very outset, the institution of *Langar* was integrally associated with the *Sangat*. This institution was of great significance. It went towards erasing social and economic inequality in a big way. Everyone irrespective of caste and creed, social status, sex and birth was to sit and eat the same food. Therefore it served as a medium of social integration between the high and the low, thereby landing a mighty blow to the caste system and untouchability. The kitchen was run with voluntary contributions made by the Guru's devotees in money or kind.

Kirtan was another institution that held great significance. *Kirtan* implies singing of the praises of the Lord, which is generally the theme of the compositions of the Guru in the accompaniment of musical instruments and in accordance with musical measures. *Kirtan* was done in congregations both in the early hours of the morning and in the evening following the conclusion of the day's work. This institution contributed substantially in fine tuning the thinking of the disciples and inducing them to work for the causes as preached by the Guru.

Guru Nanak, undertook extensive tours in the North, South, East and West of the Indian subcontinent and beyond and visited important centres of the Hindus, Muslims, Buddhists, Jains and Jogis meeting people of different races, tribes and cultural patterns in order to spread his teachings amongst them. His travels were spanned over a period of nearly thirty years.

During his first *Udasi*[1] (Odyssey) he traversed (in terms of the modern political geography of India and Pakistan) Haryana, Delhi, Uttar Pradesh, Bihar, Bengal, Orissa, Madras, Kerala, Mysore, Andhra Pradesh, Maharashtra, Gujrat and West Pakistan. The most important places visited by him were Kurukshetra, Panipat, Hardwar, Joshi Math, Gorakh Matta, Golam, Ayudhya, Prayag, Benaras, Gaya, Patna, Dhubri, Dhampur, Gauhati, Shillong, Sillhet, Dacca, Puri, Cuttock, Gantur, Kanchipuram and Tiruchirapalli. From Tiruchirapalli the Guru sailed down the Kaveri river and reached Nagapatnam, a very old port of South India. From there he proceeded to Ceylon where he visited such places as Betticola, Katargam and Sita Waka. The last named place is also called Sita Eliya from the tradition of Sita having spent her period of captivity here. At the time of Guru Nanak's visit, this place was in the Kotte kingdom of Raja Dhrama Prakarma. The inscription discovered by Dr. W.S. Karuna Ratna[2] and Parana Vitama in the famous museum of Anuradh Pura furnished a brief account of the encounter of Janakacharya (Nanak) with the Buddhist Bhikshu Dhrama Kirt-Sthavira. This inscription also informs us that Raja Dhrama Prakrama-bahu had promised to embrace Nanak's creed if he won in the debate. Nanak won. But before he could embrace Nanak's creed, the Brahmins very cleverly got arranged another public debate, this time between Nanak and Dvaja Pandita and manipulated the result in favour of the latter. In this way, they did not allow the ruler to fall under the influence of Nanak. At Manner, the Guru left Ceylon and sailed for Rameshwaram wherefrom he proceeded to Trivandrum. On his way back to Talwandi, the

---

1. According to *Miharban wali Janam Sakhi*, three *Udāsīs* were undertaken by the Guru. In the first *Udāsī* the Guru travels the places in the East and in South India. In his second *Udāsī* Northward and Westward journeys have been combined while in the third *Udāsī*, the Guru visited the places in the Punjab. *Puratan Janam Sakhi* makes mention of five journeys or *Udāsīs*. According to it, the Eastward and Southward Journeys were covered by two separate *Udāsīs* and the Guru's visit to different places within the Punjab by the fifth *Udāsī*.
2. Museum Register M. 111. According to the learned W.S. Karuna Ratna, Janakcharya was the same as Nanakacharya or Guru Nanak (Surjit Singh Gandhi, *History of the Sikh Gurus*, pp. 98-99).

Guru visited important places such as Bidar, Nanded, Baroach, Somnath, Dwarka, Girnar Rocks, Jagannath, Ujjain, Ajmer and Mathura, Sirsa, Pak Pattan and Talwandi.

The second tour took the Guru into the interior of the Himalayan region where he visited the Kangra valley, the Spiti tableland, Western Tibet, Ladakh, Kashmir and Punjab (Pakistan).

Images of Guru Nanak are said to be present in some temples of Tibet and Ladakh. There is a class of people living in this area who have substituted or added[1] the Mantra *'Om Aham, Bhadra Guru Parm Sidhi Hum'*, to the usual Buddhist Mantra, *Om Mani Padmi Hami*. It is these men in whose temples the image of Nanak has been given a permanent place. Kargil, Amarnath, Pehalgam, Mattan, Anant Nag, Srinagar, Baramula and Hasan Abdal were visited by the Guru. After that enroute to Talwandi, he sojourned at Bal Godai and Sialkot.

The Guru undertook his third missionary travel to the Muslim countries of West Asia in the garb of a Muslim devotee. Some prominent places connected with this tour of the Guru were Multan, Uch, Hinglaj, Mecca, Medina, Baghdad, Mashad, Herat, Kandhar, Kabul, Para Chinnar, Gorakh Hatri (Peshawar) and Saidpur. From Saidpur, the Guru proceeded to Talwandi and from there to Sultanpur. On the way, he came to the settlement named Kartarpur (City of the Creator) where he lived a normal householder's life for nearly 20 years. Even during this period, he undertook short tour in the Punjab. One of them, according to Bhai Gurdas, was his visit to Achal Vatala and the other to Multan and Pak Pattan. At the latter place, he met Shaikh Ibrahim while at Multan he was accorded a hearty welcome by Makhdom Bahauddin. During his tours, he gave his message to as many people as possible. His message was meant for all, irrespective of region, country, clime, caste or creed. He had a cosmic vision and earnestness to build a global society on the basis of faith in the oneness of God, unity of mankind, dignity of labour and sharing of the fruits of labour with others.

1. Sewa Ram Singh, *The Divine Master.*

On September 22, 1539 A.D. Guru Nanak passed away. According to *Puratan Janam Sakhi*, "Before Nanak's death, a quarrel arose between his Hindu and Muslim followers regarding disposal of his mortal remains. The former wished to cremate it whereas the later desired to bury it." Nanak said to them : 'Let the Hindus place flowers on my right and the Musalmans on my left. They whose flowers are found fresh tomorrow may have the disposal of the body.' After the flowers had been set on each side of him, Nanak drew his sheet over the flowers as well as over himself. Next morning, the sheet was found unchanged. When the sheet was removed, both sets of flowers were found equally fresh whereas the body had disappeared.' The version obviously seems to be a myth. But one thing which emerges is that he was loved alike both by the Hindus and the Muslim.

Before Guru Nanak breathed his last, he selected his successor and commissioned him to carry on the work he had started. The nomination of Bhai Lehna to the Guruship who became known as Guru Angad, was, in the words of Indu-bhushan Banerjee, "a fact of the profoundest significance." Trumpp writes, "The disciples of Nanak would no doubt have been dispersed and gradually disappeared as well, as the disciples of many other Gurus before Nanak, if he had not taken care to appoint a successor before his death."[1]

The period from Guru Angad Dev (Guruship 1539; d. 1552) the immediate successor of Guru Nanak, to Guru Arjan Dev, fifth in the line of succession constituted the first phase in the development of Sikhism. During this period, (A.D. 1539-1606) it made rapid strides organisationally as well as in strength and developed into a distinct community. Guru Angad during his ministry did his best to consolidate Sikhism. Guru Nanak had concerned himself more or less with the fundamentals and had left details to be taken care of by his successors. Guru Angad took care to interpret and re-emphasize the message of Guru Nanak in unambiguous terms and in a down-to-earth manner. He successfully met the challenges of *Udasis*, a sect founded by Baba Sri Chand, eldest

---

1. Trumpp, *Adi Granth*, IXX, VII.

son of Guru Nanak. Baba Sri Chand held strong belief in asceticism and renunciation (*Udas*) of the world as the correct path-way to eternal bliss and quoted Guru Nanak as the progenitor and upholder of this view. This view of Baba Sri Chand was obviously a mis-statement of the Guru's gospel. However Baba Sri Chand's impact on the masses was quite significant and wide-spread because of his heredity and the natural tendency of the Indian people to put premium on asceticism. Guru Angad, therefore took prompt steps and made it clear in unequivocal terms to his disciples that Sikhism was essentially a religion of householders. It was also declared that the *Udasis*, followers of Baba Sri Chand, even if they held faith in most of Guru Nanak's tenets were not true Sikhs. By doing so, Guru Angad, barred the door to asceticism and made the influence of Guru Nanak available not only for religious uplift but also for social regeneration. Thus *Udasism* could not become a mass movement, much less a part of the Sikh faith. By preaching vigorously the essentials of Sikhism coupled with certain other steps, the Guru tried to create distinct consciousness which went a long way in preserving Sikhism from merging into Hinduism and his disciples from being absorbed back into the Hindu masses. He collected the hymns of Guru Nanak and committed them to writing. He is also believed to have got prepared the *Janam Sakhi* of Guru Nanak by Bhai Bala. The collection of the hymns of Guru Nanak provided a focal point of piety and doctrine for those Sikhs who did not live at Khadur, the headquarter of Guru Angad Dev. Moreover, it gave definite directions to the faith of the Sikhs, besides providing a living proof of the Sikh doctrine that there was no essential difference between the Guru and his *Shabad* (Word). In addition, he made Punjabi language in *Gurmukhi* script as the vehicle of his thought and preaching. Some traditions ascribe the invention of the *Gurmukhi* script to him but one hymn of Guru Nanak's composed in the form of an acrostic shows that the alphabets already existed. The renaming of the existing *Takri* script and the instruction that it should be used for recording the Guru's hymns may well have been Guru Angad's decision. The significance of the adoption of the script and of extensive use of Punjabi language lies in the fact that the Guru rejected the foreign Arabic script and emphasised that unless the people adopted a script which was their own and which suited them as a vehicle of communication amongst themselves, their culture could not grow. Moreover, it landed a severe blow to the Brahmins who through their monopoly of the knowledge of Sanskrit had given currency to the belief that their superiority or prestige was ordained by God or gods. According to Gokal Chand Narang, "the name of the script reminded those who employed it, of their duty towards their Guru and constantly kept alive in their minds the consciousness that they were something distinct from the common mass of Hindus."

Moreover Guru Angad continued to impress upon his disciples the utility of *Sangat* and *Pangat*. Both these institutions gave a sense of unity and identity to the Sikhs. Another step of building the city of Goindwal, also played a great part in giving consciousness and distinctiveness to the Sikhs.

In the city of Goindwal, no separate ward was marked for low castes or for any particular community. Anybody could build his house anywhere. Attempts were made here in a systematic manner that Sikh values should be imbibed by the people. This is why there still persist memories that in the Sikh cities, no one could die of hunger, because in addition to *Guru ka Langar*, kitchen in each house was run as if it was *Guru's own*. The city of Goindwal indeed did a lot to shape the Sikh psyche and to propagate the Sikh ideology.

Guru Angad nominated Amar Das as his successor in 1552. He was then seventy-three years old. He held his ministry for twenty-two years until he expired in 1574. From 1540 to 1552, he had been in the company of Guru Angad Dev and had drunk deep at the fount of inspiration that Guru Angad Dev was. He had also imbibed fully the Sikh ethos and judged for himself how useful Sikhism was to bring about regeneration. Besides this, he must have gauged the extent of dangers threatening its existence and also the urgency of speedy development of the organisation of Sikhism.

The age-old reverence for the places of Hindu pilgrimage in the psyche of the followers of Guru Nanak's religion could only be removed gradually. It demanded something genuine as an alternative to assuage their misconceived notion of washing away their sins and achieving emancipation. Guru had realised that such visits of the Sikhs at Hindu places of pilgrims expose them to the guile of clever Brahmans creating all sorts of doubts in their mind beside swindling them of their hard-earned money for performing of infructuous rituals. The Guru, therefore, built a *Baoli* at Goindwal. This was a well with eighty-four steps leading down to the surface of the water. The water of this well was considered sacred, and a wash with it was regarded as an act of great spiritual merit. A tradition gradually got woven round it that whoever attentively and reverently recites the *Japuji* on every step after taking a dip in the *Baoli* would escape from the wanderings of the eighty-four lacs living creatures. The Guru fixed the first day of the Baisakhi as the day for the annual gathering of the Sikhs.

The *Baoli*, apart from catering to the need of the people for water, had deep effect on the psychology of the people. The Sikhs started visiting the place in large numbers and this afforded an opportunity to the Guru to come into close contact with them. Out of this close contact sprang the devotion for the Guru which proved to be a strong force to bind them to Sikhism. He also chose the site for a new religious centre where the construction work was started by the Guru himself and progressing rapidly under the supervision of Bhai Jetha. This ultimately became the site for the city of Amritsar.

The institutions of *Sangat* and *Pangat* received great fillip at the hands of Guru Amar Das. The Guru had issued a fiat : *"Pehle Pangat Peechhe Sangat"* (First eat together and then meet together). The fiat was implemented rigidly. When Akbar paid a visit to Guru Amar Das at Goindwal, he could not see the Guru without first taking food in *Guru ka Langar.* The *Guru ka Langar* was made a means of emphasising the unity and equality of mankind. Through this common meal the Guru demanded indirectly that all who came to him, Hindu or Muslim, Brahmin or untouchable, emperor or beggar, should lay aside their prejudices. The institution of *Langar*, in fact was a powerful device for expressing the theoretical notion of equality in a practical way. It also epitomised the cardinal faith that God was the Eternal Giver.

Besides this, the Guru preached vigorously what he stood for. He composed a large number of hymns and exhorted his followers to recite them and told them that whosoever imbibed and practised their essence would acquire divine traits. In quite a few verses, he emphasised that the Guru's *Shabad* was superior to everything else and the Sikhs were advised to use only the Guru's *Shabad* in worship.

Guru Amar Das maintained the tradition of Guru Nanak's social reforms. He condemned caste system, untouchability and the customs of *Sati* and *Purdah*. All these prevalent Hindu social customs were dehumanising and at best catered to the interests of only a particular class. He advocated equality in terms of sex, creed and caste on the basis of universal brotherhood of man. He encouraged intercaste marriages as well as widows re-marrying. He condemned idolatry both on spiritual and social grounds. Guru's God being formless and infinite was beyond description within the known vocabulary. Idolatry involving worship and deification of different gods was socially damaging as it engendered wrong consciousness about God and often gave rise to groups, each considering its deity as supreme and itself superiormost, thereby obstructing the growth of universal consciousness.

The Guru abandoned the prevailing birth and death rites of the Hindus. They were too many and too costly, beside being against the Sikh concept and Sikh spirit. The Guru advised his followers to give up these rites and in their place prescribed a simple ceremony which mostly consisted of singing of holy hymns from *Gurbani*.[1]

The upshot of all these measures was that Sikhism began to emerge as a distinct entity. In the accomplishment of his task, the Guru received great assistance from the liberal character of Akbar's policy. As was expected, the orthodox sections in the Hindu society did not take kindly to the teachings of Guru Amar Das. They complained to the Emperor more than once against his unorthodox ways. Once they even led a deputation and submitted a lengthy memorandum to the Emperor, levelling

---

1. The fact is corroborated by Baba Sundar ji's composition in *Rāg Rāmkalī* under the name of *Sadd* on page 923 of *SGGS*.

a series of charges against him. The orthodox Muslim elements also disliked the Guru's mode of preaching.

The Guru deputed his most trusted follower Bhai Jetha to the Emperor's court to answer the charges. The complaint was ultimately dismissed. A few years later, the Emperor personally waited upon the Guru at Goindwal and even ate in the common kitchen run by the devotees under the directions of the Guru. The tradition goes that the Emperor also made a land grant in the name of the Guru's daughter Bibi Bhani before his departure from there. All this gave a boost to the Sikhs and for the rest of the reign of Akbar all adversaries of the Sikhs were silenced.

The liberalism of Akbar's religious policy helped the Guru in yet another way. Muslim orthodoxy was in low spirits during the period because Akbar had withdrawn his patronage to it. It had retaliated by trying to harm the Emperor once or twice but they had met with utter failure each time. As a result, Sikhism under Guru Amar Das, and in fact for many years thereafter, experienced no difficulty from Muslim orthodoxy. Stray incidents created by a few Shaikh families settled at Goindwal however had no impact on the progress of Sikhism. At their instance, a group of young boys caused some harassment to the Sikhs, engaged in fetching water from the river Beas for the Guru's kitchen. But it was only a localised affair and the conflict seems to have arisen not from any religious cause but was probably the outcome of some local discord of a mundane nature.

The ever increasing population of the Sikhs needed sustained guidance, co-ordination of all efforts and some sort of cohesive administrative system. To this purpose the institution of *Manjis* was established. The word *Manji* literally signifies a 'cot' or a *Charpoy,* a common Indian bedstead. But here it denotes a responsible religious position conferred by the Guru upon one of his prominent devotees, or a seat of delegated authority. The Guru appointed 22[1] missionaries to

---

1. The names of the appointees are—(1) Sawan Mal, (2) Sachan Shah, (3) Paro, (4) Lallu, (5) Sadharan, (6) Khanna Chhaura, (7) Dipa, (8) Mallu Shah, (9) Kedara, (10) Mahesa Dhir, (11) Bhika, (12) Manak Chand, (13) Gangu Shah, (14) Mathu Murari, (15) Kheda Aseri, (16) Handal, (17) Beni Pandit, (18) Phirya, (19) Katara, (20) Prema, (21) Mai Das, (22) Allahyar.

carry on the work of proselytisation. Mr. Macauliffe, Indubhushan Banerjee, Kirpal Singh Narang and Hari Ram Gupta has taken *Manji* in the sense of some sort of a territorial unit which does not seem to be correct. Two explanations may be offered against the opinion of these writers considering the *Manji* in the sense of a territorial unit. The first—that they have uncritically followed Macauliffe who was probably the first person to advocate a *Manji* as a unit of territory. The second is a backward projection of a later idea. When *Masands* were appointed in the time of fourth and fifth Gurus, each *Masand* was assigned a particular area to operate in. The same analogy had been employed by our writers in the case of *Manjis* as well. Here also a good deal of responsibility for the confusion rests on the shoulders of Macauliffe. He may not have been fully familiar with Indian traditions but was very well acquainted with the traditions of the Christian church in his own country, England.[1]

The demarcation of the Sikh spiritual influence into districts or provinces, or whatever that may be, is irrelevant to the *Manji* system as conceived by Guru Amar Das. None of the Sikh writers writing before the close of the nineteenth century ever tried to impart the territorial sense to it. Whenever any reference is made by them to the institution of *Manji*, the import is invariably spiritual rather than territorial or temporal. Take, for example, Giani Gian Singh, the author of *Panth Parkash*. He refers in some detail to the grant of *Manjis* by Guru Amar Das to Bhai Manak Chand, Handal and Gangu Shah. In each sense, the grant is shown as a reward for selfless and devoted service rendered by the devotee. It may well be inferred from this that the *Manji* system was not a territorial demarcation of the Sikh spiritual empire as is commonly believed but a missionary order. The grant of a *Manji* to a person therefore meant the conferment upon him the membership of this missionary order.

Only men of recognised piety and sterling integrity were awarded the distinction of heading the *Manji*. It was also an essential qualification that they understood and practised the

---

1. For details refer to Surjit Singh Gandhi's Book, *History of the Sikh Gurus.*

teachings of the Sikh Gurus correctly. They conducted their missionary work individually as well as through *Sangats* (congregations). But they did not always confine themselves to their native places. On the contrary, whenever possible and convenient, they moved about in the countryside carrying the torch of the Guru's message. They maintained their connection with the Guru at the centre by means of a periodical visit, more often on the annual Baisakhi fair, a tradition that was started at Goindwal. Besides their preaching work, some of them, taught *Gurmukhi* script to the people and wrote *Pothis* containing Guru's hymns for free distribution among the people. Another important function performed by the *Manji* holders was to initiate fresh people into the fold of Sikhism. The method adopted was the same as was being used by the Guru at the centre. This was known as *Charnamrit*, meaning 'nectar of the foot'. This was nothing but pure water sanctified by the dip of a toe of the Guru in it. Anyone who desired to become a Sikh was administered a palmful of this sanctified water. But this method, though simple and inexpensive, presented one great difficulty. Since it was directly linked with the person of the Guru, the initiation could be performed only where the Guru was personally present. Naturally this imposed a great constraint on missionary work. This problem was solved by empowering the grantees of *manjis* to get new entrants into the Sikh fold through the administration of their own *Charnamrit*. The Sikhs thus enrolled were named *Sehling*, meaning associates. The innovation thus introduced answered an urgent Sikh need of the time and immensely helped in the spread of Sikhism.

Guru Amar Das, with his clarity of vision and his determined policy to lend a distinctive entity to the Sikhs not only established the Sikh community and saved it from a possible relapse into Brahmanical Hinduism but also paved the way for its rapid strides in future. The danger of the Sikhs yielding to the pressures of Hinduism or of falling under the spell of ascetic parasites was largely warded off. Then there was also a great deal of expansion in their ranks. In short, the Sikhs were now well-set on the road to becoming a cohesive and fast growing community with a definite ideology, and a distinct institutional structure. The benefits of the great work commenced and accomplished by Guru Amar Das were reaped by his successors, particularly Guru Ram Das and Guru Arjan Dev.

Guru Amar Das was succeeded by Guru Ram Das. Originally called Jetha, he was born in a *Sodhi* family of Chuna Mandi, Lahore on September 24, 1534. While serving along with other Sikhs in the construction of the *Baoli* at Goindwal, he attracted the attention of Guru Amar Das, and received the hand of his daughter Bibi Bhani in marriage. Thereafter he stayed with his father-in-law, and was closely associated with his ministry. He put on record many incidents connected with the struggle that his Master had with his opponents, and as such his writings are a store-house of information about the period. He had made himself so indispensable that his choice for the *Gur-gaddi* was a forgone conclusion.

In order to avoid any possible unpleasantness with the close relatives of the last Guru, he shifted his residence to *Guru ka Chak* the present site of Amritsar which had been chosen by Guru Amar Das himself and where construction work had already begun.

During his ministry, Guru Ram Das further consolidated the institutions of *Sangat, Pangat* and *Kirtan.* He also saw to the planning and construction of the new city of Amritsar. He caused *Amritsar* (Lake of Nectar) and *Santokhsar* (Lake of Contentment) to be excavated. He appointed *Masands* who performed the dual role of Sikh missionaries and collectors of devotees voluntary offerings. Each *Masand* was allotted a definite area to preach and to collect the offerings. *Masand* is a corrupted version of the Persian word *Masnad.* Though the exact number of *Masands* and their respective areas are not known, yet it is certain that very many Sikhs known for their piety and integrity were asked to function as *Masands.* In Guru Ram Das's time, the *Masands* were usually named as *Ram Dasias.* It was only in the time of Guru Arjan Dev that they began to be called *Masands* almost exclusively. In keeping with the policy of his predecessors, the Guru asked his followers to avoid singing filthy songs on social occasions such as marriage, child birth as was customary and instead, he composed hymns which were akin, to *Ghori,*

Sithnian in their poetical form to be sung on the aforesaid social occasions.

Guru Ram Das had three sons, of whom he considered Arjan Dev, the youngest, most suited to succeed him. This aroused the ire of the eldest, Prithi Chand. Nevertheless, when the Guru saw that his end was near, he nominated Arjan Dev as the fifth Guru. Guru Ram Das expressed "that as one lamp is lighted from another, so the Guru's spirit will pass into him and dispel the darkness in the world." Guru Arjan's path was beset with many pitfalls. Akbar's liberalism instead of being utilized by the Hindus to fashion new responses to the new challenges was used to rehabilitate or perpetuate the orthodox Brahmanical beliefs and caste-ridden society. Naturally, the protagonists of Hindu orthodoxy were unhappy with Sikhism.

Besides, the bulk of the people had come into the fold of Sikhism as a result of the efforts of the earlier Gurus. These people were mostly drawn from the commercial class, dwelling in towns. They possessed intelligence, wealth, organising ability and practical knowledge of the world in ample measures. The gradual entry of the peasant class into the fold of Sikhism, initially during the time of Guru Amar Das, warranted new adjustments in the body-social and the body-spiritual of the Sikh movement. It became imperative for the Guru to frame programs to harness their proverbial energy and enterprising spirit in the interest of the Sikh community and the ideals it stood for. But it was no ordinary task; because to strike harmony between a mercantile class and the peasantry was a tedious problem in view of two factors : (i) the Jats were a clan of warlike habits; (ii) there was wide divergence between the respective outlooks and interests of the two groups.

However, unbaffled by the complex nature of the problem and not withstanding the trouble fomented by his brother Prithi Chand, Guru Arjan Dev addressed himself to the task of further consolidation and extension of the *Sikh Panth*. His approach to the problem was institutional, social and psychological. Like his predecessors, he built up new townships to serve as religious centres providing cohesiveness to the nascent religion. In 1588, he completed the tasks of excavation

of two tanks named *Santokhsar* and *Amritsar*. The side walls of
Amritsar (Tank of Nectar) were made *pucca* with the voluntary
and collective efforts of the Sikhs. Having completed this tank,
he decided to build the temple, reverently called 'Darbar Sahib'
meaning the Court of the Lord, in its midst. Instead of building
the shrine on a high plinth as the Hindu architectural style was,
Guru Arjan had it built on a level lower than the surrounding
land, to make the worshippers climb down the steps to enter
it. And, unlike, Hindu temple, which had only one entrance,
the Guru provided four doors on the four sides of the temple.
These architectural features were intended to be symbolic of
the Sikh faith which aimed at building a brotherhood which
does not recognise any distinctions on the bases of caste and
creed. Its four doors[1] signified that the temple was open to all
the four castes of Hindus and to all the people of the world
from North, South, East and West. In due course, flourishing
city called Amritsar after the name of one of the tank grew up
around this Sikh shrine. The Guru himself played no meagre
role for the growth and development of this city.

Another religious centre was established at Tarn Taran.
In 1590, Guru Arjan chose the site for building this new
township in the heart of *Majha*, or mid country lying between
Rivers Beas and Ravi. Guru Arjan excavated a tank and built
a temple which formed the nucleus of the new town. The tank
was named Tarn Taran, around which the city developed. The
city too began to be called Tarn Taran. In 1594, another
township named Kartarpur was founded in the Jalandhar
Doab. To begin with, a well was dug there, which was
named *Gangsar* or the Ganges Tank. The Sikhs were advised
to regard the water of the well as sacred as the water of the
Ganges was to the Hindus. It obviously was an attempt to
wean the Sikhs away from visiting Ganges held sacred in their
psyche so far. A *Baoli* at Dabbi Bazar, Lahore was also built by
the Guru.

The Guru undertook extensive tour of the *Majha* and
Doaba regions of the Punjab. He visited Sarhali, Bhaini,
Khanpur, Khanna, Kartarpur etc. The Guru also preached in

---

1. *Khatrī Brāhman sūd vais updes(u) chau varnā kao sājhā.*   (SGGS, p. 747)

the Dakha region. He visited Khem Karan, Chunian and many other places. He paid a visit to the shrine of Guru Nanak at Dehra Baba Nanak. From there he proceeded to Barath to meet Baba Sri Chand, son of Guru Nanak. The Baba received him with great warmth and urged him to continue his mission with vigour. The Guru had started his missionary travels in 1588 and completed the same in 1594.

As a result of all these steps, the rank of the Sikhs swelled fast. To integrate them and also to collect funds for his construction works, the Guru reorganised the *Masand* system. Some of the *Masands* already appointed had shown divided loyalty or were unfit to carry on the work expected of them. The Guru gave a new dimension to the system. He issued instructions to the *Masands* to the effect that they, henceforth, would look after both the secular and spiritual affairs of the Sikhs. They would foster among the Sikhs keen interest in trade, industry and other occupation and at the same time endeavour to keep them together as members of a common brotherhood. They were also required to collect *Daswandh* one tenth part of their earnings which the Sikhs were enjoined upon to contribute to *Golak* (Guru's Treasury). *Daswandh* was levied for the maintenance of the Sikh church and to undertake works of social welfare. It was the duty of the *Masand* to send the amount thus collected to the Guru regularly and procure a receipt against that. It should, however be remembered that the *Masands* were not permitted to touch a penny out of these offerings. *Masands* were required to pay a visit to Amritsar at the annual Baisakhi fair. Thus a regular contact was maintained between the Guru and the *Masands*. At certain places, where the number of the Sikhs was too large, the *Masand* was allowed to appoint his agents called *Sangtia* or *Masandia* or *Meora*.

The *Masand* system as an institution conferred many benefits and played a significant role in the evolution of the *Sikh Panth*. It trained the Sikhs in secular affairs and introduced a sort of order to which the Sikh masses became habituated. Moreover, it attracted a large number of converts. According to Mohsin Fani, "the number of these secretaries increased everywhere so much that in the time of Guru Arjan, it became very considerable and at last there was no place in the country where Sikhs were not to be found."

On June 14, 1595 his only son, Hargobind, was born at Vadali near Amritsar where the Guru retired for some time to avoid clash with his brother Prithi Chand. The birth of a son, however, increased the hostility of Prithi Chand who now saw no chance for his own son, Miharban to become Guru. Some hymns of Guru Arjan show that a few attempts were made on the life of his son who, however, was providentially saved to grow up a worthy successor of his father.

A work of far reaching significance that would cement the Sikh brotherhood was collection of *Gurbani* of his predecessor Gurus, as well as Bhagats of *Nirgun* school and compile it into a volume after editing it and including his own compositions. This volume was prepared by Bhai Gurdas ji, an eminent Sikh scholar of the time under the watchful eyes of Guru Arjan. The volume once ready was respectfully called *Adi Granth* or *Pothi Sahib*. It was then installed in the temple that had been constructed in the middle of *Amrit Sarovar*.

Many factors impressed the Guru for taking up this step. Sikhism is essentially a religion of the *Nam*. Its most religious trait was singing of Lord's praises, to the exclusion of all other ceremonies or rituals. Seeing the importance of this practice, many clever persons had begun to mix up spurious writings with the true compositions of the Gurus. In 1594, when Guru Arjan Dev returned from the religious tours of the *Majha* tract of the Punjab, he discovered that Prithi Chand had not been idle during his absence and had begun to compile an anthology of writings in which he was inserting compositions of his own son Sodhi Miharban. The Guru who was responsible for the organisation of Sikhism on sound and firm footings had to ensure unity of belief and practice. To this end he prepared an authentic compilation of the writings of the Gurus including his own. Moreover, Guru Amar Das had left definite instructions in the 23rd and 24th *pauries* of *Anand Sahib* that the real utterances of the Guru alone should be accepted and revered by the Sikhs. Besides, if the distinctive identity of the Sikhs was to be established, it was essential that they have their own scripture. The Sikhs had been oriented to own and hold *Gurmukhi* script and Panjabi language in high esteem. There was now a genuine need that they should have a separate religious book which should hold for them the same position as the Vedas do for the Hindus, the Bible for the Christians and the *Quran* for the Musalmans.

While the Guru was busy with canonisation of *Gurbani* including *Bhagat bani,* a report was sent to Akbar that Guru Arjan's sacred anthology under preparation contained passages vilifying Islam. Passing through Goindwal[1], the Emperor stopped enroute and asked to see the work. Baba Buddha ji and Bhai Gurdas ji brought a copy of the existent manuscript and opening it randomly read some of the hymns to Emperor Akbar. The Emperor, his fears dispelled, made an offering of fifty-one gold *Mohars* to the sacred text and gave robes of honour to the two disciples and sent one for Guru Arjan.

At the Guru's request, he also remitted the annual revenue of the district to ameliorate the condition of the peasants who had been hard hit by the failure of the monsoon.

In August 1604, the compilation work was completed and the *Granth Sahib* was formally installed in the temple at Amritsar. Baba Buddha ji was appointed the first reciter or *Granthi.*

The *Granth* thus prepared was an enormous volume consisting of over 5,500 hymns. Majority of these hymns were composed by the first five Gurus including Guru Arjan Dev. In 1706 Guru Gobind Singh ji included 59 *Shabads* and 57 *Shalokas* of Guru Tegh Bahadur assigning them appropriate place in the *Adi Granth.* In addition to all this the *Granth Sahib* includes the hymns of fifteen *Bhaktas* and *Sufis,* eleven *Bhatts,* *Var* (Ballad) of Satta and Balwand, Baba Sundar ji's elegy more correctly establishing the procedure to be followed at the time of demise. It is popularly known as *Ramkali Sadd.* The completion of the Sikh scripture was a major step forward. It became the most powerful instrument in spreading the teachings of the Gurus among the masses and forging a feeling of brotherhood. More than anything else, it created community consciousness among the Sikhs. It was also a contributory factor to the emergence of the Sikhs as a separate religion with a distinct ethos of its own.

---

1. *Akbar Nama* (Persian), Vol. III, p. 809.

Under Guru Arjan Dev, Sikhism made significant headway which was not to the liking of the Muslim orthodoxy. So long Akbar was alive, his favourable attitude protected Sikhism from the fury of the Muslim orthodoxy at a time when it had still not taken firm roots in the lives of the people. The strong and efficient administration of the Emperor established a stable peace in the land, which enabled the Sikhs to make rapid progress in their mission. The liberal character of the state allowed them full freedom to formulate and execute their plans of development. The remission of land revenue by Emperor Akbar at the instance of Guru Arjan Dev made the people look up to the Guru and his Sikhs as their friend and benefactor. This opened the flood gates for large-scale new admissions to the ranks of Sikhism.

The electicism of the Emperor led to a sharp reaction among the conservative sections of the Muslim population. They viewed the Emperor's policy towards the non-Muslims as extremely dangerous both to their creed and the state because of the fear that it would encourage and strengthen the Hindus. In their opinion, any step which benefited the Hindus was anti-Islamic. The Rajput policy of the Emperor was resented for the reason that it boosted the enemies of the Muslim establishment. The emergence of the religious activities among the Hindus were regarded with suspicion. Similarly they regarded the rise of the Sikhs as a dangerous heresy which needed to be nipped in the bud.

Gradually, the above-mentioned conservative reaction gave birth to a powerful Muslim revivalist movement with its headquarters at Sirhind. It was started by a Muslim divine, Sheikh Ahmed Sirhindi Mujaddad-i-Alaf Sani for whom even a slight concession to the Hindus was an act of hostility to Islam. He advocated the view that the glory of Islam emerges in the humiliation of the infidels. About the *Jazya* taken from the infidels, he held that its real purpose was 'to humiliate them and this humiliation should reach a stage where owing to the fear of *Jazya*, they should not be able to wear good clothes, enjoy any peace of mind, be in constant dread and fear of losing their assets to the king. His views about the

Muslim Shariat (Code of Conduct) were very rigid, and he poured abuse upon everything that he did not understand or which could not fit into his ideology. He was thus the antithesis of Abul Fazal and was akin to Badauni in the desire to imprison the mind in the narrowest ideological vision. Therefore, he was a severe critic of Akbar's policy of tolerance towards the non-Muslims. He writes about the miserable conditions of the Muslims under the Emperor and calls him "an enemy of the faith of Islam."

But the orthodoxy however could not influence the policy of Emperor Akbar. The accession of Prince Jahangir to the throne, however, turned the situation; in the beginning at least in favour of those who had assailed the liberal trends in Akbar's policy. There were some powerful people at the court of Akbar who were opposed to Prince Jahangir's accession and favoured his son Khusro instead, in preference to him. Even Akbar at one time had shared the same view, feeling sore as he did at the unfilial and rebellious conduct of Jahangir or Prince Salim, as he was then called. At this critical juncture, the orthodox detractors of Akbar's enlightened liberalism came to Jahangir's rescue and smoothened his way to the throne. Thus when he ascended the throne, he not only inherited his father's prejudices against the Muslim orthodoxy but was also in a frame of mind to oblige them, should an opportunity arise. Although from the twelve edicts issued by him immediately after his accession, it is evident that he never allowed their influence to get the better of him.

The required opportunity appeared in 1606 when Prince Khusro, goaded by his frustrated ambition, rose in open revolt against his father, Emperor Jahangir, and hastened towards the Punjab in a bid to mobilize support for his cause. On the way, he paid a visit to Guru Arjan Dev at Goindwal. The Emperor gave the rebel prince a hot pursuit and reached Lahore post-haste where unfortunate Khusro was produced before him tied in chains by the commander of the pursuing army, Murtaza Khan. The occasion was marked by the award of exemplary punishments to the supporters of the rebel. At this juncture on or about 23rd May 1606, the enemies of the Guru, possibly the followers of Mujaddid-i-Alaf Sani, managed to concoct a fable connecting the Guru with Prince Khusro. They poured into the ears of the Emperor Jahangir that during the short halt of Khusro at Goindwal, Guru Arjan Dev had blessed him with a saffron mark on the forehead. This was considered as a gesture of blessing in favour of the rebel and the Guru was ordered to be arrested. No enquiry was made, and no trial held. Jahangir simply says, "I fully knew his heresies, and I ordered that he be brought into my presence; that his house and children be made over to Murtaza Khan; that his property be confiscated, and that he should be sentenced to a torturous death *Yasa-o-Siyast*."[1]

While giving an account of this affair in his Memoirs, Jahangir has advanced two reasons in justification of his action. First is the popularity of the Guru as a religious and worldly leader amongst the Hindus and even the Muslims. The second is the alleged visit of the rebel Prince Khusro to Goindwal, whom the Guru is said to have blessed with a saffron mark on his forehead.

Of the two reasons, the second was devoid of any foundation. The accusation was made practically a month after the Guru was alleged to have blessed the Prince and some twenty-seven days after the Emperor himself had crossed River Beas at that very place. This makes the whole thing a puzzle and throws a very serious doubt on the genuineness and authenticity of the report. The fact that for twenty-seven days from April 26, when the Emperor appears to have crossed River Beas at Goindwal and was encamped at Jhabal on May 23, there is no reference whatsoever in *Tuzuk-e-Jahangiri* in any way involving Guru Arjan in Prince Khusro episode or of any of his accomplices; an important factor to be taken into account. Had Prince Khusro met the Guru at Goindwal and received his blessings, it would certainly have been reported to the Emperor immediately since he was in the neighbourhood where it could have been easily verified and authenticated by eye-witnesses. If found guilty, he would have been arrested and carried a prisoner with him to Lahore. But nothing had come to the ears of Emperor Jahangir for nearly a month. Then

1. *Tuzuk-e-Jahangiri*, p. 35.

the details contained in the report are historically incorrect. The Guru was neither a politician nor in any way interested in the rebellion of Prince Khusro against his father Jahangir. As far as the *Qaska* or *teeka-mark*[1] of saffron by the Guru on the forehead of the Prince is concerned, it is on the face of it, a pure and simple concoction of some conspirator's fertile imagination to exploit the emotions against the Guru. Never in the whole history of the Sikh Gurus has there been any occasion for any Guru to anoint anyone, Sikh or non-Sikh, with a *teeka*. According to *Mehma Prakash* of Sarup Das Bhalla, the Guru felt pity upon the sad plight of the prince and provided him with food obviously from the *Guru Ka Langar* (free kitchen) open to all wayfarers (*Sakhi* No. 143-1-4). He makes no mention of any *teeka* or financial help. In view of all this, the allegation against the Guru that he was involved in propping up the cause of Khusro fails to establish itself as historically sound.

From the foregoing, one thing that clearly emerges is that the Guru's so-called participation in the rebellion directly or indirectly was merely a pretext devised for his execution. The reality seems to be that someone amongst the revivalists lodged a complaint with Emperor Jahangir implicating the Guru in Khusro affair with a view to inciting the Emperor to take action against him. Immediately after the accession to the throne, the Emperor was keen to please his orthodox Muslim friends who had stood by him first in his rebellion against his father and then against the group of Aziz Koka and Raja Man Singh who were at one stage bent upon putting the crown on his son, Khusro. He readily believed the complaint and issued the order for the execution of the Guru which took place on May 30, 1606.

Guru Arjan Dev before departing for Lahore in response to the summons of Murtaza Khan nominated his young son Hargobind as his successor. At that time, Hargobind was only eleven years old. He had been carefully trained for the high office, which under the changed circumstances, was not only a place of honour but infested with great danger as well. No

---

1. Syed Ahmed, *Tuzuk-e-Jahangiri*, pp. 25 and 34.

ordinary man was expected to acquit himself well in it. Seeing the needs of the time, his father had placed him under the care of Baba Buddha ji, a veteran Sikh, who was asked to make a 'soldier saint' out of him. He instructed him in the sacred lore and also taught him the use of offensive and defensive weapons, besides horse riding, hunting, wrestling and other martial sports. So he grew up to be an all-round personality, healthy and strong, as well as saintly and enlightened.

Guru Hargobind had to work under great strain. The martyrdom of Guru Arjan was a big shock to the people who started pondering over the issue and asking themselves the question : 'Was it right to buckle under the evil instead of combating it ?' Psychologically many people were simply stunned at the sudden change of circumstances and were in utter confusion. Mother Ganga, a tough, bold and sensible lady, felt totally confused. Baba Buddha ji and other prominent Sikhs of the time were clear in their mind that the Sikh brotherhood was now on the verge of turning over a new leaf for discharging a more significant role in the country.

Therefore, the right type of leadership was the need of the hour because any laxity or mistake could inflict incalculable harm. Psychologically the moment was crucial. There were apprehensions that the Sikhs might feel exasperated and revert to escapism and asceticism thus abjuring faith in Guru's philosophy of an active and purposeful life committed to truth and righteousness.

Two courses were now open to the Sikhs. Either to adopt a submissive stance or take a bold stand and face all the dangers with courage and conviction. The young Guru and his close counsellors decided in favour of the latter course and adopted a full-fledged program of militarization. It is believed that before his martyrdom, Guru Arjan had also sent a message urging him to sit on the *Gaddi* (Guru's seat) fully armed.

With a view to symbolising his new policy, the Guru girded around his waist two swords at the investiture ceremony—one to symbolise spiritual and the other temporal power. According to the usual custom Baba Buddha ji had brought a *Seli* (a woollen cord worn as a necklace by the former Gurus) and a turban and offered them to the new Guru to wear them. But Guru Hargobind declined to put them on and said, 'the *Seli* should be placed in the treasury to impress upon the Sikhs that it was not suited to the altered political conditions imposed upon the Sikhs'. He then addressed Baba Buddha : 'My *Seli*[1] shall be my sword-belt and I shall wear my turban with a royal aigrette.' He further told his disciples that in future in Guru's house religion and worldly concern shall be combined, the cauldron to supply the poor and the needy, and scimitar to smite the oppressors.[2]

To implement his programme, he sent a letter[3] to his *Masands* to ask his Sikhs to bring arms and horses as part of their offerings in future. He strengthened the city of Amritsar by constructing a small fortress called Lohgarh. He built the *Akal Takhat* (the Throne of the Timeless God) in front of *Sri Darbar Sahib*, where the congregation listened to the spiritual discourses besides the ballads extolling feats of heroism and matters relating to training in arms and other martial sports like wrestling et al.

He enrolled a body of 52 stout Sikhs, who formed the nucleus of his future army. Five hundred youths came from *Majha, Malwa* and the *Doaba* to offer their services in defence of their religion. They did not demand pay. The Guru gave them a horse each and weapons and formed a little army out of them. He kept up their spirits by taking them out on hunting expeditions, by arranging games and wrestling matches, and by holding symposia of material music. The morning service was held, as usual, in *Sri Darbar Sahib*, where, *Gurbani* composed by the Gurus and contained in the *Adi Granth* was sung to the accompaniment of musical instruments. Singing of *Vars* narrating the brave deeds of the folk heroes was a regular routine in the *Akal Takhat* courtyard. The Guru also gave sermons and led the congregation in prayer. In the afternoon, feats of physical valour were performed in the courtyard before the *Akal Takhat*. The Guru also granted audience to the visitors and their complaints were heard and actions taken. The Sikhs were thus encouraged to have their discords settled among

1. M.A. Macauliffe, *The Sikh Religion*, Vol. IV, p. 2.
2. *Ibid.*, p. 4.
3. *Ibid.*, p. 3.

themselves. Under Guru Hargobind was also begun the custom (which still continues) of choirs moving at night round the peripheri of *Sri Darbar Sahib* Complex, with the blare of trumpets and flare of torches, singing hymns in stirring tones. All these programmes put a new life into the drooping spirits of the Sikhs who, as the Sikh chronicle records, began to undergo rejuvenation.

The new programme as stated in the foregoing paragraph did not mark any abrupt change. It was in full conformity with the teachings and spirit of Sikhism. Guru Nanak, the founder of Sikhism, had condemned cowardice and applauded the qualities of self-respect, self-confidence and manliness. He had held justice to be the primary duty of the rulers, and had stressed their answerability to God and the people for their conduct and administration. He had expressed himself against the attitude of submission to injustice dubbing it a shameful act. In the time of succeeding Gurus, certain stray incidents had happened which awakened the Sikhs to the lurking danger. During the time of Guru Arjan Dev, one Sulhi Khan had become party to an intrigue and actually set out on an expedition against the Guru, but died condemned to flames of a brick kiln.

The need of Guru Nanak's ideology of self-respect and manliness had been realized. Guru Angad Dev ji encouraged Sikhs to develop sturdy physique. Guru Ram Das encouraged trading in horses in the belief that this would promote the qualities of good horsemanship among his followers. Guru Arjan Dev had proceeded further and was perhaps the first leader who envisaged the necessity of training in the use of arms. The Sikh tradition has it that his son and successor, Guru Hargobind, received his military instructions from Baba Buddha ji in accordance with the wishes of Guru Arjan Dev. This could be possible only if Baba Buddha ji had himself learnt the military arts in the earlier period. The tradition that Guru Arjan Dev on the eve of his martyrdom had sent instructions to his son and successor that he should sit fully armed on the *Gurgaddi* also points to the same conclusion.

Although there was nothing against the tenets of Sikhism

about the new line of policy adopted by Guru Hargobind, yet in the beginning many Sikhs could not appreciate it. But all such mis-understandings disappeared with the passage of time.

As was to be expected, the militarisation of the Sikhs by the Guru created a stir in the official quarters. The Emperor felt alarmed. He summoned the Guru to his presence. When Guru met him, he was arrested and sent as a state prisoner to the fort of Gwalior, where some other ruling chiefs were also serving their terms of imprisonment. The Guru's life in the fort was arduous. He had to live on inappropriate ration. More often than not, he even distributed that among the needy prisoners. The Guru had to safeguard himself from poison which was often administered in food to the enemies whom the Emperor considered dangerous.

The Guru's ordeal enhanced his respect in the hearts of his followers. They came in batches all the way to Gwalior and circumambulated the fort from outside, bowed their heads at the gate and returned to their homes.

The Guru's total stay in the fort of Gwalior was possibly three years from 1608 to 1611. There were two causes which prompted Emperor Jahangir to release him. First, after some time political sagacity dawned on him and he realised that without recourse to liberal religious policy it was not possible for him to maintain stability and tranquility in his vast empire. Secondly, it appears that the Emperor was greatly moved by the devotion of batches of Sikhs who made regular trips to the fort to pay homage to their respected Guru without even able to see him. They were constantly chanting holy hymns during their circumambulation.

The tradition goes that the Guru refused to be released until the 52 princes incarcerated with him were allowed to come out, each holding a part of his robe. For accomplishing this feat he is remembered as *Bandi Chhor* or 'The Deliverer'.

It is believed that the efforts of Mian Mir and Wazir Khan brought about a change in Jahangir's heart and hence-forward, more cordial relations were established between the Emperor and the Guru.

For the rest of his life, Jahangir never gave any trouble

to Guru Hargobind. On the contrary he tried to befriend him.

Having been left in peace, the Guru addressed himself whole-heartedly to further the progress of Sikh religion. During the period he was in prison, the strings of discipline had loosened and several selfish *Masands* had arrogated to themselves powers that were never vested in them. They had become corrupt and strayed from their charter of duties and proper functions. Some of them had begun to pose as *gurus* in their own right and raised a body of followers or devotees called *Sehlang*. Guru Hargobind thought it high time to penalise them and make a lesson of them to impress a sense of responsibility upon other functionaries. But this was not enough. The Guru travelled over a large part of the country and along the route of his travels, he appointed missionaries for the dissemination of the Sikh teachings. Among the most renowned missionaries were Baba Buddha, Baba Gurditta and Bhai Gurdas.

After Guru Nanak, he was the first Guru who went outside the Punjab to spread his religion. He travelled from place to place like Guru Nanak, and went as far as Kashmir in the North and Nanakmata near Pilibhit in the East. He made many converts to Sikhism. At Gujrat (in Pakistan), a very interesting incident occurred when the Guru was passing through that city. Shah Daula whose shrine is still revered by thousands remonstrated with the Guru, saying, "How can a Hindu be a Faquir ? How can you be a religious man, when you have a wife and children, and possess worldly wealth ?" The Guru replied, "a wife is man's conscience, his children continue his memory, and wealth gives him his sustenance. As for a Faquir, he is neither a Hindu nor a Musalman." He visited the places connected with the previous Gurus, and put up memorials there. He made arrangements for holding regular services in Sikh shrines.

Jahangir died in 1627, and Shah Jahan succeeded him. The accession of Shah Jahan to the throne was an event of great significance in the history of the development of Sikhism. Shah Jahan's religious outlook was narrow as compared to that of his father who after 1611 had more or less adopted liberal attitude like Akbar. It is evident from the fact that he even imprisoned Shaikh Ahmed Sarhindi, head of the *Naqshbandis*.

Shah Jahan prohibited the conversion of Muslims and ordered demolition of many temples. This brought him into conflict with the Sikhs who were determined to carry on their missionary work. The Sikhs were particularly annoyed at the desecration of their famous *Baoli* at Lahore, which was filled up and a mosque erected on the site of the free kitchen attached to it. In order to avoid an open clash with the Mughal Government in the future as also to continue his missionary activities peacefully, the Guru established a new settlement at Kiratpur on May 1, 1626. The land was donated by Tara Chand the ruler of Kahlur. The Guru sent Baba Gurditta, his eldest son, for commencing the construction of a township there. Baba Gurditta ji took Baba Sri Chand there and had the ceremony performed by him.[1] This new headquarters suited the Guru very much, firstly, because it was not far from the plains of the Punjab; and secondly, it was outside the administrative jurisdiction of the Mughal officials. Kahlur was an independent state at that time.

Still, an open clash with Shah Jahan came in 1634. In that year, Shah Jahan was hunting in the neighourhood of Amritsar. At Gumtala, one of his favourite hawks strayed away and fell into the hands of the hunting party of the Sikhs, who refused to part with it, as they did not recognise those who came to claim it. Altercation led to blows, and the royal party returned to report to the Emperor as to what had happened. A detachment of troops under Mukhlis Khan was sent to arrest the Guru and bring him to Lahore. This was the beginning of the era of discord between the two.

That the attack was sudden and unexpected may be seen from the fact that the Guru was then busy with the preparations of the marriage ceremony of his daughter Bibi Viro ji. He had no munitions of war with him. Even a gun had to be improvised from the hollow trunk of a fallen tree. The battle occurred at the site where now stands Khalsa College at Amritsar. The baggage and property of the Guru was plundered. But when Mukhlis

---

1. According to *Bhat Vahis*, the foundation was laid by Sri Chand on Baisakhi Puranmashi 1683 BK/1st May, 1626 on the tract of land donated by Tara Chand of Kahlur, a small hill state.

Khan was killed in the battle, the Mughal troops returned. The Guru returned to Jhabal, about eight miles to the south-west, where he was able to perform the marriage of his daughter. The Guru had to fight another battle at Laihra[1] (Mahraj). This time, the tussle began over the possession of two horses. A *Masand* from Kabul had brought two beautiful horses for the Guru. They were seized on the way by a Mughal official and sent to the Royal stable. They were recovered from there by an adventurous Sikh, Bhai Bidhi Chand, whose 'larking' campaigns were so humorously conceived and romantically executed that for him even the prosaic Macauliffe is constrained to pause for diversion.

Disguising himself, first as a grass-cutter and then as an astrologer-tracker, Bidhi Chand carried away the horses, one after the other, from the fort, and brought them to their rightful owner. War followed. The Guru was then moving about in Malwa, when he was attacked by a powerful army led by Lalla Beg and Qamar Beg.

The battle was fought near Mahraj on 17th Poh BK 1699 (1634). More than 1200 Sikhs were killed or wounded. Casualties on the other side including those of the commanders, were even more numerous. To commemorate his victory the Guru built a tank, called *Gurusar*, on the spot.

In 1635, the Guru went to Kartarpur where he stayed for some time. Soon after, war broke out between the Sikhs and the Mughals. This time, the cause was Painde Khan, an Afghan who was erstwhile-commander of the Sikh troops and had been dismissed on account of his haughty demeanour. He went over to the Mughal higher authorities and induced them to despatch a strong force against the Guru. So another expedition was sent against the Guru, under the command of Kale Khan, the brother of Mukhlis Khan who had been killed in the battle at Amritsar. He was assisted by Painde Khan, and Qutab Khan, the *Faujdar* of Jullundur. The Guru was besieged

---

1. Refer to *Bhat Vahi Multani Sindhi* preserved in the Department of Historical Studies, Punjabi University Patiala. Macauliffe assigns 1628 for the battle of Amritsar, 1631 for the battle of Laihra and 1634 for the battle of Kartarpur. These were accepted to be correct by later writers. We, however, have based our narrative on *Bhat Vahis*.

in Kartarpur in 1635. The Sikhs bore the brunt of the attack under the able command of Bhai Bidhi Chand, and Baba Gurditta, the eldest son of the Guru. Even Guru Tegh Bahadur who was about 14 years old then and known by the name of Tyag Mal, is said to have shown feats of valour in the battlefield. As the battle was in progress, a man with his sword drawn rushed upon the Guru. The Guru evaded the assault and by a sturdy stroke severed his head saying, 'Not so, but this is how the sword is used.' In a hand-to-hand fight, Painde Khan fell at the latter's feet. The Guru said, "You are a Musalman. Now is the time for you to say your *kalima.*" Painde Khan repentingly replied, "O Guru, thy sword is my creed and my source of salvation." Seeing his former favourite on the throes of death, the Guru was moved to pity. It is said that he shaded his face with his shield from the scorching rays of the Sun and bade him final farewell.

Painde Khan's death was followed by that of Kale Khan and consequent upon it, the Imperial army was disheartened causing a great stampede in the rank and files of the Mughal forces.

The last battle was fought between the Sikhs and the Imperial forces near Phagwara in the village of Palahi. A contingent of Royal force under the command of Ahmed Khan, son of late Ahdallat Khan made a sudden and unexpected attack on the Guru and inflicted considerable damage on his followers. In the battle, Bhai Dasa and Sohela, sons of Balu Bhatt, grandson of Mula Bhatt fell martyrs.[1] This battle was fought on 1st of Jeth 1692 BK. (1635).

Guru Hargobind fared well during all the four battles, but his aim had always been defensive. He did not acquire even an inch of territory. There was something far greater involved in these skirmishes than a mere dispute over a hawk or a horse. A new heroism was rising in the land, the object of which, then dimly seen, was to create the will to resist the might of the 'Turks'.

To avoid further clashes with the government and to carry out his plans of consolidating and spreading Sikhism, he

---

1. Fauja Singh, "Chronology of the Battles of Guru Hargobind," *Punjab History Conference Proceedings,* 1971.

shifted to Kiratpur, and continued to stay there till his death. During his stay, he in 1636 asked Baba Gurditta to appoint Almast, Phul, Gonda, and Baba Hasna as head preachers. Baba Gurditta invested them with *Udasi* robes. Almast and Baba Hasna were allotted the areas of East India and Pothohar respectively. Phul and Gonda were assigned the area of the Doaba to carry on the missionary work. All these four persons founded preaching centres in their allotted area. These were named as *Dhuans* or 'hearths', symbolising the flame of Sikhism. Besides this, the Guru sent Bidhi Chand to Bengal. Earlier Bhai Gurdas had been sent to Kabul and then to Benaras to acquaint the people with the Gospel of the Gurus.

The Guru's arrangement worked nicely and produced good results. He acquired great influence over the hill people and Rajas alike. The population of the Sikhs increased. The Guru achieved all this not withstanding the domestic tragedies. Within a few years, five members of his family, including three of his sons, died one after another. The most grievous of these deaths was that of Baba Gurditta in 1638. To add to his sorrow, Baba Gurditta's son, Dhirmal, turned against his grandfather. For a long time, Guru Hargobind could not make up his mind about his successor. He had two sons living. Suraj Mal who showed little interest in Sikh affairs and Tegh Bahadur who was too much withdrawn to be entrusted with the leadership of the fast growing community. When the time came, Guru Hargobind chose Baba Gurditta's second son Har Rai to succeed him as the seventh Guru.

From 1635 to the dethronement of Shah Jahan, nothing significant happened which showed hostility of the government towards Sikhism. This was because (i) the Mughals had come to the conclusion that the primary interest of the Sikh Gurus was to conduct peaceful propagation of the teachings and not to seek any confrontation with the government unnecessarily; (ii) the increased influence of liberal Dara Shikoh at the court of Shah Jahan mitigated to a large extent the influence of Muslim orthodoxy in policy making of the state; and (iii) Dara happened to develop happy personal relations with Guru Har Rai. Thus this period of uninterrupted peace was faithfully utilized by Guru Har Rai.

Like his predecessors, the new Guru had many noble qualities. He was tender-hearted, extremely humane in his approach, firm in his resolution, clear in his perception and wise in the execution of his plans. Compassion was the keynote of his personality. Some scholars have, inadvertently or otherwise presented him as 'passive' because he was of peaceful desposition and extremely tender in his thinking and action. They brand him as a man of retiring nature. Even the sight of accidental breaking of flowers moved him to the extent of shedding tears. But they are sadly mistaken because this trait of the Guru's personality was indeed a great factor enabling rapid progress of Sikhism towards the goals set before it.

The Guru shared his grandfather's views regarding the need of military preparedness and maintained a body of people well-trained in the military craft. He also continued his predecessor's practice of hunting expeditions as a means of military training and morale boosting.

Simultaneously, he attended to the demands of consolidation in the ranks of the community. Having been convinced of the deterioration of the *Masand* system, he set up *Bakshishs*, new missionary centres, and for their control and management appointed[1] (i) Suthrashah, (ii) Sahiba, (iii) Sangata, (iv) Mihan Sahib, (v) Bhagat Bhagwan, and (vi) Bhagat Mal. Of these, Bhagat Gir, originally a *Bairagi*, was converted to Sikhism along with his followers. He was renamed Bhagat Bhagwan and appointed to carry on with preaching work in the East, where he with the help of his followers established 360 seats for the propagation of Sikhism.

The Bhai families of Kaithal and Bagrian who were devout Sikhs since the time of Guru Hargobind were made responsible for the spread of Sikhism in the land between Rivers Jamuna and Sutlej. Bhai Pheru acted as the Guru's *Masand* in the Lamma region between Rivers Beas and Ravi. As the *Masands* or missionaries appointed by the earlier Gurus became more and more corrupt, this new order of preachers attained more prominence and were found effective in preaching Sikhism in distinct and difficult places.

1. Surjit Singh Gandhi, *History of the Sikh Gurus*, p. 334.

Guru Har Rai undertook extensive tours of the *Malwa* and *Doaba* regions of the Punjab, and due to his efforts a large number of people of these areas embraced Sikhism. During his tenure of guruship, some notable conversions were made among the land owning families of the *Malwa*. The ancestors of the ruling house of Patiala, Nabha and Jind were first converted to Sikhism during this period. "Once the *chaudharies* of some leading families of the *Malwa* were converted, the ground was well set for the rapid spread of Sikh faith in the region. The pace of progress in this direction was greatly accelerated during the periods of the ninth and tenth Gurus."[1]

The closing years of Guru Har Rai's pontificate were marked by the revival of Mughal interference in the affairs of Sikh community. There are two possible explanations of this development. First, Aurangzeb won the war of succession and ascended the Mughal throne in 1658. He was a staunch *Sunni* Muslim who thought that the resurgence of any non-Islamic movement in the country was dangerous to Islamic cause and needed to be curbed ruthelessly. Secondly, the new Emperor was angry with Guru Har Rai for the latter's open support to his elder brother and rival, Dara Shikoh.

Dara, being of Sufi persuasion, sought the company of saintly men of all denominations, that gradually resulted in his intimacy with the Sikh Guru. Sujan Rai Bhandari says that when Dara Shikoh fled across the Punjab after his defeat at the hands of Aurangzeb, Guru Har Rai, responding to his appeal for help, gathered the Sikh force estimated to be 2200 strong and tried to cover up his escape against Aurangzeb's pursuing troops. This aroused the ire of the Emperor who, on the conclusion of hostilities, summoned Guru Har Rai to Delhi to explain his conduct as well as brief him about Sikh faith. The Guru instead of proceeding personally to the capital sent his eldest son, Ram Rai, to answer the queries of the Emperor. The old charge which had been levelled in the time of Guru Arjan and dismissed by Emperor Akbar as totally unfounded was raked up again, alleging that the *Adi Granth* contained derogatory references to Islam and its founder prophet Muhammad. Baba Ram Rai failed to show firmness of

1. Fauja Singh, *Sikhism*.

character and distorted facts with a view to gain favours and avoid causing any offence to the Emperor.

Aurangzeb, on his part, used the opportunity to win over Baba Ram Rai. He was the elder son of Guru Har Rai and was likely to succeed his father. In winning him over, therefore, the Mughal ruler cherished the hope of bringing the prospective Guru under his thumb. Guru Har Rai disapproved of Ram Rai's conduct and disowning him, appointed his younger son, Baba Har Krishan, to guruship after him.

The appointment of Baba Har Krishan by his father as his successor was fully in conformity with the succession practice observed since the time of Guru Ram Das. Prior to Guru Ram Das, succession was open to the entire *Sangat* and a successor was chosen irrespective of his lineage. From Guru Ram Das onwards, the guruship assumed a hereditary character, as all such institutions in those days would tend to do. But though the choice henceforth was limited to the male member of the family of the Guru, there was no rule as to who of them was more eligible for the office of the Guru. Guru Ram Das selected his youngest son, Arjan Dev. Guru Arjan Dev had no difficulty as he had only one son. Guru Hargobind had five sons out of whom three predeceased him. The remaining two were passed over in favour of a grandson (younger son of the deceased Baba Gurditta). Guru Har Rai, as we have seen, selected his younger son, Har Krishan, in preference to Ram Rai, his elder son. Guru Har Krishan later on selected his grandfather's brother, (Guru) Tegh Bahadur, as his successor.

The question of succession, however, had led to the growth of some splinter groups within the ranks of the community, such as the *Minas* and the *Dhirmalias*. The *Minas* were descendants of Prithi Chand, the eldest son of the fourth Guru, whereas *Dhirmalias* were the descendants of Dhirmal, a grandson of Guru Hargobind. Both Prithi Chand and Dhirmal were disappointed claimants to guruship and had endeavoured to set up rival gurudoms of their own. Now a third splinter group was in the process of formation. This was to be known as *Ram Rayyas* after the name of Ram Rai. Baba Ram Rai was very sore over his supersession in the matter of succession. Being at the Imperial court and having developed good relations with the Emperor at that time, he thought that he could turn the tables upon his younger brother through the influence of Aurangzeb, and thus made an appeal to the Emperor for his intervention. The Emperor was willing to help Ram Rai because, he, for his own reasons, preferred a man of his own choice and thought that a puppet Guru would most suit his interests.

Guru Har Krishan was then summoned to Delhi. The Guru went there in 1664. He was accompanied by twenty Sikhs and his mother. On reaching Delhi, the Guru put up at the house of Mirza Raja Jai Singh (situated at the present site of Gurdwara Bangla Sahib). The Emperor was in no hurry to announce his arbitration. Possibly he was content to have both the claimants under his surveillance. According to Dr. Ganda Singh and Teja Singh, "The Emperor was convinced that the choice of the last Guru was not wrong, and he dismissed the claim of Ram Rai." It is also possible that this hesitation on the part of Aurangzeb was due to his realization of the futility of imposing an unwanted Guru on the Sikhs.

Shortly afterwards, Guru Har Krishan was stricken with small-pox. But before he died, he declared that his successor would be his 'Baba' then residing at village Bakala in the Punjab. In token thereof, he entrusted the spiritual regalia (five paise and a piece of coconut) to Diwan Durgah Mal. According to *Bhat Vahi Talaunda Pargana Jind* and *Guru Kian Sakhian* by Swarup Singh Kaushish, the Guru did not leave any vagueness in his statement and actually mentioned the name of Tegh Bahadur as his successor and commissioned Diwan Durgah Mal to take the articles of spiritual regalia to Bakala and personally offer them to the new Guru.

Guru Tegh Bahadur was the fifth and the youngest son of the sixth Guru, Guru Hargobind. He was born on April 1, 1621. As a child, he was brought up with utmost care and attention. Baba Buddha and Bhai Gurdas gave him lessons in Sikh religion and philosophy respectively. He also studied History, Arithmetic, Metaphysics, Logic, Theology, Six Philosophical systems, classics like *Bhagvat Gita, Mahabharta, Ramayana* and the basic principles of Islamic philosophy.[1] He

1. Surjit Singh Gandhi, *History of the Sikh Gurus*, p. 342. Trilochan Singh, *Guru Tegh Bahadur*, p. 7.

also became well-versed in music in which his interest lay deep—the fact which is amply proved by his poetic compositions set to different musical measures. As a young child, Tegh Bahadur owed not a little to the general environment and to his parents and teachers. He did a lot of travelling in company of his father and other members of the family. In course of these travels, he paid visits to Tarn Taran, Khadur Sahib, Goindwal and Kartarpur, and thus imbibed Sikh values. Moreover, he was an eye-witness to the battles, though not all of them which his father had to fight against the Mughals. In the Battle of Kartarpur (26th April 1635) when the Mughal forces under the over-all command of Kale Khan and Painde Khan attacked Guru Hargobind, Tegh Bahadur fought valiantly in the rear guard of the Guru's Army. His father Guru Hargobind was so much pleased that he changed his name from Tyag Mal (his original name) to Tegh Bahadur, meaning 'Hero of the Sword'.

After the Battle of Kartarpur when Guru Hargobind lived at Kiratpur, Tegh Bahadur took deep interest in the missionary activities of his father. He would often accompany his father on his hunting expeditions and missionary tours.

Immediately after the passing away of Guru Hargobind, Tegh Bahadur along with his wife Gujri and mother, Nanki had shifted to Bakala, his maternal grandparents house where he stayed up to 1664. Between 1656 to 1664, he undertook a tour of different religious places with a view to disseminate Sikhism. The most important places he visited were Kurukshetra, Hardwar, Mukteshwar, Kashi, Sasram, Gaya and Allahabad, etc. In March 1664, he waited upon Guru Har Krishan and his mother Sulakhani at the residence of Mirza Raja Jai Singh and expressed profound sense of sorrow and sympathy in their bereavement. Guru Har Krishan did not live long after that and died of smallpox at Delhi.

In the meantime, Tegh Bahadur had returned to Bakala in the Punjab. It was here that in accordance with the late Guru's instructions he was invested with Guruship. Twenty-two pretenders asserted their claims to Guruship[1] and posed

1. Koer Singh, *Gurbilas Patshahi 10*, p. 22. According to the author, many claims to the Guruship were set up.

as the legitimate successors. They set up tents and employed agents to do propaganda for them and won supporters even on payment. The most vociferous and conspicuous claimant, however, was Dhirmal who was the first to pitch the camp at Bakala. All these claimants spread utter confusion among the devotees regarding the true successor. This state continued till the impostors were completely exposed by Makhan Shah Lubana and his men. Even then, Dhir Mal did not change his ways. He hired a person named Shihan to assassinate the new Guru but the attempt failed.

On November 22, 1664, the Guru left Bakala for Amritsar to pay homage at the most revered place. He wanted to bathe in the sacred tank but the ministers of the shrine shut the doors upon him. He was not allowed to enter the holy precincts. Then, the whole of Amritsar was under the control of Harji generally known as *Mina*. The priests of *Darbar Sahib* owed allegiance to him who feared that once Guru Tegh Bahadur and his adherents entered the holy precincts, they would never leave it and drive his *Masands* out of it.

Under the circumstances the Guru thought it advisable to return to Kiratpur. Leaving Amritsar, he decided to spend some time touring the *Majha* and *Malwa* regions of the Punjab before proceeding to Kiratpur. Accordingly, he visited Khadur, Goindwal and Tarn Taran. After this, he reached Khem Karan where Chaudhari Raghupat Rai presented a mare to the Guru. In Malwa, the most important places he visited were Talwandi Sabo Ki, Maur and Maisarkhana. The Guru also visited a large number of places in Bangar, the most important being Dhamdhan, where Bhai Daggo, the local *Masand*, was asked to raise a building with a well for water supply. The Guru reached Kiratpur in May 1665. On May 13, 1665, he attended the *Satarvin* (a ceremony performed on the 17th day from death) of Raja Dip Chand of Bilaspur. The Guru stayed at Bilaspur for three days during which he expressed that he would like to build a new settlement somewhere near Kiratpur and offered to buy a suitable piece of land for the purpose. Dip Chand's wife, Rani Champa, offered to donate the site of

Makhowal, Mianpur and Sahote[1], but the Guru succeeded in prevailing upon her to accept a token amount of Rs. 500.00. On June 19, 1665,[2] the new settlement was founded at the site of Makhowal. It was named as *Chak Nanki* after the revered name of the Guru's mother. In course of time, the beautiful town of Anandpur grew up around it.

He did not stay at Makhowal for long. He set out (August 1665) on his travels eastwards through the Malwa and Bangar territory. The purpose of his itinerary was to meet the *Sikh Sangats* now spread all over the area as also to make arrangement to bring them in direct contact with him.

The Guru's mother and wife travelled with him. A considerable following of devotees also accompanied him which gave his camp the appearance of the moving court of a chief. The Guru, enroute, visited Saifabad where he was accorded a hearty welcome by Nawab Saif Khan. From here the Guru reached Dhamdhan where he was arrested by Alam Khan Rohilla as per Imperial order from Delhi. According to *Badshah Burunji* the Emperor had issued the order of arrest on the complaint of some orthodox *Ulemas*[3] and Brahmins who were feeling much upset over the new awakening which had dawned upon the people under the impact of the Guru's teachings.[4] The Guru, therefore, was arrested by Alam Khan Rohilla but through the intercession of Raja Ram Singh, son of Mirza Jai Singh of Amber, he was released and allowed to proceed on his way.

During his eastward journey, Guru Tegh Bahadur passed through some major religious centres of Hindus such as Mathura, Allahabad, Benaras, Patna etc. At Patna, he left his family and proceeded further to Bengal and Assam.

The Guru reached Dacca at the end of October 1665 passing through Godagri and Gopalpur. According to Teja Singh and Dr. Ganda Singh, 'there flourished quite a network

1. According to Kesar Singh Chhibber, Guru Tegh Bahadur bought three villages; Makhowal, Mathur and Lodhipur, originally founded as per local tradition by two Pathan brothers Makhe Khan and Kale Khan.
2. Swarup Singh Kaushish, *Guru Kian Sakhian*, Sakhi 24.
3. S.K. Bhuyan, *Badshah Burunji*, Sakhi 116.
4. *Bhat Vahi Jado Bansian*, 'Khata Bartian' as quoted by Dr. Fauja Singh in his book *Guru Tegh Bahadur : Martyr and Teacher*.

of prosperous *Sikh Sangat* all over. The Dacca *Sangat* was the *Hazuri Sangat* or the head *Sangat* of these parts with a number of others under it and in turn was controlled by the Guru from Anandpur. The Guru was accorded great respect by the people of Dacca, whose association with the Sikh faith was as old as Guru Nanak. Bhai Bulaki, the local *Masand* and Bhai Natha, the disciple of Almast, did all that they could, to make the stay of the Guru comfortable. It was here that the Guru received the welcome news of the birth of his son Gobind Rai at Patna on December 22, 1666. He wrote a letter of thanks to the *Sangat* of that place for looking after his child.

From Dacca the Guru left for Jainti hills and Sylhet (early in the year 1667) where he established a missionary centre known as the Sylhet *Sangat*. After spending the rainy season at Sylhet, Guru Tegh Bahadur moved towards Chittagong and Sondip. He passed through Sharataganj and stopped at Agartala, the capital of the present day Tripura state. From there he went to Chittagong where he stayed till the end of 1667. During his stay at Chittagong, he established a large religious centre of his faith. Guru Tegh Bahadur reached Dacca in 1668. Raja Ram Singh who had been sent by Aurangzeb to oust the Assamese Ahom King Charadwaj from Gauhati[1] which he had recently captured, met Guru Tegh Bahadur and asked him to accompany him. The Guru who had already decided upon a tour of Assam accepted the offer. Another factor that compelled the Guru to accede to the Raja's request was that the Raja held the house of Nanak in deep reverence. In 1669 the Guru stayed at Dhubri while Raja Ram Singh went ahead and camped at Rang Matti, the Mughal out-post near the frontier of Assam.

Soon after, the war between the Mughals and the Ahoms started. According to a popular tradition it was because of the Guru's spiritual power that the sorcery of the Assamese failed to have any adverse effect on the Mughal forces. After some hard fighting the Guru prevailed upon the contending parties to arrive at a negotiated settlement. According to the accord[2]

---

1. Sir E.A. Gait, *History of Assam*, p. 155.
2. *Ibid.*

the old boundaries were to be maintained. Tradition has it that as token of complete harmony, the Guru invited the soldiers of both armies to help raise a mound at Dhubri in memory of Guru Nanak's visit to the place. The Guru left Assam in the year 1670 and hastened back to the Punjab. On his return journey, he paid a flying visit to Patna to see his son. The reason for the haste was Emperor Aurangzeb's adoption of a much rigid attitude towards the Hindus and other non-Muslim communities. On April 8, 1669, he had (according to *Maasar-e-Alamgiri*) issued orders to the governors of all provinces to destroy without mercy the schools and temples of the infidels. They were strictly enjoined to put a total end to the teaching and practising of idolatrous form of worship.

Under the circumstances, the Guru thought it prudent to be with his people in their hour of agony and sufferings. On the way back, he was arrested by the Kotwal of Agra but was soon released when it was made clear that the earlier order for the arrest was no longer valid because of the intercession of Raja Ram Singh. Having visited Delhi, Lakhnaur, village Malla, the Guru reached Bakala where he was joined by his family. After sometime, he proceeded to Chak Nanki.

With the return of the Guru to the Punjab, began the period of his crowning glory. Refusing to sit idle at his headquarters, he resolved to move among his people. About the middle of 1673 the Guru left for extensive tour of the Malwa and Bangar Des. According to Bhai Santokh Singh of *Suraj Parkash*, Giani Gian Singh of *Twarikh Guru Khalsa* and *Sakhi Pothi*, the Guru visited twenty places. But a recent survey conducted under the supervision and guidance of Dr. Fauja Singh reveal that, the number of places visited by the Guru are much more. The Guru's important halts were Saifabad, Mulowal, Dhilwan, Khiva, Samana, Bhikhi, Khayale, Maur, Talwandi, Bhalenda, Backhona, Gobindpura, Bagar, Dhamdhan. The tour lasted till the end of 1674 when along with his large train of followers, he returned home to Chak Nanki (Makhowal).

During his travels, the Guru preached what may be called the ideology of *Dharma* which in the context of social and political reconstruction meant social responsibility, validity of moral values, social equality, transcending narrow considerations of creed, caste, clime, sex and colour and rejection of hereditary principles as the basis of social order or ethics. The principle of Justice formed an important feature of this ideology. The concept of justice figured prominently in the thinking of the Gurus. The scientific solution as it developed in the West in the 19th century and as we understand it today was not known then. But justice as a principle of human relationship was well known and was strongly advocated by Guru Nanak and his successors. As a matter of fact, their close identification with the lower and down-trodden classes and their constant endeavours for their welfare emanated from their commitment to social justice. The exploitation of the poor by the rich was held inhuman and unjust. But if it was bad for the strong and the rich to exploit the poor; it was equally bad for the poor and the weak to compromise with injustice and tyranny.

These ideas presented good opportunities to the lower classes like Jats etc. to improve their social status. The result was rapid growth of Sikhism both in numbers and resources.

It was an anathema to a staunch and orthodox ruler such as Aurangzeb. By nature he was a puritan in his religious views; but these bore the stamp of the *Naqshbandi* Sect of Sirhind. At that time Masum, son of Sheikh Ahmed Sirhindi was conducting a vigorous propaganda against the enemies of Islam. He was successful in his mission and through his vigorous propaganda reaped a rich harvest of converts. Aurangzeb had attended his lectures while he was the governor of Multan. Masum grew fond of the prince and on the eve of his pilgrimage to Mecca predicted that in the struggle for the throne, Aurangzeb would be victorious. After Muhammad Masum's death, his son Shaikh Saif-ud-din (b. 1639-40) was adopted by Aurangzeb as his preceptor and guide. In this way, the orthodox thought process had its full assertion during Aurangzeb's reign who under its influence tried hard to translate Shaikh Sirhindi's ideas into action. Incidentally, these actions seemed to serve the political purpose as well. Aurangzeb could justify the murders of his brothers and the imprisonment of his father on the ground of his devotion to the cause of Islam.

In 1666, the stone railing of the famous Keshav Rai temple of Mathura was razed to the ground under Imperial orders. In April 1669, a general order was issued for the destruction of all schools and temples of the Hindus. Special officers were appointed in all parts of the Empire to enforce these regulations strictly. In the field of taxation, *Jazya* and pilgrimage taxes were reimposed on the non-Muslims. In matters of conversion, a vigorous campaign was launched to convert non-Muslims to Islam. The fact that a deputation of *Pandits* appeared in the *Darbar* of Guru Tegh Bahadur in May 1675, and complained of the Government conducting a wholesale campaign of conversion is a historical testimony too strong to be ignored.

Like other non-Muslims, the Sikhs too suffered under the impact of the orthodox policy of Aurangzeb. Mirza Inayat-Ullah-Ismi tells us in the *Ahkam-i-Alamgiri* that in compliance with the orders of the Emperor and with the consent of the local *Qazi*, the Sikh temples in the town of Buriya in the parganah of Khizrabad of the Sarkar of Sirhind were demolished and a mosque raised on its site. Sayyed Zafar *Darvish*[1] was appointed incharge of that mosque to guide prayers and benedictions. Some Sikhs attacked the mosque and killed the *Darvish*. The Emperor rebuked the *Qazi* and his father who was the head of the police. Such incidents had become a common occurrence.

The Emperor with this frame of mind could ill-brook the growing influence of the Sikh religion under the inspiring leadership of Guru Tegh Bahadur.

But how did the clash come to surface ? Knowing the mind and the official orders of Emperor Aurangzeb, the Imperial Intelligence Agencies seem to have been closely watching the movements and proceedings of Guru Tegh Bahadur since his return to the Punjab. These news reporters sent exaggerated and some time distorted reports about the large gatherings and money offerings at the congregations of the Guru. The Emperor, busy as he was in quelling the Pathan

---

1. *Kalimat-i-Taiyyabat*, p. 115.

rebellion in North-Western frontier, had neither the time nor the inclination to make enquiries about the proceedings of the Guru. He was already circumspect of the Sikh movement. He, therefore, readily believed all the reports of his intelligence staff and wrote to the Governor of Lahore to arrest Guru Tegh Bahadur and ordered his detention in prison.

Some historians have opined that the cause of the execution of Guru Tegh Bahadur was the response which the Guru made to the request of the Kashmiri Brahmins on May 25, 1675. A deputation of sixteen Kashmiri Brahmins headed by Pandit Kirpa Ram, son of Arhu Ram of Mattan waited upon the Guru at Chak Nanki. They told him how they were being pressed hard to embrace Islam. The Guru was much moved by their tales of woe. He told the Brahmins to go back and tell the authorities that they would accept their conversion to Islam if Guru Tegh Bahadur was first prevailed upon to embrace Islam. Consequently the Guru left for Delhi to resolve the issue with the Mughal Emperor once for all.

From this the conclusion has been drawn by many scholars that the Guru had made up his mind to suffer martyrdom for them or for the Hindu religion alone. The advocates of this view quote Guru Gobind Singh in their support : 'Guru Tegh Bahadur did a miracle in the Kali Age by protecting the frontal mark and sacred thread of the Hindus.' But this view is not correct. To regard the appeal of the Kashmiri Brahmins as the sole cause of the Guru's execution is to lose sight of the whole historical background which preceded this event. The truth seems to be that the case of the Kashmiri Brahmins only precipitated the matter.

The Governor of Lahore passed on the Imperial order for compliance to Dilawar Khan, the *Faujdar* of Sirhind, who, in turn, asked the circle Kotwal of Ropar, Nur Muhammad Khan Mirza, in whose police jurisdiction lay Anandpur, to arrest the Guru. The order, however, was kept a secret.[1]

The Guru apprehending trouble proceeded towards Delhi on 8th July 1675, probably to meet the Emperor and

---

1. William Irvine, *Later Mughals*, p. 79. Muhammad Ahsan Ijad's *Ferukh-Siyar-Nama*. p. 31.

plead the case of non-Muslims with him; and in the event of the Emperor's unfavourable response[1], suffer the consequences. The Guru along with a few of his most devoted followers who were accompanying him was arrested on July 12, 1675 (Sawan 12, 1732 BK.) at Malikpur Ranghran near Ropar by Mirza Nur Muhammad, the Kotwal of Ropar and sent to the *Faujdar's* headquarters at Sirhind where they were kept in prison for about four months. He then received a fresh order from Aurangzeb from Hasan Abdal saying that they should be despatched to Delhi. They reached Delhi and were kept in the Kotwali of Chandni Chowk. They were offered a choice between Islam and death. On their spurning conversion, Bhai Dayala and Bhai Mati Das were boiled and sawn alive respectively on 10th November 1675. Then came Guru's turn. According to Muhammad Ahsan Ijad, he was asked to embrace Islam, and when he refused to do so, was executed on November 11, 1675.

Guru Gobind Rai (called Guru Gobind Singh after the birth of the *Khalsa*) was only nine year old when his father was martyred at Delhi. The situation which he was called upon to face was very grave for the *Sikh Panth*. The immediate effect of the execution of Guru Tegh Bahadur was gravely stunning. The intensity of the shock of Delhi executions was greatly enhanced by the absence of unity and cohesion in the ranks of the Sikhs at that time. *Minas, Dhirmalias* and *Ram Rayyas* intensified their activities and were engaged in an all out campaign of vilification against the main-stream Sikhism. The circumstances of the last decade and a half had been particularly helpful. In consequence, fissiparous and centrifugal forces had become stronger. Islamic imperial state was determined to galvanise *Dar-Ul-Harb* into *Dar-Ul-Islam*. The core of Hindu orthodoxy also did not like the mission of the Guru to strike root.

Masand system considered to be the bedrock of Sikh internal governance developed serious cracks. *Masands* started

---

1. The Emperor at that time was in the North-West frontier area. Considering the difficulties of communication in that age, it is not surprising that the Guru had no idea about the exact whereabouts of the Emperor. The normal expectation was that he would be in his capital at Delhi.

showing callousness towards the main-stream Sikhism and were often hesitant to transmit their collections from the devotees to the headquarter. In a number of cases, they exhibited the temerity to project themselves equal to the Guru claiming as much episcopal as well as organisational power as their Guru had. Many of them found it safe and profitable to line up with cultish leaders such as Dhirmal, Harji and Ram Rai.

Despite all this, there was much in the heritage of the Guru which was helpful to him. His predecessors had defined parameters of their mission. They had established institutions of *Sangat* and *Pangat* to promote Sikhism and knit the Sikhs into a strong team. Guru Arjan Dev had compiled the holy scripture, *Adi Granth*, to serve as a beacon for the Sikhs. They had initiated and evolved distinct traditions such as Sikh heroism and Sikh martyrdom, understandably to orientate the Sikhs to resolve to uphold the values. Yet the situation was complex, arduous and challenging and required the one endowed with sterling qualities, extraordinary creativeness, total commitment, boundless faith in the legitimacy of the cause and firmness of a Carlylian hero. Guru Gobind Singh was undoubtedly equal to the task.

> *I came into the world assigned with the duty of upholding the righteous every place and to destroy the wicked and the evil-minded. O Ye holy men, know it well in your hearts that the only reason I took birth was to see that the righteousness flourishes that good may live and the tyrants uprooted.*[1]

---

1. *Hum eh kāj jagat mein āe.*
   Dharam het gurdev paṭhāe.
   Jahā tahā tum dharam bithāro.
   Dusṭ dokhiyan(i) pakar(i) pachhāro.42.
   Yāhī kāj dharā hum janaman.
   Samajh lehu sādhū sab manman.
   Dharam chalāvan sant ubāran.
   Dusṭ saban ko mūl upāran.43.   (Bachittar Natak)

CHAPTER II

EARLY LIFE IN BIHAR

Guru Gobind Singh, the tenth and the last Guru of the Sikhs was born in the early hours of a cold winter morning on December 22, 1666[1] in Patna at the place where the present shrine *Takht Sri Har Mandir Sahib* stands. His father Guru Tegh Bahadur had left Punjab a few months earlier to undertake

---

1. The traditional and accepted date of birth of Guru Gobind Singh is Saturday, Poh Sudi 7, 1723 Bk viz December 22, 1666 CE. This date has been recorded by Sukha Singh in his *Gurbilas* vide page 84. *Gurbilas,* authored by Koer Singh also recorded this date as the birth date of the tenth Guru. Bhai Kahn Singh in his *Mahan Kosh* has also endorsed this date to be correct. This date has also been given in an old MSS lying in Patna gurdwara and inscribed on a commemoration tablet.

Some writers, however, are of the opinion that the Guru was born on Poh Sudi 7, Samvat 1718 Bk viz December 18, 1661. One of the protagonists of this date is Gulab Singh of Nirmala order who has recorded this date in his *Gur Parnali.* (quoted in *Gur Parnalian,* Randhir Singh, page 199). *Bansavalinama* by Kesar Singh Chhibber, p. 125 also supports this date. If we accept the later date i.e. to say 1661, then age of Guru Gobind Singh at the time of his father's martyrdom would be fourteen years. Several English writers like J.D. Cunningham and Muhammad Latif have also followed them in assigning the date of birth of the Guru.

Giani Garja Singh on the evidence of *Bhatt Vahis* and *Panda Vahis* states that Guru was born in 1661. The view has been upheld by G.B. Singh and D.R. Narang in their recent book *Correct Date of Birth of Sri Guru Gobind Singh.*

We however, do not agree with Garja Singh, G.B. Singh or D.R. Narang or any other scholar who considers 1661 as the right date of birth of the Guru, because these sources were not as reliable as they are made out to be since they suffered serious inaccuracies. Each Bhatt or author of *Panda Vahi* recorded information regarding different families who intended to seek spiritual guidance from him with the purpose of maintaining cordial relation with them. The information was often general, touching only those aspects which could benefit a particular Bhatt or his family. It was rarely specific and often far from true historically.

missionary tour of Eastern states of India. Travelling with his wife, mother and a band of devotees, the Guru arrived in Patna towards the end of the year. His wife Gujri or Mata Gujri as she was reverentially called by the Sikhs, being in an advanced stage of pregnancy, had decided to remain there for her confinement while Guru Tegh Bahadur proceeded further to Bengal and Assam.

At the time of birth of his son, Guru Tegh Bahadur was at Dacca[1] fully engrossed in missionary and organisational work. Bhai Dayal Das who appeared to have stood at the head of *Sikh Sangat* of Patna at least during the life-time of the Guru, immediately despatched a letter to him giving him the happy news. The letter was carried by Bhai Kalyan Chand. Great celebrations took place at Patna as well as at Monghyr. Guru Tegh Bahadur's well-wishers and disciples flocked to Patna to behold the son of their Guru. According to Macauliffe, "The Guru was beside himself with joy on hearing the good news, which was followed by great rejoicings. Considerable sums were given away generously as alms and charity to the poor and the needy. The accompanying Raja (Ram Singh) also participated in these joyous celebrations and at his command 'Guns were fired.' The best musicians exhibited their skills, and copious alms were bestowed."[2] A contemporary chronicle writes : "The gentle breeze of happiness blew through every home. The prayer of each heart was granted as the new moon (Gobind Rai) rose over Patna."

Kirpal Chand, the maternal-uncle of the babe and *Sangat* of Patna warmly received all those who came to have a glimpse of the son of Guru Tegh Bahadur. Everyone found something unique, something magnetic and elevating in the baby.

Mata Gujri named her son Gobind Rai in the memory of his grand father Guru Hargobind. According to Sikh tradition, when Guru Tegh Bahadur was born, Guru Hargobind prophesied that he would be blessed with a son who would defend the people against the tyranny of the Mughals.

---

1. *Hukamnama's* photostat copy can be seen in *Guru Tegh Bahadur* by Dr. Trilochan Singh facing p. 228.
2. M.A. Macauliffe, *The Sikh Religion*, Vol. IV, p. 357.

Guru Tegh Bahadur's mother is said to have reminded him of his father's words and when he departed from Patna after leaving his family, he left instructions with his wife that if they were blessed with a son, he should be named Gobind. The story probably owes its origin to the fact that Gobind Rai grew to resemble Guru Hargobind more than any of his other ancestors. He inherited not only his grandfather's features and built but his temprament also. It is not surprising that the torch of defiance that Guru Hargobind had lit was carried a stage further by Gobind Rai.

Among the very first batch of pilgrims who came to pay their obeisance to the Guru was a Muslim Faquir, who seeing the child, claimed him to be very special, a divine prodigy. In the village of Ghuram (Patiala District in Punjab), another Muslim saint of high reputation, named Sayyad Bhikhan Shah made obeisance to the East instead of West on the day of (Guru) Gobind's birth. His disciples were astonished and demurred at the *Pir's* conduct, for, no Muslim was expected to make such gesture. The noble Faquir calmed them down and explained that in the city of Patna, God has revealed Himself through a new born babe. He had not done any wrong while bowing to him who was God Himself. Gobind Das or Gobind Rai as the child was called, soon became the object of adoration and wonder at Patna. His radiant face imparted joy to the people who happened to look on him. His face shed luminosity as his smile aroused affection. He indulged in lovable pranks which charmed the people no end. He was deemed to be a shining spot where the desperate found solace, the disappointed regained hope and seekers experienced bliss. He was cynosure of all eyes and his mother and grandmother in particular were very indulgent towards him and took special care to nurture him into a wise and a brave man. Guru Tegh Bahadur, despite his pressing engagements elsewhere, kept himself in touch with the family through letters and emissaries and never forgot to write to his wife, mother and brother-in-law Kirpal Chand and *Sangat* of Patna to pay full attention to the upbringing of his son.[1]

---

1. Fauja Singh, *Hukamnamas Sri Guru Tegh Bahadur Sahib*, No. 14, p. 99.

As he crossed the age of infancy he was found to take likings to the games which encouraged his interest in sword-playing, swimming, archery, horse-riding et al. He was also exposed to the literary and religious discussions and debates that were often held at Patna at the behest of the *Sangat* of Patna in which scholars/theologians/thinkers of diverse religious and literary traditions took part. People soon realised that the child was extraordinary and destined to be a great man. His physical demeanour was, of course, most pleasing. His eyes were gay, bright and cheerful and seemed to reflect wisdom beyond his age. His assertive yet unassuming utterances and the amiable and affectionate manners made him the beloved of the people and, particularly of the neighbourhood. To the boys of his age group, there seemed something mysteriously great and inspiring about him.

The grandmother and the mother of Gobind Rai must have vied with each other in their affections for the rapidly growing child and must have been careful to see that Gobind Rai did not deviate from the path chartered by the Sikh Gurus, and preached by them for nearly 200 years. It can be safely conjectured that Mata Nanki would relate to him the stories of the greatness of his great grandfather who was the first martyr in Sikh history. She must have often reminded him that he was the grandson of Guru Hargobind who in consonance with concept of *Miri* and *Piri* challenged the mighty Mughals to an armed contest in the neighbour-hood of Lahore itself[1]. At the same time we can imagine, revered Mata Gujri telling his son of the mission of Guru Nanak and his successors and nurturing him on the philosophy of devotion to one God, implicit obedience to the Guru and the relevance of *Nam Marg* (Path of meditation on Noumen).

Gobind Rai seemed to be responsive to the efforts of his mother, grandmother and his maternal uncle; for, he showed no disinclination towards their suggestions; rather he took them very seriously. All the time, even in the midst of serious counsels, he kept buoyancy and balance and was quick

---

1. Of the four battles that Guru Hargobind fought against the Mughals, the first three were fought in Amritsar District.

enough to surprise/amuse others through a play of wit and humour that he possessed in ample measure. He took delight in breaking with pallets, the earthen pitchers of women carrying water from the well in the campus of his house. They rarely complained to his mother or grandmother. Occasionally when some of them approached the mother/grandmother with a complaint, she was politely asked to forgive him as he was too young and needed their indulgence. None, therefore, even admonished him. All found in him a streak of spiritual splendour.

As he grew up, he began to show signs of organisational ability. Whenever he participated in any game, he always played the role of a leader and his companions were ready to carry out his injunctions. He would gather around himself a bevy of his playmates, run about on the banks of the River Ganges, splash water, swim, wrestle, box and fight. He would then bring his contingent back home, give them presents and feed them.[1] Sometimes, he would divide his playmates into two groups and arrange mock fights between them, himself heading one of the groups. He wielded weapons with such dexterity and ease that none of his companions could excel him. 'Guru Gobind Singh, says Henry Court, was from his early childhood an expert, and during his early years, he had learnt archery so well that none of his companions was able to shoot arrows like him.[2] Cleansing the weapons, wiping out the dust with a handkerchief and then burning incense before them with great interest and paying them obeisance daily constituted main activities in the child's daily routine.[3] The sling shot was his favourite weapon and he relished in practising and shooting pallets with it. Gobind Rai never hesitated in ridiculing the *Sadhus* and *Yogis* who sat cross-legged in an attitude of intense devotion on the banks of the river. He would taunt them for their hypocritical unconcern for life.

---

1. Khazan Singh, *History of the Sikh Religion*, p. 166.
   Bhagat Lakshman Singh, *Guru Gobind Singh*, p. 3.
2. Major Henry Court, *History of the Sikhs* or *Sikhan de Raj di Vithya*, p. 42.
3. Koer Singh, *Gurbilas Patshahi 10*, p. 32.
   Sukha Singh, *Gurbilas Patshahi 10*, p. 37.

Often when his maternal uncle returned from hunting and related his adventures in the forest, the excitement of the chase, the frightening roar of the tiger and exhiliration after the kill, Gobind Rai was all attention to what his uncle said. He developed a liking for hunting which later became his favourite sports.

Occasionally, he overstayed his play-time and returned home late. This delayed the recitation of *Rehras*, the evening prayer. By custom the *Rehras* at Gurdwara Patna Sahib is still read after the usual canonical hour.

Pandit Shiv Dutt[1], an erudite Sanskrit scholar and a revered old Brahmin, who had earned a name in the city of Patna, discovered in the Guru the culmination of a life-time quest for inward tranquility. Earlier he had left his aristocratic home and practised austerities but he had not found what he had been seeking. Thus there was a sense of emptiness in his heart. A new awareness dawned on him when he had the glimpse of Gobind Rai. His sense of duality vanished. He felt filled to the brim. He realised that it was the end of his quest. His only desire was, that the joy that his meeting with the child Guru had conferred upon him should remain with him for ever. The child-Guru became the all-time object of his contemplation and in him he perceived the vision of the deity he had long cherished and adored. At that very place, where the Pandit used to meditate on his gods and goddesses, and which is just a stone's throw from the *Takht Sri Harmandir Sahib at Patna* has sprung a Sikh place of worship, called *Gurdwara Gobind Ghat.*

A few days later when Pandit Shiv Dutt was absorbed in meditation on the banks of the River Ganges, two visitors came to seek a favour of him. They were Raja Fateh Chand Maini and his wife Vishamra Devi, who had known Shiv Dutt for a number of years. They had everything : name, power and wealth but were issueless. This caused them much unhappiness. Pandit Shiv Dutt had divined what tormented them. He told them politely that their wish could be fulfilled if they were blessed by the heavenly child who dwelt in their vicinity. He suggested that they should open their hearts to him for seeking

---

1. Kartar Singh, *Life of Guru Gobind Singh*, p. 23.

his grace. The Royal couple found a new object of worship. Their love and yearning grew day by day.

One day, the Guru entered their palace quietly and twining his little arms around the neck of the Queen, who at that time was sitting in deep reverie with her eyes closed, called out "Mother, Mother."

The Guru's one word 'Mother' took away her life-long grief. She opened her eyes and was amazed to see Gobind Rai in her lap. The miracle that she and her husband had been praying for had happened. Both of them were overwhelmed by this gesture of the child. The action filled the Queen with immense joy and in the loving embrace she felt she had got a son in Gobind Rai. She thought that she had got what she longed for and had no need for any more son. Here was a son whom both the Raja and his Queen could love and consider as theirs. He became the light of their lives. They felt that a God-filled child had come to them through His Grace and they wanted nothing more. They were perfectly satisfied and experienced beatitude. They had realised that bliss lay not in procreation but in communion with God. They made it a routine to spend most of their time in meditation and prayers. Their home became the venue of Sikh congregation. It has been so since then and today it is one of the historical shrines at Patna. Its name is *Gurdwara Maini Sangat* and it has preserved a poniard earthen pallet, a shoe of Kinkhal, a picture of the Queen, and a volume of *Guru Granth Sahib* in which *Mul Mantar* is believed to be written in Guru Gobind's hand. Reaching home Gobind Rai announced that he had found another mother. Mata Gujri wondered and asked, "Then how will he be able to play in two laps ?" "Just as one moon plays on two pools" was the reply of Gobind Rai.

The child expressed desire to eat something and the Queen served him and his companions with *Purian* (sort of pan cakes) and roasted grams, which she had prepared for her family. The practice has come down to us (though the first thing has been omitted) and everyday roasted grams are distributed among the children early in the morning.

Among the many wellwishers of the child-Guru in Patna, there were two Muslim nobles—Rahim Bakhsh and Karim

Bakhsh[1]. They were so much impressed by the child's charisma that they donated their two gardens and a piece of fertile land—a benefice still enjoyed by the holy shrine of Patna.

There are a number of traditional accounts current even in the present times, which portray greatness of Gobind Rai. It is true that tradition is not history entirely; but it is also true that every tradition embodies at least a grain of truth and therefore is a great help in formulating authentic history. This being the case, a critical scrutiny of all the traditional accounts leave one in no doubt that Gobind Rai revealed qualities which were portents of his significant role in times to come.

There lived a proud *Mansabdar* at Patna. Wherever and whenever he rode on his elephant through the town, he expected every passerby to salute him. One day, seated on his elephant, he passed through the street where Gobind Rai was playing with his mates. The elephant was caparisoned in velvet and bore costly rings on his tusks. A crowd of people stood humbly bowing their heads to the *Mansabdar*. Someone out of his entourage exhorted Gobind Rai's playmates to salute the Nawab by raising their hands to him. When Gobind Rai heard this, he goaded to his companions to 'Grin and Grimace at the Nawab.' All the children joined in the fun. The *Mansabdar* was baffled and his temper rose. His *mahavat* however, pacified him by saying, "They are children, too innocent to discriminate between the high and the low." Gobind Rai on his part had a design in his action. He wanted his friends never to display subservience and slavish mentality. Rather they should be bold enough to scorn the arrogant and haughty.

The Guru's family resided in a spacious house especially built by the Sikhs of Patna to accomodate them. Originally the house belonged to Salis Rai[2], a rich jeweller, who was blessed by Guru Nanak when he came to Patna during his itinerary. In appreciation of the Guru and his sublime message he turned it into a venue of Sikh congregation. The house was situated on a beautiful spot on the right bank of the River Ganges.

The city of Patna like the Ganges had been a darling of the muse of history. It had the privilege of being the capital

1. Kartar Singh, *Life of Guru Gobind Singh*, p. 23.
2. Ved Parkash, *Sikhs in Bihar*, p. 95.

and heart of Mauryan Empire in the third and second centuries B.C. Even earlier than that, it was consecrated by the visit of Lord Budha, who, it is said, came here to admonish its legendary founder Ajat Satru for a sin he had committed. During the rule of Sunga Dynasty, it suffered decline but it basked in glory again during the Gupta period. Its power declined and by the seventh century it was destroyed. In 1541 it was rebuilt by an Afghan ruler and soon it regained its past splendour. It was named Patna while its earlier name was Patli Putra. Since then the city has been enjoying high status both in political and economic spheres. In the Mughal period it was the capital of the *Subah* (province) of Bihar. Towards the close of his reign[1], Aurangzeb renamed it as Azamabad . It enjoyed a very commanding position as a centre of commerce and trade. According to Bowrey, "This is a country of very great traffic and commerce, and is really the great gate that openeth with Bengal and Orissa and so consequently into most parts of India, viz from the Northern kingdoms or Empires (by land) namely, Persia, Cormania (Kirman), Georgia, Tartaria etc[2]." The eyes of the foreigners were dazzled by the prosperous trade and commerce carried on in this city. Ralph Fytch, the English traveller (1538-91) spoke of it as a great town with a trade of cotton and cloth, much sugar, very much opium[3] and several other commodities. To Sebastin Manrique (1629-43), it appeared as a town of enormous quantity and variety of merchandise, whereas Peter Mundig called it the greatest mart of that entire region. The fact is also vouchsafed by the *Hukamnamas* (Epistles) of Guru Tegh Bahadur and Guru Gobind Singh. In Guru Tegh Bahadur's *Hukamnama* numbered 5, the Guru ordained the Sikhs of Patna that they should make available a certain number of tents of different kinds like Qalandri, Rawala, Qanats, Sahet Khan, Sahela etc. In that very epistle, the Guru makes mention of two scores of turbans of very fine Muslin cloth. From a lengthy *Hukamnama* of Guru Hargobind we can discern that Patna abounded in a special

---

1. Irfan Habib, *An Atlas of the Mughal Empire*, p. 39.
2. Thomas Bowrey, *A Geographical Account of Countries Around the Bay of Bengal 1669-79*, (ed.) Lt. Col. Sir Richard Carnal Temple Bart C.I.E., p. 221.
3. Irfan Habib, *op.cit.* p. 39.

type of cloth, called *Elachy*[1] made of silk and cotton-thread. Patna also traded in fine quality of scents and this fact can be verified from the information contained in the *Hukamnama* of Guru Gobind Singh dated Asuj 10, Samvat 1749 (correspoding to 1692) directing his followers at Patna to supply him a perfumed leather.[2] According to Irfan Habib a lot of merchandise from the North-Western India including Uttar Pradesh and Bihar was navigated from here to the Eastern part of India.[3]

It also served as the centre of Islamic Revivalist Movement especially of *Naqshbandis* and *Mahdies*. Sheikh Abdul Hai son of Khawaja Chakar Hisar and Sheikh Nur Mohammad had been the guiding lights of *Naqshbandi* Movement at Patna. These remained in regular correspondence with the Mujaddid at Sirhind and made strenuous efforts to spread his mission.[4] Similarly *Mahdi* Movement, ushered in India in the reign of Feroz Shah Tughlaq, made considerable headway under the guidance of disciples of Sayyad Mohammad Ashraf Jahangir Simani at Jampur.[5] The Hindu saints, especially of *Vaishnav* persuasions, also flourished at Patna during this period.

A large *Sangat* had also been functioning here since the time of Guru Hargobind. During Guru Tegh Bahadur's time Bhai Dayal Das, Gurdas, Anantia, Bhai Sangatia, Kewal Rai, Japu Deda, Murari, Bala and Ram Rai were some of the eminent Sikhs[6] who guided *Sangats* formed at various places particularly in Bihar and at other places and developed them into a cohesive network. Even *Sangats* of Benaras, Jaunpur and Mirzapur were a part of this network. These *Sangats* had established direct links with the Guru and received instructions directly from him and not through *Masands*. Therefore, such *Sangats* were designated by the Guru as *Khalsa* or *Kaliana*

1. Ved Parkash, *Sikhs in Bihar,* p. 145. According to Hugh and Parkar the *layches* and *elaches* were so called because they were so woven as to give the appearance of a cardamom.
2. This *Hukamnama* is preserved at Sri Hazur Sahib Patna.
   Ganda Singh, *Hukamname,* No. 41, p. 142.
3. Irfan Habib, *An Atlas of the Mughal Empire,* pp. 40-41.
4. S.A.A. Rizvi, *Muslim Revivalist Movement in Northern India,* p. 227.
5. *Ibid.,* p. 74.
6. Ganda Singh, *Hukamname,* No. 22, p. 105.

(emancipated). Since quite a number of Guru's *Hukamnamas* were addressed to the Sikhs of Patna, it is not difficult to surmise that Patna enjoyed a special position in the annals of the Sikh chronicles.

The Sikhs of Bihar and especially that of Patna were economically sound. That the Gurus addressed as many as three dozen letters to them at frequent intervals, each making requisition for ready money or different articles, is a proof on one hand of a strong sense of loyalty and devotion among the followers and of their good material condition on the other. The two *Hukamnamas*—one sent to the *Sangats* of Mashiana and the other addressed to *Lashkar* (army) of Prince Azam instructing them to send 80 and 100 *Tolas* of gold respectively amply supports this fact.

On the social plane too, they appeared inclined to follow teachings of the Guru. They did not approach any court for settlement of their disputes (especially those arising among themselves) or their grievances redressed. Instead their disputes or mutual discords were usually referred to and accords arrived at by the *Sangat* which acted as arbitrator.[1] In the seventeenth century, because of the fanatical and oppressive religious policy of Aurangzeb, the Sikhs, like other non-Muslims, were feeling suffocated and were unable to live their religious life freely and fearlessly. The Guru seemed to have grown fond of the River Ganges and loved to spend hours together on its banks. Hopefully, he pondered over the mythological tales and history woven around it and reached his own conclusions. Normally a vast concourse of people comprising different classes, faiths, ethnicities, ideologies and economic interests visited Patna to have a dip in the Ganges or to conduct business. In the process they interacted with one another. The Guru, being witness to all that, must have learnt a lot which in his later years helped him to mature his plans. The Sikh affairs also did not eacape his notice.

Having been born in a family with roots firmly planted in Sikhism besides their responsibility of its propagation; he

---

1. *Hukamnama* of Mata Sundri dated 19th Kartik, Samvat 1780 as quoted in Ved Parkash, *Sikhs in Bihar*, p. 137.

learnt his first lesson at home. He also learnt through osmotic effect or by joining daily congregations held at his residence. He picked Bihari, a dialect of Hindi, in the company of his Bihari friends, and *Gurmukhi* script from his dear mother. He lisped in Bihari Hindi, acquired a taste for that language which found poetic expressions in his compositions in later years. Since many scholars, thinkers, poets and artists visited Patna to pay respects to the family of Guru Tegh Bahadur, he found a chance to mix and interact with them. As a result, he not only grew maturer but also developed interest in languages as well as in the art of versification.

In short, Guru's childhood was characterised by an intense quest, for a kind of warming up for the struggle he was destined to wage on spiritual, social and political planes. It seemed as if a commissioned soul was busy at the outset equipping itself with the arsenal needed to assault the forces of evil and darkness and to rebuild man and society afresh.

The Guru himself revealed his mission in his autobiographical narrative entitled *Bachittar Natak* :

> For this have I come into the world.
> The Lord God sent me for the protection of Right (*Dharma*)
> That I spread the truth everywhere
> And defeat and destroy the wicked and evil doers.
> For this mission have I taken birth;
> Let all holy men know this in their minds
> To spread the faith to uphold holy men,
> And to extirpate the wicked root and branch.[1]

Later events showed that though physically removed from his birth place, Guru Gobind Singh never forgot it and always cherished its sweet recollections. That he was in touch with Patna is manifest from his letters that he wrote to the Sikhs of Bihar, who too always experienced uneasiness at his

---

1. *Hum eh kāj jagat meṅ āe.*
   Dharam het gurdev paṭhāe.
   Jahā tahā tum dharam bithāro.
   Dusṭ dokhiyan(i) pakar(i) pachhāro.42.
   Yāhi kāj dharā hum janamaṅ.
   Samajh lehu sādhū sab manmaṅ.
   Dharam chalāvan sant ubāran.
   Dusṭ saban ko mūl upāran.43.   (*Bachittar Natak*)

absence from that city. Of all the people, separation from Gobind Rai was most acutely felt by the Maini's and Pandit Shiv Dutt. Time weighed heavy on them and the pangs of separation became quite unbearable. They decided to pay a visit to Gobind Rai, who had by then grown up to be a handsome youngman and was residing at Anandpur in the Punjab. He was their Master and culmination of their quest for bliss. To achieve their objective, they set out on their journey to Anandpur, not withstanding the hazards involved in the venture. The faint echoes of their intended visit had not failed to reach the Guru who rushed out of his hill abode and came as far as Ropar to receive them. They were taken to Anandpur where an enthusiastic welcome was accorded. They were simply overwhelmed. Their ego completely wiped out and they enjoyed oneness with the Master, a stage of supreme bliss or *Nirban*, the term used by Guru Tegh Bahadur in his *Bani*. Pandit Shiv Dutt, now an old man, was not destined to return to Patna as he breathed his last at Anandpur where his last rites were performed with due solemnity. The Royal couple was back home safe and sound with a copy of the *Granth Sahib*, presented to them as a token of love and respect for them. It was installed, so goes the traditional account, at a suitable place inside the palace where it still continues to be enshrined adding grace and grandeur to the said palace and a new lustre to the name and fame of those with whom it was associated.

As has been said earlier, Patna was the place much loved by the Guru. People of Patna also reciprocated this love. It was not surprising that a large number of Behari Sikhs were present in the vast congregation that met at Anandpur Sahib on 29th March, 1699, the Baisakhi day, when the Guru set afloat the Order of the *Khalsa*. The Sikhs of Patna on their return duly informed the population of Patna that they were required to receive *Pahul*.[1]

Soon after the manifestation of the *Khalsa* when the people had left for their homes, the Guru at once sent letters through his proficient messengers to all the *Sangats* including those in Patna, Rampur, Dacca and Bengala intimating them

---

1. Ved Parkash, *Sikhs in Bihar*, p. 89.

about the new developments.[1] The disciples of the Guru showed the Sikhs the orders of their Master[2], enjoining upon them to come to his presence with grown hair and other mandatory articles. The same can be corroborated from a letter of Guru Gobind Singh preserved in *Takht Sri Hazur Sahib* in Patna City. This letter dated Samvat 1758 Phagan 10 (corresponding to February 6, 1702) and addressed to Bhai Mehar Chand, Dharam Chand and Karam Chand contains the following order :

> *Recite Guru's Name; you will feel elevated. You are my Khalsa. You are to comply with a requisition of Rs. 101/- for the purchase of an elephant. The same may be sent by Hundi as soon as you see the Hukamnama. Besides bring personally everything set apart for the Guru. He will be blessed who comes armed to the court of the Guru...... The Guru will always be with him. Whatever is there for the Guru, should not be made over to anyone else. Don't have any association with the Masands and do not show any respect to them. Take any Sikh who wishes to accompany you; do not put him to inconvenience. This is my order.*[3]

From the perusal of the above *Hukamnama* it becomes amply clear that, even when the Guru was away from Patna, he continued to keep himself in touch with his followers in Bihar especially those of his birth-place and reposed full confidence in them.

He was quick enough to apprise them of the changes those were gradually taking place and often looked forward to their assistance for meeting his exigencies from time to time.

---

1. Koer Singh, *Gurbilas Patshahi 10*, p. 141.
2. Sukha Singh, *Gurbilas Patshahi 10*, p. 144 as quoted by Ved Parkash, *Sikhs in Bihar*, p. 87.
3. Ganda Singh, *Hukamname*, No. 55, p. 171, translation by the Author.

CHAPTER III

AT ANANDPUR

Guru Tegh Bahadur, immediately after occupying the apostalic seat on August 11, 1664, undertook extensive tours as Guru Nanak and his father Guru Hargobind had done. His first itinerary covered certain places in *Majha* and *Malwa*. While in the second itinerary he covered places mostly in the Eastern part of the country as far away as U.P., Bihar, Bengal and Assam. He left Assam in the year 1670. The Guru took a route different from the one he had travelled during his onward journey on account of the former being shorter. This being so, he travelled in the direction of Patna via Bongaigaon, Siliguri and Kathiar.

The journey was undertaken with a definite motive. Apart from visiting *Sikh Sangats* already established, and organising new ones across India, he knit them into a network, enabling each to have linkage or communication with others, besides direct links with the Guru. He also intended to give a definite system to the collection of offerings and their remittance to the Guru. The responsibility of this task was laid on the *Sangat* itself, which was advised to send the collections through their own persons instead of *Masands* or their deputies who upto then had earned the notoriety of misappropriating the funds. Besides, the Guru intended to satisfy his deep philosophical interest in other faiths. To better inform himself of their beliefs, he had extensive exchanges with the Mughal bureaucrats in Delhi, with Brahmin priests in Prayag (Allahabad), Buddhist pilgrims in Gaya (even though the Brahmins had long since taken over), *Sufis* in Malda and with Assam's Ahom tribesmen regarding their tantric practices. He also thought it prudent to keenly watch the working of the

Mughal government in different provinces, especially their attitude towards the non-Muslims, weaker and unprivileged sections. This vouchsafes the fact that the Guru was constantly under surveillance right from the beginning of his itinerary from Chak Nanki to the Eastern region of the country.

Returning from Assam, Guru Tegh Bahadur took a very short time to reach Patna. The Guru was in haste to come to the Punjab since during the period he was away from the Punjab, there had occurred a marked change in the socio-religious policy of Emperor Aurangzeb who had adopted a much sterner attitude towards the Hindus and other non-Muslims. On April 8, 1669, the Emperor, according to *Maasar-i-Alamgiri,* issued orders to the governors of the provinces "to destroy without remorse the schools and temples of the infidels. They were strictly enjoined to put an end to the teaching and practising of idolatrous form of worship." According to De Graff, "In the month of January 1670, all the governors and native officers received the order from the great Mughal, prohibiting the practice of pagan religion throughout the country and bring down all the temples and sancturies of idol worshippers in the hope that some pagans would embrace the Muslim religion."[1] While this general order was showing its effect in the country, the Sikhs also, according to Mohammad Hashim, Khafi Khan's *Muntakhab-ul-Lubab* "had their share of Emperor's wrath. Emperor Aurangzeb having received information about them had ordered their deputies to be turned out and places of worship destroyed."[2] And in obedience to this order, a Sikh temple in the town of Burya in the Pargana of Khizrabad of the *Sarkar* of Sirhind was destroyed and a mosque raised on the site. The Sikhs were enraged. They killed the incharge of the mosque in retaliation.

Such were the circumstances when Guru Tegh Bahadur reached Patna. The people of Patna were thrilled to see their

---

1. Sri Ram Sharma, *Religious Policy of the Mughal Emperors*; Saqi Mustad Khan, *Maasar-i-Alamgiri,* p. 81, (ed.) J.N. Sarkar, *A Short History of Aurangzeb,* p. 212.
2. Khafi Khan, *Muntakhab-ul-Lubab* II, p. 652 as quoted in J.N. Sarkar, *A Short History of Aurangzeb,* p. 212.

Guru after an absence of four years. His mother Mata Nanki and wife Mata Gujri were delighted to see him. Happiest of all was the four year old Gobind Rai, who was to meet his father for the first time. His playful pranks and precocious ability had already given to the people the impression that a new prophet was born. Guru Tegh Bahadur had repeatedly sent messages from Bengal that no one should interfere with the likes and dislikes of Gobind Rai; and no one should interfere with the freedom of this new apostle of hope.

Gobind Rai was now carried in a palanquin to meet Guru Tegh Bahadur while the prominent disciples led by Bhai Dayal Das followed him chanting hymns from the *Adi Granth*. Guru Tegh Bahadur alighted from his horse while his son came out of his palanquin. He went to his father, bowed low and touched his feet in reverence. Guru Tegh Bahadur embraced him and kissed him. The Guru was delighted to see his son about whom fascinating stories had reached him. He offered him numerous presents and gifts which he had brought from Assam and Bengal. Bhai Dayal Das was the first to go forward and touch the Guru's feet. Guru Tegh Bahadur honoured him with a robe of honour, blessed and thanked him and the *Sangat* for looking after his family so well. The place where Gobind Rai first met his father has been preserved as a garden which originally belonged to the Nawab of Patna.

Even as the Guru's family and *Sangat* were experiencing beatitude in the presence of the Guru, the latter preferred to set out for the Punjab where the Sikhs needed him the most, especially when the tidings reached him that Aurangzeb was bent upon converting the land of the Punjab into *Dar-ul-Islam* to ultimately see the whole of geographical region right from Afghanistan to Delhi Islamised.

At the time of departure, the Guru told his family that they would soon be called to the Punjab. He himself proceeded to Chak Nanki via Delhi. He reached Delhi on June 13, 1670.[1] He put up in the Dharmsala of Bhai Kalyana where disciples and followers flocked in large numbers to seek his blessings.

---

1. *Bhat Vahi Talaunda Pargana Jind.*
Fauja Singh, *Guru Tegh Bahadur : Martyr and Teacher*, p. 42.

Rani Pushpa Devi came alongwith her daughter-in-law, the wife of Ram Singh and felt relieved of her anxiety to hear the well-being of her son. She beseeched the Guru to stay for a few days in her house in Raisina.[1] Soon after, the Guru left for Lakhnaur via Rohtak, Kurukshetra and Pehoa.

In the meantime, a message from Guru Tegh Bahadur reached Patna instructing Gobind Rai, his mother and maternal uncle to come to Anandpur in the Punjab. In strict compliance of his father's message, the entire family got busy packing their belongings that included Gobind Rai's precious weapons of different varieties. "His baggage consisted of various articles such as tents, *Qanats*, *Shamianas* (canopies), *Jajim* (cloth thrown over the carpet to sit on) and Shattranjs (i.e. spotted carpets). The palanquin was embellished with gold and pearls ; hawks, camels and elephants were decorated attractively. He put all his weapons, such as *Khanjar* (daggers), *Budge* (knife), *Teg* (swords), *Katar* (scimitar), *Tope* (swivel), *Tamanche* (pistol) and *Siper* (shield) in a box."[2] In short, everything was packed up at once.

The news of intended departure from Patna spread in the whole city like a wild fire. For the devotees and admirers the moment was painful. They assembled to have a last glimpse of their beloved child, who had enraptured their minds for over five years. They waited upon him, imploring him to leave behind his beautiful cradle as a souvenir so that they might be able to console themselves by beholding it when overcome with grief. The child Gobind Rai acceded to the request of the residents of Patna and the cradle is even preserved today in *Sri Harmandir Sahib* as Gobind Rai's keep-sake, before which the high and the low make obeisance. While demanding cradle, the people of Patna seemed to be struggling to keep the child's memory evergreen. At that time, none had thought that in the times to come, Patna would be inseparably associated with the name of Gobind Rai. In the medieval period, Patna was a famous trade centre, situated as it was on the route from

1. Swarup Singh Kaushish, *Guru Kian Sakhian*.
2. Koer Singh, *Gurbilas Patshahi 10*, p. 15.
   Sukha Singh, *Ibid.*, p. 35.
   Ved Parkash, *Sikhs in Bihar*, p. 93.

Prayag to Bengal, but after the birth of Gobind Rai it also came to be looked upon as a venue like Gaya, heralding the beginning of a new phase in the socio-cultural history of India through Guru Nanak's dispensation. In the Sikhs religious consciousness, Patna acquired a special place, as they considered it sanctimonious being connected with the tenth Master. This perception of the Sikhs persisted and acquired poignancy as the time rolled on. Ultimately, Patna won the honour of being the locale of one of the five supreme seats of Sikh religious authority.

Of all the people who felt disconsolate at the departure of Gobind Rai from the city, the sorrow of Raja Maini's wife was the profoundest. She swooned and could gain consciousness only when she was consoled and cheered by the child Guru himself. A large number of people resolved to accompany him wherever he would go and it was with great difficulty that they were prevailed upon to drop the idea.[1] Even the zealots among them decided to accompany him upto Danapur where they finally bid him and his entourage a befitting farewell.

At Danapur an old lady named Pardhani[2] served *khichari* (rice and lentils cooked together) which she had cooked in an earthen pot called *handi* in Hindi. The Guru blessed her and assured her that her desire to have the Guru's *darshan* daily would be fulfilled if she continued to serve *khichari* similarly to wayfarers. The place where the Guru sat to partake of *khichari* was considered special and subsequently a shrine was built there. It was named as *Handiwali Sangat*. The shrine is now called *Gurdwara Handi Sahib*. *Handi* is said to be still preserved there.[3]

From Danapur the party moved towards the Ganges and after crossing it, reached Chhapra. From there they re-crossed

---

1. According to Koer Singh, the author of *Gurbilas Patshahi 10*, "The people returned to their houses at night when they sat silently and at the same time finding no interest in any kind of work.

2. In some accounts the name is 'Jamni'.

3. The Gurdwara is housed in a small hall with verandah on three sides and a small brick-paved walled compound in front on the bank of a seasonal stream, Son.

the river and went to Arrah wherefrom they proceeded to Dum Rao and Buxor. To reach Buxor they crossed the river again. After this, they recrossed the river to visit Sasram wherefrom they set out for Benaras and on the way passed by Mughal Sarai and Chhota Mirzapur. Jaunpur which lay to the North of Benaras was visited on the way. This was the place where Bhai Gurdas had preached and established a *Sangat*. There stands now a gurdwara called *Sangat Mridang Wali*. The tradition has it that the child Guru bestowed a *Mridang*—a musical instrument—upon one Bhai Gurbax Singh, a *Masand*, Sikh missionary of the place.[1]

From Jaunpur the party reached Benaras, a great Hindu centre of classical learning. Bhagats Kabir and Ravi Das whose hymns are included in the *Adi Granth* used to live there. Guru Nanak had sojourned here during his first round of itineraries and organised a *Sangat* (holy congregation) which had been flourishing since Guru Tegh Bahadur hallowed the place in 1666 and expressed his satisfaction at the output of local *Sangat*. Understandably, this *Sangat* welcomed the child and his entourage. It is said that both Sikhs and non-Sikhs, came in large numbers to behold the divine apostle. All were amazed at wisdom and refined conduct of the Guru's child. Gobind Rai loved scenic beauty of the place. It suited his inquisitive mind as well; for in his time the residents of this place were restive due to different socio-religious ideologies like Vaishnavism, Shaivism, Sargun Bhakti, Nirgun Bhakti, Islamic Sunnism, *Sufis* et al which converged here and were proactive to prove the relevance and truth of their respective stands.

Gobind Rai's contribution to these proceedings were though childlike, yet indicated that he was well-versed in Sikh philosophy.

It is said that at Benaras, Gobind Rai refused to accept the sacred thread when it was offered to him as was customary with the Pandits of that place.[2]

---

1. According to Gurmukh Singh, the author of *Historical Sikh Shrines*, p. 32, this *Mridang* was bestowed by Guru Tegh Bahadur.
2. *Suraj Parkash*, Ras 62, Ansu 45, pp. 2197-98.

From Benaras they headed westward for Allahabad, another great Hindu *Tirath* (place of pilgrimage) in Uttar Pradesh.[1] Gobind Rai stayed where Guru Tegh Bahadur had sojourned and where now stands a gurdwara named *Pakki Sangat*.

The party left Allahabad, crossed River Ganges for the seventh time and reached Ayudhya where stands a Gurdwara commemorating the visit of Guru Gobind Singh (as a child).[2] Gobind Rai was accorded a tumultuous welcome here and a large number of people thronged to receive divine knowledge of his dispensation.

From Ayudhya, the party proceeded to Lucknow enroute to Pilibhit and Nanakmata.[3] According to another tradition, they proceeded to Mathura and Brindaban via Kanpur, Brahmavart, Bathoor and Agra. After visiting Mathura, they set out for Pilibhit via Bareilly thus crossing River Ganges for the ninth time.[4] From Pilibhit, they proceeded to Nanak Matta which was known as Gorakh Matta before Guru Nanak's visit. It was a great centre of Yogis.[5]

From Nanak Mata, the party proceeded to Hardwar via Ram Nagar. Most of the places visited by the child Gobind Rai were centres of orthodox Hindu tradition. Side by side centres of different denominations of Islam such as *Sunni, Shite, Mahdi* functioned. Discussions must have taken place on matters ranging from deeply philosophical and metaphysical to the forms and formalism then prevalent in Hindu and Muslim societies, as also in various socio-religious groups who were outside the parameters of Islam or Hinduism. It is not difficult to strike a conclusion that Gobind Rai despite his tender age, must have formed some impressions on how different socio-religious societies or sub societies functioned and conducted themselves.

The party reached Lakhnaur probably by the end of the

---

1. Fauja Singh (ed.), *Atlas Travels of Guru Gobind Singh,* p. 10.
2. Gurmukh Singh, *Historical Sikh Shrines,* p. 323.
3. Fauja Singh (ed.), *op.cit.,* p. 11.
4. *Ibid.*
5. *Ibid.*

year 1670 (September 13, 1670).[1] Lakhnaur, now in Ambala district and situated at a distance of seven miles from Ambala city was the original home of Mata Gujri and her brother Kirpal Chand. The place is marked by the presence of a majestic Gurdwara where some sacred relics of the Guru's family are kept.

While leaving Patna after a brief visit, Guru Tegh Bahadur had informed his family members that he himself would come to Lakhnaur via Delhi where he wanted to meet Pushpa Devi, mother of Raja Ram Singh.[2] This done, he immediately left for Delhi and reached there on Harh 22, 1927 BK.[3] (June 20, 1670). When he was staying at *Dharamsala*, Bhai Kalyana, Rani Pushpa Devi alongwith her daughter-in-law (Raja Ram Singh's wife) waited upon the Guru and after paying homage to him inquired of the well-being of her son. The Guru informed her that Raja Ram Singh had achieved initial victories in Assam and consoled her by saying that he would return shortly.[4]

After a stay of two months and thirteen days under strict surveillance at Delhi,[5] Guru Tegh Bahadur left for Lakhnaur via Rohtak, Kurukshetra and Pehowa. He was accompanied

1. *Bhat Vahi Multani Sindhi* 'Khata Jalhana Balauton ka'; Vahi Pandit Neel Kanth son of Pandit Atma Ram Jeotishi, Pahewa Tirth.
   From the *Bhat Vahi* : "Guru Gobind Das ji beta Tegh Bahadur ji....Lakhnaur Aae, Pargana Ambala, Sambat 1727 Asun 9 Shukla Pakhe gail Mata Gujri ji Aae Mahal Guru Tegh Bahadur ji... .
2. *Guru Kian Sakhian*, Sakhi 26.
3. Guru Tegh Bahadur Ji Mehal Nama... Assam Pati Raja Singh Dev, Amber Pati Raja Ram Singh se baidaigi lai Dilli Bhai Kalayane Di Dharamsala me aae niwas kiya, gail dewan Durgah Mal Chhibbar, Nawab Saif Khan aae sal sataran se satais Asarh mas ki baais ko do mas teran dihon Dilli me baraje. Guru Ji Shan Nazar Bandi se mukt hoe Raja Ram Singh ke Mata Pushpa Devi se badaigi lai Madhar Desh aae." *Bhat Vahi Talaunda Pargana Jind.*
4. *Guru Kian Sakhian*, Sakhi 26.
5. *Guru Kian Sakhian* : The government surveillance referred to here in all probability was started at Agra. When Guru Tegh Bahadur reached this place on his way to Delhi in 1670, he was taken under custody and from there was brought to Delhi. This view is supported by the popular and strong tradition about Guru Sahib's arrest at Agra, if read independently of the setting of time somehow imparted to it by later writers such as Bhai Santokh Singh and Giani Gian Singh.

this time among others by Nawab Saif Khan.[1] The Nawab had been leading a hermit's life since 1669. He had followed the Guru to Assam and had met him either in Assam or somewhere else on his way back.

It was indeed a great occasion for the people of Lakhnaur. Little Gobind Rai was the cynosure of all eyes, not merely because it was his first visit to the place but also due to his magnetic looks and lovable pranks. On the auspicious day of *Dussehra* which came only a few days after his arrival there, the lovely child was seated on the cot and his elder maternal uncle Mehar Chand Subhikhi performed *sarvarna* and *Dastar* ceremonies. The colour of the turban was *Zamurdi* (green) according to Bhat Vahi.[2] Sahibzada Gobind Rai was ceremoniously dressed for this special occasion. He was carrying some arms also. A *tikka* mark of sandalwood was applied on his forehead by Mehar Chand, his maternal uncle.[3] Then followed the offerings. First of all, Jhanda, the *Masand* of Lakhnaur presented 101 *Mohars*. Many others followed suit. After that people would flock from the neighbouring areas daily and make their offerings to him by way of homage. Arrangements were made for imparting formal education to the child. Bhai Sahib Chand taught him *Gurmukhi* and Bhai Sati Das gave him lessons in Persian language. It was here that he received a homage for the second time from a Muslim Pir, Arif-ud-din. Sayyed Bhikhan Shah of Thaska (in the Patiala district of Punjab) a pious Sufi also paid his obeisance to Gobind Rai. As the story goes, he held upon his palms two earthen pots when he saw the child. The latter touched both. By this Bhikhan Shah inferred that he would treat both, Hindus and Muslims, alike. During his stay of about six months at Lakhnaur Gobind Rai visited adjoining places such as Rana Majra, about 15 miles North of Lakhnaur, Salar Gram, about ten miles North of Lakhnaur and Mardogram about four miles from Lakhnaur.[4] Besides, he

1. Saqi Mustad Khan, *Maasar-i-Alamgiri*, (ed.) J.N. Sarkar (Calcutta 1947), p. 69. Dr. Ganda Singh (ed.), *Hukamname*, pp. 108-09.
2. Fauja Singh, *Guru Tegh Bahadur : Martyr and Teacher*, p. 49, footnote 38.
3. *Guru Kian Sakhian*, Sakhi 39.
4. Kirpal Singh, *Sikh Itihas de Vishesh Pakh* (Punjabi), pp. 199-200.

visited Ambala City and the villages Bhano and Kheri.[1]

He also engaged himself in various exercises such as horse-riding and use of weapons. The Sikhs of this area presented to him steeds of high quality-breed and weapons of high calibre.[2] He also enjoyed hunting in the neighbourhood of Lakhnaur,[3] which then was surrounded by groves of trees and bushes.

After a short stay with his family, Guru Tegh Bahadur, in the company of Bhai Dayal Das, Bhai Sadhu Ram etc. left for the village Malla to meet his sister Bibi Viro. The family, however, was instructed to stay at Lakhnaur till he sent for them.

From Malla the Guru proceeded to Bakala. Shortly afterward a message was received at Lakhnaur asking all members of his family to join him at Bakala.[4]

The family proceeded to Bakala wherefrom it went to Chak Nanki in company of the Guru. How long did the family stay at Bakala is not clear. Nevertheless we have the evidence of *Shahid Bilas* by Sewa Singh that in Chet Sudi 11, 1729 BK (March 29, 1672) Guru Tegh Bahadur was definitely present at Chak Nanki.[5]

Enroute to Chak Nanki, the family visited Bhanu Kheri, Ambala, Qabalpur, Harpalpur and Kutha Kheri, which lay between Ambala and Rajpura to the West of the modern G.T. Road joining the two places.[6] From Kutha Kheri, they went straight to Ropar visiting on the way places such as Nandpur, Kalaur and Kotla Nihang.[7] From Ropar they journeyed on to Kiratpur where Baba Suraj Mal, second son of Guru Hargobind

---

1. Kirpal Singh, *Sikh Itihas de Vishesh Pakh*, pp. 199-200.
2. Kirpal Singh, *Badshah Darvesh Guru Gobind Singh*, p. 5, Chandigarh, 1999.
3. *Ibid.*
4. There is another equally strong tradition that the family stayed on at Lakhnaur till the Guru arrived at Chak Nanki and sent for them. But in case the Guru's stay at Bakala was long as we have assumed here, it is more plausible that the family proceeded to Bakala and from there went to Chak Nanki in the company of the Guru.
5. Giani Garja Singh (ed.), *Shaheed Bilas*, p. 58.
6. Fauja Singh (ed.), *Atlas Travels of Guru Gobind Singh*, p. 11.
7. *Ibid.*

was living.[1] He and his family were immensely pleased to receive Gobind Rai. After staying at Kiratpur for a couple of days the family reached Chak Nanki which was only eight kilometres away from Kiratpur.[2] They were received amidst great rejoicings. Disciples from all over the Punjab poured in to meet Guru Tegh Bahadur and to see the young prophet Gobind Rai. By that time the child had attained the age of six.

Some historians including Bhai Santokh Singh, the author of *Suraj Parkash* hold that Guru Tegh Bahadur had left for Delhi to discuss the matter with the Emperor that culminated into his martyrdom before Gobind Rai reached Chak Nanki. It is incorrect in the light of the statement of Guru Gobind Singh in his composition *Bachittar Natak* wherein he has proclaimed that when he reached the age of eight for performance of his religious duties, his father left for heavenly abode.

At Chak Nanki, Gobind Rai was fondled by nurses and he was tended very carefully.[3] He received instructions in various disciplines.[4] He had picked up the accent and dialect peculiar to the Bihari people. Most of the Sikhs who were unfamiliar with Bihari language were amused to hear him as his speech was a charming novelty to them.

Excellent arrangements were made to impart education to him. Sahib Singh, a learned Granthi continued to teach *Gurmukhi*. Qazi Pir Mohammad[5] replaced Bhai Sati Das whose services the Guru utilised elsewhere. Hari Das was appointed to teach Sanskrit. Use of arms and equestry was taught by Bajjar Singh.[6] Sango Shah the eldest son of Guru Tegh Bahadur's sister Bibi Viro gave him lessons in archery.[7]

---

1. Fauja Singh (ed.), *Atlas Travels of Guru Gobind Singh*, p. 11.
2. *Ibid.*, p. 12.
3. *Bachittar Natak.*
4. *Ibid.*
5. According to Teja Singh and Ganda Singh, the descendants of Pir Mohammad have an autographed letter from Guru with them. It was given to Pir Muhammad by Guru Gobind Singh in appreciation of his services as a teacher.
6. Lakshman Singh believes that child Gobind Rai had a very efficient Rajput tutor to train him in martial art. He does not mention his name. Khazan Singh calls this tutor Bajar Singh Rajput.
7. Trilochan Singh, *Guru Tegh Bahadur*, p. 275.

Gobind Rai's tutors in various fields were very exacting. His mastery of Braj Bhasha,[1] Persian and Sanskrit[2] languages is a proof of his early grooming in these languages. The fact that he could compose *Chandi Di Var* before the age of twenty and later dictate the whole of the *Adi Granth* at Damdama during time of great stress reveal how hard his *Gurmukhi* teacher had worked on Gobind Rai. Gobind Rai's battles were a testimony to the hard labour which his Rajput tutor had put in. Some Hindu poets and scholars had sought refuge in Anandpur. He heard them recite Vedas, Ramayana, Mahabharta and other Hindu texts. These were impressionable years and Gobind Rai developed a sensitive response to literature. Side by side he was encouraged to develop interest in sports and recreation. The games which were dear to his heart were almost the same as he had played at Patna. He would divide his playmates into two groups and with himself at the head of one, engage them in mock battles. He also enjoyed hunting and swimming.

Gobind Rai was lucky in having among his playmates Maniya, Suraj Mal's two grandsons[3], his five cousins[4], the sons of his father's sister, and Nand Chand. All of them were outstanding in one aspect or the other. Maniya (later Mani Singh) was always thoughtful and contemplative with literary bent of mind. Suraj Mal's two grandsons had an incorrigible charitable disposition. His five cousins were fearless and transparently sincere. Nand Chand[5] was extremely cool and

---

1. Guru's composition as preserved in *Dasam Granth* are mostly in Braj Bhasha.
2. His Persian composition, *Zafar Nama* and *Hakayat* reveal an excellent grounding in that language.
3. Gulab Rai and Sham Das.
4. Sango Shah, Jit Mal, Gopal Chand, Ganga Ram and Mohri Chand. They commanded units of Guru's army in the battle of Bhangani. Sango Shah and Jit Mal died fighting in the battle of Bhangani.
5. Son of an old servant of Guru Tegh Bahadur. At Paonta he acted as Dewan; was sent to Srinagar (Garhwal) to attend the marriage of Fateh Shah's daughter. His daring escape enabled the Guru know of the impending attack on Paonta. He faltered in devotion to the Guru only late in life; ran to Kartarpur; and got killed at the hands of *Dhir Malias*.
   M.A. Macauliffe, *The Sikh Religion*, Vol. V, pp. 2, 12, 15, 24, 29, 36, 41, 44, 56, 87, 89.

taciturn. All of these playmates remained Gobind Rai's favourites both in childhood and in later life.

Guru Tegh Bahadur's *Darbar* was always filled with people who yearned to listen to the words of the ninth Master for their spiritual elevation. In the service of the Guru and of his Sikhs, they found an occupation which imparted them a sense of purpose and freedom.

To Guru Tegh Bahadur's *Darbar* came scholars, poets, artists; some to seek refuge, some to feel free to develop their art, some to receive help and others to seek enlightenment.[1] The Guru welcomed them all. Bhai Mani Singh reached Chak Nanki in the month of Chet 1729 BK/March 1673 from Aliwal. He recited and explicated *Gurbani*. Many more came and took up different tasks. Thus a new society was in the process of making. Chak Nanki had become a workshop to produce men immersed in Sikh ideology who could become a beacon of hope in the gloomy environments created by an oppressive government, cruel and intolerant elite, both religious and political.

Gobind Rai's regular attendance in the *Darbar* brought him in contact with people of varied interests, with the consequences that his outlook broadened, his wit sharpened and his sensibilities were fine-tuned. He started observing and analysing happenings around him with distinct objectivity which was the product of his own experience and his understanding of what his predecessors had preached. Many questions rocked his mind : Why had his father undertaken tours of different places ? Why was the new awareness which the gospel was engendering considered anathema to the power that was ? What was the *Summum Bonum* of Sikh Gurus including his father ?

Notwithstanding convulsive moments at times, Gobind Rai on the whole led a hard but blissful life at Chak Nanki, enjoying parental affection, warmth of friends and respect of the Sikhs. He acquired knowledge in different fields, registered impressions, interacted with different people and their

---

1. According to Bhai Kahn Singh, the ninth Guru had a number of poets at Makhowal.
   Also refer to D.P. Ashta, *The Poetry of Dasam Granth*, p. 32.

ideologies. This helped him in making up his mind to determine his own cause. But such a life was not to endure for long. The events moved at such a rapid pace that very soon Gobind Rai had to undergo mortifying experience. Guru Tegh Bahadur spent the whole of the year 1671 at Chak Nanki organising and training disciples, directing the construction of the city, according to the new requirements. Early in the year 1672 or 1673, he left for an extensive tour of *Malwa* and the Banger Desh. These were the backward areas where mass conversion was carried out by local officials. These were also the areas which the saints and reformers rarely visited and the local landlords in collusion with their master exploited the poor peasants with impunity. There was scarcity of water and lack of education. The people were living in poverty, ignorance, misery and fear. Guru Tegh Bahadur went there to awaken them to their individual and collective responsibilities. Every place that Guru Tegh Bahadur visited, the compassionate Master asked the people about their difficulties and problems. Where fields were dry, he had the well dug for the people. Where there was scarcity of milk, he procured cows for them and distributed them free to the people. For the landless peasants, he procured some land and urged them to live courageously as free people in love and humility before God. In barren areas, he had the trees planted.

During this time Guru Tegh Bahadur visited as many places and houses as he could, holding the torch of spiritual wisdom in one hand and the sword of freedom from fear, hunger, and oppression in the other. He felt that only those minds which are strong in moral fervour and spirit made unconquerable by the realisation of their higher destiny were capable of struggling against injustice and tyranny and could save the people from dehumanisation. The Guru, therefore, exhorted the people to imbibe spiritual and ethical values, sink differences on grounds of birth, caste, give up all fear and face tyranny with stoic calmness. The challenge of spiritual and social malaise as well as the tyrannical absolutist rule of Aurangzeb could be met only if the people were conscious of higher spiritual and ethical values and were prepared to suffer like a sage and die like a warrior, forgetting their narrow attachments. But before one could suffer like a sage, one had to be taught to live like a warrior. The Guru repeatedly laid added emphasis on this theme through his sermons and his hymns, the burden and essence of which was : be fearless by relying on the strength and power of God; be fearless by giving up attachment to wealth, body and other earthly possessions which are transient; be fearless and be stoically indifferent to pleasure and pain, happiness and sorrow; be firm in moral purity and spirit of dedication; be wise in spiritual enlightenment and the love of humanity and God and be Godlike in flesh. "Fear no one, nor strike fear in anyone's mind."

The Guru's message and teachings awakened people to their responsibilities and grim realities of human existence and inspired them with the conviction that the spirit of self-consecration alone could liberate them from fear, greed and sub servience. Through moral and spiritual effort, every man can imbibe godlike qualities in himself, become strong enough to meet any challenge to his freedom and integrity. He can become courageous enough to strike at the root of tyranny. The boon of power, strength, and inspiration should be sought from God.

In order to see the reaction of the people to his policies, Aurangzeb had sent *Khufia-Navis* (secret-news reporters) to all the provinces. From their reports, Emperor Aurangzeb learnt that the Guru had a large following in the country. People voluntarily filled his coffer with money and he distributed it freely keeping only that much which was barely necessary. He was extremely independent-minded and was loved by Muslims and Hindus alike. He vehemently opposed all taxes like *Jazya* and was preaching the message of religious freedom and fearlessness. People addressed him as *Sacha Patshah* (The True Emperor). On May 25, 1675, a deputation of sixteen[1] leading Kashmiri Brahmins led by Pandit Kirpa Ram Dutt of Mattan (who, after adopting *Khalsa* rites took the name of Kirpa Singh

1. P.N.K. Bamzai, *A History of Kashmir*, pp. 602-03.
The author says the number of deputationists was 500.
According to *Bhat Vahi Talaunda Pargana Jind* the number was 16.

and died a martyr in the Battle of Chamkaur[1]) reached Chak Nanki. These people narrated their tragic story to Guru Tegh Bahadur : how determined Aurangzeb was to convert Kashmir into the land of Muslims and in obedience of the royal order of Aurangzeb, how cruelly Iftikhar Khan (1671-1675), the Governor of Kashmir had been carrying out the fanatical policies in the state. They begged him to be with them in their hour of distress. With all earnestness they urged, "We suffer great atrocities Master ! *Janeus* (Sacred Threads) are forcibly taken off our persons. Kins are being killed. *Janeus* weighing, a maund and a quarter are snapped in a single day.[2]

The Guru listened to the Pandit's heart-touching account of forcible conversions and the atrocities that Aurangzeb's sadistic satrap of Kashmir was inflicting on the Hindus there. Their heart-rendering tale plunged the Guru in deep thought. He had already juxtaposed the whole panorama of events since the accession of Aurangzeb with the mission of Guru Nanak and reached the conclusion that the partisan and fanatical policies of the Emperor vis-a-vis non-Muslims, particularly the Hindus and the Sikhs were totally unjustified and contrary to the concept of *Halimi Raj* (The order of the merciful) and its fundamentals such as freedom from fear, freedom of conscience, freedom of worship, acceptance of diversity of faiths, multiculturistic and multi-religious approaches.

The Guru therefore, decided to take decision, which in fact, was the culmination of his cherished convictions. To say that the appeal of the Kashmiri Brahmins was the sole reason for his decision is to lose sight of other factors. His decision was prompted by larger issue of human rights including freedom of conscience. The cause of the Brahmins was in no way absent from his mind as his son and successor, Guru Gobind Singh has made reference to it in his autobiographical

---

1. Kirpa Ram, son of Aru Ram, grandson of Narain Das, great grandson of Brahm Das, of the house of Thakar Das, Bhardwaj gotra Sarswat Brahmin (Mulal) resident of Mattan Pargana Kashmir came to Chak Nanki Pargana Kahlur on Jeth Sudi Ikadshi 1732 Bk/25 May, 1675 bringing sixteen leading Brahmins of Kashmir. Guru Tegh Bahadur the ninth Guru consoled them.
2. Koer Singh, *Gurbilas Patshahi 10*, p. 48.

composition entitled "Bachittar Natak": But whether it was an independent, sole prompting factor, is open to deliberations. Being conscious that his reference to *Tilak* and *Janeu* might be taken in a narrow sense, Guru Gobind Singh himself added at the same place that the sacrifice of his father was for *Dharma* which in the context of Indian culture covers almost every aspect of life, where the principles of justice and righteousness are involved.

Guru Tegh Bahadur sat in rapt thought brooding over the anguish and the helplessness of these men, his eyes gleaming with divine compassion as he reflected on the vastness of the agony of his countrymen. He did not believe in idolatry. Sacred threads and the sandalwood *Tilak* mark on the forehead was never part of his faith. He did not believe in Brahmanism. He and his predecessors had been preaching against it for nearly two hundred years. But could he bear to see such a bloodshed, such inhuman treatment of any section of humanity ? The Sikh, the Christian were aspiring for divine light in their own way. Every form of worship however unrefined or immature, was the yearning of the creatures of the Eternal. The whole life of the universe with his countless languages, creeds and seen and unseen realities, was an act of worship, glorifying the Creator and the Sustainer. If some Muslim or Christian divine had come with similar complaint against a Hindu tyrant, Guru Tegh Bahadur would have reacted no differently. Now the helpless Brahmins had come to him after they realised that no Hindu warrior or saint, no Hindu leader or divine, no Hindu Sanyasi or Yogi dare confront the challenge of Emperor Aurangzeb to maintain their freedom of worship and to tell him : "I will die for your freedom of worship." For God-like Guru Tegh Bahadur, every creature, ignorant or wise, black or white, theist or atheist, nature worshipper or an idolater was a precious creation of the Supreme Lord, each made according to His will and each carrying the same hidden flame of His light in soul. When anyone tried to torment, agonise, strangle, destroy and physically annihilate any section of humanity in the name of any narrow totalitarian creed or religion and politics, it was his duty to stake all his power and spirit of self-sacrifice for protecting and defending it. The woeful tales of the Brahmins moved Guru Tegh Bahadur to profound pity and compassion. Their anguish became his personal sorrow. Their gloom and suffering weighed heavily on his mind.

At this moment came young Gobind Rai who was about nine year old. Never had he seen such a gloom and eerie silence in the Guru's *Darbar*. He had never seen the calm face of his beloved father so sad and reflecting agonising sorrow. He bowed and touched the feet of his father and asked, "What has happened, dear father ? What weighs so heavily in your compassionate soul that an unusual sadness is reflected from your divine face and eyes."

The Guru replied, "Grave burden the earth carries. She will be redeemed only if a truly worthy person comes forward to sacrifice his life. Only then will the distress be expunged and happiness ushered in."[1] Young Gobind Rai told his father that there was nobody more worthy than him (Guru Tegh Bahadur).

The hint was clear. The Guru appreciated the bold reply from his son, who then was barely nine years old. He decided to offer himself for the sacrifice. Therefore, he told Pandit Kirpa Ram and his associates to go home and tell the Emperor that if he (Guru Tegh Bahadur) was converted, they all would voluntarily embrace Islam. Before they took their leave, the Guru, according to *Guru Kian Sakhian*, consoled them with the words, "Guru Nanak will protect you." The Kashmiri Brahmins as per advice of the Guru sent a petition through Zalim Khan, the Governor of Lahore to Aurangzeb that Guru Tegh Bahadur was prepared to come to him and discuss with him the subject of his religious policy. If the Emperor succeeded in converting Guru Tegh Bahadur, all the Hindus of India would accept Islam but if he failed to convert him, the campaign of forcible conversion should be ended and the freedom of worship given to all the people in the realm.[2]

This declaration of Guru Tegh Bahadur in fact was a bold attempt to demonstrate that a man convinced of the moral purpose of his religious belief had the strength to stand up to

---

1. Koer Singh, *Gurbilas Patshahi 10*, p. 48.
2. P.N.K. Bamzai, *A History of Kashmir*, p. 555.

any despot bent upon subjugating people to his will. That the inalienable right of the people to practice their own faith could not be denied to them by any ruler. In a way, it was a challenge as well. The Guru understandably challenged the arrogant assumptions of Imperial power accustomed to having its own way with shackled people. The declaration also brought to the forefront the resolve of the Sikhs to rebuild society on the bases enunciated by Guru Nanak.

The intelligence reports received by Aurangzeb apprised him of all that had happened at Chak Nanki. Busy, as he was quelling the Pathan rebellion in North-Western frontier, he had neither the time nor perhaps the inclination to make extensive enquiries about the proceedings at the Guru's *Darbar*. But he was already suspicious of the Sikh movement, which his grandfather Emperor Jahangir wished to decimate with one stroke and which was in keeping with his policy, "to put down the teachings and public practices of the religion of these misbelievers." He therefore, readily believed all the intelligence reports and wrote to the Governor of Lahore to arrest Guru Tegh Bahadur and ordered that he be fettered and detained in the prison.[1] The Governor of Lahore passed on the Imperial order to Dilawar Khan, the *Faujdar* of Sirhind for compliance, who in turn asked the circle Kotwal of Ropar, Nur Muhammad Khan Mirza, in whose jurisdiction lay Anandpur, to arrest the Guru. The order, however, was kept a secret.[2]

Guru Tegh Bahadur in the meanwhile called the assembly of *Sangat* on Savan 8, 1732 BK (July 8, 1675). He told Durgah Mal that Gobind Rai was to be consecrated as Guru and asked him to fetch customary articles used at the time of passing on succession. The Guru arrayed his son in ceremonial apparel and weapons and seated him in his own place. Durgah Mal laid the articles in front of Gobind Rai and bowed in obedience. Baba Gurditta of Baba Buddha's family applied the *Tilak* (frontal mark)[3] on Gobind Rai's forehead. Guru Tegh Bahadur then said,

---

1. *Siyar-ul-Mutakhrin.*
2. William Irvine, *Later Mughals*, Vol. I, p. 79.
   Muhammad Ahsan Ijad's, *Ferrukh Siyar Nama*, p. 13.
3. Opinions differ amongst the scholars since this is a Brahmanical ritual and all the Gurus were against such practices.

"Brother Sikhs acknowledge Gobind Rai as Guru in my place henceforth. He who does so, will receive divine reward. We must now go to Delhi." The Guru made a prayer to *Akal Purakh* for the boon of righteousness even if it means martyrdom. He then took leave of his family and the Sikh devotees. He left Chak Nanki on July 10/11, 1675. He was accompanied by Bhai Mati Das, Bhai Sati Das and Bhai Dayal Das. The first halt was at Kiratpur, where Dip Chand and Nand Chand, two sons of Baba Suraj Mal, came to pay homage. Mata Sulakhani, wife of Guru Har Rai and her daughter, Bibi Rup Kaur, were upset when they learnt that the Guru was proceeding to the Imperial capital. As says *Guru Kian Sakhian*, Guru Tegh Bahadur consoled them and asked them to accept the will of God cheerfully.

It is not precisely known as to what prompted the Guru to leave Chak Nanki. Basing his inference on the information furnished by *Ferrukh-Siyar-Nama* Irvine says that Guru intended to proceed to the River Ganges for a bath. This does not seems to be correct because according to the Sikh philosophy, taking baths at known sacred places had no spiritual or social merit and were described by the Gurus as useless rituals. The probable view seems to be that the Guru hoped to see the Emperor at Delhi to plead the case of the non-Muslims, and in the event of the Emperor's unfavourable reaction bear the consequences.[1]

As the Guru arrived at Malikpur Ranghran near Ropar to cross the river Sutlej for his onward journey towards Delhi, he was arrested alongwith his three companions by Mirza Nur Muhammad Khan, the Kotwal of Ropar on July 12, 1675 (Sawan 12, 1732 BK)[2] and was sent to *Faujdar's* headquarter at

---

1. The Emperor at that time was in the North-West frontier. Considering the difficulty of communication in that age, it is not surprising that the Guru had no idea about the exact whereabouts of the Emperor. The normal expectation was that he would be at his capital, Delhi.

2. For details see *Bhat Vahi Multani Sindhi*, 'Khata Balautan Ka' (Punjabi University, Patiala); Muhammad Ashan Ijad, *Ferrukh-Siyar-Nama*, a source quoted by William Irvine in his book, *Later Mughals I*, p. 79.
   In view of the evidence of *Bhat Vahi* the statement of Koer Singh Kalal, author of *Gurbilas Patshahi 10*, relating to the Guru's arrest in a garden near Delhi, or that of M.A. Macauliffe (V 376-77) based on *Suraj Parkash*, Ras 62 (Ansu 30-37) in respect of the Guru's arrest at Agra seems historically invalid. Thus the story of the shepherd boy as related in the above accounts appears like a fable.

Sirhind where he and his companions were detained in a narrow cell for four months awaiting further orders from the Emperor (who was at Hasan Abdal at that time) or from the Governor of Delhi.

It seems that Aurangzeb deliberately kept Guru Tegh Bahadur at Sirhind for about sixteen weeks to expose him to the guile and arguments of the Mujaddads with a view to make him relent in his faith and accept Islam. Aurangzeb, perhaps, thought that none else than[1] Shaikh Saifuddin who was the son of Shaikh Ahmed Sirhindi was better equipped to do the job. His failure, however, led the Guru's transfer to Delhi. According to Swarup Singh Kaushish, the author of *Guru Kian Sakhian* (Sakhi No. 26), on receipt of *Parwana* from the Imperial headquarters, Guru Tegh Bahadur was taken in an iron cage to Delhi. The Guru reached Delhi on Maghar Vadi 1732 BK. He was kept in the Kotwali of the city under instructions from *Subedar* of Shahjehanabad who himself acted as per instructions from Aurangzeb at Hasan Abdal.[2]

Many anecdotes about this period narrated by some writers, cannot stand the test of historical scrutiny. One of the writers refers to the meetings between Aurangzeb and the Guru and narrates graphically what transpired between them. But his story cannot be authenticated because according to investigations and scrutiny Aurangzeb, was at Hasan Abdal at that time. All the same, the tradition has a sure basis, but relates to the earlier occasion when in 1665, the Guru was arrested at Dhamdhan and produced at the Imperial court at Delhi.

Another story often narrated is regarding the escape of some Sikhs, particularly Bhai Gurditta and Bhai Uda from the

1. *Bhat Vahi Purbi Dakhni.*
2. That the Emperor was not physically present at the time of Guru Tegh Bahadur's martyrdom, has been proved by the positive evidence of *Maasar-i-Alamgiri* written by Saqi Mastan Khan serving in the administration of Aurangzeb. This was the best primary source for the study. Other contemporary sources being not very useful as *Alamgiri Nama* covers only ten years of the reign of Aurangzeb. *Muntakhab-ul-Lubab* contains no reference to the Guru. *Khulast-ut-Tawarikh* makes a very brief reference to Guru's marytrdom. *Maasar-i-Alamgiri* gives the dates on which the Emperor left Delhi for Hasan Abdal and returned from there.

prison. It says that on witnessing the martyrdom of Mati Das, other Sikhs of the Guru were petrified. They went to him at night and expressed their apprehensions. He told them that they were free to leave him. They pointed to the chains of their feet and asked how their release could be effected. Through the Guru's miraculous interception, their fetters fell off, all the prison doors stood ajar and the guards snored in the sleep of neglect.[1] It is said that at this juncture Bhai Gurditta and Bhai Uda escaped. According to yet another version; the Guru helped some other Sikhs escape because he wanted to send through them a message to his son at Chak Nanki. As the account goes they were instructed to carry the insignia of Guruship to Chak Nanki and offer it on his behalf to his son.

All these stories do not stand the test of historical scrutiny. Only three men were arrested alongwith the Guru and they all were executed. Therefore the question of helping others—even Bhai Gurditta and Bhai Uda—does not arise. Again the content of the story suffers from serious drawbacks and is contrary to the spirit of Sikhism. To give credence to the display of miracle of breaking the fetters of the Sikhs in prison is positively against the teachings of the Gurus as it is violative of God's will. Similarly, the story that the Sikhs were sent to Chak Nanki to offer the insignia of Guruship holds no ground, since the Guru had already nominated his son as his successor prior to his departure from Chak Nanki.

However, it may be agreed that there was some communication between the Guru and his son, although it was extremely difficult. This conjecture is attributed to the two slokas believed to have been exchanged between them. Guru Tegh Bahadur wrote to Gobind Rai :

> All power shattered, humanity in fetters
> nothing availeth at all.
> Nanak prays O God, save all as thou saved
> elephant on his drowning call.[2]

---

1. M.A. Macauliffe, *The Sikh Religion*, Vol. II, p. 383. The account is based on Bhai Santokh Singh's *Suraj Parkash*, Ras XI.
2. *Bal chhuṭkio baṅdhan pare kachchū na hot upāe.*
   Kahu Nānak ab oṭ Har(i) gaj jio hoh(u) sahāe.53.   (*SGGS*, p. 1429)

Gobind Rai, in reply, uttered :

"With power fetters break,
availth all in grace Divine.
All is in thy hand, O Lord, Nanak seeks Divine."[1]

Many Sikh writings on Guru Tegh Bahadur make a
reference to these *sloks* and give different interpretation of
them. Of those Dr. Trilochan Singh's interpretation which is
based on 'Bhai Mani Singh's evidence seems nearest to truth.
According to him, in his *Slokas* Guru Tegh Bahadur expressed
his deep concern over the helplessness of the people, whereas
Gobind Rai in his reply assured him his confidence to handle
the situation with God's Grace.

During the eight days[2] in Delhi Kotwali, tortures of
different kinds were inflicted on the Guru. On the first day of
the Guru's arrival, *Qazi* Abdul Wahab Vora offered the Guru
three alternatives viz., (i) to show a miracle to prove divinity
of his mission; (ii) to embrace Islam or (iii) to prepare himself
to court death. He refused to perform miracles or display
occult power saying that it was never right to interfere in
the Will of God. He also declined to accept Islam. His message
to Aurangzeb was simple. "The Prophet of Mecca who
founded Islam could not impose that on the world, so how can
you ? It is not God's Will." He, however chose the last
alternative. On Friday and Saturday attempts were made to
persuade the Guru, to show a miracle or accept Islam.
Persuasions having failed, coercion was employed to make
the Guru agree to one of the first two alternatives. During the
next four days, the Guru was subjected to severest tortures.
Hot sand was poured on his body; he was not allowed to
drink water; his three disciples and companions, Mati Das,
Dayal Das and Sati Das were done to death in front of his
eyes. Bhai Mati Das was tied to two poles and sawn
asunder. Bhai Dayal Das was boiled alive to death in a
cauldron of hot water and Sati Das was roasted alive wrapped
all-over with cotton-wool. According to *Guru kian Sakhian*, he

---

1. *Bal hoā bandhan chhuṭe, sab(u) kichh(u) hot upāe.*
   Nānak sab kichh(u) tumrai hāth mai tum hī hot sahāe.54.   (SGGS, p. 1429)
2. *Bhat Vahi Purbi Dakhni.*
   Gurū jī chār māss Bassī Paṭhānā ke bandī khāne band rahe,
   aaṭh divas Dillī Kotwālī me band rahe.

calmly uttered "*Blessed are the Sikhs; blessed is their faith.*"[1]

These cruelties could not shake the Guru. All torture to him was like a mud spray against a mountain wall. Like his grandfather, Guru Arjan Dev, he was never ruffled. Not a thought of curse or retaliation disturbed his peace; not a wrinkle of frown appeared on his shining brow. As calm as at Anandpur or anywhere else, he maintained a peace of mind that the doom of the three worlds could not have disturbed.

When the authorities saw that the Guru was determined and was in no mood to oblige them, they ordered the state executioner Jalaludin of Samana to sever his head from the body. The executioner struck, and in a flash the head lay separated from the trunk.[2] The Guru allowed his end to befall upon him without the sound of a groan. He remained wholly composed before the executioner's blow. His was no stoic fortitude but a determined gesture to force a moral issue. It was not a passive but a positive decision to confront the existing situation.

As per order of the Government, the Guru's body was to be quartered and exposed for public viewing, obviously to impart stern warning to all such people who dared go against the wishes and orders of the Emperor. Because of promptitude and timely action of the Sikhs, this could not be done. According to *Bansavalinama*,[3] a furious dust-storm raged immediately after this brutal deed was accomplished. Perhaps this was the Nature's way of manifesting her anguish over the sad event and of providing the Sikhs with cover to escape with the Guru's earthly remains. In the confusion caused by the dust-storm, a devoted Sikh, Bhai Jaita, a resident of Dilwali Gate, Delhi, who along with Gurbakhsh Singh had witnessed everything with his own eyes, rushed out of the crowd and instantaneously, disappeared with the reverend head of the Guru. He shared his secret with his neighbour Nanu, son of Bhai Bagha.[4] Bhai Uda,[5] a resident of Ladwa (near Karnal) was

1. Harbans Singh, *Guru Tegh Bahadur*, p. 78.
2. *Bhat Vahi Talaunda* and *Bhat Vahi Multani Sindhi*.
3. Kesar Singh Chhibber, *Bansavalinama*.
4. According to *Bansavalinama*, Bhai Nanu was son of Bhai Bagha and Bhai Jaita son of Agya Ram. Both lived in *Mohalla* Dilwali, Delhi. (Chain 9).
5. Bhai Uda died a martyr in the Battle of Bhangani 1688.

also taken into confidence. They decided to take the holy but sorrowful possession to Chak Nanki. They placed the sacred possession in a basket, covered it carefully and started their journey to their destination. Bhai Jaita, being the strongest, had the privilege of keeping the basket on his head for most of the time on the way. They made five halts enroute. Their first halt was at Bagpat, the second at Karnal, the third at Grain Market Ambala (Sis Ganj Ambala), the fourth at Nadha Sahib (near Chandigarh) and the fifth at Kiratpur. They left Delhi early in the morning of 13th November 1675 and reached Kiratpur on 15th November 1675.[1] The head was accorded a royal reception and was carried in a procession to Chak Nanki. The moment was very painful but Guru Gobind Rai displayed unsurpassable fortitude. He consoled his mother, relatives and the Sikhs.

He hugged Bhai Jaita and blessed him exalting his whole tribe by his meaningful utterance *Rangrete Guru Ke Bete*, i.e. Rangretas are Guru's sons.

Guru Gobind Rai performed the obsequies with dignity and reverence on 16th November, 1675. A pyre of sandal-wood was raised and extract of Roses sprinkled on the head which the young Guru took and solemnly placed on the pyre. He then repeated the preamble of the *Japji* and lit the pyre with his own hand. While the head was being cremated, the Sikh congregation sang hymns of the Guru. They called to memory and spoke of Guru Tegh Bahadur's philanthropic and self-sacrificing deeds. The *Sohila* (the last of the Sikh five prayers) was then read with a concluding benediction and *Krah Prasad* (sacred food) was distributed amongst those gathered there. When Guru Gobind Rai reached home, he ordered recitation of Guru's hymns and this was continued for ten days.

When Lakhi Shah Lubana, a rich and famous contractor with a permanent residence at Delhi and a devout Sikh, came to know of the martyrdom of the Guru, he felt much upset. Being affluent and well-respected among official circles, he decided to make use of his influence. He emptied his carts

1. *Gurdwara Babangarh*, Kiratpur, marks the place where the sacred head was received and *Gurdwara Sis Ganj*, Anandpur marks the place where it was cremated.

loaded with lime near the Red Fort and went in retreat to his
home in village Raisina. On the way, taking advantage of the
darkness and carelessness of the Mughal guards, he, helped
by his sons, Nagahiya, Hema, Hari, and Dhuma, son of Kanha
took the headless body in one of their carts to their home at
Raisina, now called Rakab Ganj, on the city's outskirts. This
was accomplished on 12th November, 1675 (Maghar Sudi 6,
1732 Bk).

Apprehensive of the Royal reprisal, Lakhi Shah and his
sons then built up a pyre inside their house and set fire to it
the same evening a little after dark.

To quote from the *Bhat Vahis Jadav Bansian* :

*"Lakhi beta Gudhu ka Nagahia, Hema beta Lakhi ke, Naik
Dhuma beta Kahne ka, Tumar Bijlaut, Guru Tegh Bahadurji
Mahall Naum......ki Lash uthai..Lae Sal Satrai Sai battis
Mangasar Sudi chhat Sukarvah ko dag dia Rai Sina Gaon adhi
ghari Rat gai."*

Lakha (Lakhi Das or Lakhi Shah) son of Godhu, Nagahia,
Hema and Hari sons of Lakhi.... and Naik Dhuma son of Lahna
Tumar Bijlaut brought the body of Guru Tegh Bahadur, the
ninth Guru.... The body was cremated in the village of Raisina
half a ghari before dark on Maghar Sudi 6, 1732 Bk.

The bodies of Bhai Mati Das, Bhai Sati Das and Bhai
Dayal Das were removed by the Sikhs and cremated on the
bank of River Jamuna alongwith the bodies of those who had
passed away in the *Dharamsal* of Bhai Kalyana in Delhi on the
very day of Guru Tegh Bahadur's martyrdom.

It is said that a little after dark, a police party arrived at
the scene in search of the body but finding the house consigned
to flames and the inmates weeping bitterly returned. After the
cremation was over, the ashes were collected, put in a
pitcher like metalic vessel called *Gaagar* in Punjabi parlance
and buried on the spot.

Lakhi Shah, and other Sikhs came from Delhi to Chak
Nanki with a part of the sacred remains which they had saved.
Guru Gobind Rai welcomed them. According to *Guru Kian
Sakhian,* he took Lakhi Shah into his embrace and hugged him
warmly in acknowledgement of his services to the Sikh

community. Lakhi Shah related the whole story and the entire *Sangat* was overwhelmed with grief and pain. Guru Gobind Rai comforted the Sikhs and advised them not to give way to grief. He called upon them to contemplate upon moral issues which were dear to the Guru for which he had fearlessly embraced martyrdom.

According to *Guru Kian Sakhian*, the Guru turned thoughtful and said, "My father accepted the Will of God as the cause most agreeable. The event will be remembered as long as the Sun and the Moon continue to shine."[1]

Guru Tegh Bahadur's martyrdom had a uniqueness of its own. It was a *Suo motto* case undertaken not to achieve any mundane or even spiritual advantage. It was done to assert the sovereignty of the moral principle or for *Dharma* as Guru Gobind Rai would vouchsafe in his composition *Bachittar Natak*. It was indeed astonishing that the children of the same Creator in whom He permeates in spirit-form are considered mutually incompatible and one segment of them namely *Sunni* Muslims regard itself superior to the others. Sadly indeed, Mughal Government denied essential freedom, the right to live, the right to hold and express their religious beliefs to the people except *Sunni* Muslims. The temples/places of worship of different sections of people were desecrated and demolished. Administrative artifices and state power were used extensively to promote the rule of suppression on a scale which was horrible. The Muslim elite and the Muslim State run by Aurangzeb had a single purpose which was to create unitary and monolithic society having only one religion that is Islam of *Sunni* variety and the form of government as suggested by *Shariat*. Such a state could not but be intolerant, unaccommodating, rigid, inflexible and imposing. It was by its very nature opposed to ethical social order and the Sikh principles of tolerance and acceptance of diversity of faith and practice. Such a situation was, therefore, unpalatable to Guru Tegh Bahadur who resolved to make sacrifice as prescription for remedying the prevalent malaise. He invited the trial upon himself to redeem the people's sufferings and left Chak Nanki to go to Imperial Delhi, determined to correct the state of

---

1. Swarup Singh Kaushish, *Guru Kian Sakhian*, No. 28.

affairs or lay down his life. The choice, his own, was the consequence of no escapist ethics, but of a consciousness in the growth of which his heritage played a significant role.

Guru Gobind Rai observed everything that happened around. Nobody else understood the moral issues involved better than him. He was fully aware that what his father had done was a moral imperative and was fully justified under the circumstances. It was a religious call as well as a social need. It was perfectly in consonance with the mission of Sikhism which was laid down by Guru Nanak in the light of God's ordainment to him at Sultanpur Lodhi and passed on to his successors one after the other. Also, it was a deed of spiritual insight and discipline of the highest order.

At the same time it bespoke of love, compassion and humility as also of Guru's determination to face the tyranny till his last breath. It was not a passive submission but a positive decision to confront an existing situation. Guru Tegh Bahadur, all through his life had preached unflinching faith in God, of His omnipotence, His concern for the mankind, His everflowing benevolence, His fearlessness, His animosity towards none, His will to uplift the people to be God-consciousness. He had also exhorted that one should neither fear nor frighten anyone and that people as a whole should endeavour to be in a position to cast their life-style as per the attributes of God. For instance, they should be compassionate, caring, ever-ready to help the needy and the helpless, and to restrain the unjust and tyrannous from doing misdeeds.

Guru Gobind Rai called his father's martyrdom a deed beyond comparison in *Kalyug* as he had suffered to uphold righteousness.[1] He in the process played no charlatan, and fearlessly cast off his bodily vesture to the suzerain of Delhi (Aurangzeb). He did what God liked and loved and, therefore, in the sphere of God, sang out shouts of adoration.

This being the perception of young Guru about his father's martyrdom, he could not be acquiescent. Many thoughts might have come to his mind. Should he gird up his loins or to defend and promote the sovereignty of the moral

---

1. *Tilak janjū rākhā prabh ta kā, kīyo baḍo kalū maiṅ sākā.*   (*Bachittar Natak*)

principles held close to their hearts by his predecessor Gurus; which were the bed-rock of Sikh religion or knuckle under ? Should he combat unrighteousness by courting death following the example of his father or by taking up arms against it ? What form of unrighteousness should he combat—political, social or spiritual ? The Guru was convinced that knuckling under tantamounted to the activities scorned by God who himself was 'smasher of tyrants' and such a conduct was in no way supportive of the universe of his vision. Nor was offering of further sacrifices considered desirable for, perpetrators of evil had lost all moral consciousness. Aurangzeb the head of the state in his foolhardiness and arrogance had circumscribed God to be the One only of the Muslims (*Rub-ul-Momin*). The *Mullahs, Ulemas* and others of their ilk had based their ethics on premises those catered only to the interests of a particular class. Similar was the plight of the elite of Hindu religion. Against this background the Guru inferred and very rightly too that arms should be taken up; of course as the last resort, to combat and destroy unrighteousness and assert the sovereignty of moral principles. The Guru considered any act whether political, social or spiritual as evil if it was violative of the divine consciousness in human mind.

Such thinking of the Guru can be corroborated by his writings. At numerous places in his compositions he expressed the ideal of a crusader on the path of God, yearning to cultivate the qualities which helped forge such a character.

It appears that he became convinced inspite of his young age when he had held his father's severed head in his hands that the flames lit by Guru Hargobind had to be stoked still further and the tyrant's injustice and cruelty had to be met by armed warriors with an iron will, thereby adding a new dimension to Guru Nanak's dictum *truth is steel*. Steel would now seal the fate of those who mocked and smothered the rights of others, to safeguard mankind from the inhumanity of the evil-doers.

The task of the Guru was stupendous and difficult, yet he addressed it with zeal, fervour, and steadfastness, as was his wont, and with the conviction which later on he vented umpteen times that he did not look for help from any quarter, nor did he believe in restorting to hoax, but he would certainly sow the seed surely to germinate into the invaluable.[1]

The way had been shown by the earlier Gurus. Guru Nanak roundly condemned the atrocities inflicted by Zahir-u-din Babar on the people of India. Guru Angad too did not acquiesce when Humayun threatened him with naked sword. Guru Arjan Dev suffered execution but did not submit. Guru Hargobind proclaimed that *Miri* and *Piri* were the two parts of the ground strategy of Guru Nanak's house and the Sikh Gurus would take care of both the temporal and religious affairs of their followers and in the process would not hesitate even to make use of force. Guru Tegh Bahadur's martyrdom was a protest against the excesses of the Mughal State. Thus Guru Gobind Singh's decision to enjoin upon the Sikhs to make use of the sword if all other means fail to liquidate the wicked and their wickedness, was not a break, but a continuation with a little elaboration of the already laid down principles.

To achieve his objective, he initiated schemes to orientate the Sikh psyche to fresh targets and to fulfilment of the teachings of Guru Nanak. He issued *Hukamnama* (religious fiat) asking the Sikhs to bring him arms of different designs and makes as offerings. The Guru's orders were obeyed with zeal. His foundries also supplied a large number of weapons. He himself bore arms and induced others to emulate his example. Many of his followers, who had served in the army of his grandfather or had been the body-guards of Guru Har Rai, flocked to him. He welcomed them and drilled them in martial arts. The Guru's *Darbar* hummed with activities of the inspired, energised and determined people.[2]

The Guru encouraged various martial and strenuous sports as a part of his programme to impart physical fitness to his people. His favourite games were splashing of water in a flowing stream, hunting and sham fights. His principal companions of this time were, Sango Shah, Jit Mal, Gopal

---

1. *Kinū nā dān rākh huṅ.*
   Kinū nā bhekh bhīj hūṅ.
   Alakh bīj bīj hūṅ.
2. Giani Gian Singh, *Twarikh Guru Khalsa*, pp. 755-59.

Chand, Ganga Ram, Mohari Chand, Gopal Rai, Sham Das, Bhai Daya Ram, and Bhai Nand Chand, an upright and favourite *Masand*.

Along with all this, the Guru took steps in order to put his Sikhs on the path of self-improvement. He enjoined upon his followers to lead a disciplined life. Later on, in one of his writings, he very tersely expressed, "I am not enamoured of a Sikh; what is dear to my heart is his disciplined life."[1] He would get up well before dawn and sit contemplating on the Eternal One. He would then come to the morning assembly and listen to the holy hymns being sung by musicians and explicate the sacred Word. The rest of the day would be spent in recitation of heroic poetry, drills and athletic competitions and in administering to the needs and problems of his disciples. The evening assembly would be followed by board and concourses which continued late into the night at which general news were discussed and stories of the preceding Gurus and the eminent Sikhs of their times narrated.

Not only this, the Guru harnessed literature and the services of literary luminaries. According to the author of *Bansavali Nama*, the Guru issued *Hukamnama* to the Sikhs in 1677 that poets, writers, painters and scholars are invited to attend his court. A large number of eminent literary figures reached the court of the Guru and rendered into a dialect of Hindi, Braj (varying round Sanskrit on one extreme and colloquial Hindi on the other), the stories of Rama and Krishna and the deeds of *Chandi* The Guru himself had a natural genius for rendering poetic composition. He bore highly artistic and elegant hand at *Gurmukhi* calligraphy, specimens of which are preserved on the leaves of some copies of the *Adi Granth* of his time and in the form of inscriptions on several of his *Hukamnamas* which have come down to us.

The Guru composed 227 *Chhands* of *Debi Path* in 1683-84 and 1106 *Chhands* of *Dasam Katha Bhagwat Ki* in 1685.[2] The former composition deals with the ventures of *Chandi* in extripating the tyrants, while the latter composition relates to the story of Lord Krishna in *Duapar Yug* as stated in *Daswan Sakand*.

1. *Rehat Piārī Mujh Ko, Sikh Piārā Nāhi.*
2. Randhir Singh, *Shabad Murat.*

Another composition of the Guru which belonged to this period was *Jaap*. In this composition he has revealed his mastery over the Sikh philosophical thought and also his keenness not to break its continuity.

The first eleven verses which set the theme could make that clear. He looks upon God as follows :

> *Chakr chihan ar(u) baran jāt(i) ar(u) pāt(i) nahin jeh.*
> *Rūp rang ar(u) rekh bhekh koū kahe na sakat keh.*
> *Achal mūrat(i) anubhau prakās(h) amitoj kahijjai.*
> *Kot(i) Indra indrān sāh(u) sāhān(i) ganijjai.*
> *Tribhavan mahip sur nar asur net(i) net(i) ban trin kahat.*
> *Tav sarab nām kathai kavan karam nām barnat sumat(i).*

Contour and countenance, caste, class or lineage, He has none.
None can describe His form, figure, shape and semblance, whatsoever,
Immovable and self poised in His being without fear.
He is the Sovereign of three worlds, the demons, the mortals and the angelic beings.
Nay, even the grass blades in the forest proclaim Him to be boundless, endless and infinite.
O, Who can count all the names that are Thy Glory
Through Thy enlightenment.
I will count all Thy Attributive names.   *(Jaap Sahib)*[1]

Gobind Rai then commenced to give the names, personal and impersonal and transcendental and immanent. It is opined that he wrote the *Jaap* on the model of Vishnu *Sahsarnama*. That might well be true but it should be remembered that his *Jaap* was in complete consonance with Guru Nanak's *Japji* and very appropriately both now constitute the morning prayer of the Sikhs. The overall impact of all this was that a process was set in to galvanise the people to think/react different from gross apathy to active involvement and action, always adhering to the cause of righteousness and universal brotherhood of humankind. Besides taking steps for fostering self-improvement and physical fitness, the Guru got prepared in March 1680, a drum under the supervision of Nand Chand, his trusted Dewan.[2] The underlying objective of the Guru was to make use

1. M.A. Macauliffe, *The Sikh Religion*, Vol. V, p. 366.
2. Harjinder Singh Dilgeer, *Anandpur Sahib*, p. 19.

of it as an aid in military training as well as in generating a sense of discipline among his followers, although it caused a lot of misgivings among the Hill Chiefs as well as Mughal officials who looked upon the drum as a symbol of Guru's assertion of sovereignty, since in the contemporary political parlance, the beating of the drum was considered the prerogative of an independent chieftain. The name of the drum *Ranjit Nagara*—a heralder of victory—was also deemed to be suggestive of the Guru's political ambition. The Sikhs called the Guru *Sacha Padshah* and his court as *Sacha Darbar*. The implications of *Ranjit Nagara* and the titles as *Sacha Padshah* were misconstrued by the Hill Chieftains and the Mughal officials. These were interpreted in temporal sense and appeared to them emblems of Guru's political ambitions. Rather these should have been seen as sounding forth a fresh song, the song of victory over evil impulses within and wicked enemies outside so that life rooted in Truth may take the new course of flood and storm.

THE GURU AND THE HILL STATES

While at Chak Nanki, the Guru had to take notice of hill states, their perception of the Sikh movement, their reactions to the Mughal Emperor, their polity and their socio-religious beliefs.

Between Rivers Sutlej and the Jamuna lay Kahlur (Bilaspur), Sirmour (Nahan) and Hindur (Nalagarh). Kahlur lay on both sides of River Sutlej. On the East of River Jamuna lay Garhwal, which was not really a part of the Punjab. Between the Rivers Ravi and the Sutlej lay very important hill principalities of Kangra, Kulu, Mandi, Saket, Chamba, Nurpur, Guler, Datarpur, Siba, Jaswan and Kutler. Between the Ravi and Jehlum several hill principalities such as Jammu, Basoli, and Jasrota existed.

All the Hill States right from the ancient times were ruled by Rajput princes, who governed their principalities on the principles of feudal polity and Brahmanical orthodoxy. In the medieval period, when the Sultans established their hegemony in the Punjab, these states were only marginally touched.

In the later medieval period, situation changed and the

Mughal Imperial system extended to the hill states more or less effectively during the reign of Akbar. The rulers of principalities officially designated as *Zamindars* were required to pay tributes. They were subject to the supervision and control of local *Faujdars* of Jammu and Kangra. These *Faujdars* were privileged to have direct access to regional governors who had been instructed to provide help as and when it was needed.

The Mughal Emperors employed force, cunning and diplomacy to keep their political hold on the hill rulers very firmly. They often resorted to the policy of divide and rule. For instance Nurpur and Foler were brought into prominence at the cost of Kangra. Even then the Mughals were only partially successful in keeping them politically subservient to them. This was because of their traditional love of independence which they had developed over past few centuries because of the inaccessibility of their areas which were hilly and difficult to traverse and their never-failing pride in their social system, which otherwise was unprogressive and ultra-conservative. The economy was sustained by the agricultural *Rathies* and semi-nomadic *Gujjars* who formed a large segment of the population. Social life was dominated by the Brahmins who were numerically more than the Rajputs whose support they utilized for rigid enforcement of caste rules and preservation of the traditional caste hierarchy.

Religion, often regarded as the most important element of refined minds, had not crossed even primitive stages of animism and idolatry. The principal deities worshipped by the people were *Siva* or *Mahadeva* and his consort. Many temples were dedicated to this deity. The dominant religion in the hills was *Shaivism*. *Puranic* literature was widely read.

The worship of goddess in her several forms—*Uma, Shyam Kumari, Shakti, Bhavani, Chandi* and *Kali* was very popular, even though worship of goddess in its terrible form was preferred. She was the family deity of the proudest of Rajputs, the Katoches of a thousand years history. The recitation of *Durga Sapt Sati* was especially esteemed for ensuing safe return from a long journey.

Tantras too, with their cult of five *Makaras*—Wine, Flesh,

Fish, Parched grams and Sexual intercourse—were quite popular and a sizeable proportion of the people appear to have belonged to this sect of *Devi* worshippers. At popular level, the worship of many minor gods was quite common. The sacrifice of animals—goats, cocks, buffaloes, at the shrines of *Shaivism* and *Shakta* deities was also prevalent. *Vaishnavism* had made only marginal inroads into hill areas. The *Pandore Gaddi* (Near Gurdaspur) was established probably in 1572 and Chiefs of Nurpur and Guler associated themselves with the *Bairagis* in 1572 By 1648, Raja Suraj Sen of Mandi had introduced *Vaishnavism* in his capital. Raja Karam Parkash, the founder of Nahan had intimate association with a *Bairagi* named Banwari Das. Temples dedicated to Vishnu, Ram and Sita were raised in Kangra and Chamba by the Chiefs of those principalities in the seventeenth century. *Vaishnavism*, however, could not become popular at common man's level. A desperate resistance was put up by adherents of the 'old' faith. The *Bairagis* of Pandore, for instance, were attacked by the *Gosains*; and biting satires in the *Vaishnavas* in certain extant drawings amply indicate the general attitude of the people towards *Vaishnavism*.[1] Belief in monotheism or monism was a far cry as also, a universal society based on social equality, non-discrimination, non-exploitation and human dignity which had formed the basis of certain religious dispensation in contemporary world.

Such being the broad parameters of the polity, society and religion in hill states, the entry of Sikhism into them could hardly be welcome. Rather it was bound to provoke opposition. Sikhism stood for an egalitarian society based on principles of social equality, honest hard labour, freedom from fear and respect for all irrespective of caste, creed, birth and status etc., all having full faith in the oneness and singularity of God and universal brotherhood.

The political formulations to which Sikhism lent validity was democracy where the people were free to participate and spurn the aristocratic exclusiveness as it was associated with the Rajputs. The economic structure recommended by Sikhism

1. J.S. Grewal and S.S. Bal, *Guru Gobind Singh*, p. 17.

was anti-feudal, democratic and egalitarian in spirit and social action.

To sum up, the politico-social model in the hill states was quite different from the model the Gurus had envisaged, championed and sponsored.

The Rajput rulers who were hand in glove with socio-religious elites of the hill states resented in particular, the social equality that Sikhism professed and offered to the low caste people and the Jats whom they treated as inferiors socially because in their reckoning, it not only ran counter to their long-upheld religious notions but also delivered a stunning blow to their whole social fabric. Thus in the face of the stout opposition of the hill states and their allies, the progress of Sikhism was bound to be slow. Chronologically the contact of Sikhism with the hilly region was peripheral upto the time of Guru Hargobind. In the times of Guru Angad and Guru Ram Das there were occasional visits of devoted Sikhs to the hilly region and of still less number of seekers to the Guru's court. Among the notables of the hilly tract, there was solitary example of Raja of Haripur who visited Goindwal to make obeisance to the Guru. The impression of the Guru as also of Sikhism which the people from the hill areas carried was that of reverence. In Guler, one of the hill states of Punjab, *Sikh Sangat* had been established through a *Manjidar*. Bhai Gurdas avers that there were *Sikh Sangats* at Sirhind and Kashmir from which it can be safely drawn that Sikhism atleast had crept into the hill states.[1]

In the time of Guru Hargobind, the penetration of Sikhism was marked and significant. This happened inspite of the fact that the Guru had to undergo incarceration, wage wars against the Mughal Islamic imperialism and face the opposition of *Minas* and recalcitrance of certain *Masands*. Hargobindpur, which Guru Hargobind founded and turned into religious centre, was situated on the route leading to Kashmir. Its proximity understandably provided a chance for interaction between the hill states and Sikhs in the plains of the Punjab. Fame of the Guru and his work had already reached the

---

1. Balwant Singh Dhillon, *Pramukh Sikh te Sikh Panth* (Punjabi), pp. 131-33.

hill states. In 1618, the Guru came to Hindur to help Dharam Chand in a military engagement which the latter undertook to oust his father Sansar Chand, who had nominated his brother as his successor, a development which Dharam Chand did not like. Most probably Dharam Chand had won the heart of the Guru in Gwalior Fort where both of them had been imprisoned. The Guru returned to his head-quarters at Amritsar after Dharam Chand ascended the throne of Hindur after the death of his father in 1618. The Guru's help to Dharam Chand was significant in as much as it sent signal atleast among the Hill Rajas that the Guru was a military force to reckon with. Since the Guru's entourage consisted of scholars, preachers and devoted Sikhs besides soldiers, people in general must have had the opportunity to interact with the Sikhs resulting in improvement of their understanding of Sikhism. The Guru must have also experienced that the hill region needed Guru's dispensation for the spiritual and social elevation of its population steeped deep in ignorance and sufferings from the worst type of conservatism. But, for almost seven years, no special efforts seemed to have been made by the Guru to advance Sikhism in that region. At last in 1627, when Jahangir died, the Guru sent his son Baba Gurditta to Hindur to establish a Sikh Centre in the territory of Dharam Chand. Apart from the general impulse of introducing Sikhism in far off hilly areas, the impending profile of political landscape also inveigled him to take this step. He had gauged that Shah Jahan, the son and successor of Jahangir, would not be as considerate towards him as Jahangir had been in the past few years and in that case a new centre outside the administrative jurisdiction of the Mughals could be useful in several ways. Baba Gurditta ji was well received in Hindur and was helped to establish a centre at the present site of Kiratpur which lay close to the border of Kahlur.

In the thirties of the seventeenth century, Guru Hargobind fell out with the Mughal officials in the Punjab and after having fought successful battles shifted his headquarter to the developing city of Kiratpur which flourished still more. Kiratpur began to radiate the light of Sikhism to the neighbouring and far off places.

This caused commotions, even convulsions among common people and the elite, some appreciating and some deprecating the Guru's ideas. In short Sikhism started influencing the people. Quite a big segment of them became empathetic towards it. The ruling elite including the Brahmins and the upper castes Hindus took to Sikhism with reservation.

In 1642, the Nawab of Ropar attacked Hindur. Dharam Chand sought Guru's help and defeated him. Even in the time of Guru Harkrishan in 1656, the Sikhs rendered help to Dharam Chand in his war with the chief of Kahlur. The Guru's sustained help to Dharam Chand seemed to have been actuated by his devotion to the Guru, the Sikh's concern for the security and stability of their headquarters, the righteousness of the cause of the ruler of Hindur and the benevolence with which Dharam Chand ruled the state.

As the time rolled on, Dip Chand (1650-1667) the ruler of Kahlur became a devotee of the Guru.[1] Guru Tegh Bahadur's arrival at Kiratpur in 1665 was considered a great event since it instilled a new confidence into the devouts, besides ushering in a new era in the relationship between Dip Chand of Kahlur and the Sikhs. Dip Chand visited the Guru to request him to settle at Makhowal within his territory not far from Kiratpur (which was in the territory of Hindur). The Guru accepted the offer. Possibly the Guru wanted to be away from jealous Sodhis of Kiratpur and to function as a common friend of Kahlur and Hindur who otherwise were rivals to each other.

The existence of Guru's headquarters in two principalities did not create any immediate complications due to various reasons. Bhim Chand who had succeeded to the Kahlur's throne after Dip Chand's death in 1667, was a minor and could not assert himself in any way. Also, there was a general stir in the hills against the Mughals in the first half of the 1670's which subsumed the mutual differences of the Chiefs of Kahlur and Hindur.

---

1. Dip Chand ruled over Kahlur state from 1650 to 1667. According to Swarup Singh Kaushish, Dip Chand's wife Champa Devi was a great devotee of the Guru. Gradually Dip Chand also developed respect for the Guru. The authenticity of this fact can be gleaned from the *Sakhi* No. 24 as incorporated in *Guru Kian Sakhian*, (ed.) Piara Singh Padam.

Within few years of his assumption of *gurgaddi*, the pontific throne, the Guru intensified his activities. Following in the footsteps of his grandfather, Guru Hargobind; he spared no efforts to disseminate Guru's message. He raised an army also and made it publicly known that he would be pleased particularly if the gifts were of use to his soldiers.[1] He followed it up by selecting a place strategically better situated than Makhowal, and set up a small establishment there.[2] The change was reflected in the appearance of the Guru's *Darbar*. The young Guru would now meet his daily congregation in a costly tent with elephants and horses as a part of the establishment. He would wear an aigrette and sit on a raised platform. The Sikhs called him *Sacha Padshah*. Princes from far off places visited Chak Nanki.[3] The whole setting was that of a regal court.[4]

One such prince was Raja Ratan Rai. In October, 1680, he alongwith his mother and select courtiers reached Chak Nanki. He was the son and successor of Raja Ram Rai who ruled state of Jaintia[5] in Assam and was a disciple of Guru Tegh Bahadur.

1. J.S. Grewal and S.S. Bal, *Guru Gobind Singh*, p. 52.
2. The foundation of Anandpur was laid by Guru Tegh Bahadur (1621-1675) on 16th June, 1665 on a piece of land covering the ruined mound of an older village Makhowal, which the Guru had earlier purchased from the Rajput hill state of Kahlur. After the Battle of Bhangani (18th September, 1688) Guru Gobind Rai returned to Chak Nanki which he renamed Anandpur after one of a ring of forts (Anandgarh) which he now undertook to raise. (*Encyclopaedia of Sikhism*, Vol. I, p. 128). Rose, however, says that Anandpur was founded in 1678 (*The Land of Five Rivers, Historical and Descriptive Sketches*, p. 213). The correct position seems to be that the piece of land of Anandgarh fort had been acquired in 1678., but Chak Nanki acquired the new name once the Guru returned to this place after the Battle of Bhangani.
3. According to Sikh tradition Rattan Chand of Assam came to Makhowal and met Guru Gobind Rai in 1680. Though the Sikh tradition has preserved the memory of only this chief coming to Makhowal, others too must have visited.
4. The Persian writers tell us that Aurangzeb wanted his *Faujdars* on the North-West to see that Guru Gobind Rai stopped practices that created the impression that the Guru was a Raja (an independent ruler). Khushwaqt Rai, *Twarikh-i-Sikhan*, S.H.R. 116, pp. 632-33; Muhammad Qasim Lahori, *Suraj Parkash II*, Rut-1, Ansu 24, p. 2294; *Gurbilas* by Bhai Sukha Singh, p. 104.
5. Sylhet at this period was divided into three principal states—Laur, Gaur and Jaintia and it is highly possible that Raja Ram Rai was a ruler of one of these states.

He was lucky enough to be in the entourage of the Guru that accompanied him on his visit to different places in Assam/ Bengal. He had no male issue and longed for a son. The Guru blessed him and his wish was fulfilled. Raja Ram Rai and his wife were immensely grateful to the Guru and always yearned to make obeisance personally. But they could not as they were constrained by circumstances. Guru Tegh Bahadur laid down his life in 1675 and since then they had been feeling morally guilty. In 1680, Raja Ram Rai passed away and he was succeeded by his son Ratan Rai who was then twelve years old. He too had developed devotion to the Guru because he had been constantly told how Guru Tegh Bahadur undertook arduous tours to awaken the people; how he made supreme sacrifice for the protection of *Dharma* and for defeating the ill-conceived design of Aurangzeb to convert Hindustan which he considered as *Dar-ul-Harb* (land of infidelity) into *Dar-ul-Islam* (land of Muslims), how through his blessing his parents begot him and how great was the aura of his splendid personality. On ascending the throne, Ratan Rai expressed his desire to his mother to visit Chak Nanki to experience the greatness of his son, Guru Gobind Rai and to receive his blessings. His mother encouraged him in his resolve.

So Raja Ratan Rai came on a pilgrimage and amongst many other valuable offerings, brought a trained elephant named *Parsadi* and a unique weapon for the Master. This elephant had a white stripe from the tip of his trunk all along his back right to the end of his tail ; he was trained to hold a fan in his trunk and wave it and to perform many other feats.

The uniqueness of the weapon lay in the fact that it could be used as a sword, a lance or a club.

The young Guru accepted the offerings and showered his benediction on the Raja. The Raja enjoyed celestial atmosphere of Chak Nanki and was highly impressed by the way the Guru conducted affairs, how he scattered joy and light in abundance, how he was working on the plans to recast man and society afresh and on bases already propounded and championed by his predecessors as also ordained to him by the Almighty.

After staying for some days, the Raja sought permission to go back to his state. The parting was soul-stirring. The Guru took him in his embrace and kissed him. The Raja touched the feet of the Guru, rubbed the dust made pious by Guru's feet and touched it on his forehead. In child-like innocence and totally overwhelmed by emotions and love of the Guru, he expressed that offerings represented his love and devotion to him and were not to be parted with. The Guru acknowledged his feelings by consoling him. The Raja along with his party started his homeward journey. On reaching home, he built a temple in honour of the Guru, whom he worshipped as a holy Divine.

The scenario at Chak Nanki reflecting exuberance, vigour and a constructive dynamism was looked upon with suspicion by Bhim Chand, the ruler of Bilaspur, who had succeeded his father who was poisoned to death in 1667 by the ruler of Kangra.

Upto the eighties, Bhim Chand had set himself on the road to realise his cherished goal. He had successfully beaten back the invasion of Mughal *Faujdar* of Kangra who intended to replace him with his uncle, Manak. Similarly his new minister Parmanand had inflicted a defeat on the *Faujdar* of Sirhind and brought laurels to his young master.

It was at this stage when his reputation stood high that Bhim Chand took notice of the Guru's activities and appraised them not in the context of the Guru's vision and his grand design, but from his own perspective or at best from the perspective of the hill states. It was not difficult for him to surmise that Guru's activities not only did not fit in the long established social and political order in the hill states, but also could pose a serious threat to his authority. *Ranjit Nagara*, maintenance of an army, infusing of new ideology into the minds of the people were regarded as an affront to him and as a prelude to establishment of a state within a state. Nevertheless, Bhim Chand decided to visit the Guru to see things for himself. The Guru received the Raja in the famous woollen tent which had been presented to him by a disciple named Duni Chand from Kabul. Other gifts presented to the Guru were also displayed. Bhim Chand was surprised at the majesty and splendour of the young Guru, at his confidence and the devotion of his Sikhs towards him. When he returned to Bilaspur, he decided to make it clear to the Guru that since Makhowal fell in his territory, he was within his rights as an overlord to levy tribute. From the Guru's point of view the question of overlordship was irrelevant because none of the Gurus had paid tribute either to Hindur or to Kahlur till then. Bhim Chand also insisted on being presented with the things of his choice as for instance *Prasadi* elephant and the unique weapon which could be used as a sword, a lance or a club beside the embroidered *Shamiana* (Canopy).

Considering the Guru's refusal to oblige him as a challenge to his authority, he attacked the Guru in 1682[1] but was beaten back. Fearing that the states on his North and North Eastern border might take advantage of his discomfiture, he hurriedly packed up and retreated. In contemplating attack on Guru Gobind Rai he had been incited by the Governors of Sirhind, Lahore and Jammu.[2]

The unexpected conflict, as it was not followed by any understanding between the victorious and the vanquished, started a period of tension both for Bhim Chand and the Guru. In this environment of suspended hostilities, constant clashes between Sikhs and Bhim Chand's soldiers were inevitable. At this juncture, a large number of *Masands* tried to dissuade the Guru from proceeding with war-like activities. The Guru declined to oblige them. Nand Chand, his maternal uncle Kirpal and all others supported the Guru in his stand. View-point of *Masands* was actuated by a fear factor and it certainly did not take into consideration the far-reaching implications of Guru's acquiescence. In case the Guru had submitted, Anandpur (Chak Nanki) would have lost its independent character which it had maintained as a religious centre and the Guru would have been forced to surmount more difficulties in the process of consummating his design. In 1685, Raja Medni Parkash of Sirmour (later known as Nahan) invited the

---

1. H.A. Rose, *A Glossary of the Tribes and Castes of the Punjab and North-West Frontier Province*, Vol. III, p. 688. Rose puts Bhim Chand's defeat in 1682.
2. Hari Ram Gupta, *History of the Sikhs*, Vol. I, p. 227, it was a challenge to the king's authority. The Gurus followed the concept of *Khalsa* and if they paid any tribute that would mean 'serving a man' whereas *Khalsa* served only God.

Guru to settle in his territory. The Guru accepted the offer and left for Sirmour. Guru himself says in *Bachittar Natak*, "After this I left Anandpur (Chak Nanki) and reached Paonta (a place in the Nahan State) situated on the bank of Kalindri (Jamuna) and partook of various activities."[1]

The great majority of the Sikhs in Guru's township in Bilaspur state accompanied the Guru. There is a strong Sikh tradition that speaks of Gulab Rai and Sham Das, the grandsons of Suraj Mal, being left behind by the Guru at Anandpur (Chak Nanki) to look after the welfare of Sikhs who did not accompany him to Nahan.[2]

Why did the Guru leave Chak Nanki ? The event, as it involved shifting of headquarters and settling in another state, was not fortuitous or just a freak; it was the product of the interplay of different factors. The first among them of course was the animosity of Bhim Chand. The Guru needed a place where he could mature his plans undisturbed, free from mundane interference from any king or such other authority. Secondly, the Raja of Sirmour had cordially invited the Guru to settle in his state, knowing full well that the relation between the Guru and Bhim Chand had gone sour. Besides devotion to the Guru, he had certain mundane motives as well. Sirmour and Garhwal were neighbouring states engaged in hostilities for several generations. Supported by the Mughal government, the former had successfully encroached upon the territory of the latter. During the reign of Aurangzeb, Sirmour received Kala Garh (near Dehra Doon) and the Doon was conferred upon Garhwal. This put the two states in dangerous proximity to each other. After Aurangzeb's departure from Delhi in 1679, two new chiefs became rulers of the two states : Medni Parkash (1684-1704) in Sirmour and Fateh Shah in Garhwal (1684-1717). The former desired to strengthen himself by accommodating the Guru in his own territory.[3] Thirdly there was the Mughal factor that prompted the Guru to shift to Sirmour. For about ten years since the martyrdom of Guru Tegh Bahadur, there had been no move on the part of the Mughals against the Guru.

1. *Bachittar Natak Steek*, p. 138.
2. Giani Gian Singh, *Shri Dasmesh Chamatkar*, p. 119.
3. Hutchinson and Vogal, *History of the Punjab Hill States*, Vol. II.

Between Guru Tegh Bahadur's execution in November 1675 and the death of Maharaja Jaswant Singh in December 1678, Aurangzeb's hands were comparatively free. The situation in the rebellious tribal areas in the North-West had improved to a large extent by the end of the year 1675. Shivaji had won victories in the South in 1676-77 but this did not deter Aurangzeb from continuing religious persecutions and military aggression in the North. He had revived *Jazya* in April 1674, with a purpose to spread Islam and eliminate infidels. Then the Rajput war drew him away to Ajmer where he established his headquarters in September, 1679 to deal effectively with the rebellion of his eldest son, Akbar, who had found shelter at the court of Sambhaji. The Emperor arrived at Burhanpur in November 1681 but never returned to the North. The Deccan became the Chief Centre of his political and military activities from 1681 onwards and Imperial policy did not concern itself with Sikh affairs for quite a long time.

If Aurangzeb had really intended to harm the Sikh community after November 1675, he had an excellent opportunity during the three years period after the commencement of Rajput war. Guru Gobind Rai was a mere boy, inexperienced and yet to mature as a statesman and a warrior-general. *Minas, Dhirmalias* and *Ram Rayyas*—the dissentient sects were active in their opposition to him. But even at the height of his religious frenzy symbolised by the reimposition of *Jazya*, Aurangzeb did not take any step particularly against the Sikhs and their religion. Instead of creating difficulties for the Guru he is credited to have directed his potential rival Ram Rai to retire to his possessions in Doon valley thereby making it difficult for him to dabble effectively in Sikh affairs. Had he really changed his mind towards Sikhism and the Sikhs ? Was he now favourably disposed towards the Sikhs ? Analysis of his religious policy towards non-Muslims makes us conclude that he was not. This soft peddling towards the Guru and his Sikhs for quite a long time was actuated first by his belief that the Guru was not in a position, at least for some time, to challenge Mughal authority in respect of its religious and political policies, and secondly, he had computed that the Guru was bound to evoke jealousy/

enmity of the hill states and would soon be bogged down in hill affairs with the likely result that he would lose the intensity, even shine of his mission.

The Sikhs, however, had no reason to expect that Aurangzeb's hostility had ceased after the martyrdom of Guru Tegh Bahadur. Khushwant Singh says, ".........the leaders of the Sikh community were concerned about the safety of Gobind, for the possibility of his being taken to Delhi as a hostage could not be ruled out. To avoid any chances, the young Guru and his entourage were shifted from Anandpur (Chak Nanki) to the mountains of Paonta, which was not only farther from Sirhind as compared to Anandpur (Chak Nanki) but also provided from the nearest Mughal centre of power a natural fortress which, because of its difficult terrain was well-nigh inaccessible."[1]

In this connection Dr. A. C. Banerjee says, "In the years following the Guru's martyrdom, the 'Turks' took no steps against the young Guru nor did he seek to destroy them. His migration to Paonta took place most probably in 1685 at the instance of Raja Medni Parkash of Sirmour. It has nothing to do with the 'dread' of the Mughal hostility which appears to have evaporated as a result of Mughal inactivity for about a decade."[2] The assessment of the learned scholar is fallacious, as on one hand it runs contrary to the very strong Sikh tradition reflecting constant lurking fear of Aurangzeb's wrath and on the other hand it lacked supportive, authentic, historical evidence.

---

1. Khushwant Singh, *A History of the Sikhs*, Vol. I, p. 76.
2. A.C. Banerjee, *Guru Nanak to Guru Gobind Singh*, p. 230.

CHAPTER IV

PAONTA PERIOD

Having taken the decision to accept the invitation of Medini Parkash, the Guru left Chak Nanki in May, 1685. Along with him were, 500 soldiers, many Sikhs, a large number of poets, scholars and musicians. His baggage consisted of a large number of horses, oxen, camel and elephants. The whole caravan of the Guru passed through Ropar, Kharar, Ramgarh, Rani ka Raipur and Bhurewala. The Guru encamped at Toka situated at foot-hills on the border of Sirmour state.[1]

At Bhurewal the Chauhan Rajput landlords who after embracing Islam were generally known as Rangars and had *Zamindari* of eighty-five[2] villages entertained the Guru and his cavalcade exactly as their ancestors had done forty years earlier in 1645 when Guru Har Rai went to Nahan by the same route.[3]

At Toka too, these people provided provisions, performed other ancillary services and prayed for Guru's benediction. The Guru's grace did descend and he blessed them with an honorific 'Bhure Shah'. A small gurdwara commemorates Guru's stay at Toka. A fair is held every year on the tenth day of Jeth (May).[4]

A couple of days later, the Raja of Nahan came to escort

---

1. Hari Ram Gupta. *History of the Sikhs*, Vol. I, p. 230.
2. Trilochan Singh, *Guru Tegh Bahadur*, p. 114.
3. Sirmour (later known as Nahan) was a mountainous tract with a steep rise from the Northwest to the Northeast with elevation of more than 11000 feet at its highest level. It is divided into two by Giri, a tributary of Jamuna.
4. *Sirmour State Gazetteer*, Lahore, 1907, p. 15.
   "The Sikhs have four Gurdwaras in the state. Paonta, Bhangani, Nahan and the fourth one is at 'Toka', but it only consists of a small platform near a well, built by Fateh Singh Ahluwalia, when he held the Naraingarh territory in the later part of the 19th century (Bikrami). About 100 *Bighas* ☛

the Guru to his capital. After a short stay at Nahan, the Raja led the Guru to a spot on the eastern limits of Jamuna which formed the boundary between Garhwal and Sirmour.

The Guru liked the place which soon acquired the name of Paonta–*Paon Than*–footstool–resting place, On July 22, 1685[1] the Guru laid the foundation of a fortress. Dewan Nand Chand Sangha of Darauli performed the *Ardas* and Ram Koer, a descendant of Baba Buddha broke the ground. The fortress was completed within a very short span of twelve days.[2] Soon a number of hutments arose around the fortress to accommodate the Sikhs. The place had idyllic surroundings and the Guru loved it because it not only catered to his aesthetical sense but also provided him a requisite place to contemplate and mature his plans.

The Raja of Sirmour was so much impressed by the Guru's bearing, valour and culture, the discipline and dedication of the Sikhs and their unswerving faith in God that he requested the Guru never to leave this place.

Meanwhile, Raja Fateh Chand of Srinagar (Garhwal) heard of the Guru's reputation and paid him a visit. As it has been pointed out, he and the Raja of Nahan were not on good terms. The Guru mediated between the two and brought them close to each other.[3] The Guru hunted big game in the surrounding forest, and once killed a tiger with a sword and a shield. He himself says in *Bachittar Natak*, "I hunted a lot of tigers, bears and antelopes in the forest of Paonta."[4] He stayed at Paonta for about three years.[5]

→ in the state are attached to the Gurdwaras. It also enjoys a *muafi* in Naraingarh Tehsil and an annual grant of 100 maunds of grain from Patiala. The income is appropriated by the descendants of the late *Pujari*.

1. Sainapat, *Sri Gursobha*, p. 15, *"Ketak Bars Bhat eh Bhae, Des Pāwṭā Sat Guru Gae, Jamma Mahal Banwai, Karat Anand Prabhu Man Bhai"*; M.A. Macauliffe, *The Sikh Religion*, Vol. V, pp. 16-17.
2. M.A. Macauliffe, *op.cit.*
3. J.S. Grewal and S.S. Bal, *Guru Gobind Singh*, p. 71.
4. *Teh ke singh ghane chun(i) māre.*
   Rojh rīchh bahu bhāṅt(i) bidāre.
   Fateh shāh kopā tab(i) rājā.
   Loh parā humso bin(u) kājā.   (*Bachittar Natak*, Chapter 8, Chaupai 3)
5. *Sirmour State Gazetteer*, 112 as cited by Indubhushan Banerjee, *Evolution of the Khalsa*, II, p. 69.

He went through the whole gamut of epic and classical literature available in Sanskrit. In the process he developed liking for the art of poetry, appropriate use of diction *Rasa*, vocabulary, meters, gunas, *dhwani* and *alankar*. The fact is amply borne by his own compositions. He also came across different currents of thoughts; as for instance six schools of philosophy, Asceticism, Budhism, Jainism et al. He also took note of the theme running through *Puranic* literature and *Gita* that a divine saviour appears from time to time to uphold righteousness, and the profiles of Rama, Krishna and goddess Durga fighting and destroying the wicked. The Guru agreed that God, Sustainer and Protector of all, shall save the world and someone or some people would fulfil the Will of God but differed with it in one respect that a saviour cannot be an incarnate of God, because He being formless cannot assume human or any other form. He on his part felt that he was commissioned by God to uphold righteousness but that was his conviction sprung out of his deep meditation on the ways of God, whom he found extirpator of the wicked and upholder of righteousness exactly like his predecessor Guru Nanak who called God as *Asur Sanghar* and a 'Nourisher'. He never appropriated to himself any divine power or presented himself as 'God'. Rather he humbly declared that he was a servant of the Supreme Being and anybody calling him God representing or embodying divine power would be consumed in the fire of hell.[1]

Guru Gobind Singh himself was a prolific writer. In 1686, he completed the composition of *Shastra Nam Mala* in the conventional literary style of the time having its model the embelemetical verses of the great Masters.[2] The true import of the composition lies in personifying the weapons and for the Guru they were the medium of worship. The weapons had been used by gods and demons alike but it was their use by the former that was significant for the Guru because they had been used in defence and for promotion of righteousness. The

---

1. *Bachittar Natak VI*, Chaupais 32 and 33.
   Jo Humko Parmeshar Uchar Haiṅ, te Sabh Narak Kuṅḍ Meiṅ Parhaiṅ.
   Mai ho Param Purakh Ko Dāssā, Dekhan Āio Jagat Tamāsā.
2. D.P. Ashta, *The Poetry of Dasam Granth*, 147.

chaupais and *dohas* of adoration which Guru Gobind Rai composed were all reserved for the weapons only when they were used by the righteous[1] for the sake of righteousness.

Almost at the same time, the Guru composed *Var Sri Bhagauti Ji ki*, popularly known as *Chandi Di Var*, the first *Var* of its kind, complete and exhaustive and in blank verse, used for the first time in Punjabi literature.[2] The Guru succeeded in making his composition a means to impart heroic spirit, an important salient of his ideology. Though the source of the composition as in *Chandi Charitra* was also the tenth *Sakanda* of *Markandeya Puran*, he related in this composition only the battle of *Chandi and Durga*. Of the fifty-five stanzas in the *Var*, forty-nine described the battle scenes; the first five and twenty-five being purely narrative and informative, helping to elucidate the situation. *Chandi's* battles were, in the eyes of Guru Gobind Rai fought on the side of righteousness.

The story of Durga has been so bedded with sentences full of jewel-like choicest words that it simply savoured marvellous, highly artistic, tastefully descriptive. He pictured Durga as the one clad in armour from head to foot, while serpents coiled around her neck hissing dreadfully at the foes. Her hand-drum makes the sound of roaring tigress. She is riding a lion and fights valorously against the *Rakhshas*-tyrants and slays *Mahikhasur* among others. Her offspring, *Kali*, bursting forth from her forehead gulps down the demons and elephants alike. Durga herself is skilled in the use of a hundred arms and gives an astounding display of her martial prowess. Herself the bulwark of righteousness, she moves back and forth fearlessly. Guru Gobind Singh sees her battle as one against sin :

> All sins you annihilate
> And righteousness You countenance
> Dangerous poison is destroyed
> And creative energy maintained.[3]

The gods themselves revere Durga as "Mother" and they

1. S.S. Bal and J.S. Grewal, *Guru Gobind Singh*, p. 75.
2. D.P. Ashta, *The Poetry of Dasam Granth*, p. 147.
3. .....*Dust Nivāran*
   Dokh Hare.....
   .....Bisv bidhunsan
   Sristi kare.   (*Dasam Granth*, p. 32)

look up to her for help in overcoming and destroying their enemy.

She in fact is represented as a moral power to challenge an oppressive system and to establish harmony, morality and justice. Her aggression is, therefore, healthy as her anger is purifying. She is paradigm for both men and women. The Guru hoped that with the literary paradigm of Durga before them, the people would overcome their weaknesses and cowardice, overthrow unjust political authorities, abolish social inequalities and ultimately forge a new structure based on just and equalitarian values. As the future events unfolded, men and women were charged with courage and moral fervour by the personal example of the Guru and by his literary resurrection of this mythological heroine.

The Guru's specific choice of Durga out of millions of gods and goddesses was significant from another point of view. She is one goddess without husband, consort or lover. She is independent. She is her own mistress. She is autonomous, capable of taking her own decision, always acting as a positive force to activise the good to dare the wicked. By attributing such characteristics to Durga, the Guru purposely gave a fresh role model in the form of a woman. This was indeed something revolutionary and breath-taking. In most cultures, the image of woman has been degraded. In *Ancient Mirrors of Womanhood* Merli Stone cites several instances from a wide variety of cultures which reveal how the patriarchal structures have attempted to suppress, alter and even erase the lustre of the female. The Summerians, for example, replaced the ancient creator goddess *Nammu* with less effective *Inana*. *Billa Debuda* in Drawing from "Mythology in Women's Quest For Selfhood" sums up this entire process while ancient mythology affirmed woman's power. Through patriarchal influence over the years, those stories have come to be 'muted', curtailed and even perverted.[1]

The Guru's treatment of Durga was completely exempt from such detraction. On the other hand her exploits had been

---

1. Nikky Guninder Kaur Singh, *The Feminine Principle in the Sikh Vision of the Transcendent*, p. 132.

fully described, rather magnified. In this recalling, Durga did not lose even an iota of her shine and fire. She was represented as a paradigm of independence, sovereignty and wholeness of a person. The exalted image of Durga which the Guru created or presented went a long way to bring about a change in the psyche of the people, especially of women. Mai Bhago from Amritsar District of Punjab was one such example when she saw how some Sikhs of her area had fled Anandpur, the seat of Guru Gobind Singh, in the face of the privations brought on by prolonged siege. She chided them for pusillanimity. She led them back to fight for the Guru, and she herself took part in the battle that ensued at Khidrana (now Muktsar). She performed extra-ordinary feats of valour and skill and the entire period is replete with heroic deeds and sacrifices of Sikh men and women like her. They all fought valiantly against the mighty forces of the rulers of day. Because of this sustained resistance, the Sikhs became a political force to reckon with within half a century of Guru Gobind Singh's death.

Yet Durga was not invoked as a goddess by Guru. Nowhere in his *Var* does the Guru professes himself to be a devotee of Durga. There is an utter absence of worship that is central to *Markandeya Purana* text. Guru Gobind Singh definitely recalled Durga but only as a figure of myth and literature, but more as someone who had dwelt and to an extent still dwelling in the psyche of non-Muslims. The Guru looked upon her and for that matter took on Ram, Krishan or any other incarnation, only as an instrument created for moral purposes. He never looked upon them as incarnation of God. He very explicitly says in *Chandi di Var*. 'The strength by which Ram killed the ten-headed Ravan with arrows was bestowed on him by God. The strength by which Krishan caught Kans by the hair and dashed him to the ground was bestowed on him by God.'

After the completion of *Shastra Nama Mala* and the *Var*, the Guru set himself to complete the unfinished composition *Krishan Avtar*. He picked up the old threads in July, 1687 and having added 1347 *Chhands* (340 *Chhands* forming the part of *Ras Mandal* and 875 *Chhands* composing *Yudh Prabandh*) upto

July 1688 BK Samvat 1745 completed *Krishan Avtar*.[1] According to Dr. S.S. Bal, "both because of theme and effect of his two earlier compositions, the part of the *Krishan Avtar* written during this period was exclusively devoted to heroic poetry." This argument makes sense.

It was natural that in this part of *Krishan Avtar* the author should use *Bir Ras* and not *Vat Sakaya* and *Shingar Rasas* which the Guru used in the earlier portions of the composition.[2] Significantly in the last verse of the composition, the Guru said that he had written *Krishan Avtar* to wage a holy war.

"The tenth story of the *Bhagwat* is rendered into the *Bhakha* with no other purpose than that of war for the sake of righteousness."

We also find the Guru saying in this composition that he was not interested in riches which could come to him from all parts of the country at his bidding but wished to die the death of a martyr. Dr. Harbans Singh very aptly puts, "His poetic intuition was notable for its sublimity of style, mystical ardour and energy. His object was twofold : to sing praise of the Timeless and to infuse new vigour into the limp mass of people. His compositions were most appropriately adapted to these purpose. Rarely has poetry in any tongue recaptured the transcendent vision in such a spirit of courage and heroism. His own literary creations apart, the Guru had gathered around him a comity of literary luminaries."[3]

Sikh tradition fixes the number of such luminaries as fifty-two which is debatable. The arrival at or departure from Guru *Darbar* depended on each individual's sweet will. Possibly the number fifty-two have come into vogue because in the historical consciousness, it had acquired some sort of respect or sanctity as the much respected *Sidhs* also numbered fifty-two. According to our discovery, the number of poets,

1. Bhai Randhir Singh, *Shabad Murat.*
   Itihasic Pattar, Vol. 5.
2. D.P. Ashta, *The Poetry of Dasam Granth,* p. 79.
3. *Hukam Nāme Sikhāṅ wāle Likhe jo Likhārī Sikh Hove so Hazūr Āve.*
                                    (*Rehat Nama Bhai Chaupa Singh*)
   Jo Brahmin Vidwān Hai Changā So Bhijwavānā
   Jo Khareb Lage so Guru Ke Gharoṅ Lānā.   (*Bansavalinama,* Daswan Charan)
   Sarup Dass Bhalla, *Mehma Parkash.*

writers and thinkers was one hundred twenty-five; one hundred poets and twenty-five thinkers or prose writers.[1] The number does not include the poets of various compositions which do not suggest the names of their authors. Understandably, the number of poets and men of parts we have identified formed only the nucleus. In fact there was a much larger number of such people. There is a strong tradition that vigorous drive was made to re-write, restate, translate parts of *Puranic* literature as well as fresh literature which had the potential of remodelling the psyche of the people to enable them uphold righteousness, resist tyranny and secure the fulfilment of divine justice.

Though the detailed account of literary compositions of different poets and writers is not known, yet some works are available. Sainapat rendered *Chanakaya Neeti* from Sanskrit to *Braj Bhasha*.[2] Nand Lal[3] composed *Bandgi Nama*, Amrit Rai, Hans Ram, Kavresh and Mangal translated *Sabha Parb*, *Karan Parb*, *Daram Parb* and *Salya Parb* respectively and were honoured with the reward of huge sums,[4] besides costly gifts. Hans Ram felt exulted at the cash of sixty thousand *Takas* given to him. Mangal, Kavresh and Amrit Rai also were over-joyed when they were given cash and gifts in recognition of their services.[5] Mangal was so excited that he called the Guru *Puran Avtar*—complete incarnate and Anandpur the abode of bliss. Pandit Jagan Nath[6] who originally embellished the court of Shah Jahan was also attracted to the Guru and came to Anandpur and wrote *Adhyatmik Purkush* saying forever good-bye to his earlier predilection of producing erotic literature. Even the avaricious and ego-bloated poet Chandan[7] was welcome to the court of the Guru. The Guru's personality changed him into a humble person and he wrote literature of the type and tenor the Guru had desired. Obviously, the leitmotif of the literature created under the sponsorship and

1. Piara Singh Padam, *Sri Guru Gobind Singh Ji de Durbari Ratan*, pp. 4-6.
2. *Ibid.*, pp. 25-32.
3. *Ibid.*
4. *Ibid.*
5. *Ibid.*
6. *Ibid.*
7. *Ibid.*

inspiration of the Guru seemed to bring about reawakening through the process of animating and articulating the best in our cultural heritage.

The Guru very wisely and aptly employed the medium of literature to impart a new orientation to the minds of the people given to passivity. For this latter purpose, he did not hesitate even to pick up themes from the ancient epics and mythology of India to produce verses charged with martial fervour.

Side by side his engagement with the creation of appropriate literature, the Guru carried on missionary activities with zeal and zest. He held congregation in the morning as well as in the evening daily at Paonta. He took religious tours to villages such as Kapal Mochan, Kalsia, Siana and Thanesar. He also visited the village Dhankoli on his way to Anandpur from Paonta. The village Lohar was also hallowed by the Guru's visit. All these places have gurdwaras in the memory of Guru's visits.

A renowned Sufi Saint Pir Badruddin (1647-1704) from Sadhaura, popularly known by his nick-name Pir Budhu Shah was fascinated by the Guru's splendid personality and came to him to feel for himself his greatness. He held a long discussion with him and was simply captivated by the Guru's knowledge of the unknown. He became his ardent devotee. The Guru, on his part, showered affection on him—so much so that on his recommendation, he enlisted 500 Pathans in his army who had been dismissed from the Mughal army for petty offences. From historical point of view, this gesture of the Guru had great significance. It signalled that in the struggle for upholding righteousness *(Dharam)* anyone irrespective of religion, status, birth and caste et al was free to take part. It is more than likely that the relationship between the Guru and the *Pir* was based on mutual respect, just as the relationship between Sain Mian Mir and Guru Arjan had been.

The Guru decided to establish a special order of his Sikhs particularly to make comparative study of religions and also to interpret classical Indian tradition in terms of the basic philosophy of Sikhism. The project thus conceived had incidental advantages as well. Since times immemorial, learning and teaching had been the monopoly of Brahmins, *Sanyasis* or *Bairagis* (ascetics) but the project of the Guru according no recognition to caste was sure to land a strong blow to the long-held monoply of class learning. Since most of the classical Indian religious literature was available in Sanskrit, the Guru found it imperative to make arrangement for the teaching of Sanskrit to his followers. He asked his court poet Raghu Nath to do the needful. He politely and diplomatically replied that he was prohibited by convention to teach the language of gods *(Dev Bhasha)* and the holy scriptures to the non-*divyas* i.e. *Shudras* and women. The Guru admonished him for his sticking to outworn ideals and concepts. Udasis also showed their reluctance to impart the knowledge of Sanskrit and of scriptures to the non-Brahmins and non-Sanyasis.

So, he selected a dozen[1] Sikhs from different classes, castes and creeds, and sent them to Benaras. Their names were (1) Karam Singh, (2) Rama Singh, (3) Ganda Singh, (4) Vir Singh, (5) Sobha Singh, (6) Dharam Singh, (7) Daya Singh, (8) Kesar Singh, (9) Mohkam Singh, (10) Gian Singh, (11) Gaja Singh, (12) Chanda Singh, (13) Saina Singh. All these chosen Sikhs studied under the guidance of Pandit Sada Manak. In the eleventh year they came back to the Guru who now had shifted to Anandpur. Guru Gobind Singh was much pleased to find that they had become really good scholars and allotted to them different duties. Pandit Karam Singh was asked to interpret hymns from *Guru Granth Sahib* in the Guru's court. Bhai Mani Singh received knowledge of six traditional schools of philosophy from him. Bhai Punjab Singh and his disciple Roucha Singh spread Sikhism in Jammu and Kashmir. In 1699 these scholars known as *Nirmalas* were administered *Pahul* and entered the order of the Khalsa. They played a significant role in dissemination of Sikhism as also in Sikh politics in the eighteenth century. Later on as the time rolled on and the number of the contemporary associates of the Guru or of his staunch followers like Bhai Mani Singh thinned, they began to evince more interest in bandying themselves as vedantic scholars than humble interpreters of Sikh philosophy. Therefore

---

1. According to Bhai Kahn Singh Nabha, only five were sent to Kashi. They were 1. Ram Singh, 2. Karam Singh, 3. Ganda Singh, 4. Vir Singh and 5. Sobha Singh, *Mahan Kosh*, p. 534.

they began to super-impose the vedantic point of view on the Sikh theological and philosophical structures. No doubt, they recited *Guru Granth Sahib* and encouraged others to do the same, yet they did not do all this as an expression of bringing into limelight the distinctiveness of Sikhism; rather as a part of Hindu tradition.[1] The trend is reflected in most of their literary composition which came into being particularly after the mid-eighteenth century. This being so the *Nirmalas* ceased to be right type of missionaries of Sikhism and thus their services to the cause of Sikhism in the later part of the eighteenth century and onward were not worthy of admiration.

RAM RAI'S RECLAMATION

Ram Rai was seventeen years old when Guru Harkrishan passed away. He did aspire to occupy the apostalic seat, but he could not achieve any success. The Sikhs could not be duped even by twenty-two impostor claimants to guruship and they accepted Guru Tegh Bahadur as their rightful Guru. Ram Rai had to resign to his fate. Instead of resorting to opposing the mainstream Sikhism by raising and strengthening a parallel antagonistic organisation, he now chose to galvanise his establishment on the model of *Udasi Sampardaya* of Baba Sri Chand ji which ultimately became one of the most prestigious missionary wings of Sikhism. Sikh tradition suggests that his change of heart came by the sudden death of Guru Harkrishan which brought a sense of remorse and repentence in his mind. He also felt upset at the execution of Guru Tegh Bahadur on 11th November, 1675 at Chandni Chowk Delhi.[2]

Guru Gobind Rai went to Paonta in Sirmour state in 1685

---

1. Surjit Singh Gandhi, *Struggle of the Sikhs for Sovereignty*, p. 571.

   The veracity of the statement can be coroborated by examining the content of most of the books produced in this period.

   Gulab Singh Nirmala who was initiated into the classical learning by Sant Man Singh, wrote *Bhasha Vrit*, 1777, *Mokhsh Panth*, 1778, *Adhyatam Ramayan*, 1782, *Parbodh Chander Natak*, 1792. The general tenor of these books is Vedantic.

2. Trilochan Singh, *Life of Guru Harkrishan*, p. 173.

and engaged himself in multiple activities, all aimed at throwing up a model man and a model society. Ram Rai who could watch for himself the Guru's activities being only fifteen miles away from Paonta was thrilled instead of feeling dejected. Ram Rai's respectful hidden feelings and affection for the eighteen year old Guru welled up and he longed to see and talk to him. Two hurdles constrained him to become public. The first and the foremost was his *Masand*s, especially Gurbakhsh and Tara, who exploited innocent disciple in his name and did not wish a rapprochement between the Guru and Ram Rai for fear of losing their loot. Secondly, Ram Rai was in the throes of hesitancy which was born out of his own mistakes, and his wilful and wrongful challenge to the Guru's instructions. After brooding and contemplating for quite a long time, Ram Rai ultimately decided to have a personal audience with him to express his remorse for what he had done. He wanted peace of mind and blessings of the Guru.

In the winter of 1686, Ram Rai sent a special messenger to Guru Gobind Rai who sought private audience for some confidential talks with him. The Guru's devotees and his personal staff showed utmost respect to Ram Rai's envoy. He was received by the Guru in a private audience where only his uncle Kirpal Chand, his Dewan Nand Chand and Bhai Daya Ram were present. Ram Rai's envoy respectfully told the Guru that his Master wished to meet him alone but for various reasons the meeting should be held somewhere outside Paonta, where he could hold some confidential talks with him and then go back to Dehra Doon on the same day. Even the day of the meeting was to be kept secret. Kirpal Chand asked, "Why does Ram Rai wish to make the meeting between the two members of the same family such a secret and highly mysterious affair? We all respect Ram Rai for the many wonderful qualities he possesses."[1] The envoy of Ram Rai could not give suitable reply except insisting on his demand.

The Guru guessed the truth and said, "I understand why Ram Rai wishes to make this meeting, a highly private affair.

---

1. *Suraj Parkash*, Ritu 2, Ansu 2.

The *Masands* of Ram Rai have become highly over-bearing and domineering. He is afraid that they might stand in the way of our meeting and foment trouble."[1] The Guru fixed next Sunday for the meeting and told the envoy that it would take place in the middle of the river (Jamuna). He would receive him in his boat.[2]

The meeting took place as scheduled in the middle of the river in a boat[3]. Ram Rai and Guru Gobind Singh embraced each with great affection and warmth. The thirty- nine year old Ram Rai showed utmost reverence to twenty years old Guru Gobind Rai. Ram Rai said in all humility,[4] "I am fortunate to have obtained a sight of thee..... When I am gone, protect my family and property. My father Har Rai used to say that someone would be born in our family and the world to restore and refit the vessels for safe conveyance of the souls. Accordingly thou hast come into the world for this special purpose."[5] Ram Rai also broached the issue of his wily and crafty *Masands* who had gone corrupt and aggressively head-strong and were hell bent to destroy him whom they thought to be a great constraint on their designs of bolstering up *Ram Rayyas* (followers of Ram Rai) as a cult. The Guru assured him his full help whenever he or his family members would call upon him. Ram Rai left the Guru's boat as a happy and gratified man. Most of his inner conflicts were resolved. He ceased to be a separate entity and for the rest of his life, he lived as a follower of Guru Gobind Rai. He did not leave any injunction in any form that he should be regarded as a Guru of a separate sect. He displayed his faith in the Guru's teachings and ran his establishment on the model of *Udasis* of Baba Sri Chand as it functioned towards the end of his life and thereafter under the guidance of Baba Gurditta ji.

On September 3, 1686, Ram Rai sat in a prolonged meditation. He asked his wife Punjab Kaur, to bolt the door from outside and not permit anyone to disturb his meditation

---

1. *Suraj Parkash*, Ritu 2, Ansu 2.
2. M.A. Macauliffe, *The Sikh Religion*, Vol. 5, p. 21.
3. *Ibid.*
4. *Ibid.*
5. *Ibid.*, pp. 20-24.

till the time he himself knocks from within.[1] The *Masand*
Gurbakhsh whose evil genius was largely responsible for Ram
Rai's estrangement with his father and confrontation with his
brother now saw his opportunity to annihilate Ram Rai and
capture the wealth and power of his Ashram. He is described
by Sewa Singh in his *Shaheed Bilas* as the most ignoble dunce,
a stupid rascal, a corpulent and haughty rogue and a bull-
headed egoist[2].

Early next morning Gurbakhsh propagated that Punjab
Kaur had killed Ram Rai and hidden his dead body in a room
and had clandestinely conspired with Guru Gobind Rai to
hand over the Ashram to the Guru. He took his people along
with him and smashed the door of the room and made the
crowd believe that Ram Rai was dead, hurling the blame on
Punjab Kaur for this heinous crime while in fact Ram Rai was
deeply engrossed in meditation and looked motionless which
was made out to be a sign of death. Punjab Kaur protested but
Gurbakhsh blinded by his nefarious ambition   hurriedly
consigned Ram Rai's body to fire and occupied the Ashram
along with its wealth.[3] Punjab Kaur sent a messenger to Guru
Gobind Rai at Paonta for help. The Guru quickly came. But
before he reached, the body of Ram Rai had been consumed
by the fire.[4] The Guru surrounded the Ashram and rounded
up the miscreants. In the skirmish that took place, fifty-two
men of Gurbakhsh were killed. Gurbakhsh managed to escape.
Guru Gobind Rai consoled Punjab Kaur and praised her
courage[5]. The Guru sent a few *Udasis* of Baba Sri Chand's
establishment to manage the affairs of the Ashram.

Exactly a year after the tragic death of Ram Rai, Punjab
Kaur decided to hold a get-together of her late husband's
admirers including *Masands* to commemorate his first death
anniversary and to offer prayer to the Almighty.

This was a critical period for Guru Gobind Rai, for, he

1. Trilochan Singh, *Life of Guru Harkrishan*, pp. 175-76.
2. *Maha Agyani, Abhimani, Tamaltang Deha, Mughad, Kukarmi, Hankari.*
3. M.A. Macauliffe, *The Sikh Religion* V, p. 22.
4. *Ibid.*
5. Vir Singh Bal, *Singh Sagar*, Chapter 6.
"You are the wife of a great scion of Guru Ram Das's Sodhi family; on
your honour rests the honour of the whole of our Sodhi family."

was expecting an invasion on Paonta by the armies of Hill Chief's.

Hoping that Guru Gobind Rai would be too busy in his defensive preparation, *Masand* Gurbakhsh planned once more to capture the Ashram. He reached Dehra Doon on 23rd August, 1688 and set himself up as the self-styled successor of Ram Rai. Punjab Kaur once again sent a messenger to Guru Gobind Rai who despatched fifty of his choicest warriors under the command of Dewan Nand Chand and Bhai Mani Singh to Dehra Doon. They reached there on August 24. Gurbakhsh used indecent language about the Guru. Bhai Mani Singh was incensed and he turned the throne-like cot of Gurbakhsh upside down with the result that his fat and bulky body rolled on the ground. In an hour's fight, most of his followers were killed while others ran away.[1] Gurbakhsh once again escaped and never again visited Dehra Doon. He rushed to Lahore and with the assistance of some Mughal officials captured Ram Rai's Ashram there. He instigated his followers in the Punjab to work against Guru Gobind Rai. The treacherous role of these *Ram Rayyas* of Punjab in which they continuously helped the Mughals and Afghans against the Sikhs was the main cause of the decision of the Khalsa Holy Order to socially boycott them who had no affiliations with the Ashram at Dehra Doon the members of which never claimed for themselves status of a cult or a sect. Indeed, it was a wonderful achievement of the Guru's missionary activities at Paonta. The opposition to the Sikh faith around Paonta and Doon valley diminished considerably.[2]

1. Trilochan Singh, *Life of Guru Harkrishan*, p. 178.
2. The relationship of Punjab Kaur with Mata Sundri and Mata Sahib Kaur were most amicable after the death of Guru Gobind Singh. It is through the help of Mata Punjab Kaur's followers that Mata Sundri was able to take Baba Kahan Singh a direct descendant of Guru Angad, out of the Mughal prison, just a day before he was to be beheaded along with other companions of Baba Banda Singh Bahadur in March 1716 in Delhi. Punjab Kaur proved to be well versed in administration and organisation of her followers. She set up a remarkable code of conduct for all future incumbents of Ram Rai's Ashram, who were to remain celibates and study *Guru Granth* and the ideals of Guru Nanak. Punjab Kaur died in 1740 (Trilochan Singh, *op.cit.*, p. 179).

Alongside, the Guru's religious and literary activities, a new paradigm of militarism emerged under his auspices. The common motifs underlying militarism are : political domination, urge for patriotic strife and acquisition of wealth. But the Guru's militarism did not recognise any of these. Nor did Guru's militarism resemble that of Spartans which expected its votaries to do anything, good or bad, for the state. The Guru's militarism in fact was *Dharm Yudh*—fight for uprooting unrighteousnes and upholding the virtuous. Rooting out un-righteousness and wickedness implies the establishment of the hegemony of Truth which in fact is another name of the Supreme Lord. For restoring righteousness, the use of arms as the last resort to destroy the evil-doers and those deviated from the path of *Dharma* could not be ruled out. Therefore Guru Gobind Rai accepted and adopted sword as the restorer of *Dharma*. Guru's affinity for this weapon for the purpose is very clearly reflected in the following couplets of *Zafar Nama*.

"When all other means have failed, it is but righteous to take to sword."[1] Since the target of upholding righteousness was divine in Guru's perception and understanding, the sword to him became a symbol of divine power as well as of dignity and worldly might. It was in this background that the Guru used the term *Kirpan* as the transcedent Lord, the Saviour and Punisher of the wicked. The Guru expressed :

> "I bow with love and devotion to the Holy sword.
> Assist me that I may be able to complete this work."[2]
> "Thy radiance and splendour dazzle like the Sun
> Thou bestowth happiness on the good.
> Thou terrifiest the evil, Thou scatterest sinners.
> I ask thy protection
> Hail, hail to the creator of the world,
> The saviour of the creation, My cherisher
> Hail to thee, O Sword !"

Such militarism was at once the need of the time and a

---

1. *Chūṅ kār az hamā hīlte dar guzasht.*
   Halāl ast burdan bā shamshīr dast.

2. *Namaskār Srī khaṟag ko karoṅ so hit(u) chit(u) lāe.*
   Pūran karo giraṅth eh(u) tum muhe karauh sahāe.1.   (Bachittar Natak)

potent instrument for the development of the country. It has been seen throughout the ages that no amount of education or religious refinement is enough, unless the refined and emancipated man, one who combines in himself wisdom and power in equal degrees has control of the commercial and industrial machine which is the state today, and control of the organised power which is the state always.

All along refining and defining the new type of militarism, the Guru was sagacious enough to develop a viable military apparatus the beginning of which had been made at Anandpur. As if defining the new form of militarism was not enough, the Guru composed a logistic support body for his army. The commanders responsible for logistic support were the most efficient. In the early career of the Guru, Jit Mal, Gopal Chand, Sango Shah and Mohri Chand held charges of Civil Defence problems of Anandpur, weapons and ammunition, war animals, food and supply portfolios respectively. Such departments and portfolios although in rudimentary form looked analogous to the present-day Army Service Corps. Also, such an administrative body foreshadowed the war council of the modern times. As a management technique, every soldier was made to realise his duties towards himself, other individuals and *Panth* as a whole. Ample care was taken that an individual soldier was not driven to shoddy substitute to bolster his ego. Ordnance Factories at Paonta and Anandpur also functioned under the military administrative set-up.

The Guru took special care for the training of his soldiers. He held regular competitions in archery, sword fighting, unarmed combat, ambush and patrolling. Large scale hunting expeditions were organised where soldiers got training to use their weapons on live and fast moving targets. Training was imparted to the cavalry to launch attack to shock the enemy to be followed by swift attack of the infantry to invest the gains of the cavalary and demoralise the enemy. The basic concept is accepted even today when armour and infantry are employed in conjunction with each other against well entrenched enemy and organised defence.

The bulk of the Guru's army consisted of the Sikhs from

Malwa and *Majha* regions of the Punjab. They took food from *Guru ka Langar* while uniforms, arms and horses were provided out of the Guru's *Golak* (contributory treasury). The soldiers belonged to all castes. A good number of Muslims were also in the Guru's army. The composite character of Guru's army was a positive proof of his altogether non-particularistic and universalistic ideal of attaining freedom of conscience, of belief and of raising a social order on the bases of principles of tolerance, acceptance of diversity of faith and religious practice.

The Guru had no fondness for mercenaries, but at times, when he felt shortage of men and instructors for imparting military training, he did not hesitate to recruit them on salary basis. He enlisted 500 Pathans at Paonta at the instance of Pir Badruddin but his experience was not pleasant. Regarding the scale of pay, not much is known. However, the Guru paid Rs. 5[1] to the officer and Rs. 1/- to the soldier, per day in the case of aforesaid Pathan soldiers. It is likely that some sort of rough registration of them was kept with the Guru. According to the author of *Suraj Parkash*, when the people gathered around the Guru, he asked them to join his army and their descriptive rolls were prepared.

The maximum strength of the Guru's army at any time has been estimated to be 20,000 and at Paonta it did not exceed five thousand. The Artillery men were very few in number although matchlock men were considerable. The horses were procured on payment as well as through offerings of the followers. The Guru's own blue horse had become a tradition on account of its agility, boldness, steadfastness and intelligence.

Forts formed a salient feature of Guru's military organisation. He built the Fort of Paonta and raised walls around the city. He regarded forts as a very potent bulwark against aggression. He took special care that the fort should be built on a hilltop or at such places wherefrom the garrison could observe the movement of the enemy forces while the enemy should not be able to move easily towards the fort. In

1. M.A. Macauliffe, *The Sikh Religion*, Vol. V, p. 20.

addition, fort should be spacious to accommodate enough soldiers, war animals and foundaries. It should have port holes on the parapets for the cannon to fire.

The battle array of the Guru consisted of a vanguard, centre or main body, right flank, left flank and reserve. During advance the Guru always took into consideration the terrain, the enemy's strength and quality of his fighting equipment. Ambuscade was a popular tactic employed by the Guru. Elephants were also valued much as a vehicle for the advance of the army. The *Prasadi* elephant was donated by Raja Rattan Chand, a Chieftain of Assam and another was sent by *Sangat* of Dacca[1].

The Guru also had a network of spies to collect information regarding enemy's forces, their deployment, their weapons and their nature of organisation. How did he train the spies is not known but it is certain that they were very efficient. On the eve of the Battle of Bhangani, it was their information which led the Guru to select the elevated place a few miles away from Paonta wherefrom the battle could be controlled and fought more effectively.

In the organisational vision of the Guru, weapons of the soldiers were also given requisite attention. In addition to the weapons he procured from his disciples, he got them manufactured in his own foundries at Paonta and Anandpur. The weapons used by the Guru were of four kinds. (1) *Mukat,* (2) *Amukat,* (3) *Mukta Mukat,* (4) *Yantar Mukat. Mukat* weapons were those which parted company of the users, as for instance arrows. *Amukat* were those weapons which remained with the users such as sword or *Katar. Mukta Mukat* weapons could be used both ways : in the hands and throwing them on the enemy. The weapons such as spears and lances fall in this category. Weapons of the fourth kind were used with the help of mechanical devices like catapult. The Guru's varied activities entailed a lot of expenditure and needed strong support at least from his own disciples. In this context, the *Masand/Manji* system could play a very important role. But the Guru was dismayed at the reticence and disinclination of the

---

1. Ganda Singh (ed.), *Hukamname,* p. 131.

majority of *Masands/Manjidars* who preferred to watch their own interests to that of the *Sikh Panth*. They not only kept for themselves the whole or a large part of *Daswandh*,[1] but also made the Sikhs skeptical about the designs of the Guru. This being the perspective the Guru got convinced that some alternative would have to be found to make the people informed of his latest activities and what Sikhism really aimed at.

The Guru's period at Paonta marked a watershed in his life. He matured his ideas and fashioned his concepts. He evolved suitable strategies to implement them. He produced requisite literature and rallied around himself the most capable persons from different corners of India to harness their wisdom in the service of his mission which he refined and defined with absolute clarity and lucidity. He gave new metaphors, new symbols and new slogans to energise, vitalise and rejuvenate the people given to mental and physical inertia. He reclaimed Ram Rai and worked in such a way that his establishment ceased to be a separate entity and functioned as if it was the *Udasi* establishment of late Baba Sri Chand. He organised his internal affairs diligently, made proper arrangements for carrying on correspondence with *Sangats* and eminent Sikhs. It is likely that the letters from *Sangats*/disciples were received and registered[2]. Similarly the *Hukamnamas* or letters from the Guru were registered before they were sent to different places. There is every possibility that the copies of the *Hukamnamas* were kept by the Guru's establishment and proper arrangements made to keep record of the amount of *Daswandh* and other offerings. He organised appropriate war machine. Lest his militaristic organisation

---

1. One tenth of the earning made obligatory by Guru Arjan Dev for the Sikhs to contribute to Guru's treasury as a token of one's thankfulness for the bounties of God.
2. Ganda Singh, *Hukamname*, p. 17. A large number of *Hukamnamas* were numbered. Besides they were written in specific form. For instance on each *Hukamnama* there is Guru's sign or instruction in Guru's hand to be followed in the context of the *Hukamnama* to be scribed by a scriber who would start his writing with ੧ਓ ਗੁਰੂ ਸਤ—*Ikoṅkār Gurū Sat*, ੧ਓ ਸਤਿਗੁਰੁ *Ikoṅkār Satgurū* or ੧ਓ ਸਤਿਗੁਰੁ ਜੀਓ—*Ikoṅkār Satgurū Jīo*.

reduces itself to an organ of tyranny, the Guru reconstructed the concept of militarism. He viewed and reviewed the policies of the contemporary government both of the Hill Chieftains and the Mughals. He also observed the objectives, the policies and the extent of the influence of *Naqshbandis* who had their centres at important places such as Sirhind, Lahore, Delhi, Agra and Jaunpur et. al. He carefully studied their theology, their social ideas and their attitude towards Sikhs and non-Muslims and liberal Muslims. He also took note of different faiths and their impact on society and made bold statements to denounce what he considered contrary to his vision. He finetuned the Sikh ideology left in legacy by his predecessor. He forged a theory of *Dharm Yudh*—struggle for rightenousness which was different from Muhammedan concept of *Jehad* and Christian concept of *Crusade* in as much as its causative factor was injustice, tyranny and unrighteousness and its goal was the establishment of a social order based on rightheousness, which was defined not in terms of any specific group, race or religion but in terms at once universalistic and humanistic.

CHAPTER V

THE BATTLE OF BHANGANI—
A VIOLENT REACTION OF HINDU ORTHODOXY

On September 18, 1688[1], the Guru fought the Battle of Bhangani against Fateh Shah and his allies. As to the circumstances which led to the battle, different versions are professed. The Sikh records state that Bhim Chand asked the Guru for the loan of *Parsadi* elephant both to assert his suzerainty and to use it on the occassion of the betrothal ceremony of his son. The Guru refused to oblige which embittered Bhim Chand who vowed to take revenge on him. Bhim Chand consulted some of his brother chieftains, Raja Kirpal of Katoch among others as to the course he should pursue to deal with the Guru for this rebuff. It was ultimately decided that this subject be finally taken up soon after the ensuing marriage of Bhim Chand's son with the daughter of Fateh Shah. Fateh Shah himself had been consulted about it. In the meantime, the Guru had retired to Paonta and became a great friend of Fateh Shah by amicably settling the disputes between him and the Raja of Nahan.

As the day of the marriage approached, the groom's marriage party started for Srinagar, the capital of Garhwal state.

---

1. Different dates regarding the battle are given by different scholars. We have based our conclusion on the versions given by typed copy of *Bhat Vahi's* (now reserved in Punjabi University Patiala) and *Bansavali Nama* by Kesar Singh Chhibber (ed. Ratan Singh Jaggi), 1972, page 124, *Shaheed Bilas* by Sewa Singh. We have rejected the dates given by Bhai Santokh Singh and *Gurbilas Patsahi 10* by Sukha Singh. Bhai Santokh Singh writes that the battle was fought in 1686. While according to Bhai Sukha Singh it was fought sometime between 1686 and 1689. *Mahan Kosh* fixes the date as April 16, 1686.

The shortest route to Srinagar passed through Paonta; but the Guru refused to give them the passage apprehending trouble from Bhim Chand who was accompanied by a large retinue of fully armed soldiers. After a lot of negotiations, the Guru agreed to allow bridegroom and a small number of his guests to cross the ferry near Paonta. The rest of the party was constrained to follow a circuitous route to reach Srinagar (Garhwal).

This made Bhim Chand desperate who waited for an opportunity to give vent to his anger. The opportunity came when the Guru sent Dewan Nand Chand[1] with rich presents at the *Tambol* ceremony.[2] Bhim Chand openly threatened that he would sever all connections with Fateh Shah and return without going through the marriage ceremony of his son if the presents were accepted. Nand Chand had to bring back all the presents to Paonta. On the way, Nand Chand was attacked by Bhim Chand's men, but he escaped unharmed. After the marriage was over, Bhim Chand held a conference with Fateh Shah and some other Hill Chiefs, such as Kirpal of Katoch, Gopal of Guler, Hari Chand of Hadur, and the Raja of Jaswal, who were there. They all decided to attack the Guru at Paonta.

From the above account, three points emerge. Firstly, the sole or the main cause was the estrangement between Bhim Chand and the Guru. Secondly, it was caused by the Guru's refusal to oblige the Raja by *loaning* of *Parsadi* elephant and then to disallow passage to the marriage party through Paonta. Thirdly, Fateh Shah was forced to wage a war under the pain of threat by Bhim Chand.

Let us examine all these points carefully before we reach any conclusion. Let us first exmine two points. If we accept the authenticity of these points, the Guru's stay in Nahan territory must have been nominal, for he left Makhowal (Chak Nanki) when the marriage of Bhim Chand's son with the daughter of Fateh Shah was impending and he came back immediately after the marriage ceremony was over. The view is upheld by the Sikh records unanimously. The Sikh Chronicler's view that Bhim Chand asked for a temporary loan of the animal on the

---

1. Dewan Nand Chand was the son of Baba Suraj Mal, one of the five sons of Guru Hargobind.
2. Giani Gian Singh, *Panth Parkash*, pp. 1419-20.

occasion of his son's marriage also points to the conclusion that even when Bhim Chand was making preparations to proceed to Srinagar to celebrate his son's wedding, the Guru was still at Makhowal (Chak Nanki). From the Guru's own account as vouchsafed in *Bachittar Natak*, we learn that he left Paonta immediately after the Battle of Bhangani. This being so, we have good reasons to believe that he made somewhat protracted stay at Paonta. Thus, it follows that the Guru must not have gone to Paonta immediately before the marriage of Bhim Chand's son. And if this is so, the entire story that the bitterness between the Guru and Bhim Chand grew as a result of the Guru's refusal to loan out elephant on the marriage of his son falls to the ground like nine pins. But it does not mean that Bhim Chand was well-disposed to the Guru. Infact when Bhim Chand grew to his adulthood and took upon himself the responsibility of running the state, he took note of the activities of the Guru at Makhowal (Chak Nanki) and became keen in asserting his authority on the establishment of the Guru. In his youthful pride he threw all caution to the wind and made an unsuccessful attack on the Guru. It is possible that Bhim Chand might have played his nefarious role in instigating Fateh Shah. But to attribute the outbreak of hostility between the Guru and Fateh Shah solely to the enmity of Bhim Chand and to consider it the major cause of the war is too much for the historical analysis to justify.

Another thing which fortifies our assumption is that in *Bachittar Natak*, practically the only reliable evidence regarding the Battle of Bhangani, there is no mention of Bhim Chand. This fact in itself is significant particularly when the Sikh tradition asserts that Bhim Chand's enmity was the main cause of the clash. If Bhim Chand had been the sole or main cause of the battle, it was improbable that the Guru would so readily return to Kahlur immediately after the battle was over.

Closely connected with this is the question—If Bhim Chand's enmity towards the Guru was not the cause or the major cause, what else then was responsible for the battle ? Cunningham[1] says that the Guru seems to have endeavoured

---

1. J.D. Cunningham, *A History of the Sikhs*, p. 61.

to mix himself up with the affairs of the half independent chiefs and to obtain a commanding influence over them, so as to establish by degrees a virtual independent principality, amid mountainous fastnesses to serve as the base of his operations against the Mughal rulers. Cunningham's statement seems partially true. It is doubtful whether the desire of the Guru had advanced to the extent of establishing an independent principality[2] but there are definite indications in the Sikh records that the Guru was interested in the affairs of the Hill Chieftains; and we feel that, this was exactly in which the genesis of the Battle of Bhangani could be found.

The invitation of Medini Parkash to the Guru to settle down in Sirmour was an act born not only of his admiration of the Guru's personality or adoration of his mission; but was also a measure which was a proof of his political sagacity and the foresight. Medini Parkash did so, because he was convinced that the Guru and his armed followers would prove beneficial for his state. In close proximity to the Sirmour state on the western side of River Jamuna was the state of Garhwal. These two neighbouring states had borne enmity towards each other for about four generations if not more.[3]

The Rajas of Garhwal had some tangible reasons to hate the Sirmour Royal-house for its being an instrument in the hands of the Mughals who had been keen on depriving the rulers of Garhwal of their independent status. Moreover, the Sirmour Rajas who were then basking in the sunshine of the Mughal favour had seldom missed the opportunity of territorial gain at the expense of Garhwal.

The enmity started as early as 1635 when Shah Jahan entrusted Najabat Khan, the *faujdar* of the country at the fort of Kangra hills the task of bringing Garhwal under Mughal supremacy. At that time, the ruler of Sirmour was Mandhaha the great-grandfather of Medini Prakash. He actively supported

---

1. A.C. Banerjee, *The Sikh Gurus and the Sikh Religion*, p. 286.
2. The Guru's own account of battles in the hills discloses no desire either for the establishment of a virtual principality or for the commencement of any military operations. He faced hostilities only where these were forced upon him.
3 *Sirmour State Gazetteer*, pp. 10-12.

Mughals and got a slice of Garhwal territory as a reward. His son Subhag Parkash and grandson Budh Parkash also nursed enmity towards the Garhwal ruler and were always apprehensive that they would retaliate to get back the territory occupied by Sirmour. In 1684, Budh Shah of Sirmour and Medini Shah of Garhwal died to be succeeded by Medini Parkash in Sirmour and Fateh Shah in Garhwal.[1]

To Aurangzeb, Raja Subhag Parkash rendered important services. He intercepted the correspondence between Dara, who was in the Punjab making frantic efforts to gain the Mughal throne and Sulaiman who was at that time a guest of Prithvi Shah, the Garhwal ruler.

With the twin purpose of bringing the ruler of Garhwal within the ambit of the Mughal influence and persuading him to hand over Sulaiman to the Mughals, Aurangzeb commissioned Ra'ad Khan to undertake the expedition. Subhag Parkash once again rendered much-needed help. As a result, Subhag Parkash got the area named Kala Khar identified in the Sirmour State with the modern area of Kalagadh[2] which lies near Dehra Doon.[3]

Subhag Parkash expired in 1664 and Budh Parkash succeeded him. During his reign (1664-1684) the Mughal government stopped meting out preferential treatment to Budh Parkash.[4] This was because Medini Shah (he was different from Medini Parkash of Sirmour (later known as Nahan) the heirapparent to the Garhwal throne had handed over Sulaiman Shah to Aurangzeb in December, 1660 and soon after when he became the Raja, had recognised the Mughal Emperor as his suzerain.[5]

In appreciation of the submissive demeanour of Medini Shah, Aurangzeb handed back the Doon to the Garhwal State.

Now the situation as it stood during Aurangzeb's reign was that with Sirmour possesing Kalagadh (Kala Khar) and Garhwal owning the Doon, the boundaries of the two rival

---

1. *Sirmour State Gazetteer*, pp. 13-14.
2. *Ibid.*
3. *Ibid.*, p. 14.
4. J.N. Sarkar, *A Short History of Aurangzeb*, Vol. III, pp. 563-65.
5. *Ibid.*

states got mixed up in such a way that Aurangzeb was able to exploit the situation to his own advantage. Though situation was explosive, yet no open conflict occurred. In 1684 Budh Parkash and Medini Shah died and they were succeeded by Jog Raj under the title of Medini Parkash in Sirmour and Fateh Shah in Garhwal.[1] Both the new chiefs were ambitious men of ability and therefore afraid of each other. While watching each other's moves on the frontier, they had to be on guard against surprise attacks. It was in this background that Medini Parkash invited the Guru to Sirmour state and allowed him to build a fort at Paonta, a place guarding the only convenient route from one state to the other.

The Guru, whose relations with Bhim Chand of Kahlur were strained, welcomed the invitation and shifted his headquarters to Paonta.

There was a likelihood of the Guru being involved in the boundary dispute if it arose between two rival states. But he tackled the problem with a finesse worthy of a great statesman and a great religious leader. He improved relations between Sirmour and Garhwal.[2] His success in accomplishing the task was no less than a miracle. It is said that the Guru also used the services of Ram Rai in getting the things straightened out.[3]

With the passage of time, the relations between Sirmour and Garhwal once again went sour. Fateh Shah decided to break the agreement and bring all the disputed territory between the two states under him by force. As a first step towards breaking Sirmour resistence, the Garhwal ruler

---

1. J.S. Grewal and S.S. Bal, *Guru Gobind Singh*, p. 71.
   Sirmour State Gazetteer, p. 15. Jog Raj was the son of Budh Parkash who was the son of Subhag Parkash.
2. The Sikh tradition very significantly preserves the memory of both Fateh Shah and Medini Parkash visiting the Guru regularly. Sometimes they would visit the Guru at the same time and accompany the Guru for *Shikar* in the Jungles around Paonta.   (*Gurbilas Patshahi 10*, p. 120)
3. Prithvi Shah and Fateh Shah appear to have had considerable faith in the spiritual power of Ram Rai. This is clearly indicated by Prithvi Shah's settling down Ram Rai at Khanabad and allowing him to build it as the nucleus of Dehra Doon and Fateh Shah confirming the possession of several villages for the support of Mahant's retinue besides allowing him to build a small centre at Srinagar itself.   (*Dehradoon Gazetteer*, p. 172)

marched towards Paonta, which was so close to the border and so strategically placed that Fateh Shah felt it imperative to break the headquarter of the Guru at Paonta. In this project, Fateh Shah was helped by the chiefs of Dadhwar and Jaswal, Gaji Chand of Chandel, Gopal of Guler and Hari Chand of Kotiwal. According to later Sikh chroniclers the number of chiefs who joined Fateh Shah stood at fifteen.[1]

The Guru was surprised at the blatantly unethical overture of Fateh Shah. In *Bachittar Natak* he write, "Fateh Shah got enraged and clashed with us without any provocation."

The Guru, however, forestalled Fateh Shah and checked the invading army on the bank of rivulet Giri.

The opposing forces met in the field of Bhangani about 6 miles to the North-East of Paonta on the plains between the Jamuna and the Giri (called Kalindri by Guru Gobind Rai in *Bachittar Natak*), not far from the city of Rajpura on the Mussoorie road. Just on the eve of the battle, four out of five hundred Pathan mercenaries under their leader Hayat Khan, Najabat Khan, Bhikhan Khan and Jawahar Khan, who had been on the Guru's pay were seduced by the Hill Chiefs by flaunting rich rewards. They deserted the Guru to join their forces. Only Kale Khan with his one hundred men remained true to the Guru. One thousand *Udasis* with the exception of their leader *Mahant* Kirpal also left the Guru. The Guru's army, composed of 2000 soldiers was thus reduced to 1000 soldiers, while the allies forces numbered 10,000, ten times more than the Guru's forces.

Even then, the Guru was unnerved, He correctly anticipated the route which the Garhwal troops would follow and occupied a hillock to check Fateh Shah's march on Paonta. He established himself on an elevation which provided him with immense tactical advantage. With the hillock in between, the bulk of the reserve, was not visible to the rival commanders,

---

1. They were Fateh Shah of Garhwal, Bhim Chand of Kahlur, Kirpal Chand of Kangra, Sidh Sen of Mandi, Gopal Chand of Guler, Hari Chand of Hindur, Kesri Chand of Jaswal, Umed Chand of Jaswan, Dayal Chand of Kotgarh, Karam Chand of Bharmour, Daya Singh of Nurpur, Gurbhaj Singh of Indaurah, Bagh Singh of Talokpur, Hari Chand of Kotiwal, Lakhu Chand of Kot Khari. Hari Ram Gupta, *History of the Sikhs*, Vol. I, p. 236.

thereby enabling the Guru's troops to undertake maneuvers unseen by the enemy.

Taking positon on a vantage point on the elevated ground he could clearly watch the deployment and movement of the enemy forces on the other side.

From the contemporary or near-contemporary records which throw light on the battle, it is difficult to comprehend clearly the way the two armies were deployed. However, the impression that emerges is that both the armies were divided into units with separate leaders making their moves under their repsective supreme commanders, Fateh Shah and Guru Gobind Rai. No elaborate war strategy was followed. Troops moved simply or in groups as directed till the leader was killed or the force felt exhausted. Then the combatants would run to the supreme commanders who would commission fresh men to take up the task.

The battle commenced with great determination on both sides. Immediately after, the five sons of Bibi Viro, Sango Shah, Jit Mal, Gopal Chand, Ganga Ram, and Mohri Chand organised an attack. They were ably backed by Daya Ram, Dewan Nand Chand and the two Kirpals : One, the Guru's maternal uncle and the other, an *Udasi Mahant*. Kirpal (*Mahant*) hit Hayat Khan on the head with his club errupting his brain from his skull like Krishna breaking the pitcher had brought the butter out of it. This was quickly followed by Sahib Chand's entry into the fray to kill the murderous Khan from Khorasan.[1] At this juncture Pir Budhu Shah alongwith his two brothers, seven sons, and 500 men arrived to add to the small reserve that Guru Gobind Rai possessed. Upto this time Fateh Shah's side was on the defensive. Then Raja Gopal and Hari Chand launched vigorous offensive. The Guru ordered Jit Mal and his men to advance. For some time the Guru's prospects looked very bleak. At this juncture, Jit Mal with his spear struck Hari Chand who fell down senseless and had to be carried off the field. In the confusion that followed, Kesri Shah Jaswalia and Modhukar Shah Dadwalia, two of the prominent chiefs of Fateh Shah's side, escaped being killed only because

---

1. According to Sainapat, Fateh Shah had so much confidence in his generals and soldiers that he expected a walkover in the battle.

the Guru's men desisted from killing the fleeing army. A general rout was clearly in sight. At this moment, Hari Chand regained consciousness and immediately became alive to the duties of a leader. He recalled the hill troops and the Pathans and the last phase of the battle started. The Guru sent Sango Shah or Shah Sangram as the Guru would call him lovingly to foil the offensive of Hari Chand. He fought hard, led his men well, killed Najabat Khan and many of his men, but only at the cost of his life.[1] The Guru who had taken no actual part in the fray till then was now stung to action. He moved forward and struck Bhikhan Shah on the face. The blow was so hard that Bhikhan Shah could not survive. Now began the great duel with bows and arrows between the Guru and Hari Chand. The Guru had narrow escape three times, but ultimately took aim and killed Hari Chand.[2] The death of Hari Chand disarrayed the hill forces and they had a disorderly retreat. The Guru's victory was complete. He very humbly attributed his success to the Grace of *Kal* (God).[3]

Fateh Shah arrived back at Srinagar in ignominy, totally crestfallen. The battle was fought for about nine hours. The Guru's Sikhs had indicated themselves in the battlefield with honour. They had displayed great skill in swordsmanship, spearing, archery, horse-riding and hand to hand combat.

Just after the battle, the Guru went to the place where lay the bodies of Sango Shah, Jit Mal and other Sikhs. He ordered the slain of both the sides to be disposed of with due honour. The bodies of Sikhs were cremated, of the Hindus were given to a watery grave in the adjacent river and of the Muslims

---

1. *Bachittar Natak VIII*, p. 20.
2. *Ibid.*, p. 25.
   Hari Chand in his rage drew forth his arrow. He struck my head with one and discharged another at me. God preserved me as it only grazed my ear in its flight. His third arrow penetrated the buckle of my waist belt and reached my body but did not injure me. It is only God who protected me knowing me his servant. When I felt the touch of the arrow, my anger was kindled. I took up my bow and began to discharge arrows in abundance, upon this, my adversaries began to flee. I took the aim and killed the young chief. (Macauliffe's Translation in *The Sikh Religion* V, p. 44.)
3. *Bachittar Natak*, "God in His grace bestowed victory on me."

buried with all solemnity. The wounded were properly tended. The dead bodies of Sango Shah and Jit Mal, and Pir Shah's sons were brought to Paonta, where they were cremated and buried respectively the next day.

On returning to the Fort of Paonta, the Guru held a *Darbar*, bestowed robes of honour and other gifts upon the valiant soldiers and generals.[1] Pir Budhu Shah requested for a comb with the Guru's hair stuck in it as the most appropriate reward. He was also given a turban and a *Hukamnama* admiring his services.[2] Those who kept themeselves away from the battle were driven out of the place. Guru himself says, "He fostered the faithful and rooted out all the wicked."[3]

The Battle of Bhangani brought into focus many aspects of importance. It bolstered up the morale of the Sikhs. it instilled a new confidence among them. It demonstrated that the kinetic power of the ideology coupled with appropriate organisation was more than a match for the massed might of princes and potentates. The Guru was convinced that the mercenaries were no subsitute for the persons imbued with the spirit of a mission. The battle also highlighted that all was not well with internal organisation of the Sikhs. The *Masands* as a group had gone corrupt and were more interested in their selfish ends than responding to the call of the Guru. Instead of performing their duty of linking the people with the Guru's message, they exploited them. This thing sparked off a question—Whether *Masand* system should be scrapped or maintained as such ? The battle was significant from another point of view. Nearly fifteen Hill Chiefs combined their military strength to attack the Guru. The combination of so many chiefs and that too within a record time was indeed astonishing for him who had done nothing to provoke them. He was not a ruler and as such did not possess any principality. To engineer such a massive attack on him was obviously uncalled for and a clear-cut case of moral turpitude.

The Guru was, therefore, constrained to think that the hill chieftains including Fateh Shah of Garhwal had been motivated

1. *Gazetteer of Himachal Pardesh Sirmour 1969*, p. 55.
2. *Mahan Kosh*, p. 264.
3. *Bachittar Natak*, Chapter VIII.

by certain ulterior design. This could possibly be the annihilation of the *Sikh Panth* which in their reckoning had the potential of destabilising their socio-political system that they had nursed and loved for so long and which had provided them with permanent position in society.

Dr. Hari Ram Gupta however opines that the Hill Chieftains were instigated by the Mughal authorities. But this view seems to be far fetched at least at this stage. There is no concrete evidence that the Mughals encouraged the Hill Chieftains to organise and to lead expedition against the Guru. The Guru, therefore, had to be wary of them while formulating his plans, especially when even the ruler of Sirmour who had professed to be his admirer preferred to remain aloof from the battle which in fact was more against him than Guru. Possibly he did not wish to be out of step with his brother Hill Chieftains when they gave the expression that they were doing all this to safeguard their politico-socio cultural heritage which the Guru's dispensation sought to demolish.

CHAPTER VI

RETURN TO ANANDPUR 1688
FIGHTING IN THE HIMALAYAN FOOT-HILLS

The Guru did not stay at Paonta for long. His stay at Paonta after the Battle of Bhangani was very short—one month and ten days, according to Swarup Singh Kaushish.[1] He left Paonta on Katak Sudi Trodsi, BK 1745 for Kapal Mochan; an ancient pilgrimage centre of the Hindus, 20 kilometres away from Jagadhari. The Guru delivered his instructions to a large number of people who had gathered there to celebrate the fair held · annually in honour of Kapal Mochan. Since that was the full moon day in Katak (28th October, 1688), the day which was believed to be the birthday of Guru Nanak, the Guru held a special congregation and honoured his Sikhs with *Siropas* consisting of a saffron coloured piece of coarse cloth.[2] During his stay at Kapal Mochan, he found time to visit Chhachhrauli and Balachour, the two villages close by to Kapal Mochan.

From Kapal Mochan, he went to Sadhaura to console, Nasiran wife of Pir Budhu Shah on the death of her two sons in the Battle of Bhangani. The *Pir* was simply overwhelmed and in a spirit of profound humility and thankfulness said, "How beneficent is God to me who enabled my sons to lay down their lives in His service."

After Sadhaura, he pitched his camp at Laharpur,[3] fifteen kms from Sadhaura. He spent over two weeks there. During

---

1. Swarup Singh Kaushish, *Guru Kian Sakhian*, p. 102, (ed.) Piara Singh Padam.
2. *Ibid.*
3. Kartar Singh, *Life of Guru Gobind Singh*, p. 81.
   M.A. Macauliffe calls this city Lakhanpur which is wrong.

this period, Pir Budhu Shah met him a number of times. From here, the Guru despatched his soldiers to Anandpur and he himself proceeded to Toka. This place is located about 12 kms. from Nahan city. It had a very picturesque location. It was skirted by dense forests which abounded in game. He decided to stay here for five days and indulged himself in chase and hunt.[1]

The Guru's next halt was at Tabra[2] in the state of Ramgarh. The Raja of Ramgarh received and served him with great devotion and hospitality and made him suitable offerings. The Guru gave him a sword with a jewelled handle. The Rani of Raipur came here to pay her respects to the Guru and to invite him to visit her house.[3] From Tabra he left for Raipur,[4] the headquarter of the state of the same name where the Rani was acting as a regent for her minor son.[5]

The Rani was a devoted disciple of the Guru.[6] The Guru himself had blossomed forth in his own beauty in her soul. She had risen above all to the unknown heights of pure thoughts. She enjoyed perfect peace as she was love-immersed, all closed in joy of his faith. She believed obeying the Will of the Guru was the highest fulfilment of her life as whatever He willed was of the highest good. Since most of the Hill Chieftains had turned against him especially after the Battle of Bhangani and the state of Raipur was hedged by all such states which had turned hostile to the Guru, Rani's ministers advised her to sap her discipleship of the Guru, which in their reckoning was like a red rag to the bullish Chieftains and could provoke them to invade and annex her state.

Rani of Raipur remained unshaken as she was one with

1. According to Bhai Kahn Singh, *Guru Shabad Ratnakar Mahan Kosh*; Giani Gian Singh, *Twarikh Guru Khalsa*, Guru Gobind Singh stayed here for a few days, on his way back from Paonta to Anandpur.
2. Kartar Singh, *Life of Guru Gobind Singh*, p. 81.
3. *Ibid.*
4. Gurmukh Singh, *Historical Sikh Shrines*, p. 305.
5. *Ibid.*, "The Rani of Raipur came here to pay her respects to the Guru and invited him to visit her house and bless her young son."
6. *Kalghidhar Chamatkar*; Kartar Singh, *op.cit.*, p. 83.

the mission of the Guru, and fully supported and subscribed to it. The worldly possessions had ceased to have any meaning for her now. She had turned a true victor, surrendering everything at the feet of her Guru and yearning only for his blessings, his presence, and his divine light. She knew, perhaps, intuitively, that while returning to Anandpur he would pay a visit to her place; although her city did not fall on the direct route from Paonta to Anandpur. The Guru too was very keen to see his disciple, both to fulfil the longing of his disciple and to assure her protection from any danger from the hill Rajas. He reached Raipur alongwith his entourage including a retinue of large number of *Khalsa* soldiers.

The Guru encamped in the spacious campus near the main gate of the fort.[1] The Rani served victuals to the Guru and his entire retinue. She attended the holy congregation, listened to the chorus of heavenly music and partook of the immortalizing Word.[2] Her body, heart and soul drank deep, now that the fount of blessings had arrived at her door. At the conclusion of the congregation, the Rani begged the Guru to hold the morning holy congregation in her palace in the fort, and honour her with his benign presence at dinner late in the evening.

The Guru accorded his consent and the congregation was held as scheduled. He also stayed in the palace till the dinner time. The Rani then made an offering of a beautiful horse with costly trappings and a purse of eleven hundred rupees.[3] All members of the *Khalsa* army accompanying the Guru received two rupees each.[4] The Guru gave her son a robe of honour, a sword and a shield. To the Rani, he gave a priceless gift.[5] It was a book of Divine Word. He told her not to have any fear either from the Rajas or from the Turks.[6]

The Guru departed from the city, and she as her disciple, remained united with him. She constructed two gurdwaras,

---

1. Kartar Singh, *Life of Guru Gobind Singh*, p. 83.
2. *Ibid.*
3. *Ibid.*
4. *Ibid.*
5. *Ibid.*
6. *Ibid.*

one where the Guru encamped and the other in the fort where he dinned.

An unusual incident took place here when Ranghars of Toda village stole Guru's camels during the night and passed them on to their relatives at village Laha where under the pressure of the village people, they had to restore them to him.

Next stay of Guru was at Mani Majra[1] where Mata Raj Kaur accorded him a hearty welcome (Maghar Sudi Dasmi BK. 1745). Therefrom he went to the village Dhakauli[2] and addressed the *Sangat* there and also met Isher Das, the *Masand* of the place. After this, he met Nihang Khan, the Zamindar of the place in proximity to the present-day Ropar city. Nihang Khan was so much touched by the gesture that he decided to dedicate all his life in the cause of the Guru. This happened on the *Amavas* of Maghar 1745 BK.[3] (1688).

A day later, the Guru visited the places such as Sirmour, Ropar, Ghanaulla, Bunga, Atari et. al. Then he arrived at Kiratpur and stayed with Mata Sulakhani. Bhai Amar Chand, the grandson of Guru Har Rai, Deep Chand and Nand Chand, the sons of Suraj Mal made their obeisance to the Guru.

In *Bachittar Natak* while the Guru gives the details of the Battle of Bhangani, he did not even allude to what made him leave for Anandpur immediately after the battle was over. According to Dr. Fauja Singh, 'Anandpur was strategically a much better place than Paonta in the state of Sirmour and that is why after about three years only, the Guru had returned to Anandpur.' But this does not explain the whole thing. The attitude of the ruler of Sirmour contributed a lot in arriving at the decision on the part of the Guru. Medini Parkash's callous indifference doubtlessly shocked the Guru. He found himself sandwitched between Fateh Shah as his avowed enemy on one side and Medini Parkash, an indifferent friend on the other. In such situation he was bound to rethink and reshape his policies.

Meanwhile Bhim Chand had also softened towards the Guru. He had seen for himself that the Guru was a force to

---

1. Swarup Singh Kaushish, *Guru kian Sakhian,* pp. 102-103.
2. *Ibid.*
3. *Ibid.*

reckon with and it was not an easy task to dislodge him from Anandpur. He had also observed that the Guru was not a jingoist, taking sadistic pleasure in waging wars, rather a harmoniser and a champion for the cause of righteousness. Besides, a member of the family of Bhim Chand had developed devotion for the Guru and his causes. It is on record that Rani Champa Devi, mother of Bhim Chand, had high regards for the Guru and took pleasure in inviting him to her home or going to him for paying her respects. This relationship had also helped to bring about harmony between the Guru and Bhim Chand. Political ambition of Bhim Chand also played its role. During Guru Gobind Rai's absence from Anandpur (Makhowal) Bhim Chand's position in the hill politics had changed for the better. Known chiefly as the head of an important state till 1635, he was now acknowledged as a great military leader. This became possible in 1686 when he had won a great victory over the combined forces of Bashahar, Mandi and Kothai who had attacked Bidhi Chand, the Raja of Kulu, the maternal uncle of Bhim Chand.[1]

Among the Hill Rajas the tradition of revolting against the Mughals was an old one, because they always regarded them as political and cultural impositions. The first wide-spread rebellion had taken place in the reign of Akbar.[2] The Rajas of Nurpur and Basu, Suraj Mal and Jagat Singh respectively had revolted in the later years of Jahangir reign and early in the reign of Shah Jahan. Perhaps believing that a concerted effort would be better rewarded, the Hill Rajas formed a confederation during the reign of Aurangzeb in 1675 and even defeated the then Mughal governor when he invaded the hills.[3] The Emperor's sudden return from the North-West had however disturbed the confederation so much that it disintegrated soon after. There were much better prospects now; for Aurangzeb had involved himself in the Maratha war in the far off Deccan while Imperial administration was fast losing its grip over the affair in the Northern region. The Hill

---

1. Hutchinson and Vogal, J.Ph., *History of the Punjab Hill States* I, 388, 462, 582, *Mandi State Gazetteer*, p. 37.
2. *Ibid.*, pp. 149-50, 225, 326.
3. *Ibid.*, pp. 205, 309.

Rajas hoped that they would liberate themselves from the Mughal yoke by concerted military action. Therefore they felt encouraged to join an union[1] which included states from all the three groups Simla, Kangra and Jammu.

Bhim Chand saw in the victor of Bhangani, a good ally, and he, therefore, sought reapproachment with the Guru which was reached, through the mediacy of the queen of Raipur. Both, the Guru and Bhim Chand entered into an agreement at Raipur.[2] The Guru now felt free to join his army which he had already sent to Anandpur and Bhim Chand was relieved of the fear of the Sikhs, to his sovereignty.

Guru Gobind Singh used the changed circumstances and the reapproachment with Bhim Chand to freely build up and strengthen his headquarter. He extended the area of Chak Nanki to cover the land of Agampura and Taragarh which he purchased from Rani Champa, heir apparent of Kahlur. He built Anandgarh fort in March 1689 from which the whole town of Chak Nanki soon came to assume the name of Anandpur—city of Bliss. Possibly, inspired by his father's unequalled serenity and tranquility under all circumstances and climes the Guru named it so. He renewed his contacts with his disciples particularly with those living in *Malwa* and *Doaba* regions of the Punjab. He despatched the *Hukamnama* far and wide calling upon the Sikhs to visit Anandpur. The Sikhs responded enthusiastically. A large number of Anandpur's inhabitants who had accompanied him to Paonta came back. Many poets, scholars and thinkers came to pay homage to the Guru. A good number of them brought their families with them and made Anandpur their permanent home. Quite a few

1. *Journal of Indian History* XXXI, II, 140, 142, cited by B.N. Goswami, *Social Background of Kangra Valley Painting*.
2. Bhai Vir Singh says that the agreement was signed at Paonta. We do not agree with his contention. He argues on the presumption that Bhim Chand led the attack on the Guru in the Battle of Bhangani but this presumption is open to objection on the ground that the Guru makes no mention of the Raja of Kahlur's participation in the Battle of Bhangani. We concur with J.S. Grewal and S.S. Bal in their view that the formality, if there was any, was effected at Anandpur, though a tacit understanding must have been reached through someone, when Guru Gobind Singh stayed with the Rani of Raipur.

traders, shopkeepers and artisans chose to settle in Anandpur. It was a star attraction for all those who loved the life-style of the Sikhs. No wonder, Anandpur began to bustle with new life. The Guru took care that those who kept themselves away from the Battle of Bhangani did not settle at Anandpur. He, however, patronised all those who distinguished themselves in his service at Paonta.[1] He had to put his own house in order, for there were people in his camp who cared little for his cause and who had followed him merely for the sake of personal profit.[2] Besides all this, he took some important defensive measures.

He built a chain of forts. In addition to the fort named Anandgarh, he built Lohgarh, Fatehgarh, Taragarh, Agamgarh (also called Holgarh)[3] and Kesgarh. Kesgarh was in the centre of this network while all others were around it. It would be grossly incorrect inference that the Guru had anti-Mughal projects in mind. Anandpur which he had made his headquarters, was situated in potentially hostile territory. Bhim Chand's attitude could change any time and the political atmosphere of the region never portended stability. It was always likely to cause flare-ups even on trivial issues among the Hill Rajas or between the Hill Rajas and the Guru. It was therefore necessary for a body of outsiders like the Sikhs to put themselves in a strong position. The Guru increased the strength of his armoury, established foundries in his forts, employed skilled workers and cast match-locks, swords, daggers and lances et al. He encouraged his people to train themselves in martial art and organised hunting expeditions. The Guru himself led many such expeditions in the surrounding forests which was very rich in wild life including leopards, bears and elephants. The area was then known as Hathout meaning abode of elephants.

---

1. *Bachittar Natak*, VIII, p. 37.
2. Indubhushan Banerjee, *Evolution of the Khalsa*, Vol. II, pp. 73-74.
3. Holgarh was in the village named Agamgarh, and therefore it also assumed the name Agamgarh vide page 19 of *Anandpur Sahib* (Punjabi) by Dr. Harjinder Singh Dilgeer.

EXPEDITION OF ALIF KHAN

Two years after Guru Gobind Rai's return to Anandpur, the combination of the Rajas consisting of Gopal Chand of Guler, Ram Singh of Jaswan, Prithvi Chand of Dhadwal, Kesri Chand Jaswal and Sukhdev Singh of Jasrota stopped paying annual tribute to the Mughals. The *Faujdars* of Kangra and Jammu, who were assigned the duty of collection of tribute, naturally sought help from the Government of Lahore. A strong contingent under Mian Khan with Alif Khan as his deputy was deputed to lead the expedition against the hill chiefs.[1]

The object of this expedition was to crush resistance in the Jammu and Kangra regions simultaneously. Mian Khan himself went to Jammu and sent Alif Khan to Kangra.[2]

Alif Khan moved to Nadaun instead of Kangra (30 Kms South of Kangra) which was apparently a *Naib Faujdari* with a small contingent of the Army to look after the Eastern part of the Kangra state. His aim was to make Nadaun his base and therefrom attack Bhim Chand to make a quick end of the challenge of Hill Rajas. His movement was quick and he thought that he would not allow Bhim Chand to have any help from outside. He selected an elevated ground and raised a wooden fortress on it.[3] Besides, he asked the *Faujdar* of Kangra to prevail upon the Hill Rajas who had joined the rebels to come with their forces to Nadaun. Kirpal of Kangra and Dayal of Bijharwal joined Alif Khan.[4]

Bhim Chand, contrary to the expectations of Alif Khan, acted with speed and alacrity. Raj Singh and Ram Singh Jaswal[5] immediately rushed to his help since their territories were very close to Nadaun. The Rajas of distant states also sent help, although they did not come themselves. Prithvi Chand

1. *Bachittar Natak*, IX, 2.
2. *Ibid.*
3. *Ibid.*
4. J.S. Grewal and S.S. Bal, *Guru Gobind Singh*, p. 87.
5. Following the *Gurbilas Patshahi 10*, Indubhushan Banerjee rightly calls him the Raja of Jaswal. This gets confirmation from the name Ram Singh appearing in the list of the Rajas of Jaswal given by Hutchinson and Vogal. See Indubhushan Banerjee, *Evolution of the Khalsa*, Vol. II, p. 81 and Appendix A.

of[1] Dhadwal sent his contingent. Sukhdev, a Gazi from Jasrota, also came to participate in the impending war. Bhim Chand specially sought help of the Guru on the occasion[2], who came in person at the head of a strong contingent equipped with bows, arrows, swords, spears and a few muskets, believing perhaps that it was a *Dharam Yudh*, because the Hill Rajas had taken up cudgels against the oppressive Mughal rule.

Though Bhim Chand had mustered a strong force, yet it was not an easy task to wrest victory. The enemy was entrenched in the fortress which though not very strong, being made of wood, yet had an assured advantage for its occupants of a cover denied to Bhim Chand. Moreover, Alif Khan's forces having been deployed on a high ground held distinct advantage over Bhim Chand's forces.

Bhim Chand launched the attack. The sharp arrows and the shots could make no impact on the enemy because of its position and struck only the wooden rafters of the fortress. Bhim Chand led another attack invoking *Hanuman*[3] for help. Kirpal fought with great determination and exhibited true valour of a Rajput. Others too fought desperately and soon the troops of Katoch were surrounded on all sides. The people of the tribes of Nanglu, Panglu, Jaswal and Guler advanced in a well planned move and on the other side, Raja Dayal of Bijharwal defended mightily.[4] At this critical juncture, the Guru played his part most effectively in the battle. He writes

1. According to Indubhushan Banerjee, he was the Chief of Mudhwar, a hill state in the Jammu region. According to Hutchinson and Vogal, the later Chiefs of Datarpur bore the suffix of Dhadwal. We feel that he was more likely to be the Chief of Datarpur. *History of the Punjab Hill States*. Vol. I, p. 212.
2. *Bachittar Natak*, IX. 3.
3. *Ibid.*, IX, 6.
4. *Ibid.*, IX, 16.
   (a) "Nanglu is a sect of Rajputs descended from Chua Mian, son of Sagar Chand, the sixth Raja of Kahlur." *A Glossary of the Tribes and Castes of the Punjab and North West Frontier Province*, Vol III, p. 156). Possibly the Panglu also is another Rajput sect of the same type.
   (b) It appears that Guler also supported Bhim Chand and this is confirmed by *Gurbilas Patshahi 10* (VII 41). It seems that the Guru is refering to the clans of Jaswal and Guleria and not to the states of those names. Guleria and Jaswal were two of the six clans of Katoch (Indubhushan Banerjee, *Evolution of the Khalsa*, Vol. II, p. 82. Footnote.

"Then this humble servant (of God) took up his gun and aimed at the heart of a Raja (Dayal). Fighting bravely he fell to the ground. Even when falling, the proud warrior in his rage shouted 'kill'. I put aside the gun and took up my bow, shot four arrows with my right hand and three with my left. I could not see whether they struck anybody or not. By that time, God turned the battle in our favour. The enemy was driven into the river....Arrows and bullets flew in abundance as if warriors were playing Holi.[1]

Alif Khan and his men fled the field.[2] They crossed the River Beas and Bhim Chand's victory was complete. The Rajas of Jaswal, Guler and other states hastened to their capitals for fear of Mughal reprisal on their respective states. Guru Gobind Rai stayed there for eight days[3] and then marched back to Anandpur with his followers. Bhim Chand and his troops remained behind at Nadaun[4] where soon after he reached an accord with Alif Khan through Kirpal Chand Katoch who acted as an intermediary. Bhim Chand and his associate Rajas settled terms of peace without consulting the Guru. The *Bachittar Natak* is completely silent about the scenario that developed after Nadaun victory but from Bhim Chand's role in later year, it appears that he and his associate Rajas had agreed to pay tribute thereby recognising Mughal suzerainty. To the dismay and anguish of the Guru, he was neither apprised by Bhim Chand while deciding to sit for negotiations with the Mughals nor was he informed of the terms arrived at.

The Guru and his followers while still on their way to Anandpur had to punish the inhabitants of Alsun[5] who had refused to sell supplies to them and displayed the audacity to ridicule Sikh religion, presumably at the instigation of certain officials of Kahlur who harboured strong dislike for the new religio-cultural model outside the Hindu context and, at least for the present, found themselves very strong because of their reapproachment with the Mughals.

1. *Bachittar Natak*, pp. 18, 19, 20.
2. *Ibid.*, p. 22.
3. *Ibid.*, p. 23.
4. *Ibid.*
5. *Bachittar Natak* IX, p. 24.

It is difficult to determine whether the village was plundered or only the slanderers were chastised. However, one thing is certain; that the village dominated by the Rajput caste and having ties of lineage with Bhim Chand had aversion for the Guru and his mission, and in the case of the reapproachment of Bhim Chand with Rajas and the Mughal government, they thought it an appropriate occasion to pick up dispute with him to please their master and to give vent to their own innate hatred. The Guru under such circumstances had no alternative but to bring the villagers to the book. Inspite of his help to Bhim Chand in the battle of Nadaun, he gained nothing; not even the goodwill of Bhim Chand. According to S.S. Bal,[1] the Guru, however, won over two friends in Raja Raj Singh and Raja Ram Singh. Raj Singh's state Jaswan lay to the North of Anandpur and watched the only route that the Mughal *Faujdar* at Kangra could take to harm the Guru at his headquarter at Anandpur. Guler lay towards the North-West of Anandpur linking it with the present district of Hoshiarpur where the Guru had a devoted following. He could not thus be easily threatened by Bhim Chand even with the Mughal support from Kangra.' The Guru severed all connections with Bhim Chand.

The experience of the ultimate outcome of Battle of Nadaun convinced Guruji that he could not hope to depend for long on the friendship of his two neighbours and therefore, he stepped up activities to build up his strength. During the next three years and nine months when he had undisturbed peace, he worked out a plan to raise a much larger armed force. He gave his army a strong social base by giving a call to his followers not only to come to Anandpur in greater numbers every year but also to make the city as their home. But the Guru's preoccupations in raising the army did not divorce him from his religious duties. Once well-settled at Anandpur, he took up the completion of his work *Akal Ustat* in 1691 which he had started writing in 1684. The composition is considered to be one of his best works and is divided into six parts. In the first part there is invocation to God who is looked upon as

1. J.S. Grewal and S.S. Bal, *Guru Gobind Singh*, p. 91, 1967.

Timeless, Omnipresent, All Steel and Supreme Nature. The second part deals with the futility of worldly pomp and power. The third part is a satire on various penances and austerities. The fourth part relates to the popular theological queries on the spiritual aspects of life and philosophy of Hindu *Shastras*. The fifth part sings the praises of *Chandi* as Primordial power. The last part is a hymn to God in all His splendour. Another composition *Charitro Pakhyan* (Triya Charitra) is believed to have been composed during this period in September 1693[1], understandably to expose the wiles of women and their perverse and unscrupulous characters and behaviours. In *Akal Ustat*, the Guru dilated on the functional attributes of God— universal in character, cutting across boundries of races, continents and languages—sustainer of all for all times. To Him "temple and mosque are the same and Rahim and Ram are not different either." All humankind has the same components of earth, ether, air, water and fire. The differences whatsoever, are only of living, dress, customs and country. 'To all, he utters nothing but the truth, that he alone attains God, who loves Him.' This composition more than any other by him spotlights the non-sectarian and non-partisan character establishing his philosophy totally in tune with Guru Nanak's teachings of universal humanism and strict monotheism.

DILAWAR KHAN'S ATTEMPT TO WEAKEN GURU'S POWER

Large congregations at Anandpur and the Guru's rapidly increasing military strength unnerved the Kangra *Faujdar* and possibly a few Hill Rajas too. Their concern was compounded when they pondered upon the influence which the Guru brought to bear upon the Hill Chiefs to take decision of stopping payment of tribute to the Mughal exchequer forthwith, and the dangerous and wider ramifications which could result if Guru's influence was not checkmated. They, therefore,

---

1. The date is given in the tale no. 405 in *Charitro Pakhyan*. The total number of tales is 404 but the last tale is numbered 405, showing thereby one tale is missing.

sought Aurangzeb's directions as to how should they proceed to arrest the menace.

The Emperor, in response to this representation, directed his *Faujdars* of Sirhind and Jammu and *Subedar* of Lahore to stop the Guru from collecting his Sikhs at Anandpur. A special order was issued in November, 1693 to the Governor of Sirhind to admonish Gobind Rai, son of Tegh Bahadur and make him abide by the instructions of the Emperor.[1] Accordingly, Dilawar Khan,[2] the *Faujdar* of Kangra began a series of attacks with the aim of breaking the Guru's power at Anandpur.

KHANZADA'S EXPEDITION—1694

In November-December 1694, he sent his son Rustam Khan refered as Khanzada in *Bachittar Natak* to curb the power of the Guru at Anandpur. He framed a plan to take the Guru by surprise. He crossed River Sutlej with a thousand soldiers under the cover of darkness at about mid-night; but just then Alam Khan,[3] a *Deoridar* of the Guru, informed him. Immediately, the *Ranjit Nagara* was sounded. The Sikhs took up their arms with alacrity and promptitude and with the zeal of a zealot arranged themselves in a battle array to give a hot welcome to the enemy. The quick formation of the Sikhs bewildered the enemy as their guns began to discharge volleys of shots and emitted murderous fire altogether terrifying them. As a result they had to reel back with their weapons unused.[4] While going back, the soldiers of Khanzada plundered village

1. *Akhbarat-i-Durbar-i-Mualla* (R.A.S.) 1/1677-79 an extract of the news letter dated 20-11-1693 in the *Akhbarat* runs as follows : News from Sirhind— Gobind declares himself to be Guru Nanak. *Faujdars* ordered to prevent him from assembling (his Sikhs).
2. According to Gokal Chand Narang, he was the Governor of Kangra, *Transformation of Sikhism* reprint 1989, p. 90. According to *Panth Parkash* he was Governer of Kashmir. The author of *Suraj Parkash* calls him Panj Hazari Sardar. Indubhushan Banerjee considers him only a Mughal officer. According to Macauliffe, he attained power in Punjab during insurrection which arose while Aurangzeb was in Deccan.
3. According to Sunder Singh the author of the *Battles of Guru Gobind Singh*, Alam Khan was Guru's *Deoridar*. According to Indubhushan Banerjee, he was Guru's attendant. Giani Gian Singh calls him Alam Shah—*Twarikh Guru Khalsa*, p. 835.
4. *Bachittar Natak*, X 6.

Barwan, stayed for some time at Bhalan and then returned to Dilawar Khan crestfallen and demoralised. Thus the Guru became victorious without a fight as he writes : "Through God's favour, the wretched fools could not even touch me, and they fled."[1] Many of the Khanzada's soldiers lost their lives while crossing the flooded ravine. The Sikhs out of gratitude upto this day call the ravine, *Himayati Nala*—a helpful brook.

HUSSAIN KHAN'S EXPEDITION—1695

The failure of Khanzada piqued Dilawar Khan to plan another expedition against the Guru. He chose Hussain Khan,[2] perhaps the ablest General with the Kangra *Faujdar* for the purpose. Hussain Khan marched with fury and looted and plundered whatever came before him. He brought Madhakar Shah, the Raja of Dhadwal to his knees, and plundered Doon. Kirpal Chand, the brother of the Raja of Kangra joined him. Ajmer Chand of Kahlur too cast his lot with Hussain, probably with a view to achieve double-purpose : winning the favour of the Mughals and annihilating the Guru and the movement he was piloting.

All the three, Hussain, Kirpal and Ajmer Chand, alongwith their armies made plans to proceed to Anandpur. Just then an incident occurred which changed the course of future development. The Guru had appraised their designs and made preparations to foil it.

At this juncture, the Guru's mother at the instance of *Masands* tendered advice that he should avert war which could prove disastrous, by making up with Hussain. The Guru, however, quietened her by bringing it home to her that he was doing nothing against His all-pervading Will. Now when Ajmer Chand of Kahlur and Kirpal had joined hands with Hussain Khan; Gopal, the Raja of Guler too proceeded to negotiate with Hussain Khan. Flattered and blinded by his successes, Hussain Khan did not deem it proper to take note of the difficulties of Gopal, the Raja of Guler and threatened

---

1. *Bachittar Natak*, X, 9, 10.
2. *Ibid.*, XI, 8.

him with dire consequences if he did not pay ten thousand rupees as war levy. Gopal pleaded his inability to pay and came back[1]. Thereupon, Hussain besieged the town of Guler. Finding that the inhabitants of the town were incapable of withstanding the rigorous siege, Gopal sought for peace but nothing less than ten thousand rupees could satisfy Hussain. In helpless state, Gopal approached the Guru who sent Sangatia along with seven other Sikhs to re-open the negotiations on his behalf. Sangatia on his own security brought the latter in Hussain's camp to negotiate but the two parties could not reach any settlement. Kirpal and Ajmer Chand began to conspire to arrest Gopal but the latter escaped in time. Kirpal lost his temper and fulminated in fury. He together with his brave commandoes Kimmat, Himmat, Hussain Khan and Ajmer Chand lost no time to attack the city. Fighting commenced with vengeance. Raja Gopal was helped by Guru's commanders, Lal Chand, Ganga Ram, Kirpa Ram and Agri Singh Brar along with 300 chosen soldiers and Raja Ram Singh of Jaswan. Hussain won a lot of applause for his valour but a sharp pointed arrow struck Hussain Khan dead. Raja Kirpal and several other brave officers such as Himmat and Kimmat fell fighting. On the side of Gopal, there was a heavy loss. Sangatia and his seven comrades were killed.[2] Agri Singh Brar also fell fighting.

Gopal came out victorious. The Guru felt jubilant and correctly remarked that the rain of bullets that was originally intended for me was showered by the Almighty elsewhere.[3] The Guru calls this battle in *Bachittar Natak* as Battle of Hussaini.[4]

---

1. The amount was exhorbitant even if he was expected to share the burden with his friend, the Raja of Jaswan. It must have been compared with the annual tribute that they paid to the Mughal government which did not exceed a few hundred rupees for either Guler or Jaswan. For the amount demanded; see *Bachittar Natak*, XI, 13 and for the annual tribute by the three Rajas to the Mughal government; see B.N. Goswami, *Social Background of Kangra Valley Painting*, pp. 57-58.
2. *Bachittar Natak*, XI, 57.
3. *Ibid.*, XIII, 69.
4. *Ibid.*

ANOTHER EXPEDITION—AUGUST, 1695

Dilawar Khan sent yet another expedition. Jujhar Singh and Chandan Rai[1] were sent to Jaswan but they could not achieve the desired result. They undoubtedly recovered Bhalan[2] (14 kms. away from Anandpur) a strategic place in the state, which had previously been captured by the Hill Chiefs and was now under the charge of Jaswan contingent. But before they could proceed further, Gaj Singh[3] of Jaswal with his contingent fell upon them. Jujhar Singh and Chandan Rai fought like lions but were soon over-powered. Jujhar Singh was killed in action and Chandan Rai fled. The enemy failed to reach Anandpur and retreated.[4] The result of the defeat of the Imperial forces had an adverse effect on the Mughal administration in the Hill area which fell in disarray much to the chagrin of Aurangzeb, who was away in Southern India to extend his sovereignty to the *Shia* states and the Marathas. The Hill Rajas took courage to withhold payment of their annual tribute in defiance of their agreement. The Sikhs hardened and emboldened their attitude towards the Imperial authority. The scenario being grave and disturbing, Aurangzeb realised that some drastic measures had become absolutely necessary and accordingly sent one of his sons, Prince Muazzam afterwards known as Bahadur Shah for the restoration of the order in hill area and for the recovery of unpaid tribute.[5] Prince Muazzam was born in September 1643. He was arrested by Aurangzeb in 1686 on the suspicion that he reached secret under-standing with the *Shia* ruler of Golconda to make use of his service later on certain occasions. He was set free in 1691. He remained viceroy of North-West region including Punjab and Afghanistan from

1. Jujhar Singh was a Rajput prince whom Aurangzeb despatched from Deccan. Chandan Rai was the deputy of Jujhar Singh. Hari Ram Gupta, *History of the Sikhs* I, p. 242.
2. Indubhushan Banerjee, *Evolution of the Khalsa*, II, 86.
3. Guru Gobind Singh mentions this name in *Bachittar Natak*. Gaj Singh was in command of Jaswan contingent. He certainly was not the ruler of Jaswan State who was Ram Singh.
4. *Bachittar Natak*, Section XII, Chaupais 1-12.
5. *Ibid.*, XIII, I, 'Sahazadah Ko Agham Madar Desh', Bhai Santokh Singh, *Sri Guru Partap Suraj Granth*, part II, Ansu 48.

1696 to 1699.[1] He resided at Kabul and occasionally visited other provinces.

    The Prince took up his position in August 1696 at Lahore[2] and from there he directed operations aimed at the Hill Rajas. He deputed Mirza Beg to teach a lesson to the Hill Rajas. He inflicted upon them defeat after defeat, plundred their country, set fire to villages, took hundreds of prisoners and in order to make example of them had them shaved clean and their faces blackened, seated them on donkeys and made an exhibition of them throughout the disturbed area.[3] Having received such a severe treatment from the Imperial troops, the Rajas realised that it was too dangerous to provoke the wrath of Aurangzeb and defy his authority. They were extremely demoralised and gave up all hope of fighting their way out to freedom. They paid their arears of tribute into the royal treasury and made abject apologies for their deviation from the path of loyalty. Even those who deserted the Guru or turned apostates or made away with the offerings collected for the house of Guru also suffered destruction and humiliation. After Mirza Beg, the Prince sent four more officers who also pursued the policy of Mirza Beg relentlessly and with equal severity.[4]

    Under these circumstances the Guru, no doubt, passed through turbulent times.[5] He, therefore decided to prepare himself to meet any future contingency. He sent *Hukamnama*[6] dated 2nd August, 1696 directing his leading disciples such as

1. William Irvine, *Later Mughal*, pp. 1-4.
2. Refer to Khafi Khan's account in Elliot and Dowson, *History of India as Told by its Own Historians*, Vol. VII, p. 153.
3. Gokal Chand Narang, *Transformation of Sikhism*, p. 91.
4. *Bachittar Natak*, XIII Chaupais 9-25.
5. The statement is amply supported by different *Hukamnamas*. One of these letters is to the progenitors of the Phulkian house in which the Guru asks for assistance. In another *Hukamnama*, addressed to the *Sangat* of Dacca the Guru acknowledges the receipt of swords, cloths and money and asks for more. Still in another letter asks for first class war elephant. (*Hukamnamas* 35-37 in the book *Hukamname*).
6. *Hukamnama* dated 2nd August 1696 (2nd Bhadon Samat 1753 BK) to Bhai Tiloka and Rama and the entire congregation under them to come to him with a force. For English translation see *Patiala and East Punjab Historical Backround*, p. 44. Also consult the book *Hukamname* by Dr. Ganda Singh, page 147, *Hukamnama* no. 43. Also see *Hukamnama* no. 42, p. 145.

Bhai Tiloka and Bhai Rupa to rush to Anandpur along with their followers. He also wrote to the progenitors of the Phulkian house asking for assitance.[1] But while taking strong measures to humiliate and demoralise the Hill Rajas, Prince Muazzam left the Guru untouched presumably he did not find any justification to proceed against him. The Guru had no principality nor did he flaunt sovereignty. Till 1696, the Guru took up arms against the Mughals only twice, for the first time at Nadaun and for the second time at Guler. In both these cases, the Guru came to the assistance of the Hill Rajas with twin objectives that the Mughals did not find opportunity to financially squeeze and socially degrade the people and did not proceed against him under the influence of the smiten Mughal officers or local elements inimical to him.

The Guru's power did not pose any threat to Mughal authority, a fact which had been amply brought home to the prince at Lahore by Mahabat Khan, the then Governor of the Punjab. Besides, the Prince himself was open-minded, liberal and particularly considerate towards saints and holyman. Understandably, Guru Gobind Singh whom he called *Dervish*— a saint (he mentioned him so in one of his royal rescripts) could not be a victim of anybody's whims or distorted thinking.

Nand Lal Goya who was a litterateur in the court of the Guru and had been in the service of the Prince formerly at Agra, also seemed to have exercised his personal influence with the Prince in favour of the Guru.[2]

Real politic also warranted good behaviour towards the Guru. The Prince had seen for himself that he had a following totally dedicated to him. That could be useful in case the struggle for the throne ensued after the death of his father who had grown very old and in view of the average longevity of life at that point of time could be expected to leave this world any time.

Certain other issues also demanded answers before we close the account of the expedition of the Prince. One— how

1. Indubhushan Banerjee, *Evolution of the Khalsa*, Vol. II, p. 166. S.S. Johar, *Guru Gobind Singh*, 1967.
2. According to *Gurbilas Patshahi 10*, this was due to the pleas of Nand Lal 'Goya' who was sympathetic to the Sikhs and was erstwhile employee of the Prince. Also refer to Indubhushan Banerjee, *op.cit.*, p. 116.

did the Hill Rajas react to the Guru under these circumstances ? Two—why did the Guru keep quiet ? Three—what has the Guru to say regarding those persons who deserted him or turned apostates or made away with the offerings that the faithful Sikhs had deposited with them.

The Hill Rajas tried to involve the Guru on their side and against the Mughals, but he did not respond because he had observed for himself that they were selfish and their actions had always harmed the Sikhs even causing demoralisation among them. However, their pressure tactics had significant effect on the internal cohesion of the Sikhs, many of whom left the Guru, some out of fear of the Mughal forces, some under the instigation of the Hill Rajas and some prompted by the urge to grab the offerings, meant for the Guru. He makes explicit mention of such people in his composition, *Bachittar Natak*. In Chaupais 5 to 8 the Guru condemns those persons who proved treacherous to his cause.[1]

In Chapter 13, he calls them opportunists sure to become penniless and desperate. In that state they would come to him for shelter and help but they would not be allowed any soft corner.[2]

Regarding his own safety and that of his followers at Anandpur he says :

> "Providence Himself protected the saints as He could not see any pain being caused to them."
> "He considered me as His own slave and saved me from all troubles by extending His hand of Grace."[3]

By not opposing the Mughal forces while they aggressed against the Hill Rajas, did the Guru not resort to the act which tantamounted to his acquiescence in Mughals' excesses ? Was it not appropriate for him to side with the Hill Rajas ?

According to Teja Singh and Ganda Singh, the prince did not touch the Guru because of some kind of understanding between him and the government. The learned scholars based their conclusion on the following statement of the Guru as recorded in *Bachittar Natak* (XIII, 9) :

---

1. *Bachittar Natak*, XIII 8.
2. *Ibid.*, XIII 12.
3. *Ibid.*, Chaupais 24-25.

Babe Ke Babar Ke Dou
Ap Kare Parmeshwar Se Aou
Din Shah Un Ko Pehchano
Duni Pat Un Ko Anumano
Jo Babe Ke Dam na de Hai
Tin Te Gaih Babar Ke Lei Hei.

Sirdar Kapur Singh has bitterly criticised the statement of Teja Singh and Ganda Singh. Writing in 'The Baisakhi of Guru Gobind Singh' he says,[1] "The learned authors make a most amazing statement about the Sikh doctrine of the Church and the states inter-relationship, which is wholly unwarranted and which is pernicious to the extreme. Neither the context hints at any such understanding, nor the text is susceptible of translation or interpretation which the learned authors have made it here. Nor, the whole Sikh history or the Sikh doctrine lend any contenance to the doctrine of ultimate and mutual exclusive dichotomy of the church and the state."The learned Sardar then gives his version of the translation which in our view reflects correct sense of the original :

Those of Baba (Nanak)
and those of Babur
God himself maketh them both
Know the former thus :
As the king of religion
Understand the latter thus :
As the secular king.
They who fail to render that,
What is due to the (house of) Baba
The minions of Babur seize them,
And make exactions upon them
And inflict severe punishments
Upon such defaulters;

In addition, their worldly goods and property are looted and taken away.

The text nowhere says, explicitly or by implication, that the church and the state 'both derive their authority from God Himself'. It clearly says, "God *maketh* them both as the instruments of His will. The word *Kare* in the text neither literally nor here can be interpreted to mean authorised; it

1 Kapur Singh, *Parasharprasna*, pp. 197-198.

simply means made by or maketh. Similarly the word *Pehchano* is not in the sense of a commandment : thou shalt recognise. It means know, identify, understand. The house of Baba means the true relgion of Earth, and the text says, understand the term to mean thus as such. Likewise *anumano* cannot and does not mean recognise and accept. It literally and here in the next stanza means, understand, see, take it as, infer that the house of Babur means the secular state."[1]

There is no doubt left by the Guru about the meanings of this text. "He says that there are two forces which claim allegiance of men's souls on earth, the truth and morality as religion, and the state as embodiment of mere utilitarianism and secular politics. The primary allegiance of man is to the truth and morality and those who fail in this allegiance suffer under the subjugatism of the earthly state unnourished by the courage and hope which is born through unswerving adherence to their primary allegiance. In this perpetual struggle between the state and the church, for exclusive possession of the soul of a man, a man of culture and religion shall not lose sight ever of his primary allegiance, and he who does so, does it at his own peril, for, by doing so, he helps give birth to times in which everything is force, politics, utility and labour, poverty and hardship, tyranny and slavery. The Guru does not assert that this perpetual dichotomy and antagonism of the Church and the state must be resolved or even that it is capable of being resolved, by the suppression or subjugatism of the one by the other; rather, he appears to recognise their eternal antagonism and in this antagonism sees the hope and glory of man, the social and political context in which the Sikh way of life is to be practised." "The church must perpetually correct and influence the state without aiming to destroy or absorb it for, as the history shows the attempt of the one to oust the other, meets with no lasting success, and each of the two antagonistic entities arises again after having been crushed in vain and both appear anew as if bound together. This is what the Guru means when he declares in the text that the House

---

1. Kapur Singh, *Parasharprasna*, pp. 197-98.

of Baba Nanak and the house of Babar, God maketh both of them and that "Those who repudiate their allegiance to the House of Nanak, suffer grieviously without hope, at the hands of the state."

In the afore-alluded excerpt from Chapter Thirteen of *Bachittar Natak* as also in the whole corpus of Chapter, he nowhere mentions even in nuances that there was any understanding between him and the Mughal government, or that the Sikh doctrine is, in essence, the care of the other world, through non-interference with the world which should remain within the exclusive domain of the secular state.

The only established fact is that the Imperial expeditionary contingents inflicted severe punishment on the rulers of different Hill states as also on their residents including those who deserted the Guru out of fear or for selfish motives or both. The Prince did not think it necessary or wise to invest the fortified town of Anandpur, the seat of the Guru. The Guru declares that the Imperial forces decided not to join issues with him.

The decision of the Prince not to touch the Guru was personal and had no connection with any directive from Emperor Aurangzeb. Nor was it the product of any understanding, tacit or avid, between the Guru and the Prince. It seemed that various factors, his understanding that the Guru was not a potential threat to Mughal kingdom, his innate respect for the sages, the Real Politic, the pleas of Bhai Nand Lal, all combined impelled the Prince to arrive at the decision of leaving him untouched.

The Guru on his part kept cool because the Prince did not distort or manipulate moral principles of the Sikhs, nor did he disturb their independent cultural and religious identities.

He did not come forward to help the Hill Rajas, firstly; because the Rajas had always been unscrupulous in their conduct vis-a-vis him and his mission; and, secondly; they bandied claim of Almighty absolutism, professedly denying the right to the Sikhs to live independently as per value-pattern as told by their Guru. At times, the Hill Rajas even threatened to oust him from Anandpur, if he and his Sikhs did not subscribe to their views regarding society and religion and did not pay annual tribute as a mark of recognition of the sovereignty of the Raja of Kahlur.

Muazzam's cowing down of Hill rulers and his departure from Lahore ended the Guru's anxiety and he felt free to engage himself in peaceful pursuits now. A phase of intense activity followed. He invited new entrants to his literary *Darbar* already enriched with the return of ths Sikhs who had been sent to Benaras in 1686.[1] He encouraged them to translate the episodes of *Ramayan* and *Mahabharat* found relevant to the mission of his new order that he was about to embark upon.[2] To leave no room for any ambiguity and doubt in comprehending the *Avtars* not only in all their glory but also in their weaknesses, such compositions as *Vishnu De Chaubis Avtar*, *Brahma Avtar*, *Uppa Avtar* were completed. In 1696 he is said to have written *Charitaro Pakhyan* mainly to divert the attention of his young disciples from sex thoughts to the noble cause, in the service of relgion and nation. *Ram Avtar* was also finished in 1698. *Bachittar Natak* was written in the first half of 1698. A perusal of his works would convince one and all that the Guru's literary activities had a purpose. He felt that the people should be vitalised to stand against injustice. No wonder then, the Guru took care to impart knowledge from the classics what was vital and morale building. He examined the conduct of *Avtars*, their strong points as well as their weakness. His purpose was to show that they were not God, all-powerful and infallible, rather personalities like others, liable to commit mistakes and prone to foibles. In *Bachittar Natak,* he seemed to recapitulate and reaffirm the message conveyed to him directly by God. In holy congregations, the theme underlying his writings was deliberated upon frequently;

---

1. These later formed the nucleus of *Nirmal Panth*. They returned to Anandpur in 1692 according to Dr. S.S. Bal and 1697 according to Khazan Singh. We consider Bal's date as correct because there is a strong tradition that they lived at Benaras for seven years.
2. We observe some of the most talented poets in Guru Gobind Singh's *Darbar* now beginning to translate parts of *Mahabharat*. Amarat Raj Sabha-Purav Mangal Shaliya-Purav and Kuresh Daro-Purav. It is difficult to say if something similar was done about *Ramayana*, but in all probability some poets had commenced translation of *Ramayana* in this period. See Bhai Vir Singh's tract *Guru Gobind Singh Da Vidya Durbar.*

and, as a result, the devout Sikhs as well as non-Sikhs who came to Anandpur felt its impact. This in turn, infused into them fresh confidence and brought them face to face with new challenges.

Among the new entrants to the *Darbar* of the Guru, the most notable was Bhai Nand Lal, son of Chhaju Mal, Mir Munshi of Dara Shikoh, who was holding post of Munshi at Ghazni. Bhai Nand Lal had served the Mughal Government in various capacities before coming to Anandpur. The Munshi of Nawab Wassaf Khan, the incharge of fort of Bhakkar, Nazim of Dina, Kehror, Fatehpur and Pargana Mahayyud-din Pur, and Naib-*Subedar* of Multan. During the regime of Aurangzeb he was turned out of Government service because of his father's cordial relations with Dara Shikoh–a facet which was unbearable for Aurangzeb. He felt much hurt and decided to involve himself totally in literary pursuits in his quest to find new themes. For solace of his disturbed mind, he decided to visit Anandpur to see the Guru, whose fame as a saviour and heralder of a new age had spread far and wide. He had known about him in his childhood when he used to visit *Sikh Sangat* at Ghazni and some other places in Afghanistan. When he reached Anandpur and saw for himself the Guru totally absorbed in his task of awakening and elevating the people, he was simply captivated. His intellect quickened, his sensibility sharpened, his moral sense purgated and heightened, his self attuned to the essence of Guru's teachings and he was transported to the stage of transcendence. He became beau ideal of a Sikh. He decided to live at the *Darbar* of the Guru. After some time i.e. in 1695, he went to Agra where he got the post of Mir Munshi of Prince Muazzam who had, just after his release from the prison assumed the charge of the *Subedar* of Agra.

He however was not destined to work at the post for long. It is believed that Aurangzeb once asked for the interpretation of an excerpt from *Al-Quran*. Various interpretations were presented to the Emperor but the version forwarded by Prince Muazzam was considered to be the most appropriate. In a public *Darbar*, Nand Lal was awarded a robe of honour and a cash prize of Rs. 500. Aurangzeb who did not like an infidel's mastery over the sacred text suggested to the Prince that such a man of learning should be converted to Islam. When the Emperor edict came to the knowledge of Bhai Nand Lal, he felt perturbed. There was only two courses left for him. He could either embrace Islam or go elsewhere. The former course was rejected by him forthwith because he had to all intents and purposes, entered the Sikh fold. The second course was more practical for him. He at once packed up, begged leave of the Prince and reached Lahore. Here he met his pupil Ghiasuddin, the *Darogha* of Agra who had come on leave to this place. Both of them reached Anandpur. Ghiasuddin returned to Lahore after some time but Bhai Nand Lal continued to stay at Anandpur upto 1705. During this period Bhai Nand Lal drank deep in the fount of Sikh spiritual thought as enshrined in *Adi Granth*. He keenly observed the Sikh way of life and understood the ultimate goal of the Sikh movement. The inauguration of the order of the *Khalsa* was also noted by him. His politic genius blossomed. He produced seven works of poetry in Persian and three in Punjabi. The first book which he presented to the Guru, bore the title *Bandgi Nama* which was changed to *Zindgi Nama* by Guru Gobind Singh. The Guru wrote the following verse at the end of the book :

Ab-e-Hai Van Pur Shud Chun Jam-e-o.
Zindgi Nama Shud, Bandgi Nama-e-o.

(When this goblet was filled with the water of life his *Bandgi Nama* became *Zindgi Nama*).

Other books in Persian were *Ghazaliat, Tausife Sana, Ganj Nama, Jot Bigas, Dasturul Insha, Arzul Alfaz*. The three books named *Jot Bigas, Rehat Nama, Tankhahnama* were in Punjabi. Except *Tausife Sana* and *Khatima* and *Dasturul Insha*, all the books whether in Persian or Punjabi depict the splendour of the Guru and his philosophy besides the devotion of Bhai Nand Lal for him. The style is excellent and speak highly of the literary attainments of Bhai Sahib.

At the same time, the Guru took care to expedite the process of acculturising his disciples in Sikh discipline. He exhorted them to attend *Sangat*, listen to and participate in *Kirtan*, and do service at *Guru ka Langar*. The Sikh's consciousness expanded and was enlightened. Anandpur, therefore, fully reflected a new religio-social model. Every home functioned as if it was *Guru ka Langar* (Lords Kitchen). Sometimes, the Guru tested his Sikhs. In the early morning of one day, the Guru disguised himself as a common pilgrim and went around the streets of Anandpur looking for a meal. The Sikhs were busy preparing the food. So they could not promise anything till they were fully prepared to receive guests. Then he reached Bhai Nand Lal's house and asked for food. Bhai Nand Lal welcomed the guest with a beaming smile and a radiant face and placed at his disposal what was available in the kitchen : butter, half-kneaded flour, half-cooked pulse and sundry vegetables. He then very humbly said, "This is getting ready and is all for you. But if you permit me, I will prepare them for you and serve you in the name of 'My Master'. Next morning the Guru told everyone that there was but one *Guru ka Langar* at Anandpur and that belonged to Bhai Nand Lal. The Guru's words of commendation were a sort of homily on *Guru ka Langar*. Every house of a Sikh should provide food to the needy in a spirit of thankfulness to God whom he/she should consider as the Primal provider of provisions. While doing so, no consideration of caste and creed et al. should circumsrcibe the minds. Sikhs should never forget to offer his thanks to the Almighty before taking or serving food. The Guru said, "If a hungry person calls at your door and you turn him away, remember that you are turning out not him but me. He who serves the poor and the needy; serves me. The mouths of the poor are the Guru's receptacles for all gifts.[1]

Anandpur presented a spectacle of perfect harmony, free from petty jealousies and parochialism. It bore the look of Heaven where all castes, creeds and colours met in the joyous *Sangat*. The focal point of the people of Anandpur was the Guru

---

1. That the Sikhs considered it their relgious duty to feed and serve all who called at their door is confirmed by the testimony of Munshi Sujan Rai of Batala, who began his book, the *Khulastut-Twarikh* in 1695-96. and finished it in 1697-98 or a year or two before the *Birth of the Khalsa*.
   "If a person turns up at their door at midnight and calls in the name of Baba Nanak, though he may be stranger or even a thief, robber or scoundrel, they serve him according to his need, as they serve a brother and a friend." Sujan Rai Bhandari *Khulastut-Tawarikh* (Pbi.), p. 81.

whom they looked upon as an enlightener, sustainer and protector.

One day there came a *Kalal* or a wine distiller a profession; held in acute hatred by the society in Punjab. He was still clinging to the wrong belief that[1] one's profession determines one's status in society. With this status complex weighing on his mind, he stood a little away from the Guru. But the Guru took him by his hand and seated him in the congregation. He hesitated and meekly admitted that he was a *Kalal*. The Guru proclaimed, No, 'You are not a *Kalal*', but *'Guru ka Lal'* [a gem (son) of the Guru]. Such was the Guru's disposition towards so called low castes. His mission was to uplift such people and give them a realisation that they were as dignified as anyone else in this world. The Guru's baptism of love, indeed, articulated them to feel free, proud and self-confident.

On another occasion, the Guru called for a glass of water. It was brought to him by a handsome lad, a scion of a rich lord. The hands fetching the glass were clean as also were water and the tumbler. The Guru held the glass in his hand for a while, and then returned the same to the young man without even sipping, and said, "My son, it seems your hands have not yet laboured in the service of the people." "No Sir, I have never worked with these hands as yet", said the boy. "Ah my boy, go and make them pure first in the service of the people."[2] The Guru's priorities were very clear, that society based on caste should be discarded forthwith and it should be reorganised on the basis of love for all, equal rights, divinity of individuals, dignity of labour and faith in the singularity and unicity of God with a commitment to improve the lot of the people.

Taboos, totems, superstitions, rituals, fastings, sacrifices, renunciation, yogism, pilgrimages, and such-like things which had often been projected as the right tools to comprehend and realise God were simply rejected as irrelevant, never to be adopted and believed upon.

---

1. It was believed that merely stepping on the bone of a dead *Kalal* would condemn one to the fire of hell.
   Puran Singh, *Ten Masters*, Chief Khalsa Dewan, Amritsar, p. 102.
2. Bhai Vir Singh, *Kalgidhar Chamatkar*; Puran Singh, *op.cit.*

A group of Hindu *Sanyasis* visited Anandpur. They expressed their views complainingly to the Master that he was not laying due emhpasis on the virtues of renunciation. The Guru replied, "My disciples are men of renunciation. In joy, their bliss is infinite and no more is needed; all things come to their hands and they use them as they need. As long as they do not go under illusion *(Maya)*, they are free and pure. If one has obtained self-realistion, then of what use, my freinds, is renunciation."[1] They were keen to extend the arguments further when he interrupted them playfully, bidding his Sikhs to put live charcoal on the lids of their coconut bowls of renunciation. And as the lac cementing the joints melted under fire, the bowls were shaken and gold coins dropped out exposing their hypocricy and double-talk.[2]

Hansa, a religious teacher of the Jains, came to the Guru perhaps to see the spiritual calibre of the Guru. He was a *pandit*, a great painter and a leading monk. He brought an offering of painting of the sunrise for Guru Gobind Singh. The Guru saw it and said, "Technically the painting is a fine piece of work. It seems painter's heart was dark and cruel. Hansa was puzzled. He sought an audience with the Guru but the Guru would not oblige him. Then one day a palanquin came to Anandpur. Seated in it was almost a living skeleton, though long ago he was a robust youngman. He was lying in a helpless condition in pursuance of his vow of self-purification. The Guru sent for him.

This youngman now half dead with his efforts of fulfilment of his vows, was once in the convent with Hansa as a *Jain Brahmchari*. Closeby to the same convent, there lived a young girl almost a child whose parents had dedicated her to the Jain temple as an offering. She and the youngman belonged to the same village and had played together in their childhood. Both loved each other at an age when they hardly knew what love was; but their guardians had seperated them, putting the boy in the temple and the girl in the convent. Hansa

1. Bhai Vir Singh, *Kalgidhar Chamatkar*; Puran Singh, *Ten Masters*, p. 101. Kartar Singh, *Life of Guru Gobind Singh*, p. 94.
2. *Ibid.*, p. 101. Kartar Singh, *Life of Guru Gobind Singh*, p. 94.

was incharge of the temple. For years, both the young boy and the girl did not see each other. Then one day while gathering flowers in the forest, they met for a moment and started talking nostalgically. This was an inexcusable sin according to the rules of the convent and the nunnery. The girl was punished by having her eyes gouged out. The boy was sent to the hills for a prolonged penance.

Hansa was responsible for all that had befallen upon the young boy and the girl. Hansa knew the whereabouts of the girl and he was asked to bring her to Anandpur. After a long search, the blind girl was brought by him to Anandpur. By this time the young *Brahmchari* had also recovered from his illness and gained full health. He was sitting in the holy assembly, and enjoying the divine *Kirtan* as the blind girl arrived in the holy congregation. The Guru looked at her as she came in front of the master. The Guru blessed her and initiated her into the *Rajyog* of *Nam*. It is recorded that she recovered her sight and that her face reflected the celestial light. The Guru's jubilance was immense and he ordered that the two disciples be tied in nuptial knot and the event celebrated there and then. The Guru's message was loud and clear. The penance and celibacy are not at all the valid means of emancipation. These are, in fact, against the order of God according to which there is no antagonism between *Prakriti* and spiritual pursuits, rather both are the attributes of the same single supreme unit, that is God. How can therefore, repression or penance which afflicts the body, be acceptable to God ? Similarly celibacy cannot be accredited as valid since it prevents and prohibits a person from taking *de-jure* part in worldly activities which are in fact the manifestation of the Divine. Hansa gave up his old beliefs—non-existence of God, duality between material and celestial world, transitoriness of the world, futility of the worldly activities, celibacy, penances and fasts—and hastened to embrace Sikh religion.

Festivals such as Baisakhi, Diwali and Holi were celebrated with great enthusiasm and care was taken that these occasions served as a means to suffuse the people with Guru's mission and the Sikh philosophy. Holi festival was so organised and celebrated that the Sikh's perception of Holi changed altogether.

They discarded the hollow belief that the festival was celebrated to express joy at the burning of Holka—a sister of Harnaksh who disliked his son Prahlad for not accepting his father's claim that he was God. In order to please her brother, Holka planned to burn Prahlad. She took him in her lap, sat in the midst of a heap of easily combustible straw. She is believed to have worn a sheet of cloth believed to be fire-proof made so through incantations. The myth also subscribes that with long and strenuous penance, she had acquired a boon that she will not be burnt by fire. But it so happened that the sheet moved aside uncovering a part of her body exposing it to the vagaries of raging fire with the result that she was burnt to ashes. The boy escaped the furious fire because a part of the sheet that had uncovered Holka's body draped over him. In the historical consciousness, the event has been considered triumph of goodness over evil; and on this account some people consider it an appropriate occasion to celebrate.

The Sikhs, despite finding the theme to their liking, did not make this story the *raison-de-etre* of their celebration of Holi festival. For them the festival symbolised loftiness of spirit and its assertiveness in the cause of humanity; very much akin to the nature in the spring blossoming forth amidst turnings and twistings. The Guru called Holi as *Hola Mohalla* and not simply a festival of colours. Each celebration at Anandpur was a lesson in inter-personal socialisation, a great aid in fostering a common natural pride and a shared sense of fraternity in social actions.

He divided the gathering at Anandpur into two groups; one part took up position in the Holgarh Fort and dug in for defence against impending attack. The other under command of the Guru made the attack. In front of the attacking party were the standard bearers. A separate flag was flying on the Fort. Both the sides were divided into various battalions. It was a mock fight without arrows and bullets. The garrison was dressed in white, while the assailants wore yellow clothes. The fighting lasted four and a half hours. Eventually the Fort would be captured through various war manoeuvres employed by the attacking force. War drums were beaten. The Cavalry units of both sides rushed upon each-other. A number of prisoners were taken by both parties. Afterwards a *Darbar* was held and conventional Holi was played joyfully. *Gulal*, rosewater, and saffron water were freely sprinkled on one another with *pichkaries* (syringes). Huge quantity of *Karah Parshad* worth Rs. 5000 would be prepared and laid in big pans on the lawns adjoining the Guru's court. The Guru would order the Sikhs to plunder it. At once all would assault the *Karah Parshad* pans. All of them jostled each other to get to the *parshad*, often resulting in rolling of a few to the laughter of others. In a moment the entire quantity would be finished. The Guru also participated in the game. He called it *Mai Holla* or a petty fight. Later on it became popular as *Hola Mohalla* which according to Bhai Kahn Singh means 'attack or place to be attacked'.[1] The occassion could not but attract the focalised attention of Bhai Nand Lal, a poet of Persian language. He also carried a pen-name of 'Goya'. He composed a poem. A free translation of the poem is reproduced here.

"Many have written about the flower of Holi in the garden of the world. It made the lips beautiful like a flower bud. Rose water, amber musk and saffron water fell like rain from all sides. The scattering of clouds of *Gulal* by the blessed hand (of the Guru) reddened the earth and the sky. The syringes filled with saffron-coloured water imparted lovely hue to the uncoloured (*Har Be Rang Ra Khaehrang-o-Bu Kard*). When my king (*Shyam*) wore the coloured neck cloth, both the worlds became happy through his kindness. One who happened to see his divine face achieved the objective of his life. Goya's heart has only one desire that he should sacrifice himself for the dust over which the Guru's devotees pass."[2]

Despite Guru's enhanced attention to peaceful pursuits,

---

1. *Kalgidhar Chamatkar,* pp. 225-26.
   Nihangs have preserved the memory of this day's mock battle. They celebrate *Hola Mohalla* at Anandpur on the following day after Holi. They wear deep blue robes, tall conical turbans, yellow girdles and enact the mock battle. Riding on horses with sparkling spears and swords and shouting their war-cries, they march, in procession. They often halt the procession for a while to display and demostrate the skill that they had acquired in the use of their personal weapons.
2. Swarup Singh Kaushish, *Guru Kian Sakhian,* p. 145, *Sakhi* No. 73.
   Hari Ram Gupta, *History of the Sikhs* Vol. 1, pp. 244-45.

he did not lose sight of the defence of his headquarters, for he could visualise the hardened attitude of the Hill Rajas towards him and assess the situation for a possible thrust of the Mughal because of their parochial stance. He, therefore, completed the construction (1699) of five forts all around the town : Kesgarh at the Centre; Anandgarh (fort of bliss) 500 meters to the East, Lohgarh (fort of steel) one kilometer to the South, Holgarh one and a half kilometer to the North. Fatehgarh, Anandgarh and Keshgarh were built on Hill tops. All were located at strategic places. Fatehgarh, Holgarh and Lohgarh were situated on the banks of a rivulet Charan Ganga. All the forts could bear the assault of big guns. They were connected with each other through skilfully constructed earth works and underground tunnels. The strongest fort was Anandgarh which exists even to date.

For water supply a huge well was dug up. It was worked by the Persian Wheel. The well and the wheel can still be seen there.

The code of conduct framed by very close associates of the Guru who had observed him and even received directions from him from time to time has the following to say in respect of discipline.

> He is not a Sikh who does not observe discipline.
> Without discipline one is just a vagabond,
> Wandering aimlessly from door to door.
> Without discipline one falls into the hellish pit.
> One who does not observe discipline is a wild creature.
> One who does not observe discipline is a defaulter.
> One who does not observe discipline cannot be happy.[1]

Therefore, hold fast to the disciplined way of life.[2] Behind feverish, literary and cultural activities there could be discerned the restlessness of a soul struggling hard to come to some important decision. To those who were intimately connected

---

1. *Rehnī rahe soī sikh merā. Oh sāhib maiṅ us kā cherā.*
   Rehat binā na sikh kahāvai. Rehat binā ḍar choṭā khāvai.
   Rehat bin sukh(u) kabhu na lahe. Ta te rehat su driṛh kar rahai.

   (*Rehatnāmā*, Bhai Desa Singh)

2. "Tankhah Nama" quoted in *Social and Political Philosophy of Guru Gobind Singh*, by Sher Singh, pp. 128-129.

with him, it must have foreshadowed some great step. The Hill Rajas and Mughal *Faujdars* however, could not have guessed what Guru Gobind Singh was thinking in those years. When they heard of the birth of Gobind's third son (Zorawar Singh) early in 1697 and of another (Fateh Singh) two years later, they might have imagined that the Guru was settling down and would pay more attention to his family life than to his people. His elder sons Ajit Singh and Jujhar Singh were born in 1687 and 1690 respectively. What was really in the offing, none, could figure out. And when at long last, its configuration was visible it was stunning, striking, perplexing and storming besides heralding of a new era where hackneyed society and its value-style would yield place to fresh social pattern based on fresh value-system.

CHAPTER VII

EMERGENCE OF THE KHALSA

Why did the Guru set up the *Khalsa* ? Did he do so to revenge the unjust persecution of his father ? Was he constrained by the contemporary politico-social scenario ? Was he coerced by the corruption and robbery of the *Masands* to take this step ? Was the Sikh mission responsible for the emergence of the *Khalsa* ?

Cunningham says, "The Guru acted......under the mixed impulse of avenging his own and his country's wrongs.[1] He became an irrepressible foe of the Mahemetan name.[2] His aim was far-reaching : 'In heart of the powerful empire, he set himself to task of subverting it.' Sir J.N. Sarkar observed that the Guru was not the person to leave his father's death unavenged"[3] and so he began the policy of 'open hostility to Islam.' Gokal Chand Narang also endorsed the view of Cunningham and concluded that the Guru's purpose was to avenge his father's death and strike a blow at the power of Aurangzeb.[4]

It is ironical that neither J.N. Sarkar nor Gocal Chand Narang made an independent inquiry. They blindly followed Cunningham and took it for granted that it was but natural that the Guru should seek to avenge his father's cruel assassination and to punish the ruler who was responsible for it. These scholars attributed ordinary human motives to the Guru neglecting absolutely the sublimity of his mission and his personality.

1. J.D. Cunningham, *A History of the Sikhs*, p. 60, (ed.) H.L.O. Garrot.
2. *Ibid.*, p. 59.
3. J.N. Sarkar, *A Short History of Aurangzeb*, Vol. III, p. 314.
4. Gokal Chand Narang, *Transformation of Sikhism*, p. 88.

The story elaborated by Cunningham appeares to have been based on Ghulam Mohi-ud-din's version of the speech of Guru Gobind Singh at Kesgarh on the Baisakhi of 1699 as recorded in his work *Tarikh-i-Punjab*. According to him the Guru is reported to have said :

"You should remember that the Musalmans have maltreated us. They have killed our ancestors. Now in accordance with the mandatory wish of my father Guru Tegh Bahadur, I cherish the desire of avenging myself upon my father's murderer."

Did Guru Tegh Bahadur express any such mandatory wish before his martyrdom ? There is no refrence to any such wish in *Bachittar Natak* which was composed not long before the creation of the *Khalsa*. According to the Sikh tradition as recorded, while in prison at Delhi, Guru Tegh Bahadur wrote to his son as under :

> All human power has failed,
> Humanity groans in chains,
> Moral efforts are of no avail,
> Lord, save them, O save
> With thy Merciful aid,
> As Thou did save
> The drowning elephant, that prayed ![1]

On receipt of this slok from his father, Guru Gobind Singh replied :

> All power is mine with thy Grace, Lord
> The fetters of bondage are broken,
> Liberty and truth everything is possible,
> Lord, everything is in Thy hands,
> Nanak craves for Thy protection and aid.[2]

Guru Tegh Bahadur reiterated perhaps in response to his son's reply.

> The Name remaineth, saints remain,
> Gur Gobind remaineth

---

1. Fauja Singh and Taran Singh, *Guru Tegh Bahadur Jiwan te Rachna*, p. 167.
2. Translation by Dr. Trilochan Singh of Slok No. 54 of Sri Guru Tegh Bahadur.

Saith Nanak, few are they who in this world
who follow the Guru's instructions.[1]

Not a single line in the foregoing advice can be taken as
the expression of any mandatory wish of Guru Tegh Bahadur
made before his martyrdom to avenge his assassination. In fact,
any such direction would have been entirely inconsistent with
Guru Tegh Bahadur's tenor of life who never lost an opportunity
to emphasise that one who is unmoved by joy and sorrow, to
whom friend and foe are alike, is a truly liberated soul.

In view of this the statement attributed to Guru Gobind
Singh by Ghulam Mohi-ud-din alias Bute Shah[2] and believed
by Cunningham and Sir J.N. Sarkar is incorrect. There is
another very cogent reason which renders the statement of
Bute Shah redundant and superfluous. Bute Shah places the
creation of the *Khalsa* soon after the execution of Guru Tegh
Bahadur and before Guru Gobind Singh's battle with the Hill
Rajas and the Mughals. This is a cut and dried case of faulty
chronology that suggests a connection between the execution
of the ninth Guru and the creation of the *Khalsa* which is far
from the truth. From this, two conclusions can be postulated.

One, Bute Shah did not verify the fact; and Second, he
did not take cognisance of the series of events that took place
between 1675 through 1699 and which could provide him
more realistic historical perspective. Similarly, the contention
that the Guru was openly hostile towards Islam is entirely
baseless. The Guru was never against Islam or for that matter
against any religion. He was an ardent votary of Love, raising
it to the status of God. It was for this reason that both Hindus
and Muslims were attracted towards him. Pir Budhu Shah of
Sadhaura together with his sons and seven hundred followers
fought hard and bravely in the Battle of Bhangani in 1688 in
which he lost two of his sons and hundreds of his disciples.
In the battle of 1702, Sayyid Maiman Khan commanded the

1. Fifty-sixth Slok of Guru Tegh Bahadur according to M.A. Macauliffe, was
   sent to Guru Gobind Rai while he himself was in prison at Kotwali,
   Chandni Chowk at Delhi, M.A. Macauliffe, *The Sikh Religion* Vol. IV, p. 385.
2. *Tarikh-i-Punjab* authored by Bute Shah was written in 1848. *Tarikh-i-Hind*
   was written by Ahmed Shah Batalia in 1818. Both historians record almost
   identically and claim that their information was based on royal news
   writer's reports.

Guru's forces engaged in fighthing against the Mughal troops. Nabi Khan and Ghani Khan in defiance of the wish of Wazir Khan, the Governor of Sirhind fearlessly and courageously helped the Guru out of his distress at Machhiwara. In *Akal Ustat* the Guru Says :

> Shaving his head one is accepted as a *Sanyasi,* another a *Jogi* or a *Brahmchari,* a third as a *Jati.*
> Some are Hindus while others are Muslims. Of the latter some are *Shias* and others are *Sunnis.*
> Man's caste should be considered as one. (*Manas Ki Jat Sabhai Ekai Pehchanbo*).
> Creator *(Karta),* Beneficent *(Karim)* are the same.
> Provider *(Razak),* Merciful *(Raheem)* are the same.
> Let no one even by mistake, suppose there is a difference.[1]
> Temple and Mosque are the same. Hindus worship and Muslim prayer are the same. All men are alike, but they are under delusion. Deities, demons, heavenly dancers, singers, Muslims, Hindus wear different dresses under the conditions of their countries. But they possess eyes, ears, bodies, made of same elements composed of earth, air, fire, and water.
> *Allah* and Unknowable *(Alakh)* are the same, the *Puranas* and the *Quran* are the same, they all are alike, it is the one God who created us all.

The Guru in his composition *Jaap* has given 735 names of God based on His traits seen in His actions/deeds out of which thirty pertain to Islam. In yet another composition of his known as *Akal Ustat* the Guru is emphatically forthright and remarked "Even by mistake deem not the God of Hindus to be different from the God of the Muslims. Worship one God recognise the enlightener. All men have the same form; and in all men the same divine light."[2]

Sujan Rai Bhandari wrote in 1698, "In their (Sikhs) eyes their own people and others as well as friends and foe are alike. They love their friends but they don't illtreat their enemies."[3]

In the presence of such a plethora of evidence, it is only appropriate to reject the view that the Guru harboured hostility towards Islam or created the *Khalsa* to take revenge of his father's execution.

---

1. *Akal Ustat,* Swayyas, p. 85.
2. *Ibid.,* p. 86
3. *Khulasatut-Twarikh,* p. 81.

The creation of *Khalsa* infact was the outcome of the interplay of different factors, some primary, others ancillary. Among the ancillary factors the first was the political scenario.

The Mughal reign had assumed the form of a purely Islamic state under Aurangzeb. Earlier, especially in the times of Babar, Humayun and Akbar, the reign could be categorised as largely Islamic, but not totally Islamic. Babur and his son were no religious bigots. Similarly Akbar's religious propensities were those of a liberal Muslim. He found no difficulty in reaching an understanding with the Hindu Rajputs and did not hesitate to determinely and boldly face the religious orthodoxy. He strived to construct bridge of understanding between the two main religious communities of India, viz., Hindu and Muslim. His order, *Din-i-ilahi* was an association of liberal-minded persons. He did not levy discriminatory taxes such as *Jazya* on the non-Muslims nor did he pass laws unfavourable to them. He did not interfere in religious affairs of any community. He was sympethatic even to Christianity and extended his patronage to the Christian missionaries. Jahangir, except for a few early years when he under the influence of the *Naqshbandis*, martyred Guru Arjan Dev, followed, by and large, a liberal religious policy and did not allow state-power to serve the cause of Islam exclusively and blatantly. Shah Jahan was comparatively less liberal and took measures which buttressed the cause of orthodoxy. But even his reign could not be designated as an Islamic state. In Aurangzeb's time, the state became 'Islamic' by and large, as the Muslim orthodoxy was in the imperial saddle and ran the show.

J.N. Sarkar a celebrated historian of the Mughal period, while explicating the nature of Muslim state says in his book *History of Aurangzeb*, Vol. III, that in Islam 'true king is God and earthly rulers are merely His agents, bound to enforce His law on land. Civil law is completely subordinated to religious law and, indeed, merges its existence in the latter. The civil authority exists solely to spread and enforce the true faith. In such a state, infidelity is logically equivalent to treason because the infidel repudiates the authority of the true king and pays homage to his rivals the false gods and goddesses.....Therefore the toleration of any sect outside the fold of orthodox Islam is no better than compounding with sins. And the worst form of sin is polytheism, the belief that the one true God has partners in the form of other deities.[1] Such a belief is the rankest ingratitude (*Kufr*).[2] Islamic Theology, therefore, tells the true believers that his highest duty is to make exertion (*Jehad*) in the path of God by waging war against infidel lands (*Dar-ul-Harb*) till they become part of the Islam. (*Dar-ul-Islam*) and their populations are converted into true believers. After conquest the entire infidel population becomes theoretically reduced to the status of slaves of the conquering army.......The conversion of the entire population into Islam and the extinction of every form of dissent is the ideal of a Muslim state. If any infidel is suffered to exist in the community, it is as a necessary evil and for transitional period only. Political and social disability must be imposed upon him and bribes offered to him from the public funds to hasten the day of his spiritual enlightenment and addition of his name to the role of the true believers..... A true Islamic king is bound to look on jubilantly when his infidel subjects cut each other's throats; for whichever side may be slain; Islam is the gainer. (*Har tarf ke shawwad, kushta sud-i-islam ast*)[3]

Aurangzeb was believer in the Islamic theory of state, the view which continued to be butterressed and strengthened by the circumstances, *Naqshbandis* and the financial needs of the state. His reputation had suffered greatly in the Muslim world for executing his brothers and imprisoning his father. The *Naqshbandis* who were headed by Masum Shaikh Saifuddin and had a wide network in the whole of Mughal empire had considerable influence on Aurangzeb's thinking, who, following them believed, that it was his religious duty to help resurgence of Islam by eliminating infidelity and heterodoxy. He also needed finance to wage his wars for escalation of Islam as well as for crushing infidelity. This could easily be procured from

---

1. The Arabic term for polyheism is *shirk* meaning 'associating other falsegods with God'. Hugh's, *Dictionary of Islam*, p. 579.
2. *Kafir* means literally covering up the truth (Regarding God) and secondily ingratitude.
3. J.N. Sarkar, *A Short History of Aurangzeb*, Vol. III, pp. 163-64.

the non-Muslims especially the Hindus including the Sikhs. For all these reasons he adopted the policy of an awed persecutor of non-Muslims as well as non-*Sunni* Muslims.

After ascending the throne, Aurangzeb hastened to convince the orthodox Muslims in the empire that they have backed the right horse. He began with puritanic measures. In the second year of his reign, he discontinued the celebration of *Navroz* (first day of the lunar year). A few years later music and dancing were prohibited. *Jharokha Darshan* was discontinued on the ground that it smacked of human worship. Several punishments were awarded for anything that was constructed by the theologians in violation of spirit of Islam. Permissible length of the beard was fixed at four fingers and offenders against this order were penalised.

But most of these restrictions were of a general nature and covered all communities. Non-Muslims were singled out for discriminatory treatment in four specific fields : public services, construction of new and repair of old temples, conversion and taxation. Regarding the discrimination of the government towards the Hindus in services, the remarks of Sri Ram Sharma are pertinent. He says that towards the end of Aurangzeb's reign, there was a small number of Hindus occupying the *Mansabs* of 1000 and above than the number of similar *Mansabdars* towards the end of Shah Jahan's reign. But the decrease in number becomes still more significant when we take into account the increase in the total number of *Mansabdars* which rose enormously in the reign of Aurangzeb. In 1657, under Shah Jahan, there were 8000 *Mansabdars* in all; whereas in 1690 the number had risen to 14556.... The percentage of Hindus in the higher rank of the state services could not have been more than half of what it was towards the end of Shah Jahan's reign. Besides, this carefully planned campaign was launched prohibiting the construction of new and repair of the old temples. In 1659, the year of coronation of Aurangzeb, he ordered that no new temple should be built. In 1666 the stone railing of the famous Keshwa Rai temple of Mathura was razed to the ground by Imperial order.[1] In April 1669 he issued a general order for the destruction of all schools

---

1. J.N. Sarkar, *A Short History of Aurangzeb*, Vol. III, p. 175.

and temples of Hindus. "Orders were now sent to the governors of all the provinces that they should destroy the schools and temples of the infidels and put an end to their educational activities as well as the places of the religion of *Kafirs*.[1] In 1669 the temple of Vishwanath at Benaras was demolished. The temple of Gopinath in Benaras too was destroyed about the same time. Similar destructions were ordered in various Rajput states such as Ajmer, Ujjain, Bengal and other provinces of the Empire. In 1674, Aurangzeb confiscated all lands held by Hindus as religious grants."

'Lest the orders go amiss, strict administrative measures were taken. He appointed officers in all the sub-divisions and the cities of the empire to enforce the regulations of Islam with the directions that destruction of Hindu temples was one of their chief duties. The *Qazis* were actually associated with the new policy. The officers were told that the reports of destructions of the temple would be looked upon as authentic only if it bore their seal and attestation.'

Like other non-Muslims, particularly the Hindus, the Sikhs too according to Khafi Khan came under the state order for their share. Their temples were destroyed and their leaders externed of repraisal.[2] Mirza Inayat-Ullah-Ismi tells us in the *Ahkam-i-Alamgiri* that in compliance with the orders of the Emperor and with the consent of the local *Qazi*, the Sikh temple in the town of Burya in the pargana of Khizrabad of the *Sarkar* of Sirhind had been demolished and a mosque had been raised on this site.[3] Sayyed Zafar *Darvesh* was appointed incharge of that mosque to guide prayers and benedictions. Some Sikhs attacked the mosque and killed the *Darvesh*. The Emperor rebuked the *Qazi* and his father who was the head of the police. According to Dr. Hari Ram Gupta, incidents of this sort had become a common occurrence.[4]

In the field of taxation the policy of discrimination was launched with greater vigour. *Jazya* and pilgrimage tax were

---

1. J.N. Sarkar, *A History of Aurangzeb*, Vol. III, p. 174.
2. *Muntakhab-ul-Twarikh*, p. 652, as quoted in J.N. Sarkar, *A Short History of Aurangzeb*, p. 212.
3. *Kalimat-I-Taiyyabat*, p. 115.
4. Hari Ram Gupta, *History of Sikh Gurus*, p. 249.

relevied, custom duties on the Muslims were fixed at 2.5 percent and in the case of the Hindus at 5 percent. It was ordered that in the Lunar year, the Muslims should pay 2.5 percent and the Hindus 5 percent on the price of their cattle.

The ruling Muslim community being in a minority, great importance was attached to conversions. Bakhtawar Khan states that Aurangzeb himself administered *Kalima* to prominent persons and adored them with *Khilat* with his own hands.[1] In March 1695 Aurangzeb had issued an edict that, all the Hindus except Rajputs will not ride on elephant, fine horses, in palanquins or carry arms.[2]

Aurangzeb was equally bigotted towards *Shia*, *Sufi* saints and liberal-minded people. In 1661 Mansur-e-Sani *Sufi* Muhammad Sarmad was beheaded for believing in *Sufi* tenets.[3]

In 1678, Diwan Muhammad Tahir was put to death for liberal interpretation of Islam.[4] Qamir, a famous theologian and a scholar from Sirhind, was hanged on the same charge. In 1683, Mir Hussain was executed in Kashmir in its tribal territory for breaking *Ramzan* fast a little before sunset.[5] In 1669 celebration of Moharram was banned. Many *Shia Imams* were executed.[6]

This policy of Aurangzeb had manifold implications, one of which was that *Mansabdars* taking cue from Aurangzeb became highly zealous and vigorous in their dealings with the non-Muslims. This apparently provided them with a way of fulfilment of their financial needs and greed, apart from dislodging the non-Muslims from the ownership of land they had occupied to be made available to the state for reallocation and distribution among Muslims.

The second ancillary factor was the religio-social scenario. Islam and Hinduism were the two major religions in India, and were divided into sects and cults. Among the Muslims, the majority belonged to the *Sunni* sect. The *Qazi*, *Muftis* and the *Ulemas* were the exponents of their faith. The ultimate

---

1. Bakhtawar Khan, *Mirat-e-Alam*, p. 159.
2. J.N. Sarkar, *A Short History of Aurangzeb*.
3. Abul Kalam Azad, *Hijat-e-Sahadi*, pp. 52-53.
4. *Maasar-i-Alamgiri*, p. 120.
5. Ghulam Ali Azad Bilgrami, *Khazan-e-Amira*, p. 328.
6. Khafi Khan, *Muntakhab-ul-Lubab* II, p. 213.

authority in their religious life was *Quran*. Besides this, *Sunna*, the sayings of the prophet also served as the principal source. The books embodying interpretation of *Quran* (*Tafsir*) were also regarded as the object of esteem by the *Sunnis*. Collection of *Hadis*, prepared by Al Bukhari and Zama Khshrri's commentary on the *Quran* named *Kashshaf* were very popular in the Punjab as also in India.

Al-Ashri's (873-93) book *Maqalat* was considered to be a good guide so far as *Sunni* ideas and institutions were concerned. As a rule, a *Sunni* ought to have faith only in the oneness of God who is all-powerful, just, majestic, inscrutable, righteous and merciful and show no regard to idol worship; observe daily prayers (*Salat*), keep the daily fast during the month of Ramzan, go on pilgrimage to Mecca (*Haj*) and give charity to his Muslim brotherhood (*Zakat*). A mere observance of these things was sufficient for one to be regarded as a pious Muslim.

Next to *Sunnis*, the most important sect of the Muslims in Punjab was that of *Shias*. The distinction between the *Shias* and *Sufis* had its roots in the dispute between the Alis and Umayyads in the year which followed the Khalafat Utman's association (35.A.H.). In its origin, it has nothing to do with the religion founded by prophet Muhammad. Rather it was occupied with the political question of the succession to the leadership of the Muslim community.[1] At first, the Alis on their side claimed that they were the legitimate *Khalifas* because they descended from the Prophet's daughter Fatima and his cousin and intimate companion, Ali. The Umayyads, on their part, claimed a nomination by the choice of the Muslims themselves and as a further title claimed worship with the Prophet as being the Hashmite family. Later, the Alis stood for the claims of the descent against all claims of right to office because of the popular choice. Besides this, among the *Sunnis*, the *Khalifa* is a political ruler essentially, while the *Shia* party regards the Prophet's successor as a religious guide and therefore preferred to designate him as the *Imam* of the Muslim community[2]. The *Shias* recognise twelve *Imams* in the line from Fatima and Ali. The last *Imam* Muhammad Ali Mahdi was believed to have

1. James Hastings, *Encyclopaedia of Religion and Ethics*, p. 117.
2. *Ibid.*

disappeared from the world in A.D. 880 and was expected to reappear to restore justice and righteousness. *Sunnis* did not recognise them. The *Shias* recognised the authority of *Quran* and prophethood of Muhammad but had no faith in first three *Khalifas*.

Ismailis and Qamirathians were the other Muslim sects in the Punjab. The Ismailis reposed faith in seven prophets ending with Jafar-us-Sadiq and Ismail. They claimed to derive teachings from a hidden source which must receive absolute obedience.[1] The laws of Shariat according to Ismaili belief were not meant for those who possessed esoteric knowledge.[2] *Quran* itself had inner meanings. They denied all divine attributes, holding that the divine essence has given forth light by which various form of intelligence and matter have been created having no real individuality. The divine essence which was alone in the beginning will be alone in the end. The initiates were taught to use speculative philosophical reasoning as a result of which doubts were raised about the systems of religions including Islam. Besides *Shias*, Ismailis and Qamirathians were generally not liked by *Sunnis*. Aurangzeb also had no soft corner for them, and so far as *Shias* were concerned, he was very bitter. There were various other sects of Islam but they had so small a following that they were virtually incapable of playing any significant role in Islamic fraternity vis-a-vis Hinduism or its sects. Besides nursing inter-sects theological and doctrinal differences, they had also differences in social outlook and approach to different problems. They, however, had one thing common between them which was their formalism, particularism, obscurantism, esoteric practices, superstitions, demeaning rituals et al in which they had plunged deep.

In the 16th and 17th centuries particularly, there emerged certain revivalist movements which created new religious orders, but even they did not hold any praxis for the regeneration of Indian Muslims or of mankind as a whole. *Mahdvis*, believing that *Mahdi*, would reappear to restore original glory to Islam and it was the duty of the Muslim to

---

1. S.G.F. Braudein, *Dictionary of Comparative Religion*.
2. J.S. Grewal, *Guru Nanak in History*, p. 68.

believe and follow him. Sayyid Mohammad of Jaunpur (Birth September, 1443) was famous *Mahdi* in India. *Naqshbandis* was another religious group. Unlike *Mahadis*, it wielded considerable influence among the Muslims even in Guru Gobind Singh's time. They believed that their Qayyum who had direct access to God and prophet Muhammad, was destined to usher in the revival and promotion of Islam, and in this process *Bidat* (innovation) and *Kufar* had to be erased by which they meant crusade (*Jehad*) should be launched against *Kafirs* who did not accept Islam of their concept, to make them accept Islam or to finish them. In the case of Christianity and Judaism which were the religions of the Book, the crusade would not operate if their followers agreed to enter into agreement. The *Sunnis* which formed the majority of the Muslims were anxious that the Muslim Shara should be observed in totality and principle of *Jehad* should be pursued vigorously with the ultimate objective of converting *Dar-ul-Harb* into *Dar-ul-Islam*. In the process, they supported and sponsored all such movements which in their reckoning could bring the goal nearer. Strangely enough, all those movements did not strive to shed off unneccessary accretions to Islam, nor did they try to coalesce different sects of the Muslims, into one unified whole with vision of seeking welfare of all. Regretfully, religion was seen as an instrument to advance particularstic interests rather than be considered a great artifice to reform individuals and corporate living. Even among *Naqshbandis*, there were groups having intra-group conflicts, as for instance, *Naqshbandis* of Delhi had differences with their counterpart at Delhi.

Sufism, another form of religious life of the Muslims in India, had also developed contradictions. According to one estimate there were *Sufis* and *Sufis*, some having faith in *Tahudi-i-Wajudi* and some in *Tahuhidi-Shuhadi*. In Social outlook they were *Sulekul* (protagonist of peace for all) but in the Indian context they could not shed off particularism and compromised with orthodox Islam, although they were hesitant to act as a fanatic and opperessive to other religions. Quite a number of *Sufi* saints such as Mian Shaikh Badruddin, Bhikhan Shah and Saif Khan had enjoyed in deep friendship with the Sikh Gurus and some Hindu Saints as well. All the same, they did not draw up any programme for lifting the mankind out of the prevailing quagmire.

Hinduism too presented a sorry spectacle. Its main forms Vaishnavism, Jogism, Saivism were at the most half-baked attempts to regenerate society. These did not conceive Reality appropriately nor did they project any social philosophy. The people brought up in these traditions grew to be good ascetics instead of being responsible citizens alive to their civic and social duties. *Tantrism* was another cult of Hinduism that held some population of the Hindus in tight grip. Regretfully this form also had debased itself to a few formulae and incantations to be muttered for attaining mundane advantages. The religious elites of both Hinduism and Islam had gone corrupt.

Corruption, immorality and vices were rampant among the *Qazis* as well as *Imams* of the mosques. They visited the hemp saloons without hesitation.[1] The theologions were shrewd enough to exploit the royal patronage to their utmost advantage. They seemed to be following the maxim "Make hay while the sunshine".[2] According to Shah Nawaz Khan, Aurangzeb himself bemoaned that in the reign of Timurids, not a single truth-loving person or an honest *Qazi* was heard of (with the exception of Murtaza Khan).

The *Qazis* of the cities and towns in concert with the governors and magistrates would sell out of greed the decrees of *Qisas* (retaliation on account of murders) for gold.[3]

The demeanour of Brahmins and other religious functionaries of various forms of Hinduism was no less better. They had become extremely self-centered and had no moral qualms. They misguided the people on matters religious and social and filled their coffers. They were also in collusion with the ruling classes to safeguard their interests as well as to promote the interests of the rulers by projecting them as the blessed personalities. Certain reformatory movements like Sufism among the Muslims, Baulism in Bengal, and the Bhakti movement in almost all parts of the country had surfaced but their impact on the society was marginal. With the passage of

---

1. *Anfasul-Arifin*, p. 9.
2. S.A.A. Rizvi, *Muslim Revivalist Movements in Northern India*, p. 411.
3. *Maasir-ul-Umara*, Vol. I, p. 237, (Persian version).

time, they had compromised their uniqueness with the orthodoxy either of the Hindu or that of Muslim variety .

About the approach and vision of different religions and sects, the remarks of *Bachittar Natak* are illuminating and pertinent. In Chapter 6 of *Bachittar Natak*, the Guru made it clear that Brahma, Vishnu, Mahesh, Dattatreya, Rishis, Sidhs, Prophet Mohammad did not improve upon the lot of this world, rather they began to present themselves as God's equals and enmeshed the people in rituals, formalism, meaningless practices. For instance saint Dattatriya taught only how to beautify ones nails and hair and Prophet Muhammed began his own cult instilling in people to call him as the sole spokesman of God.[1] "All of them were entangled in their own beliefs and could not see what the Supreme Reality was."[2]

The Guru was naturally upset at the sordidness of religious affairs. His anguish is amply visible in many of his poetic outpourings. For instance in *Bachittar Natak*, he says :

> All those previously incarnated
> Their own names having propagated
> None showed the true path
> Nor did they recognise the Almighty God.[3]

Government and religious elites being altogether uncreative, partisan, greedy, tyrannous, ego-centric held no hope to the Guru in his wish to improve the lot of the people.

No less worrisome for the Guru was disintegrative forces that had been brewing in the Sikh society and had the potential to disturb its internal organisation and cohesion. The *Masands / Manjidars* who with the strength of the *Sangats* under their respective charges constituted the pivot of Sikh organisation and had served Sikhism creditably since the time of its inception, had ceased to function appropriately. Upto the time of Guru Hargobind, Sikhism had crossed frontiers of Punjab and had won the hearts of the masses in far off regions such

---

1. *Bachittar Natak*, Chapter VI, pp. 1 to 28.
2. *Ibid.*, Chapter VI, p. 28.
3. *Sab te apnā nām(u) japāio, sat(i) nām(u) kāhūṅ na dṛiṛāio.*
   Sab apnī apnī urjhānā, Pārbrahm kāhūṅ na pachhānā.

as Bengal, Uttar Pradesh, Madhya Pradesh, and certain parts of South India, Jammu, Kashmir et al. As a result *Sangats* had been formed on a large scale often by the Sikhs themselves and sometimes by the *Masands/Manjidars* appointed by different Gurus. The members of the holy congregation were largely in touch with the Guru through *Masands* and their Deputies *(Mewaras)* although examples of *Sangat* being guided and supervised by the devoted Sikhs were not lacking. *Masands*, therefore, acquired an extraordinary influence over the *Sangat* as they were the medium through whom instructions of the Guru to the people were transmitted. The offerings of the people were also collected and then remitted to the Guru by the *Masands*, although at times, the *Sangat* sent them directly. The *Masands* kept a part of the offerings for performing their organisational, secular and episcopal duties. The system worked well for sometime but as the time advanced, its functioning became shoddy and remissly. The office of a *Masand* which in the first instance was filled by men of piety and integrity became hereditary in the families of the first incumbents, and in course of time, fell into the hands of those persons who were neither serious about their episcopal duties, nor possessed the requisite integrity in respect of financial matters. *Masands* not only took to the jobbery, misappropriation of the offerings on a large scale, but also claimed status equal to the Guru and did not hesitate to clone *Sangats*. Still they could not do much harm either to the solidarity of the Sikhs or the escalation of Sikhism, because they feared Guru Hargobind for his promptitude to take quick and strong actions.

The uncordial relationship between the state and the Gurus, the animus and provocative stance of the rival claimants of Gurudom, such as Dhirmal, Ram Rai, Miharban and his successors, particularly after Guru Hargobind, the Gurus could not pay much attention to the organisational as well as episcopal matters with the natural consequences that *Masands/Manjidars* found opportunities to be more bold, more active in pursuing their petty designs instead of serving the cause of Sikhism. This tendency was clearly manifest during the pontificate of Guru Har Rai and Guru Harkrishan. It persisted even during the period of Guru Tegh Bahadur. The fact that quite a number of them sided with Dhirmal and one of them called by the name of 'Shihan' did not hesitate even to fire at Guru Tegh Bahadur was a brazen example of *Masand's* contumacy and their recalcitrance.

Guru Gobind Rai had chartered a massive programme of rejuvenating and reshaping the society. In the process he had realised that he would have to face animosity of the Hill Rajas, conservative Hindu elements, ignorant masses, Mughal Islamic Imperialism, privileged classes, dissenting sects and his rival claimants to the guruship. To steer clear through all this, he needed unflinching devotion of the Sikhs in general and whole-hearted co-operation of the *Masands* in particular. But the latter failed him badly. They adopted many tactics to dislodge him from his chosen path. They bred doubts in the minds of his family members, and the Sikhs in general regarding the soundness of his programme and policies. When the Guru imparted military training and adopted assertive postures vis-a-vis Hill Rajas, they would at once go to Reverend mother of the Guru and prevail upon her to actively intervene and dissuade the Guru from such activities. Similarly, when the Guru decided to encounter the enemy at Bhangani, they were cynically critical. Not satisfied with their out-pouring against his plan to fight at Bhangani, they inveigled dissentients and rival claimants to the guruship to step up their nefarious activities. Many of them openly sided with them against the interests of Guru. They also involved the *Sangats* under their influence in the issues, they championed and sponsored. Resultantly, *Masands* and the *Sangats* coalesced into different groups—each group under some *Masand/Manjidar* committed to the cause other than the cause of Sikhism/Guru. Many *Masands* were bold enough to keep the offerings and *Daswandh* with themselves which they were enjoined upon to remit to the Guru. These were the people who had not only absconded with the offerings which the Sikhs had made to the Guru at Anandpur when there was a cataclysm caused by the attack of Mirza Gias Beg and four Mughal Ahadyas. Such people wielded a considerable influence in the whole of *Majha* territory and most of the *Doaba*. They seemed to have co-operated with schismatic groups among the Sikhs in many cases. An inderminate number of Sikhs were following the descendants of Guru Ram Das who had set up a rival Guru lineage. Notable, amongst them were the descendants of Prithi Chand and of Dhirmal (The elder brother of Guru Har Rai). Ram Rai, the elder brother of Guru Harkrishan had also attracted considerable following contemptuously called *Ram Rayyas* but his strength lay in the hills where Aurangzeb had granted him the territory of Dehra Doon.

Sikh chronicles are galore with examples of *Masand's* total perversity. It is often narrated that one day, a company of mimes came to the Guru's court. The Guru asked them to imitate acts and deeds performed by *Masands*. One of them accordingly dressed himself as *Masand*, the second as *Masand's* servant and the third as *Masand's* courtesan riding behind him on a horse back as he went to collect offerings for the Guru. The mimes portrayed to life the villainy and oppression practised by the *Masands*. Again we are told that a *Masand* billeted himself on a poor Sikh and demanded sweets instead of the crushed pulse and unleavened bread which formed the staple food of the host. The *Masand* took the bread, threw it into the host's face and spattered the crushed pulse on the ground. He then abused the Sikh and would not cease scolding him till the poor Sikh sold his wife's petty-coat to provide him sweets.[1] The stories may have some minor exaggerations but the substantial truth implicit in them is certified by the Guru himself. He writes :

> "If anyone goes the *Masands*, they will tell him to bring all his property at once and give it to them.
> If anyone serves the *Masands,* they will say 'Fetch and give us all thine offerings.'
> Go at once and make a present to us of whatever assets are in their house.
> 'Think on us night and day, and mention not others even by mistake.'
> If they hear of anyone giving, they run to him even at night, they are not at all pleased at not receiving.
> They put oil into their eyes and make others believe that they are shedding tears.

---

1. M.A. Macauliffe, *The Sikh Religion,* Vol. V, p. 89.

> If they see any of their worshipper wealthy, they serve sacred food and feed him with it.
>
> If they see him without wealth, they give him nothing. Though he begs for it, they will not show him their faces.
>
> Those beasts plunder men, and never sing the praise of the Supreme Being.[1]

The *Masands* had become hypocritical, avaricious, ego-centric, dishonest and were engaged in creating their own followings to cater to their own selfish ends instead of linking the Sikhs to the Guru. The latter fact was palpably taken notice of by the Sixth Nanak[2] and he designated the Sikhs who had direct link with the Guru as *Khalsa*, the pure ones, or Guru's own as the *Khalsa* lands were under the direct control of the Mughal sovereign. The Guru seemed to make use of this term deliberately so that the Sikhs might take note of the Guru's preference for the Sikhs with direct connection with the Guru. Guru Tegh Bahadur also used this term (*Khalsa*) for the Sikhs of Patna understandably to make known to them that they were preferred as they had direct linkage with him. What was implicit in all this was the fact that to be a Sikh directly of the Guru was dearer to the Guru than a Sikh linked with the Guru through the mediacy of a *Masand*.

In a way, Guru Hargobind and Guru Tegh Bahadur had indicated their aversion for *Masands* and had taken steps to enable the Sikhs to have direct links with them. In consonance with their designs, they defined the identity of a Sikh in terms of his relation with the Guru as well.

Guru Gobind Singh's perception about the *Masands* was no different from his father and grandfather, but he waited long, before he took any decisive step against them. The Guru's slow peddling in this regard seemed to have been actuated by practical considerations. Any drastic interference in their affairs was to put the whole Sikh organisation out of gear, but ultimately the Guru was roused to action. He exposed the misdeeds of *Masands* and issued *Hukamnama* to various

---

1. M.A. Macauliffe, *The Sikh Religion*, Vol. V, VI, pp. 322-323, about Guru's attitude towards *Masands*, also refer to *Hukamnamas* Nos. 46-50 from the book *Hukamname* by Dr. Ganda Singh.
2. Ganda Singh, *Hukamname*, *Hukamnama* No. 3 of Guru Hargobind, p. 67. *Hukamnama* No. 8 of Guru Tegh Bahadur, p. 76.

Sangats that they should not only stop sending their offerings and the amount of *Daswandh* through *Masands* but also avoid any social relations with them. They were asked to have direct link with the Guru. The story goes that the Guru was so much enraged at the misdemeanour of *Masands* that he had them rounded up numbering nearly 2200 and brought to Anandpur where he destroyed them in boiling oil and by other torments.[1] This does not seem to be credible as the Guru had hardly the means of laying his hands on all of them, particularly on those of out-lying districts and it seems more probable that some of them were punished, while the others were pardoned. The Guru, however, did not stop at that. He thought of abolishing *Masand* system altogether as he found it not only injurious to the community but also felt it was a great wedge between the Guru and the Sikhs. But he definitely wanted to get rid of them.

Equally disruptive and inappropriate were the activities of dissentient sects such as the followers of Prithi Chand, contemptuously called *Minas* by Bhai Gurdas, the followers of Dhirmal, commonly known as *Dhirmalias* and the followers of Ram Rai, popularly called *Ram Rayyas*. Hardas the son of Miharban and grandson of Prithi Chand, the elder brother of Guru Arjan Dev, was leading the *Minas* after his father and his grandfather. He was a contemporary of Guru Gobind Singh. He called himself the seventh Guru in succession to Guru Nanak claiming inheritance of his light and projected his sect as the mainstream Sikhism. He kept control of the central Sikh shrine Sri Harmandir Sahib and *Darbar Sahib* complex including *Sri Akal Takhat* and spared no pains to present the compositions of his father as well as sacred texts.

His real purpose was to impress upon the Sikhs that guruship after Guru Ram Das was vested in his father and grandfather and currently in his person and his followers represented mainstream Sikhism. He made applicable a code of conduct which like the writings of his father were inclined

---

1. H.A. Rose, *A Glossary of the Tribes and Castes of the Punjab and North-West Frontier Province*, Vol. III, p 72

towards Brahmanism.[1] Guru Har Rai's elder brother Dhirmal had already done his worst to gain guruship for himself and was still campaigning to attain his objective. The followers of Ram Rai had not ceased to present themselves as the representatives of Sikhism, although their progenitor, Ram Rai, had reconciled to the guruship of Guru Gobind Singh and had publicly proclaimed to his effect. They were particularly active at Lahore where their headquarter next in importance only to that of Dehra Doon was situated, and at Srinagar (Garhwal state) where some of the Ram Rai's *Masands* had decided to stay. At Dehra Doon they were wary of conducting vicious propaganda against the Guru because Punjab Kaur, wife of Ram Rai, had been converted to the Guru's mission. The example of these claimants of Sodhi family was not lost upon other members of Sodhi family and twenty-two of them were audacious enough to simultaneously claim pontific throne at the death of Guru Harkrishan. Many of the Sodhis began to consider themselves as entitled to the services of the Sikhs and appointed their own *Masands*. A great destructive force was thus let loose in Sikhism, of which *Masands* were not slow to take the fullest advantage. The greed of these aspirants for the guruship and the recalcitrance of the *Masands* fed each other resulting in development of a serious threat to the solidarity of the Sikhs, their loyalty to their Guru and the immutability and sovereignty of the Sikhs doctrine. The Guru, was obligated to take serious note of such development and therefore he denounced the *Minas*, *Dhirmallias* and *Ram Rayyas* as heretics, projecting beliefs and opinions opposed to Sikhism. He also made the Sikhs aware of their nefarious activities and issued *Hukamnamas* to *Sangat* of different regions that they should not remit their offerings and amount of *Daswandh* to him through a *Masand* or any of his agent. These should be sent directly to him or through his specially appointed emissaries.[2]

A *Hukamnama* directing Sikhs not to have any social

1. Harji, *Goshtian Guru Meharban*, Gosht No. 30, also refer to *Sodhi Harji—Jiwan Te Rachna* by Gurmohan Singh Ahluwalia.
2. Ganda Singh, *Hukamname*, No. 46.

relationship with the followers of Prithi Chand, Dhirmal and Ram Rai was also issued.[1]

Equally irritating were the deliberate distortions of the real concept of guruship. Guru Nanak was Guru because it was avowed that the guruship on Nanak was bestowed directly by the Almighty God. With Guru Angad and his immediate successors, it could not have been direct and immediate. Indeed to them the words and message of the Guru as transmitted to them were considered as Guru, Guruship being supposed to have been transmitted to them through words, and the mission that went with them. Guru Arjan also got guruship because he was transmitted the light that made his predecessors Guru, but he was at the same time the son of fourth Guru and it was from this cue that guruship began to be seen as something hereditary, a principle which actually speaking was against the concept and institution of Guru in Sikhism.

Since the hereditary principle and law of promogeniture were generally considered as adjuncts to each other by the people, Dhirmal, the eldest son of Guru Hargobind and Ram Rai the eldest son of Guru Har Rai began to dispute the succession to the pontific seat. They turned hostile to the central Sikh church and formed the rival sects and colluded with the Mughal authorities to disrupt/erode the Sikh authority. Beside this, the Guru realised that any hereditary institution particularly of socio-religious nature in an expanding society was liable to deteriorate in character and become authoritarian. There is ample evidence of Guru Gobind Singh himself showing that the *Masands* had actually turned authoritarian and used to indulge in corrupt practices that led to the exploitation of the poor and innocent Sikhs. All this convulsed his mind and he seemed to have given a serious thought to it. Accordingly, he made up his mind to abolish personal guruship and invest it with something permanent and inviolate. Much work had already been done in this direction. Now he resolved to take things to their logical end. There was the revered *Granth* well established by then as the

---

1. Ganda Singh, *Hukamname*, Nos. 49 and 50.
   M.A. Macauliffe, *The Sikh Religion*, Vol. V, p. 95.

book enshrining Divine Word of the Lord propagated through Gurus and considered as sacred as the Gurus themselves and even the Almighty.

On the matters other than spiritual, there was the institution of *Sangat* by now developed into a cohesive unit to take up responsibility of secular affairs of the Sikhs as well. The *Granth* and *Sangat,* could now take care of the spiritual and secular functions of the Guru, the revered *Granth* could take the mantle of the spiritual Guru, the *Panth* (*Sangat*) as the secular Guru and their combination as the mystic entity. But how to translate these ideas into practice was the most pertinent question.

The Guru had lived among the people of semi-independent states of Shivalik Hills and had tried hard to enlighten and awaken them to their responsibilities towards God, themselves and society. But he soon discovered that they were insensitive to any fresh call. Similarly, the Guru found the Hill Rajas holding fast to feudalistic values and totally reluctant to make efforts to introduce reforms. As a result, the people had become bereft of vigour and vitality to play any worth-while role in remoulding individuals and society as envisaged by the Guru.

The Rajputs of the present-day Rajasthan also did not hold any hope to the Guru. They had enmeshed themselves in feudal order and caste-based social structure. Not only this, they had succumbed to the Mughal hegemony and had surrendered their political and social will. No doubt, in the time of Guru, the Rathors of Marwars and Sisodias of Mewar had challenged the tyrannous Aurangzeb's religious policy of converting *Dar-ul-Harb* into *Dar-ul-Islam*, yet their cases were the product of injured vested interests and were not actuated by any higher motive or design.

Such people obviously were not fit to be the vehicle of Guru's programme of rejuvenation and regeneration. The case of the Marathas was no better. No doubt they rose against the inequitable rule of Aurangzeb under their charismatic leaders, first—under Shivaji and then under his successors, Sambha Ji, Raja Ram (Sambhaji's brother) and Tara Bai (Raja Ram's wife) and ultimately established Maratha sovereignty. Yet they were incapable of reconstruction of society anew on the bases of justice, equality, freedom. They felt satisfied with *Varan* based society clinging to feudalistic values. Their vision was circumspect and their social action particularistic. The times demanded emergence of a person with all-inclusive vision of society but they were too inelastic to expand beyond the parameters laid down by their *Dharm Shastras*. At political level, they did not look beyond Hindu *Padshahi* or *Swaraj* for Marathas. No fresh concept either of polity or of governance, society or metaphysics was thrown up by them. Such people obviously could not be helpful to the Guru who was determined to reshape society and polity in the light of his revelation.

People other than those mentioned in the aforesaid paragraphs were also taken cognizance of by the Guru. His compositions reveal that he surveyed, although mentally, the Bundhelas Arabians, the French, the Gores (people from Gaur), Qureshies of Qandhar, people of Ghazni, Bengalee, Banghshias, (people of the areas of Kohat and Qurran), Nepalese, Michinese (people of the area adjoining China), Hinguelse (people from Sind).[1] He also seemed to have critically appraised different sects including *Rafazi*,[2] *Imams*, *Siddhs*, *Naths* et al.[3] He found all of them ego-ridden and unenthused in regard to participation in the Guru's contemplated crusade against the perpetrators of Kubadh-misdeeds.

While the Guru had carried out a in-depth analysis of the people of other religions, sects and regions, he had also critically scrutinised the social complexion of his disciple. The compositions of the Sikhs had undergone a distinct change. The Jats of *Majha* and *Malwa* had entered into the fold of Sikhism in large numbers. They had brought along with them their tribal culture. Because of their profession of agriculture and their habitatism amidst war-like people for quite a long time coupled with difficult social and geographical environments, they had developed spirit of adventure and

---

1. *Akal Ustat*, Stanzas 254-255.
2. Certain Muslims who renounced their allegiance to Zaid grandson of Hussain.
3. *Akal Ustat*, Swayyas 85-86.

descernible elasticity in their character and behaviour. They had developed a natural tendency to be less rigid particularly in matters which needed adaptability. Sikhism threw no damper on all these qualities but they needed orientation towards Sikh values, especially in relation to other components of Sikhs, primarily the stock from low caste. Next to the Jats in number were the people designated as low castes in the Hindu caste-hierarchy who embraced Sikhism. Their primary need was to acquire a dignified social status and an atmosphere which should enable them to keep their head high without shame and fear. Sikhism, undoubtedly guaranteed dignified social status and condemned squarely any distinction on bases of caste et al, yet they needed to be reassured.

Opposed to both these classes were Khatris and Brahmins who inspite of their entry into the fold of Sikhism had not been able to shed their caste affiliation and could ill-brook the Jats and the so-called low-caste people being raised high in the social scale. Many of them came forward to sarcastically comment on caste-based system but majority among them were not prepared to alienate themselves from the caste-system. Further, most of the Sikhs were still in the grip of various sectarian movements such as *Nathism, Shaivism, Deviism* et al in spite of professing faith in the Guru. They also needed a brainwash.

In a nutshell, the sociological canvas bore a highly confused picture of the Sikh Society. The Guru must rub off some unacceptable contours or draw new ones to ensure the success of his Mission.[1]

The politico-socio-religious scenario being what it was, he pondered upon it in the context of his own experience, legacy which he had inherited from his predeccessors and the mission which was revealed to him directly from God. Guru Nanak, the first of his predecessors came to this world to enlighten and improve upon it and this being so, he established *Tisara Panth*, literally meaning the *Third Highway* to the ultimate reality after the two being Muslims and Hindus according to Bhai Gurdas Singh, the composer of forty-first

---

1. Surjit Singh Gandhi, *History of the Sikh Gurus*, p. 429.

var.[1] Guru Nanak is said to have experienced direct encounter with God at Sultanpur on the bank of the Behien rivulet and had a vision of Him. According to Guru Nanak, he was Transcendent, Formless, Infinite, Singular, a Unity as well as Unicity, Self-Existent, Beyond Time and Space, Beyond Enmity and Fear and the Sole Creator. He was also immanent and this being so, he pervaded everything, seen and unseen, who are related to Him as rays are related to the Sun or sparks to fire. World also partook of His immanence. Man also emanated from Him. Since He was the source of all creations, He was not detached from it. He permeated it and regulated it just as potter regulated his clay and in spirit form permeates his constructions. Therefore, He had intimate relation with nature, man, world, universe, unmanifest and manifest things. He therefore, was looked upon by the Guru as attributive in His immanent aspect; as for instance He was regarded, Merciful, Saviour, Sustainer, even Destroyer, although Guru Nanak's expressions of God convey relatively sparsely, the destructive attributes of God. He probably reckoned that presenting God as saviour of people implied destruction of the wicked.

Guru Nanak's vision of God as delineated in the foregoing paragraphs led him to remodel man and society in the light of his perception. Since God was singular, sole creator of all His creation including this world, it was not profane or irrelevant, rather it was a time bound reality and a dwelling place of God and therefore a place worth living. World being *Sargun* (immanent) aspect of God is to be held in veneration and not be condemned as veritable hell or an illusion. Also, it is not to be exploited and squandered nor is it irrelevant to the process of ascent towards God. A love bond and an active association between God and the world existed and are inbuilt. The world being reality and having infinite links with God as the immanent is a place to be lived upon to experience how God manifested himself as also to struggle to experience the ultimate ineffable vision of God. Human's destiny is to

---

1. *Var* 41, *Pauri* 16. [A Writing of Bhai Gurdas Singh (1844) included in the *Vars of Bhai Gurdas* (Bhalla)]

endeavour to discover and realise himself/herself and then experience and operate as per spirit of the attributes of God which he could do by controlling evil impulses, eliminating *Haumain* (ego) and orientating his actions as the Will of God. In simple words, the Guru expected people to regenerate themselves through appropriate actions and meditate upon God in both his Immanent and Transcendent aspects. In this context, Guru Nanak propounded and preached the following triple precepts as the basis of an ideal society.

(i)   *Kirat Karna*
(ii) *Wand Chhakna*
(iii) *Nam Japna*

Kirat Karna means that one should earn one's livelihood by honest creative labour. *Wand Chhakna* implies that one should share the fruits of one's labour with the fellow beings. *Nam Japna* denotes meditating on Lords' Name, which means that one should not lose sight of the cosmic process and the divine, permeating everything of the world. By imbibing *Nam* culture, one would not fall victim to *Haumain* which causes many evil impulses to emerge in a person. Society built on such precepts was bound to be healthy, egalitarious, non-exploitive, just, non-discriminatory, condemnatory of distinctions on the bases of cast, birth, status, creed and wealth et al. because these were the product of faulty perception of Reality/God and flawed notions regarding ultimate destiny of man, world and the nature of their relationship with God.

In the process of rejuvenation and regenerations of man and society, the Guru did not recommend any ascetic practices, pilgrimages, renunciation of the world. He rightly believed that imbibing *Nam* culture is a right type of pilgrimage. Eliminating *Haumain* and other evil impulses should be considered as the right type of asceticism and renunciation instead of resorting to fasts, penances and shunning of world et al. The Guru set a fresh ideal before the people which was to seek union with God. What he meant was that they should conform to different attributes of God which implied that they should be compassionate, kind, helpful and intolerant of injustice and oppressor or tyrants. Guru called such people

Gurmukh—the Guru-conscious, *Nirmal*—Pure, *Khalsa*—immaculately pure. In *Japji*, the Guru called such people as *Panches* and wished leadership to be comprised of them. In this context, he expressed that only those should rule who are really competent. By that he meant that they should be ethical, enlightened and Guru-God-conscious, never ever resorting to injustice and oppression and always remaining attuned to God.[1]

This mission of Guru Nanak was carried on by his successors who made it more lucid, clear and explicit through preaching, singing the compositions of the Guru, adding their own compositions to the already existing hymns of Guru Nanak. They contributed towards the development of Sikhism by adding concepts as well as praxises. The *Sangats* were established in far-flung regions. New cities like Kartarpur, Amritsar, Tarn Taran, reflecting and committed to Sikh ethos were founded. A system of *Daswandh* among the Sikhs was made prevalent. Links with the *Sangats* were forged. Central Sikh scripture was prepared. Key Sikh shrine, Sri Harmandir Sahib and fresh symbol of supreme Sikh authority both in religious and temporal affairs was created in the form of *Sri Akal Takhat Sahib* at Amritsar. It was declared clearly and unequivocally that Sikhism does not hold religious and temporal affairs exclusive to each other; rather these two are complementary. In order to resolve problems occurring in any of these two spheres, Guru's guidance would be sought. Tradition has it that Guru Hargobind made this principal conspicuous by wearing two swords on his body, one symbolising religious authority and the second symbolising temporal authority. This was continued to be dinned into the ears of the Sikhs. There was a widespread belief that it was not easy to wean them away from their age-old fixation that there existed dichotomy between spirituality and temporality, a belief that was continuously embedded in the psyche of the people by Indian religious traditions, generally speaking. All the Gurus were persistent in following the basic tenets as laid down by Guru Nanak. To quote *Sri Guru Granth Sahib* (p. 966),

---

1. *Takht(i) rājā so bahai je takhtai lāik hoī.*   (SGGS, p. 1088)

Jot Ohā Jugat Sāe Saih Kāiā Pher Palatiai. The same was the light and the methodology of all the Gurus, simply their bodies had changed. This fact was also vouchsafed by Guru Gobind Singh in *Bachittar Natak.* He said 'Sri Nanak was accepted as Angad (Guru) and Guru Amar Das was identified as Angad, Guru Amar Das was called (Guru) Ram Das and this mystery was understood by the saints only. The stupid ones could not follow it, ordinary persons considered them in different forms but some rare ones understood them as one. Those who know them are bound to attain the high spiritual stages but without understanding (the mysteries) nothing could be procured.[1] Saying this Guru Gobind Singh brings down the spiritual lineage of the Gurus to his own and thus proved in accordance with *Sri Guru Granth Sahib* that all the Gurus were one, and their thought frame was no different either. At the same time, Guru Gobind Singh observed that inspite of concerted efforts of his predecessors, people as individuals and as a social fraternity were intransigent, very slow to accept the proposed changes by the Gurus including himself. He in his compositions made no secret of his dissatisfaction with the concepts of state, sovereignty, God and his creations, the modalities of the reconstruction of society, demeanours of human beings both at individual and social level. Even prevalent religions had ceased to function properly. The elites of all religious and social fraternities had become self-centered, corrupt, greedy and protector of their vested interests. The Kings and their bureaucracies were palpably insensitive to the aspirations of the people. Misdeeds were galore. Even *Masands/Manjidars* who originally were appointed by the Guru and had done a good job, resorted to jobbery, avarice and malpractices, caring little for the laudable job of spreading the message of the Gurus.

Face to face with such scenario, blatantly unhelpful to him in the fulfilment of his mission, the Tenth Master seemed to be always in quest for some solution right from the day he assumed guruship. Whether he was at Anandpur or at Paonta

---

1. J.P. Sangat Singh, *Bachittar Natak Steek*, Chapter 5, Naraj Chhand, Stanza 7, 8, 9, 10, pp. 106-107.

or at any other place; he was persistent in his efforts to achieve his objective. He went through the whole gamut of ancient Indian literature, both religious and secular. He saw for himself the political apparatus of the Mughals and the Hill-Chiefs. He critically appraised the social and religious formations of the people along with their faiths and beliefs and himself wrote number of compositions such as *Jap, Akal Ustat, Chandi Di Var,* et al. Even a cursory study of these compositions would highlight some of his cardinal formulations. In his compositions, the Guru addressed God by various names. He calls him Attributeless, Formless, Timeless, Self-existent, Omniscient, etc. He also calls him by various attributive names such as Sustainer, Magnanimous, Merciful, Compassionate, Protector, Destroyer of oppressors, Extirpator of enemies and tyrants, Just et al. He also calls him by such names as *Sarbloh* (all steel), *Mahan Loh* (great steel), *Sarbkal* (All death), *Mahan Kal* (great death), *Asidhuj* and *Kharg Ketu* (having sword in his hand).

From all this, it is clear that Guru's faith in God was unfathomable, as also in his potential to smash the wicked as well as to bless and elevate the virtuous. From this faith flowed his confidence that He was the skipper of the ship of the destiny of the people—the task which He undertakes and accomplishes through his chosen people just as He did in *Doapar,* through Lord Krishna and in *Treta* through Lord Rama who smashed the wicked and evil forces to usher in new eras of felicity, harmony and peace. It was against this background that he considered himself as the one commissioned by the Almighty to spread His religion, to save the saints and to extirpate the tyrants. The veracity of the statement is vouchsafed by the Guru's statement in *Bachittar Natak.* The Guru says :

> I shall now tell my story,
> How God sent me into this world as I was performing penance.
> On the mountains of Hemkunt[1]
> I performed such penance that I became blended with God
> When God gave me the order,

1. J.P. Sangat Singh, *Bachittar Natak Steek,* Chapter VI, Stanza I, pp. 110, 111, 112.

> I assumed birth in this Dark age
> I did not desire to come,
> As my attention was focused on God's feet
> God remonstrated earnestly with me[1]
> And sent me into this world with the following order
> When I created this world
> I first made the demons who became enemies and oppressors
> They became intoxicated with the strength of their arms.
> And ceased to worship Me, The Supreme Being.[2]
> I became angry and atonce destroyed them.
> In their place I established gods.
> They also busied themselves with receiving sacrifices and
>   worship
> And called themselves supreme being.[3]
> I have cherished thee as my son,
> And created thee to extend my religion.
> Go and spread my religion there
> And restrain the world from senseless deeds.[4]
> Understand this, O holy men in thy hearts
> I assumed birth for the purpose of spreading the faith saving
>   the saints
> And extirpating all tyrants.[5]

From the reading of the above excerpts from *Bachittar Natak,* an impression emerges that the Guru considered himself commissioned by God to spread religion, extirpate tyrants and restrain people from committing misdeeds. He also felt inspired that he was under the direct command and protection of God. By considering himself as such, the Guru did not claim status of an incarnation of God, who according to Hindu belief assumed birth to save the saints and to destroy the tyrants. He was God's servant and slave; he was not to be guided by enmity to anyone or influenced by fear of mortals. His view of the problem resembled that of a judge punishing a criminal simply for the sake of protecting society against the unrighteous, unjust, violator of justice who threatens its foundation and block its progress.

---

1. J.P. Sangat Singh, *Bachittar Natak Steek,* Chapter VI, Stanza 5, pp. 110, 111, 112.
2. *Ibid.,* Stanza 6.
3. *Ibid.,* Stanza 7.
4. *Ibid.,* Stanza 29.
5. *Ibid.,* Stanza 43.

In complete dedication to the mission of God, the Guru addressed the problems. He reappraised the whole scenario as it existed or it was to exist in times to come. He computed his resources—historical, metaphysical, sociological and religious. He juxtaposed the results of his calculations with the ultimate configuration and destiny of people not only of India but of the world as a whole as envisaged by Sikhism, and in the process realised that a timely adjustment between the forces of evil and those of good through the use of force was an essential ingredient of the moral world. God could not tolerate the unhappiness of his saints (righteous people) who must be protected from the wicked. To this purpose, the use of force as a last resort in favour of the good was legitimate. Krishan and Ram who made use of force against tyranny and injustice had peculiar fascination for Guru Gobind Singh. The power which was manifest through human agency was God's, for, an important attribute of God in Guru Gobind Singh's view was precisely this power. It is in this context that Guru invested sword with divinity, raised it to the level of God, and Guru named God as *Bhagauti* or *Kharag Ketu* (wielder of sword). By doing so, the Guru was carrying the mission of Guru Nanak and his predecessors to its culmination. Guru Nanak called God *Asur Sanghar* (smasher of the evil-doers) along with other attributive names of God and had not hesitated to denounce Babar for his excesses and Lodhi rulers for abjuring righteous causes and the ruling and religious elites for their enormities. The strain of this action-thinking-model continued to be followed by subsequent Gurus, of course with gradually increasing emphasis depending upon circumstances and the intensity of challenges. Guru Hargobind explicitly and unequivocally, made it clear that Sikhism embraced spiritual and temporal aspects of life and the Guru's sacred duty was to guide, and direct his disciples as well as all those who make allegiance to him in both the worlds, spiritual and temporal and wore two swords one of *Piri*, symbolic of spiritual authority and the other of *Miri*, to represent temporal authority. The use of swords as symbols marked the Guru's determination to pursue his resolves at all costs and by all righteous means including the use of force, of course as a last

resort. Bhai Gurdas in his thirty-fourth *Var*, (*Pauri* XIII) says
'Just as one has to tie pail's neck while taking out water; just
as to get the jewel, the snake is to be killed; just as to get Musk
from the deer's belly, deer has to be killed; just as to get oil,
oil seeds have to be crushed; to get Kernel, coconut has to be
broken; similarly to correct senseless people, sword has to be
taken up.[1] The use of force was considered legitimate religious
act if it is to be used against unrighteousness. Guru Tegh
Bahadur, Guru Har Rai, Guru Har Krishan did not prohibit the
use of force and remained champion of righteousness throughout even against the heaviest of odds. Guru Gobind Singh,
thus did not, plough a lonely furrow. He followed the path
shown by his predecessors with the difference, that he
followed it with more vigour. He had to do this because of the
changed circumstances and the commission assigned to him
by God Himself (to extirpate the tyrants, save the saints and
spread the religion) which implied that the Guru was obligated
to improve upon the present as also to set the people on the
road of *Dharma* through new leadership comprising of saints-
lovers and crusaders for righteousness. Guru's mission was
indeed a primary impulsion, epitomic of what Sikhism stood
in terms of doctrine, society, individuals and corporate living
and ultimate destiny of mankind at global level. The praxis
was the *Khalsa*.

The Guru decided to put his plan into operation on the
first of Baisakh 1756 BK corresponding to March 29, 1699. He
sent *Hukamnama* (edict) to his followers inviting them to visit
Anandpur in full strength on the Baisakhi festival. He specially
exhorted them to come with long hair and beard unshorn.[2]

---

1. *Jio(n) kar(i) khūho(n) niklai gal(i) badhe pānī.*
   Jio(n) man(i) kāle sup sir(i) has(i) de na jānī.
   Jān kathūrī mirg tan(i) mar mukai ānī.
   Tel tilo(n) kio(n) niklai vin(u) pīre ghānī.
   Jio(n) muho(n) bhanne garī de nalīer nisānī.
   Bemukh lohā sādhīai vagdī vādānī.   (*Var* 34, *Pauri* 13)
2. The Guru sent fiats (*Hukamnamas*) to the following effect to all the *Sangat*
   wherever they were :
   The Sikhs should come to me wearing long hair. Once a man becomes a Sikh,
   he should never shave himself. He should not touch tobacco and should
   receive baptism of the sword. Sainapat, *Sri Gursobha*, Chapter V, p. 30.

The Sikhs responded by gathering in very large number at Anandpur[1] on the day of the festival (March 29). Guru Gobind Singh rose early and sat in meditation. He then appeared before the *Sangat* who hailed him with shouts of greetings. Bhai Mani Singh gave exposition of a hymn from the Holy Book. Guru Gobind Singh then stood before the assembly with his sword unsheathed and spoke : "Is there anyone here who would lay down his life for his 'Guru' and *Dharma*. It was an amazing call and no wonder his words struck consternation among the gathering. They did not know what the Guru meant and gazed in awed silence until he spoke again. Now confusion turned into fear. For the third time, Guru Gobind Singh repeated his call. Daya Ram, a Sobti Khatri of Lahore rose and said with humility, "My head is at Thy disposal, my true Lord. There would be no greater gain than dying under thy sword." He walked by the Guru to an especially improvised enclosure close by. The Guru returned with his sword dripping blood and waving it to the multitude asked for another head. This was more than anyone could endure. People started leaving the place hurriedly. Some of them rushed to complain to the Guru's mother. But when the Guru had made a third call, Dharm Dass, a Jat from Hastinapur came forward to sacrifice himself for the Guru. He too was taken to the enclosure. In the same way the Guru made three more calls. Mohkam Chand a calico printer of Dwarka, Himmat, a cook of Jagannath Puri and Sahib Chand a barber of Bidar cheerfully responded one after the other and stepped forward to offer their heads.

A while after, the Guru led the five Sikhs back from the enclosure into which he had taken them one by one. In the enclosure confidentially guarded, he had kept sets of apparels especially designed and made. Decked in saffron-coloured gorgeous toprobes with neatly tied turbans of the same colour, the glorious five walked deferentially behind their master overwhelmed with thankfulness. The Guru, himself, was attired in the same manner as his chosen disciples. The gathering considerably thinned and still in shocked muteness

1. M.A. Macauliffe, *The Sikh Religion* Vol. V, p. 91.

was puzzled further to see those whom they had thought to have been sacrificed to the Guru's sword, yet remain in flesh and blood.[1]

The Guru introduced these five to the audience as *Panj Piare*[2], "the five devoted spirits beloved of the Guru." He expressed his deep sense of gratitude for the culmination of Guru Nanak's revelation. He said that the five beloved had blessed themselves and brought glory to their faith. The Guru added that they (A Khatri, and four so-called low castes) would form the nucleus of the *Order of the Khalsa*, God's own, that he was going to inaugurate.

Then the Guru proceeded to initiate them to his new Order by a new method. The method of initiation into the Sikh fold which Guru Nanak had introduced and which had hitherto been current in Sikhism was *Charan Pahul* according to which the neophytes were served a handful of water which had been touched by the Guru's toe. During Guru Arjan Dev, this initiation rite underwent a little change. The water was not touched by the toe, but simply placed under the cot of the Guru. Evidently the idea behind the rite was to develop the sense of surrender and humility. But in the context of the changed situation this idea alone was not sufficient. Accordingly the Guru introduced another method of initiation. The Guru took water in an iron bowl, stirred it with *Khanda* a two-edged sword to the recitation of five compositions[3] : *Japji, Jaap Sahib, Sudha Sawayyas, Chaupai* and *Anand Sahib*. Revered Jito ji, wife of the Guru did not relish that the five Sikhs who had offered their heads to the Guru should be given plain water. She immediately brought a plate full of sugar puffs (*patasas* in Punjabi language) and with the approval of the Guru put them into the water. This was considered propitiatory in the sense that the initiates would henceforth be blessed with the grace

1. Harbans Singh, *The Heritage of the Sikhs*, p. 84.
2. The episode of the *Panj Pyaras*, their names and details of the preperation of *Amrit* have been recorded in *Gurbilas* literature associated with Guru Gobind Singh. See Koer Singh, *Gurbilas Patshahi Das* (1751 C.E.) (ed.) Shamsher Singh Ashok, pp. 127-139. Sukha Singh, *Gurbilas Padshai Das* (1797 A.D. pp. 90-92, personal library of Trilochan Singh).
3. *Jap(u) Ji* was composed by Guru Nanak, *Anand* by Guru Amar Dass, *Jaap, Sawayyas* and *Chaupai* by Guru Gobind Singh.

of feminine sweetness. *Amrit*, the divine nectar of Immortality, was now ready.

The nectar thus prepared was administered to all the five beloveds from the same bowl to signify their initiation into the casteless fraternity of the *Khalsa*. They sat *Bir Asan*, i.e. in the heroic posture with the left knee up and the right knee on the ground and the body weight resting on the right heel. The Guru then gave them each five palmful of *Amrit* to drink. He sprinkled it five times each on their hair, their face, and their eyes each time repeating loudly *Waheguru Ji Ka Khalsa, Waheguru Ji Ki Fateh*. Lastly, all five of them were given the steel bowl to quaff from it one by one the remaining *Amrit* in token of having become brothers. The most striking thing in the process of the preparation of *Amrit* was the substitution of the two-edged sword in place of the Guru's toe. This thing heralded a new theme that henceforth the *Khalsa* would follow the ideal of self-assertion and self-reliance alongwith the ideal of humility and self-surrender. The baptism symbolised a rebirth by which the initiated were considered as having renounced their previous occupation, *Kirt Nash*—for serving the cause of righteousness, their caste ties—*Kul Nash*—to become the family of Guru Gobind Singh and their earlier creed—*Dharam Nash* for the creed of the *Khalsa*, all rituals—*Karam Nash*—to feel unencumbered to tread the path shown by the Guru. The moment marked their complete break with their past. The baptised males and females were enjoined to affix 'Singh' (Lion) and 'Kaur' (Princess) respectively as suffix with their names.

The baptism by the double-edged sword introduced on the day of the creation of the *Khalsa* required the initiates to live a virtuous life of morally responsible actions under the discipline and code especially prescribed for them. For outward recognition, the Guru asked them to keep long hair (*kesh*) and never to cut or pluck them. In order to avoid them giving a disheveled look, the long hair on the head must be tied into a knot/bun on top of the head. Guru's love for hair was so profound that he had cautioned the initiates never ever to harm hair on any part of the body, a *Kangra* (comb) to be kept in the hair knot in order to keep them unentangled, an iron *Kara* (bracelet) on the wrist of one's master hand, a *Kirpan* (a sword) on his person and *Kachha*—a pair of short breeches. These five K's *(Kesh, Kangha, Kara, Kirpan, Kachha)* are not mere external symbols.[1] A single and pervasive leitmotif is discernable in these marks of investiture on the personality of a baptised Sikh (Singh), and this can be characterised as a sense of preparedness to uphold the ideals which the Guru had pinpointed. These symbols the decision for which was announced more through profound deliberations upon the fragile moral complexities besetting human beings than through any mystically intuited wisdom gave the Sikhs their form and identity; and are symbolic of their conduct. The long unshorn hair besides being a symbol of manliness are also symbolic of the higher state of consciousness of the wearer. The hair which the Sikhs maintain as a command of their Guru are also believed to imprint on the wearer, the investiture of spirituality, even of godliness. In Sikh scriputre, an epithet used for God is *Kesva* i.e. who wears long tresses. Let it be stressed here that God of Sikh perception is formless and it is personified only when the attributes with which He is remembered are to be explained. It is against this background that Professor Puran Singh calls hair 'a dear remembrance, an hairloom, a trust, a pledge, a love, a vow, an inspiration. Guru Gobind Singh in one of his *Hukamnamas* calls hair as the seal of Guru.

Kara was necessarily made of iron and of no other metal. The Guru called Supreme Reality as *Sarb-Loh*—All Iron. *Kara* therefore, is a constant reminder to the baptised Sikhs never to lose sight of this attribute of God as well. It had another symbolic significance. Its circular form signifies perfection. A circle is also said to represent *Dharma*. Thus *Kara* to a member of the *Khalsa* brotherhood represents a just, perfect and righteous life marked by self-discipline and self-control.

---

1. *Nishān-i-Sikhī īṅ Paṅj Harfe kāf.*
   Hargiz Nabāshid azīṅ Paṅj muāf.
   Karā Kārdo Kachh Kaṅghā bidāṅ.
   Bilā Kes Hech Ast Jumlā Nishāṅ.
   (These five letters of 'K' are emblems of Sikhism. These five are most incumbent and are steel bangle, big knife, shorts and comb with unshorn hair. Without unshorn hair, all others are of no significance).

According to Dr. Hari Ram Gupta, *Kara* was a permanent substitute of *Rakhri*, a thread tied by sisters on the wrists of brothers reminding them of their duty to keep and protect them. Similarly the *Kara* served as a reminder to the Sikhs that they had promised to be true to the Guru and the *Panth* and that promise must be kept at all costs." Another significance attached to it is a constant reminder to the Sikhs that they are not to lay their faith on any other god or goddess except the Almighty Formless One.

Kirpan is a synthesis of two words *Kirpa* (mercy or kindness) and *Aan* (honour) which signify and highlight the purpose for which it is to be used. In Sikh religious parlance the word conveys two dimensional meanings.' One, sword (*Bhagauti*) is an attributive name of the Real One in the composition of Guru Gobind Singh. Thus the wearer feels that he is ever under the protection of *Bhagauti*. Second, and which is in fact a derivative of the first, it symbolises manifestation of *Shakti* or divine power, which is to be used for protection of the saints against the demonic powers as a last resort when all other means fail to make necessary impact.

The sword was never a weapon of aggression and it was never used for self-aggrandisement. It stands for righteousness and brave action for the protection of truth and virtue.[1] In *Akal Ustat*, the Guru addressed Timeless as All-Steel. At the opening of *Bachittar Natak* the sword is addressed as a synonym for the Timeless being.

> *Namaskar Sri Kharag Ko*
> *Karon Su Hita Chit Lai*
> [Honour to the Holy sword
> I bow to it with love and devotion]

It is also conceived as God's generative function :

> *Khanda Prathmi Manai Kai*
> *Jin Sabh Sansar Upaia*[2]
> [After the primal manifestation of the sword,
> the universe was created.]

This sword was considered as synonym of God Primal

---

1. Harbans Singh, *The Heritage of the Sikhs.*
2. "Var Durga ki", *Shabdarth Sri Dasam Granth Sahib*, Vol. I, p. 174.

generative Principle, supreme power to sustain moral order and to annihilate negative forces. In this way, the Guru conveyed to the *Khalsa*, as an individual as well as a corporate body that they, as wielders of sword should cast themselves in the mould of God, Creator, Sustainer, Protector and Annihililator of negative forces.

The Sikhs stress on physical or bodily cleanliness along with inner purity warrants that their hair should be kept tidy and untangled unlike *Sanyasis*. Obivously comb is the easiest means to realise the objective. Comb also beckons cleanliness of mind and purging of body of evil thoughts. Unlike a dagger, which is associated with secret attack or hidden defence, the sword is associated with open combat, goverened by certain ethical principles. Thus sword of the *Khalsa*, male or female, is the assertion of his right to freedom. To quote Kapur Singh[1] "(The Sword) is by ancient tradition and association, is a typical weapon of offence and defence and hence a fundamental right to wear, of the free man (and woman), a sovereign individual. All governments and rulers whether ancient or modern have and do insist on wearing arms. Indeed in final analysis, a government or the state is sustained and supported by the organised might and exclusive right of possession of arms. A citizen's right to wear arms being conceded as only of a permissive and licensed character. It follows from this that the measure of freedom to possess and wear arms by an individual is the precise measure of his freedom and sovereignty. Since a member of the *Khalsa* brotherhood (and motherhood) is pledged not to accept any alien restrictions on his (or her) civic freedom he/she is enjoined upon to insist on struggle for his (or her) unrestricted right to wear and possess arms of offence and defence."

The last of the K's is the *Kachhaira* or *Kachha* a pair of breeches whose length must not come below the knee of the wearer. It is held to symbolise sexual restraint serving as a deterrent against extra marital relations and upholding the ideal of moral purity. It is also a garment which was well-suited to the eighteenth century *Khalsa*, allowing for their prowess as horsemen and as wielders of the sword.

---

1. Kapur Singh, *Parasharprasna*, or *Baisakhi of Guru Gobind Singh*, pp. 139-148.

The ceremonies that surrounded the event of the creation of the *Khalsa* are conspicuous of the absence of any mythic element. The Guru did not invoke any god or goddess of the Hindu pantheon, rather he tried to keep the entire ceremony human. He did so with the obvious aim of raising the human ingredients involved in the ceremony to the Divine level. According to Guru Gobind Singh, this can possibly be done not through the intervention of any deity but only through exalting and consecrating the human beings to be pure in thoughts and deeds. If at all any mythological element is involved, it is demythologizing the myth of churning of the ocean by gods and demons with a view to extract *Amrit* (Nectar) out of it. Guru prepared *Amrit* from pure clean water taken in a steel vessel and stirred it by a double-edged sword *(Khanda)*. *Patasas* or sugar puffs were added to it. Initially Guru Gobind Singh prepared the *Amrit* by constantly stirring the water with *Khanda* to the accompaniment of recitation of five *Banis (Jap ji, Jaap, Sawayyas, Chaupai* and *Anand)* and thereafter any five baptised Singhs *(Khalsa)* were declared elegible to perform this ceremony of preparing and partaking *Amrit*.

The five outward symbols taken together signified that the *Khalsa* both as individual and as a corporate body should be strong in body, mind and soul and develop an integrated personality. These symbols not only gave a manly bearing to the Sikhs, but a distinct identity too. These also made it impossible for them to conceal their identity in future as some Sikhs had done at Delhi at the time of Guru Tegh Bahadur's execution in November 1675.

Further, they gave the Sikhs a distinguished appearance, different both from the Hindus and the Muslims, the fact which imparted a semblance of unity, close botherhood, equality and group consciousness.

According to Dr. Hari Ram Gupta, "In those days Hindus of respectable families wore five ornaments : gold earrings, a necklace, gold or silver bangles, finger rings and a waist belt of gold or silver or a *Tragi*. The wearer felt proud of displaying his superior social position. At the same time, he saw the risk of losing these articles as well as his life in the bargain. Guru Gobind Singh provided to his followers, five jewels which were within reach of everybody down to the poor, peasant and the lowest labourer. Instead of creating fear in the mind of the wearer, his five jewels made his Singh bold, brave and awe-inspiring."[1]

To quote from a report of the proceedings, "Though several refused to accept Guru's religion, about twenty thousand men stood up and promised to obey him as they had the fullest faith in the divine message."[2] The novitiates came forward in batches to receive baptism. The first five among those who now volunteered were Ram Singh, Desa Singh, Tahal Singh, Ishar Singh and Fateh Singh. They were called *Panj Mukte* the five liberated ones by the Guru.[3] According to *Guru Kian Sakhian*, in the next row stood Mani Ram, Bachittar Das, Ude Rai, Anik Das, Ajaib Das, Ajaib Chand, Chaupat Rai, Diwan Dharam Chand, Alam Chand Nachna and Sahib Ram Koer followed by Rai Chand Multani, Gurbaksh Rai, Pandit Kirpa Ram Dutt of Mattan, Subeg Chand, Gurmukh Das, Samukh Das, Amrik Chand, Purohit Daya Ram, Barna, Ghani Das, Lal Chand Peshoria, Rup Chand, Sodhi Dip Chand, Nand Chand, Nanu Rai of Dilwali and Hazari, Bhandari and Darbari of Sirhind. Countless more batches came, each one more eager than the other. Anandpur was seized with an uncanny fervour of the spirit.[4]

According to one estimate as many as 80,000 men were baptised in a few days. The Guru called them the *Khalsa*, the pure and his very own ideal (*Isht Suhird*). The Guru also sent instructions that those who call themselves Sikhs should get themselves confirmed by receiving new baptism. The baptised Sikhs were termed as *Khalsa*.[5] In the pre-*Khalsa* period, the term *Khalsa* was restricted to such privileged Sikhs who were

---

1. Hari Ram Gupta, *History of the Sikhs*, Vol. I, pp. 274-75.
2. Harbans Singh, *The Heritage of the Sikhs*, p. 87.
3. Swarup Singh Kaushish, *Guru Kian Sakhian*, pp.120-125.
4. *Ibid.*
5. Ahmed Shah Batalia (*Tarikh-i-Hind*) and Ghulam Mohi-ud-din (*Tarikh-i-Punjab*) specifically mention twenty thousand persons accepting the new order, and in some of the modern works, the number given is 80,000. These computations appear to be no more than guess works. But it may be safely assumed that the number of persons present at Anandpur at that time ran into thousands and it was larger than the usual gathering on Baisakhi Days.

directly connected with or had access to the Gurus. In one sense, all the Sikhs were made *Khalsa*, the privileged ones directly connected with the Guru without any intermediary such as *Masands.*

In addition to the five symbols, the intitiated were to observe a difinite *Rehat* (code of conduct). They were not to cut any hair on any part of their body.[1] They were disallowed to smoke, chew tobacco or take alcoholic drinks.[2] They were not to eat the meat of an animal which had been slaughtered by being bled to death, as was customary with the Muslims. They were forbidden to have any sexual relationship with a person other than lawfully wedded spouse. They were to wear a turban and not a cap. The Guru enjoined upon the *Khalsa* to be strictly monogamous. Ragarding sexual matters, the Guru said that his father Guru Tegh Bahadur had given him these instructions which should serve as a guide to the Sikhs :

"O son, as long as there is life in the body, make this thy sacred duty ever to love thine own wife more and more. Approach not another woman's couch either by mistake or even in a dream. Know, that the love of another's wife is a sharp dagger. Believe me death entereth the body by making love to another's wife. They who think it great cleverness to enjoy others wife, shall in the end, die the death of a dog." Again the Guru declared :

> Never enjoy, even in dream, the bed of a woman other than your own wife.[3]

The most remarkable episode in this connection happened when the Guru having administered *Amrit* to the five Sikhs stood up in supplication and with folded-hands begged them to baptise him in the manner as he had baptised them in order to enable him enter the *Khalsa* brotherhood. They were amazed

---

1. Sainapat, *Sri Gursobha,* Chapter VI, 1/197.
2. M.A. Macauliffe, *The Sikh Religion,* Vol. V, p. 153. "The Guru said 'wine is bad, *bhang* destroyeth one generation but tobacco destroyeth all generations.' " Santokh Singh says that the tabacco leaf resembles the ear of a cow and so the Guru prohibited their use. (*Suraj Parkash,* 557).
3. M.A. Macauliffe, *op.cit.,* Vol. V, p. 110.
   Par nāri kī sej
   Bhūl supne hūñ na jaīyo

at such a strange request, but he silenced them saying that he too wanted to be one of them. As he was their Guru, they collectively would be his Guru. The 'five beloved' initiated the Guru to the order of the *Khalsa* according to the new rites. After this, there remained no difference between the baptised Sikhs and the Guru. They were to be his *Khalsa,* body of his body and soul of his soul, nay his otherself, his beloved ideal (*suhird*). The Guru thus merged himself in the *Khalsa* and the whole body of the *Khalsa* was invested with the dignity of Guruship. Henceforth a convention was established that five chosen/ selected Sikhs could represent the *Khalsa*. The Guru also sent instructions that those who called themselves Sikhs should get themselves confirmed by receiving the new baptism. The baptised Sikhs were termed as the *Khalsa*.[1]

The term was not without a precedence. In the pre-*Khalsa* period, the term *Khalsa* was restricted to such privileged Sikhs who were virtually directly connected with the Gurus and whose subordination to the *Masands* was simply dejure. "The word *Khalsa* in the sense of the privileged Sikhs occurs in a *Hukamnama* (fiat) issued by Guru Hargobind and also in the one issued by Guru Tegh Bahadur."[2] But with Guru Gobind Singh anyone who is baptised by the new method and abides by the instructions of the Guru was a member of the *Khalsa* brotherhood.

Apart from wearing five symbols and observing code of conduct, the Sikhs were expected not to pay homage to any external object except the *Granth,* not to recognise caste

1. The exact import of the term *Khalsa* provides an interesting study. Dr. Ernest Trumpp, the author of *Adi Granth* (1877) holds that it is an Arabic term meaning personal estate. The baptised Sikhs were the personal estate of the Guru. Cunningham writes that *Khalsa* or *Khalisa* is an Arabic derivation and has such original or secondary meaning as pure special five and Co. In the revenue records of the Sultan and the Mughals, *Khalsa* denoted the land as directly held by the crown as distinguished from the land held by the tributary Chiefs. The *Khalsa* denotes either the Kingdom of the Guru or that the Sikhs are pure chosen people. The Guru called his baptised Sikhs, the *Khalsa* because they constituted the valued property of the Guru. They were not his paid soldiers but were a body of volunteers who were ever prepared to shed their blood for him.
2. The photostat copies appear in *Hukamnamas* ed. by Dr. Ganda Singh on serial Nos. 5 and 8.

prejudices, superstitions, empty rituals, esoteric and ascetic practices. They were to have faith that the Guru was always present in the general body of the *Khalsa* and that wherever even five staunch Sikhs would assemble, the Guru is deemed to be present there. They were free to establish marriage relationship among themselves without any caste considerations. They were not to entertain any gender complex and were morally be and to consider women equal to men.

But they were not to have any social or matrimonial relations with smokers,[1] with persons who shaved their heads,[2] with those who killed their daughters as soon as they were born and with the descendants or followers of Prithi Chand, Dhirmal, Ram Rai and those *Masands*[3] who had fallen away from the tenets and principles of Guru Nanak. They were not to worship idols, cemeteries or cremation grounds.[4] They were to rise at dawn, bathe and recite *Gurbani* as enshrined in *Sri Guru Granth Sahib*. They must have faith in the singularity and unity of God.

According to a News-writer of the period, the Guru is reported to have said, "I wish you all to embrace one creed and obliterate differences of religion. Let the four Hindu castes who have different rules for each sect abandon them.[5] The Sikhs were to live a truthful life and would never allow his attention to be deviated from Immortal God. The Guru, in fact, recommended an unqualified worship of one True Lord, as it was set out by him in his *Jap, Akal Ustat* and other compositions. All beliefs, rituals or ceremonies that implied the recognition of anything but the one True Lord were categorically rejected as is evident from the following *Swayya* in which a direct reference is made to the *Khalsa*[6], his duties and beliefs :

1. Sainapat, *Sri Gursobha*, p. 31.

2. *Ibid.*

3. *Ibid.*, p. 36.

4. Bhai Nand Lal, *Rahitnama. Gor Marhī Mat Bhūl Na Jāwe* (worship not even by mistake a tomb or a relic of cremation) (Guru Gobind Singh, *Swayyas*).

5. The above address is based on the report of a news-writer sent to the Mughal court as it is vouched by the Persian Historian Ghulam Mohi-ud-din (Teja Singh & Ganda Singh, *A Short History of the Sikhs*, p. 68)

6. For translation of the relevant portions of Guru Gobind Singh's compositions, see *The Sikh Religion*, Vol. V, pp. 261-263, 306-310.

'He who repeateth night and day the name of Him
Whose enduring light is unquenchable,
Who bestoweth not a thought on any but the one God
Who hath full love and confidence in God
Who putteth not faith even by mistake in
     fasting, or worshipping cemeteries, places of
     cremation, or *Jogis* places of sepulchre
Who only recogniseth the one God and no
     pilgrimages, alms, the non-destruction of life,
Hindu penances or austerities;
And in those hearts the light of the perfect
One shineth, he is recoginsed as a pure member
     of the *Khalsa*."

SIGNIFICANCE

The creation of the new order of the *Khalsa* had manifold ramifications. It caused a great stir in the body-social of the Sikhs. Some embraced the order of the *Khalsa*, others reacted despondently. Some of the Sikhs felt cautioned against accepting the new order till written orders from the Guru were received. Some others remarked that the code was extremely tough to abide by and also incompatible with our family traditions and customs. Many explained that the code was creation of the preceptors themselves. The situation at some place led to dissensions[1] among the Sikhs while at others it resulted in tension between the Sikhs and the non-Sikhs. *Khatries* and Brahmins, by and large, remained aloof. Some of them even professed that they had faith in the religion of Guru Nanak and other Gurus; but many out of them refused to renounce the teachings of the *Vedas* and *Shastras*. They had been quite willing to pay lip service to the ideal of a casteless society; but they loathed to embroil themselves to the task of the new order with the result that many of them reverted to Brahmanism. Some just remained Sikhs, better known today as *Sahjdhari* and very few of them entered the order of the *Khalsa*.

Sainapat, a poet in the court of the tenth Master mentions two events which amply depict the attitude of certain Sikhs. One concerns a *Khatri* who openly spoke against the new order of the Guru in a congregation at Delhi. The congregation

---

1. Sainapat, *Sri Gursobha*, Chapter VII.

turned him out. He then rushed to his like-minded friend named Pritam. The Sikhs warned Pritam for siding with the discarded person. Pritam ignored the warning with impunity and convened a special conclave at Darapur where the Sikhs had gathered in a large number to enjoy a fair. Pritam and his associates prevailed upon the Sikhs to keep the matter of adopting the new order in abeyance till the receipt of written orders of the Guru. The dissentients did not stop at that. Some time later, they proclaimed at an assembly of the Sikhs arranged by them that there was nothing wrong in abiding by the religion of the ancestors and thus, they persuaded many to ignore the innovations enjoined by the Guru.[1] Meanwhile a Sikh passed away. His family members chose not to observe ceremonies of *Bhadan* (shaving off their heads). The matter evoked protests and caused a great commotion among those who did not like the divine covenant initiated by the Guru. They arranged boycott of the adherents of the new order of the *Khalsa*. Some of them occasioned a general strike in the main bazaar of Delhi to show their solidarity. Quite a number of them approached the local government officials to instigate them to take actions against such Sikhs who were determined to follow the path as chartered by Guru Gobind Singh. The government officials however, issued orders that the shops should remain open.[2]

Since the Guru had invested the *Khalsa* with status equal to his own and projected them as limb of his self, they became the most esteemed personnel and it was but logical that they assumed leadership of the Sikhs. Hitherto the leadership was in the hands of *Masands/Manjidars* or someone considered to be held in high esteem by local *Sangat* but now it passed on to the *Khalsa* self-sovereign and enjoying the status of the Guru himself. Expressed in ethnological term, the *Masands* or local leaders were mostly urban *Khatris* while the *Khalsa* consisted of the people bulk of whom were Jats and menial classes such as artisans and scavengers et al.

The *Khalsa* leadership, therefore, comprised of the latter mostly, who from the time of Manu had been denied any

---

1. Sainapat, *Sri Gursobha*, Chapter VII.
2. A literal translation of the Stanzas in *Sri Gurusobha* by Sainapat, Chapter VII.

respectable status in the caste based Hindu society. Since the *Khalsa* order repudiated castes and other distinctions on the bases of wealth, profession, culture, and creed etc., Jats and other socially neglected classes rejoiced and the *Khalsa* movement became synonymous with the rise of hitherto nelgected classes/groups/individuals.[1]

Ideologically, the *Khalsa* aimed at a balanced combination of the ideals of *Bhakti* and *Shakti* or to express it in the modern terminology the *Khalsa* was to be a brotherhood in faith and brotherhood in arms at one and the same time. The Guru's injunctions included, that the *Khalsa* should bear arms, *Kirpan* (Sword) being one and the most important of them, that they should use double-edged sword in the preparation of the *Amrit* and use of the appellation of Singh at the end of each name which signified the martial valour, the *Khalsa* was expected to inculcate. Sword became an object of reverence with the Sikhs, for it symbolised power and safety. The sentiment of the Sikhs for the Sword was so much that God was given the name of 'All Steel' by the Guru. This being so, those who worshipped sword promised exemptions from every other kind of religious rites or ceremonies and he was to be regarded as the *Khalsa* who combats in the van, who mounts on the war horse, who is ever waging war and who is perpetually armed.[2]

The Guru himself says :

> I am the son of a brave man, not of a Brahmin
> How can I perform austerities ?
> How can I turn My attention to thee,
> O Lord, and forsake of domestic affairs ?
> Now be pleased to grant me the boon
> I crave with clasped hands
> That when the end of my life cometh,
> I may die fighting in a mighty battle.[3]   *(Krishna Avtar)*

---

1. Koer Singh understands that the rise of the Jat power was the direct result of the creation of the *Khalsa*. A close study of the Chapter IX of *Gur Bilas* makes it abundantly clear that the lower classes felt a sense of pride to join the new order and in a way, they found in it the augury of new era for themselves.

2. J.D. Cunningham, *History of the Sikhs*, pp. 375-76.

3. M.A. Macauliffe, *The Sikh Religion*, Vol. V, p. 312.

As is evident from the writings of the Guru in connection with the *Khalsa,* the soldierly qualities were given place of eminence. In fact militarism was adopted as an article of faith. The Guru says :

> All steel, I am thy slave
> Deeming me, thy own, preserve me;
> Think of mine honour, whose arm thou has taken,
> Deeming me thine own, cherish me
> Single out and destroy mine enemies
> May both my kitchen and my sword
> prevail in the world.[1]

The Guru's primary concern was thus with his *Degh* (Kitchen) and his *Tegh* (Sword), the one as the symbol of service to assist the weak, the helpless and the oppressed and the other the emblem of power to extirpate the tyrants, and the *Khalsa* was the instrument that he created to achieve his two-fold purpose.[2]

All this, coupled with the new awareness of social egalitarianism had a miraculous effect on the psyche of Guru's disciples. Teja Singh and Dr. Ganda Singh have observed that; 'Even those people who had been considered dregs of humanity were changed, as if by magic into something rich and strange. The sweepers, the barbers, and confectioners who had not even touched a sword and whose whole generations had lived as grovelling slaves of the so-called higher classes became under the stimulating leadership of Guru Gobind Singh doughty warriors who never shrank from fear and who were ready to rush into the jaws of death at the bidding of the Guru.'[3] According to Gordon, 'the dry bones of an oppressed peasantry were stirred into life, and the institution of the Sikh baptismal rite at the hands of a few disciples anywhere in a place of worship, in a house or by the roadside brought about the more full and wide spread development of the new faith. In this way, within a few months, new people were born, bearded and beturbaned, fully armed and with a crusaders' zeal to build a new common-wealth. They implicitly believed

1. M.A. Macauliffe, *The Sikh Religion*, Vol. V, p. 311.
2. Indubhushan Banerjee, *Evolution of the Khalsa*, p. 118.
3. Teja Singh & Ganda Singh, *A Short History of the Sikhs*, p. 68.

that 'the *Khalsa* shall rule, their enemies will be scattered, only those that seek refuge will be saved.'

From sociological point of view, the *Khalsa* represented a new mozaic where tribal or caste affiliations had no room, nor were the superstitions, demeaning ceremonies and empty rituals given any accredition status. On the other hand, it stood for broad outlook transcending parochial prejudices. Even the differences on the basis of religion were considered irrelevant or the creations either of the ignorance or of opaque understanding. This impression emerges exactly when the Guru dinned into the ears of his disciples that the four sects of the Hindus, the Brahmins, Kashatryas, Vaish and Sudras, would like *Pan patta* (Beetleleaf), *Chuna* (Lime), *Supari* (Beetle-nut) and *Katha* become of one colour[1] when well-chewed. The *Khalsa* stood for righteousness, social equality, faith in *Nirgun* God, honest labour, and division of its fruit and repudiation of all types of exploitation. Evidently, this type of social pattern was more fit for arousing the dormant energies of the people and making them flow into the channel which fed the national stream of the country.

The emergence of the *Khalsa* was significant from another respect also. It generated among the people the longing for social freedom and ascendancy. Evidently, this pattern of society was more congenial for the dormant energies to awaken with the result that the new confidence and new aspirations began to articulate the people, admittedly the precondition for progress. Moreover, as the accent of the programme of the *Khalsa* was to transcend the artificial barriers on the basis of caste, creed, race and region, the field was prepared for the sapling of Nationalism and Universalism to take roots.

Moreover, the *Khalsa* marked the culmination of a Sikh-Guru relationship. Guru Gobind Singh expressed his feelings about the *Khalsa* in one of his *Sawayyas* popularly known as *Khalse di Mehma shabad* in which his appreciation for them is juxtaposed with his decision to do his best for them.[2]

---

1. Sir John Malcolm, *Sketch of the Sikhs*, p. 45.
2. D.P. Ashta, *The Poetry of Dasam Granth*, p. 146.
   Trilochan Singh, *Guru Gobind Singh (A brief life Sketch)*, Delhi, 1964, pp. 20-21. Trilochan Singh (and others). *The Sacred Writings of the Sikhs*, London, 1960, p. 272.

All the battles I have won against tyranny
I have fought with the devoted backing of these people
Through them only have I been able to bestow gifts
By their kindness, the store houses have been filled
I owe my education to them
By their kindness were the enemies killed
I owe my glorious existence to them
Otherwise ordinary men like me are found in millions
Service to them is pleasing to me
I do not enjoy serving any other people
Giving gifts to them is meritorious
Gifts to them prove fruitful in the next life.
Praiseworthy is this, all other gifts are futile,
My wealth my body, my soul my head,
All that is in my house is dedicated to them.

This consideration of the Guru for his creation, the *Khalsa*, should not be interpreted as a personal affair. It should be interpreted in terms of the mission of the Guru. Just as the Guru according to his own belief was the chosen instrument of God for restraining men from senseless acts[1] so his Sikhs of the *Khalsa* order were the willing agents for working out that mission. Thus the *Khalsa* was the body of mankind always at war for destroying the evil and protecting righteousness.

In addition to it, the *Khalsa* marked the completion of the evolution of the Sikh *Sangat*. In the begininig *Sangat* was merely a religious gathering of devotees functioning more or less in isolation as a body. Gradually, an increase in its functions occurred and the isolation of one from another was loosened by the forging of common links, such as the preparation of scriptures, the building up of certain religious centres, institutions of *Manjis* and *Masands* as the agencies of the central leadership and assertion of the principle of the supremacy of the Guru. With the creation of the *Khalsa* the network of semi-integrated *Sangat* was fully integrated. The investing of the *Khalsa* with supreme powers later on marked the completion of the historical process long underway. The *Khalsa Sangat* became sacrosanct because of the authority which they could now legitimately claim to have. The *Khalsa Sangat* as a collective body thus appeared to be equated with

1. S.S. Bal & J.S. Grewal, *Guru Gobind Singh*, p. 124.

the Guru himself. Through the Guru, the *Khalsa* belonged to God. (*Waheguru Ji Ka Khalsa*).

Besides this, the *Khalsa* symbolized determination to complete the social and religious revolution initiated by Guru Nanak. The successors of Guru Nanak had guided this revolution with great devotion and dexterity. Yet some lapses were conspicuously visible at the time of Guru Gobind Singh's accession. The creation of the *Khalsa* was not merely an endeavour to integrate the members of his community, it was also a powerful bid for the culmination of the mission set in motion by his predecessors in the field of social and religious life. The code of conduct prescribed for the newly created *Khalsa* was so devised as to impose a strict discipline on the Sikhs to ensure firm adherence and commitment on their part to the lofty ideals of Sikhism.

Still, from another point of view, the *Khalsa* order was significant. It marked the period of important beginnings. By the Guru's reforms, the Sikh community was not only strengthened but also converted into a great vehicle of revolution. New awareness dawned upon the Sikhs. They discovered that there was no dichotomy between man and God as man emanated from God Himself. They discarded age-old wrong notions about Reality (God) and his creations including this world. They realised that contemporary social and political constructs did not conform to the theological vision of God as experienced by the Guru, and its social reflections. As a result, they addressed themselves to build thinking-action praxis in the light of the Guru's personal examples and their utterances. The process was sure to introduce significant changes in all aspects of the society.

Taking cue from the inevitable, the forces championing status quo rallied to crush the *Khalsa*. Consequently the *Khalsa* had to launch a titanic struggle first against the Mughals and then against the Afghans who ruled over Punjab, the territory where the overwhelming majority of the Sikhs lived. The struggle continued till the *Khalsa* emancipated the land and established their sovereignty in 1765 after the conquest of Sirhind. A new form of polity replaced the old one and the concept of kingship changed as also the nature of bureaucracy.

Henceforth the king would not be an absolutist monist, rather first among the equals, dedicated to exercise the sovereignty of God as his faithful agent, always caring his creations, seen and unseen, without any discrimination. This was the reason that during the *Khalsa* rule, the welfare and protection of the people were always at the centre stage. In social sphere too, the Sikhs tried to make radical changes. They always denounced casteist approach. Other approaches which smacked of religious/social particularism were also discarded. The *Khalsa* always put premium on harmony based on recognition of the Divine in everyone. As a consequence of all this, the differences on bases of caste and creed et al in the eighteenth century were relegated to the background or ceased to be influential factors in the territories ruled by the *Khalsa*.

With the creation of *Khalsa*, a few new doctrinal developments took place. One, the *Khalsa* was united directly with the Guru since Guru in Sikhism had been equated with the Real one the *Akal Purakh* Himself. The dissolution of the institution of *Masand*, and then of personal guruship signified that the *Khalsa* was as much of the Guru as of God. The Sikh salutation, *Waheguru Ji Ka Khalsa, Waheguru Ji Ki Fateh*—literally means that the *Khalsa* belongs to the Lord (*Waheguru*) and the *Khalsa* exploits were in reality God's victories. Second, the *Khalsa* as a corporate body was equalitarian *inter se*, as well as in terms of relation to the Guru himself. In 1699, Guru Gobind Singh first administered baptism to the select five and then himself received baptism from them. By doing so he underscored the point that there was complete identification between the Guru and the *Khalsa*. The fact has been very clearly brought out in *Sarab Loh Granth* (a volume attributed to Guru Gobind Singh) as well as in a *Var* by Bhai Gurdas Singh who overwhelmed by a sense of wonderment exclaimed, "Let all of us hail and greet Guru Gobind Singh who was Guru and Disciple at one and the same time."[1] The *Khalsa* therefore, being the image of Guru and God, became the body of spiritually and socially realised individuals committed and dedicated to the 'Word' as enshrined in *Sri Guru Granth Sahib*;

---

1. *Wāh(u) Wāh(u) Gobind Singh, āpe gur(u) chelā.*

the *Jyoti* or spirit of the ten Gurus as also to work for the uplift the mankind as a whole and was apotheosised as Guru in 1708. The latter point has been repeatedly emphasised by Guru Gobind Singh and his predecessors.

Since the constituents of the *Khalsa Panth* are realised selves, they realise the essential unity of mankind, and it is only the foolish (Those who suffer from duality), who overlook the inner unity and wrangle over the outward differences.

Another doctrinal development was the concept of true democracy whose constitution was built not on law books but on the laws of love, truth and justice. In this constitution, the people inspired by the natural goodness of humanity, the spontaneous benediction of God and the Guru's mystic presence in all beings were made supreme. Its directive principle was the Principle of Happiness of all. A vital responsibility of the *Khalsa* was the maintenence of ethical values. However, the *Khalsa* democracy is different from the modern political democracy at least on two counts. One, the latter is essentially numerical or quantitative whereas the democracy of Guru Gobind Singh's vision is qualitative through his realised persons (*Khalsa*) who in turn get the job done through their representatives selected unanimously.

CHAPTER VIII

ALLEGED WORSHIP OF GODDESS DURGA

The *Order of Khalsa* was inaugurated by Guru Gobind Singh in 1699. It is believed by some scholars that before initiating the Order, the Guru invoked goddess Durga to bless him. Of all the scholars bearing such views, McLeod's remarks are the most striking because of their peculiarity. He states :

"Shivalik Hills have long been a stronghold of the *Devi* or *Shakti* cult..... The result of prolonged residence within the Shivaliks was, that elements of the hill culture eventually penetrated the Jat culture of the plains and introduced yet another stage in the evolution of the *Panth*.[1]

"In his (Guru's) writings and in those which were produced at his court, we find constant reference to the mighty exploits of the Mother Goddess, one of the most notable being his own *Chandi Di Var*.[2]

He then hastens to add another work of *Chandi Chritar* (Satasaya) from *Markandeya Puran* to the list and ends with the explication that as a result of the fusion of the two cultures, a new and powerful synthesis took shape; one which prepared the *Panth* for determinative role in the chaotic circumstances of the eighteenth century."[3]

The remarks of McLeod can be split into three parts for purpose of analysis and understanding.

    i) That the Guru had full faith in *Shakti* cult.

    ii) That the influences of Hill culture which in his

---

1. W.H. McLeod, *The Evolution of the Sikh Community*, p. 13.
2. *Ibid.*
3. *Ibid.*

perception was predominantly *Shakti* culture was so prevading that it influenced and permeated the Sikh culture which in his opinion was a Jat culture, pre-eminently.

iii) Jat culture and Hill culture when interacted with each other, a new synthesis came into being which unleashed powerful forces which helped the Sikhs to tide over difficulties that came their way in the eighteenth century.

McLeod's remarks or for that matter those of the scholars of his ilk are frivolous. Religiously, empirically and ideologically, these cannot be justified.

The *Shakti* cult in different forms had been prevalent in India, especially in its North-Western region since the ancient times. The worship of Mother Goddess was probably widely practised in the Indus Valley region. During the Aryan period doubtlessly, male Gods were predominant, but the traces of *Devi* cult can be found in Vedic literature. In this connection references can be gleaned in ample from different texts of Aryans. For instance *Dehi Sukta* in *Rig Veda* which provided the basis for the cult of *Chandi* in *Markandeya Puran* as also to a *Sukta* in the *Atharveda* (VI, 38) in which *Devi* was worshipped as immanent in the entire creation. As Aryan settlements spread in different parts of India, the concept of *Shakti* received wider acceptance and assumed subtle ramifications. According to A.C. Bannerjee, "It developed in some of the *Upnishads* and *Purans* and particularly in the *Tantras*."[1] In the North-West, the *Shakti* cult found a prominent place in the Kashmir *Saivism* as also in the philosophy of Gorakh Nath which inspired the Yogis.

Although the Yogis were primarily devotees of Siva, they were subject to strong *Tantric* influence. The *Aee-Panthis* mentioned in the *Japji* (Canto-XXVIII) as also in a contemporary work *Dabistan-i-Mazahib*, worshipped a female disciple of Gorakh Nath named Bimla Devi who was called Mai, later on corrupted into *Aee*.

In the Hill region of the Punjab where Hinduism in its most archaic form existed, the people were worshippers of Devi or Mother goddess. In Kangra alone, there were numerous local

1. A.C. Banerjee, *The Sikh Gurus and the Sikh Religion*, p. 300.

Devis (goddesses) and 360 of them were assembled together at the founding of the Kangra temple.[1] Guru Nanak's teachings had no scope for recognition of any deity-male or female. Except the Transcendental Being who is one and the only one, Formless, Inifinite, Self-existent, All effulgence, Sole Creator of all the creations of this world or of yonder Guru Nanak recognised no one else. He is Immanent in the sense that all creations emanated from Him. No part of His creation is autonomous in the sense that it is a unit apart from Transcendental Being. Everything is in control of God of Nanak. Goddess or any other deity did not have any separate entity not to speak of superiority to God of Nanak. Therefore Guru Nanak or for that matter other Gurus including Guru Gobind Singh and their disciples worshipped and obeyed God and not any deity, nor had Nanak or Guru Gobind Singh sought anything from any mortal, any god or goddess. But Guru Nanak had a direct encounter with God and had been commissioned by Him to spread *Nam* culture among people to improve upon their lot.[2]

There are no doubt references to *Tantric* philosophy and practices in *Gurbani* but these should not be interpreted as acceptance of traditional meanings. Instead these should be read as a part of the whole and explained with reference to the basic principles of the Sikh thought. For the founder of Sikhism, the ultimate stage of human experience in the spiritual world was *Sahaj* and it was not through mechanical *Tantric* practices that this blessed stage was to be reached. Not unoften two supporting statements are made to support that Guru Nanak had accepted the influence of *Tantrics* or *Shakti* cult. One of them relates to Canto XXX of *Jap Ji* : *Eka Mai Jugat Viai Tin Chele Parwan*. The second pertains to the following utterances of the Guru :

> *Khat(u) Mat(u) Dehi Man Bairagi*
> *Surat Sabd Dhun Antar Jagi.*[3]

There is no denying the fact that some terminology prevailing in *Tantric* cult has been used in various hymns

---

1. H.A. Rose, *Glossary of Tribes and Castes of the Punjab and the North West Frontier Province*, p. 318.
2. *Puratan Janam Sakhi.*
3. *SGGS*, p. 903.

composed by the Gurus as is evident from the preceding examples. Two explanations warrant serious considerations. Firstly; these terms were not used in the same meanings and connotations as used in *Tantric* cult. For example, *Mai* is not used in the sense of a creator, rather as an agent of God or as an instrument of a process ordained by Him. The exact translation of the Canto XXX rendered by Gurbachan Singh Talib, a famous exegist of Sikh scriptures is as follows :

"The universal Mother is what in Vedanta is known as *Maya*. She is progenitor of all, through the creative process ordained in the universe. This *Maya* generates not through union with God, but only through a 'process' ordained for her."

Likewise *Anhat Dhuni* et al. have no *Tantric* connotation. *Anhat Dhuni* in Sikh scripture means the experience of revelation when Light of God is revealed in the soul.[1]

In Sri Rag, Guru Nanak says :

"Throwing one's doubts aside when one meets the Guru, one hears the melodious *Anhad Shabad*. When one hears it, one's *Haumai* (egoism or pride) is destroyed."[2]

Secondly; some terms as used in *Tantric* sense were misleading to those who had not yet been able to get over the hang of their original faith. This was impinging on their psyche and causing confusion. Guru ji gave their meaning in consonance with the Sikh philosophy.

The attempt to associate Sikhism with *Tantra* becomes more pronounced in regard to Guru Gobind Singh. He has been described as a protagonist of *Shakti* cult whose interpretation of *Tantric* philosophy teaches man a new way of obtaining salvation through war. To appraise the Guru as such is to misinterpret or distort Guru's mission and approach. The *Shakti* cult has many elaborate rituals. Guru Gobind did not subscribe to that philosophy nor did he accept these rituals as necessary adjuncts of the spiritual discipline. He did not recognise pilgrimages, almsgiving, penances or austerities as legitimate means for spiritual elevation. In this perspective, the Guru cannot be described as a protagonist or a prophet of

---

1. Trilochan Singh, *Hymns of Guru Tegh Bahadur*, p. 37.
2. *SGGS*, p. 18.

Shakti cult. Nor did he enjoin a new mode of salvation through war. Salvation according to the Guru was full realisation of the unicity of God which is possible through proper discipline. War for Guru was never an end in itself rather a sacred duty in certain circumstances, the purpose being not to win salvation but elimination of injustice and oppression even by resorting to force, of course, as a last resort. The Guru uttered, "Whoever decides to abide in the *Khalsa* should not fear the clash of arms, be ever ready for the combat and the defence of his faith."[1] The emphasis on formless is in full conformity with the old Sikh Tradition. Guru Gobind Singh says :

"Take the broom of Divine knowledge in thy hand and sweep away the filth of timidity."[2] Timidity in Sikh ideology has been considered as a bar to spiritual advancement as also to the proper performance of temporal duties. In Guru Gobind Singh's scheme of regeneration, these two aspects of life are closely linked. The Guru prays to *Sarb Loh* (All Steel) "May both my Kitchen and my Sword prevail in this world." The Guru's cardinal concern was with the Kitchen and the Sword, the one, the emblem of service to the poor and helpless and the other, the emblem of power to resist and extirpate the tyrants.

Some writings of *Dasam Granth* such as *Chandi Charitar* and *Chandi Di Var* are often quoted in support of the thesis that the Guru had faith in goddess Durga. It is, however, naive to draw such conclusion on the basis of these works. In the first instance, these are translations from *Markandeya Puran* and can by no stretch suggest Guru's faith in *Devi* or *Avtars*. Secondly, the internal evidence shows that *Chandi Charitar* was written not for the exposition of Guru's faith, but to instill the sentiment of anger and courage. The author himself says, "*Chandi Charitar* has been rendered into *Bhakha* verse for the sole purpose of suffusing the moral rage and courage."[3] The entire personality of *Chandi* has been described in unique metaphors. The story of seven hundred *sloks* has been completed by the poet to show daring exploits. In the epilogue,

---

1. M.A. Macauliffe, *The Sikh Religion*, Vol. V, p. 223.
2. *Ibid.*, p. 167.
3. *Dasam Kathā Bhagaut kī Bhākhā Kar Banāe*
   Awar Bāsnā Nahī Prabh Dharam Yudh ke Chāe. (*Krishnu Avtar*)

the Guru thanked *Kirpa Sindh* (Ocean of Compassion) and not *Devi* for helping him in rendering the story of *Chandika* in *vars*. The Guru was categorical that reposing faith in gods, goddess including Durga, Brahma, Vishnu or Shiva was futile. Only faith in the singularity of God and endeavours in the light of His attributive will would uplift humankind at individual and social levels. He writes, "I do not at the outset propitiate Ganesh. I never meditate on Krishan and Vishnu. I have heard of them but I know them not. It is only God's feet I love.[1]

Chandi Di Var too was written not to worship goddess Durga but to show the ultimate triumph of righteousness over the evil forces.

From the above, it can be safely assumed that the Guru did not worship goddess Durga or had any faith in *Shakti* cult. Nor is it correct that synthesis of Jat culture and Hill culture helped the *Panth* to play a determinative role in its affairs in the eighteenth century; for, it is common knowledge that Jat culture and Hill culture had nothing intrinsically fine to offer, the former being non-existent as a separate entity, primitive and tribal, the latter being based on *Jati* and mired in feudal values and unmeaning superstitions.

But how did the story of *Devi* worship germinate and gain currency on such a large scale ? For a satisfactory answer to this question we will have to cast a glance over the historical literature.

The most important work in Sikh annals pertaining to the time of the tenth Master is *Sri Gursobha* by Sainapat, one of the court poet of Guru Gobind Singh. The work gives a detailed and realistic account of creation of the *Khalsa* on the Baisakhi day and other events of the life of the Guru. It does not make a mention of the worship of any goddess. Had it been a part of the event, Sainapat would not have missed it; rather he would have flashed it. McLeod, purposely or out of conviction, states that the work was not contemporary and he assigns 1711 A.D., as the date of its compilation. But he is wrong because

1. M.A. Macauliffe, *The Sikh Religion*, Vol. V, pp. 310-311. This excerpt is from 'Krishna Avtar' in *Dasam Granth*.

the date given in the manuscript is clearly 1701[1] which proves beyond any doubt that Sainapat was a contemporary and his was an eye wintness's account.

Apart from negative evidence of the complete absence of the story of *Devi* worship or *Hom*, Sainapat gives a positive statement indicating that "*Devi*, like other *Avtars* only indulged in egoist self-praise for her own worship and not that of God, the creator." At another place in *Sri Gursobha*, he avers, "Thousand like Dhruva, thousands like Vishnu, many like Rama, the kings, many goddesses, many Gorakhs offer their lives at his (Guru Gobind Singh's) feet." The Mughal newswriter reporting on the occasion of the *Khalsa* noted that the Guru urged his followers, "Not to adore incarnation such as Ram, Krishna, Brahma and Durga; but to believe in Guru Nanak and the other Sikh Gurus."

Sujan Rai who wrote his *Khulastut Twarikh* between 1695 and 1698 does not refer to any *Hom* in his account of Guru Gobind Singh. If the Guru had in any manner been connected with *Hom* even for demonstrating its futility, this writer would certainly have mentioned it.

Parchi Patshahi Dasvin Ki by Sewa Das Udasi (A.D. 1741/BK. 1798) and *Mahima Prakash (Vartak)* by Kirpal Dayal Singh (1798 BK/A.D. 1741) make a mention of *Hom* at the time of the initiation of *Khalsa* in a very casual way. For instance *Mahima Prakash (Vartak)* says :

"Once Guru called *Pandas* from Kashi, got the *Hom* done by them and initiated the *Khalsa Panth*."[2] The reference to *Hom* seems to suggest some sort of the ceremonial ritual in the nature of initial ceremony. It does not convey at all that the worship of goddess *Durga* was undertaken. Even the fact of the performance of the *Hom* as mentioned in the alluded works seemed to be more a fiction or imagination than a reality; for, firstly, the contemporary works are silent about it and secondly, it is too much, to expect that the Guru would

---

1. *Sammat Satrah Sai Bhai Barakh Aṭhāvan Bīt
   Bhādoṅ Sudī Paṅdras Bhaī Rachī Kathā Kar Prīt.
   (*Sri Gursobha*, Chapter 1, p. 10)

2. *Mahima Prakash (Vartak), Sakhi I*, as quoted by Bhai Vir Singh, *Devi Pujan Partal*, p. 55.

compromise on his principles for whose sake he had done so much and his father had courted martyrdom.

Among the chronicles, Koer Singh's *Gurbilas Patshahi 10,* gives the account of *Devi* worship. This work was completed in 1751 A.D. According to Koer Singh, the ritual to appease *Devi* was started in 1742 BK 1687 AD and continued till 1689 AD. During this period, Guru Gobind Singh was at Paonta and not at Anandpur. The author forgetting this fact makes bold attempt of making the *Devi* appear atop Naina Hills. Apart from making chronological mistakes, Koer Singh seems not to be careful enough to avoid contradictions in his narrative. For instance he writes that the Guru wanted every person to be treated equally but later concludes by suggesting that Brahmins should be given preferential treatment. All this makes the work of Koer Singh altogether unreliable.

Any way, the *Devi* episode was dealt in greater details in subsequent works : *Mahima Prakash* by Sarup Das Bhalla (1831 BK/1774 AD), *Gurpratap Suraj Granth* by Bhai Santokh Singh (AD 1843) et al. even as these later writers do not agree in details. Possibly the configuration of the story was determined by the fancies of individual writers. One thing, however, is irrefutable that the story originated with *Gurbilas Patshahi 10* by Koer Singh to which later on many alterations were made. This work was written four decades after the writing of *Sri Gursobha* during which period the Sikhs were engaged in a life and death struggle against the state and order on permanent basis had been issued that *Nanak Panthis* (Sikhs) should be decapitated unless they forsake their religion. In that crucial period, the Sikhs had no time to look after their spiritual heritage and only Hindu outsiders were left to indulge in it who because of their Brahmanical leanings introduced *Devi* in the *Khalsa* account partly to give credibility to their Hindu beliefs; and partly to dissociate themselves from Sikhism at least in the eyes of Muslims since being a Sikh in those days was to invite trouble.

The most decisive evidence in favour of total rejection of the story is found in the Guru's ideology as it is embodied in his own writings. He had a total commitment to the concept of *Ik Onkar* and shared the vision of transcendence with Guru

Nanak. He, therefore, could not worship any god or goddess. He says, "O man, worship none but God, not a thing made by Him. Know, that He who was in the beginning, unborn, invincible and indestructible is God."

Again without the support of the one Name "Deem all religious ceremonies as superstitions."[1] Guru Gobind Singh was an uncompromising monotheist. So he cannot be said to have worshiped *Devi* much less on the occasion of the initiation of the *Khalsa* order, for which he had been ordained by God himself.[2]

Some confusion has arisen from the Guru's use of the name *Bhagauti* by which goddess Durga has often been called. But the Guru uses it in the sense of God or of sword which is identified with God. In the invocatory lines to *Chandi Di Var*, Guru Gobind Singh remembers the Transcendental one by the term *Bhagauti—Pratham Bhagauti Simer Kei*. Here the word for the One is *Bhagauti* which means sword and God. Worship of *Bhagauti* could not, therefore, mean worship of Durga. In the *Bachittar Natak*, the Guru uses *Mahakal Kalika* which, as he says, he worshipped in his previous birth. Some writers in their haste to prove that the Guru worshipped goddess have considered *Maha Kal Kalika* as the name of goddess Durga. Such people have tried to interpret the term out of context. *Maha Kal Kalika*, in fact, is single expression meaning God and not a combination of two terms....*Maha Kal* (God) and *Kalika* (Durga).

In this context Dr. Madanjit Kaur's discovery is very significant. According to her, "Guru Gobind Singh did not stand in need of invoking *Devi* as is clear from the fact that his grandfather, Guru Hargobind, had already employed sword and fought battles with the aggressive rulers. Even Guru Gobind Singh had himself fought battles successfully at Nadaun and Bhangani to chastise the evil mongers. He therefore, did not need any new sanction from any god or goddess to sanctify or legitimise his act of the creation of *Khalsa*.

The brief discussion leads to the conclusion that the story

1. M.A. Macauliffe, *The Sikh Religion*, Vol. V, p. 325.
2. *Pragaṭio Khālsā Parmātam kī Mauj.*

of *Hom/Devi* had no historical basis. Guru Gobind Singh had nothing to do with *Shakti* cult, as it is in direct opposition to the Sikh creed whose *axis mundi* is one and the only one Transcendental and Formless God. The pronouncement of McLeod that a new synthesis came into being when Jat culture and Hill culture mingled in each other has no basis whatsoever. The story of *Devi* worship/*Hom* was only an invention of later Brahmanical-minded chroniclers or of the people who intended to justify their own degradation from the lofty principles proclaimed by the Guru to please their idolatrous neighbours.... or to ponder to their own petty interests.

CHAPTER IX

ONSLAUGHT OF HINDU CONSERVATISM AND ISLAMIC IMPERIALISM

The immediate effect of the creation of the *Khalsa* was that it brought the hostility of the Hill Chiefs in the open. In the activities of the Guru they saw a potent threat to their own religion and power.

The Guru infact, wanted peace for his new born *Khalsa* to grow and to organise itself, but in his mission and reforms, the Hill Chiefs found something fundamentally different from what they had been born to uphold. After the creation of the *Khalsa*, one of the first acts of the Guru was that the Sikhs should be baptised according to the new rites, and to this effect, he enjoined them to come to Anandpur. The Sikhs responded enthusiastically. Ever increasing number of the baptised Sikhs surcharged with egalitarian spirit and disengaged from orthodox way of life and always ready to combat the evil, seriously alarmed the Hill Chiefs. It is therefore, not surprising that the Guru's continued presence in their midst was considered a direct challenge to their feudal order and their style of living.

Besides this, the Hill Chiefs and Ajmer Chand of Kahlur in particular, had another grievance against the Guru. The ever increasing number of Sikhs who visited Anandpur created the problem of meeting their mundane needs. The Guru had no possessions except Anandpur and its suburbs which he might call his own. For provisions, the Guru depended on the voluntary contributions of his followers which usually helped meet the needs sufficiently. But in the wake of the call of the Guru to his Sikhs to receive baptism speedily, the number of the visitors to Anandpur increased manifold. At times, the supply of provisions did not match the demand. Therefore these had to be supplemented from the neighbouring villages.[1] Since the Hill Rajas, especially Ajmer Chand, the Raja of Kahlur state in which Anandpur was located, had no love lost for the Guru for the reasons adumbrated above, they did not hesitate to create troubles by inciting the people in their favour. This fact in conjunction with others as referred to earlier so worked upon the Rajas that they made up their mind to restrain the Guru.

Two of them, Alam Chand and Balia Chand, Chieftains[2] of some principality, finding their opportunity when the Guru was accompanied by a few Sikhs, fell on him. The Sikhs gave a determined fight, but because of enemy's large strength, soon started losing ground. Not long after, reinforcement under Uday Singh reached and the tables were turned. Alam Chand lost his right arm and left the field. Balia Chand was seriously wounded and his soldiers took to their heels. The Guru returned victorious.[3]

The defeat of Alam Chand and Balia Chand unnerved the Hill Rajas, who met in a council and decided to seek Emperor's help. They presented their case to him through the Nawab of Sirhind admitting that they had failed to restrain the Guru and if the Emperor did not deal with him hastily and firmly, he might find the situation uncontrollable later. According to M.A. Macauliffe, the *Subedar* of Delhi, under instructions from Aurangzeb who was at that time in the Southern part of India, despatched a force of ten thousand under his two able generals Painde Khan and Din Beg. The Hill Chiefs joined them at Ropar. The Guru met the combined forces near Anandpur. In a sanguinary battle Painde Khan was killed. Din Beg and Hill Rajas fled away.[4] They were pursued by the *Khalsa* soldiers for

1. Sukha Singh, *Gurbilas Patshahi 10*, XIII, p. 9. *Sri Gursobha*, VIII, p. 40, XI, pp. 5-6.
2. We have not been able to identify the hill states to which they belonged.
3. Swarup Singh Kaushish, *Guru Kian Sakhian*, (ed.) Piara Singh Padam, *Sakhi* 64, p. 129.
4. M.A. Macauliffe, *The Sikh Religion*, Vol. V, pp. 124-126.

some distance. A large booty consisting of horses, arms and precious baggage fell into the hands of the Sikhs.

Much chagrined and agonised, the Hill Rajas now resolved to act against the Guru independently of the Mughals. They organised a federation and gave its leadership to Ajmer Chand[1], son of Bhim Chand of Bilaspur who was the most knowledgeable amongst the Hill Chiefs with regard to the Guru and his Sikhs because of the location of Guru's headquarters in his state. He sent a message to the Guru asking him to either vacate Anandpur or pay the rent and revenue thereof since it lay in his territory. In the absence of a favourable response he would have to face Raja's wrath. The Guru rejected the demands of the Raja outrightly, and to counter his threat issued fiats to his followers to join him at Anandpur to participate in the war likely to be imposed on him. They responded in large numbers.[2] The Hill Rajas besieged Anandpur. The Sikhs took positions in the forts of Anandgarh, Fatehgarh and Kesgarh. On the first day (Bhandon 29, 1757 BK) Ajmer Chand made a forceful attack on Taragarh fortress near Anandgarh but his army was repulsed by the Sikhs led by Baba Ajit Singh, the eldest son of the Guru. On the side of the Sikhs, Ishar Singh, Kalian Singh and Sangat Singh achieved martyrdom among others.[3] A Hill Chieftain Raja Ghumand Chand suffered severe wounds during the battle.

Next day, Ajmer Chand once again mounted fierce assault on the fort named Fatehgarh. He and his allies met with stout resistance from the *Khalsa* and in the sallies organised by determined Sikhs under the able command of experienced Bhagwan Singh. The hill forces suffered heavy casualties in a five hour battle. As the sun-set approached, the fighting stopped. Jawahar Singh and Bhagwan Singh received martyrdom.[4]

On the following day with the breaking of dawn, fighting

1. Raja Bhim Chand had abdicated in 1691 soon after the reverses at Nadaun.
2. *Ibid.*, p. 126.
3. Swarup Singh Kaushish, *Guru Kian Sakhian*, p. 130, *Sakhi* 66, also see *Bhat Vahi Tumar Bijlauton ki*, extract given by Piara Singh Padam in *Guru Kian Sakhian*, p. 130.
4. *Bhat Vahi Jado Bansian ki*, 'Khata Bartie Kanauton Ka'—Also consult *Guru Kian Sakhian* by Swarup Singh Kaushish, p. 131.

resumed. Ajmer Chand launched a vigorous attack on Agamgarh this time, but failed miserably. The Sikhs lost Bagh Singh and Gharbara Singh, their veteran campaigners.[1]

Ajmer Chand now called a conference of his allies to take stock of the situation. During the meeting a different strategy was drafted to achieve success. It was decided to storm the fort of Lohgarh initially to be followed by simultaneous attack on other sides of Anandpur. The command of the troops for storming the fort was given to a very brave chieftain, Kesri Chand Jaswaria.[2] He meticulously planned his manoeuvres; one of which was that a very highly intoxicated elephant would be set against the door of Lohgarh to break it and make way for the hill forces to enter the fort. The plan though made in camera[3] leaked out to the Guru who forthwith took steps to counter it. The Guru wanted to appoint Duni Chand,[4] considered to be very bold and iron-willed Sikh, to face the elephant, but his spirit failed and he deserted the Guru.[5] Bachittar Singh, son of Bhai Mani Singh, lost not even a fraction of a second to offer his services to meet the challenge of the elephant. The Guru gave a pat on his back and handed over a specially forged spear named *Nagni* to face the intoxicated elephant.[6]

As the morning of 1st Katak dawned, the hill forces, under the overall command of Ajmer Chand, positioned themselves near the fort of Lohgarh. Kesri Chand led the force from the front. They goaded the intoxicated and well shielded elephant to the main gate of the fort. When the furious animal advanced to strike the door with all its might, Bachittar Singh, having invoked the blessings of the Guru through prayer, struck it with his spear with such a force that it pierced through the plates covering its forehead to his brain making him furious

1. *Bhat Vahi Talaundha Pargana Jind*, 'Khata Jalhane Puaron ka'.
2. Swarup Singh Kaushish, *Guru Kian Sakhian*, p. 132.
3. *Ibid.*, p. 134.
4. He was the Grandson of Bhai Salho. Refer to *Guru Pad Prem Sagar* by Bawa Sumer Singh 1882, Swarup Singh Kaushish, *op.cit.*, p. 133.
5. Swarup Singh Kaushish, *op.cit.*, p. 135, *Sakhi* 67. Bawa Sumer Singh, *Guru Pad Prem Parkash*, p. 4, (1882 A.D.)
6. *Ibid.*, p. 135, also Consult *Bhat Vahi Talaundha Pargana Jind*,' Khata Jalhanon Ka.'

with pain. The elephant lost his sense of direction and purpose. It turned back and ran pell mell trampling everything on its way, including the hill soldiers waiting to enter the citadel once the gate was broken. In the disorder that ensued, Uday Singh already astride his swift horse, sprang forward and challenged Kesri Chand. Kesri Chand astride his steed attacked Uday Singh with his sword. Uday Singh dodged the attack aside and then hit him with his sword so strongly that his body was cleaved in twain.[1] Kesri Chand having met his remesis, Ajmer Chand thought it appropriate to seek safety in retreat. Alam Singh son of Daria, Sucha Singh son of Rai Singh, Kaushal Singh son of Makhan Singh attained martyrdom in the battlefield.[2]

Fighting continued for four consecutive days but did not yield any favourable result for the Hill Rajas; rather ignominy and demoralisation fell into their lap. Any more failures in the battle might have spelt disaster for them. These could have given opportunity to some disgruntled elements in their territories to defy them, besides feeling tempted to join the *Khalsa*. Now to save face, the Hill Rajas decided upon a stratagem at the suggestion of Parmanand, the family priest of Raja of Kahlur[3] who was well known for his cunning and guile. They sent Parmanand to Anandpur with a letter. He very cunningly and stealthily placed it at the gate of Anandgarh duly tied to an image of cow with *janeu* (sacred thread). The letter stated that the Rajas sincerely regretted the losses on both sides and desired an amicable settlement immediately so that the purposeless fighting could be stopped.[4] The letter also stated that a unilateral retreat on their part would be too humiliating and mortifying in the eyes of their subjects as well as other neighbouring states and if the Guru vacated Anandpur, the siege would be raised and then he could come back and reoccupy it after some time, if he desired. According to Sainapat, they appealed to the Guru's sense of chivalry by

---

1. Swarup Singh Kaushish, *Guru Kian Sakhian,* p. 136, also consult *Bhat Vahi Talaundha Pargana Jind,* 'Khata Jalhanon ka'.
2. *Ibid.*
3. *Ibid.*, p. 137.
4. *Ibid.*

requesting him to leave Anandpur to them as the *Gao-bhat*, that is the touch of the Cow.[1]

The Guru agreed thinking that the Hill Rajas after all had realised the futility of waging a war. Probably the Guru did so because he reckoned that prolonged hostilities might induce the Hill Chiefs to approach the Mughals to come to their help.

Any way, the Guru came out of the security of the fort and stepped in the open leaving Anandpur in the hands of some of his brave and trusted men. He established himself at Nirmohgarh, a place about four kilometres away from Anandpur.

Throwing their promise to the winds the Hill Chiefs fell upon the Guru. The Sikhs resisted with all their might and the enemy had to retreat.[2]

In this battle, Dewan Sahib Singh and his band of one thousand Sikhs bore the brunt. The Dewan and some other eminent Sikhs such as Mathura Singh, Surat Singh, Deva Singh, Anup Singh and Sarup Singh laid down their lives for the Guru.[3] Then the Guru himself took the command and made so vigorous an assault that the hill forces had to lift the siege.

Ajmer Chand, now exasperated, decided to square up the issue with the Guru once for all. He decided to get aid from his suzerain, the Mughal government, and sent an envoy for the purpose.[4] It is not clear whether this appeal was made to Aurangzeb when he was in the South or to Muazzam at Kabul or to the Mughal government at Delhi, whether directly or through the *Subedar* of Sirhind. In any case, the Mughal contingents arrived shortly at Sirhind to collaborate with its *Faujdar* who had been instructed to aid the vassal chief of Bilaspur against the Guru.[5]

1. Indubhushan Banerjee, *Evolution of the Khalsa*, Vol. II, 128; *Sri Gursobha*, 45.
2. Swarup Singh Kaushish, *Guru Kian Sakhian*, p. 137, *Sakhi* 69.
3. *Ibid.*, p. 138.
4. *Sri Gursobha* (ed.) Shamsher Singh Ashok, pp. 64-65 stanza 345.
5. The Hill Rajas wrote a letter to the *Faujdar* of Sirhind asking for his help against the Guru. Kartar Singh in *Life of Guru Gobind Singh*, p. 181; *Sri Gursobha*, pp. 64-65, stanzas 345-351.
   According to Giani Gian Singh, Aurangzeb himself is said to have sent an order to Wazir Khan to proceed against the Guru. *Twarikh Guru Khalsa*, p. 915, Santokh Singh, *Sri Gur Partap Suraj Granth*, pp. 2642-48.

Ajmer Chand also succeeded in instigating Gujjars and Ranghars to fight against the Sikhs. Both these communities were Muslims and resided in a number of villages around Anandpur in his state. They were organised into clans—each clan under a head. They were habitual marauders and had often tried to plunder the Sikhs while on their way to Anandpur. Possibly, Ajmer Chand played upon their communal feelings vis-a-vis the *Khalsa* and their marauding instincts to enlist their co-operation.

The Mughal army as well as the army of the Hill Rajas joined hands at Sirhind and then moved on to achieve success in their mission. The Guru already abreast with the circumstances made appropriate preparations. Apart from retaining some *Khalsa* who would normally come to have an audience, he had invited daring men of different *Sangats* from several towns and villages, given them arms and enlisted them as his soldiers.[1] The Guru's strategy was to defend himself against the offensive stance of the enemy. The allied armies attacked Nirmohgarh from one side while Ajmer Chand attacked from the other. Their objective was to weaken the defences of the Guru. In Sainapat's simile[2], the enemy surrounded Nirmohgarh, as the stars surround the moon.' The contest lasted for about a day before the *Khalsa* could get respite from the enemy's vigorous attack. Ultimately, Guru was constrained to evacuate Nirmohgarh, probably because of the use of cannons by the Mughal *Faujdar*.[3] But before the retreating *Khalsa* army could cross the river Sutlej, they were overtaken by the allies who were naturally keen to obstruct their safe passage.[4] The *Khalsa* fought desperately for four hours[5] and eventually succeeded in crossing the river and entering the territory of Raja Dharampal[6], the Chief of Jaswan, who was an ardent admirer of the Guru. The Guru and the *Khalsa* marched towards the town of Basoli, fourty-five kms

---

1. Sainapat, *Sri Gursobha*, Chapter 9, p. 65, stanza 351.
2. *Ibid.*
3. Kartar Singh, *Life of Guru Gobind Singh*. The use of canon by the Mughal troop is not improbable.
4. Sainapat, *op.cit.*, p. 69.
5. *Ibid.*
6. *Ibid.*

from Anandpur beyond Una across River Swan, eighteen kms away on the Una-Hoshiarpur road.

The Guru had hardly left the place, when another engagement took place on the bank of River Sutlej. The Sikhs fought gallantly and forced the enemy to retreat. Sahib Singh, a noted and noble Sikh general, lost his life.

The combined forces of the Hill Rajas also crossed the river and attacked the Sikhs at Basoli. The Guru put up a formidable defence and once again the enemy was unable to subdue the Sikh forces. The battle is known as Battle of Basoli.[1]

Thereafter, the Mughal troops returned to Sirhind with unsure satisfaction of achieving although at a great cost, the limited objective of expelling the *Khalsa* from the territory of Kahlur on the Eastern side of the River Sutlej. The Hill Rajas also withdrew to their respective states.

The Guru and his family put up at the residence of the Raja while beautiful canopies were pitched in the suburb of the town for accommodating the *Khalsa* soldiers.

The Guru stayed at Basoli for some days, resting and enjoying hunting and other sports.[2] Soon, the Guru took initiative against Ajmer Chand leading incursions into his territory on the North of River Sutlej. He gradually moved towards Anandpur. At this time, the Gujjars and Ranghars of the village Kamlot attacked a party of the Sikhs who had gone on a hunting expedition. Hearing about the mis-adventure of the Ranghars against the hunting party, the Guru ordered the *Khalsa* to teach them a lesson. Uday Singh who headed the hunting party led an attack on the village. The Gujjars and Ranghars were severely dealt with. Jiwan Singh[3], a notable general, laid his life in this contest. His dead body was brought to Basoli where it was cremated with full honours.

Finding that Wazir Khan, the *Subedar* of Sirhind, had gone back, and the Hill Rajas were satisfied that they had at long last got rid of him (the Guru), the Guru, marched back to

1. Basoli fell in the territory of Jaswan.
2. Sainapat, *Sri Gursobha*, Chapter X, p. 72, stanza 90.
3. He was the son of Prem Chand and grandson of Moola, *Bhat Vahi Talaunda Pargana Jind*, 'Khata Jalhanon ka'.

Anandpur[1] and lost no time in repairing the forts and other buildings and structures badly damaged by the allied forces. He also took prompt steps to re-establish the past glory of Anandpur as the headquarters of the *Khalsa*. No wonder, the Sikhs in large numbers started surging to Anandpur to seek Guru's benedictions and also to offer their services. Meanwhile news reached Anandpur that *Sangat* of Darap region had been stripped of their belongings including their offerings for the Guru by Ranghars of Bajrur. This was beyond the liking of the Guru who ordered Ajit Singh, his eldest son, to proceed to Bajrur at once to punish the miscreants. The order was obeyed forthwith and the Sahibzada besieged the village. Chittu and Mittu, the leaders of the village were put to sword and the village was ransacked. The inhabitants were taught a lesson who never plundered or coerced the *Sikh Sangats* in future.[2]

Towards the end of the last year of the seventeenth century, the peace of Anandpur Sahib was disturbed by Wazir Khan, the *Subedar* of Sirhind, who made a surprise attack on Anandpur. The Sikhs had to evacuate the city and proceed to Bhadsali at a distance of 45 kilometers from Anandpur beyond Una across the River Swan. The Mughal forces went in pursuit and engaged the Guru's forces at Bhadsali. In the hard contest, Sahib Singh, a notable Sikh commander and a hero, lost his life. Soon after, when the din of the war diminished and tempers cooled down, the Guru returned to Anandpur[3] hopefully to renew ties with his Sikhs and to extend the area of Sikh influence.

The Guru obliged Sidh Shah, the ruler of Mandi, with his short visit in 1701.[4] He was accorded a very warm welcome by the Raja. At Mandi, the Guru interacted with other Rajas who had come there, seemingly in response to Sidh Shah's invitation. Consequently, the Rajas were convinced of the loftiness of the Guru's designs. In later years, some of them

1. M.A. Macauliffe, *The Sikh Religion*, Vol. V, pp. 128-37.
   Phir Basyo Anandpur Rajan Manian.
2. Swarup Singh Kaushish, *Guru Kian Sakhian*, (ed.) by Piara Singh Padam, p. 142, *Sakhi* 72. The date of this event is given by Kaushish as Chet Vadi Panchah Samat 1754–1700 A.D.
3. Sainapat, *Sri Gursobha*; Harnam Singh, pp. 55-57, 62-65.
4. This date is given by Khazan Singh in his book *History and Philosophy of Sikhism*, V. I.

only played a marginal role against the Guru while the Raja of Mandi had been an ardent follower and sincere admirer.

The Guru attended Rawalsar[1] fair held every year on the first of Baisakh. On this occasion the Raja begged the Guru for the perennial safety of his capital. The Guru granted the boon. The memory of this event is preserved in the tradition that the Guru got a small earthen pot (*Hāndī* in Punjabi Language) and threw it into the River Beas flowing by the side of Mandi. The vessel did not dissolve. The Guru uttered, "As my earthen vessel is safe so will remain safe your Mandi. If ever Mandi is plundered, heavenly balls of fire will burst."[2] It is obviously the blessings of the Guru that the town of Mandi continued to enjoy immunity from the Sikh intrusion till 1839, although it had long been a tributary to them from 1809. In 1840 a force under General Ventura was sent into the hills by the orders of Nau Nihal Singh, grandson of Maharaja Ranjit Singh.[3]

In 1702, Sayyad Beg and Alif Khan, two eminent commanders of the Mughals, who were going to Delhi from Lahore were tempted by Ajmer Chand through the offer of a large sum of money to attack the Guru. According to Hari Ram Gupta, they were promised a payment of one thousand rupees a day.[4]

Both the commanders marched towards Anandpur. The Guru was at that time sojourning at Chamkaur along with a few soldiers while returning from Kurukshetra. After a few skirmishes, Sayyad Beg was so much impressed by the Guru's

---

1. Rawalsar is a natural lake with floating islands about 15 Kilometres West of Mandi Town. At the time when Guru Gobind Singh visited the place, there was practically no habitation around it.
2. *Jaisi Bache Merī Hāndī*
    Waise Bache Gī Terī Mandī
    Mandī ko Jab Luṭenge
    To Asmānī Gole Chhuṭenge
    Lepel Griffin : *Rajas of the Punjab*, pp. 580-81.
    Hutchinson and Vogal, *History of the Punjab Hill States* p. 389.
    A Glossary of the Tribes and Castes of the Punjab and the N.W. Frontier Province, Vol. 1, p. 691.
3. *A Glossary of the Tribes and Castes of the Punjab and the N.W. Frontier Province,* p. 691.
4. Hari Ram Gupta, *History of the Sikhs*, Vol. I, p. 286.

charismatic personality that he thought it appropriate to join him.[1] Alif Khan had to retire inspite of his long-nursed desire to avenge his failure which he had met earlier while fighting against the Guru in Kangra hills.[2] On his arrival at Delhi, he was scolded by the higher authorities. Sayyad Beg fought in the battle on Guru's side. After the battle, he stayed with the Guru for some time. A little after this event (March 1703), Sahibzada Ajit Singh had to subdue and kill Jabar Jung a local Chaudhary of the village Bassi Kalan in the district of Hoshiarpur. The cause was that a Brahmin's wife had been forcibly taken away by the Chaudhary to satisfy his carnal desires. The Brahmin was terribly depressed and had virtually broken down morally. He ran for succour from pillar to post but none offered him any help. At last he came to Anandpur and related his doleful story. The Guru was shocked and asked Sahibzada Ajit Singh to lead a military expedition immediately against the cruel and unscrupulous Choudhary. The task was accomplished with alacrity and the woman was restored to her husband. The Brahmin and his wife were overwhelmed by the profound sense of gratitude to the Guru. Everybody at Anandpur had been convinced by now that the righteous cause was the noblest for the Guru.

In 1703, the Guru had to deal with two attacks. On both the occasions, Ajmer Chand was the architect of the campaign. On the first occasion, he attacked in association with Rajas Bhup Chand, Wazir Singh and Dev Saran.[3] On the second occasion, he sought help from Mughal *Subedar* of Delhi and then raided the Guru's citadel. On both occasions, he suffered defeat[4] and his mission remained elusive. Guru Gobind Singh's control over Anandpur[5] remained firm, to the disappointment of Ajmer Chand and to the dismay of his

---

1. M.A. Macauliffe, *The Sikh Religion*, pp. 153-54. Sayyad Beg threw away his sword and vowed never to use it against the Sikhs again. See *Sakhi Pothi*, p. 59. He fell fighting for the Guru when another imperial force under General Said Khan attacked Anandpur in collusion with the Hill Chieftains in February 1703, (*Encyclopaedia of Sikhism* Vol. IV, p. 23).
2. M.A. Macauliffe, *The Sikh Religion*, pp. 154-55.
3. *Ibid.*, pp. 153-154.
4. *Ibid.*, Vol. V, p. 154.
5. *Ibid*

associate Hill Rajas. The Mughal commanders were also nonplussed by the high morale of the Sikhs. Another remarkable thing happened in the second attack. Maiman Khan, a Mughal commander, deserted his side and joined the Guru in response to the call of his conscience. The Guru blessed him and his entry into Guru's forces boosted the morale of Sikh soldiers. At this juncture, the Guru in exultation and exuberance uttered that, "It is through them (*Khalsa*) that I have won my victories and have been able to grant gifts to others."[1]

Just about this time, presumably at the request of the Hill Rajas as well as of the local chiefs, a strong contingent of the Mughal soldiers was sent to Anandpur from Delhi to fight against the Guru. The fight was designated as *Jehad*—a crusade proclaimed against the infidels whose decimation had been made out to be a religious act of a very high order by the Muslim priestly class especially of *Sunni* hue in the medieval times of India under Aurangzeb. The Commander of the Mughal contingent was Sayyad Khan. He was joined by the Hill Chiefs along with their armies. The fight began. The Guru's five hundred regular soldiers fought heroically. Maiman Khan, Sayyad Beg and several other Muslims fought on their side. This was something strange for Sayyad Khan. Sayyad Beg and Maiman Khan both fell fighting. Sayyad Khan was a general of repute and had won many a battles. He was sure of victory and did not expect prolonged and stiff opposition. But he was amazed at the doggedness and martial expertise of the Guru's followers. His ego was hurt and he aimed a shot at the Guru that went amiss. Another attempt also failed. He was a skilled shooter and had never missed the target. But when he failed twice, he was perplexed. He had heard a lot about the greatness of the Guru and his lofty ideals from no other person than his own sister Nasiran who was the wife of Pir Buddhu Shah, a great admirer of the Guru. When he came face to face with the Guru in the battlefield, he grew contemplative. He reflected on the cause of war and got convinced that it was the working of the elements, sponsoring and upholding conspiracy of the Mughal politico-cultural

---

1. Narain Singh, *Guru Gobind Singh Retold*, p. 229.

imperialism and Hindu conservatism to protect their vested interests. Being God-fearing to the core, he decided to take side of the cause of the Guru which he looked upon as righteous, facilitating human beings, both at the individual and the corporate levels, to refashion their consciousness to enable them establish a society, free from exploitation of any kind, guaranteeing basic freedom to a man. He decided not to give a fight. Instead, he yearned for the Guru's blessings. He got down from the horse and touched the Guru's stirrup with his head and rose with light in his eyes, love and joy in his heart. He entered the discipleship of the Guru and returned to a lonely cave near Kangra to pass his days in Divine contemplation. When the Guru proceeded to Deccan 'Sayyad Khan followed him and remained with him to the last.' There were many other Muslim soldiers, who had, for love's sake, placed themselves at the Guru's disposal and fought battles for him. Their presence in the Guru's army gives a lie to the assertion of the persons like Muhammad Latif who would have us believe that the Guru was an 'irreconcilable and inveterate enemy of every Mohammedan'. He had no ill-will against any individual of whatever religion caste or creed. It was the evil system that he wanted to destroy and it was against its authors and defenders that his efforts were directed.

The Mughal government appointed Ramzan Khan in place of Sayyad Khan. He resumed the campaign with vigour. There was much bloodshed on both sides. Maiman Khan was killed. The Sikhs had to evacuate a part of Anandpur which the Mughal army plundered with impunity. Mughal army celebrated its victory by indulging in merry-making on a large scale. They drank so heavily that they became oblivious of the possibility of an attack by the vigilant Sikhs. Under Sahibzada Ajit Singh, the Sikhs fell upon them in a surprise attack causing consternation among the revellers. The Mughal army fled in different directions leaving behind all the booty they had plundered earlier from Anandpur. The reverses faced by Ramzan Khan equally upset the Emperor who was camping in Southern India and the Hill Chiefs.

After some time, the hostilities started again. The reasons were no different than the previous occasion; viz; the ever

increasing prestige of the Guru, hatred for his movement
which championed the cause of values diametrically opposite
to those of the Hill Rajas.

The latter who were in the close proximity of the *Khalsa*
at Anandpur arranged a formidable force of allies against the
Guru and atonce marched upon him. They were welcomed by
a few cannon shots from the fort of Anandgarh. They decided
to lay siege to the town instead of suffering heavy losses in an
attempt to capture it by a direct assault. Even this plan of their's
was badly foiled. They could not achieve any success against
the lightning-like sorties of the *Khalsa* cavalry whose shrewd
tactics completely discomfited them. The Hill Chiefs were left
with no alternative but to retreat. Inspite of this, the Hill Rajas
never relented in their determination to oust the Guru from
their territory. They made preparations on a large scale. The
Gujjars and Ranghars were also incited to join the war against
the *Khalsa*. They harnessed their own resources with care and
assiduity and requested the Mughal authorities,[1] for assistance.
Till then, the Mughal Governments of Delhi, Lahore, Sirhind
and Jammu had fully monitored the potentialities of the Sikhs
including their military might and were convinced that
challenge of the Sikhs was not to be brushed off as insignificant.
If it was not tackled seriously and promptly, it could assume
dangerous dimensions. It could become a potent threat to the
Mughal rule as well as to the Hill states. They, therefore,
favourably endorsed the petition of the Hill Rajas to Aurangzeb
who was at that time in South India conducting campaign
against the recalcitrant *Shia* states and the Marathas. Their
main argument was that Emperor's neglect of *Khalsa* challenge
might cost the Mughals their territory in the North-West. The
Emperor was naturally upset. He issued specific instructions
to his governors of Lahore and Sirhind to actively assist the Hill
Chieftains and to take necessary steps to force the Guru to
evacuate Anandpur. The era of comparative peace that the

---

1. We are not sure whether direct representation was made, but it is fairly
   certain that the Emperor had sent orders to the Mughal officials notably
   Wazir Khan, the *Faujdar* of Sirhind. Mirza Muhammand Harisi, *Ibratnama*;
   S.H.R. 231, 66, 67. Ahmed Shah, *Twarikh-i-Hind*, S.H.R. 1291, 383. Ganesh
   Das, *Chahar Bagh-i-Punjab*, S.H.R. 553, 158.

Guru had enjoyed in the wake of the company of Prince Muazzam had come to an end with the creation of the *Khalsa* which the Mughal Government had not taken kindly to as it read dangerous portents in it. Even then Aurangzeb slow pedalled the problem, and except rendering tentative military and diplomatic help to the Hill Rajas in their fight against the Guru, he did nothing tangible on a scale matching his power.

In all this, the Emperor being a willy politician had a design. He wanted to achieve his object of snuffing out the Sikh movement through Hill Chieftains or to get both the Guru and the Hill Rajas weakened by their infighting before taking decisive action against one or both emerging victorious out of their mutual wars. But when the news reached him that the Hill Chieftains even with the military help from his local officials had been humbled by the Guru, he became explicit, serious and overt, and issued clear instructions to his Governors. He despatched a personal letter :

"There is only one Emperor. Thy religion and mine are the same. Come to me, by all means, otherwise I shall be angry and go to thee. If thou come, thou shalt be treated as holy men are treated by monarchs. I have obtained this sovereignty from God. Be well advised and thwart not my wishes."[1]

The Guru went through the letter brought by a *Qazi* and wrote the following reply,

> *My brother ! the sovereign who had made thee Emperor hath sent me in the world to do justice. He hath commissioned thee also to do justice, but thou hast forgotten His mandate and practisest hypocrisy. Therefore how can I be on good terms with thee who persecutes the Hindus with blind hatred ? Thou recognisest not that the people belong to God and not to the Emperor, and yet thou seekest to destroy their religion."[2]

The allied forces soon advanced from Ropar side to attack Anandpur. According to Mohammad Akbar, "a fierce battle took place near Kiratpur. The Sikhs fought gallantly but were soon driven back and forced to take refuge in the fort of

---

1. M.A. Macauliffe, Vol. V, p. 165.
2. *Ibid.*

Anandgarh."[1] The allies, thereafter, encircled the Sikhs on all sides and the great siege of Anandpur began.

In this exigency, the Guru invited help from the Sikhs. He issued several letters to different *Sangats* to reach Anandpur fully armed immediately (1704 A.D. 1761 BK). One such letter was sent to Bhai Mukhia and Bhai Parsa who were asked to come with, "cavalries, footmen, gunners and daring youths."[2] The Guru divided his army into six contingents. He placed one each in five forts, while a detachment of 500 men, was kept in reserve. Anandgarh was in Guru's personal charge, Fatehgarh was entrusted to Uday Singh. Holgarh was in the command of Mohkam Singh. Guru's eldest son Ajit Singh controlled Kesgarh. His other son Jujhar Singh held Lohgarh. Ajit Singh won a great victory on the very first day by killing Jagatullah, the leader of Ranghars and Gujjars. Two heavy guns named *Baghan* (Tigress) and *Vijay Ghosh* (Victory warrant) were scaled on the ramparts of Anandgarh. They wrought havoc in the enemy ranks. In the first day fight Wazir Khan lost nine hundred men, while the Sikh loss was also immense. Even in the midst of bloodshed and high tension environment, the sublime tasks of righteousness were accorded adequate premium. At the conclusion of first day's battle, Sikhs came with faces red with anger. They lodged a complaint with the Guru against one Bhai Ghanaiya who served water even to the wounded soldiers of the enemy in the battlefield, thereby playing treachery to the cause of the *Khalsa*. The Guru summoned the alleged culprit to his presence and enquired if he had done what the Sikhs were ascribing to him. " 'Yes' and 'No' my Lord. It is true that I served water to persons who are called Turks quite as freely as to those called Sikhs. But I served no Turk or Sikh. Thou hast so enlightened my mind that I beheld thee in every human body that I saw lying wounded on the battlefield, craving for water. So I gave water to none but thee, O Master," Bhai Ghanaiya said humbly. The Guru was immensely pleased to know that his Sikh has understood the

---

1. Muhammad Akbar, *The Punjab under the Mughals*, p. 219; *Adarah-i-Adabiyat-i-Delli*, 1974.
2. Ganda Singh, *Hukamname*, p. 181, *Hukamnama* no. 60.

mission of Guru Nanak and has even displayed his understanding in his deeds.

The siege was conducted with great intensity and planned in such a manner that all ingress and egress routes for both goods and persons were completely blocked. With the logistic support being cut off, the Sikhs were put to great hardships. The position of ration stock became extremely serious and the Sikhs were driven to undertake some dangerous expedients. They sallied out to snatch provisions from the besiegers, but met with a partial success; and that too on some occasions. The allies collected their stores at one place and guarded them round the clock. The Sikhs resorted to direct assaults on the allies but they were thawarted by them. A small brook taken from River Charan Ganga for supply of water to Anandgarh was diverted by Raja of Kahlur. Civil population being hard pressed began to flee.

Having suffered extreme hardships, the Sikhs besought the Guru to evacuate the fort, but the Guru counselled them to bear patience for some more time. On perpetual insistance by some Sikhs, the Guru declared that everybody was free to leave whenever he/she wanted to.

When the enemy learnt of the distress in which the Sikhs and the Guru were placed at that time, they planned a different strategy to derive maximum advantage of the situation. They sent a message to the Guru suggesting that if he decides to abandon Anandpur, he would be allowed a safe passage. Their offer of a safe passage was treacherous, since they had planned to draw out the Sikhs from within the shelter of the township and attack them to annihilation. The Guru sensed their ulterior motive when he received the message, and therefore did not accept the offer. But some of the *Masands* and the Sikhs who were under their influence insisted that the offer of the enemy be accepted and the Anandpur abandoned. Forty of them were so vehement in their demand that they became desperate and disclaimed Guru Gobind Singh as their Guru. Then they left Anandpur in a huff. At this juncture they prevailed upon Mata Gujri to support their view-point. The Guru then thought out a scheme to expose the hypocrisy of the enemy, as also to convince his followers of their folly.

The Guru ordered a few bullocks to be laden with waste material. When all preparations had been completed, he informed the messengers of the enemy that he had accepted their proposal. They were told that the Guru's treasure would leave the township to be followed after some time by him and his people. The enemy received this information with great joy. At the appointed hour of the night, the Guru called for the loaded bullock carts tied lighted torches to the horns of the bullocks and sent them out under escort of some Sikhs. When the enemy saw the treasure bearing caravan emerging from the township, they forgot all their pledges and fell upon the escort party of the Sikhs in order to loot the treasure.[1] But their disappointment was unfathomable when they found that the carts were loaded with tattered clothes and rubbish. After exposing the ill intentions of the enemy, the Guru according to Koer Singh addressed his Sikhs in the following words :

> Never true to their words are these
> Hill Rajas, you know not their deceptions.
> They are all big cheats unworthy of trust.[2]

Wazir Khan expressed regret for the misconduct of some of his troops and delivered a letter to the Guru. This letter bearing the seal of Emperor Aurangzeb contained many assurances for the safe passage of the Sikhs out of Anandpur Sahib.[3] The followers of the Guru who were already anxious to leave the township became very vocal and active. They approached Mata Gujri and pleaded with her.[4] The Guru, however, felt that the promise of the Mughals were simply the ploys to dupe the Sikhs. He had sufficient experience of the double talk of the Mughals as well as of the Hill Chiefs.

---

1. M.A. Macauliffe, *The Sikh Religion*, Vol. V, p. 175.
2. Koer Singh, *Gurbilas Patshahi 10*, pp. 155-56.
3. According to Hari Ram Gupta the letter was delivered by Wazir Khan himself, *History of the Sikhs*, Vol. I, p. 290. *Zafarnama*, Verse 5, 13-15, Gian Singh, *Twarikh Guru Khalsa*, p. 980. Santokh Singh, *Sri Gur Partap Suraj Granth*, pp. 5843-44, 5852, 5853.
   According to Santokh Singh, Aurangzeb wrote, "I have sworn on the Quran not to harm thee. If I do, may I not find a place in God's court hereafter. Cease warfare and come to me. If thou desire not to come hither, then go wheresoever thou pleasest."
4. Santokh Singh, *op.cit.*, p. 5848.

But ultimately the Guru took a decision to evacuate the fort and the city much against his wishes and better judgement. Some scholars have wrongly surmised that the Guru's action smacked of acquiescence. In fact, the offer of safe passage was made by Wazir Khan and the Hill Rajas with the full knowledge that the Guru would never surrender. And the Guru's decision was prompted more by his determination to die fighting than by the promise held out to him by the Mughals.

The Guru evacuated Anandgarh and Anandpur on December 5-6, 1705 (Poh 6-7; Samvat 1762 BK). Just before this, he distributed his treasures as well as arms among the Sikhs and when everything was ready. Whatever could not be carried was put to fire.[1]

The moment the enemy got an inkling of the departure of the Sikhs, they forgot all about their vows and set out in hot pursuit immediately.

Skirmishes commenced from Kiratpur onwards. Realizing the impending danger, Guru Gobind Singh placed a band of 50 Sikhs under Bhai Uday Singh[2] and charged him with the responsibility of delaying the enemy's advance.[3] Bhai Uday Singh fought a bloody battle with the enemy at Shahi Tibbi. All of them perished fighting bravely, covering themselves with immortal glory. The battle lasted for two and half hours.[4]

When the battle at Shahi Tibbi was in progress, the rest of the caravan including Guru Gobind Singh had reached the bank of River Sirsa. It was almost daybreak now. About this time the news arrived that a contingent of enemy troops was fast approaching. Bhai Jiwan Singh[5], a prominent Sikh, was given a contingent of 100 Sikhs and ordered to encounter the

---

1. *Sri Gursobha* XI, 64/467; Santokh Singh, *Sri Gur Partap Suraj Granth*, 5855. The vows appear to have been most wantonly violated and to these we have poignant references in the *Zafarnama*. Sainapat also refers to violation of oath by the imperial forces.
2. Santokh Singh, *op.cit.*, p. 5848.
3. Bhai Uday Singh was the son of Bhai Mani Singh Ahiwal [*Shaheed Bilas, Bhai Mani Singh*, (ed.) by Giani Garja Singh]
4. *Sri Gursobha* XII, p. 84, 11/479.
5. Bhai Jaita's name after baptism.

pursuers. With the rest of his people, the Guru descended into
the flooded waters of the River Sirsa. The flow of water was
so fierce that many of them were drowned and many more
were swept away. Guru's family members too separated from
each other. Besides, there was a heavy loss of valuable
literature and property. It was here that the Guru's mother,
revered Mata Gujri and his two younger sons, Zorawar Singh,
and Fateh Singh, got separated and proceeded to Saheri, the
village of one of their domestic servants, Gangu Brahmin, who
handed them over to the state police at Morinda to be taken
to Sirhind[1] where they were cruelly put to death by Wazir
Khan, the governor of Sirhind, in spite of the vehement
protests of the then Nawab of Malerkotla.[2] Mata Sundri and
Mata Sahib Kaur were hurriedly led by Bhai Mani Singh
towards Delhi where they stayed in the house of Jawahar
Singh.[3] As regards the Guru himself, accompanied by his two
elder sons and a band of veteran Sikhs, he was able to reach
the village Ghanaulla[4] on the other side of River Sirsa. It was
now planned to proceed further to Kotla Nihang Khan and
pass the day safely in the residence of the Pathan Zamindar
Nihang Khan[5] who, being a sincere follower of the Guru, could
be depended upon for help even in a critical situation such as
this. Apprehending that the route ahead might be wrought
with danger, the Guru set apart a band of about 100 veterans
including Sahibzada Ajit Singh under the command of Bhai
Bachittar Singh and instructed them to march by the direct
route, whereas he along with some of his people preferred to
take the longer path along the left bank of River Sutlej. The
Guru met no resistance on the way and reached Kotla Nihang
Khan safe and sound. Bachittar Singh and his men, however,

1. Sainapat, *Sri Gursobha*, Chapter XI.
2. Inayat Ali Khan, *Description of the Principal Kotla Afghans*, pp. 13-14.
3. Lakshman Singh, *Guru Gobind Singh*, p. 105, (I have consulted 1909 edition).
4. Santokh Singh, *Sri Gur Partap Suraj Granth*, p. 5858.
5. Muslim Chief of Kotla Nihang Khan, near Ropar, in the Punjab, was a
   devotee of Guru Gobind Singh. According to Swarup Singh Kaushish,
   Guru Kian Sakhian, he with his wife and sons attended Baisakhi festival
   at Anandpur in 1699 and rendered homage to the Guru. At his request
   Guru Gobind Singh visited him in his village a month later on the occasion
   of the betrothal of his son and blessed the family.

had to fight their way through a cordon of the Ranghars of Malikpur, a village enroute and Pathans of Ropar. In the fierce fighting that took place on this occasion, majority of the Sikhs received martyrdom. The leader, Bachittar Singh, was mortally wounded and in that serious condition was carried to Kotla Nihang Khan by Sahibzada Ajit Singh.

The Guru did not want to stay at Kotla longer than was absolutely necessary. He decided to proceed further on the same day. His two elder sons, Sahibzada Ajit Singh and Sahibzada Jujhar Singh, and 40 Sikhs were to accompany him. When the night fell, the whole band set out on the onward journey. Nihang Khan detailed his son, Alam Khan to guide them to the route, they were to follow.

When Guru Gobind Singh left Kotla Nihang Khan, his object, it seems, was to proceed to Machhiwara and Raikot. At the former place lived two Pathan brothers, Nabi Khan and Ghani Khan. They had many trade dealings with the Guru and eventually had become his devoted followers. Moreover, they happened to be cousins of Nihang Khan and as such could be depended upon. The second place, Raikot, was under the control of Rai Kallha, whose daughter had been married to Alam Khan, son of Nihang Khan. Besides, like Nabi Khan and Ghani Khan of Machhiwara, Rai Kalla also had become a follower of Guru Gobind Singh. Another reason for the Guru to select this route was that the sixth, seventh and the ninth Gurus had already travelled across this area and attracted a good number of local people to the Sikh faith.

BATTLE OF CHAMKAUR

After Kotla Nihang, the village Bur Majra, became the halting place of Guru Gobind Singh and his men. Soon after their arrival there, news was received that a large body of Sirhind troops were approaching right on their heels. Immediately, the Guru decided to face the enemy at Chamkaur. He hurriedly reached his destination and encamped his entourage in a garden on the skirts of the village. He was well aware of the topography and locale of the place as he had on a previous occasion fought a military engagement here in 1702 when he was on his way to Kurukshetra.[1] The garden belonged to Rai Jagat Singh, the local landlord. The Guru sent some of his disciples to request him to let him take shelter in his *Haveli* (a spacious walled house) more like a *Garhi* (Mud Fortress).[2] Jagat Singh hesitated for the fear of the ruler's wrath but his brother Rup Chand asserting his right as a co-owner of the place allowed the Guru to use the place as he liked.[3] According to some chroniclers, the names of the owners were Bandhu, Chand and Gharlu who willingly handed over their *Haveli* to the Guru.[4] Soon after, the imperial army closed upon the place. The Pathans of Malerkotla, the Ranghers of Ropar and many Muslims of the neighbouring areas also joined it.[5] The Guru's army comprised of only forty[6] men, an infinitesimally small number in comparison to the huge army of the Mughals.[7] Besides, the Guru's soldiers were poorly equipped and had only those weapons, mainly consisting of swords, lances and *jamdhars*, which they had managed to carry during their flight from Anandpur. The allied forces attacked the *Garhi* (Mud Fortress) at day break. The Guru organised allround defence of the *Garhi*. He himself occupied a position on the top storey to observe and direct the operation as also to shoot his arrows. Out of forty men (exclusive of Guru and his two sons) about one fourth were deputed to defend the gate. An equal number was posted in the upper storey to keep a sharp watch on the enemy's movements. The rest took up their positions along the walls to keep vigil to prevent enemy scaling them. According to Mirza Inayat Ullah Khan the compiler of *Ahkam-i-Alamgiri*, the *Garhi* was attacked by 700 cavalrymen but the actual number appeared to be much large.[8]

Imperial Commanders, Khwaja Mohammad and Nahar Khan reconnoitred the Guru's arrangements and immediately

---

1. *Mahan Kosh.*
2. *Encyclopaedia of Sikhism*, Vol. I, p. 429.
3. *Ibid.*
4. Sainapat, *Sri Gursobha*, Chapter 12, stanza 473.
5. *Sri Gursobha*, (ed.) Dr. Ganda Singh, p. 52.
6. The number did not include the Guru and his two sons, Ajit Singh and Jujhar Singh.
7. *Zafarnama*, a letter addressed to the Emperor Aurangzeb.
8. Hari Ram Gupta, *History of the Sikhs*, p. 208.

Takht Sri Patna Sahib, Bihar
Birth-place of Guru Gobind Singh

Takht Sri Kesgarh Sahib, Anandpur Sahib
Guru Gobind Singh floated the order of Khalsa at this place
on the Baisakhi day of 1699 A.D.

Gurdwara Parivar Vichhora Sahib, Distt. Ropar
Situated on the bank of Sirsa where Guru Gobind Singh's family stranded
after leaving Anandpur Fort in 1704 A.D.

Gurdwara Katalgarh Sahib, Chamkaur Sahib
Martyrdom place of the elder sons of Guru Gobind Singh.

Gurdwara Fatehgarh Sahib, Sirhind
Martyrdom place of the younger sons of Guru Gobind Singh.

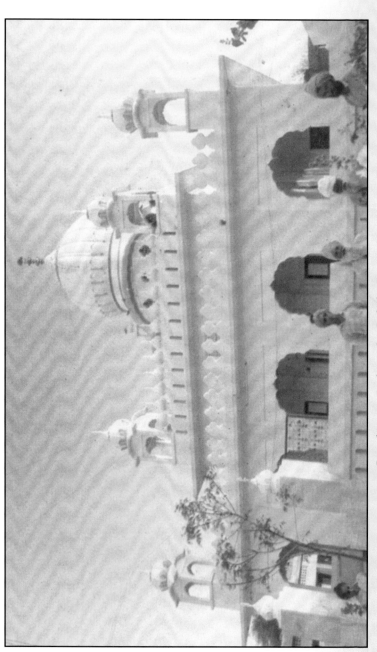

Gurdwara Lohgarh Sahib, Dina Kangar

Guru Gobind Singh wrote his famous Persian-Verse *Zafarnamah* (Epistle of Victory) to Emperor Aurangzeb from this place.

Takht Sri Damdama Sahib, Sabo Ki Talwandi (Bathinda)
The place where Guru Gobind Singh with Bhai Mani Singh as his
scribe prepared a fresh recension of Guru Granth Sahib,
popularly known as *Damdami Bir*.

Takht Sachkhand Sri Hazur Sahib, Nanded (Maharashtra)
Place of ascension of Guru Gobind Singh to his Eternal Abode.

resorted to psychological warfare. They sent their envoy to the Guru to remind him that he was to face not the paltry and undisciplined troops of the Hill Rajas but an invincible army of Aurangzeb, who was the king of kings, the asylum of the poor, the protector of the world, and it would be his sheer folly to attempt improbabilities. He should immediately renounce hostilities, make instant submission, embrace Islam and swerve infidelity.[1] The Guru's reaction to envoy's advice was of gross indifference. Sahibzada Ajit Singh, however, got provoked. He drew his scimitar and roared to the bearer of the message, "Utter another word and I will slash your head off your body."[2] The envoy though infuriated, yet remained tight-lipped. Soon he trudged back to his camp, agitated and disturbed.

The enemy then attacked the *Garhi* (Mud Fortress) with all the fury and might at their disposal. The Sikhs also gave them a blazing welcome. They rained arrows from all sides; from behind the walls, from roofs, firing ports and through every chink in the doors. Clad in black like a fly, enemy made a sudden and concerted attack. The Guru at that juncture responded to their manoeuvre very deftly. Every soldier who advanced from behind the wall was struck by an arrow and fell soaked in blood. Nahar Khan also tasted the pinch of a sharp-edged arrow of the Guru and found safety in flight. Many other Khans followed him betraying their courage and bravado. The Khawaja, seemingly the keyman of the Mughal forces, failed to muster courage to come into the open and that really was Guru's regret.[3] Many Sikhs lost their lives in the contest. They ran short of ammunition two or three hours before the sunset. Now the Guru devised another stratagem. He divided his men into groups, each of whom went out and fought the enemy with their personal weapons viz. sabre, spear, sword and lance. These groups operated in different directions one after the other to keep the enemy guessing and themselves fighting on their chosen ground. The leitmotif was

---

1. Ganda Singh, *Makhiz-i-Twarikh-i-Sikhan*, I, p. 8, also refer to Sayyed Muhammad Latif, *History of Punjab.*
2. *Ibid.*
3. *Ibid.*

that the enemy should not be able to storm the *Garhi* that day. The Guru's sons, Ajit Singh (17 years) and Jujhar Singh (15 years) led vigorous attacks and received martyrdom in the process.[1]

By the night fall, thirty-five out of the forty Sikhs, both the sons of Guru who were still in their teens fell fighting. Only five Sikhs, Daya Singh, Dharam Singh, Man Singh, Sant Singh and Sangat Singh survived. They suddenly gathered in a group, deliberated on a plan in hushed tones and then resolved to enact the scene of Anandpur in which the Guru, five years earlier, had played a double role of being the Guru and disciple at one and the same time. They told the Guru that at the moment, they were the Guru and he was a *Khalsa*. They passed a *gurmata* (resolution) ordaining the Guru to escape in the interest of the *Panth*.

They also decided that Bhai Daya Singh, Dharam Singh (The first and the second of the five beloveds) and Man Singh would accompany the Guru. Sant Singh and Sangat Singh were to stay behind to continue the fight.

The Guru who had made up his mind to die fighting had to retract from his decision and he decided to leave the mud fortress. The Guru could not but obey the *gurmata*—fiat of the five Sikhs—*Panj Pyaras*—representing the whole of *Khalsa Panth* whom he had raised to the status of Guru at Anandpur at the Baisakhi of 1699. He took off his plume, placed it before the five Sikhs went around them thrice and bowed before them. "The *Khalsa Panth* said the Guru, "Has stood well the ordeals and deserves to be crowned." He reiterated, "The *Khalsa* is the Guru and the Guru is *Khalsa*." Whenever five of you assemble with God in thy hearts, God and the Guru will be with you. The word is the Guru, and under its guidance, the *Khalsa* is the Guru."

According to Sainapat, Sant Singh was killed[2] when the Guru and his party were on the verge of leaving the fortress. Sangat Singh alone had to hold the advancing enemy at bay till his last breath. He put on the dress including plume similar to that of the Guru and positioned himself in the upper storey

---

1. *Zafarnama*, line 19-41; Hari Ram Gupta, *History of the Sikhs*, p. 208.
2. Sainapat, *Sri Gursobha*, Chapter 12, p. 70.

which the Guru had occupied during the day time. From a distance, or to an observer who had not seen the Guru himself, it was well-nigh difficult to differentiate between the Guru and Sangat Singh because he was wearing the dress akin to that worn by the Guru. The latter resembled the Guru almost. The enemy, therefore, concentrated their attention on him, mistaking him for the Guru, and, no wonder, they were jubilant when an arrow struck him dead. Historians have differed : whether it was Sant Singh or Sangat Singh or Jiwan Singh who put on the dress similar to that of Guru and successfully duped the enemy. Sant Singh could not be because Sainapat in his work *Sri Gurusobha* says that Sant Singh was killed just when the Guru and his party made a move to abandon the fortress. He also informs us that the Guru got enraged at the death of Sant Singh and very excitedly let fly arrows, causing havoc in the enemy ranks.

Bhai Jiwan Singh could also not masquerade as Guru because there is a positive evidence of *Bhat Vahi* declaring him to be a martyr in the battle on the bank of flooded River Sirsa.

This being so, it is not difficult to surmise that it was Sangat Singh who dressed up himself like the Guru and bore the brunt of the enemy's attack.

He was the younger brother of Bhai Jaita, a day younger to Guru Gobind Singh. According to Kankan, a court poet of the Guru, he had enjoyed the privilege of being the Guru's companion at Patna, and even afterward.

He is mentioned as Bangesak by Koer Singh, Shamsher Singh Ashok, a modern writer, also supports him. Sukha Singh uses the expression Bangesh in the case of Sant Singh to convey that the latter used to live in Bengal. Since in the time of Guru Gobind Singh, Patna where Sangat Singh played with Guru Gobind Singh, formed the headquarter of Suba of Bihar and not of Bengal, the usage of Bangesh to establish that Sangat Singh or Sant Singh belonged to Bengal does not carry conviction. The fact is that Bangsi or Bangesh both usages were meant to convey that Sangat Singh had connection with the people inhabiting the region called Bangesh. By the time Koer Singh wrote *Gur Bilas*, the Rangrettas, especially the band of the Sikhs under Bir Singh, had over-run the region of Bangesh in the North-Western frontier of India and many of them had settled themselves there. Like other inhabitants of this region, they began to be called Bangesar i.e. to say they belonged to 'Bangesh' region. This fact seemed to have impelled Bhai Sukha Singh to use this expression.

As per plan, all the three (Daya Singh, Dharam Singh and Man Singh) approached the enemy camps stealthily from three different directions i.e. heading towards South, East and West, undetected by skillful use of the ground and their field craft training. Just at the approach time to the camp which was coordinated, arrows from *Garhi* were discharged to extinguish burning torches of the enemy soldiers which had illuminated the *Garhi*, and its surrounding areas. While running past the enemy camp in the South, East and West, they raised loud cries individually warning that the Guru along with his soldiers was escaping. Since by now there was complete darkness, the allied forces got confused and fell upon each other killing many of their own soldiers. The allied forces deployed towards the North of *Garhi* moved towards the East and West of *Garhi* to capture the Guru. At this moment when there was total chaos the Guru moved towards the North and escaped towards the pre-decided rendezvous.

The allied force commanders unable to apprehend the motive behind the moves of the Sikhs made a forceful attack on the *Garhi* and had the satisfaction of having killed the Guru who was in fact Sangat Singh. The *Garhi* was captured. The Mughal forces joy was unbounded as they were under the impression that the Guru had been killed. But soon the euphoria evaporated when they came to know of the reality. It was not the Guru but one of his Sikhs named Sangat Singh who was killed by their arrows.

The Guru had left the fortress under the very nose of the enemy. Similarly, Man Singh, Dharam Singh and Daya Singh effected their escape. Wazir Khan and his commanders had to face utter disappointment. They won the battle but gained nothing.

Thereafter, the Mughals employed all their resources to capture the Guru but in vain. The Guru had covered long distance during the night on unfamiliar tracks. According to one assessment, the Guru covered 16 kms in two hours barefooted in unknown terrain, full of thorny bushes and reached the predetermined place before the appearance of dawn.

Thirty-seven *Khalsa* soldiers plus two elder sons of the Guru laid down their lives at Chamkaur out of spiritual conviction rather than love of worldly gain or glory. Such persons, indeed, were *Jiwan Mukt*, the ones who had the fullest realisation of God and led their lives in harmony with Guru.

According to some scholars, it were these people who are mentioned in the communitarian prayer of the Sikhs. But this view is not supported by any substantial historical evidence. Even a little reflection on the whole episode would expose its improbability. The number of martyrs at Chamkaur was only thirty-seven, three less than the forty as it is generally believed. Moreover, persons who courted martyrdom at Muktsar were in no way less resplendent than their counterparts at Chamkaur, equally courageous and eager to trudge the righteous road with their heads placed on their palms and hence their incorporation in the *Ardas* (Prayer) was doubtlessly legitimate.

CHAPTER X

THE GURU'S ESCAPE TOWARDS MALWA
A SAGA OF FORTITUDE AND SUFFERING

When the Guru reached Jandsar, a Gujjar of village Kiri recognised him and raised an alarm but to no effect.[1] The Guru moved on and reached the village Behlolpur at a distance of five kilometers to the West. From there he reached the wilds of Machhiwara. For all these days he had eaten nothing but only tender leaves of plants and wild shrubs and had nothing but only a clod of earth to rest upon. The rough and thorny paths had lacerated his limbs. His feet were blistered and cloths torn. But he was still unshaken. Reclining under a tree in a lonely jungle, the Guru sang :

> Beloved Friend, beloved God, Thou hear the servant's plight
> When Thou are not near, the comforts of cloak is ailment.
> The home is like living with serpents
> The flask is like a sharp thorn
> The goblet, a dagger, like knife of a butcher
> The tatters of my beloved are more dear
> Than the comforts with hell-like separation.[2]

(Shabad Hazare Patshahi 10)

At Machhiwara, he was joined by Dharam Singh, Man Singh and Daya Singh. But the situation was grave since the enemy was in hot pursuit. Realizing this, one Gulaba, an old

---

1. Fauja Singh (ed.), *Guru Gobind Singh Marg*, p. 44. According to Dr. Hari Ram Gupta, there were two Gujjars, Ramzu and Kala, who recognised the Guru.

2. *Mittar Piāre Nū Hāl Murīdāṅ Dā Kehnā.*
   Tudh Bin Rog Rajāiān Dā Oḍhan Nāg Nivāsāṅ De Rahnā.
   Sūl Surāhī Khaṅjar Piālā Biṅg kasāiāṅ Dā Sahnā.
   Yārḍe Dā Sānū Sathar Chaṅgā Bhath Kheriāṅ De Rahnā.

Masand of Machhiwara took the Guru and his three Sikhs to his residence. But very soon the heart within him succumbed to greed.

At this juncture, two *Pathan* brothers, Nabi Khan and Gani Khan, who used to visit Anandpur in connection with their horse-trade and had developed reverence for the Guru waited upon him. The Guru obliged them by agreeing to stay at their residence that lay close by of Gulaba at Machhiwara. Guru halted there for two days.

THE GURU'S FIRST LETTER TO AURANGZEB

During this short period, the Guru wrote a letter to Aurangzeb, popularly known as *Fatehnama*, which, in fact was a letter of admonition of Aurangzeb.

In the first three couplets of *Fatehnama* the Guru swore in the names of weapons, holy heroes of God and the Giver of kingdom to Aurangzeb, the Granter of the privilege of shielding the faithful and the low.

Then in the next few stanzas, the Guru seemed to be rebuking Aurangzeb who had been resorting to subterfuge and fraud in his dealings even with his father and brothers; how he had built an empire through loot, plunder and hypocritical acts. In couplet 6, the Guru said, "The rosary, O King in thy hand is but a snare to entrap the people unaware. When thou maketh pretend to pray wistfully, thou watch the prey."

In some other couplets, the Guru reminded the Emperor that retribution was sure to fall on him. His failure in Southern campaigns and in Mewar were to be perceived in that context (Couplet 11). He also made pointed reference to the killing of his two elder sons at Chamkaur. Through the cunning and craft holding in the same breath, he should not think that he had won (couplet 14). His *Khalsa* remains invincible and is in a position to deliver death blows to all his evil and aggressive designs.

In couplets 9 and 10, the Guru expressed that under his loving care the people had received sacrament of steel now and were determined to rid themselves of oppression, injustice and coercion.

If now Emperor dared cast his covetous glances on

Punjab, he would have to face so vehement an opposition that he would not be allowed to have a moment of respite, even a drop of water (Couplet 13).

This time, the *Khalsa* would not take the Emperor's words for granted. The Guru writes :

> No more, in us, thy words inspire
> The sort of faith thou doth desire
> We'll hence in arms correspond
> The like of thee, to them, respond.   *(Couplet 17)*

From couplet No. 18 through couplet No. 24, the Guru seems to throw a challenge to the Emperor's military might as also to his personal bravery. Regarding his personal bravery, the Guru challenged Aurangzeb that he should come into the field personally instead of depending upon recruits. The Guru very cogently brought a moral question in couplet No. 24.

> Armed with sword and the shield,
> Thou must personally take the field
> It is cowardly to fire humanity
> For thy evil aims and vanity.   *(Couplet No. 24)*

The letter[1] contained 24 couplets in all. It was in Persian verse and is a unique example of epistolary poetry. The *masanvi* metre of Firdausi and Nizami had been employed in it and the choice of words was impeccable.

Bhai Daya Singh disguised himself as a Muslim *Faquir* while his companions, Dharam Singh, Man Singh, Nabi Khan and Gani Khan masqueraded as his attendants. He was then seated in a litter and taken out from Machhiwara. They told all the inquirers that they were escorting *Uch-Da-Pir* or a high saint which by a pun would also mean the holy saint of Uch (a place near Bahawalpur now in Pakistan). At the village named Lal, a military commander had certain doubts regarding the identity of the person seated in the litter, and he made searching enquiries. Considering the answers illusive and unsatisfactory, he sent for *Qazi* Pir Mohammad of village Saloh, from whom the Guru had studied Persian, to identify the occupant of the litter. The *Qazi* certified that he was not Guru Gobind Singh. After that, Daya Singh was allowed

1. D.S. Duggal, *Fatehnama and Zafarnama.*

to proceed further to his destination fixed by the Guru.

Wrongfully though, it has often been assumed that the Guru and not Bhai Daya Singh, disguised himself as *Uch-Da Pir*. The avowal is based on the information gleaned from Bhai Sukha Singh's *Gurbilas* and *Suraj Parkash* by Bhai Santokh Singh. Regretfully, these celebrated works have not quoted any reliable historical source and have simply recorded the prevalent hearsay while the authors of these should have taken into consideration the backdrop of the event, ideology of the person involved in the event before portraying it. But the authors seem to have made a big lapse. Guru Gobind Singh simply could not take recourse to a guise to escape from danger or conceal his creedal identity. He would not simulate or evade a vowel of his identity, no matter how compelling the claims of expediency, for to do so would tentamount to disregarding his own teachings and assertion, *Kahio Prabhu so Bhakh Hun, Kahio Prabhu so Main Karon* (I say whatever God orders. I do whatever God wishes).

In this connection, it must be remembered that only a day or so earlier in his predicament at Chamkaur, the Guru had stoutly refused to leave the mud walls of the *Garhi* without first throwing clear challenge to thousands of his enemies beleaguering him and trumpeting his defiance : "The Guru now comes forth from behind the mud-walls and let him who cares and dares to obstruct his progress advance and try."

It would be a sheer travesty to assume that less than forty-eight hours afterwards, he would behave differently. The Guru was not a cyclothymic personality, given to wavering will and vacillating creed and conviction. The Guru who taught *Jujh Maron Tau Sach Patije* would never pretend to be a *Pir-i-Uch* under any circumstances whatsoever.

This statement by the Guru clinches the issue in the matter of this *Pir-i-Uch* episode showing that although the Sikh chroniclers are correct in giving almost all the material details, they erred in equating the *Pir-i-Uch* person with the Guru.[1]

---

1. That the Guru left Machhiwara in the guise of *Uch-Da-Pir* was not mentioned by *Sri Gursobha*, *Mahima Parkash* by Kirpal Singh (1798 B.K.-1731 A.D.); *Bansavalinama* by Kesar Singh Chhibber (1836 B.K.-1779 A.D.); *Gurbilas* by Koer Singh (1751 A.D.). The *Uch-Da-Pir* was first mentioned in *Gurbilas* by Sukha Singh.

Closely connected with all this is a question who was the person seated in the litter if he was not Guru Gobind Singh ? According to Sirdar Kapur Singh he was Bhai Daya Singh who assumed the guise of a holy man and who was helped to escape local military vigilance in a manner normal and honourable in such a situation, and that Sayyed Pir Mohammad had rendered true testimony as enjoined by *Koran* when he solemnly testified that inmate of the litter was not the Guru. Bhai Daya Singh had been entrusted with the task of delivering the letter personally to Aurangzeb and therefore he resorted to the stratagem of disguising himself.

Having been let off by the Mughal military commander, Bhai Daya Singh alongwith Nabi Khan, Gani Khan, Dharam Singh and Man Singh proceeded to Ghulal where the Guru had already reached as per programme carefully planned out by Gani Khan, Nabi Khan and *Qazi* Pir Muhammad. Here the Guru awarded the *Qazi*, a *Hukamnama* acknowledging his services for him. The *Qazi* then returned to his place.

From Ghulal, the Guru visited Lal. Here an orphan boy named Bhag Mal attended to all his needs. The Guru was so pleased that he blessed him and declared that he would be a person of immense fortune as his name suggested. Next sojourn of the Guru were at Katani Rampur and Kanech. At Kanech, a *Masand* named Fateh Chand avoided to welcome him as his spirit had failed out of fear of Wazir Khan. He was so much petrified that he even refused to part with his mare pretending that it had been taken away by his son-in-law.[1]

From Kanech, the Guru reached Sahnewal whose *panchayat* refused to pay respect to the Guru. When he was about to move in, the people including women of the village came forward to offer apology and to pay their respects. The Guru blessed them and went further to village Mohi near Jodhan, where-from he proceeded to Heira through village Seloani. A devoted disciple of the Guru known as Kirpal Das,[2] a name sake of the *Udasi Mahant* who had proved his mettle as a

1. Ishar Singh Nara, *Safarnama te Zafarnama*, pp. 227-228; *Guru Gobind Singh Marg*, p. 40, M.A. Macauliffe, *The Sikh Religion*, Vol. V, p. 193.
2. *Ibid.*, p. 229. *Gurdham Sangreh*, p. 137 by Giani Gian Singh.

warrior in the Battle of Bhangani lived there.[1] He accorded a warm welcome to the Guru and implored him to stay with him. Here he wrote a *Hukamnama* a letter commanding his followers to always hold Nabi Khan and Gani Khan in high esteem, for, they had rendered unto him, selfless and altruistic service.[2] The *Pathan* brothers thereafter returned to their homes, gratified and content spiritually.

There is another fact that mitigates against the literal acceptance of the chronicler's story. In the Islamic penal code, for six specific crimes, the punishment is fixed. The punishment of apostasy, which on the basis of *Qiyyas* includes false oath on the *Koran* by a Sayyed is death. There is no exercise of discretion in this. Again to abet, concealment and engineer escape of a rebel against the Islamic authority of the state is an act of high treason for which the punishment is death without discretion. Sayyed Pir Muhammad by doing what he did according to Sikh chroniclers, should have earned death at the hands of the Mughal authorities when it was disclosed that the Guru had escaped the Mughal forces. But providentially, he enjoyed a longer span of life. Similarly, two *Pathan* brothers did not attract the attention of the state authorities for committing an act of high treason on account of having aided the escape of a dangerous and a powerful enemy of the state. From this, it becomes clear that the Mughal authorities as well as the politically sensitive Muslim populace were well aware that in the *Pir-i-Uch* episode, Sayyed Pir Muhammad had testified and as such there was no such event as escape of Guru Gobind Singh in a disguise.

Guru Gobind Singh's own testimony on the point is quite conclusive. In *Zafarnama* his letter to Aurangzeb, the Guru tells the Emperor that during his progress from Chamkaur to Bathinda desert (1705), he met no impediment or harm whatsoever. God led him safely out of the enemy's cordon without a scratch on his person.[3]

From this place, the Guru proceeded to village Lamma where the people, who had already embraced Sikhism received him with utmost reverance and love.

---

1. Santokh Singh, *Sri Gur Partap Suraj Granth*, Rut 6, Ansu 48.
2. *Ibid.*
3. *Na pechīdā mue na ranjīdah tan.*
   Ke berūn khudāvurd dushman shikan.　　　　(*Zafarnama*, 44th Stanza)

From Lamma, he reached Raikot.[1] The chief of Raikot named Rai Kalha was an ardent follower of the Guru and a close relation of Nihang Khan. He was aware of the imperial orders that the Guru should be apprehended wherever he was, but he took pleasure in defying it as he valued faith in the Guru more than his life. When he came to know the sufferings the Guru had borne, tears rolled down his eyes. According to Bhai Santokh Singh, he waited upon the Guru at Seloani and requested him to visit Kot Kapura. Now when the Guru visited Raikot, Rai Kalha left no stone unturned to provide comfort to him. The Guru granted him an excellent sword in recognition of his selfless service. At the Guru's behest, he sent Nura Mahi to Sirhind to fetch news about what had happened to other members of his family.

Not long after, Mahi delivered the news of what had happened to the Guru's family members after he left Anandpur. He told that in the confusion that prevailed in the wake of Guru's departure from the city, Mata Gujri's wealth and his two sons, Zorawar Singh and Fateh Singh, aged nine and seven respectively had nowhere to go until their family cook Gangu, a Brahmin by caste, offered to take to his own village Saheri. They accompanied him to his house. Now he turned perfidious and deceitful, obviously to get some reward from the Mughals and also to possess wealth of Mata Gujri, he informed the Mughal officers Jani Khan and Mani Khan of Morinda that the Guru's mother and his two younger sons were staying at his place. The officials at once took them in their custody and carried them to Sirhind to hand them over to Nawab Wazir Khan. Gangu also went to Sirhind where his services were duly appreciated by the Mughal Governor. Mata Gujri and his grandsons were imprisoned in a tower of the fort called *Thanda Burj* meaning the Cold Tower. It was torturous for an 80 year old lady and her two grandsons to stay in it during the peak winter month. Wazir Khan who was biting his lips with anger for his failure to capture the Guru, now had

---

1. A Rajput named Tulsi Ram had been converted to Islam. A descendant of Tulsi Ram, named Rai Ahmed, founded the town of Raikot in 1648. Rai Kalha was the son of Rai Kamal Din, a brother of Rai Ahmed.

another opportunity to settle score with him, albeit vicariously and unethically by exercising his authority on the little children.

On December 9, 1705 Baba Zorawar Singh[1] and Fateh Singh were produced before Wazir Khan, who had just returned from the Battle of Chamkaur. Wazir Khan tried to lure them to embrace Islam with promises of riches and honours but they spurned the offer. He threatened them with death as an alternative at the non-acceptance of Islam, but they remained determined. A death sentence was eventually awarded to them. Nawab Sher Muhammad of Malerkotla protested on the ground that Islam does not permit such harsh punishment to children who were unable to discriminate what is right or wrong for them that it would be ethically and religiously improper to harm innocent children. Wazir Khan spurned his protest and ordered that the children be bricked alive in a wall if they still refused conversion. They were kept in *Thanda Burj* in that severe winter for another two days. On 11th December, under the orders of Wazir Khan, their punishment of brick walling them alive while standing commenced. As the masonry reached above chest height, it crumbled. On December 12, 1705, the very next day, the Sahibzadas were once again offered the choice of conversion or death. They chose the latter and fearlessly faced the executioner's sword. The aged Mata Gujri who had all along been confined in the *Thanda Burj* a little distance away breathed her last as the news of her grandsons, execution reached her. The dead bodies were kept for the night at a spot now called Bimangarh, just outside the fort wall.[2]

Mahi also narrated how revered Mata Sundri ji and

---

1. M.A. Macauliffe writes : "It is a general belief among the Sikhs that the children were bricked into a wall and suffered to die in that position but the authors of *Suraj Prakash* and the *Gurbilas* both state that the children were put to death by the sword of a Ghalzai executioner in the order of their ages." (*The Sikh Religion*, Vol. V, p. 189). Sainapat merely states that Jujhar Singh gave a fitting reply which put the Nawab and his courtiers into extreme uneasiness and that the two boys chose the path of martyrdom for the sake of righteousness as their grandfather had done (*Sri Gursobha* XI), see also William Irvine, *Later Mughals*, Vol. I, p. 88.
2. Hakim Ram Kishan, *Janam Sakhi Guru Gobind Singh*, p. 145.

Sahib Kaur ji (the Guru's wives) were escorted to Delhi by Bhai Mani Singh and lived secretly at a place where now is situated Mata Sundri College.

As the news of the ghastly events reached Todar Mal, who was a wealthy Sikh of the Guru, and was a resident of Sirhind, he hastened to the court of Wazir Khan. He had the intention of paying ransom for the children and their grandmother. But he was disappointed to find that the worst had already happened. He then approached Wazir Khan for permission to cremate them befittingly. The permission was reluctantly granted but on the condition that he would have to purchase the piece of land by paying as many gold *Mohars* as, placed closely together, would completely cover it up. Todar Mal complied with the condition and cremated the three dead bodies.[1] The Sikhs have raised a beautiful hall in the campus of Sri Kesgarh, Anandpur, in gratitude to Todar Mal's noble deed. A young and pretty girl Anup Kaur closely related to revered Mata Jito ji was captured by Sher Muhammad of Malerkotla who desired to admit her to his harem. She was taken to Malerkotla where she committed suicide instead of submitting to the carnal advances of the Nawab.

The Guru received the tragic news with amazing courage and equanimity. Mahi also hinted that there was a rumour floating in the town of Sirhind that Wazir Khan would soon lead a force in search of the Guru.

Realising that the surroundings of Raikot were not a strategically suitable place to put up a fight with the enemy, he decided to move to Lakhi Jungle. The Guru is believed to have stayed with Rai Kalha for sixteen days.[2] According to Ishar Singh Nara, his next sojourn was Lopo Gran after which he stayed at a place which is now called Alamgir. Nagahiya Singh the brother of Bhai Mani Singh presented him a beautiful horse. From this place he proceeded towards Lakhi jungle. On

---

1. On the spot where the bodies were cremated, a gurdwara (Shrine) called Jyoti Sarup was later erected. At the place where the two Sahibzadas were bricked and beheaded stands the shrine called Fatehgarh Sahib. Near the site of the Tower in which the three were imprisoned and where Mata Gujri breathed her last stands a shrine called Mata Gujri's *Burj* (Tower).
2. Santokh Singh, *Suraj Parkash*, Rut 6, Ansu 53.

the way he passed through villages of Manuke, Mehdeana, Chakkar, Takhtupura and Madhen and reached Dina.

THE GURU AT DINA

At Dina about 13 kilometers South-West of Takhtupura, a devoted Sikh Rama presented the Guru with a steed of a very high quality. He accepted it and blessed Bhai Rama. The news of his arrival at this place spread soon and the Zamindars/peasants of the area started flocking to him, some to assure him of their faith and the others just to know him and his mission. Some of the influential people who made their obeisance here were Lakhmir, Shamir and Takht Mal all the three grandsons of Jodha Rai[1] who embraced Sikhism under the impact of the charismatic personality of Guru Hargobind. Param Singh and Dharam Singh the grandsons of Bhai Rup Chand also came for audience with the Guru. Mahant Dayal Puri came all the way from Sirhind. The Guru asked the Mahant to carry out the task of spreading his message in the area around Sirhind, and in doing so, he should fear none. The Guru stayed there for quite some time.

Around this time he received a message from Aurangzeb, most probably a reply to his letter *(Fatehnama)*. The original letter of invitation is not available in any of the collections of his Rukat, Ahkam or Arqan nor do we have any details of its contents. The twenty-eighth *Sakhi* of the *Sakhi Pothi* (book) (*Sau Sakhi* MS 79) contains a brief summary of it. According to it, *Parwanas* were issued to the Guru saying, "There is only one kingdom. Seeing the *Parwana* you better come here immediately. Our religious sentiments are the same. If not, I will come myself. The awe and superiority of saintliness will then have gone. You may live in kingdom as other saints and devotees live." To this, continues the *Sakhi*, were added some words of arrogance not unusual with the style of the Royal *Parwanas* (letters) that the kingdom had been bestowed upon him by God.[2]

---

1. Bhai Jodha was a staunch devotee of Guru Hargobind. He fought on the side of the Guru when the latter came to this part of the country to raise an effective defence against the invaders. He was the Chief of Kangar, a place nearly 5 kilometers from Dina.
2. Avtar Singh, *Sakhi Pothi*, translated, printed and edited, pp. 60-61, 62-63, 112-113.

The Guru in response to the message wrote a letter bearing the title *Zafarnama* in which he underlined the perjury of the Mughal officials and the urgency of his paying personal attention to his affairs.[1] The letter was taken to the Emperor by Bhai Daya Singh and Dharam Singh in the guise of Muslim *Darveshes*.[2] They came to Agra and from there proceeded to the South through Gwalior, Ujjain and the Malwa country till at last they reached Burhanpur. From there, they finally reached Ahmednagar via Aurangabad. Daya Singh went to the *Sangat* at Ahmednagar and explained to the local Sikhs the object of his mission. He does not seem to have received any sincere assistance from the local Sikhs, some of whom were openly critical of the Guru's policy and action. Then Daya Singh made an acquaintance with a Sikh who apparently had some influence in high quarters and arranged the delivery of the letter to Aurangzeb.

ZAFARNAMA (EPISTLE OF VICTORY)[3]

Zafarnama is a letter written by Guru Gobind Singh in reply to the oral and written communication of Aurangzeb, which the Guru had received at village Dina through a *Qazi* sent by the Emperor in response to his earlier letter *Fatehnama*. This was composed in chaste Persian language at Dina itself. The letter is an excellent literary piece replete with similes and metaphors superbly used to telling effect. According to D.S. Duggal, "occupies a place of eminence in epistolary poetry of Persian." The following lines amply bear out this statement:

> With limbs and skulls of warriors killed
> The field was eminently filled
> Like so many bats and balls to play
> In the field, in heap, they lay.38. [4]   (*Zafarnama*)

---

1. *Shumā rā chu farz ast kāre kuni(n).*
   Bamūjab navishtah shumāre kuni(n).53
   Navishtah rasīdo bā guftah zubān.
   Babāyad ki kār inh bārāhat rasān.54.
   Ke kāzī marā guftah beron niyam.
   Agar rāstī khud biyārī kadam.56.   (*Zafarnama*, Stanzas 53, 54, 56)
2. Sainapat, *Sri Gursobha*, stanzas 564 to 569, Chapter XII.
3. Translation by M.A. Macauliffe.
4. *Saro pāe amboh chandā shudah*
   Ke maidān puraz goe chaughān shudah.   (*Zafarnama*, Stanza 38)

Besides being a tribute to the literary excellence, this letter is of great importance since it throws a flood of light on the Guru's approach on unethical issues, his concept of God and justice, his views regarding the duties and functions of a sovereign vis-a-vis his subjects, his outlook regarding the use of force and different historical events intimately connected with Guru's life.

In stanza No. 1 to stanza No. 12, the Guru's unshakable faith in God is amply manifest. He extols Him as Eternal, Merciful, Bounteous being, Dispenser of justice, Holy refuge, Guide, True king, Radiant, Sublime, Provider of livelihood, Wise, Care-taker of the humble, the low and the lost, Vanquisher of foes, Solution of all woes and troubles, Designer of supreme laws of nature and of the Earth, Chastiser of foes[1], Fearless, True emperor, Formless, Non-existent, Incomparable, Mightiest of all[2] (stanza 72), Carefree[3] (stanza 71), Omnipresent, Omnipotent and Omniscient.

The Guru's invocation to such a God of myriad attributes and functions instill in him a moral spirit unswerving, always inspiring him to function in the world without any fear, as also to advise and warn the people including even the Emperors to tread the righteous path.

He, therefore, boldly criticises Aurangzeb for his unethical conduct. He tells him frankly and fearlessly that he, his *Dewans* and *Bakhshis* (officials of the highest rung in Mughal bureaucracy) were liars, have no qualms and care a fig even for oaths rendered on Holy *Koran*. He himself is a defier of his religion, worshipper of mammon and a veritable pledge breaker. He also pointed out that his pledged words rendered on holy *Koran*, in fact, were snares to entrap the people. One such snare being his word that the Guru would not be harmed if he vacated Anandpur.

From stanza 19 to stanza 44, the Guru gave the account of the Battle of Chamkaur, stating how he had to face a

---

1. *Zafarnama*, Stanza 44.
2. *Khudāvaṅd ezad zamīno(ṅ) zamā(ṅ)*
   Kuniṅdeh ast her kas makīno(ṅ) makāṅ.   (*Zafarnama*, Stanza 72)
3. *Ke ū be muhāb ast shāhenshāh.*
   Zamīno(ṅ) zamāṅ sachāe pātshāh.   (*Zafarnama*, Stanza 71)

disproportionately large number of the Mughal troops and how he lost thirty-seven of his followers including his two elder sons Ajit Singh (17) and Jujhar Singh (14). In these stanzas it was also mentioned that the Guru killed Nahar Khan, a Mughal General and he and his Sikhs kept at bay the enemy for almost the whole day. Though the Mughal soldiers attired in black made furious charges, shouting and shrieking like a swarm of flies, yet the *Khalsa* held them in check. The moment anyone left the safety of his defence in an attempt to commit offence, he was laid in a pool of blood by an arrow. But how *Khalsa* only forty-three strong, tired and hungry, could hold against the countless number of the enemy. Except four all fell fighting. In the critical hours, God led the Guru out of the fort to a place of safety. The Guru did not suffer even a scratch on his person in the process.

The Guru reminded in stanza 75 that no doubt Aurangzeb had claimed four tender lives (four children of the Guru) yet the spirit of the Guru was as high as ever and the coiled cobra of deadly venom is very much alive in the form of Singhs. The Guru also warned him that, "he should be prepared for retributive justice on the Day of Judgement for all the atrocious acts committed by him. His professions of adherence to the tenets of his faith was a mere fraud, because without the least qualms, he had broken the most solemn words pledged by him on *Koran.*"

To arouse his moral conscience still more, the Guru brought forth another fact. He accused him of siding with the crafty hill chieftains who were idolaters and fought against him who was an iconoclast (metaphorically speaking) like him. The Guru in his sweep clearly hinted at the real causes that caused confrontation between the Hill Rajas and him. He also tried to hammer into the mind of Aurangzeb his unethical unrighteous and immoral conduct, simply to put him to shame, morally speaking. The Guru, while denouncing the immoral conduct of the king and his men for wanton repudiation of their own solemn words pledged by them voluntarily on their holy texts, said that if he had ever held out such solemn promises, he would have upheld their sanctity even at the cost of his life.

"Nothing could have led us astray from our self-chosen path had we sworn by the words we believe. Falter ? Never, our life be relieved."

Particular emphasis is, therefore laid on the need for an upright and ethical conduct on the part of an individual embracing the entire gamut of his life. Aurangzeb was strongly condemned not only for his dastardly designs but also for the dishonest, unethical and immoral means that he invariably employed to wrest advantages over his adversaries. In this context the Guru spoke the following words :

> You (Aurangzeb) are not sincere in your affirmations to the tenets of your faith.
> A Man who is not true to his words stands condemned and is rejected as a counterfeit coin by man and God both.

Guru Gobind Singh, therefore, raised ethical conduct to a sovereign status and made it as the true expression of the harmony of human personality with the Will of God.

Living life ethically was the keynote of the teachings of Guru Gobind Singh and was a faith with him. Therefore, fully aware about the immoral acts of Aurangzeb he wished that Aurangzeb should remould his life on ethical values. He advised him to mend himself. In case he was willing to stand by his solemn promises and statements made orally by and through written note, and his thoughts and actions were in harmony with each other, he was ready to negotiate with him. The Guru invited the Emperor to Kangar (then outskirts of Dina) where all the contentious issues would be discussed and resolved[1] (stanza 58). The Guru also hinted that he would be welcomed appropriately and presented with a valuable steed. Alternatively, the Guru left to him to find for himself the real cause of the fight.[2]

All through the letter, not a trace of hatred could be felt or found. It only depicted moral rage along with a very strong urge to reform Aurangzeb and to make him realise that whatever he had done towards him and his *Khalsa* was not

---

1. *Chi tashrīf dar kasbah kāṅgaṛ kunad.*
   Vazāṅ pas mulākāt bāham shavad.58. (Zafarnama, Stanza 58)
2. *Agar hazrate khud sitādāh shavad.*
   Bajāṅ o dile kār vāzah shavad.52. (Zafarnama, Stanza 52)

inconsonance with the Will of God. The Guru took his stand essentially on moral grounds and that is what formed the scarlet thread passing through the whole range of verses to impart coherence to them. The officials of Aurangzeb had forced an unjust war on Guru Gobind Singh and had broken their solemn vows and the honourable conduct expected of a King of Aurangzeb stature. If all this was done with the Emperor's approval, then the Emperor could not boast of being a believer in God. He should have really remembered the True Lord if in the life hereafter, he wished Him to remember the Emperor. By ignoring the dictates of justice, Aurangzeb had shown himself to be a stranger to real statesmanship as well as to the fundamental teachings of God as propagated in Islam. In possession of immense power, he should not have forgotten that power was entrusted to the ruler for protecting the innocent people and not for spilling their blood.

A very important undercurrent of *Zafarnama* was that the righteous cause must be upheld and forces championing the unrighteousness must be resisted, even with the use of arms if need arises. The sanction for the use of arms in the oft-quoted stanza of *Zafarnama*, namely :

> When the affairs are past redemption,
> By all other means of peaceful intention,
> It is just to assert the right
> Through thy sword and a righteous fight.22.[1]

Unfortunately it is not invariably understood in proper perspective. The message of the stanza is two-pronged; bloodshed should be avoided as far as possible, but at the same time, the cause should not be abandoned merely because, as a last resort, it warrants the use of force. The use of arms is allowed for a noble cause of universal validity, once all other peaceful means for resolving the crisis have been completely exhausted. A very clear implication is that, in such circumstances, the use of force, as an unavoidable ultimate necessity, must be limited to the bare minimum prominently pops out of these popular lines for all sensitive minds to take note of.

---

1. *Chūṅ kār az hamā hīlte dar guzasht.*
   *Halāl ast burdan bā shamshīr dast.*22

The *Zafarnama* contains 111 stanzas and is written in chaste Persian language. Bhai Daya Singh and Dharam Singh (according to *Gursobha* by Sainapat, Daya Singh and his five companions) were deputed to deliver the letter personally to Aurangzeb at Ahmednagar. They reached Ahmednagar after considerable difficulty and succeeded in handing over the letter to the Emperor who seemed to have been much impressed by the contents of the letter. The fact is vouchsafed by a statement of Sainapat in his treatise *Gursobha*. Mirza Inayat Ullah Khan in his compilation *Ahkam-i-Alamgiri* refers to a letter received from Guru Gobind Singh in which he had expressed his wish to meet the Emperor. Accordingly, Aurangzeb deputed a *Gurzbardar* and a *Mansabdar* Muhammad Beg and Sheikh Yar Mohammad respectively to approach Guru Gobind Singh through Munim Khan and use all diplomatic skill in persuading him to go to Emperor. If Guru Gobind Singh was to march through the territory of Sirhind, his safety was to be guaranteed, and if he needed any money for his travel that was to be supplied from the properties seized from the Guru himself. Dr. Anil Chander Banerjee, a renowned scholar of Sikhism, says, "There are reasons to think that the original text of the letter is no longer available." He bases his conclusion on two grounds; firstly, it is usual to compose diplomatic communication in the style and form of *Zafarnama*. *Zafarnama* is written in a 'dramatic form' in verse in the metre in which the Persian *Masnavis*, as also the *Shahnama*, are composed. Diplomatic letters are not composed as such. Secondly, there are statements which can hardly be attributed to the Guru, as for example the epithet "*Sarwar-i-ka-i-nat*" applicable to God only, has been used with reference to Aurangzeb.

Both the grounds are flimsy, untenable and tenuous. *Zafarnama* was not a diplomatic letter in the sense the diplomacy is often understood. Had it been so, the Guru would not have called a spade and peeled skin after skin of pretensions, fraud and hypocrisy of the Emperor, nor would he have asked him to look inwards to his own moral conscience and ponder upon the inexorable laws of God, which always go against those who are unethical in the performance of their duties. Further, it is not sound to base conclusion on a single expression. The referred expression seemed to have been a distortion effected by a copyist or by some vested interests or a substitution for some other word. Anyway anyone stray expression cannot determine the tenor of any document.

In sum *Zafarnama* was a scathing exposure of the perfidy of the Emperor Aurangzeb, his unprincipled support to the Hill Rajas, his wrong notion about sovereignty as well as about the conduct of public affairs, his distorted and smudged thinking about religion and his sadistic pleasure at the innocent killings, his hypocritical approach to God and his creation. At the same time, it was a testament of the assertion of the Guru that ethical principles were supreme in matters of public policy as well as of private behaviour, that a sovereign must protect and promote righteousness instead of terrorising the people with force, that sovereignty of morality both in the affairs of state as well as in the conduct of individual human beings should be upheld at all costs; that absolute truthfulness should be addressed to, equally by a sovereign and an ordinary citizen, that people had inherent right to resort to force as a last resort against the forces of injustice and corruptions.

From Dina, the Guru occasionally went out and visited a few places in the neighbourhood. Two such places were Manan and Bhadaur.

THE GURU IN LAKHI JUNGLE

While still at Dina, the Guru came to know that his whereabouts had become known to the Mughal government of Sirhind. From then on he started looking for some suitable place where he could best meet the challenge of the enemy. No less was his keenness to inculcate in the minds of the people the spirit of *Dharam Yudh* (war of righteousness). Against this backdrop, he decided to enter Lakhi Jungle.[1]

---

1. In Guru Gobind Singh's time and even much later, there was a dense forest in Ferozpur Area. It extended from the bank of River Sutlej near Ferozpur to the wastes of Bathinda stretching over an area of about 80 kms. ☛

He left Dina and travelled from one village to another. He visited Bander, Bargarh, Saravan. At Saravan he gave people a little practice in archery. Next, he proceeded to Jaito. Therefrom the Guru went to Kotla Maluk Das and Lambhawal wherefrom he made a dash to Kot Kapura situated 13 kms in the North. It was situated on a promontory in a big pond and was admirably suited to stand a siege or an attack. Probably, the pursuing enemy forces had come too near by now. Chaudhari Kapura, a Brar Jat and master of the fort welcomed the Guru who asked him to lend his fort for a few days. Fearing the wrath of the Mughals, he politely refused to oblige him.[1] From here he proceeded to Dhilwan Sodhian, 3 Kms from Kot Kapura where Sodhi Kaul, a descendant of Prithi Chand, the elder brother of Guru Arjan Dev, received the Guru with great warmth and cordiality. As the tradition goes, it was here that the Guru took off his blue robes which he had been wearing ever since he left Machhiwara and tearing them off into small pieces consigned them, one by one, to fire. The historic words that he is said to have uttered on this occasion are memorable :

> The blue robes have been torn off,
> And with that ends the rule of Turko-Pathans.[2]

Chaudhari Kapura, now repentant of his earlier disgraceful act, came to see the Guru and asked for his forgiveness. The Guru pardoned him and asked him to give him a good guide. He provided one Chaudhari Khan, under whose guidance the Guru marched westward in the direction of Dhab Khidrana. On the way, he passed through Ramiana, Mallan, Gauri, Sanghar and Kaoni.

Meanwhile hundreds of his followers had collected around the Guru. Among them were a large number of

---

☛ This was supposed to contain one lac trees and thus was called Lakhi Jungle. Forster says the Lakhi Jungle was secure retreat owing to scarcity of water, the valour of its people and for a breed of excellent horses called the *Jungle-Tazees*.

1. Giani Gian Singh, *Sri Guru Panth Parkash*, pp. 291-92.
2. Some scholars have doubted the veracity of the tradition on the ground that Guru could not have uttered such words because he bore no enmity against the Muslims. Certainly, the Guru did not bear enmity against Muslims or Islam, but it is also not improbable that he would not have wished the end of Turko-Pathan rule which was tyrannous.

Majhails (people of the *Majha* region) of the Punjab who came to the Guru to pay their respects and also to offer their condolences on the death of his sons and his mother. The Guru received them warmly and counselled them to keep cool. Instead of being sad and anguished, they should learn to live in the Will of God. Many poets and bards who had left Anandpur when it was besieged also came to the Guru in Lakhi Jungle. Poets sang inspiring songs, full of love from their aching hearts. It was a great reunion. The poems full of pathetic themes, went deep into the peoples' hearts.

The swarming of hundreds and thousands of the Sikhs to the Guru to reaffirm their faith in him deeply touched the sensitive mind of a folk-poet who spontaneously poured forth :

> To Lakhi Jungle repaired the *Khalsa*
> Resistless was the friend's call.
> They paused not for food or drink and rushed to the Guru
> like the buffaloes running to their master at his nod
> One waited not for another
> Such eagerness swayed their hearts
> Gone was the pangs of separation
> Perfect union prevailed
> Overwhelming was their gratefulness.[1]

It was here that one Sayyad Ibrahim much impressed by the Guru's teachings appeared in his *Darbar*. He besought the Guru for enlightenment. For years together, he had meditated but had not been able to achieve his goal. But now as he listened to his gospel, he was metamorphosed and entered the *Khalsa* fraternity by receiving *Khande-ki-Pahul* and committing himself totally to the ideals of the *Khalsa*.

According to Muhammad Latif, the number rallied around the Guru swelled to twelve thousand.[2]

In the meanwhile, when the forty Sikhs who had given

---

1. *Lakhī Jungle Khālsā, Didār Āye lagā.*
    Sun Ke Sad Māhī Dā, Mehī Pāṇī Ghāh Muto Ne
    Kise Nāl Na Raliā Kāī, Koī Shauk Paiyo Ne
    Giā Firāk Miliā Mit Māhī, Tāṅ Hī Shukar Kito Ne.
                                    (Koer Singh, *Gurbilas Patshahi 10*, p. 211)
2. Muhammad Latif, *History of the Punjab.*

up their discipleship of the Guru out of fear of death during the siege of Anandpur and in token thereof had handed over a signed disclaimer to the Guru, reached back their homes, they were chided and taunted even by their own women for deserting the Guru in his hour of difficulty. The Sikhs in general and especially those who lived in *Majha* region met in a convention at Patti[1] and expressed their deep concern at the plight of the Guru as also at the perfidy of the Sikhs who signed *Bedawa* (a disclaimer). They decided to send their representatives to the Guru to offer their condolences at the sad demise of his four sons and to suggest that they could negotiate on his behalf to bring about reconciliation between the Guru and the Mughal Government.

THE FORTY DESERTERS[2]

The public hatred coupled with their own sense of remorse at their treacherous deeds impelled them to do something to recompense for their infidelity and perjury. They, therefore, decided to meet the Guru to offer their apology who at that time was in the jungle area of the *Malwa*. They and the Sikh representatives accordingly started their march towards the Guru. The forty included Bhag Singh, Bhag Kaur's[3] brother and her husband Nidhan Singh[4] son of late Choudhari Des Raj[5] of Patti. They met the Guru between Ramiana and Khidrana. After condoling the sad and untimely death of his sons, they offered to negotiate with the Mughal Government to effect compromise between the Guru and the Mughal Government.

The Guru replied, "Friends, you have come to advise me, thinking yourselves to be wiser than I. But I am not inclined to accept your advice. You have not rightly comprehended the real spirit of Sikhism. If you had, you would not be advising me, but seeking my advice and carrying out my orders. If you had understood my ideals of life, you would have never thought of making peace between me and the tyrants. Rather,

---

1. *Suraj Prakash;* Swarup Singh Kaushish, *Guru Kian Sakhian, Sakhi* No. 90.
2. *Ibid.*
3. Swarup Singh Kaushish, *op. cit.*
4. *Ibid.*
5. *Ibid.*

you would have joined my army and fought against them. You advise me to give up fighting and seek peace with the cruel bigoted tyrants. I cannot do that. Know ye not that I have no quarrel with, or personal grudge against any man ? People are groaning under tyranny and oppression. It is to rescue them that I have taken up arms. My sword strikes at tyrants, not at meeks. It defends the weak against the strong. Come and join me in this holy task of liberating people. Your policy of co-operation and meek submission has only tightened the chains. What could you, or people like you do when Guru Arjan and Guru Tegh Bahadur were put to inhuman tortures and death respectively ? The only sorrow that I feel springs from beholding my countrymen disunited and in chains. The only desire that sits ever alert in my heart is for the unification and liberation of the down-trodden people. If you are my Sikhs follow my advice. I am sorry I cannot concur with you or accept you as my instructors in this matter."[1]

This statement of the Guru simply benumbed them. Preferring their safety to the Guru's cause they retraced their steps to their homes. The forty Sikhs who earlier had deserted the Guru at Anandpur refused to follow them. Now they were changed persons, burning with the desire to .egain discipleship of the Guru by displaying hundred percent fidelity to the noble cause of the Guru. Even Bhag Singh, one of the forty, who faltered in the initial stages of conversation with the Guru displayed his resolve to serve the cause of his master at all cost. *Mai* Bhag Kaur[2] seemed to have played a great role in keeping him on the right track. All the forty Sikhs accompanied by Bhag Kaur decided to swim or sink for the cause of the Guru. They moved on towards the Guru who by then had proceeded further alongwith representatives of *Majha* region to select a strategically suitable place to give a fight to the advancing Mughal forces who were in hot persuit of the Guru. These forty were led by Mahan Singh of the village Sursinghwala in the district of Amritsar and included Nidhan Singh[3], husband of

---

1. Kartar Singh, *Life of Guru Gobind Singh*, p. 220.
2. Bhag Kaur was the daughter of Paloo Shah and was married to Nidhan Singh, son of Des Raj of Patti.
3. Swarup Singh Kaushish, *Guru Kian Sakhian*, p. 160—Bhai Santokh Singh also vouchsafes "Sun Māī Bhāgo Sachiārī. Kul Naihar Susrāhei Ubārī."

Mai Bhag Kaur. She herself was the forty-first Sikh skilled in handling weapons and possessed determination of steel.

BATTLE OF MUKTSAR—December 29, 1705

Apprehending the advance of Mughal forces, Guru ji crossed the Lakhi Jungle to reach a place known as Khidrana[1] which was famous for its *Dhab* a sort of water pond, a natural depression in the ground which was fed by rain water. The Guru planned the defence in such a way that it should not be easy for the enemy to capture the *Dhab* which was the only reservoir for supply of water in that part of the country. He himself took up his position on an elevated maund and his Sikhs in bushes which lay around the maund and the adjoining pool of water.

The troops of Wazir Khan marched towards Khidrana spreading terror on the way.

As the forty Sikhs from *Majha* region reached in the neighbourhood of Khidrana, they came to know that the Mughal forces under the command of Wazir Khan were advancing to attack the Guru who had just encamped around *Khidrana-di-Dhab*. They deemed it appropriate to block them on the eastern side just outside Khidrana. This happened on 29th December, 1705 (Magh Vadi 10, 1762 BK).[2] In the battle that ensued these forty led by Mahan Singh and inspired by dauntless *Mai* Bhag Kaur fought heroically. In order that the enemy might not reach Khidrana, they resorted to subtle tactics. They spread loose cloth sheets on bushes to give impression to the enemy that a large force under the Guru lay encamped there.[3] They took positions in the thickets of *Van* trees (Quercus Incania) and *Karir* bushes (Capparis Incania) and readied themselves to accord hot welcome to the enemy. When the enemy's troops came near, they launched

1. *Sri Gursobha*, (ed.) by Shamsher Singh Ashok, p. 96; Sukhdial Singh, *Guru Gobind Singh Ik Sarvekhan*, p. 92. According to a tradition, the owner of this place was Khidrana.
2. According to *Bhat Vahi*, the battle was fought on Magh vadi 10, 1762 BK, but according to the local tradition the date was Baisakh 1762 BK/18 April, 1705.
3. *Malwa Desh Ratan di Sakhi Pothi*, p. 54. Also refer to *Shri Guru Tirath Sangreh*, pp. 147-48, by Tara Singh Nirotam.

so vigorous an assault that the enemy was simply amazed. The clatter of arms and din and dust of the battle-field alerted the Guru who showered arrows from his position. When the enemy distanced itself from the farthest extent of the range of his arrow, he mounted the steed and made dexterous movements to aim his arrows successfully.

The Mughal soldiers were confused and bewildered. The forty fought with rare valour and determination. They having exhausted their ammunition and quivers becoming empty of arrows were obliged to have recourse to their spears and swords. Small bands advanced, engaged the enemy in hand-to-hand fight, killed several time more than their own number, until they were completely overpowered, and killed or mortally wounded.[1] (Only Bhag Kaur was seriously injured who recovered later on) but not long before they had shown the fire of their faith and their mettle as the toughest fighters whom the experienced Wazir Khan had ever known in his life. The Mughal forces were soon in dire straits. They had already been fatigued by their long march and also by the scarcity of provisions including water. But now when they found themselves face to face with determined *Khalsa* engaged in pitched battle, they were further exhausted and exasperated. Another factor also fatigued their verve. The main body of the *Khalsa* under the command of the Guru was fresh with sufficient war materials and in control of the only source of water in the area. Better provisioned and better stationed, *Khalsa* force constituted a psychological advantage on Mughal soldiers. The net result of all this was that Wazir Khan decided not to pursue the Guru further. He thought it sagacious to feel

1. (1) Bhag Singh Jhabalia, (2) Dilbagh Singh, (3) Gharbara Singh (Kandhara Singh), (4) Darbara Singh, (5) Ganda Singh (Ganga Singh), (6) Raj Singh Khairpuria, (7) Mahan Singh Khairpuria, (8) Sital Singh, (9) Sunder Singh Jhallian, (10) Kirpal Singh, (11) Dayal Singh, (12) Nihal Singh, (13) Suhel Singh, (14) Kushal Singh, (15) Chanda Singh, (16) Sumir Singh, (17) Sarja Singh, (18) Garja Singh, (19) Boora Singh, (20) Sultan Singh (Patti), (21) Nidhan Singh, (22) Sobha Singh, (23) Joga Singh, (24) Hari Singh, (25) Karam Singh, (26) Dharam Singh, (27) Kala Singh (Kalla Singh), (28) Sant Singh, (29) Kirat Singh (Kehar Singh), (30) Gulab Singh, (31) Jadho Singh, (32) Jango Singh, (33) Bhanga Singh, (34) Dhana Singh, (35) Bhola Singh, (36) Malla Singh, (37) Mann Singh, (38) Lachhman Singh, (39) Sadhu Singh, (40) Maiya Singh (Majja Singh).

satisfied that atleast he had been successful in marginalising him.

Wazir Khan's return to Sirhind without striking the main body of the *Khalsa* force was considered a great victory among the *Khalsa*. The Guru's prestige and popularity increased manifold. His mission also received impetus. According to Colonel Ravi Batra, the Mughal force numbered twenty thousand, while[1] the *Khalsa* forces numbered only two thousand including cavalry and irregulars.[2]

After the Mughal forces had left the field, the Guru visited the scene of actual battle and with a fatherly affection went about lifting the heads of the martyrs in his lap, wiping their faces and blessing them one by one. When it was the turn of Bhai Mahan Singh to be thus caressed and blessed, the Master found that some life was still left in him. After a while, Bhai Mahan Singh opened his eyes and found himself in the lap of the Guru. He was filled with supreme joy. The Guru asked him if he had any desire to be fulfilled. Bhai Mahan Singh said, "No, Master, I have seen thee. What else or more could I desire ? But if thou has taken compassion on us here, then tear off our disclaimer." The Guru at once met his demand and uttered, "You have saved the root of Sikhism in *Majha*. You and your companions, all forty of you are *Muktas* or the persons who have the fullest and truest realisation of the self. Mahan Singh thereafter closed his eyes for eternal sleep. Then the Guru went to the place where Bhag Kaur was lying unconscious on account of her wounds.

A little medical aid revived her. She told the Master the whole story of the repentant forty. The Guru told her about the last deed of Mahan Singh how he made a request to tear off the paper bearing disclaimer.

The Guru was greatly pleased with Bhag Kaur for what she had done. She was evacuated from the battle-field and her wounds were tended to. After her recovery, Bhag Kaur chose to stay with the Guru and served as his bodyguard. She

---

1. Colonal Ravi Batra, *Leadership in its Finest Mould : Guru Gobind Singh*, p. 58.
2. Most of the troops at Khidrana were peasants and artisans. According to Muhammad Latif, the number of Mughal forces was seven thousand only.

followed the Guru to Bathinda, Rajputana, Delhi, Agra and Nanded. She led the Sikh way of life in totality. After the Guru's death at Nanded, She left for Bidar where she preached her Guru's teachings. Shortly afterward she breathed her last at Jawara 10 Kilometers from Gurdwara Nanak Jhira.[1]

The Guru's *Khalsa* gathered firewood from the forests all around and prepared a pyre whereon the dead bodies of Mahan Singh and other martyrs were cremated.

Khidrana-di-Dhab—Pool at Khidrana, also known as *Ishar Sar*, was at that time renamed as *Muktsar-Pool* of *Salvation*. The event held out a great lesson and a sublime moral. Turning back on the Guru was a blasphemy, while turning towards the Guru was a pious and meritorious act. The event also held out hope to all those who would wish to reunite themselves to the Guru as he was an Eternal Forgiver.

The Guru renovated and enlarged the tank near the field of the battle. Later on, a gurdwara was built at the cremation site of 40 *Muktas*[2], along with some other shrines raised in memory of different events connected with the battle. The area occupied by these shrines is called *Tutti Ganddhi Complex* symbolising that the breach in relationship between the Guru and his Sikhs was plugged and all lost was retrieved. The people in thousands gather together at the premises on the Ist of *Magh* every year for ablution in the sacred pond and to attend religious *dewans* (Meetings). On this day people recall the supreme sacrifice of the *Khalsa* and also the blessings of the Guru on the martyrs. They feel overwhelmed and cannot help contemplating on the sacred impulse that enabled the forty *Muktas* to achieve the high status. This way their visit to the place and dip in the tank is symbolic of getting purgated and re-linked with their Guru. In general parlance it began to be believed that a mere dip in the tank would ensure a Self-Realisation which is a false notion and contrary to Sikhism. Dip of the mind in Gurus ideology and total commitment to it even at the cost of ones life is a sure way to salvation or Self-Realisation instead of a dip of the physical being in the water.

1. L.S. Tandon, *The Sikh Review*, October 1971, pp. 26-27.
2. The sites were marked out by an 18th century *Nirmala* saint Bhai Langar Singh resident of Harike Kalan 18 kms East of Muktsar.

CHAPTER XI

DAMDAMA PERIOD

From Muktsar, the Guru moved to Rupana, Bhander, Gursar and Thehri, Bambiha, Rohila and Jangirana and Bhai Ka Kot which had been founded by Bhai Bhagtu. From there, he moved on to Kot Sahib Chand and further on to Chatiana where Brars who had fought for him demanded the arrears of their pay under the threat of blocking his onward march. But by God's grace, it so happened that a devoted Sikh of the Guru from the neighbouring area brought enough money in time which enabled the Guru to pay off all the arrears. Chaudhari Dana the leader of the Brars was extremely apologetic for the insolence and impudence of his people and refused to receive any payment for himself.

His act of self-abnegation greatly impressed the Guru who on his request immediately agreed to visit his native place, Mehma Swami. The journey lay through Ablu a place founded by uncle of Dana. Reaching Mehma Swami, the Guru encamped at the place now called Lakhisar and from there made a visit to Dana's home and several other places around. After a few days at Lakhisar, the Guru decided to go to Talwandi Sabo at the request of Chaudhari Dalla. He took the same old route and once again passing through Chatiana, Kot Sahib Chand and Kot Bhai arrived at Giddarbaha and then paying short visits to Rohilla, Jangirana, Bambiha, Bajak, Kaljhirani, Jassi Bagwali, Pakka Kalan and Chak Hira Singh reached Talwandi Sabo now called Damdama Sahib or *Takhat Damdama Sahib*. The place appealed to the Guru so much that he assumed a permanent residence there. He reached here on January 17, 1706 and stayed on till October 30, 1706. At this place, Mata Sundri and Mata Sahib Deva joined him[1] from Delhi along with Bhai Mani Singh. After obeisance and greetings Mata Sundri said, "Me Lord, where are my sons ? Where have they been left ?" The Guru, never unequivocal, consoled her and remarked, "The four sons have been offered as a sacrifice over the heads of these sons. What does it matter if we have lost four sons, while thousands like them are alive and are in thine lap and mine."

These words of the Guru had their instant effect. The mother's sadness vanished and a new realization dawned on her. She was an altogether changed person. She realised that death in the cause of righteousness is in fact a cause for rejoicing in the Will of God.

The period at Damdama was put to best possible use by the Guru. He utilised the time in laying abiding foundations of Sikhism in the *Malwa* tract. Many old and hereditary Sikhs were administered *Khande-ki-Pahul* and brought more thoroughly into the *Khalsa* fold. Dalla, the Choudhary of the Talwandi Sabo; Tiloka, the ancestor of Nabha State and Rama, the ancestor of Patiala State, were outstanding examples. Besides, new converts were also made in large numbers. According to Trumpp, their number swelled to one lakh twenty thousand.[2]

Talwandi Sabo attracted large crowds from far and near and presented the spectacle of a new Anandpur. The Sikh devotees and others who came and assembled here had been estimated at more than ten times the number of people at Anandpur.[3] The Guru made a number of trips to important places nearby. In one trip he visited Bhagi Bhander, 3 kms North of Talwandi Sabo, Kot Shamir, 3 kms further North and Chak Bhai Ka, about 10 kms from Talwandi Sabo to the North. At the last-named place, the Guru was given a warm reception by one Rai Singh, grandson of Bhai Bhagtu. On another occasion, he went to Bathinda city and stayed there for seven days. While coming back to Talwandi Sabo, the Guru visited Mahima and Bhakri, both located North of Bathinda. On some other occasion, he visited Tala Pind about 16 Kilometers to the

1. Bhai Vir Singh, *Kalghidhar Chamatkar*, p. 757.
2. Trumpp, *Adi Granth*, p. XCII.
3. Fauja Singh (ed.), *Guru Gobind Singh Marg*, p. 27.

South. At Kewal, Chaudharies, Rama and Tiloka waited upon him.

Guru Gobind Singh was equally awake to the spiritual need of the people living at far off places. To this purpose, the Guru appointed preachers like Bhai Pheru.[1] Punjab Singh[2] and Rocha Singh[3] having been baptised at Bathinda were appointed to disseminate Sikhism in the areas of Pothohar, Kashmir, district of Hazara and Muzaffrabad. They and their successors strove hard to awaken the people to the *Khalsa* way of life. All available records vouchsafe the veracity of this fact. The Guru also made efforts to organise preaching work in Sind and Rajasthan. Bhai Kanahiya and his associates did commendable work in Sind, presently a province in Pakistan.

Alongwith his work of administering *Khande-ki-Pahul* to the Sikhs, the Guru spared no efforts to transform the little culture which had gripped the minds of the people. It was exactly because of this that in his discourses to various *Sangats*, he dwelt at length on the futility of totems, esoteric practices, caste-distinctions as well as caste considerations, superstitions, grave-worship and many other social and religious prejudices. The Guru did all this to persuade the people to attach themselves at mental level with better cultural roots.

To make the preaching effective and to keep it on the right track, it was found essential that a cadre should be raised to do the job. This also necessitated the correct interpretation of the compositions enshrined in *Guru Granth Sahib*. The Guru interpreted the scripture himself and asked some of his devoted disciples to understand its true meaning and impact. According to Baisakha Singh[4], sixty persons acquired mastery

1. Baba Pheru Singh, received *Pahul* on the Baisakhi of 1699; preached Sikh religion in Kashmir and other hill areas around.
2. Punjab Singh, Birth 1672 at Nand Har-Shahar, father's name Hari Ram Shah, a great scholar of Persian and Sanskrit, member of the band of preachers of Pheru Singh, received *Khande-ki-Pahul* from Guru Gobind Singh at Damdama, nominated successor to Pheru Singh after his death in 1736. Preached in the areas of Muzaffrabad, Poonch and Srinagar.
3. Rocha Singh, Birth 1688 in village Kausa (Hazara District in Pakistan); Received *Khande-ki-Pahul* from Guru Gobind Singh and preached in Hazara District, Kashmir.
4. Vaisakha Singh, *Malwa Sikh Itihas*.

over the subject. The most important out of them was Bhai Mani Singh. Besides this, the Guru created two Orders, one of the *Nirmalas* and the other of the *Gyanies*. No doubt, the Guru, while at Paonta, sent eleven members to Benaras to learn Sanskrit and acquire knowledge in Hindu Philosophical systems. These men were named *Nirmal* meaning pure, yet the *Nirmala* order was set afloat at Talwandi Sabo. The purpose was to interpret Indian religious thought and history in terms of the world-view of Sikhism.

The order of the *Gyanies* also came into being under the direct inspiration of the Guru and that too at Talwandi Sabo. The underlying objective was to raise a group of persons competent enough to interpret *Gurbani* correctly. Guru Gobind Singh interpreted the verses enshrined in *Sri Adi Granth* and took steps so that a number of persons might acquire proficiency to do the same. Bhai Mani Singh was the first person who received this training from him. He laid the foundation of the order of *Gyanies*. This class later on did a lot to ensure correct exposition of the Sikh scriptures as it was passed on to its head by the Guru himself. The two chief headquarters of this order have been at Damdama (Talwandi Sabo ki) and at Amritsar.

Another important and abiding contribution of the Guru during this period was to prepare afresh the final recension of *Sri Adi Granth*[1]. According to Giani Gian Singh, Bhai Mani Singh was appointed amaneusis. Everyday two watches of time were fixed for the purpose of preparing the scripture. As the Guru dictated, so recorded Bhai Mani Singh. The project was completed in several months. A new volume of the original *Granth* was prepared in this way. This is how that volume came to be known as *Damdami Bir* recension.[2]

---

1. Some scholars aver that the Guru reproduced the whole *Adi Granth* from memory and completed it by adding to it the hymns composed by his father. That the hymns of the ninth Guru were incorporated here is contradicted by the fact that there is a copy of the *Holy Granth* at Patna bearing the date 1748 BK (1691), containing the hymns of Guru Tegh Bahadur in their proper places. There is another copy found at Dacca which was written earlier than this, in 1675, in the first year of Guru Gobind Singh's accession.

2. Giani Kirpal Singh, *Sri Gur Panth Parkash*, pp. 1678-80.

The averment of certain scholars that the *Granth* was named so, because it was originally written at Talwandi Sabo, also known as Damdama is not correct.

Prior to Guru Gobind Singh, three recensions had gained currency and prevalence. These were Bhai Gurdas recension, Bhai Banno recension and Lahore recension. Bhai Gurdas recension was original and authentic as it was completed by Bhai Gurdas ji under the able guidance of Guru Arjan Dev in 1604. But because of certain extraneous influences and certain vested interests, Banno's recension and Lahore recension were prepared and each of them was passed on as the original. In Lahore recension the *Dhunis* which had been specified to be used while singing *Vars* in Bhai Gurdas recension were deleted because presumably its framers did not wish the Sikhs to be aroused under the impact of *Dhuni*-based *Vars* in view of the biased attitude of the Mughal government towards the Sikhs.

Examination of the manuscript of the Lahore tradition has revealed that a significant number of them originated in the Kiratpur area during the period of Guru Har Rai (1644-1661 A.D.). This tradition continued to be popular in some section of the *Panth* right upto the beginning of the nineteenth century. The solitary and the only copy of the Lahore tradition that was written in the early nineteenth century is held at the British Library in London.[1] This contains a solitary couplet attributed to Guru Har Rai. It comes after the *Mundavani* as follows :

ੴ ਸਤਿਗੁਰ ਪ੍ਰਸਾਦਿ ॥[2]
ਸਲੋਕ ਮਹਲਾ ੭ ਸ੍ਰੀ ਗੁਰੂ ਹਰਿਰਾਇ ਜੀ ਦਾ ਬੋਲਣਾ
ਜਿਨਿ ਕਉ ਸਤਿਗੁਰੁ ਦਇਆ ਕਰੇ ਤਿਨ ਰਖ ਚਰਨੀ ਲਾਇ ॥
ਨਾਨਕ ਤਿਸ ਬਲਿਹਾਰਣੈ ਜਿਨ ਗੁਰੁ ਡਿਠਾ ਜਾਇ ॥

The introductory formula in the beginning of this couplet (the voice of Sri Guru Har Rai) clearly shows that the Lahore recension was quite different from the Kartarpur recension and hence could not claim authenticity and originality.

---

1. British Library London, MSOR 2748.
2. By the grace of the eternal one, the true Guru Slok Mahalla 7 'The voice of Sri Guru Har Rai'. Those on whom the true Guru bestows his benevolence, are kept in his refuge. I am devoted to those, Nanak, who go to have a glimpse of the Guru.

Likewise Banno recension was also passed on as authentic, while it was not at all so. Firstly, it contained spurious material, as for instance, *Gosht Maler Nal* and *Ratan Mala*, a composition of 25 stanzas in Raag *Ramkali*. The alluded to apocryphal *Slokas* of Guru Nanak under both the headings have themes which have nothing to do with Sikh ideology. The first set of *Slokas* under the heading *Gosht Maler Nal* reflect discussions with a Muslim audience about creation while the stanzas of *Ratan Mala* give exposition of *Hath Yoga* technique which obviously cannot be the work of Guru Nanak. It is definitely an *Udasi* account which was edited out of the *Kartarpur Bir*, as prepared by Bhai Gurdas under the dictation of Guru Arjan Dev. According to Professor Sahib Singh, this recension was prepared by *Handalis* in association with *Udasis*.

The first Banno Bir as it is found[1] today is believed to be prepared in 1642 when the centre of Sikh activities had already shifted under Guru Hargobind from Amritsar to Kiratpur in the Shivalik Hills. The Banno version became prevalent during the second half of the century. Possibly it was brought into existence by *Handalis, Udasis* and *Bhatt* interests.

Alongwith Lahore version and Banno version, Bhai Gurdas version was also prevalent. But different recensions had created a lot of confusion whose persistence was sure to provide pretexts for different vested interests to organise dissent or schism.

Guru Gobind Singh soon after the assumption of Guruship took steps to set at rest any controversy or confusion caused or likely to be caused by vested interests including the Mughal government. He made an attempt to standardise the text of *Sri Adi Granth* and thus correct the problem of the circulation of unauthentic recensions. Although he approached Dhirmal's descendants at Kartarpur to obtain the (original) *Adi Bir,* he did not succeed in persuading them to part with the same. A number of copies of this recension, however, were available at that time alongwith two other versions of the *Adi Granth.* He used these to prepare the authorised and authentic version of the *Sri Adi Granth* at a resting place (Damdama) in Anandpur

---

1. Sahib Singh, *Adi Bir Bare,* pp. 176-81.

in the last quarter of the seventeenth century. He also included in it the *Bani* of Guru Tegh Bahadur.

The Damdami recension is believed to have been lost or drowned in the flooded River Sirsa when the Guru had to evacuate Anandgarh under unfavourable circumstances. Now at Talwandi Sabo, also called Damdama, the Guru got the authorised form re-prepared. The motivating factors to the Guru were the same, generally speaking, as, for instance, to uphold the integrity of *Gurbani*, to block the ingress of spurious compositions in the name of Nanak, to deprive schismatic groups to find their legitimacy on the basis of scriptural differences.

There was another factor that seemed to have had impact deeper than any other factor at this point of time. Since the emergence of *Sri Adi Granth*, the Gurus had been emphasising that this was the embodiment of the 'Word' which God Himself, out of His Grace, bestowed upon Guru Nanak and which each Guru passed on to his successor, thereby raising each of them to the status of a Guru. This implies that even the Guru was Guru because word was enshrined in him. Various verses of Gurus very clearly vouchsafe that 'Word' is Guru.[1]

On account of this comprehension, *Sri Adi Granth* was without any doubt the Guru. The enlightened Sikhs regarded *Sri Adi Granth* as such but this idea/belief had not yet been institutionalised formally and consequently many Sikhs were still in the grip of confusion. Hence the dire need of preparing authorised version of *Sri Adi Granth*. In this connection, we must draw our attention to the hidden but nefarious designs of Dhirmal's descendants, who went a long way to motivate the Guru to prepare the final form of *Sri Adi Granth*. Finding that the recension prepared at Damdama at Anandpur had been lost during the turmoil after the evacuation of Anandgarh, they reckoned that now, because of strains and stresses besetting the Guru's future career, it would not be possible for him to prepare another recension, and thus it would be easier

1. Guru Ram Das, *Sri Guru Granth Sahib, Rag Nat Narayan*, p. 982. *Rag Kannra*, p. 1310.

for them to lay their claim to Guruship since Bhai Gurdas recension believed to be the authentic one, was with them. It was against this backdrop that the Guru sent his request through his special emissary to descendants of Dhirmal[1] to lend Bhai Gurdas recension. But they refused point blank to part with the same.

The Guru now decided to prepare the authentic version afresh and then to institutionalise it. Already on the momentous Baisakhi of 29th March, 1699, he had merged his physical personality in the *Khalsa*, thereby exalting the *Khalsa* equal to the Guru authorising it to operate in the world as per light of the Word.

Having raised *Khalsa* equal to the status of Guru to work in the world, it was only logical to institutionalise *Sri Guru Granth Sahib* the embodiment of 'Word as the Guru eternal'. And to do so it was imperative that the authorised version of *Sri Adi Granth* should be prepared. The Guru, therefore, did the needful and installed it at Damdama (Talwandi Sabo). Bhai Mani Singh was asked to start its reading from the beginning to end. The commencement hymn received by him is recorded in *Guru Kian Sakhian*[2]. This was the Guru Arjan Dev's composition in *Raag Todi* :

> To Thy protection have I found my Lord
> Give me the gift of Thy name, of Thy praise
> So in harmony may I dwell,
> Easing the unease of mind
> At Thy door have I at last thrown myself
> No other refuge do I know
> Rescue this worthless one, O Lord.
> Bring me not to account;
> By this concession alone could I be saved
> By Thy support are all sustained
> Slave Nanak follows in the
> Footsteps of holy saints,
> Liberate me, O Lord, here and now.[3]

---

1. Dhirmal was summoned to Delhi by emperor Aurangzeb and was imprisoned in the fort at Ranthambore, where he died on 16th November, 1677.
2. Swarup Singh Kaushish, *Guru Kian Sakhian.*
3. *Sat(i)gur āio saran tūhārī.*
   Milai sūkh nām(u) har(i) sobhā chintā lahe hamārī.1.   (SGGS, p. 713)

At the conclusion of the recitation *Karah Prashad* was distributed.

According to Ishar Singh Nara[1], the celebrated author of *Zafarnama and Safarnama*, the Guru dictated two copies; one to Bhai Mani Singh and the other to Bhai Gurdas.[2] One was kept at Damdama Sahib (Talwandi Sabo) and the other at Takht Sri Sachkhand Hazur Sahib. The finalisation of *Sri Adi Granth* was celebrated with appropriate ceremony and thanksgivings. The ink and reeds used in transcribing the *Granth* was cast by the Guru into the pool close to the tent under which the work had been in progress. The Guru said that Damdama would be 'Kashi of the Sikhs' and become famous as a seat of learning. He foretold that many would study here and become learned.

The Guru collected a galaxy of scholars, poets and men of letters at the place.[3] Once again, literature began to be created to inspire the people to be awake to new realities. Literary meets were arranged to bring into focus the process of resurgence as it had been started by the Guru as also to give fillip to the production of literature to serve both as mirror of the environment and a guide to the future generation. Arrangements were also made to impart education to the people. Sukha Singh, the author of *Gurbilas Patshahi Dasvin*, says that in addition to the extension of patronage to scholars of different disciplines, he encouraged the people to study at the *Ashram*.[4] The tradition revolving round *Sikhan Sar* testify to the ardent desire of the Guru to educate the masses of this area. It will not be wide of the mark that the Guru was doing all this under the conviction that literature being produced

---

1. Ishar Singh Nara, *Safarnama te Zafarnama*, p. 307.
2. He was, most probably, Gurdas who later wrote *Ramkali Var Patshahi Dasvin*. There had been four eminent personalities in Sikh history bearing name of Gurdas. The first one is celebrated Bhai Gurdas Bhalla. The second Gurdas was an attendant of Guru Tegh Bahadur while the third one was among the progeny of Bhai Bahlo who later went over to the Ram Rai's sect. The fourth one was Gurdas Singh supposed to be the writer of *Ramkali Var Patshahi Dasvin*.
3. C.H. Payne, *A Short History of the Sikhs*, pp. 41-42. "Secure in his new retreat Gobind re-established his court, and surrounded himself with all the pomp and circumstances of Royalty." Damdama became the centre of Sikhism and a place of resort for learned men from all parts of the country.
4. Also consult Koer Singh, *Gurbilas Patshahi 10*, p. 232.

under Sikh inspiration would help the people to regain elan vital, so essential for any society to move further on the road to integrated progress. It is against this background that the Guru aspired to see 'Talwandi Sabo Ki' emerge as a great centre of learning like Kashi (Benaras) a renowned Hindu centre of learning. 'New Kashi' of the conception of the Guru was to symbolise aspirations of the new generation. The Guru also made efforts to procure the copies of the composition, forming part of this huge *Granth, Vidya Sagar*, which had been lost in the waters of flooded Sirsa. This task was partially accomplished later on by Bhai Mani Singh who collected writings of the Guru and compiled them into what came to be known as the *Dasam Guru ji ka Granth* the book of the Tenth Master, in the third decade of the eighteenth century. At this time, the art of calligraphy was at its creative best and the *pothies* prepared here were much sought after.

Along with the above activities, the Guru continued to give military training to his followers and succeeded in rallying around himself a considerable number of armed disciples ever ready to lay down their lives for the ideals of the *Khalsa* without any desire of pecuniary advantage. Efforts were also made to inculcate among the Sikhs the spirit of resistance to injustice and unrighteousness wherever and whenever they happened to come across. Various methods such as hunting, and mock fights were organised to make the people courageous. The Guru laid added emphasis on alertness and discipline. According to Dr. Indubhushan Banerjee, the Guru's strength seems to have increased to a great extent, as, besides regular followers he had also taken some Dogras and Brars in his service.[1] Koer Singh, the author of *Gurbilas Patshahi 10*, also testifies to this fact. According to him, "the Guru would distribute gold and silver coins everyday and countless soldiers would get attracted to him."[2]

---

1. Indubhushan Banerjee, *Evolution of the Khalsa*, Vol. II, p.138.
2. Koer Singh, Everyday would the Guru distribute gold and silver coins; countless soldiers were thus attracted to the place.
   C.H. Payne, *A Short History of the Sikhs*, pp. 41-42, "Numberless new recruits joined the ranks of the *Khalsa* and the position of Gobind Singh became stronger than ever before."

Wazir Khan, the *Subedar* of Sirhind, was going all out in his efforts to snuff out the *Khalsa* movement and to arrest or kill the Guru. This attitude is clearly manifest in his two messages to Chaudhari Dalla. The gist of the messages was that Dalla should arrest the Guru or else his territory would be plundered and he would be punished severely. Dalla's reply was that of a person surcharged with the mission of translating the *Khalsa* ideals into reality. He said, "I will by no means have the Guru arrested to please thee. Nay, I will defend him with my life." Zabardast Khan, the Viceroy of Lahore, was also averse to the Sikh cause. He plundered a party of Sikhs on their way to make offerings to the Guru.

In the face of this attitude of the Mughal officials of Lahore province and Sirhind, the Guru intensified his military activities. He repeatedly made exhortations to the Sikhs to bear arms and diligently practise their use. He said, "Now the times have altered and the Sikhs are obliged to defend themselves. He has established *Khalsa* order, and whosoever desired to abide in it should not fear the clash of arms, but be ever ready for the combat for the defence of his faith." At the same time the realisation of *Nam* was still the chief object of the Sikh adoration.

Shortly after, the Guru received the tidings of Imperial emissaries deputed to convey Aurangzeb's wish for a personal meeting. Guru Gobind Singh's letter to Aurangzeb appears to have produced the desired effect. In the *Ahkam-i-Alamgiri*, the receipt of a letter from Guru Gobind Singh to the Emperor is acknowledged besides the issue of orders to Munim Khan (the deputy *Subedar*) at Lahore to conciliate Guru Gobind Singh, and also making of satisfactory arrangement for his travel towards South. This may be seen in the same compendium— *Ahkam-i-Alamgiri*.[1] That Aurangzeb was anxious to meet Guru Gobind Singh is evident from the *Ahkam*, though it is not clear, why ? Possibly after having pursued *Zafarnama*, a new awareness may have dawned on him under whose impact he invited

---

1. According to the author of *Ahkam-i-Alamgiri*, he immediately sent through Muhammad Beg a *Gurjbardar* or mace bearer and Sheikh Yar Muhammad a *Mansabdar*, a firman to Munim Khan deputy governor of Lahore, asking him to make peace with the Guru.

the Guru to find an enduring solution to the Sikh problem. He, in turn, also welcomed the opportunity and planned to move to Ahmednagar where Aurangzeb had been residing. He left Talwandi on October 30, 1707.

The tremendous success achieved by the Guru in this area, despite heavy odds was due to several factors. One among them of importance may be his decision to leave the hills and to come into the interior of Punjab which was the real base of his strength. Anandpur, notwithstanding its strong fortification, suffered from inherent weakness, for the population around, consisting mostly of the conservative and caste-ridden Rajputs, was hostile to the Sikhs. They caused him harassment and impediments day in and day out. On the other hand, when the Guru entered the Punjab plains the people around were helpful, co-operative and were willing to rally under his banner, should the call come from him. This made all the difference. Closely allied to that was the second factor, viz. the impact left by the previous Gurus on the people of these areas during their visits. The 6th, 7th and 9th Gurus had, one after the other, conducted extensive tours across this area and left a deep imprint on the minds of the people. Guru Gobind Singh route through this area was dotted with the places which had already been visited by his predecessors, as for instance, Bur Majra, Ghulal, Lall Kalan, Katana, Bassian, Chakkar, Takhtupura, Patto Hira Singh, Bhagta Bhai ka, and Lambhawali, had all been sanctified by Sikh Gurus previously. The third important factor was the valuable support provided by some of the influential Zamindars of the area, prominent among them being Nihang Khan, Rai Kalha, Chaudhari Kapura, Chaudhari Dana, Chaudhari Dalla, Chaudhari Rama and Chaudhari Taloka. At that time the Mughal Empire was facing a serious agrarian crisis.[1] As a result, the Zamindars were asserting themselves. Their increasing strength was a great helping asset for Guru Gobind Singh. The next important factor was difficult terrain of the jungle Desh. Last but not the least was the Guru's charismatic personality which could turn adversity into a fortune and discomfiture into a triumph. But

---

1. Refer to Irfan Habib's book, *Agrarian System in India-Asia*.

for his powerful and towering personality, even the best of circumstances would have yielded no fruit.

It was for the first time that the Emperor truly came to know about the personality of Guru Gobind Singh and appreciated his situation. He felt persuaded to adopt a conciliatory attitude and ordered Wazir Panah Munim Khan, Deputy Governor of Lahore to write a letter to the Guru to be dispatched through Muhammad Beg *Gurz-bardar* and Yar Muhammad *Mansabdar*. Therein Munim Khan was desired to conciliate the Guru and invite him to his headquarter and then, having conveyed to him the Royal firman, to send him to the Emperor at Ahmednagar accompanied by a trusted officer of his own alongwith the above mentioned *Gurz-bardar* and *Mansabdar*. And whenever the Guru arrived in the neighbourhood of Sirhind, wrote the Emperor, Wazir Khan was to provide him with an escort and see him off safe beyond his own territories. Munim Khan was further instructed to soothe the Guru if the latter had any secret or open suspicions and to pay to him out of his attached properties as much as he desired for his travelling expenses. With this letter *Gurz-bardar* and the Guru's envoy Bhai Daya Singh together moved to the North.[1]

---

1. Inayatullah Khan 'Ismi', *Ahkam-i-Alamgiri; Insha-i-Farsi*, II, pp. 429-30. *Sri Gursobha*, XIII, pp. 38-40.

CHAPTER XII

FROM DAMDAMA TO AGRA

The Guru left Damdama (Talwandi Sabo) for the Deccan on Kartik Sudi 5, 1763 Sammat (October 30, 1706). He waited for Daya Singh's return to Talwandi Sabo for some time, whom he had sent to Aurangzeb at Ahmednagar to deliver his letter *Zafarnama;* but he had not received any communication from him or his companion Bhai Dharam Singh. He, however, had received news that Bhai Daya Singh had to face a lot of difficulties, caused by the obstructionist tactics of *Subedar* Wazir Khan's hired persons who were specially deputed to scuttle the attempts of Bhai Daya Singh to meet the Emperor to deliver the letter personally. The *Subedar* did so because he thought that if Bhai Daya Singh could have an audience with the Emperor and succeeded in delivering the letter, it would arouse the moral conscience of the Emperor causing a lot more harm to him.

The Guru also got the inkling that the letter had been delivered and its contents had moved the Emperor.

Sensing change in the mood of Aurangzeb, he decided to move towards Deccan even before Daya Singh could reach Damdama (Talwandi Sabo). The most important factor that prompted him to take this decision was the fast failing health of the Emperor who was about ninety-one in 1706 and had been overtaken by illness. The Guru deemed it appropriate to go to Deccan himself and settle the affairs with the Emperor for which purpose Bhai Daya Singh had been sent with the letter.[1]

Though the exact number of Sikhs who accompanied the

---

1. Sainapat, *Sri Gursobha*, XIV, pp. 2-6.
   Sakhi Pothi , No. 105, p. 116.

Guru toward Deccan is not known, yet, on the basis of
accounts available to us, it is not difficult to surmise that it was
quite large. Among them, a few notables were Man Singh, Ram
Singh and Fateh Singh of Bhagtu family, Dharam Singh and
Param Singh, the grandsons of Bhai Rupa. Rai Dalla also
accompanied the Guru. As the Guru proceeded further, some
of them went back to their homes, but even then the hard core
was quite large : Mani Singh, Bhupat Singh from Amritsar,
Sodhi Kanwal Nain from Dhilwan, Udey Karan, Gurdas Singh
from Daburji, Bhai Bajjar Singh from Sodhara, Ram Singh and
Tilok Singh from Phul, Godaie Singh from Bhucho, Dan Singh
with his son from Ahlu, Ram Kaur from Ramdas.[1]

Enroute to Deccan, the first halt of Guru Gobind Singh
was at village Kewal.[2] Then the Guru sojourned at village
Jharori, wherefrom he proceeded to village Jhanda.[3] When the
night fell, Fateh Singh and his brother Ram Singh left the
Guru's camp. Rai Dalla placed his offerings comprising two
gold bangles and one double-edged sword and slipped out of
the Guru's camp to return to his native place. These people did
so because they could not shed their attachment with their
assets and their kith and kins. Some others too left the Guru
fearing the discomforts of the arduous journey.

The Guru was surprised at the actions of Dalla particularly,
because he had decided to prepare him for certain other tasks.
When at dawn, he asked where Dalla was, someone amongst
his followers said, "There is no Dalla-Malla, there is only Allah
and the Guru," the theme being that, at that point of time, he
was all alone, determined to carry out his mission in spite of
high risks involved in the process.

The Guru remained calm and continued to march
towards his destination.

He reached the township of Sirsa[4], now in the State of
Haryana. People expressed their love and respect for the Guru
by serving him and his Sikhs. In the course of granting

1. Swarup Singh Kaushish, *Guru Kian Sakhian*, p. 187.
2. Fauja Singh, *Atlas Travels of Guru Gobind Singh*, p. 18.
3. M.A. Macauliffe, *The Sikh Religion*, Vol. V, p. 226; Ishar Singh Nara, *Safarnama and Zafarnama*, p. 8.
4. Fauja Singh, *op.cit.*, p. 18.

audienec to his Sikhs, he was told that one goldsmith named Gulab Singh had been imprisoned in an underground cell by Nabi Bakhsh, the Chaudhary of the village Khaudal. He had done so since Gulab Singh had refused to comply with the order of the Chaudhary to offer his daughter to cater to his carnal desires. The Guru mounted his steed and taking five Sikhs with him marched to the place. They freed Gulab Singh and chided the Chaudhary who out of fear prostrated at his feet. He forgave him and instructed him to shun terrorising the people. After visiting some neighbouring places such as Gobindpura, he came back to Sirsa.

From there, he reached Nauhar.[1] The people of this town were the votaries of Jainism. Instead of practising the high ethical principles of their religion, their whole emphasis lay upon the rejection of non-vegetarianism, which they thought was the only way to the path of bliss and social reconstruction. The Guru exposed the hollowness of their thinking and tried to make them understand the theory and practice and the ultimaticity of 'Non-violence'. Vegetarianism or non-vegetarianism are irrelevant to the process of building a good society as well as good individuals.

From Nauhar, he proceeded to village Bhadra.[2] where he was affectionately received by a Rajput family. The next halt of the Guru was at village Sahewa. During the course of travels, Dharam Singh and Param Singh carried the weapons and clothes of the Guru. They had resolved to prepare a fresh cot for him at his every halt.

Thence from, the Guru proceeded to Bahaduran. He now gave a horse each to Dharam Singh and Param Singh to enable them function more effectively. Thereafter he reached Sahena from where he proceeded to Madhu Singhnai. Bhai Ram Singh, a scion of Bhai Bhagtu, lost heart and beat a hasty retreat. The Guru sent his horseman thrice to dissuade him from leaving him but he remained adamant.

After this he reached Pushkar Raj[3], a place of pilgrimage

---

1. M.A. Macauliffe, *The Sikh Religion*, Vol. V, p. 226.
   Fauja Singh, *Atlas Travels of Guru Gobind Singh*, p. 18.
2. *Ibid.*
3. M.A. Macauliffe, *op.cit.*, Vol. V, pp. 227-228.

and worship of Brahma. The place earlier had been made hallowed with a visit by Guru Nanak. Pandit Chetan Misar who was the incharge of the place gave a detailed account regarding Guru Nanak's visit. He fell at the Guru's feet, received *Khande-ki-Pahul* and joined the *Khalsa* brother-hood. In the neighbour-hood of Pushkar Raj, the Guru was asked a serious question about his dress, which neither looked Hindu nor Muslim. The Guru impressed upon them that his mission was both for the Hindus and Muslims and transcended all types of particularism. Therefore his dress exuded uniqueness of its own.

After this, he reached Narain Pur[1] also known as Dadu Dwara where the saint Dadu had lived and flourished. His shrine, by this time, had come under the charge of Mahant Jait Ram. While passing by his sepulchre, the Guru saluted the eternal resting place of Dadu by lifting an arrow to his head. The Sikhs accompanying him took exception to it and asked him why should *Tankhah* not be imposed on him for violation of his own teachings. One of them, Man Singh quoted the Guru's own verse *Gor Marhi Mat Bhul No Mane* (worship not even by mistake cemetries). The Guru at once accepted his guilt of religious misconduct and expressed his willingness to undergo any *Tankhah* (a religious punishment) that the *Khalsa* brotherhood may award him. He was awarded a penalty of a sum of Rs. 125, a part of which was spent on *Guru Ka Langar* and the rest on the purchase of a canopy to cover the place where food was served. Jait Ram was astonished at the dress and demeanour of the Guru and remarked in surprise, "Lord, no doubt, you have saved Hinduism but your mode of thinking and style of living were not appropriate." Daduji used to say,

> Dadu, surrender thy claim to every worldly things, pass thy days without claims.
> How many have departed after trading in this grocer's shop (which is the world).[2]

The Guru retorted :

> Assert thy claim in the world
> Extirpate the wicked who doeth thee evil.

---

1. M.A. Macauliffe, *The Sikh Religion*, Vol. V, pp. 227-228.
2. *Ibid.*, Vol. VI, pp. 227-28.

The *Mahant* quoted two other couplets of Dadu;

> Be satisfied with this Kal Age.
> If anyone throws a clod or a brick at thee,
>   lift it on thy head.[1]

The Guru would not admit the last line and altered it thus :

> If anyone throws a clod or a brick at thee
> Angrily, strike him with a stone.[2]

"Daduji was an ascetic and at best did everything for his own liberation. On the other hand, the Guru's house is people's house. He believes in balanced and integrated development of the people both at individual and social levels. Sikhism promises riddance from all types of social, cultural, political and religious tyrannies. When Jogis, Brahmins, Khatries, Vaish, and others could not do anything to uplift the people, *Sikh Panth* came into being. We are committed to reconstruction of a society based on dignity of labour, truth, sharing of wealth and having complete faith in *Akal Purkh*." Jait Ram understood the import of the Guru's message and mission and expressed his agreement with him. He was so overwhelmed that he requested him to have meals at this *Ashram*. The missionary in him again burstforth. "You believe in strict vegetarianism, while we have no such prejudice. Whatever suits our soul and body, we take. We can't help serving meat to our hawks who can't do without it."

Regarding granting of arms to the *Khalsa*, the Guru explained that :

"The age is full of evils. The wicked rule in it and cause suffering to saints and holy men. Tyrants, therefore, deserve to be punished. They will not refrain as long as they are pardoned. O, *Mahant*, they who bear arms, who remember the true name and sacrifice their lives for their faith shall go straight to paradise. Therefore I have established the *Khalsa* religion (brotherhood), given my followers arms and made them heroes."[3] After this the Guru reached Kalot via Lali and Magharoda.

---

1. M.A. Macauliffe, *The Sikh Religion*, Vol. VI, pp. 228-29.
2. *Ibid.*
3. *Ibid.*, pp. 229-31.

Bhai Daya Singh and Dharam Singh on way back from Deccan met him and related to him their experiences in the Deccan. The Emperor's *Gurz-bardar* and *Mansabdar* had gone ahead towards Delhi with the *royal firman* for Munim Khan while Bhai Daya Singh and Dharam Singh came to the Guru. At Bhagaur, about 70 miles North-East of Udaipur city the headquarter of a Parganah in the erstwhile Udaipur State, the Guru heard the news of the death of Aurangzeb at Ahmednagar on the 28th of Zi-Qada 1118H (February 20, 1707).[1]

A small skirmish in the neighbourhood of Bhagaur, a day or two before the Guru's march out from there in which the two Zamindars and a couple of Sikhs were killed is said to have taken place on March 17-19, 1707.[2] The Guru's decision to stop moving further towards South was warranted by the changes in political scenario. Aurangzeb having gone from the scene for ever, further march towards the South would not serve any purpose as he would not be able to build bridges of understanding and reconciliation between the Sikhs and the Mughal government nor could he arrange that the guilty *Subedar*, Wazir Khan, was appropriately punished. He therefore, decided to wait and watch.

The war of succession among the late emperor's sons had begun. Prince Muazzam (Bahadur Shah) was in Jamraud, a few miles away from Peshawar when his father died. Azam Shah (Tara Azam) who was in Deccan with his father at the time of his death assumed command of the Imperial army and proclaimed himself as the next Emperor.

Bahadur Shah too marched from Jamraud to assert his claim to the throne. He left Jamraud in the last week of March, 1707, and reached Peshawar on the last day of the month. Munim Khan his trusted Governor at Lahore, had kept the troops in readiness for the long awaited war of succession and welcomed Muazzam who was formally declared Emperor before he entered Lahore. Collecting men and money from the officials of the Mughal government in that part of the Empire, he reached Delhi by end of May. Wazir Khan, the *Faujdar* of

---

1. *Sri Gursobha*, Stanza 622.
2. Garja Singh (ed.), *Shaheed Bilas*, p. 72.

Sirhind, had contributed eight lakhs. Mohammad Muazzam left Delhi in the first week of June, took possession of treasures at Agra and moved towards Dholpur to confront Azam Shah, his rival claimant to the throne, who alongwith a huge army and his very intelligent and valorous son, Bidar Bakhat, was fast marching to this place.

On the way to Delhi, Muazzam, who had first-hand knowledge of the Guru's valour and his influence in the Punjab, especially among the Sikhs, thought it appropriate to seek his help, partly to avoid any Sikh trouble while he was busy in war of succession, and partly to use the Sikhs in his cause. The Guru's contemporary Sainapat in *Sri Gursobha* says that the Guru was approached for help by Muazzam's emissaries.[1] Bhai Jodh Singh, in his work *Sri Kalghidhar Hulas* says that Prince Muazzam deputed Nand Lal to persuade the Guru to join with his Sikhs promising at the same time on behalf of Bahadur Shah that he would look into and redress grievance, he might have against his house.[2] The Guru read the letter and also listened to the pleadings of Bhai Nand Lal. Though he was not sure of Bahadur Shah keeping his words once victory was his, yet he decided to help him.

While reaching this decision, the Guru seemed to have been prompted by certain considerations. First, Bahadur Shah was a generous, munificent and extremely good-natured prince. His tolerance and amiability were in great contrast to the bigotry and hypocrisy of his predecessor, Aurangzeb. The Guru had himself seen that in spite of his father's instructions, he had refused to act against the Guru in 1695. The Guru, therefore, thought that if he won the battle of succession, he would be more amenable to liberal influences, especially his own. Secondly, as per law of primogeniture, which was prevalent among the Mughal rulers, Bahadur Shah being the eldest of the three living brothers (Muazzam, Azam Khan and Kam Bakhsh) had a moral right to the throne of his father. Thirdly, Nand Lal held out full assurance on behalf of the Prince. Besides the Guru thought of influencing Bahadur Shah

---

1. Sainapat, *Sri Gursobha*, (ed.) Shamsher Singh Ashok, p. 114.
2. Jodh Singh, *Sri Kalghidhar Hulas*, pp. 203-05.

in the same way as he had envisaged a possible change of heart in the case of late emperor, Aurangzeb.

According to the author of the book *Mulakat Da Parsang*[1], Bahadur Shah personally called upon the Guru at Delhi on May 20, 1707 to implore him to assist him in his difficulty. The Guru agreed and deputed Kuldeepak Singh as a liaison officer who remained with the emperor upto the end of the Battle of Jajau on June 8, 1707. He also decided to send two or three hundred Sikh soldiers under the command of Bhai Dharam Singh to side with Bahadur Shah, as a token of his moral support.

At Delhi the Guru first stayed in a house located behind Humayun's tomb. The site is now marked by the Gurdwara known as 'Damdama Sahib'. As a token of love for a so called low caste of Delhi and to acknowledge and honour the valorous deeds of Bhai Jaita, the Guru shifted to the colony of cobblers called *Mochi Bagh*. The cobblers (*Mochis*) served the Guru with great devotion. The Guru was so much impressed by their high conduct that he changed the colony's name to Moti Bagh, the Garden of Pearls. A Gurdwara stands at this place. It lies on the Ring Road now called Mahatma Gandhi Road. When the Guru was in Delhi, a goldsmith supplicated for the boon of a son. He waited on him a few times. One day when the Guru was on his way to hunt in the neighbouring jungle, the goldsmith followed him along with the Sikhs. They had not gone far, when they saw a woman leaving a newly born male child in the bushes. The Guru asked the goldsmith to adopt the child but he did not. Later, the child was adopted by Mata Sundri the revered wife of the Guru who named him Ajit Singh.

The armies of Azam and Bahadur Shah clashed with each other on June 10, 1707 at Jajau, 24 kilometres from Agra. The fierce fire of joint armies of Bahadur Shah and the Guru wrought havoc in the ranks of Azam Shah and Bidar Bakhat. Bidar Bakhat was killed in action while Azam also fell victim to an arrow immediately after.

---

1. *Punjab, Past & Present* XVII-I, April 1983, Guru Gobind Singh—the Last Phase by Ganda Singh, p. 4, see footnote.

Bhai Jodh Singh in *Kalghidhar Hulas* and Giani Gian Singh in *Twarikh Guru Khalsa* hold that the Guru also reached the battle- field to assure Bahadur Shah a victory.[1] According to Bhai Jodh Singh, the Guru told the Prince,"Have faith, you will triumph.[2] Guru's word never goes in vain". The same author adds that the Guru pushed his horse near Azam's elephant and killed him with his arrow.[3]

Muazzam inquired whose arrow had killed Azam. When the arrow was pulled out of his dead body, it was found to carry a gold-tip that the Guru had always attached with his arrows. After the defeat and death of Azam and his son, the Guru left for Delhi forthwith without even meeting the Emperor.

Bahadur Shah who now became the undisputed Emperor of India honoured the Sikhs who had taken part in the battle and gave precious gifts to each of them. He sent Bhai Dharam Singh to Delhi with a letter expressing his gratitude to the Guru for the help which he had rendered in the battle. The Emperor also invited him to Agra.

The residence of the Guru at Delhi became the focus of the Sikhs and non-Sikhs. He held congregation of the Sikhs twice daily. He himself visited Gurdwara Sis Ganj Sahib in Chandni Chowk, where his father, Guru Tegh Bahadur, was martyred on November 11, 1675. The Guru also paid a visit to the site of Rakab Ganj where Guru Tegh Bahadur's headless body had been cremated by Lakhi Shah Lubana by setting his house on fire. The Guru raised a Gurdwara at that spot as a memorial to the unparalleled sacrifice of his father.

One day, he went to the jungle near Humayun's tomb for hunting. As chance would have it, Bahadur Shah who had made a hurried visit to Delhi, happened to be close by. One of the Emperor's elephants got excited and rushed towards the Sikhs who got panicky. The Guru asked the Sikhs to keep cool. In the meanwhile the Guru patted a trained he-buffalo which charged at the elephant striking fear in its mind, who, as a sequal, turned back. The Emperor felt sorry for the

1. Giani Gian Singh, *Twarikh Guru Khalsa*, Part I, (Pbi), pp. 1078-1080.
2. *Ibid.*, pp. 1078-1081.
3. *Ibid.*

inconvenience caused by the elephant and expressed his indebtedness to the Guru. Gurdwara Damdama stands at the place which had been made sacred by the visit of the Guru.

After about a month's stay at Delhi, the Guru made preparations to leave for Agra in response to the invitation of the Emperor. He made appropriate arrangements for the stay of Mata Sundri at Delhi under the protection of the Sikhs. Mata Sahib Kaur, however, importuned him to allow her to accompany him. The Guru yielded to her request, ultimately.

On the third day after his departure from Delhi, he arrived at Mathura and encamped at Suraj Kund on the bank of River Jamuna.[1] He made a tour through Brindaban and visited all its famous places. Then he proceeded further to Agra.[2] He established his camp 12 kms short of Agra and about 6 kms from Bahadur Shah's camp.

Shortly after, Khan-i-Khanan, Munim Khan the Prime Minister invited the Guru to his palace situated in a beautiful garden. The Guru alongwith his brave Sikh soldiers, reached there. Munim Khan, Khan-i-Khanan and Prime Minister, accorded the Guru a hearty welcome and received him with all the honour due to his position and status of a 'Guru'. He told Guru ji that he had done a great favour to him by coming out to his place granting him an opportunity of his sacred glimpse.[3] The Guru came back and laid his camp nearby the same day. As the night fell, heavy rain poured down. The next day, he made a rapid reconnaissance and selected a garden where he and his followers decided to camp.[4]

The daily routine at the camp was that of a true *Khalsa*. Congregations were held twice a day where knowledge about Sikhism was imparted to the hordes of people who came to the camp from far and near.

On July 23, 1707 Bahadur Shah invited him to his court. The Guru and his Sikhs moved to the Royal presence. He was accompanied by his Sikh soldiers, but at the gate of the palace of the Emperor, he instructed them to stay back except

---

1. Sainapat, *Sri Gursobha*, p. 118, (ed.) Shamsher Singh Ashok.
2. *Ibid.*
3. *Ibid.*, p. 119.
4. *Ibid.*

one Sikh whom he took alongwith him to the place where the Emperor met him. The Guru was fully armed, impressively dressed with an aigrette fixed on his turban. His face looked resplendent[1] and his bearing charismatic. The Emperor thanked the Guru for his help in the battle and offered valuable presents to him. He distributed the presents to his Sikhs as well, just as he had done to his other generals. He honoured the Guru as a revered saint and requested him for his continued company as frequently as possible.[2] He was accompanied by two to three hundred horsemen and some more Sikhs on foot.[3] As a token of his respect for the Guru, the Emperor presented him with a rich robe of honour including a jewelled scarf, a *Dhukh Dhukhi* and an aigrette worth sixty thousand rupees. According to the long established custom, the Guru was to wear the robe of honour in the Royal presence. But he did not do so, rather asked one of his followers to carry it to his camp.[4] The Emperor did not mind this demeanour of his, for he treated him as a holy saint and not as his subordinate or dependent. According to Khazan Singh, another present of one lakh rupees was offered for Mata Sundri and sent to Delhi.[5]

The Guru stayed there for about five months. During this period the Emperor met him quite often, and sought solace from him. Their discussion often revolved around two subjects; religion and Sikh-Mughal relations.

One day, when the Guru was sitting with the Emperor, a Sayyed with a fantasised mind from Sirhind, in a bid to poison the mind of the Emperor against the Guru said to him, "Your Holiness, all the *Pirs*, Prophets and God incarnations have demonstrated their prowess through miracles. What do you say to that?" The Guru lifted his hand and pointed

1. Sainapat, *Sri Gursobha*, p. 112.
2. *Ibid.*, p. 121.
3. Khafi Khan, *Muntakhab-ul-Lubab*, p. 652.
4. Sainapat, *op.cit.*, p. 121; Ganda Singh, *Makhiz-i-Twarikh-i-Sikhan*, p. 82.
5. A news-letter of the Court of Bahadur Shah dated July 24, 1707 says 'Gobind-Nanak, according to orders fully armed interviewed the Emperor and offered one hundred gold coins. He was granted a robe of honour including a jewelled scarf, a *Dhukh Dhukhi*, an aigrette. Khazan Singh, *History of the Sikh Religion*, p. 201, Also consult Giani Gian Singh, *Twarikh Guru Khalsa*, Part I (Pbi.), pp. 1083-84.

towards Bahadur Shah and said, "He is a living miracle. He who wields the political power can do what he likes."

"No, Your Holiness, I mean the other miracles," Sayyed said again.

"The other miracle is this one." Just as he said it, he tossed a gold coin on the floor. "It can procure anything in the world, any person, any value ? Is it not ?"

The Sayyed was trying to play the game of proving the Guru to be an inept person, so as to lower his esteem and respect in the eyes of the Emperor. He, therefore, requested him again. "Will your Holiness show us some miracle, which you can perform ?[1]

"Yes", broke out the Guru like a warrior, with eyes red and pulling his sword out of his scabbard, "This is the highest of all the miracles." It takes the life out of the tyrant, can upturn the thrones and makes the Emperors helpless wanderers the next day.[2] The Sayyed thus became speechless with fear and his eyes cast on the ground.

The Emperor who was listening to the questions and answers with great interest reprimanded the questioner for his impudence. "No, No Excellency" he said, "You should not mind this impertinence on the part of the courtier."

As this news travelled, everyone was amazed at the fearlessness of the Guru even in the presence of the Emperor of the land in whose presence it was just not possible for anyone to appear around, much less draw the sword.

On some other day, Bahadur Shah said to the Guru, "There is no faith better than ours. Why should not those who want to escape hell embrace it." The Guru replied, "Your Majesty, it is not the stamp but what is under it that makes a coin worth while. Even if a counterfeit coin has your Majesty's creed imprinted upon it, no one will exchange it with even a low cost article in the market. So also is the case of faith. It is not the label but the contents of an individual that is pleasing to God, and which determines who is to be consigned to hell and who to heaven. I believe in one God, not two or

1. M.A. Macauliffe, *The Sikh Religion*, Vol. V, pp. 230-32.
2. *Ibid.*, p. 232.

three, and for me no one is an infidel save one who denies His presence."[1]

Views on many more issues touching different subjects must have been exchanged between the Guru and the Shah, but alas, there was no biographer to record them for the posterity to benefit.

What exactly transpired between the Guru and the Emperor during their meetings, we are not in a position to know; but even then circumstantial evidence and the *Hukamnamas* of the Guru help us establish a few facts. The visit of the Guru at first to *Khan-i-Khanan*, the Prime Minister, and then to Emperor Bahadur Shah himself, had evidently a much greater significance than ordinary courtesy call. The Guru had left the Punjab for the Deccan at the invitation of Aurangzeb for a personal interview with him. The only subject that could be discussed between them was the Mughal-Sikh relations—the causes of their estrangement, the ways and means of a peaceful solution of their problems and the implementation of the decisions arrived at between them. That alone again could be the subject of the Guru's talks with the *Khan-i-Khanan* and Emperor Bahadur Shah at Agra. The opportunity that had unfortunately been lost owing to the death of Aurangzeb had presented itself under cordial circumstances. The meeting with the Prime Minister and the Emperor had taken place in a very friendly atmosphere. Both were grateful to the Guru for his ungrudging response to their appeal for help in his struggle for accession to the throne and were happy over the success. Since no reliable details of discussions with them are available in any of the extant contemporary records, Persian or Punjabi, it connot, therefore, be said with certainty as to what hopes were held out to the Guru by Bahadur Shah. But there is no denying the fact that the Guru was hopefully looking forward to a satisfactory conclusion of his negotiations with the Mughal Emperor and soon expected to return to Anandpur.

Regarding the objectives which the Guru had in his mind while negotiating with Bahadur Shah, many illogical and

---

1. M.A. Macauliffe, *The Sikh Religion*, Vol. VI, pp. 232-34.

flimsy conclusions have been drawn. Accordingly to M.A. Macauliffe, "The Guru egged up by the spurt of revenge wanted Wazir Khan to be sentenced to death as per Muslim law. Dr. Hari Ram Gupta[1] also opines similarly and according to him, the Guru wanted Wazir Khan of Sirhind, Sucha Nand, Diwan of Sirhind, Gangu Brahmin of Kheri, Jani and Mani of Morinda, Shams Khan of Bajwara, Mukarram Khan of Jalandhar and Dilawar Khan of Lahore to be delivered to him."

Both the scholars seems to have erred. They have not cared to consider the mission and his central tendency, nor have they based their conclusion on some reliable evidence. Harbouring revenge or taking resort to the revengeful acts was in sharp contrast to the personality and mission of the Guru. Revenge is an evil impulse and engenders hatred. Secondly, it has never solved any problem—much less the problem of improving human relationships and understanding. From the perusal of *Zafarnama* and other writings of the Guru, it is almost certain that the Guru did not want anything more from Bahadur Shah than was normally required, that the unjust and the oppressors of the people be removed from office or transferred to distant places to create peaceful conditions in the country. It was fundamental to Sikh religion that punishment was no solution to reform the sinner. The Guru had brought about the ethical awakening in Emperor Aurangzeb through his exemplary conduct and sacred words sent in the form of *Zafarnama*. Now he had all the hopes to change the attitude of Bahadur Shah who happily was made of nobler and sublimer stuff as compared to his father. In all likelihood, the issue of his resettling at Anandpur was also broached by the Guru.

The Guru's point-of-view seemed to have elicited affirmative response from the Emperor, but Hill Chiefs of Shivalik and Wazir Khan, the *Faujdar* of Sirhind were not amiable to the development.

Therefore, the Guru issued instructions in the first week of October, 1707 to his Sikhs in the Punjab to join him fully armed on his arrival in Kahlur. To this fact, we have a very reliable piece of documentary evidence in the Guru's own letter, dated October 2, 1707 addressed from the neighbourhood of Agra to the Sikhs of Dhaul. Translated into English, the letter reads as follows :

FROM THE TENTH GURU

To the Sangat of Dhaul. You are my Khalsa. The Guru shall protect you. Repeat Guru, Guru. With all happiness, we came to the Padshah. A dress of honour and a jewelled Dhukh Dhukhi worth Sixty thousand was presented to us. With the Guru's grace the other things are also progressing (satisfactorily). In a few days, we are also coming. My instructions to the entire Khalsa Sangat are to remain united. When we arrive in Kahlur, the entire Khalsa should come to our presence fully armed. He Who will come shall be happy........ Sammat 1764[1], Kartik 1st.

The letter points to some other aspects, besides giving reference to the Guru's visit to Emperor Bahadur Shah, who presented to him a costly dress of honour. The other aspects could only be the friendly negotiations for a change in the century-old hostile attitude of the Mughals towards the Sikh Gurus. From the attitude of the Emperor during the interviews, the Guru seemed to have formed the impression that his negotiations would soon be concluded to his satisfaction, facilitating his early return to Anandpur. The only elements to be adversely affected, directly or indirectly, by the implementation of the peaceful settlement between the Emperor and the Guru were the Hill Rajas of the Shivalik and Nawab Wazir Khan of Sirhind. To meet any emergency that might be created by them on his return to Anandpur and in Kahlur state, the Guru had asked the Sikhs to join him fully armed. The irrefutable evidence of the letter also repudiates the conjecture that the Guru had left the Punjab either in despair or to arouse the Rajputs and Marathas against the Mughals. If the accidental change in the circumstances due to Prince Kam Bakhsh's rebellion in Hyderabad had not taken the Guru to the Deccan along with the Emperor with whom the negotiations referred to above were still in progress, he would have returned to the Punjab in all probability.

---

1. Ganda Singh, *Hukamname*, p. 186, *Hukamnama* No. 63.

CHAPTER XIII

FROM AGRA TO NANDED

But the Guru's expectation of an early return to Anandpur, where he could pick up the old threads of his programme and continue with his mission, proved to be a wishful thinking. No doubt, the Emperor's gestures of good-will towards the Guru were impressive, yet he was wary of agreeing to his demands. With the issue of succession to Mughal throne not finally settled, he could ill-afford to antagonise the Muslim fundamentalist's lobby at the court by going against the interest of Wazir Khan who had the solid backing of the *Naqshbandies*, then led by Khalifa Saifuddin and had contributed handsomely to the war fund of the Emperor. At the same time, he could not afford to offend the Guru who had a considerable following of his devoted disciples, scattered all over the Punjab, possessing the potential to disturb peace in the North-West. Nor could he vex the Hill Chiefs who were also a potent political factor with the capacity of creating trouble. Therefore, he was sagacious enough to realise that Guru's presence near the court was preferable to his dangerous freedom in the Punjab. But simultaneously, he was careful enough not to let his real calculations be known to him, atleast for the time being. His polite and kind demeanour towards him was all the more impressive for its political, albeit negative advantage, to the new Emperor. To the Guru, he gave the impression that when the affairs of succession were finally settled, he would favourably consider his demands. Political conduct of the Emperor, generally speaking, portended status quo so far as the relations of the Mughals with non-Muslims were concerned. On December 7, 1707 he sent orders to Sarfraz Khan the Imperial Kotwal of Delhi to see that no Hindu go about on a palanquin and Arab and Iraqi horses. They should not visit the courts wearing rings in their ears and beards shaved. The realisation of *Jazya* and pilgrim tax continued as it was prevalent in the period of Aurangzeb.[1] The contemporary poet of Delhi. Mir Jafar Ali Zatalli also condemned, although in different context, that to take up service under Shah-e-Muazzam is to lead the life of a beggar and disgrace.[2] Such conduct of the Emperor was indeed a malediction and not much good could be expected of him.

In view of all this, there was very little hope that Bahadur Shah would do something in favour of the Guru.

The Guru had also smelt the rat, but he did not still break off with him. Perhaps, he was yet under the impression that after dealing with the disturbances, the Emperor would do the needful.

According to Dr. Hari Ram Gupta, "The Guru's residence in the Imperial camp was a fatal mistake committed by him. The entire Mughal court was anti-Hindu and anti-Sikh. The Guru was looked down upon as a rebel punishable with death. Wazir Khan was a hero for them, fit to be rewarded rather than punished. His representative was always in attendance at the court. He must have reported the matter to his master. The Guru's influence with the Emperor was looked down upon by one and all. Every courtier was alert to see that no harm came to Wazir Khan, while intrigues and machinations to harm the Guru were set afoot in right earnest."[3]

Dr. Gupta's portrayal of the scenario is sufficiently correct phenomenologically; but the Guru was possessed with a mission : to bring about a change in the hearts of the fanatasised people and to give them a lesson in humanism as also propel them to follow the course towards reconstruction of a society whose members were bound by the scarlet thread of love for each other, co-existing on the basis of mutual respect, equality and faith in *Name* permeating all things, living and non-living. He had achieved some success in this

---

1. V.S. Bhatnagar, *Life and Times of Sawai Jai Singh*.
2. Mir Jafar Ali Zatalli, *Kuliyat* (ed.) *Gar Shewa-e-Gadai Nakhawa i.e. Talib Kuni Naukrie-Shah-Muazzam Khan.*
3. Hari Ram Gupta, *A History of Sikh Gurus,* p. 317.

direction, the proof of which lay in his admiration by a large
number of Muslims including Pir Budhu Shah, Gani Khan and
Nabi Khan et al. Even Aurangzeb, the arch-fundamentalist had
to grow soft towards the Guru when he received his letter
Zafarnama which was, in a way, also, an attempt to awaken
divinity in the Emperor. The Guru, therefore, was not
discouraged, much less disappointed to work for his mission,
even in the midst of hostile atmosphere. And the ray of hope
had always been there, because Bahadur Shah respected and
listened to him. If at the end, Bahadur Shah did not accede to
the warrants of the Guru, that forms a story in itself with a
moral of its own. Infact, Bahadur Shah could not extricate
himself from the syndrome of Muslim fundamentalism in spite
of the divinely inspired forces of humanism as symbolised by
the Guru.

Nevertheless, the Guru's apostolic approach forbade him
to leave Bahadur Shah in a huff.

Emperor Bahadur Shah lived at Agra in peace till
November 12, 1707 when he had to go to Rajasthan as
disturbances had broken out there.[1] The Emperor reached
Amber (Rajasthan) on January 20, 1708. Raja Jai Singh
Kachhwah had taken side of Azam Shah in the battle of
Jajau and therefore had earned disfavour of the Emperor.
Now Bahadur Shah occupied Amber and confiscated the
property and belongings of Raja Jai Singh. Then he handed
over the country of Amber to Bijal Singh, Jai Singh's younger
brother, who had already served under Prince Muazzam
when he was Viceroy of Kabul.[2] After settling the affairs at
Amber, Bahadur Shah advanced to Jodhpur via Ajmer. After
a short sojourn at Ajmer during which he offered his prayers
at the mausoleum of Khwaja Muinuddin Chisti, he proceeded
towards his objective Jodhpur, the capital of the state of the
same name, which, after the expiry of Aurangzeb, had been

1. According to *Hadiqat-ul-Aqulim* of Murtaza Husain Bilgrami (pp. 127-28),
   some of the Imperial officers had for some time been clamouring for *Jagirs*
   and salaries and Bahadur Shah had very little money in the treasury at
   the time of his succession. At this juncture *Khan-i-Khanan* Munim Khan
   suggested to the Emperor to annex the territories of Kachhwa Rajputs.
2. William Irvine, *Later Mughals*, p. 46.

occupied by Ajit Singh, the posthumous son of Jaswant Singh who had been actively assisted by his faithful general and patron Durga Das.[1] The whole ethnic stock of Rathor Rajputs had rallied around Ajit Singh. After a lot of diplomatic exertions and show of strength, Ajit Singh was prevailed upon at long last to wait upon the Emperor and accept his suzerainty.[2]

The Jodhpur problem being thus to all appearance satisfactorily disposed of, the Emperor retraced his steps from Mairtha, a town near Jodhpur, and returned to Ajmer.[3]

On the second day of April, 1708 the march towards Chittor and Ujjain was resumed. On the 12th day of April 1708, the camp was not far from Hussainipur.

On the 14th April, 1708, Rana Amar Singh Sisodia sent a letter expressing reverence for the Emperor and an offering of twenty-seven gold coins. This gesture of the Rana assured the Emperor of the peaceful settlement of a large part of Mewar never accepting the legitimacy of the Mughal rule.

When the next day dawned, the Emperor was informed that the Rana had taken flight to the hills doubting the sincerity of the Emperor. Bahadur Shah felt much upset at the Rana's volte face, but thought it politically expedient to first combat with his younger brother, Kam Bakhsh, who had proclaimed his own sovereignty of the Mughal rule instead of acquiescing in that of Bahadur Shah.[4]

In Rajasthan, an uneasy calm had been prevailing. Sisodies, Rathores, and Kachhwahs, the most important ethnic segments of Rajputs who had been smarting under the fundamentalists rule of Aurangzeb, were in a mood to assert themselves, and if possible, to assume independence. This type of mood was manifest when on 30th April, 1708, Bahadur Shah was at the town of Mandeshwar. Maharaja Ajit Singh, Raja Jai Singh Kachhwah and Durga Das Rathor took to flight, throwing open challenge to the Mughal authority in

---

1. William Irvine, *Later Mughals*, p. 47.
2. *Ibid.*, pp. 47-48.
3. *Ibid.*, p. 49.
4. *Ibid.*, p. 1708.

Rajasthan which Bahadur Shah had recently established.[1]

The Guru did not start his march alongwith Bahadur Shah immediately when he left Agra. He stayed back and joined him at Ajmer between March 24 and April 2nd alongwith his trusted Sikhs. He saw for himself how the Rajput princes reacted to the advances of Bahadur Shah and with what great difficulty, the Emperor could secure superficial and temporary calm. He must have also noted how Aurangzeb's rabid fundamentalism had engendered innate hatred for the Mughal rule equally among the Rajput commonality and the elites.

Even in the midst of mirk and dross, the Guru's nobility shone forth and its lustre enlightened who-so-ever came to his sublime presence, or to the assemblies of the Sikhs, held twice daily.

On April 2, 1708 an incident accrued. According to Abdul Rasul[2], author of *Tarikh-e-Muazzam Shah*, written in 1708, Emperor Bahadur Shah was halting at Chittor. Guru Gobind Singh was with him. There was a child whom the author called 'son of Guru Gobind Singh'. He was anxious to see the fort of Chittorgarh. He took fifty to sixty comrades with him and made a dash to enter the fort. The guards at the gate obstructed their entry into the fort. A scuffle ensued and the guards were killed. At this, strong contingent of troops (*fauj-e-digar*) sprang from Kamingah, place of ambush. A bloody fight took place. The son of Guru Gobind Singh like a furious tiger struck down men with his sharp sword and fell dead by the side of his companions. Abdul Rasul's mention of the son of the Guru did not imply his real son. His real sons, all four of them, had already obtained martydom; two having been bricked alive in the wall of Sirhind fort and two martyred at Chamkaur. The learned author erred because he mistook some other boy whom the Guru had treated with great love and affection as if he was his foster father. Sainapat[3] calls him Zorawar, son of Mata Sundri while Fauja Singh says he was the son of a

1. William Irvine, *Later Mughals*, Vol. I, p. 48.
2. *Tarikh-i-Muazzam Shah*, Persian MSS, Rampur Library, extracts reproduced by Ganda Singh in *Makhiz-i-Twarikh-i-Sikhan*, pp. 76-81.
3. Sainapat, *Sri Gursobha*, XVII, p. 123.

carpenter of Bassi Pathana near Sirhind.[1] On April 30, 1708, the
Emperor was at Mandeshwar and sojourning at different
places. He reached the bank of the River Narbada in the
second week of May, 1708. A news-letter of Imperial Court
dated May 13, 17 and 10, says, *"Ba Wazir Khan Keh, Pisran-e-
Khurd Guru Gobind Singh Ra Kushtah Bud Adawat-e-Qalbi
Darand."* (They cherished genuine enmity towards Wazir Khan
who had killed the younger sons *(pisran)* of Guru Gobind
Singh. The news-letter mentions sons *(pisran)* in plural and not
one son in singular.[2]

While the Imperial camp halted on the bank of River
Narbada, a Muslim trooper killed Man Singh[3], who was
renowned for his sagacity, faithfulness, total dedication to
the Guru and his cause. He was one of the three who escaped
the battle of Chamkaur and had pitted his lot with the
Guru in all his predicament. The Guru was much upset
naturally. The Emperor ordered that his murderer be seized
and handed over to the Guru for punishment. The Guru
forgave him and let him go scotfree, understandably to make
him and all those of his ilk realise that the Guru's house was
incorrigibly merciful because mercy being the quality of God
could engender vital forces in a sinner to shun committing sins
again. This merciful act of the Guru evoked spontaneous
admiration among the Muslims as well as among all the right-
thinking people for him. The Guru's popularity enhanced
immensely.

The Guru and the Emperor crossed River Narbada on May
17, 1708. During his halts enroute, he and the Emperor had their
separate camps. According to Khafi Khan, the historian of the
time, the Guru was proceeding towards Southern India with
Emperor Bahadur Shah at the head of two or three hundred
horsemen and also infantry men armed with spears.[4]

---

1. Fauja Singh, *Atlas-Travels of Guru Gobind Singh*, p. 19.
2. Ganda Singh, *Makhiz-i-Twarikh-i-Sikhan*, p. 84. Also refer to *Naurang-i-
   Zamana* by Abdul Rasul.
3. Koer Singh, *Gurbilas*, pp. 49-51.
4. Ishar Singh Nara, *Safarnama and Zafarnama*, pp. 404-06.
   Khafi Khan *Muntakhab-ul-Lubab*, Asiatic Society II, p. 652. *The History of
   India as Told by Its Own Historians* by Elliot and Dowson, Vol. VII, p. 413.

By the end of June, Bahadur Shah reached Burhanpur, situated on the River Tapti.[1] The Guru's entourage also followed him. The place where the Guru stayed, was known as *Khooni Bhandar*—the Bloody Spot because six cruel lions had been killed there once.

He was very warmly received here by the people. Sikhism had already made its niche in the psyche of a considerable section of its population.[2] At this place, a number of missionary centres of *Suthre Shah* and *Udasies* were doing work of proselytisation for quite a long time.[3] Bhai Gurdas in the 30th *Pauri* of *Eleventh Var*, had clearly referred to Bhai Tirath, Hardas and Dhir et al. all engaged in missionary work at Burhanpur with the result that a large number of people had embraced Sikh religion.[4]

The Sikhs of Burhanpur were simply thrilled at the Guru's arrival. They built a beautiful two-storeyed building for his stay and comfort, and also made extensive arrangements for the holy congregations to be held. The Sikhs residing in the neighbouring areas of the city also did not lag behind in offering their obeisance to the Guru as also derive benefit from his sermons and presence. A Maratha writer, Sainapat, who is the author of *Sri Guru Sahai* says, "Guru came to this area for preaching and liberation. People of all shades and religious groups attended his congregations and listened to his discourses." His holding of assemblies and imparting religious education has also been vouchsafed in *Twarikh Bahadur Shahi*.[5] All these witnesses prove beyond doubt that, while journeying alongwith the Emperor, the Guru did not lose sight of his main concern which was the spiritual and ethical elevation of mankind.

The Guru stayed at Burhanpur for twenty days.[6] During this period apart from meeting his Sikhs and non-Sikh

---

1. *Muntkhat-Twarikh (ii)*, p. 618. Sainapat, *Sri Gursobha*, Vol. XVI. pp. 122-23.
2. *Ibid.*, pp. 404-06.
3. *Lashkar bhāī Tīrathā Guālier suinī Haridās(u)*
   Bhāvā Dhir(u) Ujjain vich(i) sādh saṅgat(i) gur(u) sabad(i) niwās.
4. *Melā vaḍā Burhān pur(i) sanmukh sikh sahaj pargās.*
5. Refer to *History of India as Told by Its Own Historians*, Elliot and Dowson Vol. VII, p. 566 and also refer to *Muntakhab-ul-Lubab*.
6. Giani Gian Singh, *Panth Parkash*, p. 319.

devotees, he stole time to visit Raj Ghat, a place on the bank of River Tapti, made sacred by Guru Nanak's visit earlier as also to have interface with other spiritual luminaries. Mahatma Jiwan Das, and an aged holy personage who had chosen to be an *Udasi* in order to devote his exclusive attention to proselytise Sikh faith and had already experienced the thrill of being close to Guru Hargobind and Guru Tegh Bahadur, (He waited upon Guru Tegh Bahadur in Assam on the bank of River Brahmputra) came to the Guru to seek divine illumination. The Guru in His Grace blessed him and illumined his consciousness. Bhai Santokh Singh says[1],

> "God's knowledge dawned on him and he went into ecstasy. He realised One Supreme Soul sustaining the whole universe."

People called him Atam Das, a slave of Supreme Soul. The Guru also met *Mahant* Jait Ram of Dadoo Dwara who per chance was there. Jogi Jiwan Das and the *Mahant* told the Guru about one *Bairagi* Madho Das and his great occult powers.[2]

The Emperor, who had left Burhanpur after a stay of a day or two, now wrote to the Guru to join him. According to Giani Ishar Singh Nara, Bahadur Shah did not want that the Guru's influence among the people should increase. The Guru being embodiment of transparent sincerity, uprightness and truthfullness, did not doubt the Emperor and left Burhanpur. On the way, he sojourned at Jainabad, Balapur and Akola. Thereafter he first stayed at Banera and then at Amravati. From here the Guru first proceeded to Hingoli. At some distance from this place, he caught up with Bahadur Shah and camped at a distance of two three miles from the Emperor's camp. Both Bahadur Shah and the Guru followed the route via Malikpur, crossed Ban Ganga on August 13[3], 1708. In the beginning of September 1708, both halted at Nanded a place of pilgrimage on the River Godavari and about a hundred and fifty miles to the North-East of Hyderabad.

Throughout the journey from Agra to Nanded, the Guru

---

1. Santokh Singh, *Sri Gur Partap Suraj Granth*, Ain 2, Ansu 69.
2. Fauja Singh, *Atlas Travels of Guru Gobind Singh*, p. 20.
3. William Irvine, *Later Mughals*, p. 59.

utilised his time for the propagation of his mission.[1] Dr. Ganda Singh writes that at times, the Guru was not seen in either of the two camps for days together even for a whole week and was busy suffusing the people with the philosophy of Sikh religion.[2] On the way, he also acquired first-hand perception of men and material around.

George Forster in his letter XI in *A Journey from Bengal to England* (published, London, 1798 Vol. I pp. 262-63) vouchsafes, "He (Guru Gobind Singh) even received marks of favour from Bahadur Shah who being apprised of his military abilities gave him a charge in the army which marched into the Deccan to oppose the rebellion of Kam Buchish (Kam Bakhsh)." Many of the later historians including Elphinstone[3] held the same opinion. Elphinstone asserted that Forster's account was confirmed by Khafi Khan. But this is not correct. Khafi Khan says that, "Guru Gobind Singh accompanied Bahadur Shah with 200-300 horse men carrying spears and some infantry."[4]

His exact words were :

Dar āyyām ki bahādar shāh pādshāh mutwajja haidar ābād gardīdand gobind nām az sar grohān ān kaum badnām ba-hazūr rasīdāh ba do sad seh sad swār nezādār wa piādāh dar rakāb rafākat namūd

There is no ambiguity about the words *Rafaqat namud* which only means accompanied and nothing more. The events in the life of the Guru do not lend any support to the aforesaid statement. At Agra we find him ordering the dress of honour presented to him by the Emperor to be carried away by a follower instead of carrying it himself in the Royal presence according to the prevailing court etiquette and practices. This

---

1. He was in the habit of constantly addressing assemblies of worldly persons, religious fanatics and all sorts of people. (Elliot and Dowson, *History of India as Told by Its Own Historians*, Vol. VII, p. 566.
2. *Tarikh-i-Bahadur Shah*, "Guru Gobind Singh, one of the descendants of Nanak had come into the districts and accompanied the royal camp. Elliot and Dowson, *op.cit.*
3. Elphinstone, *History of India* (fifth edition) p. 679.
4. Khafi Khan, *Muntakhab-ul-Lubab*, Asiatic Society, II, 652; Also see the translation of *Muntakhab-ul-Lubab* by Khafi Khan in *The History of India as told by Its Own Historians*, p 413.

was a rare privilege never allowed to officials or the servants of the state. Again, during his southward march, Guru sometime separated himself from Bahadur Shah's camp for a number of days to carry on his missionary work. *Twarikh-i-Bahadur Shah* tells us that "Guru Gobind, one of the grandson's of Nanak, had come into these districts to travel and accompanied the royal camp. He was in the habit of constantly addressing assemblies of worldly persons, religious fanatics and all sorts of people."[1]

This could certainly not have been permitted to an employee of the state especially when he was proceeding on a military expedition against a threatening rebellion. There is yet another strong evidence against Forster's wrong conclusion. On the 5th Ramzan, 1120H, November 7, 1708, a month after the demise of the Guru, a report was made to the Emperor Bahadur Shah "regarding the disposal of moveable property of the Guru; Gobind Nanak. It was of considerable value and according to rule (applicable to Imperial officials and servants of the state) ought to be confiscated. The Emperor remarked that he was not in want of the goods of a *Darvesh* and ordered that the whole should be relinquished to the heirs."[2] *The Akhbar-i-Darbar-i-Mualla* (Rajasthan State Archives) has one entry on November, 1708, wherein the Emperor is reported to have said, "The Imperial Treasury will not flourish with these goods. It is the property of *Darveshan* (saints). It should not be interfered with." Here also the Emperor did not consider the Guru as a state servant.

The Guru chose to stay at Nanded, and gave up the idea of accompanying Bahadur Shah any further. He selected a congenial spot for his residence over-looking the river. Soon a colony sprang up around his abode which began to be called 'Abchal Nagar' the city Eternal. The last days of his earthly life were spent here in all the wondrous glow of Sikh ways as it

---

1. Elliot and Dowson, *The History of India as told by Its Own Historians*, Vol. VII, p. 566.
2. *Bahadur Shah Nama*; William Irvine, *Later Mughals*, Vol. I, p. 90. *Akhbar-i-Durbar-i-Mualla*, 9th of Ramzan, November 11, 1708, wherein the Emperor is recorded to have ordered : "The Imperial treasury will not flourish with these goods. It is the property of *Darveshan*, religious people, saints, it should not be interfered with.

had begun at Anandpur and had been kept aglow all through. Anandpur was reproduced in the Deccan again.

Why did the Guru give up the idea of proceeding further with the Emperor ? Why did the Guru select this place in particular ? Contemporary evidence does not throw much light on these questions. But circumstantial evidence does help us to reach some conclusions. The Guru was associated with Bahadur Shah from Agra to Nanded for over a period of about fifteen months (July 1707 to October 1708). Understandably, he was continuing old negotiations hoping that a satisfactory conclusion would soon be reached but in the process, he realised that it was far from reality. Bahadur Shah had shown marked amenability to come under the influence of Muslim orthodoxy, still spearheaded by *Naqshbandis* and Sayyed of Burhans who were averse to the award of any punishment to Wazir Khan, one of their coterie, or to any settlement between the *Khalsa* and the Mughal state. The Guru, therefore, thought it advisable to detach himself from Bahadur Shah since no fruitful results were accruing.

Even then the Guru could have chosen some other place to reside but he did not. The reason hitherto advanced is that he wanted to see Banda in order to use him as his instrument to wage a war against the tyrannous Mughal ruler of the Punjab, as also against the Hill Chiefs. This view is not plausible. Firstly, Banda was not personally known to the Guru. The Guru had only heard of him through the *Mahant* of Dadoo Dwara.[1] Guru could not be sure that he would give up his ascetic life and follow his mission. Secondly, the Guru's activities at Nanded do not subscribe to this view as these were aimed at establishing Sikh headquarter at that place to spread Sikh gospel in the whole of Deccan peninsula. The city of Nanded, about 240 kms from Hyderabad, was originally called Nau Nand Dehra because it[2] is said that nine *Rishis* dwelt there

---

1. Mahant met the Guru at Dadoo Dwara at Narayana, 14 miles to the west of Jaipur city.

2. M.A. Macauliffe, *The Sikh Religion*, Vol. V, p. 236. The author of the *Periplus of the Erythrean Sea* identifies it with ancient city of Tagara. In the middle of the 4th century, it was a capital of a small kingdom. Ruins of ancient edifice and dilapidated pillars of temples speak volume of its spiritual importance.

in pre-historic times. It had assumed the status of an important pilgrimage centre, as apart from its associations with the *Rishis*, it was the abode of different *Ashrams* (camps) of Vaishnavites, Saivites, Lingayats and *Bairagis* et al. In the fitness of things, the Guru seemed to have considered it to enter into dialogue with the leaders of these holy camps to know their reactions and ultimately to convert them to his ideology, if possible.

Without much loss of time, the Guru started addressing congregations besides offering usual daily prayers.[1] He soon became the focus of attention of the people who thronged to him to have a glimpse of his divine personality and also to be suffused with his soulful ideology.

He stayed at Nanded for about a month during which period he was relentless in his pursuit to promote the cause of Sikhism. Through his life-style and his vigorous preachings, he tried to awaken the people to enable them discriminate between dross and vital. He organised hunting expeditions in the environs of River Godavari to articulate the people to lead active and courageous life instead of drowsing in passivity and sloth. *Shikar Ghat Gurdwara* at Nanded enshrines the memory of this aspect of Guru's activities.

He regularly attended and addressed the holy assemblies both in the morning and late afternoon. These assemblies were largely attended. Thousands of people flocked to him. The Guru inculcated among them a new spirit through the recitations from *Sri Adi Granth* and through sermons. Small *pothies* (booklets containing hymns from *Sri Adi Granth*) were prepared under the overall supervision of Bhai Mani Singh and distributed among the disciples. Some copies of *Sri Adi Granth* were also prepared and given to the most deserving disciples to be read out to the people even in the absence of the Guru. Bhai Mani Singh who had acquired in-depth knowledge of Sikh scripture from Guru Gobind Singh held discourses explicative of *Gurbani*, and of the Sikh way.

Of the many disciples who came to the Guru, Sayyad Khan was one of the most important one. He came all the way from Kangra hills to see the Master. One day in the full

---

1. Sainapat, *Sri Gursobha*, p. 128.

assembly of the disciples, a messenger arrived from the Punjab and gave a letter to Sayyad Khan. He opened the letter and passed it on to the Guru. It was from his sister Nasiran and it was a song, an epic telling how the Emperor's minions had ransacked Sadhaura treating Pir Budhu Shah as a rebel. Today Shah Sahib is no more amongst us. Nasiran Said, "And it is now my turn." These eyes had not seen the Beloved yet, but they have drunk of beauty in *Dhayanam*. There is no sorrow. It is the inner joy blossoming up in the fullness of a willing death."

As the letter was read, the Guru closed his eyes and blessed Nasiran. The Guru never forgot his devotees, always inspired them with ideals which never allow a man to die even after the extinction of physical frame. Bhai Nand Lal, one of the counsellors of Bahadur Shah also attended upon the Guru. He enjoyed the blessings of the Guru's sacred presence. He told him the Emperor's point of view but never went beyond his official duties.

The Guru in his resolve to propagate his mission utilised the service of *Dhadies* fully. Nath Mal was one such *Dhadi* out of the many in the Guru's court. He sang *Vars* to the accompaniment of *Dhad* a musical instrument to highlight the achievements of the Sikh Gurus and their Sikhs. Generally, he sang in Punjabi but at Nanded all those who attended the congregations were not Punjabi-knowing people. Quite a large number of them, particularly the Muslims, understood and spoke Persian. To make them understand the Guru's mission, Nath Mal sang ballads (*Vars*) in Persian language also. One such ballad known as *Amarnama* composed under the name of the Guru himself in the first person, has come down to us through the son of Bhai Fatta, the seventh descendant of Nath Mal.[1]

A perusal of this ballad gives us, although only an outline

1. Ganda Singh translated this ballad into Punjabi. This has been published by S.G.P.C., Amritsar.
   (Piara Singh Padam's book titled *Zafarnama* contains this ballad. This ballad according to the author has two sections. He titles one as *Safarnama* and the other as *Amarnama*. It is believed that *Amarnama* was put to black and white round about the death of the Guru.)

what constituted the essence of the Guru's teachings. Nath Mal says that the Guru pitched his camp in a grave-yard which caused great tumult among the Muslims of the locality. The Guru's discreet silence and luminous personality over-whelmed and quietened them. This event under-lined the point that the Guru attached no importance to the graves and did not regard them as sacrosanct. Nath Mal further adds that the Guru killed goats on the day of solar eclipse, gave alms and rewards to the people irrespective of caste and profession et al, issued injunctions to the Sikhs not to seek guidance from Brahmins, threw the costly pearls into the River Godavari given to him as offering by Bahadur Shah, exhorted the Sikhs to have *Khande-Ki-Pahul* irrespective of the age gender or social status. The Sikhs came out victorious in the clash between Banda's followers themselves. The Guru succeeded in bending Banda to his Will.

From all this, it can safely be surmised that the Guru did not like superstitions attached with the solar eclipse, abhorred the society recognising differences on the basis of caste and wealth. He strongly upheld rational approach and commitment to build egalitarian society whose members were suffused with the faith in the one-ness of God and Brotherhood of mankind. Further more, he wished for the Sikhs to have *Amrit* (Nectar) of double-edged sword to enter into the *Khalsa* Brotherhood, which according to him was at once a pattern and instrument, to present and promote the cause of Gurus.

The Guru deliberated upon different problems of various aspects of society with different persons including those holding important positions in various religious orders flourishing then at Nanded and other places in the South. In the course of these deliberations, the Guru seemed to have made deep impact on all and sundry. Possibly many people around Nanded who are now a days better known as *Banajaras* embraced Sikh religion after having been impressed by the effulgent personality of the Guru and the ideology he sponsored.

Urged by his success and the sense of mission, the Guru established apostalic seat of Sikhism in the South at Nanded to organise the proselytising work in a better way. The ideal of setting up this appostalic seat first flashed across the Guru's mind when he was travelling in the *Malwa* region of the Punjab. According to the *Sakhi Pothi*, once when the Guru expressed his desire to go to the South to establish the aforesaid seat, a Sikh sarcastically said why go to that hellish place which is Deccan. The Guru quipped, "Don't speak in such a way about Deccan. It is dear to me and I have work to do there." Anyway the idea then was only in a nascent form. It sprouted and matured when the Guru's proselytising activities met with success and that too in a remarkably short time.

Another notable feature of Nanded activities was the Guru's unabated concern regarding the people who were suffering fresh wave of oppression and cruelty in the Punjab perpetrated by Wazir Khan and his orthodox henchmen, especially in the context of the indifference shown by Bahadur Shah towards the Guru's demand of persecuting him. Should he compromise with the oppression and the Sikh dispensation, according to which evil must be fought at any cost and the wicked must be punished without remorse, if all other means fail ? The Guru decided never ever to relent and could not help thinking of means to bring the oppressors to task. He had some infantry and two or three hundred horsemen equipped with lances. He had a great following in the Punjab and very influential and faithful batches of Sikhs around him who had kept support between the Sikhs and Guru. At this juncture some events took place which proved very significant in the history of the Sikhs. Sometime after his arrival at Nanded the Guru repaired to the *Bairagis* monastery on the bank of River Godavari on September 3, 1708. It was a solar eclipse[1] day held sacred by the Hindus who generally spend it in ablutions, propitiations and charities. *Bairagi* Madho Das as per custom had gone to the river to have a holy bath and to offer prayers.[2]

The Guru laid himself on his couch to wait for him while the Sikhs killed a he-goat and started roasting its meat. This act of the Sikhs was abhorrent to the disciples of Madho Das who were Vaishnavite vegetarians. They, therefore, became

---

1. Dhade Nath Mal, *Amarnama*, (ed.) Ganda Singh.
2. *Ibid.*

furious and ran to inform Madho Das of all that had happened in the *Ashram*. He deputed five of his disciples, known as *Birs*, to chastise the Sikhs for their acts of sacrilege. But to the Sikhs, the solar eclipse was nothing more than a natural phenomenon and the cooking of meat in no way profane. There was, therefore, an unpleasant exchange of hot words and blows and the *Birs* were beaten back by the followers of the Guru. The Banda's disciples then worked upon the credulous Hindus to go to the Emperor to lodge a complaint against the Guru. The Emperor's response was of total indifference, since the complaint was frivolous. Madho Das then came to the *Ashram* angrily but seeing the Guru all his anger disappeared. He felt a strange sense of exhilaration at Guru's sight. With very slow and measured steps showing utmost reverence, he approached the Guru and fell at his feet apologetically.[1]

The following dialogue is also recorded in Ahmed Shah Batalia's *Zikr-i-Guruan Wa-Ibatida-i-Singaan Wa Mazb-i-Eshan* :

Madho Das : Who are you ?

Guru Gobind Singh : He whom you know.

Madho Das : What do I know ?

Guru Gobind Singh : Think it over in your mind.

Madho Das (after a pause) : So, you are Guru Gobind Singh.

Guru Gobind Singh : Yes.

Madho Das : What have you come here for ?

Guru Gobind Singh : I have come here so that I may convert you into a disciple of the Guru.

Madho Das : I accept it.

The Guru perceived what was yet vital in the youthful ascetic and relumed it with promethean fire. He availed himself of this psychological moment, dressed him like a Sikh and administered to him the immortalising draughts, the *Khande-ki-Pahul* of the *Khalsa*. The Ex-*Bairagi* was now given the new name of Banda Singh. Throughout his life and afterwards, he was popularly known and recorded by the

---

1. Dhade Nath Mal, *Amarnama*, (ed.) Ganda Singh.
   Ahmed Shah Batalia, *Tarikh-i-Punjab*, p. 11; Ganesh Das, *Risalah-i-Sahib Numa*, pp. 186, 187., Muhammad Latif, *History of the Punjab*, p. 299.

historians by his self-conferred title of Banda or Banda Bahadur.[1] In an instant, he was a changed man. He was now no longer a *Bairagi*. He had now become a full-fledged Sikh, a disciple of Guru Gobind Singh, a member of the *Khalsa* brotherhood. He had now found a true preceptor and saviour in Guru Gobind Singh who became the focus of all his religious devotion. His monastic establishment was at once dissolved and he followed the Guru to his camp to prepare for a new mission—a new life. Within days, he acquainted himself with the early history of Sikhism, the lofty ideals of the Gurus and their efforts to raise a nation of 'Saint Warriors'. He also heard how Guru Arjan Dev and Guru Tegh Bahadur fell prey to the injustice of the ruling classes. The doleful tale of the cold-blooded murder of the Guru's younger sons---Zorawar Singh and Fateh Singh—who were bricked alive in a wall at Sirhind and were then mercilessly butchered to death for their refusal to abjure their faith, drew tears from his eyes and drove him into a sort of frenzy.

Finding Banda in a frame of mind to act to resist oppression and tyranny, the Guru gave him five arrows from his own quiver as a token of victory. A council of five *Pyaras* (beloved ones), consisting of Bhai Binod Singh, a descendant of Guru Amar Das's family, his brother Ram Singh, Binod Singh who descended from Guru Angad, his son Kahan Singh and Fateh Singh[2] were appointed to assist him as also to provide corporate leadership to the *Khalsa*. Twenty more Singhs were nominated to accompany him to the theatre of their future activities. A *Nishan Sahib* (flag), a *Nagara* and a dress were bestowed on him as emblems of temporal authority. The secret of his success lay, he was told, in personal purity and chastity and in the propitiation of the *Khalsa* who were to be regarded as the Guru's very self. Thus raised to the position of *Jathedar* or leader of the *Khalsa* and strengthened by the Guru's

1. Dhade Nath Mal, *Amarnama.*
2. Giani Gian Singh, *Panth Parkash* 4th edition, pp. 327-28, (Gurmukhi); *Twarikh Guru Khalsa*, Vol. I, p. 352, as quoted by Dr. Hari Ram Gupta, *History of the Sikhs*, Vol. II, p. 6. According to Ratan Singh Bhangu, the council of five Sikhs comprised Binod Singh, Kahan Singh, Daya Singh, Sunam Singh and Baj Singh.

Hukamnamas or letters to the Sikhs all over the country to join in his expedition, Banda Singh left for the Punjab to initiate and carry on the campaign against the cruelty and injustice of the Mughal government.

The commissioning of Banda by the Guru to lead the Sikhs against the unjust rule of the Mughals in the Punjab was not taken kindly by Bahadur Shah, who despite being in a hurry to go to Hyderabad to suppress the revolt of his brother, Kam Bakhsh, did not find it advisable to leave the Guru alone. He had the mistaken belief that the Guru's death would be a fatal blow to his scheme of brewing revolution in the Punjab. He, therefore, entered into a conspiracy with the two *Pathans*, Gul Khan alias Jamshed Khan and his brother Ata Ullah, already hired[1] and deputed by Wazir Khan to put an end to the fabulously rich life of the Guru.[2] Sainapat states that they paid several visits to the Guru and attended his prayer meetings, evidently to avoid suspicion and to look for a favourable opportunity to attack him. At last one evening when the Guru was enjoying siesta and his attendant was drowsing, one of the *Pathans* surreptitiously crept in to his tent and stabbed him with a dagger on his left side a little below the heart. But before he could deal another blow, the Guru despatched him to hell with his sword and his fleeing companion (Ata Ullah) was put to death by the Sikhs who heard the commotion and came running to the Guru's tent.[3]

In order to keep up his friendly stance the Emperor immediately sent expert surgeons to attend him. One of them, it is said, was an English man called Cole. The wound got healed in a few days, although outwardly. Guru Gobind Singh resumed his task of addressing the congregations. There were rejoicings among the *Khalsa* at Nanded that God had saved their beloved Guru. In a *Swayya* composed by the Guru, his gratitude to God for protecting his life is aptly expressed. Not even the innumerable weapons of all the enemies can inflict

---

1. The view is supported by the *Chatur Jugi* an old manuscript written by Bhagwan Singh and discovered by Dr. Bhai Vir Singh.
2. Ganda Singh, *A Short History of the Sikhs*, p. 74.
3. Sainapat, *Sri Gursobha*, Chapter XVIII, pp. 8-18, 128-129, 777-783.

a fatal on those who seek refuge in God. But sometime later, the Guru was testing a bow. When he stretched it powerfully, it caused the raw wounds to open up again and bleed profusely.[1]

A couple of days later, Mata Sahib Kaur was sent back to Delhi to join Mata Sundri. Bhai Mani Singh was detailed to accompany her. On the 7th October, 1708, the Guru uttered a spirited *'Wahe Guru Ji Ka Khalsa, Wahe Guru Ji Ki Fateh'* to bid his farewell to the Sikhs, whom he liked so much and who loved him above everything. As the Sikhs fervently responded with *'Wahe Guru Ji Ka Khalsa, Wahe Guru Ji Ki Fateh'*, he immersed himself in the divine light. Thus passed from the earthly scene a great teacher, a great regenerator of mankind, the anointed messenger who revealed God's ways and will to the people and showed by personal example, the ultimate possibilities of the human soul for compassionate as well as heroic actions and for suffering in vindication of the highest truth and values known to man. The Sikhs made preparations for the obsequies. The sacred body was placed on the pyre raised inside an enclosure formed of tent walls and the fire was lit amidst the chanting of the holy hymns. The *Sohila* was then recited and *Karah Prasad* distributed. Bereft of the physical appearance of the Guru, the Sikhs felt an agonising emptiness, they had not known in the history beginning from Guru Nanak.[2] But they remembered the words of the Guru who had blended himself into the *Khalsa*. The sense of indwelling of the Guru in *Granth* and *Panth* meant the presence of Guru in the collective body of the *Khalsa*. It gradually reassured them and filled in the vacuum.

A day before the end came, he asked for the sacred volume of the *Sri Adi Granth* to be brought before him. To quote *Bhatt Vahi Bhason Pargana Thanesar* :

Guru Gobind Singh Ji Mahal dasam, beta Teg Bahadur Ji ka, pota Guru Hargobind Ji ka, Parpota Guru Arjan Ji ka, bans Guru Ram Das Ji ki, Surajbansi gosal gotra Sodhi khatri Basi Anandpur, pargana Kahlur, Muqam Nanded, Godavari des

---

1. Sainapat, *Sri Gursobha*, pp. 131, 776-83.
2. *Ibid.*, p. 131, verses 34, 35.

Dahan samvat satran sai painsath, Katik mas ki chauth, Shukla
pakkhe, Budhwar ke dihun Bhai Daya Singh se bachan hoya
Sri Granth lai aye. Guruji ne panj paise, narial agey bheta rakh
matha teka. Sarbat sangat se kaha, mera hukam hai, meri jagah
Sri Granth Ji ko jano. Jo Sikh janega tis ki ghal thaen paegi,
Guru tis ki bahuri karega Sat Kar man-na.'

"Guru Gobind Singh, the tenth Master son of Guru Tegh
Bahadur, grandson of Guru Hargobind, great grandson of
Guru Arjan, of the family of Guru Ram Das Surajbansi Gosal
clan, Sodhi Khatri, resident of Anandpur Parganah Kahlur,
now at Nanded in the Godavari country in the Deccan asked
Bhai Daya Singh on Wednesday, Katik Chauth, Sukla Pakh.
Samvat 1765 BK/October 6, 1708 to fetch *Sri Granth Sahib*
(Damdama Sahib Wali Bir). In obedience to his orders, Daya
Singh brought *Sri Granth Sahib*. The Guru placed five paisa and
coconut before it and bowed his head before it. He said to the
sangat, "It is my commandment, own *Sri Granth* Ji in my place.
He who so acknowledges it will obtain his reward. The Guru
will rescue him. Know this as the truth."

These utterances were unique and had a far reaching
implications. The Guru put an end to the institution of
personal Guruship by asking the Sikhs to regard *Sri Adi Granth*
as their spiritual Guru after him. The *Khalsa* had already been
invested with the status of Guru, now both *Khalsa* and *Sri Adi*
Granth were raised to the Status of Guru.

Other documents authenticating this fact are a letter
issued by Mata Sundri Ji and Devraja Sharma's *Nanakacandrodya*
Mahakavyam, an old Sanskrit manuscript which has been
recently published by Sanskrit University Varanasi. Even
a cursory glance at the letter of Mata Sundri makes it clear
how the Sikhs after Guru Gobind Singh believed that the
Guruship had passed to the *Shabad* (word) as contained in
Granth Sahib. "None in human form after the ten Gurus was
to be acknowledged by the Sikhs as Guru. Those, who
like Banda Singh's or Ajit Singh's followers called their
leaders as Gurus were committing a mortal sin. All other sins,
says the letter, could be forgiven by repeating the Guru's

Name, but not the sin of believing in yet another living Guru
after the Ten Masters of the Sikh faith.[1]

The Second document referred to above also records
Guru's proclamation that 'The Scripture' would be the Guru
henceforth him. While the Master lay on his death bed, Bhai
Nand Lal came forward and asked the following question,
"Who shall be our teacher now ? Whom shall we salute and
see and what shall be the source of our discourses ?" The
Master replied, "*Sri Granth* which itself is the doctrine of the
Guru shall be your teacher. This is what you should see; this
is what should be the source and object of your discourses."
The original in Sanskrit reads as follows. :

> NanadLalas Tada Prcchat Ko Asmkam adhuna Guruh
> Kam Namena Ca Pasyema Kasmai Varta, Vadema Ca
> Uce Gurustu Yusmakam Grantha Eva Gururmatah
> Tam Nameta Ca Pasyeta Tasmai Varta Vedeta Ca
> *(Nanakacandrodaya, Mahakavyam XXI, 227-29)*

The personal guruship was thus ended by Guru Gobind
Singh himself. Succession now passed on to the *Granth* and
the *Khalsa* in perpetuity. This was most significant development
in the history of the community. According to Dr. Harbans
Singh, "The finality of the Holy Book was a fact rich in religious
and social implications. *Guru Granth Sahib* was acknowledged
as the medium of the Divine revelation descended through the
Gurus. It was for Sikhs the perpetual authority, spiritual as
well as historical. They lived their religion in response to it.
Through it they were able to observe their faith more fully,
more vividly. It was central to all that subsequently happened

---

1. The letter is reproduced in the book *The Heritage of the Sikhs* by Harbans
   Singh, pp. 97-98. English translation of the *Hukamnama* is as under. The
   original letter is now in possession of Bhai Chet Singh of the village of
   Rupa, to whose ancestors it was addressed,
   Dasāṅ Pātshāhīāṅ Tak Jāmai Paidhe
   Yārvīṅ Bārvīṅ Chau Baṅdā Ajita
   Vagairā Te Aitkād Lai Aunā Hatiyā Hai.
   Hor Hatiyā Guru Japan Nāl Dūr
   Hosan, Par Ih Hatiyā Gunāh
   Bakshīaigā Nahī Jo Manukh Ke Jāme
   Upper Aitkād Kareṅge.
   (Extract from the original letter).

in Sikh life. From it the community's ideals, institutions and rituals derived their meaning. It constituted the regulative principle for its aspiration and action, the integral focus of its psyche."[1]

Sainapat, writing within three years of the Guru's death gives us a simple account in the climax of the evolution of the *Panth*.

"A day before his death, the Sikhs asked him as to the form he was adopting (or the person whom he was nominating to succeed him). In reply, he said that the *Khalsa* is his physical self and that to them he has granted his role and that the Eternal and limitless Word uttered with the Lord's light is the Supreme Master—*Sat Guru Hamara*."[2]

Bhai Nand Lal in his *Rehatnama* elaborates this point. He quotes Guru Gobind Singh saying that the Guru had three *Rupa* (Forms) : (1) *Nirguna* (attributeless) i.e. the formless spirit of which the human soul was but a small part; (2) *Guru Shabad* i.e. the word of the Guru incorporated in *Sri Adi Granth*; and (3) *Sarguna*, the visible *Khalsa*, absorbed in *Gurbani*.

Another close associate of the Guru, Bhai Chaupa Singh records in his *Rehatnama*. The Guru's commandments are as follows :

"All the Sikhs are hereby commanded to obey the *Granth* as the Guru. The essence of the new system was that no individual would henceforth be recognised as the Guru. Henceforth the *Khalsa*, inspired and guided by the Word (*Gurbani* incorporated in the *Granth*) would be the physical and spiritual controller of the *Panth*." According to Giani Gian Singh, "The Guru opened the holy book, placed five paisa and a coconut before it, bowed before it, then went round the sacred scripture five times, bowed every time and declared it as the Guru for all times to come."[3]

The abolition of personal Guruship was anticipated but not accomplished at the Kesgarh assembly in 1699. There the Guru accepted for himself not only formal institution into the

1. Harbans Singh, *The Heritage of the Sikhs*, pp. 110-11.
2. Sainapat, *Sri Gursobha*, Chapter XVIII, p. 132, Verses 41 to 44.
3. Giani Gian Singh, *Twarikh Guru Khalsa*, pp. 355-56.

Khalsa but also the discipline of the new fraternity. In this way, he merged his own personality in the *Khalsa*, surrendering his high office. While hardpressed in the mud fort of Chamkaur, the five Sikhs representing mystically the whole *Khalsa* asked the Guru to escape in order to save his life for more important tasks of the *Panth*. The Guru had to honour the verdict of the *Khalsa* (Guru), thereby affirming that the supremacy of the *Khalsa Panth* was unchallengeable. This already established fact was openly canonised by the Guru on 6th October, 1708, while he passed the succession to the holy book, *the Guru Granth*. He declared to the Sikhs at the time of his death that the Word as embodied in the *Granth* would be the Guru after him. The soul of the Guru would henceforth be in the *Granth* and the body in the *Panth* (*Khalsa*). Where there are five Sikhs as representing the *Khalsa*, there the Guru will be in body, and with the *Granth* present, the Guru will also be present in spirit.

MOTIVES BEHIND GURU'S TRAVEL TO THE SOUTH

The Guru's motive in going to the Deccan alongwith Bahadur Shah inferred by different writers are as under :

1. Bute Shah and Malcolm say that he went to Deccan because he despaired at terrible reverses and bereavement of his personal family and the Sikhs which had been his lot and wanted a change.

2. Some writers say that the Guru joined the Mughal service. Cunningham says that the Guru received a military command in the valley of Godavari. According to Forster, Bahadur Shah being appraised of his military qualities gave him a charge in the army which marched into the Deccan to oppose the rebellion of Kam Bakhsh.[1] William Irvine also thinks that the Guru joined the Mughal army.[2]

3. Quite a few writers state that the Guru having found that it would be difficult to gather afresh an army strong enough to challenge and rout the Imperial forces decided to arouse the Rajputs and the Marhattas to fight against the Mughal tyranny.

---

1. Forster William, *A Journey from Bengal to England*, pp. 262-63.
2. William Irvine, *Later Mughals*, p. 90, (ed.) J.N. Sarkar.

Before arriving at definite conclusion, we will have to examine all the theories stated above. The view of Bute Shah and Malcolm that dejection and despair overwhelmed the Guru and in order to have a change he left for the South, is evidently unfounded, as it does not fit in with the Guru's personality much less the teachings of Guru Nanak that he was ordained to propagate regardless of consequences—personal or corporate. Indeed, his whole life is a lesson in fortitude, courage and high spirits. As a child of nine years, he lost his father and stood face to face with formidable Mughal Empire which was at its zenith; but even that failed to have any depressing effect on his tender yet mighty heart. He saw his dearest Sikhs killed before his eyes, sent his two eldest sons into the valley of death at Chamkaur; but even those things could not plunge him into gloom. When his wife asked him where his four sons were, his reply was characteristic of his fundamental attitude to these things. He stated :

> *"What then if the four are gone ?*
> *They yet live, and shall ever live;*
> *Millions of our dear brave sons."*

Certainly no trace of grief or despair in all this. Besides this, the tenor and tone of his letter *Zafarnama* testifies to the attitude of the Guru towards suffering. In fact, he openly threatened the Emperor while he wrote "what though my four sons have been killed, my younger son, the *Khalsa* remains behind like a coiled snake. What bravery is it to quench a few sparks of life ? Thou art merely exciting a raging fire still more." Nowhere and at no time was the Guru despondent. He was always active in the pursuit of his ideals.

Thus in the presence of such unimpeachable evidence, it is absurd to repose faith in the Dejection Theory.

The second view that the Guru went to the Deccan as an employee of Bahadur Shah is also far from truth. Cunningham who has given currency to this theory states that the Guru received military command in the valley of Godavari. He bases his conclusion on the evidence of some writers of Sikh history, namely Forster and Khafi Khan. On examination of the references cited by Cunningham we ascertain that he had little or no acquaintance with the original works of any Sikh writers. He alludes to *Bachittra Natak* and at another place *Gurbilas* of Bhai Sukha Singh. But all these accounts do not subscribe to the theory that the Guru took up service under Bahadur Shah.

So far as the authorities such as Forster and Khafi Khan are concerned, a close scrutiny of these also leads to the conclusion contrary to the service theory. Forster writes that "Guru Gobind Singh received marks of favour from Bahadur Shah who, being apprised of military qualities, gave him a charge in the army which marched into the Deccan to oppose the rebellion of Kam Bakhsh."[1] For this account, he relies on some historical tracts whose authors he names not. We have tried our best to discover those writers of the Sikh history but have failed. We think that Forster might have made use of some distorted versions of the accounts of Khafi Khan or those of some detractors of the Guru. Anyway, in the absence of any authentic information, it is difficult to maintain that the Guru took up the employment of Bahadur Shah.

Khafi Khan too does not corroborate the view of Cunnigham, although he, being a religious bigot, was in the habit of seeing everything through the myopic eyes. He describes the Guru not as a servant but a companion of Bahadur Shah. He uses the word *Rafaqat*[2] for the Guru an abstract noun of *Rafiq* which means companionship or company. Obviously, it does not connote any difference of status between the persons concerned. Thus the service theory finds no support from the statement of Khafi Khan. It appears that service theory originated from an intentional or accidental mistranslation of Khafi Khan's passage.

A modern writer, Muhammad Latif while upholding the service theory, quotes Malcolm. But on perusal of Malcolm's book *Sketches of the Sikhs*, it has been found that he too held a diametrically opposite opinion. Nowhere in his book he

---

1. Forster himself is conscious of his shortcoming. On page 253 of his *Travels* he admits that he has no substantial authority from whom he could deduce the history of the Sikhs.
2. Khafi Khan, *Muntakhab-ul-Lubab*, Text 651-52; *The History of India as Told by Its Own Historians*, Vol. VII, p. 413. Also refer to page 341 of this book.

lends credence to this theory. Hence Latif's view is without any foundation or at best an attempt to stain the unalloyed courage of the Guru.

Service theory can also be rejected in the light of the ideology and ideals of the Guru. The memory of the wrongs that had been inflicted on him and on his people were too fresh in his mind to have reconciled him joining the army of oppression. Nor, as Dr. Gokal Chand Narang writes, 'can the service theory be reconciled with the Guru's commission of Banda Bahadur to the leadership of the Punjab *Khalsa*'.[1]

Similarly the view that the Guru accompanied Bahadur Shah to Deccan for he wanted to arouse the Rajputs and the Marhattas to contribute their might to end the Mughal tyranny is at once far-fetched and a mere figment of imagination. Had the Guru gone to this errand, he would have tried to see some groups of the Marhattas or of the Rajputs to assess their strength and their will to offer a common combat front against the Mughal might. Since the Guru did not do anything of the sort, it is clear that he had no such intention or a mission. No doubt in Khafi Khan's accounts one gathers that the Guru addressed the congregation of the people who gathered around him daily; but it does not seem probable that the Guru preached sedition or revolt against the Mughal Government. If that be so, it would not have been possible for the Guru to spend so much time in the company of the Emperor.

Having negated the oft-held views, the issue of the real motive of the Guru of accompanying Bahadur Shah to the Deccan still remains unresolved. We think that after his meeting with the new Emperor who had given him an honourable reception, the Guru wrote to his followers in the Punjab and conveyed his appreciation of what had passed between him and the Emperor. In his letter, Guru Gobind Singh made a very significant allusion to the purpose of his meeting with Bahadur Shah. After remembering the jewelled scarf and the *Khillat* presented to him by the Emperor, the Guru expressed his satisfaction with other matters too. He then informed the *Khalsa* that he would return to them in a few

---

1. Gokal Chand Narang, *Transformation of Sikhism*, p. 97.

days, enjoined the Sikhs to remain devoted to one another and come fully armed to his presence on his return to Kahlur.[1] The Guru seems to have believed that he would soon get justice or succeed in prevailing upon the Emperor to follow the liberal policies, enable him return to Anandpur and to punish the *Subedar* of Sirhind for his excesses. The *Hukamnama* to this effect certainly epitomises a fresh approach to the problems. As a matter of fact, throughout this period Aurangzeb lived far away in the South at Ahmednagar, and it is possible that he might not have been kept fully and truly informed regarding the affairs in the Punjab. Although the later Sikh records speak of frequent appeals to the Emperor by Hill Chiefs and thus give the impression that the whole campaign was being conducted with the full knowledge of the Emperor yet considering the distance of Emperor's stay from the Punjab and poor means of communications and transportation, their view may be accepted with reservation.

In view of this, it is plausible that the cause of the trouble was primarily the local officials particularly Wazir Khan, the *Subedar* of Sirhind, who did not brook the popularity of the Guru on account of religious as well as Imperial reasons. The Guru in his reckoning was not only a great hurdle in the process of the consummation of the objectives of *Naqshbandis* as also of Aurangzeb but also heralded a new socio-political structure which clashed with the structure based on *Shariat* of which the Mughal state under Aurangzeb was a great champion. The crime of Wazir Khan in particular was so heinous and of so brutal a character that the Guru would have been false to himself and his ideals if he had not made efforts to bring the accused to appropriate task. He could not resort to armed conflict any longer because of the dissipated resources. Therefore the only way left to him was to resort to diplomacy. Thus, it is quite understandable that this was the purpose for which the Guru sought to see the Emperor. The death of Aurangzeb foiled him in his efforts for a while, but he was consistent and persistent in the present course drafted out by him. It was this

---

1. *Hukamnama* to the *Sangat* of Dhaul, dated Oct. 2, 1707; *Sri Gursobha*, XIth, p. 35.

very purpose for which he extended his moral support to Bahadur Shah and kept himself in the Emperor's train.

The Sikh records, more or less, are definite that this was the object for the consummation of which he joined Bahadur Shah. This thing is also quite clear from the Guru's *Hukamnama* (fiat) of October 2, 1707 wherein it is written 'the old negotiations that had brought him so far, were then in progress and he soon expected to return to the Punjab.[1] But it appears that the Emperor started for Rajputana (12th November, 1707). The Guru had to accompany him to keep up the tempo of on going talks. The Emperor, however avoided the Guru under one pretext or the other. Shortly after, the Guru discovered that his efforts for honourable reconciliation had failed and the Emperor was not sincere in his overtures. He then commissioned Banda Singh to achieve by force what he had failed to accomplish on appeal to justice.

THE GURU'S EARTHLY CLOSE

The Guru breathed his last On 7th October, 1708 as a result of the stab wound by a certain *Pathan*. Many views have been expressed regarding the circumstances of his assassination. Bhai Sukha Singh in his *Gur Bilas*[2] states that two *Pathan* youths who were the sons of Painde Khan whom Guru Hargobind had killed in the Battle of Kartarpur, came to the Guru. One day, the Guru gave one of them the sword which had been presented to him and said that a man who had sword in his hand and saw the enemy of his father or grandfather before his eyes and yet failed to avenge the wrong had been born in vain. The youngman hesitated; but after a few days when he went to see the Guru, his sense of responsibility and valour was again aroused. He struck the Guru; his third blow penetrated into the Guru's body. Upon hearing the commotion a Sikh rushed in and seeing the misdeed of the *Pathan* severed his head. The wound was stitched up; but it could not heal

---

1. *Hukamnama* to the *Sangat* of Dhaul. We have met the Emperor with all success and received a robe of honour and a jewelled necklace worth Rs. 60,000 as a gift. We are returning shortly. Be at peace with one another. When we come to Kahlur let all the *Khalsa* come armed.
2. Sukha Singh, *Gurbilas Patshahi 10*, Bhasha Vibhag, 1989, pp. 432-34.

causing loss of blood, which resulted in the death of the Guru ultimalety.

The story, when put to critical analysis, fails to stand on its ground. A son of Painde Khan who died in 1634 was by no means a youngman in 1708. Moreover, to arouse the young *Pathan* first to kill the Guru and then to see him being killed by the Sikhs is such an incongruity inexplicable by any norm of logic.

Another variant of the story has been given currency by Cunningham.[1] In their variant, the name of Painda Khan has been dropped and we are introduced to a *Pathan* merchant who had sold horses to the Guru at Anandpur. One day, when the Guru was out of funds, the *Pathan* came and asked for immediate payment. The Guru asked him to come on some other day. He (the *Pathan*) used an angry gesture, and his utterings of violence provoked the Guru to strike him dead. The body of the slain Pathan was removed and buried, and his family reconciled to the fate of his head. But his sons nursed their revenge, and availed and opportunity of fulfilling it. They succeeded in stealing upon the Guru's retirement, and stabbed him mortally when asleep and unguarded. Other writers such as McGregor[2] state that the Guru realised his mistake shortly after and as a recompense for the fate of the victim, the Guru showed special considerations to the widow and brought up her son as a father would do. When the boy grew up to manhood, he is said to have been incited by the Guru himself to strike him. The boy did it, with fatal results for the Guru. Trumpp also believes in this version and to give a rationale to it, states that the Guru had been disgusted with life and wanted to end it.

The version also cannot stand the test of historical methodology. The authors of this version unanimously state, the Pathan, the father of the assailant, was killed by the Guru after escaping from Chamkaur. The Guru's escape from Chamkaur took place in December, 1705. He reached Nanded in September, 1708. Obviously during this period of three

---

1. J.D. Cunningham, *A History of the Sikhs*, pp. 9, 73.
2. McGregor, *Hisotry of Sikhs*, Vol. 1, pp. 99-100.

years (approximately) the son of the *Pathan* who was a child as it is asserted could not have grown into manhood, fully trained in the use of arms, capable of attacking the Guru who was known for his physical strength and skill in the handling of arms. The assertion that the Guru who was in the grip of abject dejection invited the attack on himself is altogether absurd, because in that case, he could not have stitched up his wounds properly and carefully attended to. Moreover, if he had lost all hopes and was completely disappointed, he could not have commissioned Banda Singh to do his job.

Furthermore, in recent years fresh light is thrown by a *Hukamnama* according to which no demand for immediate payment was put before the Guru. In fact a *Pathan*, who had certain claim on the Guru met him, but that he made no demand for any money, but actually refused to do so when reminded of it by the Guru.[1]

Another version of the story is given by Macauliffe : 'More probable is the account given in *Twarikh-i-Bahadur Shahi*. The Guru was in the habit of addressing assemblies of worldly persons constantly, religious fanatics, and indeed all varieties of people. One day, an Afghan who frequently attended these meetings was sitting listening to him, when certain expression which were disagreeable to his ears of the faithful tell him the Guru's tongue. The Afghan was enraged and regardless of the Guru's dignity and importance, stabbed him twice or thrice with a poniard.'[2]

This version also suffers from serious abberations. There is implicit in the version that the Guru spoke against Islam. This fact cannot be true because there is nothing in the life and writings of the Guru to show that he had any kinds of hatred for Islam. According to Kartar Singh, "The story is a concoction of a zealous and a loyal Muhammadan. By inventing this story he has detracted from the Guru's glory by depicting him as

---

1. The *Hukamnama* which the Guru granted to the *Pathan* for his good behaviour is still preserved by the descendants of *Pathan*. Refer to *Life of Guru Gobind Singh*, p. 263 by Kartar Singh.
2. *Twarikh-i-Bahadur Shahi* as contained in *The History of India as Told by Its Own Historians* by Elliot and Dowson, pp. 566-67.

rash and indiscreet in his speech and inimical to Islam. He has
glorified the murderer by representing him as acting in
religious wrath aroused by the Guru's words; and he has
completely absolved the Emperor and Wazir Khan of having
any hand in the affair."

From the perusal of *Sri Gursobha* by Sainapat, one of the
fifty-two poets of the Guru's court and Chatur Jugi, the correct
version has come to light. Sainapat states that one day a *Pathan*
came to the assembly that met daily around the Guru. The
Pathan carried murderous intentions latently. He could not
have his chance because of overwhelming strength of Sikhs
present there. He came again after two or three days and
thereafter frequented the place more often. One evening he got
his opportunity and struck the Guru with his dagger. He tried
to repeat his attack the second time but before he could do it
he was despatched to the world beyond. The Guru then called
for his Sikhs who hurried to him. Two confederates of the
assailant who were waiting for him outside the tent became
victims of the swords of the Sikhs. The Guru's wound was
immediately stitched and dressed up. After a few days it
appeared to have healed up. But when the Guru tried to raise
himself, the stitches gave way. The wound was sewn up again
but after three or four days, i.e. to say on October 7, 1708, the
Guru breathed his last.

No doubt Sainapat's account seems more realistic, sober
and free from any inconsistency, yet he does not disclose the
identity of the person and the motive which prompted the
Pathan to do the nefarious act. Here Chatur Jugi, Khushwaqt
Rai and Bakht Mal come to our rescue. The man was a hireling
of Wazir Khan of Sirhind who was the real abettor of the crime.
As the Guru moved with Bahadur Shah, Wazir Khan got
apprehensive of the intentions of the Guru. He knew what
would happen to him if peace was made between the Mughals
and the Sikhs. The Emperor had already shown an inclination
to help the Guru at the expense of the Nawab. He had granted
a *farman* in favour of the Guru upon Wazir Khan for the
payment of Rs. 300 a day. Wazir Khan was now in fear of his
life and could not rest until he had got rid of Guru Gobind
Singh for good. Accordingly, he deputed a young *Pathan*

named Jamshed Khan, to assassinate the Guru, who having gathered necessary information from the Guru's wife at Delhi, proceeded to Nanded and accomplished the assigned job.

Bhai Vir Singh auther of *Kalghidar Chamatkar* says, that Bahadur Shah was personally involved in the killing of the Guru. Our probe into the historical circumstances also leads to this very conclusion. The Emperor was enraged with the Guru who, he feared, might raise the struggle against the Mughals while camping in Hyderabad. It was for this reason that though in a hurry to reach Hyderabad to suppress the revolt of his brother Kam Bakhsh, he continued staying at Nanded and was not leaving the Guru alone. Bahadur Shah had the mistaken belief that the Guru's death would be a fatal blow to his scheme of engineering the revolution in Punjab. He therefore entered into a conspiracy with the two *Pathans*, Gul Khan alias Jamshed Khan and his brother Ata-Ullah already deputed by Wazir Khan to put an end to the life of the Guru. The following historical facts testify to the involvement of Bahadur Shah in the conspiracy to kill Guru Gobind Singh.

On October 28, 1708 the Emperor ordered that a dress of mourning be presented to the son of Jamshed Khan Afghan who had been killed by Guru Gobind Singh. The imperial news-letter of Bahadur Shah's court records :

> *Keh Guru Gobind Singh Rai Jamshed Khan Afghan ra bajan Kushtah bud Khillat-e-Matami bapisar-i-Khan Mazkur Mrahmat shud.*[1]

Jamshed Khan was not a *mansabdar* or a high dignitary entitled to high honours by the Emperor. He was a spy of Wazir Khan in the disguise of a soldier in attendance upon the Sayyed who was also deputed by the Governor of Sirhind.

Two days later, on October 30, 1708, the Emperor ordered for the grant of a robe of mourning to Guru Gobind Singh's family.

The news-letter of the court states 26 Shaban year 2,

---

1. *Akhbarat-i-Darbar-i-Mualla*, dated 24 Shaba, second year of Bahadur Shah (Oct. 28, 1708) quoted by Dr. Ganda Singh in *Makhiz-i-Twarikh-i-Sikhan*, p. 83.

Oct. 30, 1708. Guru Gobind Rai Nanak-*panthi Khillat-e-Matami-Pi-Dar Badehand*.[1]

It means that the Emperor treated Jamshed Khan and Guru Gobind Singh on equal status, thereby confirming that Jamshed Khan enjoyed the patronage of the Emperor.

"On November 17, 1708 it was represented that the deceased Guru had left huge property." How should it be disposed ?[2]

It was ordered that such chattles would not replenish the Imperial treasury. "This was the property of a *Darvesh* (saint). There should be no interference with it."[3]

The Emperor's refusal to attach the property of the Guru against the will of his courtiers shows his cunning diplomacy. It was purely an eye-wash and cover up of his complicity in the impious fraud.[4]

1. *Akhbarat-i-Darbar-i-Mualla*, quoted in *Makhiz-i-Twarikh-i-Sikhan*, p. 83.
2. William Irvine, *Later Mughals*, p. 90.
3. *Hukam shad azīn amwāl*
   Khazānā-e-bādshāhāṅ mehmūr Ṅami-shwad
   Māl-e-darveshāṅ ast-mazāham nā shwad.
4. Hari Ram Gupta, *History of the Sikhs*, p. 330.

CHAPTER XIV

CULMINATION AND BEGINNING

The period of Guru Gobind Singh was at once a period of culmination as well as beginning. It marked the culmination because the concepts, organisational structure and goals of Sikhism became clear and concrete and elaborated to their logical end. This obviously brushes aside the views of some scholars who hold that the tenth Guru stood apart from Guru Nanak.

On conceptual plane, Guru Gobind Singh was monotheist of the type of Guru Nanak. As with all the Gurus, God with him was a living experience, a primal force who creates, recreates and takes care of his creations; but in His social functions, the Guru regarded Him smasher of the tyrants, 'All-steel', Protector and Saviour of the righteous. This was obviously the logical development of the concept of God. Guru Nanak once mentioned God as "The killer of the unrighteousness." This function of God continued to be hinted by Guru Ram Das and Guru Arjan also. But it fell to the tenth Guru to express it more elaborately, clearly, explicitly and unequivocally and frequently. This function was not the result of thinking in an ivory tower. It was rooted in the social pattern which the Gurus were striving to finally emerge. A community of house-holders would illbrook God who is not connected with them and does not protect them against the violators of peace and destroyers of life and property.

Guru Gobind Singh in *Akal Ustat* says :

"Thou art the Protector of life and the giver of all prosperity
Thou art the cure of all sorrows and sufferings"
"I bow to Him
Whom I see here as a warrior fully armed,
and there as a scholar seeking pure knowledge."

That God helped and protected his dear ones or the good, and destroyed the evil was an old recognised strand of Sikh metaphysics. Guru Gobind Singh not only laid more emphasis in this strand than was the case before but also evolved the idea further. He envisaged God as a mighty, invisible and invincible warrior armed to the teeth and ever ready to use his powers in support of the good.

This institution of Guru also touched its culmination point during the period of Guru Gobind Singh. Guru had acquired a place of great importance in Sikh religion from the very beginning. The predominant personality of the Guru established a nucleus around which *Sikh Panth* could rally.

Yet still in another respect in which the tenth Guru brought to completion development of an important old institution was the evolution of the Sikh scripture. Guru Arjan Dev had done a great job by authenticating the diverse compositions and preparing a single holy book for the benefit of his people. But since then, the work had remained where it was left. Guru Gobind Singh included in it the compositions of his father and put the seal of finality on it. Subsequently, this finalised version of *Sri Adi Granth* was invested with the Guruship and named *Sri Guru Granth Sahib*.

Besides, he completed the evolution of the institution known as *Sangat*. In the beginning, it was merely a religious gathering of devotees, functioning more or less in isolation. Gradually there was many fold increase in its function, and the isolation of one from the other was lessened by the forging of common links, such as building up certain religious centres, institution of *manjis* and *masands* as the agencies of the central leadership and the assertion of the principle of the supremacy of the Guru. Guru Gobind Singh raised them to the state of *Khalsa* thereby investing them with the rights and powers of dealing with the Guru directly instead of through some agency. According to Dr. Fauja Singh, "With the foundation of the *Khalsa*, the network of semi-integrated *Sangat* was fully integrated." The investing of the *Khalsa* with supreme powers marked the completion of the historical process long underway.

The institution of Guruship also touched its zenith and culminating point under the direction of Guru Gobind Singh.

Throughout the development of Sikhism in the pre-Gobindian period, the Guru had been assigned a place of predominance and significance. Guru Nanak regards the Guru as an absolute necessity. He highlights this point in so many verses. As a matter of fact in Guru Nanak's system, the Guru formed the pivot on which everything else revolved. The disciple was asked to tread the path Divine, to remain ever content within His Will and to obey His commands. But in these matters, as in everything else, the Guru was to point out the right path. He was to interpret the Will of God, and the commands of the Almighty were also to issue forth through the medium of his ordainments. The Guru, therefore, was to be implicitly obeyed. In *Sri Guru Granth Sahib*, this fact is emphasised again and again. We can glean a large number of verses from the compositions of Guru Amar Das, Guru Ram Das and Guru Arjan Dev enjoining upon the Sikhs to obey the Guru in letter and spirit. Guru Ram Das says :

> [1]Sikhs of the Guru and friends, walk in God's way.
> Faithfully obey what the Guru preacheth.
> Hear, servants of God and brethren, serve the Guru very promptly.
> Tie up service to the Guru as Thy travelling expenses to God.
> Think not of to-day or to-morrow.

Sikh tradition is also eloquent on this point. Bhai Gurdas who lived in the late 16th century says in his exposition of the essence of the Sikh religion, "The Sikh who receiveth the Guru's instruction is really a Sikh. To become a disciple must be like a purchased slave, fit to be yoked to any work which may serve his Guru. Love none but the Guru; all other love is false.[2]

A natural consequence of such teaching was the unquestioning devotion of the Sikhs to their spiritual head. The author of *Dabistan* who had frequent intercourse with Guru Har Gobind narrates a story how a certain Guru praised

---

1. *Gursikh mīt chaloh gur chālī.*
   Jo gur kahai soī bhal māno(ṅ) har(i) har(i) kathā nirālī.
   Har(i) ke saṅt sunoh(ṅ) jan bhāī gur sevioh beg(i) begālī.
   Satgur(u) sev(i) kharch har(i) bādhoh mat jāno(ṅ) āj ki kālī.   (SGGS, p. 667)
2. M.A. Macauliffe, *The Sikh Religion*, Vol. IV, pp. 244-63.

a parrot and a Sikh immediately went to its owner and offered to barter his wife and daughter for the bird. This story and many others of this type which we cannot afford to narrate here on account of the paucity of space, testify one thing for sure that the Sikhs had developed utmost devotion for their Guru. Sujan Rai of Batala wrote in 1696, "The reliance which this sect (Sikhs) has on its leader is seldom seen in other sects. If a way-farer arrived at mid night and takes the name of Baba Nanak, he is treated as a brother."[1]

The implicit faith in a common superior, knit the Sikhs together like soldiers of the regiment. The predominent personality of the Guru supplied the nucleus around which the *Sikh Panth* could gradually arise. Under the leadership of Sikh Gurus, the Sikhs evolved a sense of corporate unity which found expression through their behaviour and institutions such as *Langar* and *Sangat*.

But what was the sense in which the Guru was held upto the period of Guru Gobind Singh. The Guru was understood in three ways : The Guru was God, he was the voice of God, and he was the 'word', the Truth of God. A large number of verses can be quoted in support of the aforesaid three senses in which the Guru was held.

If we go deeper, we will find complete identification of apparently different senses. The following passage amply proves our point :

"The word is Guru and the mind (which is focussed on it continually) is the disciple. By dwelling on the ineffable one, on Him the eternal Guru-Gopal, I remain detached, it is only through the word that I dwell on Him and so through the Guru, the fire of ego is extinguished.[2]

The passage quoted above gives the meaning of forty-fourth verse of *Siddh Gosht* that brings out this identity not just with the pronouncement that the Word is the Guru but also with reference to the Guru-Gopal. God Himself is Truth.

---

1. *India of Aurangzeb*, p. 91.
2. *Sabad(u) gurū surt(i) dhun(i) chelā.*
   Akath kathā le raho nirālā.
   Nanak jug(i) jug(i) gur gopālā.
   Ek(u) sabad(u) jit(u) kathā vīchārī.
   Gurmukh(i) haumai agn(i) nivārī. 44. (SCCS, p. 943)

Closely connected with the above definition of the Guru is the question "Were the Sikh Gurus not Gurus ?" They were Gurus by all visions because they were the perfect personalities embodying 'The Truth' and conveying only the Truth. Their persons, in themselves, were not Gurus. This fact the Gurus themselves brought home to the people by example, and precepts.

It is stated in the old *Janam Sakhi* that when Guru Nanak finally resolved to make Bhai Lehna his successor, he placed five paisa before him and bowed before him. In the *Tikke di Var* (Coronation Ode) we are told that "Guru Nanak's bowing to Bhai Lehna (Guru Angad) reversed the order of things." It shows that from the very beginning the impersonal character of guruship had been recognised. The physical personality of the Guru was detached from the spirit of Guruship which was to be regarded as one, indivisible and even continuous.

The fact that the name Lehna was changed to Angad must be regarded as equally significant. Speaking of Angad must be regarded as equally significant of the nomination of Angad to the Guruship. The Coronation Ode says, "He had the same light, the same ways, he merely changed his own body." This idea is stressed again and again in the Sikh writings. The guruship was something apart from the personality of Guru and this would explain how the successive Guru could be regarded identical.

Mohsin Fani says, "They (the Sikhs) believe that when Nanak bade farewell to this world, his spirit became incarnate in the person of Angad. Angad at his demise transmitted his soul into the body of Amar Das in the same manner who further conveyed his spirit into the body of Ram Das; whose soul transmitted in the person of Arjan Mal. In short, they believe that, with the transfer of soul into Lehna (Angad), Nanak the first became Nanak the second and so on, to the fifth in the person of Arjan Mal. They believe that whoever does not recognise in Arjan Mal the true Baba Nanak, is an infidel. In their hymns and compositions all the Gurus designated themselves as Nanak. Even in private correspondence they signed as 'Nanak'." This thing was even observed by the author of *Bahadur Shah Nama* who called Guru Gobind Singh as 'Guru

Gobind Nanak'.[1] Guru Gobind Singh himself declares that all Gurus were one and that without understanding this vital aspect of hierarchy, perfection could not be attained. Guru Gobind Singh says :

> Nanak assumed the body of Angad......
> And made his religion current in the world
> Afterwards Nanak was called Amar Das
> As one lamp is lit from another—7
> The holy Nanak was revered as Angad

> Angad was recognised as Amar Das,
> And Amar Das became Ram Das,
> The pious saw this, but not the fools—9

> Who treated them all distinct;
> But some rare persons recognised that they were all one.
> They who understood this obtained self-realisation.[2] — 10

Guru Gobind Singh was not only fully conversant with the different stands of the concept of Guru but also subscribed to them.

For some time, the Guru did not effect any change. Then quite a few developments that had taken place prompted him to review the existing system. One was the nature of relationship between the Sikhs and the Guru. Dr. A.C. Banerjee says, "The importance attached to the Guru, did not, however, create a community depending on autocratic leadership. The ideal of brotherhood was an active principle from the very beginning. As a result, the Sikh community was governed by principles of equality and democracy. The individual Sikh was exalted to a position almost to that of the Guru himself. Guru Ram Das said :

> To those who obey the will of the Guru,
> I am sacrifice
> I am ever a sacrifice to those who served the Guru.

Quite a large number of verses can be gleaned to prove the veracity of the aforesaid point.

The next important development was, that the unity of Sikhs as a community was being disturbed by the emergence

---

1. William Irvine, *Later Mughals*, Vol. I, p. 90.
2. *Bachittar Natak*, Chapter V, *Pauris* 7, 9, 10.

of the impostor Gurus of dissentient sects and the degenerate *Masands*. To keep the Sikhs united, was the most important need of the hour as well as for posterity. This aspect lurked in his mind when he took the momentous decision of making changes in the institution of the Guru. On the Baisakhi day of 1699, he made a pronouncement to the effect that henceforth, the *Khalsa* was his form, limb of his limbs and breath of his breaths. He invested the *Khalsa* with the dignity of Guruship. In the Kesgarh assembly, Guru received baptism from five worthy Sikhs. When they were astonished at his demand, he said, "The *Khalsa* is the Guru and the Guru is the *Khalsa*. There is no difference between you and me. As Guru Nanak seated Guru Angad on the throne, so have I made you also a Guru."

The investing of Guruship on the *Khalsa* was a step of great benefit to the Sikh community. It seems that the abolition of the Guruship had a logical connection with the Guru's war against sectarianism within the Sikh community. The sects owed their origin to the ambition of the disappointed candidates for the guruship. It was not enough to boycott the existing sects, but the emerging of new sects must also be prevented. The abolition of personal Guruship was obviously an efficacious remedy of the disease. Furthermore, to impart divinity to each individual of the *Khalsa* organisation was, to instil confidence, establish democratic functioning of the *Khalsa* brotherhood and the unity amongst them.

But this development was the culmination of the process that had commenced with the inception of Sikhism. The Guru could impart Guruship to the *Khalsa* because essence of Guruship being truth or word was impersonal as well. And to the *Khalsa* he gave Guruship because, the Sikhs had already been exalted to a status equal to the Guru. Guru Gobind Singh was able to transmit Guruship to the Sikhs because there was no elective principle involved in the selection of the Guru. Each Guru was nominated by his predecessor. He could snap the human link, but the idea of new links had been propounded and expounded by the earlier Gurus.

Guru Gobind Singh effected another change in Guruship on the eve of his departure for his heavenly abode at Nanded when he spoke to his disciples that they should also regard *Sri*

Guru Granth Sahib as their Guru along with the *Panth* (*Khalsa*). The injunction that the *Granth* should also be considered, as 'Guru' was also the culmination of the development underway. Word (*Shabad*) had already been given the status of Guru by all the Gurus. If the relative emphasis is a good guide to some conclusion, we can say that this point was more frequently stressed by Guru Arjan Dev. Guru Gobind Singh, obviously comprehended the correct import and significance of this point. This being so he updated and thus completed *Sri Adi Granth* by including the verses of Guru Tegh Bahadur in it and made categorical statement investing *Sri Adi Granth* with Guruship. The development could be effected because of the impersonal character of Guruship and the mystic identification of the Guru with the Word, the facts which were emphasised upon from the beginning of Sikh History.

Guru Gobind Singh also carried forward the social and religious aspects of the revolution launched by Guru Nanak. The successors of Guru Nanak had guided the revolution with great devotion and ability. Yet much more was needed to be done in this context. The creation of the *Khalsa* by Guru Gobind Singh was not merely an endeavour to integrate the members of his community; it was also a powerful bid to carry to culmination his predecessor's resolutions in socio-religious life of the society. The code of conduct prescribed for the newly-created *Khalsa* order was so devised as to impose a strict discipline on the Sikhs, adherence of which would raise the Sikhs to the lofty ideals of Sikhism.

THEORY OF STRUGGLE (*DHARAM YUDH*)

The clear-cut formulation of the *Dharam Yudh* theory was also the work of Guru Gobind Singh. This theory can also be interpreted as the Theory of Progress. This theory in rudimentary form was already existing. The Gurus preceding Guru Gobind Singh followed it not only in their day-to-day life but also preached it through their sacred compositions. The vitriolic comments of Guru Nanak on the contemporary political and social systems were obviously indicative of the struggle raging in his mind to establish a new politico-social-set-up.

The cheap and senseless imitation on their part of their ruler's ways, with no other object than that of placating them was exposed as an act of servility and submission to a tyrant. It was dubbed as an act of shameful cowardice. Compromise with injustice or tyranny was thus shown as a great evil and fearlessness or heroism against tyranny a great virtue. According to Guru Arjan Dev, in the fight between good and evil, God's support would always be on the side of good, for, He is verily the smiter of the evil and the wicked and since times immemorial has been the unfailing protector of the good as against their enemies.[1] Guru Ram Dass says : "In all *Jugas* He has been creating savants and in all *Jugas* has their honour been protected by Him. Harnaksh the tyrant was smashed by Him and Prahlad the victim saved. The arrogant and the foul-tongued were forsaken while favours were showered upon Namdev.[2] Guru Arjan depicts Sikh devotees as *Mall* or *Pehlwanra* (wrestlers) in the wrestling bouts between good and evil.[3]

It was exactly to highlight this type of thinking that Guru Arjan Dev in his parting message to his son advised him to wear two swords, one symbolising *Shakti* and the other *Gian*[4] through *Bhakti*. Guru Hargobind, on his part, addressed himself to the tasks of shaping the minds of the people to rise and fight against injustice and un-righteousness. He collected arms, trained his people in the art of warfare by organising regular training exercises and roused them to a sense of fervent heroism by precept as well as by example. He also fought a few successful skirmishes with Mughal forces in which he and his men displayed extra ordinary valour. All this led to the building up of a glorious and never-to-be-forgotten tradition of heroism.

This tradition of upholding righteousness was further enriched by the ninth Guru. By his sacrifice he not only

1. *Sākat nindak dusht khin mahe bidārian.* (SGGS, p. 517)
2. *Her(i) jug(u) jug(u) bhagat ūpāyā. paij rakhdā āiā Rām rāje.*
   Hernāksh dusht har(i) māriā Prahlād tarāiā.
   Ahankāriā(n) nindakā(n) pith dei, Nāmdeo mukh(i) lāiā. (SGGS, p. 451)
3. *Haun gosāin dā pehalwānarā. Main gur mil(i) uch dumālarā.* (SGGS, p. 74)
4. *Lehne dharion chhatar(u) sir siftī amrit pīvdai.* (SGGS, p. 966)

vindicated his faith in his stand, but also taught a lesson that oppression must be resisted. The sacrifice of the Guru blazed a new trail in so far as it was a commitment to an open struggle against the organised oppression of the state.

This then was the ideology which Guru Gobind Singh had inherited. He so modified it that it became a theory of struggle which would not only explain its aims but also boost the morale of the participants. He named this theory *Dharam Yudh*. The theory finalised by the Guru had the following adjuncts :

(i) that God was eternal protector of the good against the oppressors. He was also the mightiest warrior;

(ii) that it was morally justified to wage war against the evil forces and tyranny;

(iii) that the use of force was justified against oppression and oppressors of all kinds.

This is why the Guru was motivated to raise the importance of weapons as they constituted the vehicle of success and power. Weapons were depicted as decorating the person of the Almighty Himself thus partaking of the attribute of divinity. In consequence, they were entitled to all respect and veneration. The chief of them, the sword, was called *Khal Dal Khandan* (scatterer of the armies of the wicked), *Sukh Santa Karnan* (protector of the saints), *Durmat Darnan* (scourage of the evil), *Jag Karan* (creator), *Sant Ubharan* (saviour) and *Pratparan* (sustainer). Although the force was of primordial importance in Guru Gobind Singh's theory of *Dharam Yudh*, it should not be confused with militarism. In militarism, force is employed for the sake of force, aggression and self-aggrandisement, but the Guru allowed its use only for a noble cause, just enough to correct the malady like a surgeons knife and that too as a last resort.

It is the moral duty of the people to wage war against evil. Guru Gobind Singh professed openly that he had been ordained by God to extirpate the evil and uphold the good. In this context evidence of Bhai Nand Lal is of great importance. He says :

> Rakh-i-Adl o Insaf Afrokhtah
> Dil-i-Jabar o bedad ra Sokhta

> Bina-i-Sitam ra Bar Andikhta
> Sar-i-Ma dalat ra bar Afrokhta

"He brightened up the force of equity and justice and burnt down the heart of tyranny and inequity. He uprooted the foundation of cruelty and lifted the head of justice."

The theory of *Dharam Yudh* of the Guru has been expressed very beautifully in the following excerpt from his composition *Krishnaavtar.*

> Glory to noble souls who on their earthly way
> Carry upon their lips the Name of the Lord,
> And ever contemplate deep within hearts
> Knowing that the body is a fleeting vesture,
> They make the Lord's song, they make the Lord's Name
> A boat to carry them over life's rough ocean,
> They wear as a garment that is as a fortress serene detachment,
> Divine knowledge is the light of their minds
> Their cleaver's broom in their wise hands
> is the broom of wisdom
> With it they sweep all cowardice and all falsehood.

The contemporary source such as *Sri Gursobha* also lends evidence to the theory of *Dharam Yudh* when he says :

> For this was the *Khalsa* created
> To fight the evil to smite the wicked
> And to get rid of crisis.

Dharam Yudh as preached by Guru Gobind Singh was "not a fight to protect or promote the interests of a particular sect or creed and therefore is to be distinguished from the Christian crusade of medieval period and the Muslim *Jehad* of the familiar variety. Nor was it a religious war in the usual sense of the term. It was a moral war waged for the victory of good over evil, for the triumph of righteousness over tyranny and oppression. His concept in traditional ethical terms was analogous to the mythological character of Goddess Durga's fight with the demons Mahikhasur, Sumbh and Nisumbh; to Lord Rama's fight with Ravan of Lanka or to Lord Krishna's struggle with Kans. It was based on dynamic view of religion which in its essence was a social catalyst. The Guru viewed religion as something commitedly concerned with the problems of society and as it had a vital role to play in human affairs it must work for healthy flow of social or collective life and must of necessity contend against the ills hampering the smooth and unhindered mainstream of its existence. But the revolutionary role that the Guru visualised for religion was not to be stinted in any way by harnessing it to the narrow interests of any particular religious creed or dogma. On the contrary it was to be conducted with a view to promote the general good of the society.

Furthermore, the political and social ideals were concretised and institutionalized. Before Guru Gobind Singh, it was not so. It is to his credit that he was forthright, and clear in putting forth his views on social, political and cultural matters.

But the period of Guru Gobind was not merely a period of culmination. It was also a period of a mighty beginning. By his reforms and under the impact of his dyanamic and magnetic leadership, the Sikh Community was not only strengthened but also converted into a powerful force of revolution and progress.

CHAPTER XV

A MULTIDIMENSIONAL PERSONALITY

When we picture to ourselves the whole gamut of the life and achievements of Guru Gobind Singh, he appears to us a gigantic personality with myriad layers; each layer being unique and beautiful in its own way. The all-round impression that emerges is that he was perfect in all respects and in whatever capacity he was called upon to play his part, his was the pursuit for excellence. He was extremely handsome with sharp features and with well-proportioned body. His face sparkled like full moon. The general effect of his personality was imposing, over-bearing and inspiring. His personal virtues were innumerable. He was cultured, decent, humane, sweet, responsive and tolerant. Straightforwardness, truthfulness and fearlessness were other hallmarks of his personality. He would never resort to underhand means, treachery and corruption for the achievement of his objects. Another important trait of the Guru's splendid personality was his equipoiseness. Nothing could ruffle him. He had to leave Anandpur, his hearth and home, he got separated from his companions and life-partners and his dear sons; he could, with great difficulty, save himself from the murderous fire of the Mughal artillery; his two younger sons were bricked alive at Sirhind, yet he remained composed and balanced.

To crown it all, he would not relent from his resolve. He even took the most strenuous *situations* as part of the game. He recompiled the final recension of *Sri Adi Granth*, after he had suffered a great loss at the hands of the combined forces of the Mughals and the Hill Chiefs. Obviously, he was *Sthit Pragya* or a perfect *Karm yogi*.

Besides this, the Guru was fearless and courageous.

Zafarnama the letter written to Aurangzeb is a living testimony to the marrow-deep fearlessness and moral courage of the Guru. He wrote to Aurangzeb "I shall strike fire under the hoofs of your horses; I will not let you drink the water of the Punjab—what use it is to put out a few sparks when you raise mighty flame instead." Not only this, the Guru in this letter calls the Emperor a crafty and deceitful fox.[1] He warns him of the nemesis which lay in store for him.

As a child, he aroused affection of his parents and elders. As father and house-holder, he showered filial kindness on his children. The innocent smiles of his children moved him and he felt thrilled when his children did something which was laudable. He did not miss anything which was essential for their healthy and all-round growth. He cared for his household and made all possible arrangements for providing comforts to his family members. He always attended to his household duties. His family was an ideal one. He functioned his family unit not as a dictator but as a co-partner or as the first among the equals. The family of his concept was not patriarchal in the sense often understood, it was a unit suffused with the spirit of harmony, equality and democracy. He believed in monogamy and advised his disciples to follow his advice. Polyandrous and polygamous families were contrary to his concept of family.

Similarly as a general or as a leader he was unequalled, Such men are born rarely who starting from a scratch could prepare a formidable army in a short time, which could challenge the mighty power of the time. Dr. Indubhushan Bannerjee's expression at this point is worth-noting : "In the *Bachittar Natak* the Guru is rather modest with regard to his own performance and, as it is to be expected, attributes his successes to the Will of the Almighty. But from whatever little he says, it is not difficult to see what an accomplished archer he was and how unperturbed and dauntless he could be even in the midst of raining death." In forming an estimate of the military abilites of Guru Gobind Singh it must not be forgotten for a moment that there was a tremendous disparity in terms of resources between enemy and his forces. But the amazing

---

1. *Zafarnama*, 24, 45.

thing is not that he lost but he could fight for so long. The defence that he extemporised at Chamkaur was excellent. With only forty devoted companions, he kept at bay for several hours a formidable strength of the enemy troops. This feat has hardly a parallel in the military history of the world. The sharp and discerning eye with which he chose the spot where the battle could be fought to his advantage leaves no doubt as to his tactical genius. The wisdom with which he raised forts at Anandpur and the quality of military training for which he made arrangement at the place bespeaks high of the standard of military leadership that he provided. The Guru was a great military planner as well. Every battle that he fought, he had framed a definite plan. This is amply clear from the way he had put up a stout defence with only forty Sikhs against surging mass of human heads. No odds however heavy they might be, dampened his valour and resolve. No personal danger made him shirk his duty. Wounds only stirred him to greater exertion.[1]

When he was called upon to assume the leadership of the ever increasing Sikhs, the circumstances were not congenial. The Government headed by Aurangzeb was not in a mood to tolerate any movement, much less the Sikh movement which was committed to usher in an era of liberalism in politics, social affairs and religious field. Aurangzeb was so much determined in his resolve that he did not feel hesitant even to execute those who were liberal or who had sympathy for liberal movement. Sarmad and a score of Muslim *Sufis* and Guru Tegh Bahadur had to suffer execution because of their liberal views in the sphere of religion and social system. The internal administrative organisation of the Sikhs known as *Masand* system had also gone rotten. The *Masands* being corrupt and extremely selfish, were most illfit to weave the community into a compact socio-politico-religious group. Because of certain factors which had been operating since long, the Hindu masses were completely demoralised. Hill Rajas were more interested in their feudal interests than in their people. The Sikhs had yet to come out of the shock they had

---

1. Indubhushan Banerjee, *Evolution of the Khalsa*, Vol. II, p. 159.

suffered in the wake of the unjust execution of Guru Tegh Bahadur. Besides this, the age factor also did not favour the Guru. The Indian tradition long accustomed to holding the greybearded as wise and mature had to be convinced that the ripeness had no perennial link with the age. Guru's resources, were also very scanty.

It is really amazing that the Guru, not withstanding all these adverse factors succeeded in creating his following and then lead them in such a way that they became instrument of progress not only of the community to which they belonged but also of their country—even of whole mankind. In this process, he exhibited remarkable insight into the human nature, their psychological reactions and responses to different problems and challenges, and into the social mechanism then existing.

He exploited and harnessed all that was vital among the people. He employed theology, literature, poetry and philosophy to prepare the mind of the people to serve his purpose. Through training and education, he succeeded in transforming the psyche of the people. This was the reason that the stock who was considered to be the dreg of humanity was made to long for freedom and for doing brave deeds. As a matter of fact, the potentialities which lay dormant under the killing weight of the Mughal despotism and the outworn social system as imposed by Hinduism, were awakened and forged into a dynamic force to live and die for the sake of truth and righteousness.

Still, the Guru did not allow his following to develop narrow religious patriotism. He exhorted them to enlarge their vision to awaken to the ideals of establishing the rule of the virtue all over the world. In this context the Sikh movement was different from the Maratha movement which was more of revival of their past glory. Sri Aurobindo Ghosh says, "The Marathas revival inspired by Ramdas's conception of the Maharashtra *Dharma* and cast into shape by Shivaji in spite of the genius of the Peshwas could only establish a military and political confederacy. Their endeavour to found a nation could not succeed because it was inspired by a religious patriotism that failed to enlargen itself beyond its own limit and awaken to the idea of united India." "The *Sikh Khalsa*, on the other hand, was astonishingly original and a novel creation with its face turned not to the past but to the future." "His (Guru's) aim as a leader was not to lead the people in the context of contemporary circumstances but also to make them conscious of their role, even in the times to come." He enjoined upon his followers that they were the soldiers of *Akal Purakh ki Fauj* (Army of the Almighty) and they should continue to strive to see that a society, where there is no exploitation and no discrimination on the basis of cast, creed, clime, wealth, birth and sex and there is freedom of expression, of adopting any profession and where everyone has a right to hold his head high and where mutual love for each other is established.

The Guru was faced with a very daunting task of giving a suitable reply to different challenges without resorting to atrocities and meanness. A suitable reply he gave without relegating the moral values. Some scholars have given the name of crusade to the struggle of the Guru and his followers against the tyrannous contemporary rule; but it is incorrect. It would be derogatory to give the name crusade to wars fought by the Gurus. It was a sublime attempt perhaps made for the first time in human history to fight forces of evil without losing the human values.

His contribution to the domain of thought was also of immense value. In fact, he was a creative thinker. He did not believe in the purely idealistic tradition of the country according to which it was held that the material world was unreal and the instruments of knowing it; that is to say, perception and experience are also unreal. And that what we see, perceive or experience is either illusion or ignorance. These views were constantly and deliberately hammered by Indian philosophers, notable among them being Nagarjuna and Shankar. According to them, we out of ignorance or illusion consider natural things as real. They illustrate their point by giving the example of a snake and a rope. They hold that sometime rope is perceived as a snake. Just as illusion or ignorance creates the impression of rope being snake, similarly the natural things which are as unreal as rope-snake are illusory. These thoughts when percolated down to the common man often made him doubtful even about their existence. Its social effect was to search reality somewhere else with the result that this philosophy, instead of bearing an imprint of progress, began to be used by the clevers as a mean to distract the attention of the people from the material world.

This type of working did not fit in the practical world. In one's practical life, one has to run for water when thirsty. He has to eat food and wear clothes. It is of no use laughing at it all as banal talk. The problem posed was a serious one. The evidence of practical life could not be overlooked. The snake perceived in the rope might not harm philosopher's contemplation but not so if the snake is seen through the smoke.

The Guru was convinced that the tradition tightly gripping the minds of the people will not explain the things correctly, and to their conviction. The evidence of practical life could not be just over-looked, and in fact on the basis of this evidence, it was not difficult for the Guru to surmise that the grand theoretical structure so laboriously built up by idealists would not be in a position to hold in the context of the world.

He, therefore, did not accept it in toto. He accepted this much that the ultimate reality was something—may be named as God—who is formless, deathless, beyond space and time, self-existent, all Enlightenment; but he did not believe in the fact that all the things perceived, seen and experienced in this world are illusory. Illusion there is but that is because of the faulty experience or faulty perception, not that the world, the whole world is illusion. From this it should not be concluded that the Guru began to believe in the other extreme i.e. to say that materiality is everything as it has been experienced and propounded by the Charvak school of thought or by the Marxist school of thought. The Guru regarded material things a reality and wanted that men should endeavour to improve their material world. For that matter the struggle of the Guru revolved around the establishment of the rule of the virtuous and the elimination of the evil-doers. But for the Guru it was not everything. He wanted his followers to struggle and strive to be Reality-like. Even in the midst of the material battles he stole time to sit and mutter 'Thou art, Thou art' the only reality. He preached genuine love for 'Reality', but unlike idealists, the

A Historian's Approach to Guru Gobind Singh

Guru exploded the myth that the love for it was not a force meant to be unsuccessful in this world. On the contrary, he said that it was meant to be successful only in this world, for, outside it, there was nothing except God. If a *Jivatma* manages to get free of this vortex of life and death, it gets merged straight in the Lord. Thus, love means nothing for that world where everything is merged in the Lord. Love was a force meant for this world i.e. to say the *Dharam Khand*. This was indeed a revolutionary idea for the practical world. By giving this idea, the Guru sought to win the earth back for the man. This is certainly one of the most important reasons that the Sikhs are not other-worldly. A Sikh looks upon the world as a genuine place to live, enjoy and to elevate himself. The social projection of this type of thinking on the part of the Guru was healthy and the *Khalsa* whom he created in his own image, became inspired group of men surcharged with the spirit of participating in the world to improve and ensure its progress.

Besides this, the Guru's idea of keeping up 'living separateness' also exacts praise. He asks his disciples to keep themselves in 'living separateness' (as long as the *Khalsa* keeps up its living separateness, it will enjoy all my prestige). By living separateness, he meant that his disciples having raised themselves to the ideals he had set for them, should be conscious of it and ever remain vigilant that they were not swallowed up by the environment whose improvement was yet to be effected. This was a unique contribution, because it has been observed that the cultural-pattern which gives up its living separateness and neglects its self-defence is bound to be swallowed up.

His ideas about religion were also striking and tinged with the revolutionary fervour. He repeatedly pointed out that his religion did not consist in turning increasingly towards veiled stones, nor in approaching altars or in throwing one self-prostrated on the ground, nor raising the hands before gods, or deluging the temples with the blood of the beasts, not in keeping vows, but in beholding the height of God within a peaceful soul, in dedicating one's mind, heart and soul to the service of humanity, which is the highest manifestation of the spirit of God.

Ascetics who eat dirty food are no better than filth eating swines.
Yogis who pride in besmearing themselves with ashes
Are no better than donkeys and elephants that bespatter
themselves with dust.
Recluses who retire to the grave-yards
Are no better than jackals howling in the crematory
Monks who live in remote monastries
Are like owls living in deserted houses;
Anchorites waste life in vows of silence;
In what way are they better than the deer who lives and dies
in silence in the forest.
What avails giving five calls in the name of religion
The Jackal cries time and again in the bitter cold at night
Without enlightenment and divine knowledge
The fool sinks into the pit of hell
How can one attain divine wisdom
Without faith, love and devotion.   (*Akal Ustat*)

It is an admitted fact that continuity in progress can be
assured if the people at the helm of affairs of the society are
not allowed to form a privileged class. It has been observed
that such people are thrown up to lead a society by the society
itself. Then they become privileged and concentrate their
energies to safeguard their privileges instead of identifying
themselves with the interest of the people as a whole. Such
people arrest the progress. The Guru correctly understood all
this. In *Bachittar Natak* he exposes different saints and leaders
coming up on the stage of the world and instead of leading
it to a higher destination delimit their activities and form their
respective coteries, caring little for the welfare of the human
race as a whole. The Guru bemoans that the truth, (the Guru
used the word *Par Brahma*) is abjured and falsehood is
followed (*Par Brahm Kineh Na Pechana*). Humanity thus is not
benefitted. The Guru constantly endeavoured to keep his
action and teaching continuously linked with progress and
turned his face against the privileged people. This he did
before Rousseau wrote his *Social Contract* and 150 years before
Marx formulated his *Manifesto*. The Guru said :

All the battles I have won against tyranny,
And I have fought with the devoted backing of these people.
Through them only have I been able to bestow gifts.
Through their help I have escaped harm.

> The love and generosity of these Sikhs have enriched my heart
> and love;
> Through their grace I have attained all learning.
> Through their help, in battles, I have slain many enemies.
> I was born to serve them, through them I reached eminence.
> What would I have been without their kind and ready help ?
> There are millions of insignificant creatures like me.   *(Swayyas)*

Guru Gobind Singh was the first prophet in he world history to identify himself completely with the will and destiny of the people and to give them a place higher than the highest. By doing this, he made them creative. Lest they should become privileged class or vested interest themselves, he filled their minds with the spirit of cosmopolitanism. He uttered to them :

> All men have the same human form
> In all men blazes the same divine light.   *(Akal Ustat)*

When the Order of the *Khalsa* was ushered in on the Baisakhi day of 1699, many Brahmins and Khatri followers murmured unpleasantries but the so-called condemned race rejoiced. The murmurs of the twice-born increased and many took their departure but the Guru exclaimed that the lowly should be raised and that hereafter the despised would dwell next to him. The big ladder with which the Guru used to raise the people high was in the form of self dignity of men. "Tremendous change was effected in the whole tone of national character. Even those people who had been considered as dregs of humanity were changed as if by magic, into something rich and strange."

"The last apostle of the Sikhs effectively roused the dormant energies of the vanquished people and filled them with a lofty, although fitful longing for social freedom and national ascendency, the proper adjuncts of that purity of worship which had been preached by Nanak."[1]

MISSION OF GURU GOBIND SINGH

In *Bachittar Natak* the Guru says :
I shall now tell my history,
How God brought me into the world as I was performing penance.

---

1. J.D. Cunningham, *A History of the Sikhs*, p. 75.

On the mountain of Hemkunt.......
I performed such penances that I became blended with God........
When God gave me the order
I assumed birth in this Kal Age
I did not desire to come,
As my attention was fixed on God's feet
God remonstrated earnestly with me
And sent me into this world with the following order :
When I created this world
I first made the demons who became enemies and oppressors.
They became intoxicated with the strength of their arms.
And ceased to worship Me, the Supreme Being....
I became angry and stone destroyed them.
In their place I established gods :
They also busied themselves with receiving sacrifices and worship,
And called themselves supreme being......

I have cherished thee as my son
And created thee to extend my religion
Go and spread my religion there,
And restrain the world from senselessness......

Understand this, ye holy men, in your souls
I assumed birth for the purpose of spreading the faith,
saving the saints.
And extirpating all tyrants.

From the reading of the above excerpt from *Bachittar Natak*, it emerges that Guru considers himself commissioned by God to spread God's religion, to save the saints and to extirpate the tyrants.

The Guru throughout his life lived to fulfil this mission. He never shirked upholding goodness even at the risk of his life. There is not a single example of dichotomy between his mission and his action. Even in the field when the enemies were unflinching in their determination to destroy his disciples, he would not waver in upholding the principle of goodness and nobleness. This aspect was clearly visible in his attitude, in his thinking and in his actions.

In fact this thing was the central theme of Guru's actions. Battles he fought but did not occupy even an inch of territory— his purpose being only to teach a lesson to the unjust enemy. He used his sword and allowed his followers to use it too, but only for the protection of the poor and the helpless. All his wars were of the nature of *Dharam Yudh*, the fight for *Dharma—* righteousness. He never allowed the moral content to disappear from his actions.

Bhai Kanahiya gave water to a soldier belonging to the enemy's camp. The Sikhs got infuriated at him and reported the matter to the Guru. To the surprise of all, the Guru patted him and said that he had recognised the Truth.

Irvine and other scholars, mostly belonging to the 18th century state that the Guru's precepts prohibited all friendship with Muhammdans. This is obviously wrong. The Guru perfectly understood that he was fighting against the Mughal Empire which was unjust and had lately become tyrannous. His fight was against tyranny and not against the Muslims as such.

Some Muslims such as Pir Buddhu Shah who sacrificed two of his four sons for the sake of the Guru were amongst his best friends. The Guru might not have been able to effect his escape from Machhiwara without the help of Ghani Khan and Nabi Khan. Gough is absolutely right when he remarks that the Empire rather than Islam was the object of his animosity.

Irvine and many other scholars have jumped to the wrong conclusion because in the circumstances of the eighteenth century, the fine distinction referred to above, was difficult to maintain and it ceased to be valid for all practical purposes. The Mughal Government had become rotten to the core and it was becoming futile to expect any justice from its officials any longer. One trouble led to another and the Sikhs soon found themselves in the midst of a never-ending discord with the Muslim rulers. This struggle inevitable coloured the views of the later writers and principles were attributed to the Guru, which find no support in his life and writing.[1]

Nor did he fight for the protection of the Hindus. Bulleh Shah says in one of his couplets that if Guru Gobind Singh had not taken birth, most of the Hindus (particularly those of Northern India) might have embraced Islam.

---

1. M.A. Macauliffe, *The Sikh Religion*, pp. 296-301.

Similarly Bhai Santokh Singh asserts "*Malechas* (Muslims) would have flourished, and Hindus would have been ruined and the religion of the *Vedas* and *Purans*, would have been drowned."

True that Hinduism was saved; but it happened as a part of a bigger scheme of Guru Gobind Singh. Aurangzeb, with all his might, was determined to convert *Dar-ul-Harb* into *Dar-ul-Islam* (the land of the faithfuls). By arming his disciples and arousing them to resist the Mughals, the Guru set an example for anyone to understand that even the fear of Aurangzeb and the temptations held only by him had failed to attract them to his faith.

It is, therefore unfair to think that the Guru could have been the sworn enemy of a community or a class.

The Guru was cosmopolitan in outlook and believed in the evolution of composite culture consisting of the best that was there in different types of traditions in this country or countries. The Guru spells out his point-of-view in the following lines.

"The temple and the mosque are the same; the Hindu worship and the Musalman pray to the same; all men are the same; it is through error they appear different... Musalmans and Hindus adopt their customary dresses of their different countries. All men have the same eyes, the same ears, the same body, the same build, a compound of earth, air, fire and water."

"*Allah* and *Abhakh* are the same, the *Purans* and the *Quran* are the same; they are all alike; it is the one God who created all."

The only thing that may be mentioned against the above belief of the Guru is the vendetta that he pursued against Wazir Khan of Sirhind but that was a different matter altogether. To let Wazir Khan go unpunished would have been to compromise with the very basis of his creed which was (as already mentioned), that tyrants must be punished. Yet while believing, however, in his divine-ordained mission, he took care to see that his followers did not fall into the old Hindu weaknesses of deifying their leader. He emphatically asserted that he was human, and that to attribute divine honorofic to him would be blasphemous :

> Whoever says I am the Lord
> Shall fall into the pit of Hell
> Recognise me as God's servant only
> Have no doubt whatever about this
> I am a servant of the Supreme,
> A beholder of the wonders of this creation.
>
> (*Bachittar Natak,* VI *Pauri* 32)

The Guru was a builder par excellence. He identified and understood the exact nature of the challenges and fashioned suitable response to them. The society was in the throes of caste prejudices, feudalistic tendencies, economic inequities, injustice, particularism, obscurantism, despotic tendencies, Islamic imperialism and inter-religious-group tensions.

All these forces had sapped the vitality of the people. The Guru fashioned a fitting response to these challenges. He made efforts to inculcate democratic ideas, spirit of social and economic equality, sense of justice, besides building the national will to fight and resist evil in any shape. A few half-hearted attempts had already been made by *Sufis* and *Bhaktas*, but the real beginning had been made only by the Sikh Gurus. Guru Gobind Singh brought about their culmination. He did not stop at preaching and setting his own example but he set afloat an organisation to preserve, perpetuate and consummate his programme. The organisation he evolved was the *Khalsa*.

The creation of the *Khalsa* speaks volumes of the organising genius of the Guru. It was at once a social pattern, an instrument to further the cause of Sikhism, a culmination of what the previous Gurus had conceived and preached, a vision to be translated into reality in future. Nanak disengaged his little society of worshippers from Hindu idolatry and Mohammedan superstitions and made them free of their religion and moral influence. Guru Amar Das preserved the infant community from reducing itself into a sect of escapists or ascetics. Guru Arjan gave his followers written rules of conduct and civil organisation increasingly. Guru Hargobind added to it the use of arms and a military system; Guru Gobind Singh bestowed upon it a distinct political existence and inspired them with the desire of being socially free and mentally independent. But a mass of wax figures, bearing the same hallmark and dressed up in the same fashion could not form an effective machine. He, therefore, declared that the Sikhs were under the special protection of God, His own and wherever five of them were present, Divine presence was deemed to be there.

They were further impressed upon with the idea that they were born as blessed souls to conquer all evil-doers as the soldiers of the Almighty. The Guru was an embodiment of hope and confidence of His blessings, and his followers were saturated with the same belief. The new salutation among the Sikhs was to be *Wahe Guru Ji Ka Khalsa, Wahe Guru Ji Ki Fateh* (The *Khalsa* is His own and all their victories are His). A strong conviction of one's being the chosen instrument of God and the confidence it inspires, are the strongest guarantees of success. That the Guru had given these guarantees to his followers, was indeed a significant act of confidence building.

They were asked to eschew caste and tribe-prejudices and entertain the ideals of democratic equality thereby enabling them to achieve unity which is the first step towards evolution of nationalism and cosmopolitanism. He supplemented this moral force by some other ordinances which are as under :

(1) All the Sikh names were to bear a common suffix of 'Singh' among the males and 'Kaur' in case of females, as they do upto now.

(2) All had to adopt one form of salutation, *Wahe Guru Ji ka Khalsa, Wahe Guru Ji Ki Fateh*.

(3) There was to be no external object of homage except the revered *Sri Guru Granth Sahib*.

(4) The Guru fixed upon Amritsar as the chief theo-political place of the Sikhs; and that town had ever since been the Mecca of the followers of the Guru.

(5) "The Guru was a philosopher" says Cunningham, "and understood fully how the imagination of men could be wrought upon." He thoroughly realised hypnotising power of certain external forms and symbols and knew well what an inspiration, men often receive from a change in their outward appearances. He made it a rule that the Sikhs should keep five *Kakars* i.e. to say *Kesh*—Hair, *Kangha*—Comb, *Kirpan*—Sword, *Kara*—Steel bracelet and *Kuchh*—Nicker brocker.

According to Gocal Chand Narang, "These observances

at once singled out the genuine Sikhs from the mass of the lukewarm Hindus and produced a cohesion in the internal body of the *Khalsa* which was in a short time to make a strong *Panth* of them."[1]

Guru Gobind Singh's attempt and desire to make the masses creative, articulate and wide-awake led him to uphold democratic values. In fact this tendency had been the root theme of Sikhism since its inception and also during the stewardship of Guru Gobind Singh. It was strengthened still more and instructions were issued not only to preserve it but also to make it part of social consciousness of the people. The Guru abolished *Masand* system which in course of time had outlived its utility. *Masands* had started impinging on the freedom of thinking and action of the people by acting in an authoritarian manner. By raising the status of the *Khalsa* to that of the Guru, by impressing upon the people that they all were the offspring of the Creator, by rejecting distinctions based on family, tribe, caste or class, birth or creed, and by regarding women as equal partners of men in the march of mankind towards progress, the Guru obviously clarified and demonstrated his stand for democracy and democratic values.

Thus the Guru preached the principle of equality of men and women, of abolition of special privileges, of removal of caste prejudices, of acting on *Gurmata* et al. These cannons upheld by Guru Gobind Singh are nothing practical aspects of the theory of democracy. It shows that Sikhism of the Gurus is democratic both in essence and orientation. But the Guru's concept of democracy was slightly different from the modern concept. While it is correct that Sikhism is democratic in essence and orientation, it must be clearly understood that the basis of modern political democracy is essentially numerical, while, the kind of democracy visualized by the Guru is qualitative, depending upon the decision of the people, noble and wise in spirit. Without this basis, the edifice of the Guru's vision cannot be raised.

---

1. Gokal Chand Narang, *Transformation of Sikhism*, p. 82.

CHAPTER XVI

GURU GOBIND SINGH'S LITERARY ACTIVITIES
WITH SPECIAL REFERENCE TO *DASAM GRANTH*

Guru Gobind Singh's literary heritage was very rich. Right from Guru Nanak, all the Gurus were literary luminaries themselves and the lovers of learning. Their contribution to the literary world was invaluable. The poetic compositions which they produced and which are incorporated in *Sri Guru Granth Sahib* are eloquent testimony to the high level of their literary skill. Guru Gobind Singh inherited this tradition, moulded it to suit his purpose and enriched it with his own compositions besides encouraging many poets and scholars to come forward with their compositions. In fact the Gurus, much more Guru Gobind Singh, employed literature to the service of mankind. With its help they tried hard to shape the psyche of the people to enable them face the challenges for all times to come. Guru Gobind Singh himself has given indication of his objective in one of the stanzas of *Krishna Avtar*. He says :

> "*I have rendered in the vernacular the tenth chapter of the Bhagwat with no other purpose than to arouse desire for a holy war. (a righteous war of the Lord).*"[1]

Quite a large number of compositions were produced by the Guru himself and many were produced by the court poets or writers at the Guru's instance.

---

1. From this, it should not be concluded that the Guru was a revengeful militarist. His war constituted battles for self-protection and righteousness. His poetry as well as his conduct shows love for peace and harmonious fellowship, which sometimes extended to his former enemies.

It is said that at Anandpur and Paonta, 99 poets and scholars worked under his direct inspirations and encouragement.[1] They produced literature covering a wide range of topics, forms and thoughts. Although the bulk of literature was, in fact, the reproduction and recreation of the past heroic characters, its possible aim was to bring alive whatever vital was lying dormant in our social consciousness. This is why it exuded optimism. Yet there is no greater fallacy than to assume that the literature produced by the court poets of the Guru was confined to uphold the aforesaid theme only. They in fact, wrote and translated works on varied themes including state-craft and personal frailties of human beings and state matters. But certainly no work dampened the spirit or spread the gloom.

These men of letters formed an integral part of the establishment of the Guru. They discussed, deliberated, analysed and evaluated in an atmosphere of freedom and fearlessness. They provided leadership to the people in the domain of thoughts and shaped their opinion too. Himself a great thinker and builder, the Guru rarely missed any opportunity to attend their meets and was always anxious to accredit them. The whole thing looked like Plato's academy wherein each scholar was engaged in the pursuit of truth. To ensure that they are not distracted by the financial hardships, each one of the 126 scholars was paid handsomely.[2] The Guru loved men of arts and men of letters and he spared no pains to assemble them at Anandpur.[3]

As the tradition goes and as the contemporary and semi-contemporary records aver, a good number of compositions of the court poets were compiled in the form of a *Granth* known as *Vidya Sagar*. The compositions of the tenth Guru were also compiled in a separate volume.

These books were lost during the crossing of River Sirsa

---

1. Piara Singh Padam, *Guru Gobind Singh Ji de Darbari Ratan*.
2. *Ibid.*, Hem Raj was given ten thousand *takas*. Kavresh praises Guru for his liberal grant calling this sum euphemistically 'urea of rupees'. Hir Bhat also received handsome amount.
3. *Hukamnāme Sikhāṅ Val Likhe jo likhārī Sikh Hove so Hazūr Āve* (*Rehatname*, Bhai Chaupa Singh).

which was then spate, after the Guru and his entourage had evacuated Anandgarh and were on their way to Chamkaur. The Guru made attempts to collect his lost compositions, the copies of which, it was hoped, were in possession of his devoted disciples. But he could not achieve results due to short span of time for which he was destined to live after the Battle of Muktsar.

The task of reproducing the works of Guru Gobind Singh was undertaken seriously after his death by his companion and disciple, Bhai Mani Singh. He worked constantly for about a decade on this project and finished it in 1721 or in 1726. He was able to get some copies from the Guru's Sikhs and other followers and filled the blanks from his memory.

After the Sirsa episode, the Guru, however, did not give up his interest in literary activities. He arranged literary workshop—One in the Lakhi Jungle[1], in which quite a large number of poets and writers participated and the other at Talwandi Sabo where a galaxy of scholars and poets gathered and were stimulated to create compositions to set in motion the process of the mass-awakening. A lot of literature was created there and circulated. Arrangements were also made to impart education to the people. Sukha Singh, the author of *Gurbilas Patshahi 10*, says that in addition to the extension of patronage to the scholars and writers, the Guru encouraged the people to study at the *Ashram*.[2]

DASAM GRANTH—A Compendium of Guru Gobind Singh's Compositions.

It is not possible to give exact details of the compositions of Guru Gobind Singh because much was lost to the future generations owing to political turmoil that the Guru had to face. However, *Dasam Granth* is, in fact a collection of different

1. Piara Singh Padam in his book *Guru Gobind Singh ji de Darbari Ratan* has given the list of 126 poets out of which Behari Lal Das, Khiali Adha, Tado Rai, Fat Mal, Keso, Bhagtu are some who attended the meeting of the poets in Lakhi Jungle.
2. He also includes in the list eleven scribes and clerks who worked in the establishment of Guru Gobind Singh. The list is still incomplete and more research work is required to find out the missing names.

compositions ascribed to the Guru. A brief account of these compositions is as under :

1.	*Jaap*	199 verses
2.	*Akal Ustat* (incomplete)	271½ verses
3.	*Bachittar Natak*	
4.	*Chandi Charittar, Ukt Bilas*	262 verses
5.	*Chandi Charittar*	233 verses
6.	*Var Sri Bhagauti Ji*	55 verses
7.	*Chaubis Avtar of Vishnu*	
8.	*Mehdi Avtar*	5297 verses
9.	*Brahma Avtars*	343 verses
	(Scholar of geniuses)	
10.	*Rudra Avtars*	498 verses
11.	*Gyan Prabodh* (incomplete)	336 verses
12.	*Shabad Hazare*	12 verses
13.	*Swayyas*	33 verses
14.	*Shastra Nam Mala*	
15.	*Triya Charitra Pakhyan*	7046 verses
16.	*Zafarnama*	111 verses
17.	*Hakayat*	757 verses

Total Number of verses in *Dasam Granth* are 17,377

Dr. Trilochan Singh has classified the works of Guru Gobind Singh under the following heads :

(a) Philosophical works comprising *Jaap Sahib, Akal Ustat, Gyan Prabodh, Swayyas, Shabad Hazare.*

(b) Historical works and literature of power. Under this head Dr. Trilochan Singh includes *Bachittar Natak, Chaubis Avtar of Vishnu, Mehdi Avtar, Avtars of Brahma and Rudra. Triya Charitra Pakhyan, Zafarnama, Hakayat, Chandi Charittra,* all three versions, *Shastar Nam Mala.*

1. *JAAP*

This is the introductory invocation of the *Granth* and is a part of daily regimen of Sikh prayer. It contains 199 verses. It was composed before 1699. Because it was one of the compositions recited at the time of the Sikh baptismal ceremony on the Baisakhi day of 1699. It has been written after the manner of *Vishnu Sahsar Nama*, a composition which forms a part of *Sikkand Puran*. As in *Vishnu Sahsar Nama*, thousands names of Vishnu which bring out his different attributes have been given, similarly *Jaap* was composed to supply to the Sikhs with similar number of epithets of the Creator. According to C.H. Loehlin, there are actually about 950 names in the *Jaap*. In most of the 199 verses, God has been described in negative terms. Among 950 names, there are seventy-five names used in Muslim scriptures, only a few of these being *Rahim*, *Karim*, *Razak* (Nourisher), *Arun* (Pardoner), *Salamai* (Peaceful), *Allah*, *Nirsharik*, *Husnul-chirag*, *Gharibul-Niwaz*, *Kamal-Karim*, *Rajual-Rahim*, *Bhishtul-Niwas* and many others.

A scrutiny of the names of God would lead us to conclude that He was everything to the Guru. He is a negative as well as a positive force. Every activity is his activity and everything in this world is His own projection and manifestation. Everything is not God, yet he is in everything. He has no form or feature, no caste or image, beyond description, incomprehensible, having no sign, mark or garb. God of Guru Gobind Singh is no particular entity giving rise to social particularism. He is absolute, infinite, signless, formless–all sparks (*Jyoti*) lights.

He 'is all, in all and for all.'

The *Jaap* being an invocation of the Ultimate Reality is placed in the *stotra* poetic form. All the verses are in the form of rhymed couplets and the metres and the words used are the most expressive and most appropriate. The metre known as *Bhujang Prayat Chhand* has frequently been used by the Guru in this composition. Besides *Bhujang Prayat*, other metres like *Rual(i)*, *Ek Acchari*, *Bhagwati* have also been used.

2. *AKAL USTAT* (PRAISES OF THE TIMELESS)

Akal Ustat is one of the best works of the Guru both from the point of view of subject-matter and literary qualities. *Akal Ustat* means 'Praises of the Immortal'. This composition is undoubtedly a creation of the Guru himself. The Guru envisions God as supreme in all respects, uses all types of epithets to praise Him. One can find negative as well as positive epithets but the crucial theme always remains the same i.e. God is all powerful and supreme. The new thing which strikes one while scrutinising the composition is that God has been addressed as *Sarbloh*—All steel, *Sarb Kal*, All Death, *Mahaloh*—Great steel, *Kharagketu*—having a sword as a sign on His banner.

In *Akal Ustat* the Guru touches varied topics. He makes copious use of Indian mythology but mythological figures and events in his hands are transformed into living characters engaged in the work of raising the true spirit according to the plans of the Guru. He is careful lest he is misunderstood as upholder of Hindu practices, and this being so, he strikes upon them with extraordinary force and vigour. The Guru also touches upon the topic of religion in this composition. His religion is the religion of *Nam*. It is absurd to say that he strives to nationalise God or religion. He clearly and vehemently opposes the idea of the chosen people or a blessed nation.

> *The Arab of Arabia, The French of France.*
> *The Quareshies of Qandhar meditate on thy Name.*

In the *Akal Ustat* the Guru has revealed a close knowledge of the people like the Gurkhas, the Chinese, the Manchurians, the English, the Arnesians, Georgians and Romans.

The Guru commences *Akal Ustat* with invocation to God, who is called All Steel and ends it presenting the Hindus and the Muslims, in fact people of the World over, as seekers of the same God whose blessings they cherish.

The composition *Akal Ustat* is not so named in any of *Dasam Granth* recension. The composition is, in fact untitled, but it carries at its end the words *Ustati Sampurnam* (eulogy concludes). Since the Ultimate Reality has been often referred to *Akal* by the Guru, the composition which is heavily eulogistic of the Ultimate Reality came to be known as *Akal Ustat*.

There is hardly any evidence to determine the date and place of its composition. According to D.P. Ashta, " *Akal Ustat* was composed not in one sitting, but its different parts were composed at different times and were later on compiled together."[1] However the fact that a certain section of it, i.e. ten *Swayyas* comprising verses 21-30, is traditionally recited at the time of Sikh baptismal ceremony undoubtedly proves that *Akal Ustat* was composed before 1699.

The composition comprises 272 verses, the last verse being incomplete and it is composed in twelve different metres, such as *Chaupai* (10), *Kabit* (44), *Swayyas* (20), *Tomar* (20), *Laghunaraj* (20), *Bhujang Prayat* (30), *Padhari* (38) including the last incomplete verse, *Totak* (20), *Naraj* (20), *Ruaal* (20), *Diragh Tribhangi* (20), and *Dohira* (10). The language of the composition is Braj with occasional interspersing of words from Arabic and Persian.

3. *BACHITTAR NATAK—APNI KATHA*

Bachittar Natak Granth was the name given to *Dasam Granth* by Bhai Mani Singh. According to the celebrated author of *Shabad Murat*, it is the name given to *Apni Katha*, *Avtars of Vishnu*, *Avtars of Brahma*, *Avtars of Rudra*. But somehow this name, has incorrectly been used to denote only *Apni Katha*. In this composition there are 371 verses. This composition is very important for a student of history, sociology, Indian mythology and religion. Here is a graphic description of wars of *Bhangani* and *Nadaun*, of the mission of the Guru, and of the rationale behind the martyrdom of Guru Tegh Bahadur. A sketchy account of the Guru's early life is also available. While recording the events of his past life and dwelling on the mission for which he has been commissioned to this world, he demonstrates the racial consciousness. The composition a sort of sketchy autobiography written in rhymed verses is an exquisite exposition of the Guru's mission. The Guru records, "I assumed birth for the purpose of upholding *Dharma*, saving the Saints and destroying tyrants."[2] Like any other autobiography this also is an incomplete life story going as far as the advent of Prince Muazzam (later Emperor Bahadur Shah) on the scene at the head of a large contingent (Canto 13).

---

1. D. P. Ashta, *The Poetry of Dasam Granth*, p. 37.
2. *Dharm chalāvan sant ubhāran, Dushṭ saban ko mūl upāran.*

It is generally believed that it was composed at *Anandpur* sometime before the Baisakhi day (29th March) of 1699 because the creation of the *Khalsa* and the events thereafter find no mention in it. The language is mainly *Braj* with a sprinkling of words from other languages such as *Avadhi* and *Rajasthani*.

The Real One is eulogised in this composition by His names like *Sri Kharag*, *Bhagwati* and so on. In a way the Guru perceived *Reality* not only as Creator of everything in phenomenal world, but also as an embodiment of *Shakti* which annihilates hordes of the wicked. Lest this is mistaken for a mere abstraction, he highlights *Reality* as concerned with the affairs of this world. According to him, He had been sending messengers to this world to take care of it by restraining people from misdeeds and setting them on the path of spiritual and moral progress. In this context, he states that 'he took birth to annihilate the wicked and protect the righteous (VI, 43). Undoubtedly, the events of the Guru's life in this world stand testimony to his endeavour to fulfil the task assigned to him by the Divine. Against this background it can be safely assumed that the *Reality* of Guru Gobind Singh's perception is not above or in-different to what happens in the human world but is ever active for the spread of righteousness, justice and equality. The work comprises a total of 471 verses in fourteen Cantos composed in twelve different metres such as *Chaupai* (162 verses), *Bhujang Prayat* (113 verses), *Rasaval* (90), *Dohra* (38 verses—the figure includes two verses of *Dohira Charni* also), *Naraj* (33), *Madhubhar* (12), *Swayya* (11), *Totak* (6), *Chaupai* (1), *Arill* (1), and *Padhari* (2), *Tribhangi* (2). *Chaupai* is the metre used more often because it is the most suitable for descriptive and epic poetry and is commonly used in larger composition.[1]

CHANDI CHARITTAR UKATI BILAS OR CHANDI CHARITTAR I, CHANDI CHARITTAR II AND CHANDI DI VAR OR VAR SHRI BHAGAUTI JI

There are three versions of the story of *Chandi* in *Dasam Granth*. All three are from *Markandeya Purana*. All three run

---

1. *Punjabi Sahitya Kosh*, pp. 268-69.

with the gore of the battles between goddess *Durga* and the Demons, possibly an allegory of the battles between good and evil. Dr. Trilochan Singh says, "While the *Bachittar Natak Granth* gives the history of the Aryan Period, *Chandi Charittar* and a considerable portion of the *Sarab-Loh Granth* gives the history of the Pre-Aryan period. *Chandi* is a pre-Aryan deity still worshipped over a considerable part of India. Guru Gobind Singh gave these translations to inspire the worshippers of *Chandi* with heroism and revolt against the tyranny." The first two versions of *Chandi Charittar* are in Braj while *Chandi Di Var* is in Punjabi. Dr. D.P. Ashta says, "It is the first *Var* of its kind in Punjabi" and rates it one of the first examples of Punjabi poems. The opening verses of the Punjabi version now form part of the *Ardas* or daily supplicatory prayer of the Sikhs. The verses run as under :

> Meditate first on the primal source of energy (God) and then turn your thoughts to Guru Nanak.
> Angad Guru, Amar Das, each with Ram Das, be our protector, remember Arjan and Hargobind and then remember Sri Harkrishan whose very sight dispels all sorrows.
> Think of Tegh Bahadur
> So will all the nine treasures throng thy door
> May they, the Gurus, be our guides,
> Our protectors in all places.

It will not be out of place to emphasise, that the Guru did not worship goddess *Chandi*. He simply recalled *Chandi* as a character, capable of inspiring people to protect righteousness courageously and persistently. His invocation to *Siva* in *Chandi Charittar Ukati Bilas* must not be misunderstood as invocation of the goddess (*Siva* is also the name given to the wife of *Siva*); In fact *Siva* has been used as an attributive name of the Ultimate Reality which is singular. "The *Puranic* narrative from where the Guru selects the *Adhbhut* (wonderful) *Katha* or *Lila* (story) of *Chandi* has for the Guru no historical or religious meaning nor does he ever deify the goddess in his compositions. In fact, all the invocations to the goddess by various gods in the *Puranic* account are absent from the Guru's considerably condensed versions.[1] The Guru's specific choice of *Durga* out

---

1. Dharam Singh, *Dynamics of the Social Thought of Guru Gobind Singh*, p. 60.

of millions of gods and goddesses was significant. She is one goddess without a husband, consort or lover. She is independent. She is her own mistress. She is autonomous, capable of taking her own decisions, always acting as a positive force to activate the good to dare the wicked. By attributing such characteristics to *Durga*, the Guru purposely gave a fresh role model in the form of a woman. This was indeed something revolutionary and breath-taking. She is also the only goddess who subsumes the many and various powers of gods who individually and collectively lacked the strength to face the challenge of demons, but only as a figure of myth and literature to be utilized to euphorize the people with new aspirations, ideals and hopes. The Guru looked upon her and for that matter on Ram, Krishan or any other incarnations as mere instruments created for moral purposes; he never looked upon them as incarnations of God. He very explicitly says in *Chandi Di Var*, that the strength with which Ram killed the ten-headed Ravan with arrows and Krishan caught Kans by hair and dashed him to the ground was bestowed on them by God. Indeed God himself created *Durga* to destroy the demons through her instrumentality.

The unique character of *Durga*, her determination to eradicate and finish wickedness or demonic forces fitted well in the grand design of the Guru to rebuild a fresh society based on righteousness. He made her serve a paradigm to be emulated by one and all, to overcome weakness and cowardice and to abolish unjust political authorities and social inequalities and to forge a new structure based on the egalitarianism, equality, justice and freedom.[1] Very clearly the Guru's rendering of *Chandi* narrative was not a pure adaptation of the mythical *Puranic* story in it. *Chandi* was presented not as a mythical person but as a symbol of divine *Shakti* doing heroic deeds which the Guru describes in images drawn from everyday life. "The intermixing of the extraordinary with the ordinary created an uncommon artistic effect. A special message seems to imply in all this, that everyone has the inherent potential to re-enact the *Chandi* legend in this very life and in this very world.

1. Gurinder Kaur, "Durga Recalled by the Tenth Guru" in *The Journal of Religious Studies*, Vol. XVI, No. I, II, p. 69.

This *Var* comprises of a total of fifty-five *Pauris*. As in the case of other literary *Vars*, both martial and spiritual in content, this one is also in *Pauri* a poetic metre, with only a few *Dohiras* (couplets). It gives an account of six engagements in three battles out of four, two lost by Indra and two won by *Durga*. The story begins with Indra, crest fallen and a refugee approaching *Durga* with a tale of woe beseeching her to help him get back his kingdom from the Demons, Mahikhasur, Sumbh and Nisumbh et al. Of the fifty-five stanzas, forty-nine are devoted to the description of scenes from three battles, the first five and the twenty-first being purely narrative and informatory helping to elucidate the situation. It is thus poetry of action as is Walter Scott's Battle of Bannockburj and the Flooden field. It is imbued with martial spirit, being a description of martial display of scenes of actual fighting. In the words of Dr. Mohan Singh Dewana, "Guru Gobind Singh decided to press poetry into the service of both spirituality and the fight for freedom. To instil heroism into the people. He resang for them the glorious heroic achievements of their war gods and goddesses, their human ancestral victors on the battlefield and their folk heroes." Through this *Var* as also through *Chandi Charittar* I and *Chandi Charittar* II, he wanted to give the message of *Shakti* which in fact infused a new life in the suppressed people of the Punjab. Besides, the Gurus gave a new conception of their Creator, the conception of *Sarb Loh*, All steel, of whom *Bhagwati*, *Durga* or *Chandi* was a symbol.

The *Chandi Charittar Ukti Bilas* is comprised of eight chapters consisting of 233 verses in all. A liberal use has been made of *Swayya* and *Dohra* in this composition. Out of the total 233 verses, 214 and eighty are in *Swayya* and *Dohira* metres, seven each in *Sortha* and *Kabir*, two each in *Totak* and *Puneh* and one in *Rekhta* metre. The dominant *Ras* is *Rudra* and the language is Braj.

Of the eight chapters, the first comprises twelve verses— all invocatory to the Divine. The next two chapters retell *Chandi's* battle with demons and her final victory over Mahikhasur demon. The following five chapters narrate the story of several battles which *Chandi* fought against the commanders of Sumbh and Nisumbh and finally with them.

402 A Historian's Approach to Guru Gobind Singh

The last section declares the re-establishment of the hegemony of gods as a sequel to the victory of *Chandi*. The gods, according to the perception of Guru, were not supernatural beings. They were called as such as they performed good deeds. All those who did misdeeds were called 'demons' by the Guru.

Chandi Charittar II, another composition about the exploits of *Chandi*, comprises eight sections and 262 verses. Eighteen different metres are used in its composition out of which *Bhujang Paryat* (70) and *Rasaval* (69) have been put to maximum use. Other metres used include *Naraj* (26), *Chaupai* (20), *Dohira* (14), *Beli Brindam* (11), *Ruaal* (9), *Sangit Madhubhar* (9), *Madhubar* (8), *Sangit Bhujang Prayat* (7), *Ruaval* (6), *Kualka* (4), *Totak* (4), *Bijai* (2) and *Sortha Sangit Naraj, Bridh Niraj* and *Manohar* (one each). As in *Chandi Charittar Ukti Bilas*, the Guru also tells the story of *Chandi* and her battles, giving a vivid picture of all the events interlaiding them with similies and metaphors. The details however do not strictly conform to the *Markandeya Puran* which forms the source of the story.

CHAUBIS AVTAR

This composition comprises of 5297 verses. It relates to twenty-four manifestations of the deity Vishnu . These twenty-four incarnates are : (1) *The fish*, (2) *Tortoise*, (3) *Lion*, (4) *Narayan*, (5) *Mohani*, (6) *Bear*, (7) *Nar Singh*, (8) *Bawan*, (9) *Paras Ram*, (10) *Brahma*, (11) *Rudra*, (12) *Jalandhar*, (13) *Vishnu*, (14) *Shashayi*, (15) *Arhant Dev*, (16) *Man Raja*, (17) *Dhanantar*, (18) The *Sun* or *Surya*, (19) The *Moon* or *Chandrama*, (20) *Rama*, (21) *Krishna*, (22) *Nar*, (23) *Budh*, and (24) *Neh Kalanki*. Among these twenty-four incarnations the story of Krishna is the longest (2492 verses), followed by that of Rama (864) and Neh Kalanki (588). Other accounts are quite brief. At the head of this composition, Guru Gobind Singh has prefixed what might be called a prologue to his work, which elucidates Guru's views on the doctrine of incarnation. The Guru declares that Primordial Being, also called *Bhavani*, is the sole Creator of the entire phenomenal and non-phenomenal world. All beings are the manifestations, in spirit, of the Creator. All these twenty-four incarnations were His creation but not Him who failed to realise Him.

MEHDI MIR

Mehdi Mir is a post script to the *Chaubis Avtar*. The composition runs into eleven quatrains. All of them are in *Tomar* metre. *Mehdi Mir* destroyed *Kalki* because the latter had become too powerful and haughty to distinguish between right and wrong. Now the *Mehdi Mir* himself became proud and regarded himself equal to God. To destroy him, *Kal* sent an insect which crept into his ear causing pain that proved fatal to him. While composing the story of *Mehdi Mir*, the Guru's purpose seemed to be that God's might is unchallengeable and whosoever indulges in un-righteousness, is punished. God is the Supreme Reality and all incarnations including *Mehdi Mir* were his creations who basked in glory as long as they functioned as per His will.

According to D.P. Ashta, the idea of versifying *Mehdi Mir* seemed to have come from the writings of the *Shia* sect of Islam.

BRAHMA AVTAR AND RUDRA AVTAR

Chaubis Avtar is followed by a composition known as *Avtars of Brahma*, which are *Balmik, Hashap, Shukra, Bachais, Vyas, Kalidas*. It consists of 343 verses. This account is followed by an account of eight kings. After this, another composition *Rudra Avtar* is included in *Dasam Granth*. In this composition the stories of two incarnations of *Rudra, Data* and *Parasnath* are told. Both *Brahma* and *Rudra Avtar* compositions begin with the Guru's comment that after *Brahma* and *Rudra* fell victims to *garb* (egocentricity), they had a fall. *Brahma* was directed by *Kal* (Supreme Reality) to take seven births in human form on this earth and serve mankind to free himself from the process of transmigration. Likewise, *Rudra* was directed by the Absolute to take human birth because he had become too proud.

While composing such compositions, the purpose of the Guru seemed to be to draw the attention of the people to one cardinal fact that these incarnations were the creations of the Supreme Reality and not His co-equal or co-eternal. They were subject to death, rise and fall like other human beings. They were important because they were enlightened. Dattatreya was a great ascetic and was greatly responsible for the emergence of twelve schools of *Yoga* and the ten schools of *Sanyasis*.

Another incarnation of *Rudra* was also unique. He grew to be a great warrior and a King but had the never-ending quest for Truth. Ultimately, he reached the conclusion that Reality can be realised only if one dispels ignorance and achieves *Bibek* (True knowledge).

GYAN PRABODH (Consciousness of Knowledge)

Gyan Prabodh is another ambitious composition which is incomplete. A valuable part is probably lost for ever. In its style and language, it is as perfect and grand as *Akal Ustat*. Out of 336 verses, 125 give the introduction. At the end of introduction, the Guru gives general plan of the book which give a progressive evolution of religion in four stages; (1) *Raj Dharam* (religion through political service), (2) *Dan Dharam* (religion of charity), (3) *Bhag Dharam* (religion through pious life of house-holder), (4) *Moksh Dharam* (religion of seeking salvation).

RAMKALI PATSHAHI DAS OR *SHABAD HAZARE*

There are ten verses in *Dasam Granth*. These verses exhort men to worship only one God and not His manifestations or His creation. "Worship non-else except Creator, not even His creation." The true ascetic is to consider his home as the finest and be an *Udasi* at heart to have continence instead of matted hair and uncut finger-nails, daily religious duties, the Name is to be the ashes applied on the body." Minor deity images have also been subjected to criticism.

These *shabads* are traditionally called *Shabad Hazare* or *Hazare Shabad* or *Hazare ke Shabad*. Cunningham is of the opinion that these were originally intended to be a thousand verses. Barjinder Singh believes that these verses were addressed to the Guru's *Sangat* or followers who had come from the district of Hazara (now in Pakistan). There is another view that since these *shabads* depict pangs of *Hijar* (separation) of love-torn soul of the Guru, these are named *Hazare*—the word being abberated version of *Hijir*. According to *Sankhshipta Hindi Shabad Sagar*, Nagari Parcharni Sabha IV Edition, the word *Hazare* carried the meaning of 'a fountain'. Using this fact as their base, some scholars have ventured to conclude that as these *shabads* gushed forth as if from a spiritual fountain, sprinkling soothing drops on the restless souls of the Guru's disciples, they came to be known as *Shabad Hazare*.

Whatever reasons may be assigned to the name *Shabad Hazare*, the fact remains that this is invaluable and beautiful short composition, bringing out love and plight of a devotee feeling pangs of separation from God. These are also exquisite, in terms of poetic, art, musicality, serenity and thoughtfulness.

SWAYYAS

Swayyas is a four-line stanza. There are thirty-three four-lines stanzas in *Dasam Granth*. The topics of these *Swayyas* are the meditation on the name of God, satire on ascetic practices and superstitions, true divinity and false divinity, rapport between the *Khalsa* and Guru, and true religion and false religion. The text carries the signature of *Mukh Vak Padshahi 10*.

SHRI SHASTAR NAM MALA PURAN (The Necklace of the Names of Weapons)

As the name indicates, this work gives us the names of weapons of war which are praised as deliverers. The composition runs into 1318 verses. Various weapons are given fanciful names. Among the simpler of these are the names of arrows. *Tupak*, a kind of fire arm, occupies larger space probably because it was reckoned to be the deadliest of all weapons. Many of these names of weapons are listed in the form of riddles, so much part of the Punjabi folklore and dear to the people's heart. These seem to be resolved in somewhat devious ways, for example :

> "Think hard and take the sword 'trangani' (stream). They say 'ja char' (grass eater), then think of the word 'naik' (Lord). At the end say the word 'Satru' (enemy). Lo ! Good friend, you have thought of the word meaning 'tupak' (gun)."

The reason only seems to be that each thing mentioned is the enemy of the next; the grass-eater is the deer (*ja* is what is produced by the moisture of the stream, *char* is to graze); the Lord and the master of the deer is the tiger, the enemy of tiger is the gun."

There is quite a store of such riddles. The value of these riddles is to keep up the interest of the people in weapons of war.

CHRITRO PAKHYAN (Tales of the Deeds of Women)

Chritro Pakhyan means 'stories of deeds and adventure of women as heard from others'. *Pakhyan* means 'a short tale' (refer to Apte's Sanskrit dictionary) and *Charitra* means 'life', biographic account, adventure, habit, behaviour, acts and deeds. So it is wrong to translate *Chritro Pakhyan* as tales of the wiles of women as *Charitra* does not mean what it is often, madeout to be. The composition is in fact an anthology of stories of today. The stories resemble the stories of Boccassio's *Decameroon* so closely that some of the stories of *Triya Charitra* appear to have been taken from *Decameroon* which were probably conveyed to the Master by the Italian and Portuguese travellers. The Dutch, the Portuguese and Britishers of East Indian Company were well established and had their offices at Amritsar and Lahore during the times of Guru Gobind Singh and Guru Hargobind. There are two stories in the *Dasam Granth* from Portuguese accounts and there are about two concerning Englishmen interfering in the Indian states. So these stories serve the same purpose as do the modern short stories.

The prevalent idea, that all the stories are about the wiles of women is wrong. As a matter of fact there are about fifteen stories in which there are no women character at all. There are a number of stories in which men betray women who are only passive sufferers (stories No. 55, 85, 75 & 108). There are a good number of stories about the outstanding bravery of some women. They have been shown best in politics, battlefields and in the feats of adventure. The character of the women as shown in *Charitra* No. 165 is the noblest one that any human life can present. There are tales describing the use of temples as meeting places for sexy lovers (88, 124, 146, 260, 283, 362 etc.)

There are tales of young girls concealing illegal pregnancies. There are stories of rich ladies keeping poor he-men such as sweepers (24) and gardeners (14) as lovers. Such things are not uncommon even today and form popular subjects for the story writers of modern times. There are stories of ideal lovers for the love of whom Guru Gobind Singh has nothing but praise.

Damyanti, Hir Ranjha, Sohni Mahiwal, Mirza Sahiban, Yusuf Zulekhan and Dropti are treated as ideal lovers and extract praise from the Guru.

There are 7555 verses in this composition and form the largest part of *Dasam Granth*. The date of its completion is Bhadon Sudi Ashtam 1753 BK/September 1692. Total number of tales are 404 which may be divided into categories such as tales of bravery, of devotion, the deceitfulness of women, and the perfidy of men.

At the end of the last tale there is a prayer to God, known as *Benti Chaupai* (prayer in *Chaupai*) in twenty-six stanzas which is highly philosophic and completely detached from the topic of the *Charitro Pakhyan*. The vocabulary style and thought are similar to those of the Guru's devotional and other works. This composition is one of the five *Banis* read at the time of preparation of *Khande-Ki-Pahul*. It has also been a part of the *Rehras* (evening prayer) recited daily by the Sikhs.

ZAFAR NAMA (Epistle of Victory)

The *Zafarnama* (Epistle of Victory) bearing the signature title *Sri Mukh Vak Patshahi 10* was written in February 1705 at Dina, a village in the Southern part of the Punjab in a reply to the invitation of Aurangzeb to the Guru. The composition is in Persian language. It is in poetry and not in prose. Although it was written when the Guru had suffered significant set-backs during his *Dharm Yudh*, yet it betrays no such feeling. In fact the title *Zafarnama* which means 'letter of victory' symbolises the optimistic spirit of the Guru. The letter is of immense value for a student of history. It refers to the perfidious behaviour of the Mughal officials, the unequal contest at Chamkaur, the bricking alive of the two younger sons of Guru Gobind Singh in the walls of Sirhind Fort, the unflinching faith of the Guru in the victory of the good. The tone of the letter reminds us that its writer is convinced of justness of his cause and of achieving victory ultimately. Various facts of the Guru's religious faith can also be identified in the letter. It has 111 verses. The Guru reminds Aurangzeb again and again of the justice-loving God and the value of the moral principles. The Guru upbraids Aurangzeb for breaking oath taken on the holy *Quran* by the officials on his behalf. This refers to the treachery of his generals in the Battle of Anandpur when, after promising safe conduct to the Guru's forces for leaving the city, they attacked them and looted their baggage, only to find that the Guru had anticipated treachery and filled the sacks with rubbish. He calls the Emperor the Oath Breaker (*Paiman-i-Shikan*).

HIKAYAT

Hikayat—comprises eleven stories in the Persian language, written in Gurmukhi characters. They are placed at the end of *Dasam Granth* after the *Zafarnama*. Several of these tales are Persian duplicates of some of the tales found in *Charitro Pakhyan*. *Hikayat* 4 is *Charitra* 52; *Hikayat* 5 is *Charitra* 267; and 9 is *Charitra* 290.

Of these eleven tales, the first is that of King Mandhata who nominates, after a trial, his fourth son as his successor. The second tale relates how at the death of King of China, his ministers took up the work of administration with perfect co-operation among themselves. The third tale is about Chhatra Mathai who forced Subhatta Singh into marriage with her after defeating him in a battle. The fourth story relates to the perfidy of *Qazi's* wife who had murdered her husband with a view to entering the *harem* of Raja Suba. In the fifth story the brave daughter of a Prime Minister saves his father from the clutches of his enemies and then whips him for his folly. The sixth tale is about a virgin queen who bore a child but abandons him to escape shame. After a long time she discovered that he was alive. Then she manages to adopt him as her heir-apparent. Next two tales are about the infidelity of two queens to their respective husbands. The ninth tale relates how a prince elopes with the daughter of his Prime Minister. In the tenth tale, a woman of high rank steals two horses to offer them to her lover. The last *Hikayat* concerns an impetuous woman who murders her fiance, lest he should betray her. In the *Dasam Granth* these *Hikayats* bear no heading.

POETIC ART OF GURU GOBIND SINGH

Wrapped in the classical style of his times, his poetry is rich in metaphors, abounding in beauty of sound and overbrimming with poetic niceties of diction and thought.

The metres are as full of variety as the subjects he treats. He has handled over a hundred and fifty types of metres and forms of Hindi, Persian and Punjabi measures of versification with remarkable efficiency. The bewildering variety of metres is not employed just at random. Each metre seems to have been very thoughtfully selected to contribute to the mood of the verse by its own peculiar rythm. Out of a total number of 150 metres used in the *Dasam Granth* over one hundred metres have their origin in Sanskrit, Prakrit, Apabhransa and old Indian languages. The remaining metres, either new or traditional ones, appear under new names to suit the flow of narration. Guru Gobind Singh invented new metres such as *Aj Ba, Akra, Akva et al.* Keeping the contents in view, he gives many alternative names to some of the metre. In *Dasam Granth,* the *Chaupai* metre has been used to the maximum followed by *Dohira* and *Swayya.* While describing the battle scenes, the Guru makes extensive use of metres such as *Kabit, Swayya, Pandhistaka* and *Bishnupada. Swayya* had been hitherto used for sensuous poetry, but Guru Gobind Singh used it with consummate artistry for heroic poetry.

Words never fail him. His masterly touch transmutes the leaden metal of common words into pure gold. At times, he makes use of words which if taken out of context crumble down to nonsense poly-syllables, yet in their own context they rather look indispensable. A master of many languages, he always uses the right word at the right place, and he does not care whether it is a Persian or a Sanskrit word, and Arabic or a Punjabi word, a Hindi word or one of his own coinage. In fact, many of his compound word e.g. *Raz-ul-Nidhen*, or *Karman-Karime* are a serene co-mingling of Hindi, Sanskrit, Arabic and Persian like the Sikh culture itself which is a happy admixture of the Aryan and Semitic cultures.

The Guru embellishes his poetry with alliterations apart from making use of rich imagery and right type of words. The alliterations are never forced upon the verse; nor do they, in any case, impinge upon the thought-content. They come as naturally as leaves come to a tree. The Guru decorates his poetry with many other devices as well. The following popular quatrain for example, abounds in anti-thesis. In fact, everyone of its lines contains one :

> Ever since I held thy lotus feet
> None else my eyes behold
> That Ram and Rahim
> The Purans and the Muslim Books
> Say much but I heed them not.
> The *Simrities, Shastras, Vedas,* many secrets
> they profess to have but never do I behold.
> It's all Thy grace, my saviour All thine,
> Not a whit is more.
> Thy 'feet' as against my 'eyes' as
> against 'not' 'many' as against 'none' are vivid
> contrasts building up delightful antithesis.[1]

The Guru's poetry is very musical. He knows which form of music is right for a particular moment. If he is telling you a romantic story (*Shringar Ras*), the words play a mild tinkle of sweet bells. If he is writing an ode describing a battle scene (*Vir Ras*) the words will resound with the rythm of drums.

If he is versifying a sad mood he will very skilfully muffle the drums. Whether the Guru writes long poems or short poems, epics of prayer-sermons, his skill as a poet always touches the highest water-mark. Infact the Guru's poetry is a real beauty and a 'joy' forever, more so because it comes straight from the springboard of heart. Wrapped in the holy sentiments of love, it enraptures all those who study it.

---

1. *Pāeṅ gahe jab te tumre tab te koū āṅkh tare nahīṅ āniyo.*
   Rām Rahīm Purān Kurān anek kaheṅ mat ek nā māniyo.
   Simrat Sāstar Bed sabai bahu bhed kahaiṅ hum ek nā jāniyo.
   Sri aspān kripā tumrī kar(i) mai na kaheo sab tohe bakhāniyo.

NAME OF THE COMPILATION

The name *Dasam Granth* became prevalent in recent times. Bhai Mani Singh's compilation is named as *Bachittar Natak*. The *Dasam Granth* available at Moti Bagh, Patiala also bears this name. The recension of Patna is named *Sri Granth*. The *Granth* printed at Guru Khalsa Press, Amritsar bore the name *Dasam Granth Sahib Ji* for the first time and since then it has been in vogue. The exact number of the verses composed by Guru Gobind Singh is not known. Recently a note of Guru Gobind Singh was found by S. Randhir Singh which in its original form has been given by the learned scholar in his book *Shabad Murat*. According to this note, the Guru composed 1, 27, 255 verses excluding those of *Zafarnama* and a few others. All the verses had been composed (excepting *Zafarnama*) upto 14th June, 1698 and this was also the day when the compendium of all these verses had been prepared. Kesar Singh Chhibber says :

> *"Small book (Granth) was got ready by the Guru himself at his place in 1755 BK. This book was loved by the Guru who wrote it himself. The Sikhs requested that this should be appended with Adi Granth. The Guru replied that Adi Granth was 'Granth Sahib' and this book was just a book presenting his mood."*
> *(Charan Chaudhvan, Bansavali Nama)*

DIFFERENT RECENSIONS

There are three better known recensions : one is with Gulab Singh Sethi of Delhi, the other is at Harmandar Sahib at Patna and the third is at Punjab State Archives, Patiala.[1] The version authorised by the Singh Sabha and is generally available in print, closely follows the version ascribed to Bhai Mani Singh. The sequence of contents is not the same in all the three compilations. In the compilation available at Patiala, the compositions such as *Chandi Charittar* II and *Var Durga Ki*, are not included. *Sahsar Sukhmana, Var Kaus Ki, Var Bhagauti Ki* are not there in the compilations of Bhai Mani Singh.

---

1. Originally it was at the *Gurdwara Sahib Shahi Samadhan*, Sangrur. It was procured by Maharaja Raghbir Singh. On the author's request, it was taken to the State Archives, Patiala.

We, however, have given the description of the compositions as included in the *Dasam Granth* printed by the Singh Sabha.

AUTHENTICITY OF THE WRITINGS IN THE *DASAM GRANTH*

Whether all the contents in the present volume of *Dasam Granth* are authored by Guru Gobind Singh is a question that has remained unanswered so far. The mere fact that the works are compiled in one volume does not prove anything, much less the authorship of *Dasam Granth*.

Immediately after the compilation of the *Dasam Granth*, controversy regarding its authorship surfaced. After Bhai Mani Singh's execution, the Sikhs took the Granth for examination and approval to Talwandi Sabo in the present district of Bathinda in the Punjab. The place was chosen with a purpose, for, it was deemed safe and several scholars had been living there ever since they had joined Guru Gobind Singh at this place.

While this discussion was going on, Mehtab Singh of village Mirankot arrived at Damdama (the name given to Talwandi Sabo by the Sikhs) from Bikaner. He had vowed to kill one Massa Ranghar, a high profile Mughal official who had desecrated Hari Mandir Sahib at Amritsar by converting it into a dancing hall, and was on his way to Amritsar to carry out his mission. He saw for himself the heat that the controversy over the authorship had produced. Out of his deep faith or probably to avoid wrangling and their attendant adverse effect on the solidarity of the Sikhs, he pledged in the presence of all those present in the conclave that if he succeeded in his mission and returned safe to Damdama, *Dasam Granth* would remain in one volume as Bhai ji had arranged it. If on the other hand Massa killed him, the *Granth* might be arranged according to the wishes of the objectors. Mehtab Singh slew Massa Ranghar and returned safe and the *Granth* was not touched. The story is palpably unconvincing because the killing of Massa Rangar or returning alive of Mehtab Singh and taking a decision to keep various compositions in one volume or in independent booklets are mutually exclusive, that is to say, there is no dependence of one on the other. The truth seems to be that since in the wake of the assassination of Massa Ranghar, the reign of terror for the Sikhs was unleashed by Zakariya Khan, the then Governor of the Punjab, the conclave of Sikhs at Talwandi Sabo deferred the issue of screening different compositions to determine their authorship. As a result of this, the quest for adequate answer to the question slowed down atleast for the time being; but did not die out; rather it continued to stir and stare. Off and on objections were raised regarding the authorship of *Dasam Granth*. Giani Gian Singh in his work *Panth Prakash*, Sarup Das Bhalla in *Mehma Parkash* made out to doubt the authenticity of different texts in *Granth*. In 1918 Bhasaur School refused to attribute the authorship of *Dasam Granth* to Guru Gobind Singh and published a book, *Dasam Granth Nirnay* in this context. In 1973 the S.G.P.C. issued a letter No. 36672 registering the opinion of *Jathedar* of *Shri Akal Takhat* and *Singh Sahiban* that *Charitro Pakhyan* was not the work of Guru Gobind Singh. In the World Sikh Sammelan 1995 the issue was on the agenda but because of the fear of likely flare-up among the Sikhs over this issue, it was rather abandoned. The World Sikh Council constituted a special committee of ten experts (including the author of the present work) to scan thoroughly all aspects of the issue and give judgement. The *Rashtriya Sikh Sangat*, an outfit of *Rashtriya Soyam Sewak Sangh* averred that all the compositions including *Charitro Pakhyan* are the work of the tenth Guru. Their conclusion is motivated, a sort of ploy to create confusion among the Sikhs regarding their Eternal Guru or to create wrong impression among them that they are a sect of the Hindus.

Till recently no definite decision has been arrived at, a lot of discussion notwithstanding. The position stands as it was immediately after the compilation of the *Granth*. There are two sections of the Sikhs : one holding that the whole of *Dasam Granth* was the creation of Guru Gobind Singh and the second pleading that only a part of the *Granth* was authored by the Guru.

We on our part believe that compositions like *Jaap, Akal Ustat, Bachittar Natak, Var Shri Bhagauti Ji Ki, Gian Prabodh,*

Shabad Hazare, Teti Swayyas, Khalsa Mehma require no second opinion regarding their authorship. Almost all the scholars agree that these works were authored by Guru Gobind Singh. There are, however certain interpolations and certain misplacements. For instance *Chhands* No. 211 to 230 in *Akal Ustat* are out of place and probably belong to the *Chandi Charittar II*. The last *Chhand* of *Akal Ustat* is not complete. *Gyan Prabodh* too has been left incomplete. There are several questions raised in *Dohiras* 201 to 210 of *Akal Ustat* to which no answer is available in the text suggesting that *Dohiras* carrying answers were deleted, perhaps deliberately and were replaced by those which were out of tune with the general tenor of the composition. Regarding the authorship of *Chandi Charittar Ukti Bilas, Chandi Charittar* the Second, *Chaubis Avtar, Brahma Avtar, Rudra Avtar, Charitro Pakhyan* and *Hakayat*, there are serious objections. About *Chandi Charittar* the First and Second, they are adaptation of certain portions of *Markandeya Puran*. They are loaded with material which evokes devotion for goddess Durga instead of God as perceived by the Guru. Besides their central message is not in consonance with Sikh religion. The third adaptation that is to say *Chandi di Var*, the first of its kind written in Punjabi seems to be the creation of Guru Gobind Singh because its message is clear that the wicked must be punished and the righteous upheld at all cost. The compositions such as *Chaubis Avtar, Brahma Avtar* and *Rudra Avtar* cannot claim the authorship of the Guru. In the first instance in the text itself we find names such as Ram and Sham as the author of the texts, and secondly the subject matter is not such that was needed to be written by Guru Gobind Singh. Even on a casual glance, one gets the impression that concept of incarnation which the Guru repudiated in his so many other writings was upheld and sponsored.

What we have opined in the aforesaid paragraphs is only provisionally correct. The correct picture will emerge only after doing the following :

1. Different copies of *Dasam Granth* may be compared with the ones available as manuscripts. The exercise will help us to identify interpolations/distortion if any and may even

offer clues to the identification of genuine authors of different compositions.

2. A thorough study of poetic forms and language used in *Dasam Granth* has to be made before conclusions are drawn to judge what sense a particular idea/expression or word had at the time of Guru Gobind Singh. By doing this, we will be able to judge what exactly Guru wanted to convey. Decoding of *Dasam Granth* is therefore, very important.

3. The ideology of Guru Gobind Singh created furore— even confusion among the Brahmanical priestly class. They adroitly resorted to various means, although vicariously, to distort, dilute and defile the Sikh ideology. Out of various means they employed, two were conspicuous. One was to forge linkage of Sikhism with Hindu sacred literature, and the second was to pass irrelevant even vulgar literature as Sikh literature to tarnish the image of the Sikh religion. For instance *Charitro Pakhyan* and *Hakayat* are such compositions that have not even the remotest relationship with the Sikh ideology, although very cleverly to give these compositions a look of genuineness *Benti Chaupai* which was in all probability the creation of the Guru was interpolated. Surely this composition could not have been written by the Guru. About *Charitro Pakhyan* and *Hakayat*, it is very safe to aver that these could not be the creation of the Guru by any measure. How could the Guru, so busy a person, find time to compose compositions which formed nearly one third of *Dasam Granth* and that too for describing wiles and vices of women for whom he had no prejudice and regarded them equal and respectable as a male.

Part II

GURU GOBIND SINGH'S VISION OF METAPHYSICS, POLITY AND SOCIAL IDEALS

CHAPTER XVII

GOD, UNIVERSE AND MAN

In *Akal Ustat*, a composition of Guru Gobind Singh marked for its poetic and lyrical beauty, besides its rich thought content, there are a few lines which reveal that the Guru understandably in deep contemplation experienced Supreme Reality, as Remarkably singular and Omniscient, Omnipresent, All-powerful, Sole creator and poured out such words as *Tu hi*, *Tu hi*,—Thou art only Thou art. Which he went on reciting sixteen times. It is reported that after uttering 'Thou art' for sixteen times, the Guru went into silence wondering over the Immensity and Immeasurability, Infinity, Transcendence, Immanence, Absolutelessness, Incomprehensibility, Creativeness et al. of the Supreme Reality, which he reverentially addresses as *Akal*, perhaps to show his vigorous sentiments or to impress upon people that God is beyond time while everyone else is subject to its effect. It seems the Guru views and reviews in his imagination kings and their kingdoms, generals and their armies, forts and garrisons, all engrossed and enmeshed in their paraphernalia and filled in with egoity, forgetting that these are temporary phases of life; just appearances, transitory and mortal, at best relative realities. He exclaimed :

> Emperors intoxicated with tall, stout, beautifully painted elephants having golden trappings; with millions of horses bounding,
> Like deer and fleeing faster than wind, with strong armies before whom countless heads bowed down;
> But what mattered because in the end they departed just blank,
> They conquer countries and beat their drums victoriously,
> Thousands of horses neigh and many elephants trumpet aloud.

The number of such Kings in the past, present and the future connot be counted.
But without knowing their real Master, the Lord, they felt lost in the end.[1]

Such a God, the Supreme Reality, was everything to the Guru; pinnacle of his spiritual endeavour, his societal purpose, his ethical conception and longings,—nay for everything that he aspired for, to remodel himself and the human kind so that both of them reflect in their aspirations and conduct, at macro and micro levels, the ways of God of his experience and conceptions.

With the realisation of this Supreme Reality with its myriad attributes and dimensions, the Guru went into reverie and poured out names expressing helplessness of human mind to encompass His reality. In the composition *Jaap* and *Akal Ustat* these flow into verse with the movement of a tempestuous torrent. The opening lines of the *Jaap* strikes the keynote of the whole composition.

Without sign or mark and beyond caste and category;
His face and feature, shape and form none can tell,
Beyond mutability, sensitiveness, illumined, of illimitable might.
The Lord Supreme of million of Indras, King of Kings,
Lord of three universes, of Gods, men and demons;
His infinite Glory each leaf and grass blade proclaims.
Who may recount the roll of His names ?
Content, the human spirit with mention alone of His attributes ![2]

In exuberant imagination issuing in His realisation, Guru could not help calling God by such epithets/adjectives as *Arup* (formless), *Anup* (incomparable), *Alekh* (indescribable), *Ajai*

---

1. *Māte matang jare jar sang anūp utang surang swāre.*
   Kot turang kurang se kūdat paun ke gaun ko jāt nivāre.
   Bhārī bhujān ke bhūp bhalī bidh(i) niāvat sīs na jāt bichāre.
   Ete bhae tu kahā bhae bhūpat(i) ant ko nānge hī pāen padhāre.
2. *Chakra chihan ar barn jāt(i) ar pāt(i) nahin jeh.*
   Rūp rang ar rekh bhekh koū kaih na sakat keh.
   Achal mūrt(i) anubhau Prakāsh amitoj kahijjai.
   Kot(i) Indra Indrān sāh(u) sāhān ganijjai.
   Tribhawan mahīp sūr, nar asūr, net(i) net(i) ban trin kahat.
   Tav sarb nām kathai kavan karm nām barnat sumat(i).

(invincible), *Aganj* (indestructable), *Anam* (nameless), *Atham* (unbounded), *Akarm* (unbounded by actions), *Anil* (immaculate), *Asarg* (uncreated), *Ajat* (without category), *Ajal* (ever emancipated).

These and many more such attributes or epithets are surely the product of the mind deeply immersed in spiritual contemplation, strongly equipped to express in appropriate terms the infinite nature of the Lord.

As if the Guru was not satisfied with such epithets cast in negative form, to express God of his understanding, he uses more epithets positive in form and redolent of emotional and mystical experiences to express such attributes particularly, as the human spirit has apprehended in its communion with the Infinite.

In Guru Gobind Singh's compositions, such attributive names are somewhat more elaborate, understandably to enable one to apprehend and experience His singularity, His unicity, His fatherhood and His comprehensibility.

Late Prof. Gurbachan Singh Talib discovered another reason. According to him "In all likelihood, it was done to provide a thesaurus of names of the Lord to replace the names of the gods and goddesses of the traditional pantheon conceived to be personalities apart from the Supreme Lord, the Creator".

Since God, or Supreme Reality, is the real reality and the source of manifest and unmanifest, created and not created universe, and all activities including human and non-human emanate from Him and guided by His Will/*Bhana*/*Hukam*, it is imperative to launch a further probe into the nature of the Supreme Reality.

In *Sri Guru Granth Sahib*, as well in *Jaap* and *Akal Ustat*, the most important compositions of Guru Gobind Singh, Unity of Reality has been repeatedly emphasised. *Dasam Granth* like *Guru Granth Sahib* opens with the word *Ik Oankar*, Guru Gobind Singh in his *Hukamnamas* make frequent use of this word. From all this it is not difficult to surmise that the concept of unity of Reality occupies a centre stage in Sikh ontology. The word *Ik Oankar* is a compound of three words. i.e. *Ik*, 'O' (or *Om*) and *Kar*. The word *Om* stands for Supreme

Reality. In the Upanisadic literature, the word *Om* has been used to convey the means of meditation as well as the object of it. R.D. Ranada, an authority on Upanisadic literature[1], amply supports this view. In the Sikh scripture, this word is invariably prefixed with '1' and suffixed by *Kar*. The prefix '1' is used specifically but in a different character. The Guru apparently wanted to lay stress on the fact that God was singular or the Only One. Toward off any ambiguity, above numeral was used since it could not be interpreted differently like words and phrases. Beside denoting oneness of the Supreme Reality, '1' (Written as ੧) also was epitomic of metaphysical value, symbolising the unitary nature of God. The suffix *Kar* indicates the creative aspect of *Om*—Supreme Reality which does not remain static but becomes dynamic and sustainer of the manifest material world. In the words of Dr. Sher Singh "God is creator, the sole cause manifesting through Will and manifested as word in subtle form and as world in a gross form.[2] There are numerous references in the hymns of Guru Gobind Singh to the effect that the Real One is the sole creator (*Sarb Karta*) and preserver of all (*Sarb Pale*). The spirit of Ultimate Reality is a form of forms (*Samastul Sarupe*) as well as all pervasive (*Samastul Niwase*). Thus the word *Ik Oankar* taken together would mean the one Reality which has created the entire manifest phenomenon and which simultanaeously permeates it.

GOD'S SELF-EXISTENCE

In *Mool Mantar*, (Credal Statement) God has been described as *Saibhang*, Self-existent. God alone possesses self-existence, while everything else derives its being from the One Being. All things receive existence from Him. Nothing is so perfect that it could or would exist apart from or independent of Him. The following utterances of Guru Gobind Singh are very significant in this respect. He says :

> Thou O Lord !
> Pervading spirit in four quarters,

---

1. R.D. Ranada, *A Constructive Study of Upanisadic Philosophy*, p. 246.
2. Sher Singh, *Philosophy of Sikhism*, p. 168.

Enjoyer in four directions,
Self-existent and abiding in glory,
Even united with everyone
Pilot at two crossings, birth and death;
Embodiment of grace and compassion
Ever so near to everyone
Deeply concerned with humanity
Everlasting is Thy treasure and glory.   *(Jaap, 199)*

By laying stress on His self-existence, He placed God at a very high and unique pedestal in total contrast to gods and goddesses, whose existence is questionable and are non-entities. According to Dr. Trilochan Singh, God's self-existence is not a mental abstraction; it is something very personal. He is the source of life, of physical life as its Creator, and Spiritual as its final reward. Because 'He' is God, remains steadfast and changeless.[1]

GOD IS INFINITE, ETERNAL AND ABSOLUTE

Guru Gobind Singh regards God as perfect and complete Being. In this sense, He is self-sufficient and subject to no limitations, which do not issue from His Will *(Hukam)* and He Himself is the undisputed cause of all finite existences. Some scholars have wrongly surmised that the infinite was comparable to what Vedantic thinkers thought. But this is not correct. The Guru did not apply material means to explain the infinite nature of God. By the Infinite, he meant the perfect and complete Being, never to be measured at all.

Similarly when he says that God is eternal, he does not mean duration, or a subject of tenses but it means that God is beyond time. The Transcendental-self of God is timeless. The mundane time process is a sheer illusion, the reality of which is timelessly, perfect whole. The idea of the eternal God filling endless time is devoid of spiritual value. He is eternal because he is raised above the time process and is the ultimate condition of existence of such a process, and is therefore not subject to it.

The absolute in Sikh theology means transcendent. *Nirankar* in contrast to the Immanent. The Universe as a system

---

1. Dr. Trilochan Singh's article "Theological Concepts of Sikhism."

is not Absolute as is conceived by pantheists, nor God identical with the Universe. The Universe is a creation of God and it is at His mercy. God is Absolute in the sense that He is the unconditioned source of all creations, which are finite. He is absolute because He is a Being, perfect and complete. God is spirit/light. As God is Being Itself *(Apai-Ap)*, He is in no way subject to change or dissolution like all material things. He is Spirit and Light and cannot be compared to anything outside Himself, nor can it be comprehended by mind. Since God is perfect, He is *Parmjyoti* (Pure Light).

The Guru beautifully portrays his perception of God in the sense of Spirit Light in his following verses :

> His Name is contemplated
> In all the fourteen worlds;
> He is Primeval Light and eternal Being
> Creator of all the worlds
> Supreme is He in beauty
> Pure is His form
> He is Infinite and Perfect Being.
> Lo ! He is the essence of all religions,
> He is the spirit that pervades all
> He is the glory of all
> He is the light of all.[1]   *(Jaap, 83, 113)*

God reveals Himself to prophets as light eternal. Perfect vision is the vision of God's Light and Beauty. Flawless perfection is the perception and hearing of His unstruck music.

GOD'S OMNIPOTENCE, OMNI-PRESENCE AND OMNISCIENCE

Guru Gobind Singh like his predecessor Gurus strongly believed that God is Omnipotent, Omnipresent and Omniscient. God manifested His all-powerfulness by bringing into being all existences including this world. He is *Sarb-Karta* (creator of what exists) and *Sarb Harta* (destroyer of all). The Sikh Gurus in their teachings enshrined in *Sri Guru Granth Sahib* profusely

---

1. *Lok chaudah ke bikhai jag jāp-hī jinh jāp.*
   Ād(i) dev anād(i) mūrat(i) thāpio sabai jinh thāp(i).
   Parm rūp punīt mūrat(i) pūran purkh apār.
   Sarb bisv rachio suyambhav garan bhanjanhār.

admire His incomprehensible strength. According to them, "He (God) sees divine powers like Brahma, Vishnu and Shiva at work but they cannot see Him. They do not know His mystery and power.[1] Therefore they should have no significance in a man's life who should ever seek the *Nirankar*, He is *Agadh* (unfathomable), *Akarm* (unbounded by action), *Athan* (unbounded). God is Omnipotent since He has the power to invest the content of His Will with reality, and the whole realm of His existence is constantly sustained by His activity. Guru Gobind Singh, in the sense, uttered :

> Almighty, Lord of millions of celestial kings,
> Thou art Lord of the three worlds.
> Gods, men and demons, and even the blades of grass declare thee beyond all things in nature
> Thou art the pardoners of sins,
> The King of kings,
> The Provider of means
> And the Giver of livelihood.
> Faith in God would suffer a severe jolt if the object of its trust was wrestling with difficulties which He could only partially overcome.
> The limitations of which are willed by God are not defect.
> Good and evil, the true and the absurd are a part of His creation governed by the Laws created by Him. He is responsible for the creation of evil by the side of good, but He is not responsible for its existence in society, for man is free to choose one or the other.

> Those who seek Thy sanctuary,
> Lord, wielder of sword of Justice,
> Their tormentors die in sorrow and pain;
> Those who seek refuge at Thy feet,
> From perils and straits, they are saved.   *(Benti Chaupai 21)*[2]

Guru Gobind Singh did not believe any Heaven as God's abode. The Lord is totally free and was never bound by spatial limitations. God is Omnipresent and Immense—not only by Knowledge and Power but also by Nature. His eternal spirit pervades in all beings.

---

1. *Jap Ji, Pauri* 30.
2. *Je asedhuj tav sarnī pare. Tin ke dusht dukhat hue mare.*
   Purakh Javan pug pure lihāre. Tin ke tum sankat sab tāre.

On the mounition is God,
In the caves is God
On the earth is God
In the sky is God.52.
Here is God
There is God
In the world is God
In the firmament is God.53.   (*Akal Ustat*, 52-53)[1]

The attribute of omnipresence of God implies that Being of God is not separate from His activity. God is everywhere in the sense that He permeated and pervaded everything and He makes His working felt everywhere. He is *Samast-ul-Niwas* (all pervasive).

Thou art the primal Being who never began unborn, endless.
Worthy of all praise, revered in three worlds,
Luminous, mysterious, all prior and above all thou art preserver, destroyer, ultimate death of all, Immovable and happy, Thou resideth in every place.   (*Akal Ustat*, 79)[2]

Thou hast no name, home or caste, no form colour or mark,
Thou art the Primal Being beyond all, birthless, primal and perfect.
Thou art placeless, without a guise appearance or mark, without attachment,
Thou pervadest everywhere in the form of love.
                    (*Akal Ustat*, 80)[3]

God being the self-conscious Will and the constant ground of the medium in which all existences and spirit act, reference to Him possesses a meaning for Him. All objects in fact are expression of His Will and remain dependent on Him. Objects have no independent sovereign identity. Omniscience always refers to and finds support in the conception of

1. *Gire Harī. Gufe Harī. Chhite Harī, Nabhe Harī.52.*
   Īhaṅ Harī. Ūhāṅ Harī. Zimīṅ Harī. Zamāṅ Harī.53.
2. *Ādi rūp anād(i) mūrat(i) ajon(i) purkh apār.*
   Sarb mān trimān dev abhev ādi udār.
   Sarb pālak sarb ghālak sarb ko pun(i) kāl.
   Jatra tatra birāj-hī avdhūt rūp rasāl.79.
3. *Nām thām na jat(i) jākar rūp raṅg na rekh.*
   Ādi purakh udār mūrat(i) ajon(i) ād(i) asekh.
   Des aur na bhes jākā rūp rekh na rāg.
   Jatra tatra disā visā hue phailio anurāg. 80.

Omnipotent. The whole creative process is conditioned by His Will.

> He knoweth what is within every heart
> And the sufferings of the good and the bad.
> From a tiny ant to the huge elephant,
> His mercy, the Lord bestows on everyone.   *(Benti Chaupai)*[1]

> He is agrieved when His saints are grieved
> And happy when his saints are happy.
> He knoweth everyone's sufferings
> And every secret of man's heart.
> He is searcher of all hearts.   *(Benti Chaupai)*[2]

Once while talking to Bhai Nand Lal, Guru Gobind Singh said, "Before He hears the trumpet roar of an elephant, the cry of an ant reaches Him. Guru Gobind Singh, in fact, wanted to convey that God is all-knowing, all seeing, and nothing is beyond his gaze.

> "In my folly, I thought that Thou were far,
> But no deed I do, can ever be out of Thy sight.
> Thou who art all seeing all things Thou seest."

Besides viewing Essence attributes, the Guru is equally vocal so far as God's action attributes are concerned.

Bhai Gurdas says, "If a man walks one step towards God, the Lord comes a million steps towards him".[3] To Guru Gobind Singh, the Lord pervades and permeates everywhere in the form of Love.[4] He is the sublimest love.[5] He loves all *(Smast-ul-Aziz)*. He beareth love to all *(Saneh Sabho)*.[6] He showers affection on all and loves them genuinely *(Aziz-ul-Niwaz)*. God's love should not be taken as an act. It is a principle of all acts. God is present in every creature in the form of soul

---

1. *Ghaṭ ghaṭ ke antar kī jānat. Bhale bure kī pīr pachhānat.*
   Chītī te kunchar asthūlā. Sab par kripā drishṭ kar phūlā. 11.
2. *Santan dukh pāe te dukhī.*
   Sukh pāe sādhun ke sukhī.
   Ek ek kī pīr pachhāne.
   Ghaṭ ghaṭ ke paṭ paṭ kī jāne. 12.
3. *Charan saran gur ek paindā jāe chal.*
   Satgur(u) koṭ(i) paindā āge hoe let hain.
4. *Jatra tatra disā visā hue phailio anurāg.*   *(Jaap Sahib)*
5. *Namo prīt prīte.*   *(Jaap Sahib)*
6. *Deh bihīn saneh sabo tan reh birakt ageh achchal hai.*   *(Akal Ustat)*

which manifests itself in virtuous deeds. He manifests Himself through love that He executes in every heart. It is because of this love, present in every heart as a creative principle that the whole unfolds. In the love of God, all other loves are rooted. It was perhaps what prompted Guru Gobind Singh to exclaim, "Those who love, they realise God."[1] The mysterious are ways of God who is ineffable (*Agochar* and *Agadh*).

The ultimate state of love is that the lovers should feel and experience Him always and everywhere attached with Him by a profound fraternity.

This state has been artistically poetised by Bhai Nand Lal Goya in his famous composition *Diwan-i-Goya* (27, 28, 36). He himself was a beloved of the Guru, ever yearning for the Guru's sacred glimpse. He says :

— The beloved has merged into my soul.
— No love except the love of God lasts.
— All except those whose love is transient.
— In which ever direction Thou seest.
— Thy eyes shed Grace and Light.

> In all directions Thy holy sight
> showers the rains of life,
> God is Omnipresent,
> But where are the eyes
> That can see Him everywhere.

God's love manifests itself as grace and mercy. Even to the sinners, he is merciful if they shed their sinful acts and resolve to tread the righteous ways. Guru called Him *Dayalam;*[2] *Karim-ul-Kamal* and *Kripalan*[3]. He is ever merciful to the poor, the distressed and His servants.[4]

His favours work wonders. When God showers His grace, the dumb would recite six *Shastras*, the cripple would climb mountains, the blind would see and the deaf would hear.[5] Grace in Sikh parlance means an expression of God's

1. *Jin prem kīo tin he prabh(u) pāeo.*   (*Sudha Sawaiye*)
2. *Sadā sarb dā sidh dātā diālaṅ. 60.*   (*Jaap Sahib*)
3. *Kripālaṅ sarūpe kukarmaṅ pranāsī. 73.*   (*Jaap Sahib*)
4. *Karunāliya hai(ṅ). 171.*
   Karunākar hai(ṅ). 175.   (*Jaap Sahib*)
5. *Bachittar Natak II.*

mercy more than one deserves. Humanly speaking His love is immensely greater than His Justice. In fact, God's mercy is inexhaustible and showers like rain. His anger is transitory and that too to awaken one to tread the righteous path. God's loving kindness endures for ever. There is no end to the God's love, as He is 'Home of mercy'[1], 'Ocean of mercy'[2] and favour.

In the God's love, man finds His true identity. His love lives in us all and can be uncovered from under the clouds of egoity, selfishness and ignorance through His grace. Since all human beings owe their existence to God's creative activity emerging out of His *Will/Hukam*, refusal to live and not abide by His *Will* tantamounts to refusal of fullness of one's existence. The falseself always hankers after an existence outside God's *Will* and Gods' love, outside of reality and outside of life. The presence of an iota of God's love in our heart alone leads us to a spiritual rebirth. It is this love of Him for man which bridges the chasm between the two, and also between man and man.

CREATOR AND DESTROYER

Guru Gobind Singh recalls God as a Creator as well as a Destroyer. Only God has existence from Himself and therefore, all things existing outside of God have in God, the reason for their existence. The Guru calls God by the name of *Sarb Karta* (Creator of all that exists), *Sarb Harta* (destroyer of all), *Agham Ogh Harta* (destroyer of evil and sin), *Khal Dal Khandan* (destroyer of bands of barbarians), *Ari Ganjan* (destroyer of foes), *Dusht Daman* (destroyer of tyrants and wicked). The sword is the symbol of His might.

This being so, God is not insensitive or indifferent to values. He is moved by the sufferings of the good and the virtuous, as much as by the love and devotion of man. He protects the righteous, the saints and prophets unless He wills

---

1. *Karunāliya hain. Ar(i) ghāliya hain.*
   Khal khandan hain. Maih mandan hain. 171.   (Jaap Sahib)
2. *Bisvambhar hain. Karunāliya hain.*
   Nrip nāik hain. Sarb pāik hain. 181.   (Jaap Sahib)

that their suffering and martyrdom should secure and establish a higher purpose. To protect the righteous is His *Birad* (moral duty). Even to redeem the repentant sinner is the task of God *(Patit pavan her birad tuharo)*. Thus God's Will is sovereign. God's transcendent perfection also means that God is self-sufficient and *Niranjan* (blemishless). In this strain, Guru Gobind Singh, in his *Akal Ustat* and *Jaap* invokes God by naming him *Dushtan ke Hanta*[1] (perisher of wrong doers, the tyrants and oppressors), *Ghanim-ul-Kharaj*[2] (expeller of tyrants), *Hirasul Fikan*[3] (destroyer of fear), *Riputapan* (destroyer of the enemies). Guru recalls God as a preserver by epithets such as *Sarbang Data* (Giver to all), *Sarbang Bhukta, Sarbang Jugta* (All receive their food and guidance from thee), *Gun Gan Udhar* (Store of virtues and bountiful), *Karan Kunind Rozi Dahind* (cause of all causes, provider of meals and livelihood). *Razak Rahim* (merciful giver of bread), *Chatra Chakar Varti* (filler of the whole universe), *Chatra Chakar Bhugte* (feeder of the whole universe).

Even a casual glance at varied names of God that Guru Gobind Singh uses in his compositions would convince one that he had a special fascination for His martial names. His conceiving of God as such marks no novelty—much less deviation from the perception of God of his nine predecessors from Guru Nanak to Guru Tegh Bahadur. But certainly there was particular emphasis on this characteristic by him, perhaps because of his firm resolve to be pro-active and wage a struggle against the oppressors of his time. In this struggle he made God his only support. In meditating on this idea of God, he naturally gave a significant emphasis on His heroic attributes. Thus he recalls God as *Asi-Pan* (wielder of sword). *Sarag Pani* (holder of Bow), *Sri Kharag* (the sacred sword), *Bhagauti* (the sword, *Sarb-Loh* (all steel), *Maha Kal* (Supreme Lord of Time the Eternal), *Prabh* or *Prabhu* (The Lord), *Kal* (Time of all-Time), *Mahakalika* (Divine might to destroy evil), *Kharagdharam* (Holder of sword), *Sarangdhar* (Holder of a quiver), *Kharag Panam* (Holder of a sword), *Asiketu, Kharagketu* (all meaning

1. P.C.H. 405 (382).
2. *Jap, 153.*
3. *Ibid.*

with sword on His flag), *Sastra Pane* (Holder of offensive weapons), *Astra Pane* (Holder of missile weapons called *Astra* i.e. 'O' Mighty destroyer), *Astra Mane* (Keeper of Astra i.e. mighty destroyer). The Guru also calls Him as *Sarb Loh* (All-Steel), *Sarb-Kal* (All death). The Guru was so much impressed by God's heroic qualities that he calls and invokes Him as *Tarwar* (sword), *Tir* (Bow), *Saithi* (spear) as Lord of hosts and the smasher of evil-minded.

Guru Gobind Singh's repeated invocation to God by such names as were evocative of His heroic qualities especially as a destroyer of evil and succour of the Right was no shift from the perception of God of his predecessor Gurus. In fact, the Guru was following in their footsteps with the only difference that he used such names with marked fervour. In *Sri Adi Granth*, which contains the hymns composed by the Gurus preceding Guru Gobind Singh, God is often invoked by names expressive of His heroic aspects. *Murari* (destroyer of demon, Mur), *Madhu Sudan* (destroyer of demon, Madhu), *Asur-Sanghar* (Smasher of demons), *Gur Sura* (The Heroic Lord), *Bhai Bhanjan* (despeller of fear). The theme is constantly running through the compositions of all the Gurus, where God extirpating tyrants and intervening to preserve the saintly and the innocent. This aspect of God was therefore well emphasised by the Gurus preceding Guru Gobind Singh, but it acquired poignancy and sharpness at the hands of Guru Gobind Singh who developed special fondness for this aspect of God. The *raison-d-etre* was that in Guru's vision, God was a Creator as well as Destroyer and in His latter capacity it was only appropriate that He should be heroic in His actions, against all those who violate His *Will/Hukm*. In this perspective, the Guru enjoined upon to be always ready to wage struggle against the forces of evil and unrighteousness and to see that righteousness prevails at any cost.

SUPREME REALITY IS DYNAMIC

The Guru's conception of reality is not static as is *Purasa* in the Sankhya-Yoga system, nor is it passive like Braham of Shankar's conception. The metaphysical system of Shankara considers the created elements a mere shadow or illusions

(Maya), whereas dynamic spiritual continuum of Guru Gobind Singh's conception stresses the real historical dimensions of the development of consciousness, social ideals and human society as a whole. The Reality of Guru Gobind Singh's conception is neither static nor passive. It is dynamic and in that state it creates that which did not exist earlier, but in the sense that the Supreme is solely responsible for the creation of diverse forms of the manifest world and its myriad forms which are even in flux and in a process of creation and annihilation. All such forms are only partial manifestation of dynamic Reality governed by the creative principle *Hukm*.

The concept of creation by the *Akal Purakh* is different from the process of creation associated with human beings. For example, a potter needs well-kneeded earth to create and shape earthen vessels. But *Akal Purakh* needs no extraneous material to shape different forms of manifest Reality. He creates out of His being *Sarab Bisav Rachio Suambhav (Jaap,* 79). In this way the eternal conscious Being of *Akal Purakh* is immanent in the manifest multiple units which causes their ontological identity though seemingly they are distinct as manifest forms. How did the creation take place ? Was it some specific agency or factors that undertook it or compelled the Creator to do the job ? There is no specific agency or factor. There is His *Will/Hukm* that creates and sustains His whole creation. But no creation is separate from the Supreme. In fact it permeates all the phenomenon as spirit or light. Every living being, from the smallest insect to the huge animal *(Hast Keet ke Bich Samana—Akal Ustat)* emanate from the creative force of *Akal Purakh*. Even gods and so-called incarnates are no exception to this rule and thus they cannot claim equality—much less identity and status with *Akal Purakh*. At the most they can be regarded as good human beings because of their enlightenment and realised selves. Being subject to *Kal* i.e. time or death, they make their appearances in this phenomenal world only for a specific task and period in history and finally subsumed into *Kal*. Guru Gobind Singh uses the word *Kal* frequently and even calls God as *Kal* for the reason that it not only symbolises destructive aspect but also includes creative as well and in this sense, it refers to the dynamic principle of creation, sustenance and destruction. There is no place where *Akal Purakh* does not permeate. He is here and there, on the earth and the sky.

> *Iha Hari, Uha Hari*
> *Zamin Hari, Zaman Hari.*   *(Akal Ustat, 53)*

In the fire, air, water, earth and everywhere *(Agni bae jale thale maih Sarb thaur niwas) (Akal Ustat,* 188).

The manifest world in all its entirety is not only a part, of Supreme Reality, but is always related to it. Guru Gobind Singh makes this abundantly clear in the following hymn from *Akal Ustat.*

> "From one fire, millions of sparks arise and in course of rising remain separate,
> Yet they again merge in the same fire.
> From one heap of dust innumerable particles of dust occupy the expanse in a distinct way
> And yet they again unite with the dust. From one stream millions of waves arise
> And yet these, being of water, again become water.
> Similarly all sentients and non-sentients have emerged from the One Universal Being,
> Yet having sprung from Him, they all are bound to be blended again in Him."[1]

Dr. Dharam Singh, while analysing this relation draws our attention to a very significant fact. He says, "This essential oneness of the creation and the creator leaves no place for dualism. The Guru rejects both the static metaphysical system of Vedanta and the semitic concept of transcendental (impersonal) nature of God. The *Sankhya* theory of dualism between *Purasa* and *Prakriti* is also rejected. Unlike these metaphysical systems the

---

1. *Jaise ek āg te kanūkā koṭ(i) āg uṭhe,*
   Niāre niāre hue kai pher āg meiṅ milāe(ṅ)ge.
   Jaise ek dhūr(i) te anek dhūr(i) pūrat hai.
   Dhūr ke kanūka phir dhūr(i) hī samāe(ṅ)ge.
   Jaise ek nad te taraṅg koṭ upjat hai,
   Pān ke taraṅg sabhai pān hī kahāe(ṅ)ge.
   Taise bisv rūp te abhūt bhūt pragaṭ hue.
   Tāhī te upaj sahhai tā(ṅ)hī meiṅ samahe(ṅ)ge. (87)

Sikh dynamic ontology on the other hand encompasses the
'Otherness' of created elements within all-comprehensive
structure of non-dual Reality and, on the other, identifies with
itself qua spirit, all sentient and non-sentient elements. The
latter are visualised as manifest units of the Real One. Thus the
entire manifest phenomenon becomes instrinsically one with
Reality and is realised as relative Reality."

So another fact is that behind all this manifest diversity
can be seen the non-dual unity of metaphysical Reality. When
the one becomes many as a result of self-willed manifestation,
the non-dual character of Reality is not affected.

Seen from this dynamic quality of God, it is not difficult
to conclude that world like all other creations was created by
God. Before creating the universe, God alone existed in His
Transcendent state. When He willed to create, there was an
emanation and afflux of Primal utterance called in Sikh
scripture *Kavao* (utterance). This *Will* to create, emanating in
the form of unstruck music or sound is also called *Shabad*.[1] Out
of this *Shabad* emerged the ground of materiality called in
theological terminology *Dhundukara*[2], which generally is
translated as Chaos. From this unknown darkness veiling His
being which also now was changing into becoming emerged
the existential elements : fire, water, earth, ether and air. In it
pervaded the sixth unseen principle of His Being. His all-
pervading Light forming the immanent spirit which sustains
creation. The universe was not created in six days but it took
millions of years.

How does this process take place ? God Wills and then
the whole creation is the result. His willing is creation; He does
not need any extraneous help or material to create.

In this process, God manifests Himself under His own
Will and pleasure. Guru Gobind Singh in his *Chaupai* refers to
the unfolding and refolding expansion and construction
process of creation. Says Guru Gobind Singh :

---

1. *Utpat(i) parlau sabde hovai, Sabde hī phir opat(i) hovai.*
   [Creation and dissolution take place through the Word (Logos). After
   dissolution creation again takes place through Word (Logos)].
   (SGGS, pp. 117, 1033)
2. Bhai Gurdas, *Var* I.

When God expanded His might
Vast universe came into being.
When he starts pulling it inward
Everything will merge into Him again.

According to some exegetes, this refers to the theory of evolution and devolution. In this process, the basic element of Force, the soul or the *Jiva*, the entity created by individuation, *Haumain* enters into a long series of appearance and disappearances. In *Sri Guru Granth Sahib*, this idea is expressed by Guru Arjan Dev very clearly in his *Rag Gauri* where he refers to eighty-four lakhs forms of existence through which man has to wander about. He exhorts the man to make all efforts to unite himself with the Lord of the Universe.

World thus is the emanation of God Himself who in spirit/light permeates and sustains it. The whole inclusive of every object living or non-living through spirit/light is connected with the Supreme Reality and in essence, is a part of it, which is all inclusive and all embracing. To call world a mirage, illusion or a shadow is a case of palpable misunderstanding. It is a reality not in the sense of Supreme Reality which is eternal and ultimate absolute but it is certainly not false, that a man should run away from it. He should regard it as environment in which man must interact with others to develop his personality. For that purpose he and his colleagues must improve it and convert it into a house in which man can establish and follow righteousness. This world often called *Maat Lok* is not to be discarded as an abode of evil or a jungle of wild creatures and demons. In *Asa Ki Var (Pauri I)*[1] the Guru says :

"First God created His ownself and created the Name. Then He created His *Qudrat* (Nature) in the midst of which He seated Himself with fondness. O, God; Thou art the bestower and creater and being pleased thou expandest. Thou art omniscient and give and take life just by a word. Thou

---

1. *Āpīnai āp(u) sājio āpīnai rachio nāo.*
   Dūī kudrat(i) sājīai kar(i) āsan(u) ḍiṭho chāo.
   Dātā kartā āp(i) tū(n) tus(i) deveh kareh pasāo.
   Tū(n) jānoī sabsai de laiseh jind(u) kavāo.
   Kar(i) āsan(u) ḍiṭho chāo.

enjoyeth all the game seating Himself in the midst of everything."

> That is why Guru Nanak says,
> Thy regions and universes are true/Thy world's creations are true.
> Thy deeds and thoughts all are true.
> Thy command and courts are true.
> Thy orders and utterances are true.
> The grace and its expressions are true.
> The force and its expressions are true.
> Their qualities and their appreciations are true.
> Thy might, O, True Lord, is true.[1]

Nanak, true are those, who contemplate on Him but false are those, who do not do so. They come and go. Guru Angad Dev calls the World as "Chamber of the True One, The True One resides therein." Guru Amar Das says, "This entire Universe that we see is manifestation of God and it can be seen as such by spiritually awakened. It is a place for awakening the spirit which can be done by living in this world in all earnestness and achieving the ideals in community, in global fraternity."

Guru Gobind Singh believed in non-dual and dynamic nature of Reality, which in its transcendent state is only "unmanifest effulgent spirit" *(Abiyakti Tej Anabhav Parkash)*— *Akal Ustat.* It is not made of five elements. It is also conceived as Eternal Light *(Achal Parkash)* or the Light of Light *(Tej Teja).* This formless or absolute or Transcendent Reality becomes immanent when this spirit manifests itself through its symbolic expression of light or light becomes manifest in all other lights. "This is how, as Says Guru Gobind Singh, the *Parm Jyoti* (Supreme Spirit Supreme Light) becomes *Sarab Jyoti* (Universal spirit) and *Parmatma* becomes *Sarbatma.*

The spiritual manifestation of the Divine, however, is not selective or exclusive. All beings, irrespective of their class, colour, status, ethnicity, caste and creed are His manifestation.

---

1. *Sache tere khaṅḍ sache brahmaṅḍ. Sache tere lo sache ākār.*
   Sache tere karne sarb bīchār. Sachā terā amar sachā dībān.
   Sachā terā hukam sachā farmān(u). Sachā terā karam(u) sachā nīsān.

(*SGGS*, p. 463)

He pervades equally in elephant as well as in an ant, of course brightly in human beings. Of all the species, the human specie is evaluated highest and is vouchsafed succinctly by Guru Arjan Dev in *Rag Asa* :

"O Man, other species are subservient to you. On this earth, thou art the overlord of them all."[1]

It is only among the human that the soul can aspire for and attain union with the Supreme Soul. In *Akal Ustat* the Guru gives a long list of beings, some wicked, some virtuous, some high and some low, some readers of *Puran* and some of *Kok Shastra*, some believers and some infidels, some celibates and some promiscuous, some beggars and some benevolent. In all of them permeates 'Divine spirit' but they are good or bad because of their deeds they do here and now. Those who do good deeds are gods and those who perform misdeeds are demons. By good deeds is meant those deeds which help one uncover the inner light or *atma* as an essence which is a manifestation of the Divine and are ethical and steps to take one to the next stage of progress of man towards self-illumination.

From this, it can be surmised that there are degrees of godliness in different variations. It is difficult to say with any certainty as to what things appeared first and how they developed when God willed to expand, emanate or manifest. But from the perusal of *Gurbani* impression emerges that there is general pattern, some kind of evolution ascending or progressing or in simple terms becoming more and more divine. Undoubtedly everything, in essence, is God and is made out of Him but essentially quality of divinity manifested in them is in lesser or greater degree. There is matter organic and inorganic. Among the organic things, there are species in which the cosmic mind is less developed and there are others in which it is more developed. The soul element is omnipresent but its contact with the body results in the creation of mind which under the influence of the three *Gunas* mixed in countless proportions give rise to countless forms and degrees of development.

---

1. *Avar jūn(i) terī panihārī, is dhartī pe terī sikdārī.*

A Historian's Approach to Guru Gobind Singh

Such a person who identifies himself with soul or divine light or *Atma* within enjoys oneness with *Akal Purakh—Har harijan doe ek hai (Bachittar Natak* VI. 60). This concept differs from the Islamic belief. *Allah* infuses *Rooh* in the non-sentient matter but still remains transcendent vis-a-vis material reality. It is also different from the Hindu doctrine of incarnation (*Avtarvad*) according to which the Divine Himself takes human or other forms.

The precepts of Divine manifestation and the essential oneness of man with the Divine are germane to the doctrine of spiritual unity and ethnic equality of mankind. All things being the manifestation of the One are equal not only in His eyes but also among themselves.

To realise *Akal Purakh* or to feel oneness with Him would mean to serve His immanent manifestation in the mundane world including man. Altruistically this type of service of mankind or the whole manifestation is possible only if there is unselfish love. The cultivation of unselfish love has been accorded a very high status in the scheme of Guru Gobind Singh who vehemently recommends the path of love for Divine Realisation and rejects all formalism as mere sham, absolutely of no use for this purpose. In *Sri Guru Granth Sahib,* we find *Seva* (altruistic service) and *Simran* (remembrance of Divine Name) considered as the best and the only means for God-Realisation. When the Guru says that only those who love realise the Divine *(Prabh Paio),* it does not mean a deviation from or contradiction of the fundamental philosophical beliefs of his predecessors because both the views are essentially the same. *Nam Simran* in Sikhism does not stand for a mere mechanical repetition of One or the other attributive name of the Divine as it used to be in the earlier Brahmanical and *Sufi* traditions. Here it means the realisation of Divine presence in all beings and at all places.

That man has always been the centre of attention even of the Divine has been made clear by Guru Gobind Singh in *Bachittar Natak.* He as the Immanent does not remain indifferent or insensitive to the human situation and He intervenes in human affairs whenever the forces of evil get upper hand over the forces of righteousness. His intervention is through the instrumentality of human beings chosen for the specific mission. He himself was one such human being born with the specific mission of extirpating the wicked and exalting the virtuous and the righteous. Understandably such human beings are attuned to God's *Will* and are ever ready to suffer and endeavour making the divine qualities of equality, love, justice, altruism prevail in the empirical world.

There are some thinkers who emphasise that body of man is something to be discarded. They consider it a prison of soul which is immortal and part of God's whole thereby hindering its union with the universal soul. But this view is totally rejected in Sikhism. The soul comes to the world with the birth of a being. It is only when *Akal Purakh* places the eternal light or spirit in body that man is born in this world. The body, though a transitor and relative reality, is nevertheless significant because it serves as a vehicle or means for the Divine spark based therein to try and merge with its Original Source i.e. *Akal Purakh*.

In fact, body serves as a mean to enable man realise the Real One in this very life which implies complete identification with the Divine Will. Undoubtedly body perishes like all material things but the process of its transmigration always takes place. It is in this context that all the Gurus including Guru Gobind Singh have full regard for body and required his followers to take care of it.

The idea of man being in essence the manifestation of Divine has been beautifully and lucidly illustrated by Guru Gobind Singh with some very appropriate metaphors and similes. Just as with the dawn of the day the light merges in illuminating the darkness, and the darkness dissolves itself into the light in such a way that it loses all its trace, in the same way, Reality manifests itself in all beings (*utkarkh*) and in the end all these beings completely and finally submerge themselves into the Reality (*Akarkh*). While creating or manifesting Himself *Akal Purakh* does not exercise discrimination, investing particular individuals or groups with superiority. This being so, all differences on the basis of caste, creeds or classes et al. are rejected as irrelevants in the Guru's scheme of things.

As it has been made clear in foregoing paragraphs, according to Guru Gobind Singh the entire phenomenal world owes its existence to one *Sarba Krit*—creator of all (*Jaap* 183). When the manifest Reality willed Himself to be immanent the whole of material world come into being (*Kin Jagat Pasar*) including all the fourteen realms and the beings who inhabit them (*Sarb Bisv Rachio Suyambhav*). The creation by *Akal Purkh* has been of His own will and of His own self—*Sarb Bisv Rachio Suyambhav* (*Jaap*, 79). *Akal Purakh* pervades through the entire creation. His oneness with the creation implies the effulgence of the Divine Light in all the fourteen realms—*Lok chatur das joti prakasi* (*Akal Ustat I*). Just as all beings are His manifestation, the Divine presence can be felt at all places. *Akal Purakh* pervades and permeates every place—*Sarb thaur bikhai rahio* (*Akal Ustat*, 182).

This belief of the Divine presence everywhere and in every being is central to the Sikh belief in the Divine concern for the amelioration of the whole mankind.

Various compositions of the Guru are galore with references that support and affirm this belief. In an invocatory verse in the beginning of *Bachittar Natak*, the Guru invokes *Sri Kal* in the following words :

> Hail to the creator as well as the ameliorator of the Worlds.
> (*Bachittar Natak* 1.2)[1]

Thus it is clear that phenomenal world is to be improved upon. By whom ? By no one other than man who is the principle yet part in the process of creation capable of knowing that he has reached a particular stage of the creative process and can take steps to evolve upwards to the next stage. This is the stage of the *Brahm Gyan* or the God conscious or God filled man.

"This God-conscious man is animated with an intense desire to do good in the world (*Brahm giani parupkar umaha*). By and large the aim of the highest religious discipline has been taken and accepted as the attainment of abiding and self-sufficient identity with or propinquity to God. It was thus, thought in terms of utilising the God-consciousness for transforming and spiritualising the life on earth and

---

1. *Jai Jai Jag Kāran*
   Srisht Ubāran...

transformation of humanity. It is this stance of Sikhism which is the true prototype of the sophisticated philosophy of the modern Hindu sage Aurobindo Ghosh, though there might be no direct indebtedness to Sikh thought. Those, however, who know basic and resolutionary trends of human thoughts of this kind, are capable of influencing men and minds, far separated by distance and time without contact or casual connection from its original appearance may perceive no difficulty in seeing the nexus between the two.

"The true end of man", says Kapur Singh, "is not such a vision of God that ends in reabsorption of the individual into Absolute Reality, but the emergence of a race of God-conscious men who remain earth aware and thus operate in the mundane world of the phenomenon with the object of transforming and spiritualising it into a higher and ampler place of existence."

The order of the *Khalsa* which Guru Gobind Singh founded is epitomic of such thinking. It was intended to be a body of men who by practising discipline of *Naam* reach the stage of *Brahm Gyani* and are pledged to ensure, by every legitimate means including control of political power the coming into existence or the prevailment and the preservation of a World society vitalised continuously by the affiliation of the truths of religion, open, tolerance and catholic sustaining a creative world culture, consistent with the spiritual dignity and the spiritual goal of men.

Against this backdrop, asceticism has been denounced and discarded by Guru Gobind Singh and house-holders' life has been exalted. As a concomitant to it, it was made rather imperative that world should be improved upon by annihilating evil and spreading righteousness. The Guru's own example amply bears it out. He himself fought battles to root out evil and tyranny so that righteousness is protected, promoted and establishes upper hand over evil. He called such actions the ordainments of *Akal Purakh*.[1]

Such being the nexus between the world and man which are relative realities, it is not difficult to draw the conclusion

1. *Jāhe tahāṅ tai dharm(u) chalāe.*
   Kabudh(i) karan te lok haṭāe.   (*Bachittar Natak*, VI, 29)

that the Guru affirmed the reality of historical action. According to Guru Gobind Singh, man must act for the betterment of the social phenomenon. However, this action ought not be inspired by any subjective or selfish motive. It should be altruistic and aim at the well-being of general masses irrespective of considerations on ground of caste, creed, status and birth et al. Such actions because of their very nature reflect the ethical values of equality, justice, altruism et al.; because these, in turn, spring from the realisation of essential unity between *Akal* and His creation.

CHAPTER XVIII

SIKH POLITY

Before determining the pattern of Sikh polity we will have to find answers to certain important questions : (i) Did indulgence in politics fall within the jurisdiction of Sikh religion; (ii) Did the Guru take interest in political affairs; (iii) Did political power or basic moral issues form the fulcrum of the interest of the Gurus ?

So far as the first question is concerned, our reply is that politics fell within the jurisdiction of the religion of the Gurus. This fact can be deduced by moral as well as historical arguments. The Gurus as is evident from their utterances, wanted to establish an order where goodness should prevail and unrighteousness eliminated; and where people should have absolute faith in the oneness of God. To make the people righteous, the Guru laid emphasis on the discipline of the individuals as also of the groups. In *Jap* Guru Nanak spells out the steps which one should take to regenerate oneself. It then becomes the moral endeavour of the regenerate to make the society righteous.

The regenerated persons are variously known in Sikh religious literature. Guru Nanak calls them *Gurmukhs*, Guru Arjan Dev addresses them as *Brahm Gyani* and Guru Gobind Singh has named them *Khalsa*. Now what is righteousness ? The Guru, somewhere explicitly and somewhere implicitly, explains that what is not based on justice, fellow-feeling, liberty and equality is unrighteous or oppression. But how to ensure righteousness ? Obviously some agency is needed and in fact since the inception of the civilized society, the need has continuously been felt.

It was this need to which state and politics owe its

existence. As a matter of fact, need to translate certain moral issues have always been the determinant of the nature and the pattern of the political power. In tribal society, the *panchayats* or patriarch of a tribe was the symbol of power. When the society transcended that stage, the oligarchy became the wielder of the power. Oligarchy gave place to Monarchy when the former outlived its utility. The changes in the society on moral and social planes always effected corresponding changes in the polity or the agency to wield political power.

The Sikh Gurus who were committed to certain moral issues which formed the basis of the society of their concept could not help take interest in politics. But their interest was not simply an expression of their anguish for the political unrighteousness. It had moral dimension also. For a proper appreciation of Guru Nanak's response to the events in question, the *Babar Vani* verses must be considered together. In these, Guru Nanak mentions the sufferings caused by war and explains that all this has happened because of the people's blind pursuit of wealth and riches. Because of wealth, it went hard with many. Wealth cannot be amassed without sins and it does not accompany the dead. Indeed, "He who is destroyed is first deprived of his virtue."[1]

It is thus clear that Guru Nanak's response to war and to sufferings caused by war is not only an ample expression of his rage but also involved a moral issue, the issue of the importance of virtue in the nation's healthy growth and stance.

Historical references in *Sri Guru Granth Sahib* also go to prove that political affairs were not alien to the Guru's religion. Guru Nanak's familiarity, even interest in contemporary politics, may be inferred from his expression in his verses such as : *Sultan, Patshah, Shah-i-Alam, takht, taj, hukm, malik, sikdar, qazi, chaudhari, muqqaddam, raiyat.* Guru Nanak also makes use of the references such as court, palaces, royal canopy, elephants, armour, cavalry trumpets, treasury, coins, mint, salary, taxes and revenue-free land.[2]

---

1. *Jis no āp(i) khuāe kartā khus(i) lae changiāī.*   (*SGGS*, p. 417)
2. The relevant verses occur in *Sri Rag (Astpadian), Rag Gauri (Astpadian), Rag Asa, Japji, Rag Vadhans (Chhant and Alahnian), Var Majh* etc.

Furthermore, in one of his hymns, Guru Nanak, in a general reference, called the rulers as 'blood sucking *rajas*'.

> The *rajas* are lions and the *muqqaddams* dogs;
> They fall upon the *raiyat* day and night.
> Their agents inflict wound with claws (of power)
> And the dogs lick blood and relish the liver.[1]

A condemnation of the contemporary rule is unmistakable here. It may be pointed out, however, that Guru Nanak's attack is not directed against the ruler as 'Muslims' or as 'Hindus'. In fact, the bracketing of the *Muqqaddams* (who mostly were non-Muslims) with the *Rajas* strongly suggests that Guru Nanak adopts the standpoint of common people, the *Raiyat*, as against ruler and their subordinates or agents. In another verse, Guru Nanak appears to assume a close connection between the holders of political power and the respective professions of their faith; he also notices 'discrimination' against those who do not belong to their faith. Guru Nanak says :

> The *Ad Purakh* is called *Allah*,
> Now that the turn of the Shaikhs has come;
> The gods and their temples are taxed
> Such is now the custom.[2]

The successors of Guru Nanak also had full knowledge of the contemporary political affairs. As Guru Arjan assumed pontification and took some steps to consolidate Sikhism, Jahangir began to view him with suspicion. Guru Arjan was also responsive to the political stands of the state. Perceiving the reaction that his activities had evoked in Government circles, the Guru embarked upon the course of preparing his people to face the challenges, polemical as well as physical, with determination and wisdom. On the eve of his departure for Lahore in response to the summons of Jahangir, Guru Arjan left a message for his son (Guru) Hargobind that he should sit on the throne determinedly and maintain as much army as he

1. *Rāje shīh(ṅ) muqqaddam kute. Jāe jagāean baiṭhe sute.*
Chākar nehdā(ṅ) pāin ghāo. Rat(u)pit(u) kutiho chaṭ(i) jāho.
(SGGS, p. 1288)
2. *Ād(i) purakh ko Allah kahīai sekhāṅ āī vārī.*
Deval devatiāṅ kar(u) lāgā aisī kīrat(i) chālī.
(SGGS, p 1191)

could afford. The message was an epitome of the active interest of the fifth Guru in politics. A little earlier than the moment referred to above, the fifth Guru advised Bhai Bidhi Chand and Bhai Pairana to join the personal staff of Hargobind and hinted that their martial qualities would be utilized fully in the period of his son. Guru Hargobind's open adoption of the policy of *Miri* and *Piri* had left absolutely no doubt that the political affairs were not extraneous to the teachings of the Sikh Gurus. So is the case of Guru Har Rai and Guru Harkrishan. Guru Har Rai's keen interest in the welfare of Prince Dara bears out our aforesaid assertion. Guru Tegh Bahadur's execution and Guru Gobind Singh's wars against the Mughals and Hill Rajas also point to the conclusion that the Gurus were as much alive to the contemporary political happenings as to their moral and spiritual objectives. In *Bachittar Natak* XIII, 9-10, Guru Gobind Singh writes :

> Those of Baba (Nanak) and those of Babar
> God Himself makes them both know the former thus;
> as the king of Religion.
> Guess the later then as worldly king.
> They who fail to render that
> what is due to the (House of) Baba
> The minions of Babar seize them and make
> exactions upon them
> And inflict severe punishments upon such defaulters;
> In addition, their worldly goods and
> property are looted and taken away.

In these lines the Guru says in unambiguous terms that there are two forces which claim allegiance of men's souls on earth. The Truth and Morality as Religion, and the state as embodiment of mere utilitarianism and secular politics. The primary allegiance of man is to the truth and morality, and those who fail in this allegiance, suffer under the subjugation of worldly state, unnourished by the courage and hope which is born through un-swerving adherence to the primary allegiance. In this perpetual struggle between the state and the church for exclusive possession of the soul of man, a man of culture and religion shall not lose sight ever of his primary allegiances. He who does so does it at his own peril, for, by doing so, he helps give birth to times in which everything is force, politics of utility and poverty. The Guru does not assert that this perpetual dichotomy and antagonism of the church and the state must be resolved, or even that it is capable of being resolved by the suppression or subjugation of the one by the other. Rather, he appears to recognise their eternal antagonism and character and in this antagonism sees the hope and glory of man; the social and political context in which the Sikh way of life is to be practised. The Church must perpetually correct and influence the state without aiming to destroy or absorb it, as the history shows that the attempt of the one to oust the other meets with no lasting success. Each of the two antagonistic entities surface again after having been crushed in vain and both appear as if bound together. This is what the Guru means, when he declares in the text, that the house of Baba Nanak and the house of Babar, God makes both of them and those who repudiate their allegiance to the house of Nanak suffer grievously, without hope at the hands of the state. Obviously the Guru's corpus of thought also includes also the matters which are essentially political.

ORIGIN OF SOVEREIGN POWER

Having decided that the Guru's moral order does not exclude political matters, the next question which arises is "Did the Gurus have some definite idea of polity ?"

The Gurus were not political philosophers in the sense Plato and Rousseau were. Therefore we do not find any particular political thesis in their writings or utterances. All the same, there are hints scattered in their writings which give quite distinct picture of the polity visualized by him. The cornerstone of the polity was that the sovereignty must reside in the minds of the people. The Guru says, "The Guru's sovereignty is full of twenty measures, but that of the *Sangat*, as the mouth piece of the people is of over-riding paramountcy, of twenty-one measures. This dictum repeatedly occurs throughout the Sikh literature from the earliest times as the basic principle of organisation and excercise of power, in the Sikh society, Guru Nanak, in the sixteenth Canto (*Pauri*) of *Jap* says the *Panch* must be recognised in the organisation of power (literally in the court). The *Panchas* alone are fit to occupy seats of supreme authority for exercise of power.

The *Panch* here connotes 'people of five directions, meaning thereby people of the four directions of the compass and the people residing at the centre, the venue of the assembly.' It was in exegesis of this text of *Sri Guru Granth Sahib* apparently, that Guru Gobind Singh while glorifying the *Panj Pyaras* declares, "I am ever present unseen, in the collective deliberations of the *Panchas* and there is no higher guidance on earth besides."[1] According to Guru Gobind Singh, "The spirit of the people is the spirit of the God. When anyone causes suffering to the people, God's wrath falls on him."[2] Once when a very prominent Brahman, Kesho Datt, visited Anandpur, he felt insulted for not being given privileged treatment. He condemned outright and cursed, what he called the low-caste crowd of the Sikhs who were treated better than the *Brahmins* and *Kshatriyas*.

Guru Gobind Singh calmly replied, "Do not blame me for ignoring you, for all are equal in my eyes. I will send you beddings and other things you need, but do not say a word against my inspired disciples."[3] Then glorifying the people, who were condemned by the *Brahmins*, the Guru said :

> All the battles I have won against tyranny
> I have fought with the devoted backing of these people
> Through them only have I been able to bestow gifts
> Through their help I have escaped.....
> The love and generosity of the Sikhs
> Have enriched my heart and home.
> Through their grace I have attained all learning.
> Through their help in battle, I have slain my enemies
> I was born to serve them, through them I reached eminence
> What would I have been without their kind and ready help ?
> There are millions of insignificant people like me
> True service is the service of these people;
> I am not inclined to serve others of higher castes.
> Charity will bear fruit in this and the next world
> If given to such worthy people as these
> All other sacrifices and charity is profitless

---

1. Kapur Singh, *Parasharprasna,* p. 349.
2. *Khālak Khalk Kī jānkai, Khalk dukhāvai nah. (Tankhahnama).*
3. *Sikhism and Indian Society,* Indian Institute of Advance Studies.

From head to foot, whatever I call my own
All I possess or carry, dedicate to these people.[1]

Guru Gobind Singh wrote this unique *Ode to the Khalsa people* glorifying their innate strength and power merely sixty years before Rousseau wrote his *Social Contract* and about 150 years before Marx formulated his *Manifesto*. For the Gurus, the people were the prophets of future; they were the first to point in world history that the fate of future civilization was not in the hands of mighty individuals but in the hands of the morally and spiritually awake people.

By people, he does not mean people of a particular society, religious group or social organization; rather the people in general, the people of the whole world, the whole mankind. According to Dr. Trilochan Singh, "The concept of society is found in two senses in the writings of the Sikh Gurus." It is generally synonymous with human society. It is also used in a limited sense for religious groups. When, for example, Guru Nanak criticises the dirty practices of the Jains, he does not condemn the religion but only the social aspect of this religious society. When Guru Nanak says, "The age is a drawn sword, the kings are butchers, goodness hath taken wings and flown; in the dark night of falsehood, I see not the moon of Truth anywhere."[2] He is not speaking of the ruler of any particular state or country but of the world situation at that time. In his writings, Guru Gobind Singh addresses the whole human society. Even if he refers to a particular person or group, the lesson is for the whole mankind. Guru Amar Das has made it clear; *Parthai sakhi maha purkh bolde, sanjhi sagal jahane'* "When sages speak about a particular person, the moral is for the whole humanity."[3]

Even the national cultures which divide people are regarded by the Gurus as superficial and artificial. The reasons assigned by Guru Gobind Singh for such differences are : *Nyare, nyare, desan ko prabhao hai;* different social attitude of countries have created these differences.

---

1. Guru Gobind Singh, *Dasam Granth*, translated by Dr. Trilochan Singh.
2. *Kal kāti rāje kāsāi dharm pankh kar uḍariā.*
   Kūṛ amāvas such chandramā disai nāhīṅ keh chaṛiā.   (SGGS, p. 145)
3. Trilochan Singh, "Social Philosophy of Guru Gobind Singh," article published by the Indian Institute of Advance Studies, Vol. IV, 1967.

Prof. J.S. Bains, in his article 'Political ideals of Guru Gobind Singh' says that, "In conformity with the teachings of Guru Nanak, the tenth Guru had argued that authority in every sphere ultimately derives its validity from God and not from any human source." In support of his thesis the learned professor writes, "In the *Zafarnama* which was addressed to Aurangzeb, the Guru had mentioned that God is the True Emperor of Earth and beyond and that He is the Master of both the worlds." He (the Guru) dilated on this point with more clarity when he said :

> The successors of both Baba Nanak and Babar
> Were created by God Himself.
> Recognize the former as spiritual
> And the latter as a temporal ruler.

According to the learned professor a similar idea was portrayed by the Gurus when they uttered the following words :

> By His (God) *hukm* are all things formed
> Not one is blessed, save by his *hukm*
> by His *hukm* alone nature doth run her course
> All serve beneath His *hukm*, and none may act without it
> Under Thy *hukm*, O God, hath all been done
> and naught of itself alone.

We, however, do not agree with the Professor who in our view, has not been able to correctly interpret the verses of Guru Gobind Singh. The original text nowhere says, explicitly or by implication that the church and the state 'both derive authority from God Himself.' It only says 'God maketh them both' as the instruments of His Will. The word in the text, *kare* neither literally, nor here can be interpreted to mean 'authorized'; it simply means made by or maketh. Similarly the word *pehchano* does not mean in the sense of a commandment—thou shalt recognize. It means, know, identify, understand, perceive. The (house) of Baba means the true religion on Earth, and the text says, understand the term to mean thus as such. Likewise *Unmano* (understand) cannot and does not mean 'recognise' and 'accept'. It literally and here in the text means understand, see, guess, infer, that the house of Babar means, the secular worldly state.

That the people were held to be the wielder of sovereign powers in Sikh polity can be seen from the examples of the Gurus. Once the Guru saluted the sepulchre of Dadu in Rajasthan. The Sikhs objected to this act of the Guru on the ground that it was not in conformity with the fundamental Sikh tenets and did not hesitate awarding *Tankhah* (religious punishment) to the Guru. The classic example of the high esteem in which the Guru held the Sikhs was when after selecting the 'five loved ones', he partook the holy water at their hands, thereby giving the *Khalsa* the pride of having selected their leader. This emphasis on popular basis of sovereignty and its equation with divine mandate was a unique idea and may be considered as a distinct contribution to democratic theory.[1]

The next issue before us is, how the sovereignty should operate. The Gurus seemed to be aware of this problem. They evolved various organizations for the people's sovereignty to be exercised. The most important among them is the institution of *Sangat*.

Sangat means an assembly or a union of men meeting together at a common place for perusal of a common activity mostly related to the divine order. One of the main teachings of the Guru to all those who brought faith in them was to form *Sangats*. Wherever Guru Nanak went, the Sikhs built a *Dharamsala* where they met everyday and sang the praises and the glory of Lord. When the *Sidhas* asked Guru Nanak to show them miracles, the Guru replied, "I have no power for miracles. I derive all my power from the divine word (*Bani*), and the *Sangat*. Away from *Sangat*, there is not a mole of support to me."[2] Anyone irrespective of caste, creed and clime can become the member of the *Sangat*. All services can be performed by the Sikh and non-Sikh devotees except the functions of baptism which can be performed by the ordained *Khalsa* who has lived up to the ideals. *Sangat* is not merely a gathering of

---

1. Kapur Singh, *Parasharprasna*, p. 324.
2. *Sidh(i) bolan(i) sun(i) Nānaka tuh(i) jag no karāmāt dikhāī.*
   Kujh(u) vikhāleṅ asāṅ no tuh(i) kioṅ ḍhil awehī lāī.
   Bābā bole Nāthjī as(i) vekhan(i) jogī vast(u) na kāī.
   Gur(u) saṅgat bānī binā(ṅ) dūjī oṭ nahī hai rāī.42.   (Bhai Gurdas ji, *Vār* I)

worshippers nor is it just a forum for seeking personal salvation and blessedness, but it has stood for the total re-orientation of life of the individuals and society towards a creative purposeful existence. This being so, all the discussions concerning every aspect of man's life—from fair dealings in business and from disputes to inner conflicts of the soul and the priests were referred to *Sangat*. *Sangat* was respected and considered so important that even the Gurus used to submit to its decisions. Guru Arjan refused the marriage of his son Hargobind with Chandu's daughter because *Sangat* of Delhi had decided so.

In fact, the decision of the *Sangats* have always been considered based on reasons, dispassion and unbiased deliberations, the verdicts of a composite higher self, subordinating the petty considerations of the composite lower self, *'Man Niwan Mat(i) Uchchi Mat(i) ka Rakha Aap Wahe Guru.'* Such decisions are considered to be the decisions of God who guides men to logical inferences which are not overcome by personal or emotional considerations. Such an atmosphere prevails among the members of the *Sangat* sitting at a place which has assumed the name *Gurdwara* (Dharamsal during Guru Nanak's period), literally meaning the door of the Guru.

The idea of *Sangat* is very old in India and if its etymology is traced, it was grounded in the polity of the early Indo-Aryans. There is a mention of *Samiti*, or a folk assembly in *Rig Veda* where there is a prayer for 'a common assembly and a common policy.' In *Atharva Veda* also, the aforesaid assembly has been spoken of. *The Atharva* declares that 'this *Samiti*, (the Sikh equivalent of which is the *Sangat*) is a daughter of God.' The institution of *Sangat* continued to serve the society till it got smothered under the weight of monarchical institutions.

As regards the constituents of *Sangat*, it may be said that it is composed of the people, sincere, truthful and honest, dedicated to the Guru's cause which is no other than the cause of the whole people. *Sangat*, like the *Sangh* of the Buddhist and the *Samiti* or *Sabha* of the Indo-Aryans, is no *Sangat* if its members are not well-meaning and honest. The members who do not speak and act bonafides, are no honest members, and the honest and well-meaning members are those who are not swayed by bias or favour and who speak out truthfully and fearlessly and are guided by the Guru spirit.

So far as the mode of functioning of Sangat is concerned, it is very simple and straightforward. There is always a congregation in the presence of Guru-persons or eternal Guru, Granth Sahib. At the end of the prayer the aggrieved person would stand up with his hands folded and submit his complaint to the gathering or he could make a report to the Granthi (reciter of the scripture) of the Gurdwara who would arrange to convey it to the Sangat. The Sangat may take a snap decision or may decide upon some other procedure to satisfy the complainant. The other procedure could be formation of a sub committee of five noble souls (Panch) who would deliberate on the complaint and arrive at the decision. Mohsin Fani, a contemporary of the sixth Guru, and a traveller from Iran, was amazed at the amount and intensity of one's faith in the Sangat. He found that a Sikh would stand up and submit with his folded hands to the Sangat that he is sinful and the Sangat should pray to God, the Guru, to pardon and forgive his misdeeds and grant him salvation. His inner conflicts were removed and he enjoyed peace of mind. If he lived the remaining life with caution, he was sure to die a happy man.

Sangat's working is a two-way activity. Every member of the Sangat should have faith in it and every person who sits in the Sangat should be a disciplined citizen of the Guru's kingdom. Thus there should be perfect rapport between the complainant and the collective will of the Sangat. The complainant should feel that his own voice is also a part of the people's voice and the Sangat is not only his own self, enlarged and widened, but because of its nature of collectivity, it has gained a high degree of divinity and hence its decision will be just and true.

PANTH AND GURMATA

Next to Sangat, at local level, there were regional or circle Sangats. During the time of Guru Tegh Bahadur, there was a

Bari Sangat at Dacca whose duty was to guide the local *Sangat* as also to devise plans to ensure that the Guru's commands are disseminated to the people and problems arising were solved.

No account of the operation of sovereignty is complete without reference to the institution of *Panth*.

Panth from Sanskrit *Patha, Pathin* or *Patham* means literally a way, a passage or a path and figuratively, a way of life, religious creed or culture. In Sikh terminology word *Panth* stands for Sikh faith as well as those who tread on the path of that faith, that is the Sikh people as a whole. It represents the invisible mystic body composing all those who profess Sikhism as their faith and en-compassing lesser bodies, religious as well as political, claiming to represent the whole of the Sikh population or any section of it. *Panth* for the Sikhs is the supreme earthly glory having full claim on their allegiance. It transcends any of its components and functional agencies.

A further dimension to the concept of *Panth* was brought about by Guru Gobind Singh. He introduced the initiation of Sikhs into *Panth* through administration of *Pahul* prepared by double-edgeds. Bhai Gurdas Singh's *kabit*, 'transformed *Sangat* into *Khalsa*'.[1] The *Panth* was now identified with the Guru himself, "The *Khalsa* is my life and soul." The *Panth*, now called *Khalsa Panth*, was the *Guru Panth*. Guru Gobind Singh at the time of his death declared *Adi Granth* as the Guru eternal for the Sikhs. The lineage of living Gurus came to an end and the *Guru Panth* became the corporate body of the Sikhs under the guidance of *Guru Granth*. By virtue of its status the concept as well as the fact that *Panth* as a corporate being was a sovereign power, it got further strength and affirmatiom.

The occasional meets of the whole *Panth* is a long standing tradition in the history of the *Khalsa*. In those days of the Gurus, *Sikh Sangat* in small representative *Jathas* (Bands) used to come from all the Sikh centers and listened to the Guru's word for some days. At these annual conclaves, the Guru also gave instructions about the propagation of the Sikh

1. *Gur sangat kīnī Khālsā....*

jiwan jugati (way of life). When Guru Gobind Singh passed guruship on to *Adi Granth* and the *Panth*, the institution of *Panth* acquired unique importance and no wonder the Sikhs began to look upon, it as the apex organisation.

After the capture of Baba Banda Singh, the Mughal rulers began persecution of the Sikhs with renewed vengeance. The Sikhs organised themselves into *Jathas* and fled to local or far-off jungles, hills or deserts of *Malwa*. Irrespective of the blockade by the enemy, the Sikhs would come to Amritsar at least twice a year on Diwali and Baisakhi days. Such conclaves began to be known as *Panthic* congregation. It is well known that in these conclaves very important decisions were taken which played a significant role in the history of the Sikhs.

GURMATA

The decision of the *Panth* taken in the presence of the Guru (after Guru Gobind Singh, *Guru Granth* and *Guru Panth*). was called *Gurmata*. The first *Gurmata* is said to have taken place during the time of Guru Hargobind. Sohan Kavi, for example, uses the term *Mata* in his work *Gurbilas Padshahi Chhevin* in the sense of a resolution. It related to the resolve of the Sikhs to fight against the Mughal troops detailed from Lahore to stop the activities of Guru Hargobind which the Mughal *Subedar* considered an incipient threat to Mughal government. The prefix 'Guru' to *Mata* was not fixed at that time, although it was much revered and respected and regarded as Guru's decision because, since the inception of Sikhism, it had been embedded in the Sikh psyche that *Sangat* is the abode of the Guru. Sainapat, who was a court poet of Guru Gobind Singh has left an eye-witness account of the activities of the Guru in his work *Gursobha*. He refers to a *Mata* arrived at by *Panchas* of a certain locality where the Sikhs of the locality were asked to receive *Khande-Ki-Pahul*. Although he does not prefix 'Guru' to the word *Mata*, his narrative means the same thing. In December 1705 at Chamkaur, the five Sikhs symbolically representing the authority of the *Panth*, adopted a *Mata* ordering Guru Gobind Singh to vacate the mud fortress of Chamkaur and save his life to carry on his mission. The

Guru who was initially reluctant to vacate simply acquiesed in what the *Panj Pyaras* did. At Naraina, when the Guru saluted the sepulchre of Dadu by pointing his arrow at it, the *Khalsa* objected and took a decision to award religious punishment to the Guru, for doing an act which was violative of Sikh doctrine. The Guru most willingly presented himself for punishment and admired his disciples for their right thinking and courage.

The Guru all along especially after the creation of the *Khalsa* endeavoured hard to project the *Khalsa Panth* and *Panj Pyaras* as a source of authority. He made it clear whenever he found an opportunity. When the Guru was on the verge of leaving for his heavenly abode, he reaffirmed that all the affairs of the *Panth* would be regulated before *Sri Guru Granth Sahib* by the council of five beloved ones chosen by the committed *Khalsa*. The verdict was to be called *Gurmata*. It was to be adopted by the assembly of the *Khalsa* unanimously. Its implementation was binding on the whole *Panth*. Any infringement was to be considered sacrilegious.

Some scholars especially non-Indians have stumbled on the facts and have drawn wrong conclusion regarding the meeting for *Gurmata* as the 'Greatest Council' of the Sikhs. James Brown used the term 'Grand Diet' for *Gurmata* and Forster referred to *Gurmata* as the 'Grand Convention of Sikhs'.

All these views betray ignorance or faulty perception of the facts. Historical evidence is available in abundance to testify that *Gurmata* was decision or a resolution adopted by the body of the *Khalsa* present at one time at a given place. The statement of Ratan Singh Bhangu and later its endorsement by scholars such as Dr. N.K. Sinha and Dr. Ganda Singh have finally settled the issue that *Gurmata* was a decision taken unanimously by the assembly of the *Khalsa* in the presence of *Sri Guru Granth Sahib* and it was called so because the tenth Guru vested the gurship joinly in *Khalsa Panth* and the *Adi Granth*.

Usually *Gurmatas* were passed at *Sri Akal Takhat* (Amritsar) but under special circumstances, these could be passed anywhere. The essential condition being the assemblage of the Sikhs in the presence of *Sri Guru Granth Sahib*. According to

Ratan Singh Bhangu, the leaders of *Khalsa* could determine any place for the meeting of the *Khalsa Panth* and adopt resolutions. It does not follow, however, that most important *Gurmata* were not adopted at *Sri Akal Takhat* in Amritsar. During the eighteenth century, Amritsar had become the most important centre for the collective activities of the *Khalsa*. When the leaders as well as their followers came to visit the *Darbar Sahib* at the time of Baisakhi and Diwali, matters of importance concerning the *Sikh Panth* could be discussed and resolved. Since the decisions were taken in the presence of The Guru by the *Panth*, *Gurmata* besides being the decision became symbolic form of authority oᶠ the collective will of the whole *Khalsa*. *Gurmata* (decision) could be arrived at local level as well. In that case, local *Sangat* would gather in the presence of the Guru and take decision. Such decisions *(Gurmatas)* had as much sanctity as the *Gurmata* reached at *Panthic* level.

PANJ PYARAS

Panj Pyaras, literally meaning the five beloved ones was the name given to the five Sikhs, Bhai Daya Singh, Bhai Himmat Singh, Bhai Dharam Singh, Bhai Muhkam Singh and Bhai Sahib Singh who were so designated by Guru Gobind Singh on March 29, 1699 at the historic congregation at Anandpur Sahib and formed the nucleus of the *Khalsa* as the first batch to receive at his hands *Khande Di Pahul* after they had proved their total commitment to the Guru person, Guru Gobind Singh, his ideology and his cause. The Guru then sought baptism from them whom he had just then baptised. The event symbolised the equation of the Guru with *Khalsa* whom they were representing. Earlier, only the Guru and his nominated *Masands* could initiate one into the faith through the ceremony of *Charan Pahul* but now the Guru as well as the *Khalsa* could do so. These chosen five in fact acted on behalf of the Guru in the latter's physical absence and enjoyed all powers. It is this equation between the two which Bhai Gurdas Singh *highlights* when he proclaims that great is Guru Gobind Singh who is both Guru and a disciple.

The event signalled many things. It signified that the

Guru and the *Panj Pyaras* and for that matter, the whole of the *Khalsa*, were one in spirit and therefore coequals. There exists no difference even on temporal plane in terms of authority, ideology and cause. Implied in this was the motivation provided to the *Khalsa* to initiate people to the order of the *Khalsa* and do other things on the Guru's behalf. Following their example, any five baptised Sikhs who followed *Khalsa* discipline could constitute *Panj Pyaras* at any place and at any time but less in the presence of *Sri Guru Granth Sahib*. Infact the institution of *Panj Pyaras* was neither fixed or exclusive. The Guru was believed to be present among them and their collective wisdom implied the Guru's wish. In the perception of Dr. Dharam Singh, "the Guru created a very viable alternative for the institution of person Guru. Understandably, the *Panj Pyaras* became the cynosure of the Sikhs, a symbol of authority temporal as well as spiritual, an institution to project and radiate Sikh values as well as to operate affairs in the light of the Guru-spirit. *Panj Pyaras* have collectively acted as supreme authority representing the *Guru-Panth*.

In 1705, the Guru, his two sons and forty Sikhs put up stout resistance to the Mughal forces whose number was manifold more than the Guru's soldiers. The Guru's ranks thinned further and if the resistance had been continued, the Guru might have suffered grave consequences. At this juncture five Sikhs waited upon him in the form of *Panj Pyaras* and commanded him to leave the mud fort of Chamkaur for some safe place. The Guru had to submit to the dictates of the *Pyaras*. By doing this, he reiterated the doctrine of collegial leadership in the direction of state policies. The collegiality of leadership means that all party matters are accomplished by all party members directly or through representatives who all are subject to some rules. The collegial leadership now is popularly known as *Panch Pardhani*. It does not mean that the five can appropriate into themselves the power, the authority, the temporal sovereignty in the *Guru-Panth*. It can have significance on the sense of *Sangat* attuned to the Divine in the holy presence of *Sri Guru Granth Sahib* spontaneously choosing five Gur-Sikhs, deliberating upon or resolving some issue but without acting as autocrats.

According to Dr. Sher Singh when mutual discussion, persuasions or understanding each other's points of view did not help the assembly, the *Sangat* or the *Panchayat* to arrive at some definitive decision; then the Five were selected unanimously to give their decision after giving proper hearing and giving due thought at *Panthic Meets*, even when there was no concern, *Panj Pyaras* were selected to give judgement which was considered sacred and was binding on all. The decisions so arrived at were considered sacrosanct and binding on all parties.

FORM OF GOVERNMENT

Having given the main features of the Sikhs polity as developed upto Guru Gobind Singh, we have reached the stage where it is not very difficult to judge the form of Government as envisaged by the Gurus.

Monarchical political structure does not fit in the concepts of the Gurus and Sikh polity. When the Sikh religion was being evolved, there were the Hindu monarchs as well as Muslim. The institution of the Hindu monarchy is very old. In the *Rig Veda*, the monarchy appears as the only and the normal form of government. In the *Aitreya Brahmana,* supplement of the *Rig Veda* it is asserted that the law can never overpower lawlessness except through a monarch. "In the war between *devas* and *asuras, asuras* were victorious. The *devas* opined that it was on account of our having no king that *asuras* had defeated us. They all then agreed to have a king." *Rig Vedic* tradition accorded divine sanction, for, in the *Manav Dharam Sastra*, it is laid down that God Himself created the king to protect people from lawlessness. Since the King ruled by divine right, he was a God, unamenable to the control or opinions of the people as far as the theory goes and therefore;

"Even an infant king must not be despised, as though a mere mortal, for he is a great god in human form."

The king to be formally invested with god-head must, however, be anointed, with the *Abhiseka Ceremony* by the Brahmin priest, for an unanointed king is an unlawful king whom the gods do not favour. An unanointed king is a term of contempt in Hindu politics, and it is declared that such barbarous customs are the hallmark of dirty Westerners and foreigners. According to *Arthshastra* of Kautalya, 'a single wheel cannot turn and so, government is possible only with assistance.' In this way *Arthshastra* recommends that a king should appoint ministers and listen to their advice.

Elaborating the concept of the Hindu monarchy, Sirdar Kapur Singh says, "This is the eternal triangle of Hindu monarchy, the god king, the priestly Brahmins and the ministers by royal choice. Here is a king who has no legislative powers and whose function is to uphold the social structure of *Varanasram Dharma* as laid down in the Brahmanic sacred texts, whose formal installation is dependent upon the approval and good-will of the hereditary priestly class of Brahmins, and who is constantly surrounded by a cliche of ministers of his own creation, who tend to usurp powers and replace him. This Hindu polity ensures a static conservative society which abhors social progress and change as intrinsically undesirable and dangerous, for the *Manavdharama Sastra* bids a citizen 'to walk in that path of good and virtuous people which his father and grandfather followed; while he walks in that, he will not suffer harm.' It further ensures that this society is upheld by an autocratic king, who rules only by divine right but as a divine being, answerable to no mortal on earth, as far the theory goes. As a necessary consequence this form of government ensures the intellectual leadership of the Hindu society to the priestly Brahmins who are exhypothesis wedded to the *Varnasram Dharma*, the four-fold economic-political structure of the Hindu social pyramid."

Obviously the Hindu monarchy as declared above according to which the ruler is divine is alien to Sikh polity, in the sense that it is a part of the Divine. He/She is not divine in the sense that he is infallible. Sovereignty does not reside in one man, rather it belongs to people as it emerges out of them. The Sikh polity does not recognise any exclusive priestly class to anoint the king. According to the Gurus, there can be no loyalty to super-individual state if there is no rule of law or no permanent civil service. Morever the four-fold economic-political structure of the Hindu society has no place in the Sikh political scheme. The Sikhs throughout their formative period from Guru Nanak to Guru Gobind Singh were continuously made to realise that they formed the microcosm of macrocosm and if they regenerated themselves and practised the programme as laid down by the Gurus, they were very honourable, and collectively they were as good as the Guru himself, even superior to him. By passing on physical guruship to the *Panth*, the Sikhs were made fully responsible and divine. Such people fully awakened to their inherent potentialities and responsibilities could not but afford the democratic spirit. The idea of deifying any individual or glorification of any person which might lead to the growth of personality cult was rejected as irrelevant to the Sikh way of governance. The institution of *Langar, Sangat* and the *Khalsa* have also nourished and sustained democratic ideals. The Sikhs for the greater part of the eighteenth century were zealous about holding the democratic ideals aloft. The authority of *Fatu-Hat-Nama-I-Samadi* avers that Banda Singh was not unhampered while taking important decisions at crucial moments and their struggle by his own followers. He bowed to the majority decisions of the Sikhs while deciding about the offer of a negotiated settlement made to them by Abdus Samad Khan.

Islamic monarchy was also in no way better than Hindu monarchy. In the Islamic monarchy as it existed in India contemporaneous of the Gurus, the king assumes the status of Prophet Mohammad's apostle instead of that of God, though by no means less exalted, as is apparent from the claim, which the Mughal Emperors made for themselves of being *Zilli-Illahi*, the shadow of *God on earth*. The laws of the static conservative society which he is required to uphold are derived from the *Koran* and the *Hadith*, instead of the *Vedas* and the *Dharamshastras*, and the hereditary intellectual leadership of the Brahmins is replaced by the arrogant presumptions and prerogative of the *Ulemas*. Likewise the Islamic monarch has his ministers selected and appointed by Royal arbitration who are absolutely subservient to him.

Muslim type of monarchy also did not fit in the framework of the polity of the Sikh Gurus for those very reasons which did not qualify Hindu monarchy.

The Gurus evolved a new form of government to which Guru Gobind Singh gave the name of *Khalsa Raj*—Divine kingdom; though its five beloved ones who happened to belong to five castes and five regions of India : Bhai Daya Singh, a Kashatariya, belongs to Punjab; Bhai Mohkam Singh, a washerman from Dwarka (Gujrat); Bhai Sahib Singh, a Barber from Deccan; Bhai Dharam Singh, a *jat* from (U.P.) and Bhai Himmat Singh, a Cook from Jagannath Puri in the Eastern India. He thus, in a unique way, secured an inter-regional unity of India. He made all the representatives to eat from the same pan and the Guru himself also ate from the same container. The attempt at inter-regional unity and inter-communal identity besides being a divine act was also a political weapon. The Guru was planning for the establishment of the *Khalsa Commonwealth*. Corresponding to these five regional representations, he also established five regional seats of authority, for Eastern India, the throne of Patna, for the Deccan the throne at Nanded (Hazur Sahib), for the Panjab, at *Akal Takht Sahib* at Amritsar, for the hilly Himachal at Anandpur and for the Southern Punjab in Takht Damdama Sahib. Five regions of India, five seats of authority, five representative beloved ones, thus wise the Guru wanted to establish the Republic of the Five.

Sikh polity as it is based on Sikh doctrine, Sikh ethical code, the response of the Guru to various challenges seems to have the following obligations to defray :

1. It shall strive to propagate, to uphold and to make it a basic that there is inviolable sovereignty of the human person. If God is the true sovereign *(Sacha Patshah)* in the spiritual and temporal realms, then as a creation of God, man/ woman partakes of the sovereignty of the Divine.

2. In consonance with this adumbrated understanding, man/woman is entitled to freedom of worship, freedom of expression, freedom of conscience, freedom from fear and freedom to pursue any interest.

The martyrdom of Guru Tegh Bahadur was symbolic of the assertion of the fundamental right to freedom of conscience with related freedoms of religion, belief and practice both on individual and corporate levels. The freedom with the Guru was not an empirical expediency in religiously heterogeneous society, but a transcendent value described by Guru Gobind Singh as *Dharma* in *Bachittar Natak*, characteristic of multi-religious, multi-cultural and multi-ethnic society that Sikhism sought to evolve as the composite integrated Indian/global society based on religion and political pluralism. It was in furtherance of this historical mission that the fifth Guru envisaged a nonsectarian, non-communal, all inclusive integrated polity wherein there would be no room for religious, social or political exclusiveness.

"All are co-equal partners in their common wealth with none as excluded and alien."[1]

3. It shall restructure society on equalitarian bases. It shall reject the concept of hierarchical fixity as the tradition-honoured principle of social organisation reflected in caste system which in its turn had to follow orthodox law of *Karma*. It shall also discountenance other differences based on creed, wealth, race et al., and instead, it would lend full recognition to worth and merit of each individual who is viewed in Sikhism as the very macrocosm of God. It shall see that individual is not reduced to the status of a mere ego in a machine or a mere honey gathering insect on a beehive. It is for this reason that Sikhism conceives of the religious evolution of a man as a necessary and integral pre-requisite and condition of its march towards the ideal society.

In this perspective, it would not be out of place to remark that the baptismal ceremony introduced by Guru Gobind Singh had deep sociological implications. It provided a new formative principle, process and channel of vertical mobility to the lower classes and castes in their own right on an equalitarian basis, assuredly in sharp contrast to the traditional process where by a lower group having circumstantially gained power or wealth would try to simulate the customs, manners, ritual and even caste denominations of the higher castes for acceptance on a higher rung in the hierarchical ladder.

It shall respect and promote pluralism—religious as well as social, for; Sikh polity is not only grounded in Sikhism but

---

1. *Sabhe sānjhīwal sadāin, koī na disc bāhrā jio.*

it has also sprouted and nourished by it. In this connection we quote rather extensively from Dr. J.S. Ahluwalia's lecture which he delivered at the University of California to illustrate our point and find legitimacy. He says, "Different revelations of the spirit (God-Spirit) are like the variety of different seasons which refer back to the same sun."[1]

For Sikh religion, all revelations of God are equally valid, having been given to man relative to the variables of time and place. This rules out any room for dogmatic assertion of fullness and finality of any single religious revelation as well as religion totalitarianism which is not accepted in Sikhism. "All revelations being relatively valid, no 'ISM'—religious or secular, can claim to be the sole way to God, the exclusive path to salvation, Guru Amar Das utters, "The world is ablaze O Lord ! Shower your benediction. Through whichever door it can be delivered, save it that way." Similar approach has been practised and pleaded by Guru Gobind Singh. This accounts for the basis and significance of religious, pluralism. From here it follows that unity of different religious or the global ethnic, need not be artificially conceptualised on the basis of the lowest denominator common to all religions. It can rather be realised spontaneously on the basis that different religions are different stages of the revelation of the one divine spirit manifest in different forms in different faiths.

The conception of religious pluralism in Sikhism envisages to provide a positive basis not only for co-validity and co-existence of different faiths in dynamic interaction with each other, but also for equality and co-existence of different religions at social level and their co-participation in the national body politic of their respective countries. Here co-participation of the religious ethno-religious or simply ethnic groups or—of the minorities based on religion, region, ethnicity etc. means co-participation in their corporate capacities, through their own political organisation representing the social collectivities with their respective self-identities

---

1. Numerous are the seasons emanating from one sun,
   Numerous are the guises in which the creator appears.
   ਸੂਰਜੁ ਏਕੋ ਰੁਤਿ ਅਨੇਕ ॥
   ਨਾਨਕ ਕਰਤੇ ਕੇ ਕੇਤੇ ਵੇਸ ॥

   (*SGGS*, p. 12)

which in no case should be diluted, homogenised or sublated into an overarching secular nationalism of the western type as adopted by the third world countries. Closely related and connected to the concept and model of pluralism is the ideal of Universalism to which *Khalsa Republic* shall deem itself committed. Universalism in Sikhism is based and rooted in the divinity of man which partake the divinity of God. Sikh religion, therefore is not an ethnicity specific or region specific or community specific religion."

The different ethnicity of the first five Sikhs initiated into the *Order of the Khalsa*, the sacrament of the holy *Amrit* by Guru Gobind Singh mean that Sikh dispensation was not bound down to a particular ethnicity. Guru Gobind Singh in his composition *Akal Ustat* refers to different people in terms of their ethnic identities suggesting that they are not exclusive, rather fragments of Divinity, each fragment being whole in itself and a part of the whole; and ever striving to realise that whole through love as a value and as the destiny.

The whole of the Earth planet being revered as 'mother' in Guru Nanak *Jap Ji*, there is no specific holy land or a 'promised land.' This type of understanding, *Sarbat Da Bhala* (betterment of the whole universe) is remembered in daily Sikh congregational prayer, taking in its embrace such universal issues as human rights, gender equality, the empowerment of the lowest suppressed and marginalised sect of society etc.

(4) Next important feature of the *Khalsa Republic* was to assume that every individual must engage himself/herself in honest productive labour and there shall be no exploitation of a man by another man with capital or spi or spiovery. The accumulated wealth shall not be employed as the instrument of exploitation and there shall be no privilegentia based on the white collar and gift of the gab.

Khalsa Republic is expected to achieve all this including those listed in the foregoing paragraphs not through coercion and imposition but through transformation, possibly through genuine religious projection of the basic attitudes of the individuals transformation that progressively destroys narrow selfishness. This is the moral imperative for the *Khalsa State*. It is not a supra individual identity as Hegel thought, to which obedience of an individual is due and for which an individual may be sacrificed.

It shall not be, as it cannot be a theocratic state. Firstly, in Sikhism, there is no cannonised priestly class. Secondly, the source and sanction of secular law lies in the society expressed through the will of the people. Thirdly, Sikhism does not discriminate against individual or group on the ground of creed, caste, sex or class. All are equally entitled to a place in *Such Khand* via any religious path of their choosing and faith. In fact Sikh polity is neither communal nor unitarian in character. This being so, religious unitarianism as well as religious totalitarianism is repugnant to the spirit of Sikhism. Nor shall it assume the character of communal state. The reasons are not far to seek. Firstly, it goes against the multi-religious, multi-communitarian, pluralistic society which finds validity and sanctification in Sikhism. Secondly, Sikhism does not entertain co-related concepts of *Chosen People* and the *Promised land* to those in Jewish tradition where God is said to have promised to Ibrahim to give his descendants the land of Canaan (now Israel) for an ever-lasting possession. Thirdly, "The *Khalsa* baptised by Guru Gobind Singh symbolises a generic sociological category representing the full fledged sovereign Society, and not any particular sect or group."

CHAPTER XIX

SIKH SOCIAL IDEALS

A close study of the life of Guru Gobind Singh, his precepts and his utterances would lead us to the conclusion that the Sikh social ethics has four pronounced ingredients. These are social equality, universal-brotherhood, seeking good of all (altruism) and social service. These ingredients are inter-related and interactive. Altruism and social service are, in fact, practical measures to realize universal brotherhood, the actualization of which in its turn, depends on the extent to which the principle of social equality is realized in the conduct of those who form the social fabric. This concept is rooted in the belief that the whole matter is a unity and the moral world is that where this principle is crystallized in day to day life. The Guru's concern for this unity was very acute and had been so vital a motivating force that he was very vocal and copious in his comments upon the contemporary social institutions which instead of unifying mankind on the principle of social equality propped up the inequitable and inquisitional social organisations and social ethics. In the process he made critical examination of the contemporary historical condition in India with a view to highlighting the problem of social equality in all its aspects in the contemporary context as also to suggest fresh formulations.

The Gurus preceding Guru Gobind Singh had condemned and rejected the social organization of Hinduism which has been described by Sh. S.K. Maitra as the objective morality of the Hindus. The Gurus had been equivocal and vocal in their statement that complete equality among people was to be the fundamental principle required to regulate the social relationship. They were vehement in ridiculing and invalidating the claims and make-beliefs that there existed differences among people in terms of their physical conditions and those twice born are specially blessed by God making them superior to others. Guru Amar Das went to the extent of labelling the caste system as 'an abnormality and a ritual perversity in an otherwise healthy society.' Equally categorical and forthright were they, in exploding the myth, being cherished since long that different parts of the Primordial Being gave rise to different caste, thereby making each caste a divine creation and the caste system, a divine ritual-mechanism. In the grand scheme of Sikhism to attain the ideal of self-realization both at micro and macro levels, caste was considered absolutely irrelevant—rather a hurdle to become one with the identity of Almighty. It was laid down that men of low caste need not wait to be born again in the next higher caste for the attainment of liberation and spiritual realization. Not birth but deeds ultimately determine the purity of life.

Guru Gobind Singh subscribed to what his predecessor Gurus had determined and eslablished. He carried forward the work they had commenced or had conceived to be done. The Guru spared no pains to strengthen the institutions of *Guru Ka Langar* (Guru's free kitchen), *Sangat*, *Kirtan* as they were great levellers and unifying agencies.

The unique contribution of Guru Gobind Singh was his conceiving of society to be built outside the parameters of Hindu rituals, ethics and the Hindu ritual organizational set-up. The society of his vision was based on social equality built on the recognition of light of the Divine in all beings in equal measure and of such configuration that was absolutely free from caste stratification or any other social or religious difference. The sole endeavour of this society would be to march continuously to realise self and then work under its guidance to make this mundane world, which is in fact the emanation of God, worth-living and worth for His grace. The Guru gave the name *Khalsa*—absolutely pure or Gods own— to such a society.

The Guru declared caste a taboo in the *Order of the Khalsa*. Guru Gobind Singh declared categorically, "There is no consideration of caste or membership of *Varnas*." He is all sympathy for the down-trodden and the so-called low-caste people. He remarked,

"True service is the service of those people, I am not inclined to serve others of higher castes. Charity will bear fruit, in this and the next world, if given to such worthy people as these. All other sacrifices and charities are profitless. From top to toe whatever I call my own, all I possess or carry, I dedicate to these people." It was in this context that Guru Gobind Singh spoke, "Consider all mankind of one caste alone."[1]

This was beyond the tolerance of the Brahmins who despite long association with the Guru and his ideology could not enlarge their consciousness. The Guru noticed all this and even recorded, *"Hearing this the learned Brahmin was amazed. Malice boiled in him and anger burnt as briskly as straw burns in flame. He could not bear the thought that by such levelling of castes, the Brahmins might lose their livelihood. The Pandit wept and wailed at the plight of his neglected Order."*

Again in *Akal Ustat* Guru Gobind Singh expresses, "There is no consideration of caste or of *Varna*." In *Bachittar Natak* Chapter VI, Verse 34, the Guru declared, "I shall not adopt the ways of any creed, but shall sow the seeds of pure love of God."[2] The *Panj Pyaras* (The Five Beloved) who were baptised into the *Order of the Khalsa* included those people who, according to the *Varna Order*, belonged to the so-called lower castes. The theory of separate duties for different castes was replaced by the same ethical and religious duties for all men. Thus, the fundamental equality of all men was ensured by free and voluntary admission to the *Order of the Khalsa*.

When the Brahmins refused to educate some Sikhs which included persons of the so-called lower castes, the Guru at once sent his disciples to Kashi, the seat of Hindu learning in India in the medieval period, to receive education and then to serve as preachers without any consideration of caste-distinctions. Bhai Nand Lal, the court poet of Guru Gobind Singh, has recorded in his *Rehatnama* that the Guru had decided to merge four *Varnas* into one and lead them to God.

---

1. *Mānas kī jāt(i) sabhe ekai pehchānbo.*
2. *Kahio prabhū su bhākh(i) hon. Kisū na kān rākh(i) ho(n).*
   Kisū na bhekh bhīj hon. Alekh bīj bīj ho(n).34.

One day there came to his court a *Kalal* or a wine distiller of Punjab. *Kalals* were held in acute hatred by the society, still clinging to the wrong belief that profession determines the status. Suffering from the status-complex in the contemporary Punjabi/Indian society, he stood a little away from the Guru. But the Guru took him by his hand and seated him in the *Sangat* (congregation) by his side. He hesitated and meekly said that he was a *Kalal*. The Guru proclaimed 'You are not *Kalal'* but *Guru Ka Lal* (a Ruby or son of Guru).

On 2nd November, 1675, Bhai Jaita, the sweeper, known as *Rangretta* (a man of low caste) carried the sacred head of Guru Tegh Bahadur from Delhi to Kiratpur where Guru Gobind Singh, Mata Gujri and Reverend Mother Nanki came to receive it to carry it in a palanquin to Anandpur. Guru Gobind Singh greeted Bhai Jaita affectionately and blessed his whole clan by conferring on it the honorific *Rangrette Guru Ke Bete* (Rangrettas are the Guru's sons). Significantly, the Guru's utterance embodied a message that the deeds determined the status and not the caste/profession or birth. The Guru's priorities from the day one were very clear that society based on caste/birth should be discarded and a fresh one be reconstructed on the bases of love for all, equal rights for all, divinity of individuals, dignity of labour and faith in the singularity and unicity of God with a commitment to improve upon the lot of the people.

EQUALITY IN TERMS OF DIFFERENT RELIGIONS AND NATIONALITIES

When Guru Nanak addressed himself to the task of shaping the society as per his conception, many religions such as Hinduism, Islam, Christianity, Jainism etc. were prevalent in the country. We understand religion at normative level is an attempt to instil harmony among the people to enable them improve their living as also to understand the secrets of the creation vis-a-vis God and his human beings. All religions, in fact, at the time of their birth or rise, project the *modus operandi* as stated above, but as times pass on, they fall victim to the parochialism of spirit or the narrow social political views of the people whom they profess to elevate. It was because of this that in Guru's times, the religious groups were at loggerheads with one another. The followers of Islam especially the *Sunnis* were committed to safeguard the interests of their own sect and they enjoyed sadistic pleasure in torturing the votaries of other religious groups particularly the Hindus. The idea of *Dar-ul-Harb* is indicative of this fanatical attitude. The Hindus, in their turn, fared no better. They did not appreciate the good points of Islam and Islamic culture—rather they branded the Muslims as *Malechhas*—the profaned. There were very few persons among the Hindus and Muslims known as *Sufis* and Saints who understood the real role of religion but their number was slender and their voice was not heard in the din and noise of the communal clamour. If there were no riots on a large scale, it was either because of passivity of the Hindus or out of their fear of Imperial Muslims or because of the fact that Muslims were happy at their achievements. Christianity and other religions also did not prepare the psyche so as to enable people to appreciate and respect diverse religio-cultural paths. But the need of the hour was the development of peoples' flexible attitude, towards all religions and religious groups along with their social and culture projections. The profile of the response could be visualized in the teachings of the *Bhaktas* particularly of the 14th and 16th centuries. Perhaps being earlier attempts their expressions were not forthright and their views were not categorical.

It fell to Nanak to show the right path to the people lost in the vortex of sectarian squabbles and group ferocities. He eschewed the idea of any one religion or revelation enshrined in itself the exclusive secret or knowledge of the Godhead. On the other hand, he held that God in His mysterious ways give knowledge of Truth to various people in various forms. No one can claim to hold exclusive key to salvation or by whatever names the biggest spiritual ideal is designated.

Guru Gobind Singh expressed himself more effectively and exhaustively on this theme. He regarded all human beings as the children of the same father. The following extracts from his composition *Akal Ustat*, speaks volume of the Guru's conviction and assort vainness on the same.

The Hindus and the Muslims are all one though they may have different habits under the influence of different environments. They are also compounded of the same four elements—earth, air, fire and water. The *Quran* and the *Purana* praise the same God. They all are from one form, and one God had made them all.[1]

The Guru had a vast vision of humanity consisting of variety of races, religions, ideologies and different in appearances but symbolizing unity in plurality in the sense that each of them partakes of the essence, and thus is noble and respectable. In this perspective, the strife stalking the relationship between different people was irrelevant and totally meaningless. The Guru, therefore, made earnest attempts to bring home to his followers or to his prospective audience that the creed labels and geographical considerations should be tanscended to assert fundamental equality. According to Kapur Singh, "Sikhism fully recognizes that the search for a fundamental unity of religions or the attempts at the religious raproachment have their limitation, for there are fundamental differences in the conceptions of Reality and attitude towards the world, permanently impeding a real and lasting synthesis between basically incompatible elements preaches frank and unreserved dialogue between various religions and the human groups that owe allegiance to these religions so as to arrive at the experience that transcends religious particularism and realizes a base of identity underneath all modes of religious expression. As a corollary thereof, Sikhism favours a plural, free, open, and progressive human society. God-oriented, non-aggressive but firm and ever-ready to combat rise and growth of evil through organized resistance and forwarding, yet non-ambitious."

EQUALITY IN TERMS OF PRECEPTOR-DISCIPLE RELATIONS

On March 29, 1699, the Baisakhi day, the tenth Guru floated the Order of the *Khalsa*. He administered *Pahul* to the

---

1. *Devatā adev jachch gandharb Turk Hindū.*
   Niyāre niyāre desan ke bhes ko bhramāu hai.
   Ekai nain ekai kān ekai deh ekai bān.
   Khāk, bād, ātish au āb ko rulāo hai.
   Allah abhekh soī Purān au Kurān oī.
   Ek hī sarūp sabai ek hī banāo hai.86.

five Sikhs who unhesitatingly responded to the call of the Guru to offer their heads thereby fulfilling Guru Nanak's injunction to "enter the quarter of love with their heads on the palms of thy hands."[1]

Guru Gobind Singh honoured them with the title of Guru's Five Beloved Ones. They are ever remembered in the daily prayer of the Sikhs along with his four martyred sons, an honour which with characteristic generosity of Guru Gobind Singh, the unique, the mighty, could confer on sons of the spirit not less dear to him than the sons of his flesh. Just after their baptism, the Guru himself made a request before his disciples to baptize him likewise. This indeed was a unique and deeply meaningful action unparalleled in the world history. Nowhere else has it been seen that the founder of a faith has put himself in such a position of humility and begged of the disciples to confer upon him the faith by giving him what he has already given to them. The significance of this act is deep and abiding. On the basis of this act lay two ideas very crucial for democracy : one, an intellectually apprehended idea which recognized the value and sanctity of the individual personality and places its faith in the capacity of a man's soul to grasp and pursue the good, and the second, the Master not only showed himself to be humble in spirit, thus giving the lesson which he and his predecessors had preached for generations but demonstrated also his identification with his disciples. The disciple, if he/she be true at heart and have dedicated himself to the Master's mission is worthy enough to take Guru's place and in Guru's words, "To meditate on the Name himself and to lead others towards such meditation, their own faces bright with the light divine, they bring salvation to countless others." It is when the Guru has identified humbly with disciples of such devotion and purity that it is just and right for him to change places with them. The Guru loves such disciples as they love him. Both became part of the flame exuding sameness or identification. Love being the base of identification is the seed of development which may be called democracy, equality or by any other name

---

1. *Jao tao prem khelan kā chāo. Sir dhar talī galī merī āo.*
   It mārg pair dharījai. Sir deejai kān na kījai. (SGGS, p. 1412)

political. But all such labels are inadequate, for they lack the dimension of spiritual love, which is the true basis of such relationship.

GENDER EQUALITY—STATUS OF WOMEN

In Sikhism, the issue of the status of women has been tackled from many angles. Scriptural support has been extended in favour of woman that she is not at all inferior to a man. Guru Nanak says, "From the woman is our birth, in the woman's womb are we are shaped. To the woman are we engaged and to the woman are we wedded. Woman is our friend and from woman is our family. If woman dies, we seek another; women are the bonds of the world. Why do we call women evil who give birth to kings. From the woman is the woman, without woman there is none, except God the creator. Verily, society the home, and the country where there is a true woman of divine virtues, are honoured, and become dignified and exalted in the *Darbar* of the True One."[1]

From this spiritual authority, it is clear that woman was assigned the status, in no way, inferior to a man. In fact home, society and country are honoured only if woman is held in esteem.

The Gurus in some of their compositions address themselves in feminine gender in relation to God. God himself acts as a woman. Metaphysical argument is also harnessed to impress upon the people that woman occupies equal status to man. It is held that since all mankind is emanation of God, it is ridiculous and unjust to deny equality to woman. Guru Arjan says, "Thou art my father thou art my mother", *(Tūṅ merā pitā tūṅ hai merā mātā)* he does not make use of Mata—

---

1. *Bhaṅḍ(i) jamīai bhaṅḍ(i) nimīai bhaṅḍ(i) maṅgan(u) vīāh(u).*
   Bhaṅḍauh hovai dostī bhaṅḍauh chalai rāh(u).
   Bhaṅḍ(u) muā bhaṅḍ(u) bhālīai bhaṅḍ(i) hovai baṅdhān(u).
   So kio maṅḍā ākhīai jit(u) jameh rājān.
   Bhaṅḍauh hī bhaṅḍ(u) ūpjai bhaṅḍai bājh na koe.
   Nanak bhaṅḍai bāharā eko sachā soe.
   Jit(u) mukh(i) sadā sālāhīai bhāgā(ṅ) ratī chār(i).
   Nanak te mukh ūjale tit(u) sachai darbār(i).   (SGGS, p. 473)

Mother—in feminine gender, thereby pointing out that physical differences also have no meaning in determining the status of women.

Against the background of spiritual-cum-metaphysical thoughts vis-a-vis woman as delineated above, Guru Gobind Singh discussed further the status of women. He did not regard 'woman' as hurdle or obstruction on the path of ultimate goal of self-realization. He rejected ascetisicm or renunciation as the pre-requisite and regarded householder's life if led in a righteous manner, superior to that of an ascetic, and was not contradictory to the Moral Order. In fact, in the reckoning of the Guru, the Moral Order was meaningless if it was not to be realized in this world. To regard woman a 'temptress' or 'seductress' or 'unclean' was preposterous in his eyes. Guru Gobind Singh's remarks in this context were pertinently magnificent. The discipline of *Sannyas*, (renunciation) consists of going to the forest after leaving one's home, getting the hair matted and performing ablutions, growing long nails, getting instructions from the Guru Yogi, applying ashes on the whole body. Instead of all these Yogic rituals, the Guru says, that one should live in one's house and develop moral virtues and remember God. One should enjoy all gifts of nature with moderation. A home can provide the environment of a forest if one is anchorite at heart. Countenance will be better than a Yogi's matted hair which is nothing but hypocrisy. Instead of getting instructions from a Yogi, one should listen to one's own inner self—*Atam Updesho*. One can see one's real self and soul of the world and can realise the Supreme Being in his own home by eating frugally, sleeping frugally, coupled with qualities of love, mercy and forbearance, by practicing mildness and patience and by keeping away lust, wrath, covetousness, and obstinacy from one's mind.[1]

---

1. *Re man aiso kar(i) sanyāsā.*
   Ban se sadan sabai kar(i) samjhoh man hī māhe udāsā.1. Rahāo.
   Jat kī jaṭā jog ko majjan nem ke nakhun baḍhāo.
   Gyān gurū ātam updesoh nām bhibhūt lagāo.
   Alap ahār sulap sī niṅdrā dayā chhimā tan preet(i).
   Seel saṅtokh sadā nirbāhebo hvaibo trigun atīt.
   Kām krodh haṅkār lobh haṭh, moh na man mo liāvai.
   Tab hī ātam tat ko dursai param purakh kah pāvai. (*Ramkali Patshahi*-10)

Family being the smallest but the most important social unit was sure to draw the attention of the Guru. A close study of the utterances of the Gurus would show that they all recognized this institution as the most fundamental salient of our social structure but they wanted a change in its conceptual structure and in the relation between different members of the family. The Guru never viewed this institution either as patriarchal unit or matriarchal unit because he never recognized the supreme authority of the eldest male member or the eldest female member in a family. He, on the other hand, wanted harmonious relationship among the members of the family on equal terms. In his views the principle of division of work and responsibilities was the right basis of relationship between different members of the family, and this being so, its each member was as important as the other. Father was a father only if he performed the duties bestowed upon him by divine order, and mother was ordained to function as a mother. From the point of procreation, either sex is equal, and in fact, it is co-operative effort of both the partners that procreation takes place. In no case, either sex, individually or conjointly, with the opposite sex can create anything, which is the miracle of God but an ability that He has vested in both parents equally.

The institution of family is very closely knit with marriage, which to a great extent, is the fulcrum of family, as also its adhesive. This is why at all places where people began to make conscious effort to grow as a civilized group, marriage was considered to be a sacrament. Indians were no exception to it. Guru Gobind Singh also recognized the fact and regarded marriage very sacred and an act deserving God's benediction. It is really an irony that bridegrooms regard themselves superior to their brides, and do not feel abashed at their demands of dowry and other favours. Sikhism has condemned this attitude of the males and have regarded both of them two flames of the same light *(ek jyoti doe murti)*. The variegated customs, which have grown around marriage, are meaningless accretions. Sex, of course, is a natural act of husband-wife relationship for furtherance of creation but to treat sexual gratification as the chief object of marriage tantamounts to reducing oneself to animal level. The Guru says that the marriage should not be regarded as a union of bodies. If it is so, then this union may break at any level. Bodies go on changing and with the passage of time deterioration sets in physical beauty. Therefore he says that marriage instead of being a union of bodies should be a union of souls, of minds, leading to love of each other's qualities and care for each other's well-being.[1] It is only in this context, which is at once moral and spiritual that marriage is *Anand*. *Anand* is different from pleasure although marriage signifies a physical relationship but ideals are embodied into it when it goes beyond a mere sensory experience. The word *Anand* indicates a physical immanence as well as a spiritual transcendence. The withdrawal from the physical by the ascetic monk was substituted by the realization of transcendence of *Anand*. The fulfilment was thus more meaningful and more valuable.

Guru Gobind Singh conceived in this unit of society a partial realization of God, as in the establishment of the *Khalsa* he had conceived a total realization of the Supreme Being. All the social units in the *Khalsa Order* are really the evolutionary stages of the manifestation of God, of the *Sargonisation* of the *Nirguna,* of the actualization of the possible of the potential. The first and the foremost step is the intimately fastened tie of man and woman in marriage. God manifested in this universe through the principle of His will which appeared in opposites : *Haumai* and *Nam,* individuation and universalisation. This bi-polar nature of reality continues till we reach the moral man as the higher achievement. The combination of man and woman in the highest moral order is the unity of bipolarity, the first achievement of ultimate *Anand*. Mating is a universal characteristic but mating in the moral order is possible only in man, hence *Anand*. Thus marriage in Sikhism has a metaphysical, moral and spiritual base.

It is against this background that Guru Gobind Singh rejected polygamous views. The polygamous or polyandrous marriages would run counter to the spirit of equality between

---

1. *Vār Marū Mohallā 3.* (SGGS, p. 1086)

the genders. Only monogamous marriages fit in the conceptual and operational framework of the institution of family. Guru Gobind Singh has roundly condemned sexual adultery. In the 21st Chapter of *Charitro Pakhyan,* it is described that when once a woman, on pretext of seeking initiation to Guru's discipleship succeeded in getting audience with him, she made advances, and the Guru quipped :

"How can I forsake my married life and play fond with you. How shall I face the judge on the day of judgement."

He addressed her as daughter and child to awaken in her sense of morality. He also reiterated his father's advice to her. He said, "When I had become a little grown-up, then my father, my Guru, my guide got a pledge from me. That so long there is a breath in me; I shall cherish ever increasing love with my wife and shall not, not even by mistake in a dream, share the bed of any other woman."

"Coveting other woman is playing with a dagger in disguise. Such an indulgence is a virtual death. Such a man deserves the death of a dog."[1] There can be no separation between husband and wife. The tie is fundamentally final. The couple, under the guidance of the Guru will overcome lapses and lacunae with conscious and continuous efforts and will learn to create harmony, adjustment, not just co-existence but fusion of minds and souls. A family is a *Khalsa* in miniature. It is a *Sangat,* a commune, the smallest unit and the first step towards the actualization of God in society in the form of *Khalsa.* The principle of this actualization is stated in : Ik Sikh, Doi Sadh Sang, Panjin Parmeshwar. Guru Gobind Singh with his characteristic vigour and clarity implored his disciple, "Treat every woman except one's own wife as a sister, daughter, or mother according to one's age." The Guru laid special emphasis on this both from social and spiritual aspects. In times of contemporary turbulent conditions, opportunities were likely to arise which could tempt the stronger to molest/ humiliate the ladies of the weak or the defeated and thus it was considered essential to issue such injunctions. Since family

1. *Dasam Granth,* pp. 838-842 as quoted by Dr. Sher Singh in his book *Social and Political Philosophy of Guru Gobind Singh.*

was conceived as a fundamental unit and central to the spiritual-social rise of a man—its sanctity was to be maintained at all costs and hence the dictum *Eka nari jati* (man with one wife is a true celibate). The status of woman in Sikh family is as respectable as that of a man. Both wife and husband forms a single coherent growing/harmonious whole marching in togetherness, towards the highest ideal displaying their commitment to strengthen social relationships in spirit of love and harmony.

Guru Gobind Singh, proclaimed the futility of going to the forests in search of God or to seek there a union with Him. A call for return to home and family was powerfully made by him. A new ethics of family relations was held high in place of the earlier social ethics, which supported withdrawal from the family as the necessary condition for freedom from bondage.

Female Infanticide

The practice of female infanticide has been denounced in Sikhism as it negates the ethical norms, spiritual and social equality of human beings. The origin of this practice has been traced to various causes. A scholar suggests that 'in Rome, Greece, Arabia, India and China, women of the upper classes, relieved by the males of the hard tasks both as an effort to keep them young and as a sign of rank became an economic burden and consequently infanticide fell mainly on the females."[1] It is also held that the difficulty of arranging a dowry for daughters as well as meeting other demands of the bridegroom and his family contributed to the selection of female children for infanticide in China and India. Further the origin of this custom is traced to the Ancestor Cults.[2]

According to A.M. Hocart "The ancestor cults in Greece, Rome, India and China could be transmitted only through the males and this also led to the destruction of girl infants.[3]

Obviously, all the causes itemized above have either originated due to the perversion of human mind or in the

1. A.M. Hocart, 'Infanticide', *Encyclopaedia of the Social Sciences* (ed.) E.R.A. Saligman and A. Johnson, Vol. VII, pp. 27-28.
2. *Ibid.*
3. *Ibid.*

appropriation of privileges by males or in the deep-rooted superstitions. Guru Gobind Singh like his predecessors did not give credence to any of the causes and averred that infanticide was immoral and therefore despicable. In one of his fiats to the *Khalsa* he made it an unpardonable sin and enjoined upon his followers not to regard the persons indulging in it as Sikhs. In *Rehat Nama* by Bhai Prehlad Singh, it is stated, "He who is a Sikh and deals with one indulging in female infanticide would be led to disaster ultimately." In another formulary, it is said, "Sikhs should not entertain even in mind the relationship with those indulging in female infanticide."[1]

UNIVERSAL BROTHERHOOD

The ideal of social equality is not the ultimate aim of the ethics of Sikhism. The equality may be maintained without feeling affection or regard for the person who is held to be equal but such bare equality would not be enough because it does not conform to the ideal of humanistic morality. Therefore it is essential that it should be doped with idea of spiritual unity of mankind. Thus the material content to the social ethics in Sikhism is provided from the same premises of spiritual unity which was used for proping up human equality. Guru Gobind Singh's ideas in this regard are very expressive. He says, "As out of a single fire millions of spark arise in separation but come together again when they fall back in the fire; as from a heap of dust, particles of dust swept up fill the air, and then fall in the heap of dust; as out of single stream countless waves rise up, and being water, fall back in the water again; so from God's form emerge animate and inanimate things and since they arise from Him, they shall fall in Him again." The Guru in this statement asserts that everyone ought to treat everyone else as member of the same human brotherhood. Earlier, his predecessor Gurus had also made such assertions. Guru Arjan Dev says, "Thou art our only father, we are all thy children."[2] He was much pained at the

---

1. Desa Singh, *Rehatnama*.
2. *Ek pitā ekas ke hum bārik, tu mera gur hāī.*   (*SGGS*, p. 611)

attitude of 'duality' of certain people and had to make a very significant remark that true meeting with the Guru implied abandonment of the sense of duality. In fact the Guru equates the meeting of the Guru with the demolition of the walls of 'otherness'—the other being a cosharer of the same source of emanation and a part of the same spiritual order. The universal brotherhood is thus linked together by bonds stronger than family or national affiliations. In Guru Gobind Singh's vision, "The whole humanity is one. That a man is to be honoured not because he belongs to this or that caste or creed but because he is a man, an emanation of God whom God has given the same senses and the same soul from Himself as to the other men.[1] The Guru disliked the segmentation of the humanity on grounds of different modes of worship, appearances, castes, creeds and wished the people to cultivate right perspective and understanding so that they might be able to appreciate that there is an essential unity of human kind. Without realising this truth, "fools have wrangled and died over discussion of these differences."[2] They are incapable of realising that one should "Recognise the whole of humanity as one in spirit."[3] According to J.S. Ahluwalia, "Sikh religion is universal. It is not an ethnicity specific, region specific or caste specific religion. The different ethnicities of the first five Sikhs initiated into the *Order of the Khalsa* through the sacrament of holy *Amrit* by Guru Gobind Singh mean that this religion is not bound down to particular ethnicity. Guru Gobind Singh in his composition (*Akal Ustat*), refers to different people in terms of their ethnic identities co-worshipping God. Contemporary ethnicised Punjabiaised form of Sikhism is just one of the possibly many more determinate forms of Sikh religion flowing out in other ethnic contexts. New ethno-religious species, developing out of the parental genus would really make a religion embodying universalism and upholding as one of its cornerstones. Sikhism is also not tied down to a

---

1. D.P. Ashta, *The poetry of Dasam Granth*, p. 190.
2. *Kart birudh gae mar(i) mūṛā.*
   Prabh ko raṅg(u) na lāgā gūṛā.20.   (*Chaubis Avtars*)
3. *Akal Ustat*, 87.

particular region, though the Punjab is the natural habitat of Sikhism where it has grown during the last five hundred years. The whole of Earth planet having revered as 'mother' in Guru Nanak's *Japji, (Pavan guru, pani pita mata dhart mahat...)* there is no specific holy land or promised land conceived as such in Sikhism." According to Professor Avtar Singh, "The argument of the Guru seems to be that brotherhood is a reality but is not visible because of the pall of ego or *Haumai* (individuation). Once this partitioning pall is removed, the relationship should be visible clearly. As a matter of fact, the whole of social ethics of the Sikhs is oriented towards the demolition of this (false) wall of separation, and the realisation of order and still wider identification is indicative of the progressive realization of the ideal."

The greatest hinderances to the realization of the ideal of universal brotherhood are slander and enmity. So far as slander is concerned, Guru Gobind is profuse in his utterances against this evil. Like his predecessors for instance, Guru Arjan regards *Nindak* the person who does not find peace here and hereafter.[1] Slandering others amount to putting their filth into one's own mouth.[2]

This evil causes mutual distrust and suspicion among the smaller social groups but may also poison the social relationship among much larger groups like different religions. Social value of the slanderer is negative as he is not considered trustworthy. He is, in fact, a sick member of the society. Enmity is the desire to cause harm and pain to others. Guru Arjan Dev says, "Why entertain enmity. God pervades everywhere. Enmity puts premium on the sense of otherness which the Guru wished to eradicate to enable one to realise identity of the spirit among all people."

Evil has to be fought but it must be done without any feeling of enmity towards other persons. Bhai Nand Lal says, "Injury to any person is an injury to the Creator. He is the soul and life of creation." God being the sublimest love (*Preet preete–Jaap*, 68), breathes love to all (*Puran prem ki preet sabare—Akal*

---

1. *Arṛāve billāvai niṅdak(u).*
   Pārbrahm(u) parmesar(u) bisariā āpnā kītā pāvai niṅdak(u). (373)
2. *Par niṅdā par mal(u) mukh sudhī agn(i) krodh chaṅḍāl.*(15)

Ustat, 244) and pervades everywhere in the form of love (*Jaap*, 80). It becomes, therefore, imperative for a disciple to shed sense of enmity and cherish and enjoy divine love."

ALTRUISM—CONSIDERING THE WELFARE AND HAPPINESS OF ALL

In Sikhism, another social ideal is the welfare and happiness of others before one's own. This ideal in the modern parlance is known as altruism. This ideal has been adequately praised in Sikhism. Bhai Gurdas says, "The test of a good man is that he seeks the welfare of others always. The bad man is selfish. He does no good to others. An altruist is far away from egocentricity. His is a heart always anxious to serve anybody without accepting or deeming any reward whatsoever. He/she regards altruism as an opportunity to receive divine sanctification since the Creator is present in His creation. Naturally any altruistic activity done in a spirit of selflessness takes one nearer to God. Altruism implies love and concern of human beings for others and thus enables them to completely moralize themselves. The Gurus, therefore, had always stressed on *par-upkar* (Good service to others) as the cardinal virtue, and true to this spirit almost all the moral codes *(Rehatnamas)* compiled by contemporaries or semi-contemporaries of Guru Gobind Singh affirmed this aspect. The compiler of *Prem Sumarg* says, "When food is ready, pray for someone to come and share your food so that your food may be sanctified." If a needy person turns up, consider him/her to be an answer to your prayer. In case no one comes, you ought to go out and seek out someone and if by chance no one is available, lay aside some food to be served in emergency. Bhai Chaupa Singh in consonance with this strain required the Sikhs to consider altruistic service to the needy as 'rendition to the Guru'.

CHAPTER XX

EPILOGUE

Guru Gobind Singh's earthly life spanned nearly forty-two years. During this period his accomplishments were many-fold and had a deep impact on the contemporary society. His personal example and his ideology both were a watershed in the history of mankind. He brought to culmination and perfection what his predecessors had preached, practised, up-held and then institutionalised the same, so that these might continue to play their role in the Society. He improved upon the inistitutions of *Guru Ka Langar, Sangat* and *Kirtan* et al. The conceptual frame-work, in respect of some of them, were made more comprehensive, more clear and even more wide-ranging. For instance *Sangat* was connoted as *Panth* and *Guru Ka Langar* became the mainstay of Sikh economic edifice. He abolished *Masand* system that had outlived its utility and it had become rife with corruption, loose morals, unscrupuloussness, jobbery and schismatic activities of its officials. Instead he established a wide network of *Sangats* connected directly with the Guru or *Bani*. Such *Sangats* that had linked themselves with the Guru without any intermediary were known as *Khalsa*. The individuals also were referred to as such if they too forged direct links with the Guru. To keep such *Sangats* and individuals vibrant and firm in their faith in the Guru, the Guru sent his special agents off and on. They were however asked to be guided by the *Word* as enshrined in *Sri Guru Granth Sahib*. These steps engendered compactness and solidarity among the Sikhs besides strengthening their bond with the Guru and his ideology. This being the perspective, sects such as *Ram Rayyas, Minas, Dhirmalias* could not substantially harm the Sikh religion as well as Sikh society.

As the compactness of the Sikhs grew, they ceased to be a force hostile to the growth of Sikh movement, ideologically as well as socially.

Lest this contemplated compactness go loose and astray, he institutionalised it on the 29th March, 1699 on the Baisakhi day. He set afloat a new *Order* to be called *Khalsa* consisting of people—males/females, knit together in the love of the Almighty and the commitments to be new men and women with new vision of society, transcendental in their out-look and actions. They would be free from the bondages of lineage and social-spiritual inheritance, believing in oneness of God, His fatherhood of mankind and unity of mankind on basis of spiritual and social equality as their faith, ever seeking guidance from no one other than Guru Gobind Singh and *Sri Guru Granth Sahib*. Each *Khalsa* like the *Khalsa* as a social category was expected to behave, believe and act as per the norms, laid down by the Guru for the *Khalsa* brotherhood to be observed at macro level. Such institutionalised form of the *Khalsa* was obviously a novel social model of society as well as of an individual; whose field of action was neither confined to any geographical boundaries, nor a race or a creed but the whole mankind. *Khalsa* ideals were therefore cast and moulded on ethics which did not recognise any social or religious boundary and political particularism, but was rooted in ecumenical conscience—transformed as such by the message of the Guru that urged the *Khalsa* to base it on the spiritual vision of the Guru typified in the following utterance, "He is Father and we all are His children." It was in this background that he never occupied any territory even though he could do so. Later on when the *Khalsa* had to wage war against the Mughals and the Afghans, the dominant impulse was to establish such a society that might reflect the lofty teachings of the Guru.

Such doings were obviously no ordinary achievements. These were certainly historical milestones. The list of Guru's achievements is not exhausted with what has been registered above. His contributions to metaphysical thought were a landmark. He propounded the concept of Reality with more clarity and forthrightness. His relationship with man and universe brought out clearly its distinctiveness and differentiation vis-a-vis other prevalent concepts and traditions. The Guru wrote a full poem *Jaap* in which he enumerated numerous names of God, each one symbolising one of His attributes. One gathers impression that Guru's God was absolute and also attributed. He was transcendental and immanent at the same time. He in His immanent aspect as a spirit permeates and pervades the whole universe. In the Guru's thinking, the absolute-in-itself is indeterminate, but it also becomes determinate as *Karta Purkh*. This being so, the absolute has determinate relationship with man and the phenomenal reality with His world of time and space. It was under the impact of this conviction that the Guru used many names for God which reveal that God functioned in the world among the terrestrial beings and for certain purposes which were not only spiritual but mundane as well but always within a certain design. From this, it also follows that the Guru's Supreme Reality admits Supreme Being not as a determinate being or as a creative spirit but also the reality of determinate things in the realm of becoming. Thus the Guru reckoned that world and God had organic relationship expressed in unity of spirit in which the individual retains his subjectivity and individuality. Man of the world being emanation of God and determinate beings, could not be valueless as had been held for a long time in Indian idealistic tradition. Rather they had a role to play to achieve certain goals. To be righteous and to establish righteousness at all costs, and so see that the whole world followed righteousness was an article of faith with the Guru.

In the *Vedantic* tradition of Indian thought, the identity of the individual self and the universal self means only the identity of the two in their abstract beingness and not in their organic wholeness. *Atma* is a part or form of *Brahma*. The identity relationship between the two being that enclosed in space and outer, unbounded external space. The enclosedness of space corresponds to the embodiment of *Brahm-Atma* in human form. Salvation here would obviously mean the knowledge that the inner and outer are identical in nature. This is self-transcendence to a state of abstract being, where the self loses its organic existentiality, its subjectivity and its *Namrupa* individuality. In Ramanuja's *Theistic Vedanta* also, the determinate *(Namrup)* existential reality of the self is sought to be merged into the absolute as an inflowing river becomes one with the ocean without retaining its distinctiveness. In Sikhism this is not so. Individual and the absolute have an identity but it is in nature of an organic relationship expressed in the unity of spirit where individual retains its individuality as also its subjectivity, the two forms being united in the oneness of spirit and certainly not dualistic or antagonistic. Self-transcendence here means self-realisation in union with God.

"The human state, being the body form is therefore not a fall. It is a *Karmic* punishment, in the shape of separation from *Brahman*. It is rather a God-given opportunity which the self through self-realisation has to transform from an 'object' into 'subject' full of self-consciousness and will-power. He comes to partake the qualities of the Divine given by the ethical attributes of Godhead in *Jaap*. He, as such, becomes prepared as a self-conscious instrument for realising the Divine Will on earth. A prior identity of spirit between the self and the absolute becomes an identification of the individual and the Divine Will. At this stage the victory of a man in righteous action as a categorical imperative is seen as the victory of the Divine *"Wahe Guru Ji Ka Khalsa Waheguru Ji Ki Fateh."* The righteous actions are to be performed imperatively on planet Earth, which is not to be shunned and treated abhorrently. Rather it should be respected as the veritable field for man to realise the self within as part of Self. The self-realisation or realising reality is different from that which is understood and made out in Indian idealistic tradition. *Brahma* is not only *Sat Chit* but *Anand* also, which means a state of harmony, calmness, equilibrium and equipoise. In fact this characteristic of *Brahma* flows from its homogeneity given by underlying spatial conception of time. Therefore it has no historicity. In individual life the principle of harmony takes the form of *Nirvana* in Budhism and *Smadhi* in Yoga. The corresponding state in Sikhism being *Sahaj Avastha* but with a qualitative difference. This is not a state of passive but a dynamic active equilibrium which in fact means orderliness of cosmos. That orderliness which comes into being in consonance with *Hukm* or Divine Will. Such will is not static and is always at work both from outside and inside human beings, impelling them to move towards a purposeful direction. In the Guru's thinking, matter in some mysterious union with consciousness conceives and comes to partake of the three principles namely organisation, development and disintegration which operate the universe from within thereby making it an autonomous world with inherent temporal processes, programmed for God's design. The external will, having once charged into universe, works as the internal law *(Hukm)* of the autonomous world. "What he willed, He put into the world once for all."

From this, it follows that in Sikhism the process of change is religiously valid. All changes or developments are also accepted as real. It was created in consonance with *Hukm* that permeates it as a spirit. Certainly material world is not permanent but it is not unreal at the same time. Thus perceived permanence (The continuation of a thing in its original state of being all the time) is no more equated with Reality.

Metaphysical thoughts of the Guru especially about Reality, man, universe and their inter-relationship formed the foundation for a fresh model of society, value pattern and polity that were markedly novel. These were progressive and highly conducive to the onward development of mankind at all levels, local, national and international. God, man and society began to be looked upon as bound together in organic wholeness.

The Universe, time and space being both creation and abode of the Divine, came to be looked upon as real. The self in relation to God retained its *Namrup* existentiality. The union with Divine meant the union of spirit and not the self-submerging unity of substance. Salvation thus came to be seen as self-realisation in the absolute sense and not self-annihilation. The self, in relation to society, kept intact its individuality and no more was required to be subsumed under holistic categories of society (say of caste). The innate goodness of man was stressed upon. Evil was derived not from the aboriginal sinful nature of man or the *Karmic* recompense, or the state of embodiment of dissociated *Atman* in phenomenal form. It was rather traced back to the contingent imperfection and perversion of social system, with a belief in the essential perfectibility of society through collective, organised social effort.

In consonance with such thinking, the Guru redefined and redesigned the role which one was expected to play as an individual and as a component of the society. As an individual, he must purgate himself of the evil impulses and elevate himself by fine tuning himself/herself with the Supreme Reality to realise that he was a part of the same as a ray of light is no different than as its source. Full realisation of the Self would mean state of equipoise or of bliss. But he is not to treat himself aloof from the creation. He should feel and realise that the Divine spirit residing in him is also permeating in his fellow beings. To reach this stage he was required not to resort to miracle, wrong beliefs, rituals, fasts, pilgrimages, egoistic activities but to meditate, contemplate and realise the all-pervading spirit of God within and to act in the light thereof. By pleading and exhorting as such, the Guru, once for all, broke the unnecessary fetters and shackles of clericalism, *Karam-Kand*, outmoded, hackneyed religio-social formulations especially about Reality and his relation with human beings. Perhaps for the first time, in the history of religions in India, the Guru very explicitly put forth that in the process of self-realisation and self-illumination, one need no intermediary and the only course is the elevation of man through self-effort not outside this world but within it.

Since self-effort on earth cannot be an isolated act, one has to take care of the people around. Since all have spirit of God within them, there should be natural affinity between one another, something that has to be discovered and realized. This spiritual realization is the foundation of a model society in the reckoning of the Guru. Therefore the Guru suggests umpteen times through his compositions and actions that one should not lose sight of this fact while working and functioning in the world. It was from this perspective that the Guru squarely and roundly condemned caste system, being discriminatory in its functioning. This system was also denounced for its being wrongly considered Divine and therefore predetermined and confirmed for all times. The upward movement of the lower sections into the higher levels of society could only be through a cultural process named as *Sanskritisation* by M.K. Srinivas. According to it, a lower caste, having circumstantially acquired wealth or power would be admitted into the higher structure of the caste bound society only after he gives up its original identity, emulate and adopt the caste denominations, identity and behaviour pattern of the higher castes. The Guru totally rejected this approach. He provided social equality, moral sanctity, and veritable mobility for the so-called lower classes and sections of society in their own right and with their own self-identity.

Denying equality in terms of sexes, classes and professions, was also rejected by the Guru as grossly unspiritual and totally violative of Sikh social ethics. The ultimate goal of Sikh social ethics was to build egalitarian, harmoneous, non-exploitive, free from fetters of clericalism, superstitious society. A society that is filled with and fired by the mission to strive both at individual and corporate levels to enable people feel confident and filled with the spirit of elevating the standard of the community (*Sarbat Da Bhala*).

In Sikh parlance such society was the *Khalsa* society whose each member was designated *Khalsa*. It was formally brought into existence on the Baisakhi of 1699. *Khalsa* was a model of humanity on the lines of divinity and the *Khalsa* society was the model society as the Almighty had ordained. The Guru was so proud of it that he exclaimed that God Himself has created it out of his own *Will*. *Khalsa* as an individual also filled the Guru with sense of satisfaction—so much so that Guru considered him as his own limb and his own life.

And very rightly the Guru perceived as such. Was it not *Khalsa*, an ideal being, committed to the ordainment of the Guru and pledged to their implementation till their last breath ? Was not the *Khalsa* society a model society pledged to act and cast itself in social ethics as propounded by the Guru ? It was not to work on any narrow particularistic principle for a particular region or country—rather it was to work for God's cause whose notion and arena of action had been clearly delineated by Guru Gobind Singh. Any cause of righteousness was God's cause and righteousness in the Guru's reckoning was anything that helped people to blossom and fructify in the light of the supreme Spirit. Obviously actions which aim at the destruction of the evil forces or obstruct the progress of the *Khalsa* society to its cherished destination are righteous. Such actions include even the use of arms albeit as a last resort. In this context, the Guru's views were clear and are embodied in the following verse of *Zafarnama.*

> *Chun kar az hama hilte dar guzasht.*
> *Halal ast burdan ba shamshir dast.*

"When all means fail, it is legitimate to make use of sword."

The *Khalsa* society was the objectification of what the *Khalsa* stood for, an organization of the *Khalsa*, a model social pattern, a methodology of revitalising decadent society and civilization, the latter being the discovery of Arnold Toynbee who regarded *Khalsa* society as a proper response to the decaying Indian civilization but which unfortunately could not come out of its womb. But it did signify many important points.

Firstly—it considered itself sovereign, fearless and free, accountable only to God; Sovereign of the Sovereigns. It rejected the notion of political sovereignty vesting either in the king as his Divine right, or in a state or in any party. Instead it favoured sovereignty to vest in the collectively expressed will of the people.

Secondly—it was averse to homogenization of group identities into monastic uniformity. On social level, this means that a group has an inviolable right to participate in its corporate capacity in the body politic of the society or to express it otherwise. *Khalsa* society would accord full respect to religio-cultural and political pluralism.

Thirdly—each member of the *Khalsa* society was made to feel that he/she was not different from the Guru. In fact, the Guru demonstrated perfect equality between the Master and Disciple by receiving *Pahul* at the hands of his disciples and by implication awarding Divine status to man.

The step was unique and unparalleled because never

before in the history of any religion or nation, master had ever declared Master-Disciple identity discrimination. On this account Bhai Gurdas Singh became lyrical and could not help praising the Guru as *Waryam Akela* (Hero Unique) and Master-Disciple, incomparable and unsurpassable. The Guru sanctified common humanity condemned and despised for millennia by those code-makers who chose to forget the common origin of man from the Divine essence and invented instead a new fiction whereby the poor labouring folk were ordained to be born servitors in this world and condemned to a place away from redemption in the world hereafter.

The *Khalsa* society as profiled above was very clear about the Reality of God. His omnipotence, His relationship with man, its ultimate goal of improving the lot of the whole mankind through righteous deeds, its unflinching faith in the protectiveness of God, its being model in its objectives and configuration, its individual and social ethics, its democratic vision, its unique polity which vested sovereignty in the people, its equalitarianism, its universalistic outlook.

From its very inception *Khalsa Panth* came into clash with all those forces—which clashed with the *Khalsa* ideals. It had to face Mughal state believing in absoluteness of the power of its sovereign who was committed to implement *Shariat* in toto, and convert the whole of India into the land of Islam. In such a state, non-Muslims were subjected to a variety of severities so that they might feel constrained to embrace Islam. After a long drawn-out fight, the *Khalsa Panth* succeeded in thwarting their nefarious designs in the Punjab, the region where it had entrenched itself. It had to fight another enemy in one of the renowned invader and statesman of Asia, Ahmed Shah Abadali. Against him too, the *Khalsa Panth* achieved remarkable successes. At least in the region from the Khaiber to the suburb of Delhi, people were made to breath the air of freedom. Also, it had to face violent opposition from the orthodox Hindu elements who too vehemently opposed the *Khalsa* ideals. The Guru had to fight battles against the Rajput rulers of Hill states of Shivalik and Kumaon regions of the Himalayas who spearheaded Hindu conservative elements. At long last, the Guru succeeded in blunting the edge of their orthodoxy when many of them entered the *Khalsa Panth*. The Hindu conservatives by and large, stopped opposing the *Khalsa Panth* openly and violently but the change in their attitude reflected more of expediency than the appreciation of their ideology.

All through the difficult period of trials and tribulations, the *Khalsa* society showed remarkable courage, spirit of sacrifice, extraordinary resoluteness, very high standard of morality and personal character. These facts find appropriate attestation even from a person who was an enemy of the *Khalsa*. He was *Qazi* Nur Mahammad who came to India with Ahmed Shah Abdali's seventh invasion of the country (1764-65) and was an eye-witness to the Sikh battles with the invader. In his poetic account of the Durrani's invasion, in Persian language, he referred to the Sikhs in a rude and derogatory language but could not at the same time help proclaiming their many natural virtues. He said : "Do not call them 'dogs' (his contumelious term for the Sikhs), for they are lions, and are courageous like lions in the field of battle. If you have to learn the art of war, 'come and face them in the field.' They will demonstrate it to you in such a way that one and all will praise them for it. Singh is a title (a form of address) for them. If you do not know the Hindustani language, I shall, tell you that the word 'Singh' means a lion. Truly, they are like lions in the battlefield and in times of peace, they surpass *Hatim* in generosity."

"Leaving aside their mode of fighting, there was another point in which they excel all other martial people. In no case would they slay a coward, nor would they put an obstacle in the way of a fugitive. They do not plunder the wealth and ornaments of a woman, be she a well-to-do lady or a maid-servant. There is no adultery among these 'dogs'. They do not make friends with adulterers and house breakers."

Ultimately they succeeded in the establishment of their sovereign state. Their success was due to the inspiration of the Gurus and their ideology of guaranteeing all round integrated development of individuals as well as of the whole man-kind. This fact is amply borne by the different coins issued by Banda Singh Bahadur and Sikh *misaldars*. They had been issued in the name of the Guru. The inscriptions in Persian, the official language of the day, stated.

By the Grace of the True Lord is struck the coin in the two worlds. The sword of Nanak is the guarantee of all desires and victory is of Guru Gobind Singh, the King of the kings.

The reverse carried an inscription (in Persian) in praise of the new capital described as 'city of peace'. An official seal was introduced for authentication of state documents. It had an inscription (in Persian). *The Kettle and Sword (symbols of Prosperity and power) and victory and ready patronage have been obtained from Guru Nanak and Guru Gobind Singh.*

The *First Khalsa Sovereign* state was formed by Banda Singh Bahadur in the Punjab which was destroyed by the Mughal power. Even this reverse did not break the morale of the Sikhs which had its nourishment from the *Khande-ki-Pahul* of Guru Gobind Singh. They again rose and re-established their sovereignty, this time under *Misaldars* who after some time instead of working in the light of the teaching of the Guru succumbed to the temptation of behaving like absolute monarchs displaying all evils of the decadent Mughal rulers. The result was that their territories were grabbed by one of them, Maharaja Ranjit Singh.

His was a monarchy which was in reality an aberration because a military monarchy was far from anything that the tenth Guru had contemplated. Neither the *Misl* Chiefs nor the Maharaja respected the spirit of selection based *Panch Pardhani* democracy which was the essence of Guru Gobind Singh's concept.

The military monarch could not liquidate the spirit and the vision of the model society, that the Sikhs had inherited from Guru Gobind Singh and his predecessors. When the political system organized by Ranjit Singh broke down after his death, Sikh soldiers realised the gravity of the situation and their religious consciousness led them to the conclusion that the *Khalsa* alone, not the selfish and short-sighted nobility, guided by the tradition of the *Misl* period or the puppet swayed by court intrigues, could save the sovereign state. The old democratic tradition, submerged for more than half a century reasserted itself. The army, organized in *Panchayats*, assumed the charge with deliberate intention of doing what the leadership had failed to do. That they would fail was inevitable. They were not strong enough to resist the combined onslaught of British Imperialism and the self-seeking Sikh aristocracy. But through their efforts, the essence of Sikhism based in Guru Gobind Singh's ideology emerged triumphant even though the Sikh state succumbed to an alien power. Their ideals, vision of society and sense of mission never allowed the *Khalsa* to be passive. Rather they were actuated to be ever dynamic participant in the activities of the world for the righteousness to prevail. This finds its testimony in Akali Movement (1920-25) which was essentially movement against the evils that had plagued the *Khalsa Panth* rendering it static and unprogressive. It was also against those who helped the evil designs to continue and corrode the import of the Guru's ideology. Their participation in freedom struggle of India was also epitomic of their faith in the Guru's ideology which clashed with the oppressiveness of the Imperial structure of the British colonial rule. In the present day world, the *Khalsa Panth* in spite of various allurements and entanglements continues to be stirred by Guru Gobind Singh's example and his mission.

The Guru's ideological impact was not confined to his followers alone. It touched a vast spectrum of people, even beyond the land of the five rivers, in the whole sub-continent. The Guru's vitriolic comments on Hindus' understanding of Reality and His relations with human beings, their social philosophy and social formulation and their recognition of rituals and ceremonies etc. as the legitimate artifices for regeneration and ultimate emancipation caused a ferment among many of the Hindus who when juxtaposed their cherished institution and concepts with those of the Guru found substance in what the Guru said. Naturally, they re-evaluated their religious and social heritage against the background of their sad plight to bring about necessary changes in their thought pattern as well as in their social structures. The result was that caste system, Hindu ritual-system and many other ceremonies were considered meaningless and irrelevant to the integrated growth of the society and thus were blatantly questioned. The Hindu traditional religious elites, the Brahmins were thoroughly exposed as totally ignorant and unprogressive, who since long had shackled the human spirit in unnecessary labyrinth of artifices to cater to their own selfishness and to maintain their high status. They also questioned the sacred literature including various *Dharamshastras* that propped up Hindu social and political structures.

The awakened Hindus reacted in two ways : Firstly, many of them entered the fold of Sikhism. This happened in the Punjab and its peripheries where Sikhism was originated and matured under the personal care of the Gurus. Secondly, quite a large number of them were prompted to reform the Hindu society. Their feelings were amply reflected in the Hindu literature of the medieval times. Much of the literature exposed malaise in the Hindu society and the key causes of the same. Their general observation was that apart from the oppression of the Muslim imperialists aiming at destruction and dislocating of Hindu society and religion, the inner causes such as irrelevant social institutions and the rigid clerication et al confused spiritual thinking, especially about Reality and His relationship with the world were no less responsible for it. Quite a number of the Hindu scholars from various corners of India reached Anandpur, Paonta and Talwandi Saboke. They re-wrote old classics including *Ramayan*, *Mahabharta*, *Krishanavtar*, *Chandi Charitar I*, *Chandi Charitar II*. Their main thrust seemed to be to present the characters in these classics not as divine beings but as heroes committed to the righteous causes and living in the world like other mortals. *Krishna Avtar*, *Ram Avtar*, *Chandi*—all were heroes in the sense that they upheld the cause of goodness even at the risk of their lives. The underlying purpose of these writers was to make the people feel self-dependent, bolder and courageous by themselves and to feel free from beliefs and the shackles of the irrelevant social and religious institutions.

This emphasis led to the emergence of certain fresh religio-social formulations and formations. In religious and social spheres, the rigid caste-heirarchy began to be challenged both as social organisation and a spiritual artifice. Idol worship began to be questioned. The multitude of gods and goddesses began to be questioned as the possessors of absolute powers.

Instead, God as the Supreme diety began to be apprehended as their Creator as also of all other things in the world. Such a scenario was visible in the hymns of *Bhakti* Saints and their followers. In certain parts of India, these notions led to the rise of new social and political movements. *Satnamis* of Narnaul (in present-day Haryana) and the rise of Marhattas under the inspiration and leadership of Shivaji and Peshwa were such examples.

This trend has continuously been buttressed. As late as twentieth century, Rabinder Nath Tagore, Swami Vivekanand and Aurobindo Ghosh—considered wise men among the Hindus—admired Guru Gobind Singh for showing paths to Hindus to preserve their identity through reforming themselves. It is altogether another matter that they did not take notice of the new premises of the Guru's formulations to form a new variety of humanity named *Khalsa* by the Guru.

The Muslims also could not escape the impact of the Guru. The Muslims of *Sufi* persuations saw very many valid points in his teachings. Quite a number of them for instance, Bhikhan Shah, Pir Budhu Shah and Pir Mohammad, Nahar Khan, Gani Khan and Nabi Khan turned highly appreciative of the Guru and took pleasure in rendering help to him even in the most critical moments. *Sunni* Muslims especially those under the influence of *Naqshbandis* were highly fidgeted at the *Khalsa* dispensation as it clashed with their long cherished political and social concepts and practices. They expressed themselves in taking rigid position vis-a-vis the Sikhs with the result that instead of reforming themselves, they made resolve to put an end to the *Khalsa Panth* which they labelled as Biddat. It was unfortunate that Indian Muslim Society displayed no tractability to make corrections in their thinking and behaviour. Rather it clung more tenaciously to their beliefs in *Shariat, Dar-ul-Islam* and *Jehad* in the sense of crusades against non-Muslims to convert them to Islam or to extirpate them. This approach made the energies of the Muslims flow into channels that led them to involve themselves in purposes either unattainable or highly destructive. In the Indian context where the majority of people were non-Muslims and had been sufficiently stirred or got awakened, the end results were insignificant. From the point-of-view of higher Islam, this approach absolutely served no purpose. The cause of one-ness of God and Brotherhood of mankind was not advanced even a bit.

Inspite of the lapse of centuries since the mission of Guru Nanak-Guru Gobind Singh was unfolded, the relevance of the mission had not abated. It is, perhaps, the only model that can suitably form the nucleus of global society which in these days is considered to be the need of the times. It is increasingly felt that the future of the world lies neither in nationalism, racialism, regionalism, religions, or communism, nor in internationalism which is more or less, a political arrangement at global level. The future lies in the globalisation which implies universal, ethical, political and religious values, pooling of material and non-material resources and their equitable distribution among the people. Various strategies are being worked out to achieve such a globalisation. Even U.N.O. is involved in such exercises. Special conclaves are being organised in different regions and it is being emphasised that all human beings in essence are part of Essence that is God, and they are not opposite to one another. Economists and political scientists are also busy moulding and shaping certain structures to work out global norms at political, social and economic levels. In such pursuits Guru Gobind Singh's mission, his ethics, his vision of society and economy can serve as a beacon. The fact had been realised, although dimmly in certain quarters, and hopefully in the coming future, world would be attracted towards Guru Gobind Singh for guidance and inspiration.

APPENDIX–A

Poets and writers of *Darbar* of Guru Gobind Singh

1. Bhai Mani Singh Dewan
2. Bhai Nand Lal Goya
3. Bhai Chaupa Singh
4. Bhai Daya Singh
5. Pt. Kirpa Ram
6. Nanua Bairagi
7. Bhai Ramkuir
8. Devidas
9. Lakhan Rai
10. Bhoj Raj
11. Tansukh Lahorie
12. Chandersen Senapati
13. Kashi Ram
14. Prahlad Rai
15. Amrit Rai Lahorie
16. Mangal Rai
17. Hansram Bajpai
18. Kunwresh
19. Tahkan Das
20. Chand
21. Aniraj
22. Sukhdev
23. Brind
24. Girdhar Lal
25. Alam Shah
26. Nand Ram
27. Hari Dass
28. Gopal
29. Dharam Singh
30. Gurdas Singh
31. Gurdas Guni
32. Bhai Feru
33. Brahm Bhatt
34. Heer Bhatt
35. Sunder
36. Sharda
37. Sudama
38. Hussain Ali
39. Chandan
40. Dhanna Singh
41. Ramdass
42. Brij Lal
43. Mir Chhabilla
44. Mir Mushki
45. Keso Bhatt
46. Desa Singh Bhatt
47. Narbad Singh Bhatt
48. Kirat Singh
49. Nihchal Fakir
50. Pindi Lal
51. Nand Lal
52. Mallu
53. Kalua
54. Ballu
55. Ballabh
56. Allu

57. Madhu
58. Udrai
59. Thakur
60. Mandass Bairagi
61. Eshar Dass
62. Mathradass
63. Ramchandra
64. Madan Giri
65. Rai Singh
66. Sukha Singh
67. Maha Singh
68. Harijass Rai Hazoori
69. Pt. Raghu Nath
70. Pt. Mithoo
71. Madan Singh
72. Dhyan Singh
73. Mala Singh
74. Bidhi Chand
75. Khan Chand
76. Birkha
77. Rawal
78. Sheikh
79. Sahib Chand
80. Dharam Chand
81. Alam Singh
82. Nanu Rai
83. Nand Chand
84. Daya Ram Purohit
85. Ram Singh
86. Karam Singh
87. Ganda Singh
88. Vir Singh
89. Jaina Singh
90. Daya Singh
91. Dharam Singh
92. Himmat Singh
93. Mohkam Singh
94. Sahib Singh
95. Ram Singh
96. Deva Singh
97. Tehal Singh
98. Isher Singh
99. Fateh Singh
100. Lal Dass Khiali
101. Adha
102. Jado Rai
103. Fatt Mal
104. Keso Guni
105. Bhagat
106. Asha Singh Musudi
107. Sena Singh
108. Mani Singh Musudi
109. Bal Gobind
110. Phate Chand
111. Fateh Chand
112. Nihala
113. Bala
114. Darbari Singh Chhota
115. Gharbari Singh
116. Durbari Singh
117. Hardas
118. Ram Rai
119. Sital Singh Bahurupia
120. Roshan Singh
121. Pakhar
122. Shiha Singh
123. Ram Singh
124. Chhauna Singh
125. Bulaka Singh
126. Sahib Singh

APPENDIX–B

Contemporary Hill Chiefs

Source : *History of the Punjab Hill States*, 2 Vols., by Hutchinson, J. and J. Ph. Vogal

KANGRA

Vijay Ram Chand	1660-1687
Udai Ram Chand	1687-1690
Bhim Chand	1690-1697
(Kirpal Chand, who is frequently mentioned in the *Bachittar Natak*, was his brother)	
Alam Chand	1697-1700
Hamir Chand	1700-1747

KAHLUR (Bilaspur)

Dip Chand	1650-1667
Bhim Chand	1667-1712
Ajmer Chand	1712-1741

HINDUR (Nalagarh)

Sansar Chand	?-1618
Dharam Chand	1618-1701
Himmat Chand	1701-1704
Bhup Chand	1704-?

SIRMOUR (Nahan)

Karam Chand	1616-1630
Mandhata Parkash	1630-1654
Subhag Parkash	1654-1664
Budh Parkash	1664-1684
Mat Parkash	1684-1704
Hari Parkash	1704-1712

MANDI

Shayam Sen	1664-1679
Gaur Sen	1679-1684
Sidh Sen	1684-1727

NURPUR

Raj Rup Singh	1646-1661
Mandhata	1661-1700
Dayadhata	1700-1735

JAMMU

Bhupat Dev	1625-1650
Hari Dev	1650-1675
Gajai Dev	1675-1703
Dhrub Dev	1703-1717

GARHWAL (Srinagar)

Prithi Shah	?-1662
Medni Shah	1662-1684
Fateh Shah	1684-1717

GULER

Rup Chand	1610-1635
Man Singh	1635-1661
Bikram Singh	1661-1675
Raj Singh	1675-1695
(Gopal of the *Bachittar Natak*)	
Dalip Singh	1695-1730

JASWAN

Anirudh Chand	1588-1589

He was succeeded by Samir Chand,
Man Singh, Ajaib Singh, Ram Singh,
Ajit Singh and Jaghar Singh. Of these,
Ram Singh was certainly a contemporary
of Guru Gobind Singh.

KULU

Jagat Singh	1637-1672
Bidhi Singh	1672-1688
Man Singh	1688-1719

APPENDIX–C

Sermon given by Guru Gobind Singh on the Baisakhi of 1699

Guru Gobind Singh delivered a very inspiring speech while addressing the mammoth gathering at Anandpur Sahib on the Baisakhi day of 1699. Mr. Max Arthur Macauliffe (1837-1913) attributed the source of this information to the report of a contemporary news-writer of the Mughal court and for this, he depended upon Ghulam Muhai-ul-Din's book *Tarikh-i-Punjab* written in 1848. According to Dr. Ganda Singh, the report was first inscribed in *Tarikh-i-Hind* written by Ahmed Shah Batalia in 1818.

We reproduce here below the original text in Persian and its transcription in Gurmukhi script along with its english translation by Dr. Harnam Singh Shan.

Original Text in Persian Script

همه ها در یک مذهب در اید

که دُوئی از در میاں بر خیزد۔

وار چهار برنے قوم بُود

از برہمن و چهتری و شُودر و وَیش۔

که هر یکے را دھرم شاستر دین علیحده مقرر است۔

آں را ترک داده بر یک طریق سلُوک نمائند

وهمه برا برند

ویکے خُود را بر دیگرے ترجیح نه دهند۔

و آں عملے کیش از میاں بر داشته۔

ترقی بیابند۔

همہ ہا در یک مذہب درآید

آں کہ درویدوشاستر تعلیمے آں ہا

تاکید مزید رفتہ است

از خاطر بدر کند۔

وسوائے از گورو نانک و خلیفائے اُو

بردگر از سنادیدے بہنمود

مثل رام کشن و برہما دیوی وغیرہ

اعتقادہ نہ نمائند۔

وپاہلے من گرفتہ

مردماں ہر چہار برن

در یک ظرف بخر ند واز یک دیگر اصلاح برند۔

ہم چنیں سخنہاۓ بسیار گفتند۔

چوں مردماں بشنیدند

بسیار از برہمناں و چھتریاں بر خاستند و گفتند

کہ مانذہب کہ گورو نانک و ہمہ گورواں بداں قایل نہ شدُ باشند۔

ومذہب کہ مخالفِ وید وشاستر بود ہر گز قُبول نے کنیم۔

ومذہب کہنار اکہ پیشینہ نگاں اقدام نمُودہ اند۔

بگفتہ کو دکے از دست نہ دہیم ایں گفتہ بر خاستند۔

مگر بست ہزار کس رضا داد ند

و مطابقت بر زباں آوردند۔

Original Text in Gurmukhi Script

ਹਮਹ ਹਾਦਰ ਯਕ ਮਜ਼ਹਬ ਦਰਆਇਦ
ਕਿ ਦੂਈ ਅਜ਼ ਦਰਮਿਆਂ ਬਰਖਜ਼ਦ।
ਵਾਰ ਚਹਾਰ ਬਰਨੇ ਕੌਮ ਹਨੂਦ,
ਅਜ਼ ਬ੍ਰਹਮਨ ਵ ਛੱਤ੍ਰੀ ਵ ਸ਼ੂਦ੍ਰ ਵ ਵੈਸ਼
ਕਿ ਹਰ ਯਕੇ ਰਾ ਧਰਮ-ਸਾਸਤ੍ਰ ਦੀਨ ਅਲਹਿਦਾ ਮੁਕਰਰ ਅਸਤ।

ਆਂ ਰਾ ਤਰਕ ਦਾਦਹ
ਬਰ ਯਕ ਤਰੀਕ ਸਲੂਕ ਨੁਮਾਇੰਦ।

ਵ ਹਮਹ ਬਰਾਬਰੰਦ
ਵ ਯਕੇ ਖ਼ੁਦ ਰਾ ਬਰ ਦੀਗਰੇ ਤਰਜੀਹ ਨ ਦਿਹੰਦ।
ਵ ਆਂ ਅਮਲੇ ਕੇਸ਼ ਅਜ਼ ਮੀਆਂ ਬਰਦਾਸ਼ਤਹ,
ਤਰੱਕੀ ਬਯਾਬੰਦ।
ਹਮਾ ਹਾਦਿਰ ਯਕ ਮਜ਼ਹਬ ਦਰਾਇਦ
ਆਂ ਕਿ ਦਰ ਵੇਦ ਵ ਸ਼ਾਸਤ੍ਰ ਤਾਲੀਮੇ ਆਂ ਹਾ,
ਤਾਕੀਦੇ ਮਜ਼ੀਦ ਰਫ਼ਤਹ ਅਸਤ,
ਅਜ਼ ਖ਼ਾਤਿਰ ਬਦਰ ਕੁਨੰਦ।
ਵ ਸਿਵਾਏ ਅਜ਼ ਗੁਰੂ ਨਾਨਕ ਵ ਖ਼ਲੀਫ਼ਾਇ ਉ
ਬਰ ਦਿਗਰ ਅਜ਼ ਸਨਾ ਦੀਦੇ ਹਨੂਦ
ਮਸਲ ਰਾਮ ਕਿਸ਼ਨ ਵ ਬ੍ਰਹਮਾ ਦੇਵੀ ਵਗ਼ੈਰਾ
ਇਅਤਕਾਦ ਨਾ ਨੁਮਾਇੰਦ।
ਵ ਪਾਹੂਲੇ ਮਨ ਗਿਫ਼ਤਹ
ਮਰਦੁਮਾਨੇ ਹਰ ਚਹਾਰ ਬਰਨ
ਦਰ ਯਕ ਜ਼ਰਫ਼ ਬਿਖ਼ੁਰੰਦ।
ਵ ਅਜ਼ ਯਕ ਦਿਗਰ ਇਸਲਾਹ ਬਰੰਦ।"

ਹਮ ਚਿਨੀਂ ਸੁਖਨਹਾਇ ਬਿਸਯਾਰ ਗੁਫ਼ਤੰਦ।
ਚੂੰ ਮਰਦੁਮਾਂ ਬ ਸ਼ਨੀਦੰਦ
ਬਿਸਯਾਰੇ ਅਜ਼ ਬ੍ਰਹਮਨਾ ਵ ਛੱਤ੍ਰੀਆਂ ਬਰਖਾਸਤੰਦ ਵ ਗੁਫ਼ਤੰਦ,
"ਕਿ ਮਾ ਮਜ਼ਹਬੇ ਕਿ ਗੁਰੂ ਨਾਨਕ
ਵਾ ਹਮਹ ਗੁਰੂਆਂ ਬਦਾਂ ਕਾਯਲ ਨਾ ਸ਼ੁਦ ਬਾਸ਼ੰਦ।
ਵ ਮਜ਼ਹਬੇ ਕਿ ਮੁਖ਼ਾਲਿਫ਼ੇ ਵੇਦ ਸ਼ਾਸਤ੍ਰ ਬਵੱਦ,
ਹਰਗਿਜ਼ ਕਬੂਲ ਨਮੇ ਕੁਨੇਮ।
ਵ ਮਜ਼ਹਬੇ ਕਹਨਾ ਰਾ ਕਿ ਪੇਸ਼ੀਨਾ ਨਿਗਾਂ ਇਕਦਾਮ ਨਮੂਦਹ ਅੰਦ,
ਬਗੁਫ਼ਤਹ ਕੋਦਕੇ ਅਜ਼ ਦਸਤ ਨ ਦਿਹੇਮ।"

ਈਂ ਗੁਫ਼ਤਾ ਬਰਖ਼ਾਸਤੰਦ,
ਮਗਰ ਬਸਤ ਹਜ਼ਾਰ ਕਸ ਰਜ਼ਾ ਦਾਦੰਦ,
ਵ ਮੁਤਾਬਕਤ ਬਰ ਜ਼ੁਬਾਂ ਆਵੁਰਦੰਦ।

Its Translation into English

"All should come into the fold of one creed
so that the difference among them may disappear.
And all the four castes of Hindus,
(viz. the Brahmins, Chhatris, Vaishas and Shudras)
for each of whom the *Ved, Shastras,*

should abandon those altogether;
follow one path and
adopt one form of adoration (of God).
They should consider one another as equals;
and no one should think himself preferable to another.
They should leave aside all those rites and customs,
and be progressive in their pursuits.
The notion about pilgrimages, like that to the Ganges etc.,
which are enjoined and emphasised in the *Vedas* and
Shastras, should be removed from the mind.
With the exception of Guru Nanak and his spiritual
successors,
none of the Hindu deities,
Such as Rama, Krishna, Brahma and Devi, etc.,
are to be adored.
After receiving my *Pahul* (Baptism of the Double-edged
sword),
men of all the four castes
should eat out of the same vessel
and reform one another."

He (Guru Gobind Singh) said
many more such things.
When the people heard those,
many of the Brahmins and Chhatris got up and said :
"They would never accept the religion
which Guru Nanak and the other Gurus did not adopt,
and which was opposed to the teachings of *Vedas* and
Shastras
On the other hand
they would not give up the ancient religion
which their ancestors had believed in,
at the bidding of just a boy."

Saying this, they left.
In spite of that, twenty thousand men
accepted the Guru's gospel
and pledged to act upon it.

BIBLIOGRAPHY

Abdur Rasul, Maulvi, *Tarikh-i-Muazzam* (Persian), Rampur Library, M.S.

Abul Fazal, *Akbar Nama* (Persian), Lucknow, 1883.

Ahluwalia, Jasbir Singh, *Metaphysical Postulates of Sikhism*, Godwin Publishers, Chandigarh, 1976.

— —, *Sikhism Today*, Guru Gobind Singh Foundation, Chandigarh, 1987.

Akhbarat-i-Durbar-i-Mualla (Persian).

Alamgir Nama (Persian).

Arfi, Narajan, *Ranghretian da Itihas* (Punjabi), Literature House, Amritsar, 1993.

Archer, John C., *The Sikhs*, Princeton University Press, New Jersey, 1946.

Ashta, Dharam Pal, *The Poetry of Dasam Granth*, Arun Prakashan, New Delhi, 1959.

Athar Ali, *The Apparatus of Empire*, Aligarh Muslim University, 1985.

Attar Singh, *Travels of Guru Tegh Bahadur and Guru Gobind Singh*, English Translation of *Sakhi Pothi*.

Avtar Singh, *Ethics of the Sikhs*, Punjabi University, Patiala, 1970.

Aqil Das, *Halat-i-Aurangzeb* (Persian).

Badehra, Ganesh Das, *Chahar Bagh-i-Punjab* (Persian), edited by Kirpal Singh, Khalsa College, Amritsar, 1965.

Bal, Vir Singh, *Singh Sagar* (Punjabi), edited by K.K. Bansal, Punjabi University, Patiala, 1998.

Bamzai, P. N. Kaul, *A History of Kashmir*.

Banerjee, A.C., *The Sikh Gurus and the Sikh Religion*, Munshiram, Manoharlal, Delhi, 1983.

— —, *Guru Nanak to Guru Gobind Singh*, Rajesh Publications, New Delhi, 1978.

Banerjee, Indubhushan, *Evolution of the Khalsa, 2 Volumes*, A. Mukherjee and Company, Calcutta, 1947.

Batalvi, Ahmed Shah, *Tarikh-i-Punjab* (Punjabi), Translation by Gurbakhsh Singh, Punjabi University, Patiala, 1969.

Batra, Colonel Ravi, *Leadership in its Finest Mould : Guru Gobind Singh*, S.G.P.C., Amritsar, 1979.

Bhai Nand Lal Granthavali (Punjabi), edited by Ganda Singh, Punjabi University, Patiala.

Bakht Mal, *Twarikh-i-Sikhan* (Persian).

Beale T.W., *An Oriental Biographical Dictionary*.

Bhalla, Sarup Das, *Mehma Parkash* (Punjabi), Bhasha Vibhag, Patiala, 1971.

Bhandari, Sujan Rai, *Khulastut-Twarikh* (Punjabi Tr.) Punjabi University, Patiala, 1972.

Bhat Vahi Jadobansian (Hindi), Punjabi University, Patiala.

Bhat Vahi Multani Sindhi (Hindi), Punjabi University, Patiala.

Bhat Vahi Talaunda Pargana (Hindi), Punjabi University, Patiala.

Bhat Vahi Purbi Dakhni (Hindi), Punjabi University, Patiala.

Bhat Vahi Tumar Bijlauton Ki (Hindi), Punjabi University, Patiala.

Bhangoo, Ratan Singh, *Prachin Panth Parkash* (Punjabi), Khalsa Samachar, Amritsar, 1926.

Bowrey, Thomas, *A Geographical Account of Countries Around the Bay of Bengal 1669-78*, edited by Lt. Col. Sir Richard Cainal Temple Bart C.I.E., Hakluyat Society, Cambridge, 1905.

Bute Shah, *Twarikh-i-Punjab* (Persian).

Chaupa Singh, *Rehatnama* (Punjabi).

Court, Major Henry, *History of the Sikhs* or *Sikhan de Raj di Vithya*, Reprint, Languages Deptt. Punjab, Patiala.

Chhiber, Kesar Singh, *Bansavalinama Dasan Patshahian Ka* (Punjabi), edited by P.S. Padam, Singh Brothers, Amritsar, 1997.

Cunningham, Joseph Davey, *A History of the Sikhs*, Reprint, Satvic Books, Amritsar, 2000.

Danishmand Khan, *Tarikh-i-Bahadur Shah* in Elliot and Dowson Vol. VI and VII.

Dara Shikoh, *Sakinat-ul-Auliya* (Persian).

Dardi, Gopal Singh, Translation of *Sri Guru Granth Sahib*, World Sikh University Press, Delhi.

— —, *Guru Gobind Singh*, National Book Trust, India, 1966.

Daulat Ram, *Sahib-i-Kamal Guru Gobind Singh* (Punjabi), Lahore 1918, Reprint by Gurmat Sahit Charitable Trust, Amritsar, 1999.

Dharam Singh, *Dynamics of the Social Thought of Guru Gobind Singh*, Punjab University, Patiala, 1998.

Dhadi, Nath Mal, *Amar Namah* (Punjabi Tr.), 1708, Translation by Ganda Singh, S.G.P.C., Amritsar, 1953.

Dhillon, Balwant Singh, *Pramukh Sikh te Sikh Panth* (Punjabi), Singh Brothers, Amritsar, 1997.

— —, *Early Sikh Scriptural Tradition*, Singh Brothers, Amritsar, 1999.

Dhillon, D.S. and Bhullar, S.S., *Battles of Guru Gobind Singh*, Deep and Deep Publishers, Delhi, 1990.

Dilgeer, Harjinder Singh, *Anandpur Sahib* (Punjabi), Shromani Gurdwara Parbandhak Committee, Amritsar, 1999.

District and States Gazetteers of the Undivided Punjab, Four Volumes bound in two, Low Price Publications, Delhi, Reprinted in 1993.

District Gazetteers: Amritsar (1883 and 1892-93); *Ferozepur* (1883-84); *Gupran Wali* (1883-84); *Sialkot* (1895 and 1928)

Elliot and Dowson, *History of India as Told by its Own Historians*, 1866-67 Vol. VI, VII.

Fauja Singh (ed.), *Atlas Travels of Guru Gobind Singh*, Punjabi University, Patiala, 1968.

Fauja Singh et al., *Sikhism*, edited by L.M. Joshi, Punjabi University, Patiala, 2000.

Fauja Singh, Gurbachan Singh Talib, *Guru Tegh Bahadur : Martyr and Teacher*, Punjabi University, Patiala.

Fauja Singh and Taran Singh, *Guru Tegh Bahadur Jiwan te Rachna* (Punjabi), Punjabi University, Patiala, 1987.

Fauja Singh, *Hukamnamas Sri Guru Tegh Bahadur Sahib*, Punjabi University, Patiala.

Forster, George, *A Journey from Bengal to England*.

Ganda Singh, *Makhiz-i-Twarikh-i-Sikhan* (Persian), Amritsar.

— —, *Nanak Panthis* Translation from *Dabistan-i-Mazahib* (Persian).

— —, *Hukamname* (Punjabi), Punjabi University, Patiala, 1967.

Gandhi, Surjit Singh, *Sikhs in the Eighteenth Century*, Singh Brothers, Amritsar, 1999.

— —, *History of the Sikh Gurus*, Gurdas Kapur and Sons (P) Ltd., Delhi, 1978.

Gazetteer of Bilaspur.

G.B. Singh, *Sikh Relics in Eastern Bengal*.

Gian Singh, Giani, *Twarikh Guru Khalsa*, Bhasha Vibhag Punjab, Patiala, 1967.

— —, *Panth Parkash* (Punjabi), Bhasha Vibhag, Punjab, 1970.

Grewal, J.S., *Guru Nanak in History*, Panjab University, Chandigarh, 1969.

Grewal, J.S. and Bal S.S., *Guru Gobind Singh*, Panjab University, Chandigarh, 1967.

Gordon, General John J.H., *The Sikhs*, London 1904, Reprint in 1970, Languages Department, Patiala.

Griffin, Sir Lepel, *Rajas of the Punjab*, Languages Deptt., Punjab, Patiala, 1970.

Gupta, Hari Ram, *History of the Sikhs*, Vol. I, Munshiram Manoharlal, New Delhi, 1984.

Gurmukh Singh, *Historical Sikh Shrines*, Singh Brothers, Amritsar, 1995.

Guru Gobind Singh, *Dasam Granth* (Punjabi).

Guru Gobind Singh, *Zafar Namah* (Persian) English Translation by Trilochan Singh.

— —, *Fateh Namah* and *Zafar Namah*, (English Translation by Devinder Singh Duggal).

Guru Gobind Singh Marg, Language Department, Patiala.

Harbans Singh, (ed.), *The Encyclopaedia of Sikhism*, 4 Vols., Punjabi University, Patiala.

— —, *Guru Tegh Bahadur*, Manohar, Delhi, 1994.

— —, *The Heritage of the Sikhs*, Manohar, New Delhi, 1994.

Harbans Singh (Dr.), *Deg Tegh Fateh*, Hazoor Printing Press, Chandigarh, 1986.

Hugel, Baron Charles, *Travels in Kashmir and the Punjab*, London, 1845.

Hutchinson, J., and Vogal, J. Ph., *History of the Punjab Hill States*, 2 Vols., Government Printing Press, Lahore, 1933.

Inayatulla, Mirza, *Ahkame-i-Alamgiri* (Persian).

Irfan Habib, *An Atlas of the Mughal Empire*, Oxford University Press, 1982.

Irvine, William, *Later Mughals*, Vol. I, II, Reprint Oriental Books Corporation, New Delhi.

Jodh Singh and Dharam Singh, *Sri Dasam Granth*, Text and Translation into English, Vol. I and Vol. II, Gurdwara Board Takht Sach Khand Sri Hazur Abchal Nagar Sahib, Nanded, 1999.

Jodh Singh, *Varan Bhai Gurdas*, Text and Translation, Vol. I and Vol. II, Vision and Venture, Patiala, 1998.

Jaggi, Ratan Singh, *Dasam Granth da Pauranik Adhyan* (Punjabi), New Book Co., Jalandhar, 1965.

Kanhaiya Lal, *Tarikh-i-Punjab*, Punjabi tr. Jit Singh Sital, Punjabi University, Patiala, 1968.

Kapur Singh, *Parasharprasna or The Baisakhi of Guru Gobind Singh*, Jullundur, 1959.

Kapur, Prithipal Singh and Dharam Singh, *The Khalsa*, Punjabi University, Patiala, 1999.

Karam Singh Historian, *Amritsar Di Twarikh* (Punjabi).

Kartar Singh, *Life of Guru Gobind Singh*, Lahore Book Shop, Ludhiana, 1951.

Khafi Khan, *Muntakhab-ul-Lubab* (Persian).

Kharak Singh and others, *Fundamental Issues in Sikh Studies*, I.O.S.S., Chandigarh, 1992.

Khazan Singh, *History of the Sikh Religion*, Reprint, Languages Deptt. Punjab, Patiala, 1970.

Khushwant Singh, *A History of the Sikhs*, Vol. I, Oxford University Press.

Kirpal Singh, *Sikh Itihas de Vishesh Pakh* (Punjabi), Shromani Gurdwara Parbandhak Committee, Amritsar, 1995.

— —, *A Catalogue of Punjabi and Urdu Manuscripts*, Khalsa College, Amritsar, 1963.

Koer Singh, *Gurbilas Patshahi 10* (Punjabi), ed. Punjabi University, Patiala, 1986.

Lakshman Singh, Bhagat, *A Short Sketch of the Life and Work of Guru Gobind Singh*, Tribune Press, Lahore, 1909.

Latif, Syed Muhammad, *History of the Punjab*, 1889 A.D.

— —, *History of Lahore*.

Macauliffe, M.A. *The Sikh Religion*, 6 Vols. Reprint, Satvic Books, Amritsar, 2000.

Malcolm, Sir John, *Sketch of the Sikhs*, London, John Murray, 1812.

Manmohan, *History of Mandi State*, Lahore, 1930.

Marenco, Ethne K., *The Transformation of Sikh Society*, 1974.

McLeod, W.H., *The Evolution of the Sikh Community*, Oxford University Press, 1975.

— —, *Sikhism*, Penguin Books, 1997.

Mohsin Fani, *Dabistan-i-Mazahib* (Persian), English Translation by Umrao Singh Shergill.

Muhammad Akbar, *Lahore Past and Present*, Punjab University Press, 1952.
— —, *The Punjab under the Mughals*, Lahore, 1948.
Muhammad Farman, *Hayat-i-Mujaddad* (Persian), 1958.
Nabha, Kahn Singh, *Guru Shabad Ratankar Mahan Kosh* (Punjabi).
Nara, Ishar Singh, *Safarnama te Zafarnama* (Punjabi), 1979.
Narain Singh, *Guru Gobind Singh Retold*, Pingalwara, Amritsar.
Narain Singh, *Waryam Ikela* (Punjabi), Guru Nanak Mission, Patiala, 1972.
Narang, Gokal Chand, *Transformation of Sikhism*.
Narotam, Pundit Tara Singh, *Guru Tirath Sangreh* (Punjabi).
Nayyar, Gurbachan Singh, *Sikh Polity and Political Institutions*, Oriental Publishers and Distributors, New Delhi, 1979.
Nayyar and Sukhdial Singh, *Guru Gobind Singh : Yatra Asthan, Prampravan te Yad Chinh* (Punjabi), Punjabi University, Patiala.
Nikky Guninder Kaur Singh, *The Feminine Principle in the Sikh Vision of the Transcendent*, Cambridge University Press, 1993.
Nur Muhammed, Qazi, *Jang Namah* (Persian) completed in 1765.
Nur-ul-Hasan, "Sayyed Sheikh Ahmed Sirhindi and Mughal Politics," *Proceedings Indian History Congress*, 1945 VIII.
Padam, Piara Singh, *Dasam Granth Darshan* (Punjabi), Kalam Mandir, Patiala, 1998.
— — (ed.), *Guru Kian Sakhian* by Swarup Singh Kaushish, Reprint, Singh Brothers, Amritsar, 1995.
— —, *Sri Guru Gobind Singh Ji de Durbari Ratan* (Punjabi), Kalam Mandir, Patiala, 1976.
— —, *Rehatname*, (Punjabi) Reprint, Singh Brothers, Amritsar, 1995.
Parmanand, *Sri Guru Gobind Singh Ji Ka Charittar*, Lucknow, 1904.
Pashaura Singh, N. Gerald Barrier (eds.), *Sikh Identity : Continuity and Change*, Manohar, New Delhi, 1999.
Patwant Singh, *The Sikhs*, Harper & Collins Publishers, 1999.
Payne, C.H., *A Short History of the Sikhs*, Reprint, Department of Languages, Patiala.
Punjab History Confrence Proceedings, Sixth Session, Punjabi University, Patiala, 1971.
Punjab State Gazetteer Faridkot State, Vol. XVI;
Punjab State Gazetteer Vol. ck Mandi and Suket States with maps, Lahore, 1908.
Puran Singh, *Spirit of the Sikh*, Part II, Punjabi University, Patiala, 1980.
— —, *Guru Gobind Singh*, Guru Gobind Singh Foundation, Chandigarh, 1966.
— —, *The Book of the Ten Masters*, Reprint, Singh Brothers, Amritsar, 1995.
Quresh, I.H., *A Short History of Pakistan*, University of Karachi, Reprint 1985.
Randhir Singh, *Udasi Sikhan Di Vithia* (Punjabi), Shromani Gurdwara Parbandhak Committee, Amritsar.
— —, *Itihasik Pattar* (Punjabi), 1953-54, Sikh History Society, Amritsar.

Randhir Singh, *Shabad Murat* (Punjabi), Shromani Gurdwara Parbandhak Committee, Amritsar.

Rizvi, Sayyad Athar Abbas, *Muslim Revivalist Movements in Northern India in the 16th and 17th Centuries.*

Rose, H.A., *A Glossary of the Tribes and Castes of the Punjab and North-West Frontier Province,* Lahore, 1911-19.

Rose, D; *Land of the Five Rivers and Sikhs,* 1875.

Rukat-i-Alamgiri (Persian).

Sahib Singh, *Adi Bir Bare* (Punjabi), Singh Brothers, Amritsar, 1970.

— —, *Guru Gobind Singh,* Raj Publishers, Jullundur, 1970.

Sainapat, *Sri Gursobha* (Punjabi), edited By Ganda Singh, Punjabi University, Patiala, 1969.

Sangat Singh, J.P., *Bachittar Natak Steek* (Punjabi), Singh Brothers, Amritsar, 1991.

Santokh Singh, Bhai, *Sri Gur Partap Suraj Granth,* Amritsar 1955, annotated by Bhai Vir Singh.

Sarkar, Sir Jadunath, *A Short History of Aurangzeb,* M.C. Sarkar and Sons, 1930.

— —, *Assam and the Ahoms.*

— —, *Anecdotes of Aurangzeb.*

— —, *History of Aurangzeb,* Vol. III, Orient Longman, First Edition 1928, Delhi.

Saqi, Mustad Khan, *Maasar-i-Alamgiri* Punjabi Tr. Fauja Singh, Punjabi University, Patiala, 1977.

Seva Singh, *Shaheed Bilas* (Punjabi), edited by Garja Singh, Punjabi Sahitya Academy, Ludhiana.

Sewa Ram Singh, *The Divine Master,* edited by P.S. Kapur, ABS Publications, Jalandhar, 1988.

Shabdaarth Dasam Granth Sahib (Punjabi), Punjabi University, Patiala, 1973.

Sharma, Sri Ram, *Religious Policy of the Mughal Emperors,* Bombay, 1962.

Shashi Bala, *Sikh Metaphysics,* Singh Brothers, Amritsar, 1999.

Sher Singh, *Political and Social Philosophy of Guru Gobind Singh,* Sterling Publishers (P) Ltd., Delhi, 1967.

Sikh Religion and Human Civilization, edited By Dr. Jodh Singh, Punjabi University, Patiala, 1999.

Sinha, N.K., *Rise of the Sikh Power.*

Sirmour State Gazetteer, Punjab Government Publication, Lahore, 1939.

Sohan Lal, *Umdat-ul-Twarikh* (Persian), Lahore, 1885.

Sukha Singh, *Gur Bilas Patshahi 10* (Punjabi), Bhasha Vibhag, Patiala.

Teja Singh, *Sikhism, Its Ideals and Institutions,* Reprint, Khalsa Brothers, Amritsar, 1951.

Teja Singh & Ganda Singh, *A Short History of the Sikhs,* Reprint, Punjabi University, Patiala, 1999.

Thakur Singh, *Sri Gurdwara Darshan* (Punjabi), Amritsar, 1923.

Talib, Gurbachan Singh, *The Impact of Guru Gobind Singh on Indian Society*, Guru Gobind Singh Foundation, Chandigarh, 1966.

Tek Singh, *Chatur Jugi* (Punjabi), Bhai Vir Singh Private Collections, Amritsar.

Trilochan Singh, *Ernest Trumpp and W.H. McLeod as Scholars of Sikh History, Religion and Culture*, International Centre of Sikh Studies, Chandigarh.

— —, *Guru Tegh Bahadur*, Delhi Gurdwara Management Committee, Delhi, 1967.

— —, *Life of Guru Hari Krishan*, Delhi Gurdwara Management Committee, Delhi, 1980.

— —, *Hymns of Guru Tegh Bahadur*, Delhi Gurdwara Management Committee, Delhi.

Ved Parkash, *Sikhs in Bihar*, Janki Prakashan, Delhi, 1981.

Vasvani, T.L., *In The Sikh Sanctuary*, Madras, 1922.

Williams, G.R.C., *Historical and Statistical Memories of Dehradoon*, Roorkee, 1874.

Yusaf Husain, *Glimpses of Medieval Indian Culture*, Bombay, 1957.

INDEX

Abadali, Ahmed Shah 492, 493
Abdul Rasul 335, 336[fn]
Abdus Samad Khan 461
Ablu 303
Abul Fazal 39
Achal Vatala 23
Afghanistan 81, 171, 179
Agamgarh 162, 254 (See also Holgarh)
Agampura 161
Agartala 58
Agra 85, 86[fn], 144, 179, 180, 288, 302,
    316, 322, 323, 324, 325, 328, 330,
    331, 333, 335, 338, 339, 341
Agya Ram 102[fn]
Ahdallat Khan 49
Ahiwal, Mani Singh, Bhai 269[fn]
Ahlu 317
Ahluwalia, Fateh Singh 124[fn]
Ahluwalia, Gurmohan Singh 208[fn]
Ahluwalia, J.S. 464, 481
Ahmed Khan 49
Ahmed Shah 264[fn]
Ahmednagar 288, 293, 314, 315, 316,
    321, 357
Ajaib Chand 228
Ajaib Das 228
Ajat Satru 73
Ajit Singh, Sahibzada/Baba 188, 253,
    259, 261, 263, 266, 270, 271,
    272[fn], 273, 274, 290, 323, 334, 350
Ajit Singh, the posthumous son of
    Jaswant Singh 334
Ajmer 23, 122, 196, 333, 335
Ajmer Chand 169, 70, 251, 252, 253,
    254, 255, 256, 257, 258, 260, 261
Akali Movement 495
Akbar 27, 28, 29, 37, 38, 39, 46, 112,
    122, 193, 266[fn]
Akola 338

Al Bukhari 198
Alam Chand 252
Alam Khan 168, 168[fn], 271
Alam Singh 255
Alamgir 286
Ali 198
Alif Khan 163, 164, 165, 260, 261
Alis 198
Allahabad 55, 57, 79, 85
Allahyar fn 29
Almast 50
Alsun 165
Amar Chand, Bhai 159
Amar Das, Guru 26, 27, 28, 29, 30, 31,
    32, 33, 36, 216, 222[fn], 347, 366,
    368, 369, 388, 399, 436, 449, 464,
    468
Amarnath 23
Ambala 86, 86[fn], 88, 103
Amber 57, 333
Amravati 338
Amrik Chand 228
Amrit Rai 131
Amritsar 32, 34, 35, 36, 37, 43, 47, 48,
    48[fn], 56, 68[fn], 115, 129, 182[fn], 215,
    298, 306, 308, 317, 389, 406, 411,
    412, 455, 456, 457, 462
Anandgarh (fort) 162, 187, 253, 255,
    264, 266, 267, 269, 393
Anandpur 57, 58, 62, 77, 79, 82, 90,
    97, 103[fn], 117[fn],129, 131, 132, 133,
    140, 142, 157, 157[fn], 158, 159,
    160, 161, 162, 163, 165, 166, 167,
    168, 169, 171, 173, 174, 177,
    178[fn], 179, 180, 181, 183, 184,
    185, 186[fn], 204, 207, 221, 228,
    248, 251, 252, 253, 254, 256, 257,
    258, 259, 260, 261, 261[fn], 262,
    263, 264, 265, 266, 267, 268, 269,

270[fn], 272, 274, 279, 284, 286, 296, 297, 298, 304, 308, 309, 314, 328, 329, 330, 331, 341, 349, 350, 357, 359, 376, 378, 392, 408, 448, 457, 462, 470, 496 (*See also* Chak Nanki, Makhowal)

Anant Nag 23

Anantia 74

Andhra Pradesh 22

Angad/Angad Dev, Guru (Bhai Lehna) 24, 25, 26, 44, 108, 114, 209, 347, 368, 399, 436

Anik Das 228

Anup Kaur 286

Anup Singh 256

Anuradh Pura 22

Apte 406

Arabia 479

Arhu Ram 62

Arif-ud-din 87

Arjan Dev, Guru 24, 32, 33, 34, 35, 36, 37, 38, 39, 40, 41, 42, 44, 52, 53, 64, 102, 108, 132, 143[fn], 193, 207, 209, 222, 295, 298, 307, 308, 310, 347, 349, 350, 364, 365, 366, 371, 372, 388, 399, 435, 437, 443, 445, 452, 480, 482

Arjan Mal (Previous name of Guru Arjan Dev Ji) 368

Arrah 84

Aru Ram 94[fn]

Ashok, Shamsher Singh 222[fn], 256[fn], 275, 299[fn], 322[fn], 325[fn]

Ashta, D.P. 91[fn], 126[fn], 127[fn], 130[fn], 236[fn], 396, 397[fn], 399, 403, 481[fn]

Assam 57, 59, 66, 79, 80, 81, 86, 117, 117[fn], 118, 338

Ata Ullah 348, 362

Atam Das 338

Atari 159

Atma Ram Jeotishi, Pandit 86[fn]

Aurangabad 288

Aurangzeb 52, 53, 54, 58, 59, 60, 61, 63, 73, 75, 80, 81, 92, 93, 94, 95, 96, 99, 101, 105, 106, 107, 117[fn], 118, 121, 122, 123, 149, 150, 160, 168, 168[fn], 171, 171[fn], 172, 177, 179, 189, 193, 194, 195, 196, 197, 199, 201, 205, 210, 256, 256[fn],

262, 264, 265, 268, 268[fn], 273, 279, 280, 282, 283, 287, 288, 289, 290, 291, 292, 293, 294, 310[fn], 313, 314, 316, 321, 322, 323, 328, 329, 332, 333, 334, 335, 357, 377, 378, 387, 407, 408, 450

Avtar Singh, Professor 287[fn], 482

Ayudhya 22, 85

Azad, Abul Kalam 197[fn]

Azam Khan 75, 322, 324

Azam Shah (also known as Tara Azam) 321, 322, 323, 333

Azamabad 73

Aziz Koka 41

Babar 108, 177, 193, 446, 447

Bachais 403

Bachittar Das 228

Bachittar Singh, Bhai 254, 270, 271

Backhona 59

Badauni 39

Badruddin, Shaikh 200

Bagar 59

Bagh Singh 151[fn], 254

Bagha, Bhai 102, 102[fn]

Baghdad 23

Bagrian 51

Banda Singh Bahadur, Baba (*See also* Madho Das) 138[fn], 341, 344, 346, 347, 348, 350, 356, 358, 360, 455, 461, 493, 494

Bahadur Shah (also known as Prince Muazzam) 171, 322, 323, 324, 325, 326[fn], 327, 328, 329, 330, 332, 333, 333[fn], 334, 335, 336, 337, 338, 339, 340, 341, 343, 344, 345, 348, 353, 354, 355, 356, 358, 361, 362, 362[fn], 397

Bahaduran 318

Bahauddin, Makhdom 23

Bahawalpur 280

Bahlo, Bhai 311[fn]

Bains, J.S. (Prof) 450

Baisakha Singh 305

Baj Singh 347[fn]

Bajak 303

Bajjar Singh, Bhai 89, 317

Bajrur 259

Bajwara 329

Bakala 54, 56, 59, 88, 88[fn]
Bakht Mal 361
Bakhtawar Khan 197, 197[fn]
Bal Godai 23
Bal, S.S. (Dr.) 113[fn], 117[fn], 125[fn], 127[fn], 150[fn], 161[fn], 163[fn], 166, 166[fn], 178[fn], 237[fn]
Bal, Vir Singh 137[fn]
Bala, Bhai 25, 74
Balachour 156
Balapur 338
Balia Chand 252
Balmik 403
Balu Bhatt 49
Balwand 37
Bambiha 303
Bamzai, P.N.K. 93[fn], 96[fn]
Ban Ganga 338
Bander 295
Bandhu 272
Banerjee A.C. (Dr.) 123, 123[fn], 148[fn], 242[fn], 242, 293, 369
Banerjee, Indubhushan (Dr.) 11, 24, 30, 125[fn], 162[fn], 163[fn], 164[fn], 168[fn], 171[fn], 173[fn], 235[fn], 256[fn], 312, 312[fn], 377, 378[fn]
Banghshias 211
Banno, Bhai 307, 308
Bannockburj 401
Banwari Das 113
Baramula 23
Bareilly 85
Bargarh 295
Barjinder Singh 404
Barna 228
Baroach 23
Bart, Richard Carnal Temple (Sir) 73[fn]
Barwan 169
Bashahar 160
Basoli 111, 257, 258, 258[fn]
Bassi Kalan 261
Bassi Pathana 336
Bassian 314
Basu 160
Batala 181[fn], 367
Batalia, Ahmed Shah 191[fn], 228[fn], 346, 346[fn]
Bathinda 283, 294[fn], 302, 304, 305, 412
Bathoor 85

Battle of Kartarpur 55
Beas (river) 34, 40, 51, 165, 260
Behari Lal Das 393[fn]
Behlolpur 278
Benaras 22, 50, 57, 74, 84, 85, 133, 178, 178[fn], 196, 306
Bengal 22, 50, 57, 66, 73, 79, 81, 83, 118, 196, 201, 203, 275
Beni Pandit 29[fn]
Betticola 22
Bhadaur 294
Bhadra 318
Bhadsali 259
Bhag Kaur, Mai (Mai Bhago) 129, 297, 298, 298[fn], 299, 300, 301
Bhag Mal 282
Bhag Singh 297, 298
Bhagat Bhagwan/Bhagat Gir 51
Bhagat Mal 51
Bhagaur 321
Bhagi Bhander 304
Bhagta Bhai ka 314
Bhagtu, Bhai 303, 304, 318, 393[fn]
Bhagwan Singh 253, 348[fn]
Bhai Ka Kot 303
Bhai Rama 287
Bhaini 34
Bhakkar 179
Bhakri 304
Bhalan 169, 171
Bhalenda 59
Bhalla, Sarup Das 41, 130[fn], 248
Bhandari 228
Bhandari, Sujan Rai 52, 181, 192, 247
Bhander 303
Bhanga Singh fn 300
Bhangani 90[fn], 102[fn], 117[fn], 124[fn], 142, 145, 147, 148, 151, 154, 156, 157, 159, 161, 161[fn], 162, 191, 204, 249, 283
Bhangu, Ratan Singh 456, 347[fn], 457
Bhani, Bibi 32
Bhano 88
Bhanu Kheri 88
Bhardwaj 94[fn]
Bharmour 151[fn]
Bhasaur 413
Bhatnagar, V.S. 332[fn]
Bhika 29[fn]

Bhikhan Khan 151
Bhikhan Shah 67, 87, 153, 200, 497
Bhikhi 59
Bhim Chand 116, 119, 120, 120[fn], 121, 145, 146, 147, 150, 151[fn], 159, 160, 161, 161[fn], 162, 163, 164, 164[fn], 165, 166, 253, 253[fn]
Bhola Singh 300[fn]
Bhucho 317
Bhup Chand 261
Bhupat Singh 317
Bhurewala 124
Bhuyan, S.K. 57[fn]
Bidar 23, 302
Bidar Bakhat 322, 323
Bidhi Chand, Bhai 48, 49, 50, 446
Bihar 22, 72[fn], 73, 74[fn], 75, 75[fn] 76, 79, 275
Bijal Singh 333
Bijharwal 163, 164
Bikaner 412
Bilaspur 56, 111, 119, 120, 121, 253, 256
Bilgrami, Ghulam Ali Azad 197[fn]
Bilgrami, Murtaza Husain 333[fn]
Bimangarh 285
Bimla Devi 242
Binod Singh, Bhai 347, 347[fn]
Bir Singh 275
Boccassio 406
Bongaigaon 79
Boora Singh 300[fn]
Brahm Das 94[fn]
Brahma 202, 246, 247, 402, 403, 414, 425
Brahmavart 85
Brahmputra (river) 338
Brar, Agri Singh 170
Braudein, S.G.F. 199[fn]
Brindaban 85, 325
British Library (London) 307, 307[fn]
Buddha, Baba 37, 42, 43, 44, 46, 54, 97, 125
Buddhu Shah, Pir 132, 152, 154, 156, 157, 191, 262, 333, 343, 386, 497
Budh Parkash 149, 150, 150[fn]
Budh Shah 149
Budha, Lord 73
Bulaki, Bhai 58

Bunga 159
Bur Majra 271, 314
Burhanpur 122, 288, 337, 338
Burhans 341
Burya 80, 196
Bute Shah 191, 191[fn], 353, 354
Buxor 84

Calcutta 87[fn]
Calcutta, Manjit Singh 13
California 464
Ceylon 22
Chak Bhai Ka 304
Chak Hira Singh 303
Chak Nanki 59, 62, 80, 81, 88, 88[fn], 89, 91, 92, 94, 94[fn], 97, 98, 100, 103, 104, 105, 117, 117[fn], 118, 119, 120, 121, 123, 124, 161 (*See also* Makhowal, Anandpur)
Chakar Hisar, Khawaja 74
Chakkar 287, 314
Chamba 111, 113
Chamkaur 94, 260, 271, 277, 279, 281, 283, 285, 289, 335, 336, 353, 354, 359, 378, 393, 407, 455, 458
Champa Devi, Rani 56, 116[fn], 160, 161
Chand 272
Chanda Singh 133, 300[fn]
Chandan, poet 131
Chandan Rai 171, 171[fn]
Chandel 151
Chandigarh 103
Chandni Chowk 134
Chandu 452
Charadwaj 58
Charan Ganga (river) 187, 267
Chatiana 303
Chatur Jugi 361
Chaupa Singh, Bhai 352, 392[fn], 483
Chaupat Rai 228
Chet Singh, Bhai 351[fn]
Chetan Misar, Pandit 319
Chhachhrauli 156
Chhaju Mal 179
Chhapra 83
Chhatra Mathai 408
Chhibber, Kesar Singh 57[fn], 65[fn], 102[fn], 145[fn], 281[fn], 411
China 211, 408, 479

Chisti, Khwaja Muinuddin 333
Chittagong 58
Chittor 334, 335
Chittu 259
Chua Mian 164[fn]
Chuna Mandi, Lahore 32
Chunian 35
Cormania 73
Cunningham, J.D. 11, 65[fn], 147, 147[fn], 148, 189, 189[fn], 190, 191, 230, 234[fn], 353, 354, 355, 359, 359[fn], 384[fn], 389
Cuttock 22

Dabbi Bazar, Lahore 34
Daburji 317
Dacca 22, 57, 58, 66, 77, 172[fn], 306[fn], 454
Dadhwar 151
Dadoo Dwara 338, 341, 341[fn] (*See also* Narain Pur)
Dadu 319, 320, 451, 456
Dadwalia, Modhukar Shah 152
Daggo, Bhai 56
Dalla, Chaudhary/Rai 303, 304, 313, 314, 317
Damdama Sahib 303, 304, 305[fn], 306, 307, 308, 310, 311, 311[fn], 316, 412 (*See also* Talwandi Sabo Ki)
Damyanti 407
Dan Singh 317
Dana, Chaudhary 303, 314
Danapur 83
Dara Shikoh 50, 52, 149, 179, 446
Darapur 233
Darauli 125
Darbara Singh 300[fn]
Darbari 228
Daria 255
Dasa, Bhai 49
Data 403
Datarpur 111
Dattatreya 202, 403
Daya Ram, Bhai 109, 135, 152, 221
Daya Ram, Purohit 228
Daya Singh, Bhai 133, 151[fn], 274, 276, 278, 280, 281, 282, 288, 293, 315, 316, 321, 347[fn], 350, 457, 462
Dayal, Raja 163, 164, 165
Dayal Chand 151[fn]

Dayal Das, Bhai 66, 74, 81, 88, 98, 101, 104
Dayal, Kirpal Singh 247
Dayal Puri, Mahant 287
Dayal Singh 300[fn]
Deccan 316, 317, 321, 328, 330, 341, 350, 353, 354, 355, 356, 462
Deep Chand 159
Dehra Baba Nanak 35
Dehra Doon 121, 135, 138, 149, 150[fn], 205, 208
Delhi 22, 52, 54, 55, 57, 59, 62, 63, 63[fn], 79, 81, 86, 86[fn], 98, 98[fn], 99, 99[fn], 101, 102, 102[fn], 104, 105, 106, 123, 134, 144, 190, 200, 227, 232, 233, 236[fn], 252, 256, 260, 261, 262, 264, 270, 286, 302, 304, 310[fn], 321, 322, 323, 324, 325, 326, 331, 332, 349, 362, 411, 452, 470, 492
Des Raj, Choudhari 297, 298[fn]
Desa Singh 228, 480[fn]
Dev, Raja Singh 86[fn]
Dev Saran 261
Deva Singh 256
Dewana, Mohan Singh (Dr.) 401
Dhade Nath Mal 345[fn], 346[fn], 347[fn]
Dhadwal 163, 164, 164[fn], 169
Dhakauli 159
Dhamdhan 56, 57, 59, 99
Dhampur 22
Dhana Singh 300[fn]
Dhankoli 132
Dharam Chand 78, 115, 116, 228
Dharam Singh, Bhai 133, 274, 276, 278, 280, 282, 287, 288, 293, 316, 317, 318, 321,323, 324, 457
Dharam Singh, Dr. 13, 300[fn], 399[fn], 433, 458
Dharampal, Raja 257
Dharm Dass 221
Dharmsala 81
Dhaul 330, 357[fn], 358[fn]
Dhillon, Balwant Singh, Dr. 13, 114[fn]
Dhilwan 59, 317
Dhilwan Sodhian 295
Dhir 337
Dhirmal 50, 53, 56, 64, 203, 204, 205, 207, 208, 209, 231, 308, 309, 310, 310[fn]

Dholpur 322
Dhrama Kirt-Sthavira 22
Dhrama Prakrama-bahu 22
Dhruva 247
Dhubri 22, 58, 59
Dhuma 104
Dilawar Khan 62, 97, 167, 168, 169, 171, 329
Dilbagh Singh 300fn
Dilgeer, Harjinder Singh (Dr.) 110fn, 162fn
Dilli 86fn (*See also* Delhi)
Dilwali 228
Din Beg 252
Dina 179, 287, 287fn, 288, 291, 294, 295, 407
Dip Chand, Raja 56, 98, 116, 116fn, 228
Dip Chand, Sodhi 228
Dipa 29fn
Dowson 172fn, 336fn, 337fn, 339fn, 340fn, 360fn
Dropti 407
Duggal, D.S. 280fn, 288
Dum Rao 84
Duni Chand 119, 254
Durga 126, 127, 128, 129, 241, 245, 246, 247, 249, 374, 414
Durga Das 334
Durgah Mal, Diwan 54, 86fn, 97
Durrani 493
Dutt, Kirpa Ram, Pandit 93, 228
Dvaja Pandita 22
Dwarka 23, 221, 462

East Indian Company 406
Elliot 172fn, 336fn, 337fn, 339fn, 340fn, 360
Elphinstone 339, 339fn

Fat Mal 393fn
Fateh Chand (a masand) 282
Fateh Chand, Raja 70, 125
Fateh Shah 90fn, 121, 145, 146, 147, 149, 150, 150fn, 151, 151fn, 152, 152fn, 153, 154, 159
Fateh Singh 188, 228, 270, 284, 285, 317, 347
Fatehgarh Sahib 162, 187, 253, 266, 286fn

Fatehpur 179
Fatima 198
Fauja Singh, Dr. 49fn, 52fn, 57fn, 59, 67fn, 81fn, 85fn, 87fn, 88fn, 89fn, 159, 190fn, 278fn, 304fn, 317fn, 318fn, 335, 336fn, 338fn, 365
Ferozpur 294fn
Firdausi 280
Forster William 340, 353, 353fn, 355, 355fn

G.B. Singh 65fn
Gait, E.A. (Sir) 58fn
Gaj Singh 171, 171fn
Gaja Singh 133
Gaji Chand 151
Ganda Singh 133
Ganda Singh, Dr. 54, 57, 74fn, 78fn, 87fn, 89fn, 133fn, 142fn, 143fn, 172fn, 206fn, 208fn, 209fn, 230fn, 231fn, 235, 235fn, 266fn, 272fn, 300fn, 323fn, 326fn, 330fn, 335fn, 336fn, 339, 343fn, 345fn, 346fn, 348fn, 362fn, 456
Gandhi, Mahatma 323
Gandhi, Surjit Singh 30fn, 51fn, 54fn, 134fn, 212fn
Ganesh Das 264fn, 346fn
Ganga, Mother 42
Ganga Ram 90fn, 109, 152, 170
Ganga Singh 300fn
Ganges (river) 75, 83, 85, 98
Gangu Brahmin 270, 284, 329
Gangu Shah 29fn, 30
Gani Khan 279, 280, 282, 283, 333, 497
Gantur 22
Garhwal 111, 121, 148, 149, 150, 151, 151fn, 154
Garja Singh, Giani 65fn, 88fn, 269fn, 321fn
Gauhati 22, 58
Gaur 117fn
Gauri 295
Gaya 22, 55, 79, 83
George Forster 339
Georgia 73
Ghanaiya, Bhai 266
Ghanaulla 159, 270
Ghani Das 228

Ghani Khan 192, 271, 386
Gharbara Singh 254, 300[fn]
Gharlu 272
Ghazni 179, 211
Ghiasuddin 180
Ghosh, Aurobindo 379, 441, 497
Ghulal 282, 314
Ghulam Mohi-ud-din 190, 191, 228[fn], 231[fn]
Ghumand Chand, Raja 253
Gian Singh 133
Gian Singh, Giani 10, 30, 59, 86[fn], 108[fn], 121[fn], 146[fn], 157[fn], 168[fn], 256[fn], 282[fn], 295[fn], 306, 324, 324[fn], 326, 337, 347[fn], 352, 352[fn]
Gias Beg, Mirza 204
Giddarbaha 303
Giri 124[fn]
Girnar Rocks 23
Gobind Rai/Singh, Guru 9, 10, 12, 17, 37, 58, 62, 63, 65, 65[fn], 66, 68, 69, 69[fn], 70, 71, 72, 72[fn], 73, 74, 76, 77, 78, 81, 82, 83, 84, 85, 85[fn], 86[fn], 87, 88[fn], 89, 89[fn], 90, 91, 92, 95, 96, 98, 100, 101, 103, 104, 105, 106, 108, 110, 113[fn], 117[fn], 118, 120, 122, 123[fn], 125[fn], 126, 127, 127[fn], 129, 131[fn], 133, 134, 135, 136, 137, 138, 138[fn], 139, 151, 152, 157[fn], 160, 161, 161[fn], 168, 168[fn], 171[fn], 173, 175, 178[fn], 180, 183, 188, 190, 191, 191[fn], 200, 204, 206, 207, 208, 209, 216, 219, 220, 221, 222[fn], 223, 224, 225, 227, 230, 231[fn], 233, 235, 236, 238, 239, 240, 241, 243, 244, 245, 246, 247, 248, 249, 250, 260[fn], 267, 269, 270[fn], 271, 275, 280, 281, 282, 283, 288, 291, 292, 293, 294[fn], 305, 305[fn], 306, 306[fn], 307, 308, 311[fn], 312[fn], 313, 314, 315, 317, 323[fn], 335, 336, 339, 339[fn], 340, 342, 346, 347, 348, 349, 350, 351, 352, 355, 356, 361, 363, 364, 365, 367, 368, 369, 370, 371, 373, 374, 375, 376, 377, 384, 386, 387, 388, 390, 391, 393, 393[fn], 394, 395, 398, 399, 401, 402, 406, 407, 409, 411, 412, 413, 414, 415, 419, 421, 422, 423, 424, 425, 427, 429, 430, 431, 432, 433, 434, 436, 438, 439, 441, 442, 443, 446, 448, 449, 449[fn] 450, 454, 455, 457, 459, 461, 462, 463, 464, 465, 466, 467, 468, 469, 470, 471, 473, 475, 476, 477, 478, 479, 480, 481, 482, 483, 484, 485, 490, 494, 495, 497, 498
Gobindpura 59, 318
Godagri 57
Godaie Singh 317
Godavari (river) 338, 342, 344, 345, 353, 354
Godhu 104
Goindwal 26, 27, 29, 31, 32, 37, 39, 40, 55, 56, 114
Golam 22
Gonda 50
Gopal Chand 90[fn], 108, 140, 146, 151, 151[fn], 152, 163, 169, 170
Gopal Rai 109
Gopalpur 57
Gorakh Hatri (Peshawar) 23
Gorakh Matta 22, 85
Gorakh Nath 242
Gordon 235
Goswami, B.N. 161,[fn] 170[fn]
Goya, Nand Lal 173
Graff, De 80
Greece 479
Grewal, J.S. 113[fn], 117[fn], 125[fn], 127[fn], 150[fn], 161[fn], 163[fn], 166[fn], 199[fn], 237[fn]
Gujrat 462
Gujrat (Pakistan) 22, 46
Gujri Ji, Mata 55, 66, 68, 71, 81, 86, 86[fn], 267, 268, 270, 284, 285, 286[fn], 470
Gul Khan 348, 362
Gulab Rai 90[fn], 121
Gulab Singh 65[fn], 300[fn], 318
Gulaba 279
Guler 111, 113, 114, 146, 151, 151[fn], 163, 164, 165, 169, 170, 170[fn], 173
Gumtala 47
Guninder Kaur Singh, Nikky 128[fn]
Gupta, Hari Ram 30, 120[fn], 124[fn], 151[fn], 155, 171[fn], 186[fn], 196, 196[fn], 225, 227, 228[fn], 260, 260[fn], 268[fn], 272[fn], 274[fn], 278[fn], 329, 332, 332[fn], 347[fn], 363[fn]

Gurbakhsh 135, 137, 138
Gurbakhsh Singh 102
Gurbaksh Rai 228
Gurbax Singh, Bhai 84
Gurbhaj Singh 151[fn]
Gurdas, Bhai 23, 36, 37, 46, 50, 54, 74,
    84, 114, 207, 220, 307, 308, 310,
    311, 311[fn], 337, 366, 427, 434[fn],
    483
Gurdas Singh 311[fn], 317
Gurdas Singh, Bhai 212, 213[fn], 239,
    454, 457, 492
Gurdaspur 113
Gurditta, Bhai/Baba 46, 47, 49, 50,
    53, 97, 99, 100, 115, 136
Gurinder Kaur 400[fn]
Gurmukh Das 228
Gurmukh Singh 84[fn], 85[fn], 157[fn]
Gurnam Kaur, Dr. 13
Gursar 303
Guru ka Chak 32
Gwalior 45, 115, 288

Hadur 146
Handal 29[fn], 30
Hans Ram 131
Hansa 183, 184
Har Krishan, Guru 53, 54, 55, 220
Har Rai, Guru 50, 52, 53, 98, 108, 124,
    136, 159, 203, 205, 208, 220, 307,
    307[fn], 446
Harbans Singh, Dr. 102[fn], 130, 222[fn],
    225[fn], 228[fn], 351, 351[fn], 352[fn]
Hardas 207, 337
Hardwar 22, 55, 85
Hargobind, Guru 42, 43, 44, 45, 46,
    49, 49[fn], 50, 51, 53, 55, 66, 67, 68,
    68[fn], 73, 74, 79, 88, 107, 108, 114,
    115, 117, 146[fn], 202, 203, 206,
    206[fn], 209, 215, 219, 230, 249,
    287, 287[fn], 308, 338, 349, 350,
    358, 372, 388, 399, 406, 445, 446,
    452, 455
Hargobindpur 114
Hari 104
Hari Chand 146, 151, 151[fn], 152, 153,
    · 153[fn]
Hari Das 89
Hari Ram Shah 305[fn]
Hari Singh 300[fn]

Harike Kalan 302[fn]
Haripur 114
Harji 56, 64, 208[fn]
Harkrishan, Guru 116, 134, 134[fn], 203,
    205, 208, 399, 446
Harnaksh 185, 372
Harnam Singh 259[fn]
Harpalpur 88
Haryana 22, 497
Hasan Abdal 23, 63, 99, 99[fn]
Hansa, Baba 50
Hashap 403
Hashim, Mohammad 80
Hastinapur 221
Hayat Khan 151, 152
Hazara 305, 305[fn], 404
Hazari 228
Hazur Sahib 311, 462
Hem Raj 392[fn]
Hema 104
Henry Court 69, 69[fn]
Herat 23
Himachal 462
Himmat 170, 221
Himmat Singh, Bhai 457, 462
Hindur 111, 115, 116, 120, 151[fn]
Hindustan 118
Hinglaj 23
Hingoli 338
Hir Bhat 392[fn]
Hir Ranjha 407
Hira Singh, Patto 314
Hocart, A.M. 479, 479[fn]
Holgarh 187, 266 (*See also* Agamgarh)
Holka 185
Hoshiarpur 166
Hugh 74[fn], 194
Humayun 108, 193, 323, 324
Hussain Khan 169, 170
Hussaini 170
Hussainipur 334
Hutchinson 121[fn], 160[fn], 163[fn], 164[fn],
    260[fn]
Hyderabad 330, 338, 341, 348, 362

Ibrahim, Sayyad 296
Ibrahim, Shaikh 23
Ijad, Muhammad Ahsan 62[fn], 63, 97[fn],
    98[fn]
Inayat Ali Khan 270[fn]

Index 523

Inayat Ullah Khan, Mirza 272, 293, 315[fn]
Inayat-Ullah-Ismi, Mirza 61, 196
Indaurah 151[fn]
India 16, 22, 22[fn], 66, 74, 79, 96, 108, 143, 171, 200, 242, 263, 264, 276, 324, 336, 379, 386, 399, 452, 461, 462, 479, 493, 495, 496
Indra 401
Irfan Habib 73[fn], 74, 74[fn], 314[fn]
Irvine, William 62[fn], 97[fn], 98[fn], 172[fn], 285[fn], 333[fn], 334[fn], 335[fn], 338[fn], 340[fn], 353, 353[fn], 363[fn], 369[fn], 386
Ishar Singh 228, 253
Isher Das 159
Ismail 199

Jabar Jung 261
Jadho Singh 300[fn]
Jafar-us-Sadiq 199
Jagan Nath, Pandit 131
Jagannath Puri 23, 221, 462
Jagat Singh, Rai 160, 272
Jagatullah 266
Jaggi, Ratan Singh 145[fn]
Jahangir (also knows as Salim) 39, 40, 41, 45, 74, 97, 115, 160, 193, 445
Jai Singh, Raja 54, 55, 57
Jainabad 338
Jainti 58
Jaintia 117, 117[fn]
Jaipur 341[fn]
Jait Ram, Mahant 319, 320, 338
Jaita, Bhai 102, 102[fn], 103, 275, 269[fn], 323, 470
Jajau 323
Jalaludin 102
Jalandhar 34, 329
James Brown 456
James Hastings 198[fn]
Jammu 111, 112, 120, 133, 161, 163, 164[fn], 168, 203, 264
Jamraud 321
Jamshed Khan 348, 362, 363
Jamuna (river) 51, 104, 111, 124[fn], 136[fn], 148, 325
Jandsar 278
Jangirana 303
Jango Singh 300[fn]
Jani Khan 284, 329

Japu Deda 74
Jasrota 111, 163, 164
Jassi Bagwali 303
Jaswal 146, 151, 151[fn], 163[fn], 164, 165
Jaswal, Kesri Chand 151[fn], 163, 254, 255
Jaswal, Ram Singh 163
Jaswan 111, 151[fn], 163, 166, 170, 170[fn], 171, 171[fn], 257, 258[fn]
Jaswant Singh, Maharaja 122
Jaswaria, Kesri Chand 254
Jaunpur 74, 84, 144, 200
Jawahar Khan 151
Jawahar Singh 253
Jehlum 111
Jetha, Bhai 29
Jhabal 40, 48
Jhabalia, Bhag Singh 300[fn]
Jhallian, Sunder Singh 300[fn]
Jhanda 317
Jind 52
Jit Mal 90[fn], 108, 140, 152, 153, 154
Jito ji, Mata 222, 286
Jiwan Das 338
Jiwan Singh 258, 269, 275
Jodh Singh, Bhai 322, 322[fn], 324
Jodh Singh, Dr. 13
Jodha, Bhai 287[fn]
Jodhan 282
Jodhpur 333, 334
Jog Raj 150[fn]
Joga Singh 300[fn]
Johar, S.S. 173[fn]
Johnson, A. 479[fn]
Joshi Math 22
Jujhar Singh 171, 171[fn], 188, 266, 272[fn], 274, 285[fn], 290
Jullundur 48

Kabir 84
Kabul 23, 48, 50, 119, 172, 256
Kachhwah, Jai Singh 333, 334
Kahan Singh (Son of Bhai Binod Singh) 138, 347, 347[fn]
Kahlur 47, 47[fn], 94[fn], 111, 115, 116, 116[fn], 120, 147, 150, 151[fn], 161, 161[fn], 164[fn], 165, 169, 178, 251, 252, 255, 258, 267, 329, 330, 349, 350, 357, 358[fn]
Kaithal 51

Kala 278[fn]
Kala Garh 121
Kala Khar/Kalagadh 149
Kala Singh 300[fn]
Kalal, Koer Singh 98[fn]
Kalaur 88
Kale Khan 48, 49, 55, 57[fn], 151
Kalian Singh 253
Kalidas 403
Kalindri (modern Jamuna river) 121, 151
Kaljhirani 303
Kalki 403
Kalot 320
Kalsia 132
Kalyan Chand/Kalyana, Bhai 66, 81, 86, 104
Kam Bakhsh 322, 330, 334, 339, 348, 353, 355, 362
Kamaldin, Rai 284[fn]
Kamingah 335
Kamlot 258
Kanahiya, Bhai 305, 386
Kanchipuram 22
Kandhar 23
Kandhara Singh 300
Kanech 282
Kangar 287[fn], 291
Kangra 12, 13, 19, 23, 111, 148, 151[fn], 161, 163, 166, 167, 168[fn], 169, 242, 243, 261, 263, 342
Kanha 104
Kankan 275
Kanpur 85
Kans 129, 374, 400
Kaoni 295
Kapal Mochan 132, 156
Kapur, Prithipal Singh (Prof) 13
Kapur Singh, Sirdar 175, 175[fn], 176[fn], 226, 226[fn], 282, 441, 448[fn], 451[fn], 460, 472
Kapura, Chaudhary 295, 314
Karam Chand 78, 151[fn]
Karam Parkash, Raja 113
Karam Singh 133, 133[fn], 300[fn]
Kargil 23
Karim Bakhsh 71
Karnal 102, 103
Kartar Singh 70[fn], 72[fn], 156[fn], 157[fn], 158[fn], 183[fn], 256[fn], 257[fn], 298[fn], 360, 360[fn]

Kartarpur 23, 34, 48, 48[fn], 49, 55, 90[fn], 215, 307, 308, 358
Karuna Ratna, W.S. 22[fn]
Kashi 55, 133[fn], 247, 312, 469
Kashmir 23, 93[fn], 94, 94[fn], 114, 133, 168[fn], 197, 203, 242, 305, 305[fn],
Katana 314
Katani Rampur 282
Katara 29[fn]
Katargam 22
Kathiar 79
Katoch 145, 146
Kausa 305[fn]
Kaushal Singh 255
Kaushish, Swarup Singh 11, 54, 57[fn], 82[fn], 99, 105[fn], 116[fn], 156[fn], 156, 159[fn], 186[fn], 228[fn], 252[fn], 253[fn], 254[fn], 255[fn], 256[fn], 259[fn], 270[fn], 297[fn], 298[fn], 310[fn], 317[fn]
Kautalya 460
Kaveri 22
Kavresh 131, 392[fn]
Kedara 29[fn]
Kehar Singh 300[fn]
Kehror 179
Kerala 22
Kesar Singh 133
Kesgarh 162, 187, 190, 253, 266, 286, 352, 370
Kesho Datt 448
Keshwa Rai 195
Keso 393[fn]
Kewal (a village) 305, 317
Kewal Rai 74
Khadur Sahib 25, 55
Khafi Khan 12, 80, 80[fn], 172[fn], 196, 197[fn], 326[fn], 336, 336[fn], 339, 339[fn], 354, 355, 355[fn], 356
Khaiber 492
Khairpuria, Mahan Singh 300[fn]
Khairpuria, Raj Singh 300[fn]
Khalafat Utman 198
Khalifa Saifuddin 331
Khan, Chaudhary 295
Khanabad 150[fn]
Khanna 34
Khanna Chhaura 29[fn]
Khanpur 34
Khanzada (*See also* Rustam Khan) 168, 169

Kharak Singh, Dr. 13
Kharar 124
Khaudal 318
Khayale 59
Khazan Singh 69fn, 89fn, 178fn, 259fn, 326, 326fn
Kheda Aseri 29fn
Khem Karan 35, 56
Kheri 88, 329
Khiali Adha 393fn
Khidrana (now Muktsar) 129, 295, 297, 299, 299fn, 301, 302
Khiva 59
Khizrabad 61, 80, 196
Khorasan 152
Khushwant Singh 123, 123fn
Khushwaqt Rai 117fn, 361
Khusro 39, 40, 41
Khwaja Mohammad 272
Kimmat 170
Kirat Singh 300fn
Kiratpur 47, 50, 55, 56, 89, 98, 103, 103fn, 115, 116, 265, 269, 307, 308, 470
Kiri 278
Kirpa Ram 62, 94fn, 96, 170
Kirpal Chand 66, 67, 86, 120, 135, 145, 146, 151, 151fn, 152, 163, 164, 165, 169, 170
Kirpal Das 282
Kirpal Singh 87fn, 88fn, 281fn, 300fn
Kirpal Singh, Giani 306fn
Koer Singh 10, 55fn, 65fn, 69fn, 78fn, 82fn, 83fn, 94fn, 96fn, 222fn, 234fn, 248, 268fn, 275, 281fn, 296fn, 311fn, 312, 312fn, 336fn
Kohat 211
Kot Bhai 303
Kot Kapura 284, 295
Kot Khari 151fn
Kot Sahib Chand 303
Kot Shamir 304
Kotgarh 151fn
Kothai 160
Kotiwal 151fn
Kotla Nihang Khan 88, 270fn, 271
Kotte 22
Krishna 109, 126, 129, 152, 217, 219, 246, 247, 400, 402

Kuldeepak Singh 323
Kulu 111
Kumaon 492
Kurukshetra 22, 55, 82, 85, 260, 272
Kushal Singh 300fn
Kutha Kheri 88
Kutler 111

Lachhman Singh 300fn
Ladakh 23
Ladwa 102
Laharpur 156
Lahore 39, 47, 62, 68, 97, 120, 124fn, 138, 144, 163, 168, 172, 178, 208, 221, 260, 264, 307, 313, 313fn, 315, 321, 329, 406, 445
Laihra 48, 48fn
Lakhanaur 59
Lakhanpur 156fn
Lakhi Jungle 286, 294, 296, 295fn, 299, 393, 393fn
Lakhisar 303
Lakhmir 287
Lakhnaur 59, 82, 85, 86, 86fn, 87, 88fn
Lakhu Chand 151fn
Lakshman Singh, Bhagat 10, 69fn, 89fn, 270fn
Lal 280, 282
Lal Chand 170
Lali 320
Lall Kalan 314
Lalla Beg 48
Lallu 29fn
Lambhawal 295
Lamma 283, 284
Langar Singh, Bhai 302fn
Lanka 374
Latif, Muhammad 65fn, 263, 273, 296, 296fn, 301, 346, 346fn, 355, 356, 356fn
Laur 117fn
Lehna, Bhai (Guru Angad Dev) 24, 368
Lepel Griffin 260fn
Lodhipur 57fn
Loehlin, C.H. 395
Lohar 132
Lohgarh 162, 187, 254, 266
London 236fn

Lopo Gran 286

Lubana, Lakhi Shah 103, 104, 105, 324

Lubana, Makhan Shah 56

Lucknow 85

Macauliffe, M.A. 10, 30, 43[fn], 48[fn], 66, 66[fn], 90[fn], 98[fn], 100[fn], 110[fn], 125[fn], 136[fn], 137[fn], 141[fn], 153[fn], 156[fn], 191[fn], 205[fn], 206[fn], 209[fn], 221[fn], 229[fn], 234[fn], 235[fn], 245[fn], 246[fn], 249[fn], 252, 252[fn], 259[fn], 261[fn], 265[fn], 268[fn], 282[fn], 285[fn], 288[fn], 317[fn], 318[fn], 319[fn], 320[fn], 327[fn], 328[fn], 329, 341[fn], 360, 366[fn], 386[fn]

Machhiwara 192, 271, 278, 279, 280, 281[fn], 295, 386

Madanjit Kaur, Dr. 249

Madhakar Shah 169

Madhen 287

Madho Das (previous name of Baba Banda Singh Bahadur) 338, 345, 346

Madhu 431

Madhu Singhnai 318

Madhya Pradesh 203

Madras 22

Magharoda 320

Mahabat Khan 173

Mahal 86[fn]

Mahan Singh 298, 299, 301

Maharashtra 22, 379

Mahayyud-din Pur 179

Mahdi, Muhammad Ali 198

Mahesa Dhir 29[fn]

Mahesh 202

Mahi 285

Mahikhasur 374, 401

Mahima 304

Mahraj 48

Mai Das 29[fn]

Maiman Khan 191, 262, 263

Maini, Raja 83

Maisarkhana 56

Maitra, S.K. 467

Maiya Singh 300[fn]

Majja Singh 300[fn]

Makhan Singh 255

Makhe Khan 57[fn]

Makhowal (Chak Nanki/Anandpur) 57, 57[fn], 59, 91[fn], 116, 117, 117[fn], 120, 146, 147

Malcolm, John 236[fn], 353, 354, 355

Malda 79

Malerkotla 270, 272, 285, 286

Malikpur 63, 98, 271, 338

Malla Singh 300[fn]

Malla (village) 88

Mallan 295

Mallu Shah 29[fn]

Maluk Das, Kotla 295

Man Singh 41, 274, 276, 278, 280, 282, 317, 319, 336

Man Singh, Sant 134[fn]

Manak 119

Manak Chand, Bhai 29[fn], 30

Manan 294

Mandeshwar 334, 336

Mandhaha 148

Mandhata 408

Mandi 111, 113, 151[fn], 160, 259, 260, 260[fn]

Mangal 131

Mani 329

Mani Khan 284

Mani Majra 159

Mani Ram 228

Mani Singh 317

Mani Singh, Bhai (alias Maniya) 90, 91, 101, 133, 138, 221, 254, 270, 286, 304, 306, 310, 311, 312, 317, 342, 349, 393, 397, 411, 412

Mann Singh 300[fn]

Manu 233

Manuke 287

Mardogram 87

Marx 383, 449

Mashad 23

Mashiana 75

Massa Ranghar 412, 413

Masum 60

Mathu Murari 29[fn]

Mathur 57[fn]

Mathura 23, 57, 61, 85, 195, 325

Mathura Singh 256

Mati Das, Bhai 63, 98, 100, 101, 104

Mattan 23, 62, 93, 94[fn]

Maur 56, 59

McGregor 359, 359[fn]
McLeod, W.H. 241, 241[fn], 242, 246, 250
Mecca 23, 60, 101, 198
Medina 23
Medini Parkash 120, 123, 124, 148, 149, 150, 150[fn], 159
Medini Shah 149, 150
Mehar Chand 78, 87
Mehdeana 287
Mehdi Mir 403
Mehma Swami 303
Mehtab Singh 412
Mewar 279
Mian Khan 163
Mian Mir, Sain 45, 132
Mianpur 57
Mihan Sahib 51
Miharban 36, 203, 207
Mir Hussain 197
Mir Munshi 179
Mirankot 412
Mirza Beg 172
Mirza Sahiban 407
Mirzapur 74
Mirzapur, Chhota 84
Mittu 259
Mohari Chand 109
Mohi 282
Mohkam Chand 221
Mohkam Singh 133, 266, 462
Mohri Chand 90[fn], 140, 152
Mohsin Fani 35, 368, 453
Monghyr 66
Moola 258[fn]
Morinda 270, 284, 329
Muazzam, Prince (*See also* Bahadur Shah) 171, 173, 178, 179, 256, 265, 321, 322, 324, 333, 397
Mudhwar 164[fn]
Mughal Sarai 84
Muhammad Beg 293, 313[fn]
Muhammad Harisi, Mirza
Muhammad, prophet 52, 198, 199, 200, 202, 461
Muhammad Qasim 117[fn]
Muhammad Sarmad 197, 378
Muhammad Tahir, Diwan 197
Muhkam Singh, Bhai 457
Mukarram Khan 329

Mukhia, Bhai 266
Mukhlis Khan 47, 48
Mukteshwar 55
Muktsar 129, 277, 299, 302[fn], 303, 393 (*See also* Khidrana)
Mula Bhatt 49
Mulowal 59
Multan 23, 60, 179
Multani, Rai Chand 228
Munim Khan 293, 313, 313[fn], 315, 321, 325, 333[fn]
Mur 431
Murari 74
Murtaza Khan 39, 40, 41, 201
Mussoorie 151
Muzaffrabad 305, 305[fn]
Mysore 22

Nabha 52, 304
Nabha, Kahn Singh (Bhai) 65[fn], 91[fn], 133[fn], 157[fn], 186
Nabi Bakhsh 318
Nabi Khan 192, 279, 280, 282, 283, 333, 386, 497
Nachna, Alam Chand 228
Nadaun 163, 165, 166, 173, 249, 253
Nadha Sahib 103
Nagahiya 104, 286
Nagapatnam 22
Nagarjuna 380
Nahan 113, 120, 121, 124, 124[fn], 145, 149, 157
Nahar Khan 272, 273, 290, 497
Naik Dhuma 104
Najabat Khan 148, 151, 153
Namdev 372
Nanak, Guru/Baba 17, 18, 19, 20, 21, 22, 22[fn], 23, 24, 25, 26, 28, 35, 44, 58, 59, 60, 68, 72, 79, 83, 84, 85, 94, 96, 106, 107, 108, 110, 123[fn], 126, 138[fn], 156, 167, 168[fn], 177, 181[fn], 191, 207, 209, 212, 213, 214, 215, 219, 222, 222[fn], 231, 232, 238, 243, 244, 247, 249, 267, 307[fn], 308, 309, 319, 338, 339[fn], 340, 349, 354, 364, 366, 367, 368, 369, 370, 371, 388, 391, 399, 430, 436, 443, 444, 445, 447, 449, 450, 451, 452, 461, 465, 470, 471, 473, 474, 494, 498

Nanak Jhira 302
Nanakmata 46, 85
Nand Chand 90, 98, 109, 110, 120, 159, 228
Nand Chand, Dewan 125, 135, 138, 146, 152
Nand Har-Shahar 305[fn]
Nand Lal, Bhai 11, 131, 173[fn], 177, 179, 180, 181, 186, 231[fn], 322, 343, 351, 352, 373, 427, 469, 482
Nanded 23, 302, 331, 338, 340, 341, 342, 343, 344, 345, 348, 349, 350, 359, 362, 370, 462
Nandpur 88
Nanglu 164
Nanki, Mata 55, 68, 81, 470
Nanu, Bhai 102, 102[fn]
Nanu Rai 228
Nara, Ishar Singh 282[fn], 286, 311, 311[fn], 336[fn], 338
Narain Das 94[fn]
Narain Pur (also known as Dadu Dwara) 319
Narain Singh 262[fn]
Naraina 456
Naraingarh 124[fn], 125[fn]
Narang, D.R. 65[fn]
Narang, Gokal Chand 26, 168[fn], 172[fn], 189, 189[fn], 356[fn], 389, 390[fn]
Narang, Kirpal Singh 30
Narbada, River 336
Narnaul 497
Nasiran 156, 262, 343
Nath Mal 343, 344
Natha, Bhai 58
Nauhar 318
Nazim 179
Nidhan Singh 297, 298, 298[fn], 300[fn]
Nihal Singh 300[fn]
Nihang Khan 159, 284, 314
Nihang Khan, Zamindar 270
Nihang, Kotla Khan 270
Nirmala, Gulab Singh 134[fn]
Nirmohgarh 256, 257
Nirotam, Tara Singh 299[fn]
Nisumbh 374, 401
Nizami 280
Nur Mahammad, Qazi 493
Nur Mohammad, Sheikh 74

Nur Muhammad Khan, Mirza 62, 97, 98
Nura Mahi 284
Nurpur 111, 112, 113, 151[fn], 160

Orissa 22, 73

Padam, Piara Singh 116[fn], 131[fn], 156[fn], 252[fn], 253[fn], 259[fn], 343[fn], 392[fn], 393[fn]
Painde Khan 48, 49, 55, 252, 358, 359
Pairana, Bhai 446
Pak Pattan 23
Pakistan 22, 23, 280, 305, 305[fn], 404
Pakka Kalan 303
Palahi 49
Paloo Shah 298[fn]
Panah Munim Khan, Wazir 315
Pandore 113
Panglu 164
Panipat 22
Panjab 462
Paonta 121, 123, 124, 124[fn], 125, 132, 134, 135, 137, 138, 140, 141, 142, 143, 145, 146, 147, 150, 150[fn], 151, 154, 156, 157[fn], 158, 161[fn], 162, 248, 306, 392, 496
Para Chinnar 23
Param Singh 287, 317, 318
Parana Vitama 22
Paras Ram (Avatar) 402
Parasnath 403
Pardhani 83
Parkar 74[fn]
Parmanand 119, 255
Paro 29[fn]
Parsa, Bhai 266
Patiala 48[fn], 52, 67, 87, 98[fn], 145[fn], 411, 411[fn]
Patli Putra 73
Patna 22, 57, 58, 59, 65, 65[fn], 66, 67, 68, 70, 72, 73, 74, 74[fn], 75, 76, 77, 78, 79, 80, 81, 82, 86, 90, 275, 411
Patti 297, 298[fn]
Payne, C.H. 311[fn], 312[fn]
Pehalgam 23
Pehowa 86
Persia 73
Peshawar 321

Peshoria, Lal Chand 228
Peshwa 497
Peter Mundig 73
Phagwara 49
Pheru Singh, Baba/Bhai 305[fn]
Phirya 29[fn]
Phul 50, 317
Pilibhit 46, 85
Pir Badruddin 132, 141
Pir Mohammad 89[fn], 280, 282, 283, 497
Pir Shah 154
Plato 19, 447
Poonch 305[fn]
Pothohar 305
Prahlad 185, 372
Prayag 22, 79, 83
Prehlad Singh, Bhai 480
Prem Chand 258[fn]
Prema 29[fn]
Pritam 233
Prithi Chand 33, 36, 53, 205, 207, 209, 231, 295
Prithvi Chand (Raja of Dhadwal) 163
Prithvi Shah 149, 150[fn]
Punjab 11, 22[fn], 23, 34, 36, 39, 47, 52, 54, 55, 59, 61, 65, 67, 77, 80, 81, 82, 87, 89, 111, 114, 115, 129, 138, 141, 149, 161, 168[fn], 171, 173, 182, 198, 199, 202, 238, 242, 270[fn], 280, 296, 314, 322, 328, 329, 330, 331, 341, 343, 345, 348, 356, 357, 358, 362, 377, 401, 407, 412, 413, 462, 470, 482, 492, 494, 496
Punjab Kaur 136, 137, 138, 138[fn], 208
Punjab Singh 133, 305, 305[fn]
Punjab State Archives 411
Puran Singh 182[fn], 183[fn], 224
Puri 22
Pushkar Raj 318, 319
Pushpa Devi, Rani 82, 86

Qabalpur 88
Qamar Beg 48
Qamir 197
Qandhar 211
Qayyum 200
Qurran 211
Qutab Khan 48

Ra'ad Khan 149
Raghbir Singh, Maharaja 411[fn]
Raghu Nath 133
Raghupat Rai 56
Rahim 167, 410
Rahim Bakhsh 71
Rai Ahmed 284[fn]
Rai Kalha 271, 284, 284[fn], 286, 314
Rai Singh 255, 304
Raikot 271, 284, 284[fn], 286
Raipur 157, 157[fn], 158, 161
Raisina, village 104
Raj Kaur, Mata 159
Raj Singh 163, 166
Raja Ram 210
Rajasthan 210, 305, 333, 334, 335, 451
Rajasthan State Archives 340
Rajpura 88, 151
Ram 113, 129, 167, 219, 400, 410, 414
Ram Das, Guru 32, 33, 53, 114, 137[fn], 205, 207, 309[fn], 349, 350, 364, 366, 368, 372, 399
Ram Kaur 317
Ram Kishan, Hakim 285[fn]
Ram Koer 125, 228
Ram Nagar 85
Ram Rai, Baba 52, 53, 54, 64, 74, 122, 134, 135, 137, 138, 143, 150, 150[fn], 203, 207, 208, 209, 231, 311[fn]
Ram Rai, Raja 117, 117[fn], 118
Ram Singh 133[fn], 228, 317, 318, 347
Ram Singh, Raja 57, 58, 59, 66, 82, 86, 86[fn], 163, 163[fn], 166, 170, 171[fn]
Rama, Chaudhary 314
Rama 109, 126, 172[fn], 247, 304, 402
Ramdas 317
Rameshwaram 22
Ramgarh 124, 157
Ramiana 295, 297
Rampur 77
Ramzan Khan 263
Ramzu 278[fn]
Rana Majra 87
Ranada, R.D. 422, 422[fn]
Ranbir Singh, Dr. 13
Randhir Singh, Bhai 65[fn], 130[fn], 411
Rang Matti 58
Rani ka Raipur 124

Ranjit Singh, Maharaja 260, 494
Ranthambore 310[fn]
Ratan Rai, Raja 117, 118
Rathor, Durga Das 334
Rattan Chand 117[fn], 142
Ravan 129, 374, 400
Ravi (river) 34, 51, 111
Ravi Batra, Colonel 301, 301[fn]
Ravi Das 84
Rawalsar 260, 260[fn]
Rizvi, S.A.A. 74[fn], 201[fn]
Rocha Singh 305, 305[fn]
Rohila (village) 303
Rohilla, Alam Khan 57
Rohtak 82, 86
Rome 479
Ropar 62, 63, 77, 88, 97, 98, 116, 124, 159, 252, 265, 270[fn], 271, 272
Rose, H.A. 120[fn], 207[fn], 243[fn]
Rousseau 383, 447, 449
Rup Chand 228, 272, 287
Rup Kaur, Bibi 98
Rupa, Bhai 173, 317
Rupa (a village) 351[fn]
Rupana 303
Rustam Khan (*See also* Khanzada) 168

Sachan Shah 29[fn]
Sada Manak, Pandit 133
Sadharan 29[fn]
Sadhaura 132, 156, 191, 343
Sadhu Ram, Bhai 88
Sadhu Singh 300[fn]
Sagar Chand 164[fn]
Sahena (village) 318
Saheri 270, 284
Sahewa 318
Sahib Chand 87, 152, 221
Sahib Kaur/Sahib Deva, Mata 138[fn], 270, 286, 303, 325, 349
Sahib Singh 258, 259
Sahib Singh, Bhai 457, 462
Sahib Singh, Dewan 256
Sahib Singh, Professor 308, 308[fn]
Sahiba 51
Sahnewal 282
Sahote 57
Said Khan 261[fn]

Saidpur 23
Saif Khan 57, 86[fn], 87, 200
Saifabad 57, 59
Saifuddin, Masum Shaikh 60, 99, 194
Saina Singh 133
Sainapat 11, 31, 125[fn], 152[fn], 220[fn], 229[fn], 231[fn], 232, 232[fn], 233[fn], 246, 247, 255, 257[fn], 258[fn], 259[fn], 270[fn], 272[fn], 274, 274[fn], 275, 285[fn], 288[fn], 293, 316[fn], 322, 322[fn], 325[fn], 326[fn], 335[fn], 337, 337[fn], 342[fn], 348, 348[fn], 349[fn], 352, 352[fn], 361, 455
Saket 111
Salar Gram 87
Salho, Bhai 254[fn]
Saligman, E.R.A. 479[fn]
Salim, Prince (*See also* Jahangir) 39
Saloh 280
Samana 59, 102
Sambha Ji 122, 210
Samukh Das 228
Sangat Singh 253, 274, 275, 276
Sangat Singh, J.P. 216[fn], 217[fn], 218[fn]
Sangata 51
Sangatia Bhai 74, 170
Sangha 125
Sanghar 295
Sango Shah 89, 90[fn], 108, 140, 152, 153, 154
Sangrur 411[fn]
Sansar Chand 115
Sant Singh 274, 275, 300[fn]
Santokh Singh, Bhai 10, 59, 86[fn], 89, 100[fn], 145[fn], 171[fn], 229[fn], 248, 256[fn], 268[fn], 269[fn], 270[fn], 281, 283[fn], 284, 286[fn], 298[fn], 338, 388[fn], 387
Santokhsar 32, 34
Saqi Mastan Khan 99[fn]
Saqi Mustad Khan 80[fn], 87[fn]
Saravan 295
Sarfraz Khan 331
Sarhali 34
Sarhindi, Shaikh Ahmed 46
Sarja Singh 300[fn]
Sarkar, J.N. 80[fn], 87[fn], 149[fn], 189[fn], 189, 191, 193, 194[fn], 195[fn], 196[fn], 197[fn], 353[fn]
Sarup Singh 256

Sasram 55
Sati Das, Bhai 87, 89, 98, 101, 104
Satta 37
Sawan Mal 29^{fn}
Sayyad Beg 260, 261, 261^{fn}, 262
Sayyad Khan 242, 243, 262, 263
Sayyed Zafar 61, 196
Sayyid Mohammad 200
Sebastin Manrique 73
Seloani 282, 284
Sethi, Gulab Singh 411
Sewa Ram Singh 23^{fn}
Sewa Singh 88, 137, 145^{fn}
Shah Daula 46
Shah Jahan 46, 47, 50, 115, 131, 148, 160, 193, 195
Shah Nawaz Khan 201
Shah Sangram 153
Shahi Tibbi 269
Shahjehanabad 99
Sham 414
Sham Das 90^{fn}, 109, 121
Shamir 287
Shams Khan 329
Shan, Harnam Singh, Dr. 13
Shankar 380, 431
Sharataganj 58
Sharma, Devraja 350
Sharma, Sri Ram 80^{fn}, 195
Sher Muhammad 285, 286
Sher Singh, Dr. 187^{fn}, 422, 478^{fn}, 459
Shihan 56, 204
Shillong 22
Shiv Dutt, Pandit 70, 77
Shiva 246, 425
Shivaji 122, 210, 379, 497
Shukra 403
Sialkot 23
Siana 132
Siba 111
Sidh Sen 151^{fn}
Sidh Shah 259
Siliguri 79
Sillhet 22
Simla 161
Sind 211, 305
Singh, Roucha 133
Sinha, N.K. (Dr.) 456
Sirhind 60, 62, 74, 97, 99, 114, 120, 123, 144, 168, 168^{fn}, 192, 196, 197, 228, 238, 256, 256^{fn}, 258, 259, 264, 264^{fn}, 270, 271, 284, 286, 287, 293, 294, 313, 315, 322, 326, 329, 330, 336, 347, 357, 361, 362, 387
Sirhind Fort 407
Sirhindi, Sheikh Ahmed Mujaddad-i-Ala/Sami 12, 38, 39 60, 99
Sirmour 111, 120, 121, 123, 124, 124^{fn}, 134, 148, 149, 150, 159
Sirsa 23, 317, 318, 393
Sirsa, River 269, 270, 275, 309, 392
Sisodia, Rana Amar Singh 334
Sita 113
Sita Eliya 22
Sita Waka 22
Sital Singh 300^{fn}
Sobha Singh 133, 133^{fn}, 300^{fn}
Sobti Khatri 221
Sodhara 317
Sodhi, Kanwal Nain 317
Sodhi, Kaul 295
Sohan Kavi 455
Sohela 49
Sohni Mahiwal 407
Somnath 23
Sondip 58
Spiti 23
Sri Chand, Baba 24, 25, 35, 47, 47^{fn}, 134, 136, 137
Srinagar (Garhwal) 90^{fn}, 125, 145, 146, 147, 150^{fn}, 153
Srinagar (Kashmir) 23, 305^{fn}, 146
Srinivas, M.K. 490
Sube, Raja 408
Subeg Chand 228
Subhag Parkash 149, 150^{fn}
Subhatta Singh 408
Sucha Nand 329
Sucha Singh 255
Suhel Singh 300^{fn}
Sujan Rai, Munshi (of Batala) 181^{fn}, 367
Sukha Singh, Bhai 10, 65^{fn}, 69^{fn}, 78^{fn}, 82^{fn}, 117^{fn}, 145^{fn}, 222^{fn}, 252^{fn}, 275, 276, 281, 281^{fn}, 311, 355, 358, 358^{fn}, 393
Sukhdev Singh 163, 164

Sukhdial Singh 299[fn]
Sulaiman Shah 149
Sulakhani, Mata 55, 98, 159
Sulhi Khan 44
Sultan Singh (Patti) 300[fn]
Sultanpur Lodhi 23, 106, 213
Sumbh 374, 401
Sumer Singh, Bawa 254[fn]
Sumir Singh 300[fn]
Sunam Singh 347[fn]
Sundar ji, Baba 28[fn], 37
Sunder Singh 168[fn]
Sundri, Mata 75[fn], 138[fn], 270, 285, 303, 304, 323, 325, 326, 335, 349, 350
Suraj Kund 325
Suraj Mal, Baba 50, 88, 90, 98, 121, 146[fn], 159, 160
Suraj Sen, Raja 113
Surat Singh 256
Surinder Pal Singh, Prof. 13
Sursinghwala 298
Suthrashah 51
Sutlej (river) 51, 98, 111, 168, 258, 270, 294[fn]
Swan (river) 258, 259
Sylhet 58, 117[fn]

Tabra 157
Tado Rai 393[fn]
Tagara 341[fn]
Tagore, Rabinder Nath 497
Tahal Singh 228.
Takht Mal 287
Takhtupura 287, 314
Tala Pind 304
Talib, Gurbachan Singh, (Prof.) 244, 421
Talokpur 151[fn]
Taloka, Chaudhary 314
Talwandi 22, 23, 59
Talwandi Sabo Ki (also called Damdama) 56, 303, 304, 306, 307, 309, 312, 393, 412, 413, 496
Tandon, L.S. 302[fn]
Tapti (river) 337, 338
Tara 135
Tara Azam (also known as Azam Shah) 321
Tara Bai 210

Tara Chand 47, 47[fn]
Taragarh 161, 162, 253
Taran Singh 190[fn]
Tarn Taran 34, 55, 56, 215
Tartaria 73
Tegh Bahadur, Guru (*See also* Tyag Mal) 37, 49, 50, 53, 54, 54[fn], 55, 57, 57[fn], 58, 61, 62, 63, 65, 66, 67, 67[fn], 73, 74, 76, 77, 79, 80, 81, 82, 84, 84[fn], 85, 86, 86[fn], 87[fn], 88, 89, 90[fn], 91, 92, 94, 94[fn], 95, 96, 97, 98, 99, 99[fn], 100, 101, 102[fn], 103, 104, 105, 106, 116, 117, 117[fn], 118, 121, 122, 123, 134, 168, 190, 190[fn], 191, 191[fn], 204, 206, 206[fn], 220, 227, 229, 230, 298, 306[fn], 309, 311[fn], 324, 338, 347, 349, 350, 371, 378, 379, 397, 399, 430, 446, 453, 462, 470
Teja Singh 10, 54, 57, 89[fn], 174, 175, 231[fn], 235, 235[fn]
Thakar Das 94[fn]
Thanda Burj 284, 285
Thanesar 132
Thaska 87
Thehri 303
Thomas Bowrey 73[fn]
Tibet 23
Tilok Singh 317
Tiloka 172[fn], 173, 304
Tirath, Bhai 337
Tiruchirapalli 22
Todar Mal 286
Toka 124, 124[fn], 157
Toynbee 15
Trilochan Singh, Dr. 54[fn], 66[fn], 89[fn], 101, 124[fn], 134[fn], 137[fn], 138[fn], 190[fn], 236[fn], 244[fn], 394, 399, 423, 423[fn], 449, 449[fn]
Trumpp, Ernest 24[fn], 230[fn], 304, 304[fn], 359
Tughlaq, Feroz Shah 74
Tulsi Ram 284[fn]
Tumar Bijlaut, Lahna 104
Tyag Mal (earlier name of Guru Tegh Bahadur) 49, 55

U.N.O. 498
Uch 23

Uda, Bhai 99, 100, 102
Udaipur 321
Udari, Charanjit Singh, Dr. 13
Udasi, Sewa Das 247
Uday Singh 252, 255, 258, 266, 269, 269[fn]
Ude Rai 228
Udey Karan 317
Ujjain 23, 196, 288, 334
Umayyads 198
Umed Chand 151[fn]
Una 258
Uttar Pradesh/U.P. 22, 74, 79, 85, 203, 462

Vadali 36
Vaisakha Singh 305[fn]
Ved Parkash 72[fn], 74[fn], 75[fn], 77[fn], 78[fn], 82
Ventura, General 260
Vidyarthi, Devinder Singh 12
Vir Singh 133, 133[fn]
Vir Singh, Bhai 161[fn], 178[fn], 182[fn], 183[fn], 247[fn], 304[fn], 348[fn], 362
Viro, Bibi 47, 88, 89, 152
Vishamra Devi 70

Vishnu 113, 202, 246, 247, 395, 425
Vivekanand, Swami 497
Vogal 121[fn], 160[fn], 163[fn], 164[fn], 260
Vora, Abdul Wahab 101
Vyas 403

W.S. Karuna Ratna, Dr. 22
Wassaf Khan, Nawab 179
Wazir Khan 45, 192, 256[fn], 258, 259, 264[fn], 266, 268, 268[fn], 269, 270, 276, 282, 284, 285, 286, 299, 300, 301, 313, 316, 321, 329, 330, 331, 332, 336, 341, 345, 348, 357, 361, 387
Wazir Singh 261
World Sikh Sammelan (1995) 413

Yar Muhammad, Sheikh 293, 313[fn], 315
Yusuf Zulekhan 407

Zabardast Khan 313
Zakariya Khan 413
Zalim Khan 96
Zatalli, Mir Zafar Ali 332, 332[fn]
Zorawar Singh 188, 270, 284, 285, 347

G